Pathways
Literature for Readers and Writers

Perfection Learning®

EDITORIAL DIRECTOR   Julie A. Schumacher
EXECUTIVE EDITOR   Carol Francis
SENIOR EDITOR   Gay Russell-Dempsey
DESIGNER   Tobi S. Cunningham
IMAGE RESEARCH   Anjanette Houghtaling
PERMISSIONS   Meghan Schumacher, Oliver Oertel

COVER ART   Color Blocks #55 © Nancy Crow,
                     1994.
                     41" x 43"
                     photo by J. Kern Fitzsimons

3 4 5 RD 11 10

#29992

Softcover   ISBN-10: 0-7891-7478-2
             ISBN-13: 978-0-7891-7478-9

Hardbound ISBN-10: 0-7569-8100-x
             ISBN-13: 978-0-7569-8100-6

Pathways
Literature for Readers and Writers

Perfection Learning®

UNIT TWO *Family Ties*

UNIT THREE *The Forces of Nature*

UNIT FOUR *Other Worlds*

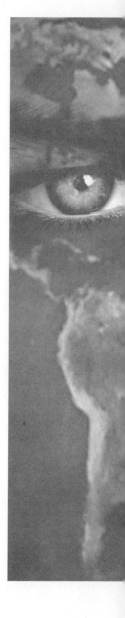

UNIT FIVE *Crossing Borders*

UNIT SIX *Echoes from the Past*

UNIT SEVEN *The Dark Side*

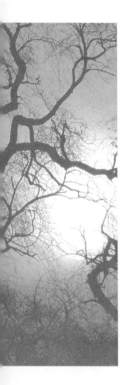

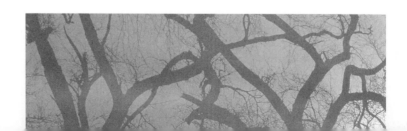

To The Student

Literature for Readers and Writers

The subtitle of this literary anthology is "Literature for Readers and Writers." Literature for readers may be a familiar concept to you, but what about literature for writers? To answer that question, think back to your younger grades. What do you remember best from your classes? If you are like most people, you probably remember the subjects about which you wrote compositions or reports. Writing about something has a way of "making it your own." When you have to take something in—through reading or through visual learning—digest it inside yourself, and then present it back to readers in a personalized form, you really come to know it. That holds true for topics in science and social studies and any number of other subject areas.

Writing and the subject of literature, though, have even deeper connections. The authors of the literature you read have gone through the same process of taking things in—life experiences, the wanderings of the imagination—and trying to digest and present them back to readers in as clear a way as they can. When you write about literature, you mirror, to some extent, the process that the authors use. As you do, you can begin to appreciate how an author's mind works, and that appreciation can deepen your enjoyment and understanding of what you read.

One of the features of this book is a special selection at the end of each unit called Writers on Writing. These pieces provide insight into the authors' writing process.

Your Writer's Notebook

This book has several different kinds of activities to broaden your experience as a writer and as a reader of literature. Your companion through these activities will be your Writer's Notebook. **Before** you read a selection, you can use your notebook to write about your reading expectations and predictions, or to remind yourself what you know about the author or subject. **While** you read, you can keep track in your notebook of any questions that you have, any parts that you especially enjoyed, any parts that confused or troubled you, and any parts that reminded you of something in your own life or something in another book you have read. **After** you read, you will find writing activities in the book that will help you digest what you have read. Each after-reading lesson recommends a graphic organizer for you to copy into your Writer's Notebook to use to get your thoughts straight, and then suggests a writing activity based on the notes in your organizer to help make the ideas your own.

Kinds of Writing

In your Writer's Notebook, you will be doing several different kinds of writing. One is **exploratory** writing. The purpose of this writing is to help you discover your responses to and thoughts about what you have read. You are the only audience for this kind of writing—as you write, you are having a conversation with yourself.

Another kind of writing you will be doing is **creative** writing. The purpose of this kind of writing is to help you discover your own powers as an author, a poet, or a playwright. You may be asked to write a story, a dialogue, a play, or a poem. In the process, you will also be discovering the kinds of issues authors, poets, and playwrights must deal with when they create their works. Those discoveries will help you appreciate the literature you read.

Finally, you will be doing formal, **academic** writing. This is the kind of writing that you are often assigned in school. You are no longer writing for just yourself to discover ideas; you are writing to express to other readers the ideas you have thought about and digested. In your Writer's Notebook, you will sometimes be asked to do activities that are smaller tasks within the larger task of writing a formal paper.

Writer's Workshops

Each unit ends with a four-page activity called A Writer's Workshop that guides you through the process of writing a polished composition intended for other readers. The kind of composition you work on will be related to what you have read and already written in that unit. For example, the first unit includes several autobiographical narratives and focuses on the theme of "passages." So the workshop activity for that unit guides you through the process of writing your own autobiographical narrative about a passage you have experienced.

· · ·

Writing is one of the most satisfying pathways into literature. May your journey along it be rewarding.

UNDERSTANDING FICTION

Short Stories and Novels

The two main types of fiction are short stories and novels. How do they differ? Short stories can usually be read in one sitting, have fewer characters, and take place in a limited setting. They generally have just one theme, unlike a novel, which is multi-themed. Both types of fiction contain the following basic elements.

Plot   The plot is the action of a story—what happens in it. As one old saying has it, the writer gets the hero up a tree and then gets him back down again. A good plot shows how one event leads to another, which causes another, and so on until the story ends. A problem or **conflict** is needed to move the story forward. No "trouble" equals "no story"!

But fictional conflict doesn't necessarily mean things blowing up. In fiction, a conflict means that the main character wants something, and someone or something is in the way of getting it. The "opponent" can be anything from a raging hurricane to a picky math teacher. And some conflicts occur from within. Perhaps the main character wants to be popular, but his or her basic nature—shy and awkward—makes that goal difficult. Inner conflicts can be the worst kind.

In a well-made story, the conflict builds until there is a **climax**, or high point of the action. Here the bully is confronted, or the inner demon is conquered. In the story's **resolution**, the conflict sorts itself out.

Character   As a reader, you keep turning the pages of stories mainly because you are interested in what happens to the characters. Writers create believable characters by describing their actions, speech, thoughts, feelings, and interactions with others. There are **round characters**—characters who are drawn realistically and seem capable of change—and **flat characters**, who are undeveloped.

Setting   A story's setting includes the time period and location in which the events of the plot occur. A setting can actually influence the plot and characters, sometimes even becoming a character itself. When nature is given human characteristics—an angry sea, a forbidding forest—setting is being used as a character.

Theme   The theme is the underlying meaning or message of a story. A *story* is about a particular character and what happens to him or her. The *theme* of the story is more universal. Usually, the theme is not directly stated. The reader must interpret what the author is saying through careful reading and analysis.

UNDERSTANDING NONFICTION

Nonfiction sounds like it might be the opposite of fiction, or that it might be anything *other* than fiction. In fact, much nonfiction uses many of the tools of fiction—vivid storytelling, characters, and settings—to write about true things. Like fiction, it relies on specific details, colorful images, and sometimes dialogue to make the writing come to life. Although it often reads like fiction, everything in it is expected to be true.

Nonfiction includes writing about the sciences, arts and culture, sports, adventure, travel, family, and personal life. Memoirs, biographies, and even literary book reviews fall under the heading of nonfiction. It comes in the shape of essays, diaries, and excerpts from longer works and can be either formal or informal. The most common kinds of nonfiction are listed below.

Autobiography   An autobiography is the story of someone's life, written by the person him- or herself. Events in the writing are true, but they are colored by the author's memory as well as by the writer's wish to look "good" to readers. Autobiographers can emphasize incidents or leave them out entirely depending on the impression they want to create.

Biography   This is also a true story about a person's life, but it is written by someone else. Usually, biographers do a great deal of research on their subject before they begin to write.

Essay   An essay is a short, multi-paragraph piece of writing that focuses on one topic or idea. Much of the writing you do for school will be essay writing. Essays differ depending on the writer's purpose. Some are **persuasive** and try to convince others to change their mind about an issue and accept the writer's point of view. **Personal** essays are informal pieces that present the writer's thoughts and feelings. An **expository** essay is more formal in tone and structure. The purpose of this type of essay is to present information and ideas.

Articles   Articles may be long, short, humorous, serious, formal, or informal. Their purpose is to provide factual information to the reader. Examples include newspaper and magazine articles and entries in encyclopedias.

Nonfiction writing is a product of the writers' unique voices and the choices they make when presenting their subjects. If two people write an essay about the same topic, the results will probably be very different. Imagine two essayists describing a chili cook-off. One writer thinks the event is absurd; the other takes it to heart. The first writer focuses on chili's weirdest ingredients—such as chocolate—and pokes fun at how seriously the competitors take themselves. The second writer depicts the event as a cooking Olympics of creativity.

UNDERSTANDING DRAMA

While plays are written to be performed, and this is certainly the best way to enjoy them, you can still experience drama by reading it. This is a great way to practice your visualizing skills. As you read a play, try to see the characters moving through the scenery and imagine how they sound.

In a good play, nothing is left to chance. Each character, change of scene, and line of dialogue is chosen carefully. Plays are more narrowly focused than novels and movies, with fewer characters, less action, and usually one dominant theme. Here are the main elements of drama.

Cast of Characters The list of a play's characters is found at the beginning of a play. The playwright might add the briefest description; for example: **Lord Capulet,** *Juliet's father.* When you are reading the play, refer back to the cast of characters as often as necessary until you are familiar with everyone.

Acts and Scenes An act is a large division of a full-length play, sometimes separated from the other act or acts by an intermission. A scene is a section of the play that occurs in one time and place. Each act may have one or several scenes. As you read a scene, try to visualize the set as well as the characters on the stage.

Dialogue Dialogue refers to the words that characters speak to each other. In drama, great characters are defined by the quality of their dialogue—the juicier, the better. In a script, a character's words directly follow his or her name. This manuscript style helps the actors learn and keep their lines straight. When you are reading a character's lines, try to imagine what that person looks like and how he or she might speak.

Stage Directions Stage directions are exactly that—instructions for the people who are putting on the play. The directions are usually printed in italic type. They describe the setting and tell actors where and how to move or say their lines. Some playwrights like to provide detailed descriptions of the scenery, lighting, costumes, and sound. Others leave such decisions for the play's director, actors, and production crew. Don't skip the stage directions when you are reading a play—they provide valuable information about the playwright's intent.

UNDERSTANDING POETRY

A poem expresses ideas and feelings in a compact form. To get to the heart of a poem's meaning, ask yourself questions like these:

- Who is writing this, and to whom? What does the title mean, and what is the **subject**? What is the **setting**?
- What **word choices** does the poet make? Might some words be **symbols**?
- What **imagery**, or word pictures, does the poem contain?
- What **theme** does it all suggest—what central idea?
- What **sound devices** occur?

When you first look at a poem, notice its shape. Unlike prose, a poem's lines don't always stop or start at the margins of a standard page. Where each line ends is a clue to how it is supposed to sound. A poem is often made up of **stanzas**: rhythmical units of lines. The stanzas in a poem generally have lines with a similar rhyme pattern.

Rhyme refers to identical or similar sounds that are repeated (hat/cat/rat). Rhymes are the music of poetry, a source of play for the poet and delight for the reader. And while rhyme is an important feature of older verse, many modern poems do not have any rhyme at all.

Rhythm means a repeated pattern of beats or accents ("SHE sells SEA shells, DOWN by the SEA shore").

Comparisons are important to poetry, especially **personification, metaphors**, and **similes**. This **figurative language** allows words to mean something other than their literal definition. A rose is almost never just a rose in poetry. When in bloom, it may be compared to a sweetheart's beauty. And when it is withered, poetically speaking, it may refer to death.

After considering the words and meaning of any poem, you need to look at its "mechanics." **Sound devices** are techniques used to create rhythm and emphasize certain sounds in a poem. Some of the most common include:

- **Alliteration** The repetition of similar letters or sounds at the beginning of close words. Peter Piper picked a peck of pickled peppers. Warm, wet, walks are wonderful.
- **Assonance** The repetition of vowel sounds in stressed syllables. The time is ripe for this assignment.
- **Consonance** The repetition of consonant sounds in stressed syllables. Brad had a hard head. Stir the batter, mother.
- **Onomatopoeia** A word that imitates the sound it represents. Buzz, whiz, shush, kerplunk.
- **Repetition** The technique of using repeated elements in a poem to give it rhythm. A **refrain** is a repeated line or a stanza.

Rites of Passage

He looked down into the blue well of water. He knew he must find his way through that cave, or hole, or tunnel, and out the other side.

Doris Lessing, from "Through the Tunnel"

TOWARDS THE HILL, Ken Danby, 1967

1

BEFORE YOU READ

The Bass, the River, and Sheila Mant

Oranges

Meet the Authors

W. D. Wetherell Wetherell was born in 1948. He lives with his family in Lyme, New Hampshire, near the banks of the Connecticut River—the river that forms the border between New Hampshire and Vermont, the river in the story "The Bass, the River, and Sheila Mant." He has written several books—novels, collections of short stories, nonfiction—as well as travel articles that have appeared in *The New York Times*. His lifelong fondness for the Connecticut River inspired him to create the anthology *This American River: Five Centuries of Writing About the Connecticut River*. He is also active in local and regional efforts to protect the river.

Gary Soto Mexican American writer and poet Gary Soto (born 1952) grew up in a poor neighborhood in Fresno, California. He turned to writing when he was a freshman at Fresno State University, where he discovered the power of contemporary writers and poets. He has never stopped writing. One of his most recent projects is a collection of love poems for adolescents called *Partly Cloudy: Poems of Love and Longing*. For more on Gary Soto, see page 390.

Build Background: Coming-of-Age Stories

In a coming-of-age story, the main character undergoes an adventure or some inner struggle that is part of the character's growth and development. Sometimes the adventures are violent and teach cruel lessons about how the world works. Sometimes the struggles are internal, involving only the character, the choices he or she makes, and lessons learned as a result of the choices.

The story you are about to read is a coming-of-age story. In it, a fourteen-year-old boy experiences a dramatic but hidden struggle between something he cares about and something he thinks he wants.

- At what times have you hidden your own feelings or interests because you were afraid of what others might think?

- Think of times you have been torn between something you always enjoyed as a child and some new interest.

The Bass, the River, and Sheila Mant

W. D. WETHERELL

THE BASS, THE RIVER, AND SHEILA MANT

W. D. Wetherell

There was a summer in my life when the only creature that seemed lovelier to me than a largemouth bass was Sheila Mant. I was fourteen. The Mants had rented the cottage next to ours on the river; with their parties, their frantic games of softball, their constant comings and goings, they appeared to me **denizens** of a brilliant existence.

denizens
inhabitants

"Too noisy by half," my mother quickly decided, but I would have given anything to be invited to one of their parties, and when my parents went to bed I would sneak through the woods to their hedge and stare enchanted at the candlelit swirl of white dresses and bright, paisley skirts.

Sheila was the middle daughter—at seventeen, all but out of reach. She would spend her days sunbathing on a float my Uncle Sierbert had moored in their cove, and before July was over I had learned all her moods. If she lay flat on the diving board with her hand trailing idly in the water, she was **pensive**, not to be disturbed. On her side, her head propped up by her arm, she was observant, considering those around her with a look that seemed queenly and severe. Sitting up, arms tucked around her long, suntanned legs, she was approachable, but barely, and it was only in those glorious moments when she stretched herself prior to entering the water that her various suitors found the courage to come near.

pensive
dreamily
thoughtful

These were many. The Dartmouth heavyweight crew[1] would **scull** by her house on their way upriver, and I think all eight of them must have been in love with her at various times during the summer; the coxswain[2] would curse at them though his megaphone, but without effect—there was always a pause in their pace when they passed Sheila's float. I suppose to these **jaded** twenty-year-olds, she seemed the incarnation of innocence and youth, while to me she appeared unutterably suave, the **epitome** of sophistication. I was on the swim team at school, and to win her attention would do endless laps between my house and the Vermont shore, hoping she would notice the beauty of my

scull
row

jaded
made dull or
cynical by
experience

epitome
ideal example

---

1 **Dartmouth heavyweight crew:** one of the rowing teams at Dartmouth College

2 **coxswain:** team captain

Unit One Rites of Passage

flutter kick, the power of my crawl. Finishing, I would boost myself up onto our dock and glance casually over toward her, but she was never watching, and the miraculous day she was, I immediately climbed the diving board and did my best tuck and a half for her and continued diving until she had left and the sun went down, and my longing was like a madness and I couldn't stop.

It was late August by the time I got up the nerve to ask her out. The tortured will-I's, won't-I's, the agonized indecision over what to say, the false starts toward her house and embarrassed retreats—the details of these have been seared from my memory, and the only part I remember clearly is emerging from the woods toward dusk while they were playing softball on their lawn, as bashful and frightened as a unicorn.

Sheila was stationed halfway between first and second, well outside the infield. She didn't seem surprised to see me—as a matter of fact, she didn't seem to see me at all.

Sheila was stationed halfway between first and second, well outside the infield. She didn't seem surprised to see me—as a matter of fact, she didn't seem to see me at all.

"If you're playing second base, you should move closer," I said.

She turned—I took the full brunt of her long red hair and well-spaced freckles.

"I'm playing outfield," she said, "I don't like the responsibility of having a base."

"Yeah, I can understand that," I said, though I couldn't. "There's a band in Dixford tomorrow night at nine. Want to go?"

One of her brothers sent the ball sailing over the left fielder's head; she stood and watched it disappear toward the river.

"You have a car?" she said, without looking up.

I played my master stroke. "We'll go by canoe."

I spent all of the following day polishing it. I turned it upside down on our lawn and rubbed it with chamois until it gleamed as bright as aluminum ever gleamed. About five, I slid it in the water, arranging cushions near the bow so Sheila could lean on them if she was in one of her pensive moods, propping up my father's transistor radio by the middle thwart[3] so we could have music when we came back. Automatically, without thinking about it, I mounted my Mitchell reel on my Pfleuger spinning rod and stuck it in the stern.

---

3 **thwart:** seat in a canoe

I say automatically, because I never went anywhere that summer without a fishing rod. When I wasn't swimming laps to impress Sheila, I was back in our driveway practicing casts, and when I wasn't practicing casts, I was tying the line to Tosca, our springer spaniel, to test the reel's drag, and when I wasn't doing any of those things, I was fishing the river for bass.

Too nervous to sit at home, I got in the canoe early and started paddling in a huge circle that would get me to Sheila's dock around eight. As automatically as I brought along my rod, I tied on a big Rapala plug,[4] let it down into the water, let out some line and immediately forgot all about it.

It was already dark by the time I glided up to the Mants' dock. Even by day the river was quiet, most of the summer people preferring Sunapee or one of the other nearby lakes, and at night it was a solitude difficult to believe, a corridor of hidden life that ran between banks like a tunnel. Even the stars were part of it. They weren't as sharp anywhere else; they seemed to have chosen the river as a guide on their slow wheel toward morning, and in the course of the summer's fishing, I had learned all their names.

I was there ten minutes before Sheila appeared. I heard the slam of their screen door first, then saw her in the spotlight as she came slowly down the path. As beautiful as she was on the float, she was even lovelier now—her white dress went perfectly with her hair and complimented her figure even more than her swimsuit.

It was her face that bothered me. It had on its delightful fullness a very dubious expression.

"Look," she said. "I can get Dad's car."

"It's faster this way," I lied. "Parking's tense up there. Hey, it's safe. I won't tip it or anything."

She let herself down reluctantly into the bow. I was glad she wasn't facing me. When her eyes were on me, I felt like diving in the river again from agony and joy.

I pried the canoe away from the dock and started paddling upstream. There was an extra paddle in the bow, but Sheila made no move to pick it up. She took her shoes off and dangled her feet over the side.

Ten minutes went by.

---

4 **Rapala plug:** a popular lightweight fishing lure designed by Finnish fisherman Lauri Rapala

"What kind of band?" she said.

"It's sort of like folk music. You'll like it."

"Eric Caswell's going to be there. He strokes number four."

"No kidding?" I said. I had no idea who she meant.

"What's that sound?" she said, pointing toward shore.

"Bass. That splashing sound?"

"Over there."

"Yeah, bass. They come into the shallows at night to chase frogs and moths and things. Big largemouths. *Micropterus salmoides*,"[5] I added, showing off.

"I think fishing's dumb," she said, making a face. "I mean, it's boring and all. Definitely dumb."

Now I have spent a great deal of time in the years since wondering why Sheila Mant should come down so hard on fishing. Was her father a fisherman? Her **antipathy** toward fishing nothing more than normal **filial** rebellion? Had she tried it once? A messy encounter with worms? It doesn't matter. What does, is that at that fragile moment in time I would have given anything not to appear dumb in Sheila's severe and unforgiving eyes.

She hadn't seen my equipment yet. What I *should* have done, of course, was push the canoe in closer to shore and carefully slide the rod into some branches where I could pick it up again in the morning. Failing that, I could have **surreptitiously** dumped the whole outfit overboard, written off the forty or so dollars as love's tribute. What I actually *did* do was gently lean forward and slowly, ever so slowly, push the rod back through my legs toward the stern where it would be less conspicuous.

It must have been just exactly what the bass was waiting for. Fish will trail a lure sometimes, trying to make up their mind whether or not to attack, and the slight pause in the plug's speed caused by my adjustment was tantalizing enough to overcome the bass's inhibitions. My rod, safely out of sight at last, bent double. The line, tightly coiled, peeled off the spool with the shrill, tearing rip of a high-speed drill.

Four things occurred to me at once. One, that it was a bass. Two, that it was a big bass. Three, that it was the biggest bass I had ever hooked. Four, that Sheila Mant must not know.

antipathy
distaste

filial
befitting of a son or daughter

surreptitiously
in a way intended to escape observation

---

5 *Micropterus salmoides:* the species name for largemouth bass. *Micropterus*, from Greek, means "small fin"; *salmoides*, from Latin, means "trout-like."

"What was that?" she said, turning half around.

"Uh, what was what?"

"That buzzing noise."

"Bats."

She shuddered, quickly drew her feet back into the canoe. Every instinct I had told me to pick up the rod and strike back at the bass, but there was no need to—it was already solidly hooked. Downstream, an awesome distance downstream, it jumped clear of the water, landing with a concussion heavy enough to ripple the entire river. For a moment, I thought it was gone, but then the rod was bending again, the tip dancing into the water. Slowly, not making any motion that might alert Sheila, I reached down to tighten the drag.

While all this was going on, Sheila had begun talking, and it was a few minutes before I was able to catch up with her train of thought.

"I went to a party there. These fraternity men. Katherine says I could get in there if I wanted. I'm thinking more of UVM or Bennington.[6] Somewhere I can ski."

The bass was slanting toward the rocks on the New Hampshire side by the ruins of Donaldson's boathouse. It had to be an old bass—a young one probably wouldn't have known the rocks were there. I brought the canoe back out into the middle of the river, hoping to head it off.

"That's neat," I mumbled. "Skiing. Yeah, I can see that."

"Eric said I have the figure to model, but I thought I should get an education first. I mean, it might be a while before I get started and all. I was thinking of getting my hair styled, more swept back? I mean, Ann-Margret?[7] Like hers, only shorter."

---

6 **UVM or Bennington:** University of Vermont or Bennington College, also in Vermont

7 **Ann-Margret:** a popular red-haired actress in the 1960s and 1970s

She hesitated. "Are we going backwards?"

We were. I had managed to keep the bass in the middle of the river away from the rocks, but it had plenty of room there and for the first time a chance to exert its full strength. I quickly computed the weight necessary to draw a fully loaded canoe backwards—the thought of it made me feel faint.

"It's just the current," I said hoarsely. "No sweat or anything." I dug in deeper with my paddle.

Reassured, Sheila began talking about something else, but all my attention was taken up now with the fish. I could feel its desperation as the water grew shallower. I could sense the extra strain on the line, the frantic way it cut back and forth in the water. I could visualize what it looked like—the gape of its mouth, the flared gills and thick, vertical tail. The bass couldn't have encountered many forces in its long life that it wasn't capable of handling, and the unrelenting tug at its mouth must have been a source of great puzzlement and mounting panic.

Me, I had problems of my own. To get to Dixford, I had to paddle up a sluggish stream that came into the river beneath a covered bridge. There was a shallow sandbar at the mouth of this stream—weeds on one side, rocks on the other. Without doubt, this is where I would lose the fish.

Me, I had problems of my own. To get to Dixford, I had to paddle up a sluggish stream that came into the river beneath a covered bridge.

"I have to be careful with my complexion. I tan, but in segments. I can't figure out if it's even worth it. I wouldn't even do it probably. I saw Jackie Kennedy in Boston, and she wasn't tan at all."

Taking a deep breath, I paddled as hard as I could for the middle, deepest part of the bar. I could have threaded the eye of a needle with the canoe, but the pull on the stern threw me off and I overcompensated—the canoe veered left and scraped bottom. I pushed the paddle down and shoved. A moment of hesitation . . . a moment more . . . . The canoe shot clear into the deeper water of the stream. I immediately looked down at the rod. It was bent in the same, tight arc—miraculously, the bass was still on.

The moon was out now. It was low and full enough that its beam shone directly on Sheila there ahead of me in the canoe, washing her in a creamy, luminous glow. I could see the lithe, easy shape of her figure. I could see the way her hair curled down off her shoulders, the proud, alert tilt of her head, and all these things were as a tug on my heart. Not just Sheila but the aura she carried about her of parties and casual touchings and grace. Behind me, I could feel the strain of the bass, steadier now, growing weaker, and this was another tug on my heart, not just the bass but the beat of the river and the slant of the stars and the smell of the night, until finally it seemed I would be torn apart between longings, split in half. Twenty yards ahead of us was the road, and once I pulled the canoe up on shore, the bass would be gone, irretrievably gone. If instead I stood up, grabbed the rod, and started pumping, I would have it—as tired as the bass was, there was no chance it could get away. I reached down for the rod, hesitated, looked up to where Sheila was stretching herself lazily toward the sky, her small breasts rising beneath the soft fabric of her dress, and the tug was too much for me, and quicker than it takes to write it down, I pulled a penknife from my pocket and cut the line in half.

With a sick, nauseous feeling in my stomach, I saw the rod unbend.

"My legs are sore," Sheila whined. "Are we there yet?"

Through a superhuman effort of self-control, I was able to beach the canoe and help Sheila off. The rest of the night is much foggier. We walked to the fair—there was the smell of popcorn, the sound of guitars. I may have danced once or twice with her, but all I really remember is her coming over to me once the music was done to explain that she would be going home in Eric Caswell's Corvette.

"Okay," I mumbled.

For the first time that night she looked at me, really looked at me.

"You're a funny kid, you know that?"

Funny. Different. Dreamy. Odd. How many times was I to hear that in the years to come, all spoken with the same quizzical, half-accusatory tone Sheila used then. Poor Sheila! Before the month was over, the spell she cast over me was gone, but the memory of that lost bass haunted me all summer and haunts me still. There would be other Sheila Mants in my life, other fish, and though I came close once or twice, it was these secret, hidden tuggings in the night that claimed me, and I never made the same mistake again.

Oranges GARY SOTO

The first time I walked
With a girl, I was twelve,
Cold, and weighted down
With two oranges in my jacket.
December. Frost cracking   5
Beneath my steps, my breath
Before me, then gone,
As I walked toward
Her house, the one whose
Porch light burned yellow   10
Night and day, in any weather.
A dog barked at me, until
She came out pulling
At her gloves, face bright
With rouge. I smiled,   15
Touched her shoulder, and led
Her down the street, across
A used car lot and a line
Of newly planted trees,
Until we were breathing   20
Before a drugstore. We
Entered, the tiny bell
Bringing a saleslady
Down a narrow aisle of goods.
I turned to the candies   25
Tiered like bleachers,
And asked what she wanted—
Light in her eyes, a smile
Starting at the corners

Of her mouth. I fingered   30
A nickel in my pocket,
And when she lifted a chocolate
That cost a dime,
I didn't say anything.
I took the nickel from   35
My pocket, then an orange,
And set them quietly on
The counter. When I looked up,
The lady's eyes met mine,
And held them, knowing   40
Very well what it was all
About.

Outside,
A few cars hissing past,
Fog hanging like old   45
Coats between the trees.
I took my girl's hand
In mine for two blocks,
Then released it to let
Her unwrap the chocolate.   50
I peeled my orange
That was so bright against
The gray of December
That, from some distance,
Someone might have thought   55
I was making a fire in my hands.

AFTER YOU READ
The Bass, the River, and Sheila Mant / Oranges

Think and Discuss

1. Wetherell wrote, "A story isn't about a moment in time, a story is about *the* moment in time." Which moment in time is this story about?

2. The passage from childhood to adulthood involves learning many lessons—about yourself, about others, and about the world. What lesson does the main character learn in "The Bass, the River, and Sheila Mant"?

3. Think about the two **characters** in the story: the narrator and Sheila Mant. In your Writer's Notebook, create a character map similar to the one below for each character. You may find you need to add more traits for the narrator's map and fewer for Sheila's map.

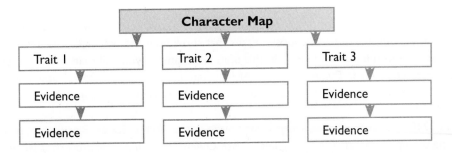

4. "The Bass, the River, and Sheila Mant" is a **first-person narrative**. What are the advantages of having the main character tell his own story?

5. Think about times you have you faced a choice between two appealing options. What and how did you choose?

6. What "rite of passage" do both "The Bass, the River, and Sheila Mant" and "Oranges" represent?

Write to Understand: Character Sketch

Use your character map for the narrator to write a character sketch. Your sketch should tell the most important traits of the narrator and how these traits are revealed through his thoughts and actions. When you've finished your character sketch, exchange your work with a partner. Discuss any differences in the traits you and your partner identified.

BEFORE YOU READ

from *I Know Why the Caged Bird Sings*

Meet the Author: Maya Angelou

Maya Angelou was born Marguerite Johnson in 1928. At the age of three, she was sent to live with her grandmother in Stamps, Arkansas. There she learned what it was like to be an African American girl in a world controlled by whites. She wrote about that world in her first work of literature, *I Know Why the Caged Bird Sings*, from which the selection that follows was taken. Angelou has written five other autobiographical works, as well as poetry, plays, and essays. In 1993, in rhythmic tones that reflected her background as a dancer, Angelou read her poem "On the Pulse of the Morning" at the inauguration of President Bill Clinton. She became only the second poet in U.S. history to recite an original work at a presidential inauguration.

Build Background: Setting in Autobiography

What makes you who you are? Certainly genetic background plays a role, as does family environment. People's identities are also tied to the time and place in which they grow up, so writers of autobiographies choose details that show how the time and place influenced them as they formed their identity. In this unit, for example, you will read autobiographical selections set vividly in Los Angeles and Afghanistan in the 1990s, in a dingy basement in a small Minnesota town in the 1950s and, in the selection that follows, in Arkansas in the year 1940.

In 1940, the races were still largely separated in the United States. Black athletes were among the first to cross the "color line." Jesse Owens, the runner who brought glory to the United States at the 1936 Olympics, and Joe Louis, the heavyweight champion boxer, were national heroes for both black and white America. But in other fields of endeavor, most African Americans remained locked out.

- What else do you know about racial segregation and the South in 1940?

- In what ways might the time and place of your growing up set limits on your future?

Actress Constance Good in the 1978 movie *I Know Why the Caged Bird Sings*

from *I Know Why the Caged Bird Sings*

MAYA ANGELOU

from *I KNOW WHY THE CAGED BIRD SINGS*

Maya Angelou

This book is dedicated to
MY SON, GUY JOHNSON,
And all the strong
black birds of promise
who defy the odds and gods
and sing their songs

The children in Stamps trembled visibly with anticipation. Some adults were excited too, but to be certain the whole young population had come down with graduation epidemic. Large classes were graduating from both the grammar school and the high school. Even those who were years removed from their own day of glorious release were anxious to help with preparations as a kind of dry run. The junior students who were moving into the vacating classes' chairs were tradition-bound to show their talents for leadership and management. They strutted through the school and around the campus exerting pressure on the lower grades. Their authority was so new that occasionally if they pressed a little too hard it had to be overlooked. After all, next term was coming, and it never hurt a sixth grader to have a play sister in the eighth grade, or a tenth-year student to be able to call a twelfth grader Bubba. So all was endured in a spirit of shared understanding. But the graduation classes themselves were the nobility. Like travelers with exotic destinations on their minds, the graduates were remarkably forgetful. They came to school without their books, or tablets or even pencils. Volunteers fell over themselves to secure replacements for the missing equipment. When accepted, the willing workers might or might not be thanked, and it was of no importance to the pregraduation rites. Even teachers were respectful of the now quiet and aging seniors, and tended to speak to them, if not as equals, as beings only slightly lower than themselves. After tests were returned and grades given, the student body, which acted like an extended family, knew who did well, who excelled, and what piteous ones had failed.

Unlike the white high school, Lafayette County Training School distinguished itself by having neither lawn, nor hedges, nor tennis court, nor climbing ivy. Its two buildings (main classrooms, the grade school and home economics) were set on a dirt hill with no fence to limit either its boundaries or those of bordering farms. There was a large expanse to the left of the school which was used alternately as a baseball diamond or a basketball court. Rusty hoops on the swaying poles represented the permanent recreational equipment, although bats and balls could be borrowed from the P.E. teacher if the borrower was qualified and if the diamond wasn't occupied.

Over this rocky area relieved by a few shady tall persimmon trees the graduating class walked. The girls often held hands and no longer bothered to speak to the lower students. There was a sadness about them, as if this old world was not their home and they were bound for higher ground. The boys, on the other hand, had become more friendly, more outgoing. A decided change from the closed attitude they projected while studying for finals. Now they seemed not ready to give up the old school, the familiar paths and classrooms. Only a small percentage would be continuing on to college—one of the South's A & M (agricultural and mechanical) schools, which trained Negro youths to be carpenters, farmers, handymen, masons, maids, cooks and baby nurses. Their future rode heavily on their shoulders, and blinded them to the collective joy that had **pervaded** the lives of the boys and girls in the grammar school graduating class.

pervaded
spread
through every
part

Parents who could afford it had ordered new shoes and ready-made clothes for themselves from Sears and Roebuck or Montgomery Ward.[1] They also engaged the best seamstresses to make the floating graduating dresses and to cut down second-hand pants which would be pressed to a military slickness for the important event.

Oh, it was important, all right. Whitefolks would attend the ceremony, and two or three would speak of God and home, and the Southern way of life, and Mrs. Parsons, the principal's wife, would play the graduation march while the lower-grade graduates paraded down the aisles and took their seats below the platform. The high school seniors would wait in empty classrooms to make their dramatic entrance.

---

1 **Sears and Roebuck or Montgomery Ward:** two important mail-order houses in the United States from whose catalogs people could order, by mail, everything from clothing to housewares and farm equipment

In the Store I was the person of the moment. The birthday girl. The center. Bailey[2] had graduated the year before, although to do so he had had to forfeit all pleasures to make up for his time lost in Baton Rouge.

My class was wearing butter-yellow piqué dresses, and Momma launched out on mine. She smocked the yoke into tiny crisscrossing puckers, then shirred the rest of the **bodice**. Her dark fingers ducked in and out of the lemony cloth as she embroidered raised daises around the hem. Before she considered herself finished she had added a crocheted cuff on the puff sleeves, and a pointy crocheted collar.

bodice
the upper part
of a dress

I was going to be lovely. A walking model of all the various styles of fine hand sewing and it didn't worry me that I was only twelve years old and merely graduating from the eighth grade. Besides, many teachers in Arkansas Negro schools had only that diploma and were licensed to impart wisdom.

The days had become longer and more noticeable. The faded beige of former times had been replaced with strong and sure colors. I began to see my classmates' clothes, their skin tones, and the dust that waved off pussy willows. Clouds that lazed across the sky were objects of great concern to me. Their shiftier shapes might have held a message that in my new happiness and with a little bit of time I'd soon **decipher**. During that period I looked at the arch of heaven so religiously my neck kept a steady ache. I had taken to smiling more often, and my jaws hurt from the unaccustomed activity. Between the two physical sore spots, I suppose I could have been uncomfortable, but that was not the case. As a member of the winning team (the graduating class of 1940) I had outdistanced unpleasant sensations by miles. I was headed for the freedom of open fields.

decipher
decode;
understand
something
puzzling

Youth and social approval allied themselves with me and we **trammeled** memories of slights and insults. The wind of our swift passage remodeled my features. Lost tears were pounded to mud and then to dust. Years of withdrawal were brushed aside and left behind, as hanging ropes of **parasitic** moss.

trammeled
confined or
restrained

My work alone had awarded me a top place and I was going to be one of the first called in the graduating ceremonies. On the classroom blackboard, as well as on the bulletin board in the auditorium, there were blue stars and white stars and red stars. No absences, no tardinesses, and

parasitic
living in or
on another
organism

---

2 **Bailey:** her brother

Unit One   Rites of Passage

my academic work was among the best of the year. I could say the preamble to the Constitution even faster than Bailey. We timed ourselves often: "WethepeopleoftheUnitedStatesinordertoformamoreperfectunion . . ." I had memorized the Presidents of the United States from Washington to Roosevelt in chronological as well as alphabetical order.

My hair pleased me too. Gradually the black mass had lengthened and thickened, so that it kept at last to its braided pattern, and I didn't have to yank my scalp off when I tried to comb it.

Louise and I had rehearsed the exercises until we tired out ourselves. Henry Reed was class valedictorian. He was a small, very black boy with hooded eyes, and long, broad nose and an oddly shaped head. I had admired him for years because each term he and I vied for the best grades in our class. Most often he bested me, but instead of being disappointed I was pleased that we shared top places between us. Like many Southern Black children, he lived with his grandmother, who was as strict as Momma and as kind as she knew how to be. He was courteous, respectful and soft-spoken to elders, but on the playground he chose to play the roughest games. I admired him. Anyone, I reckoned, sufficiently afraid or sufficiently dull could be polite. But to be able to operate at a top level both with adults and children was admirable.

His valedictory speech was entitled "To Be or Not to Be." The rigid tenth-grade teacher had helped him write it. He'd been working on the dramatic stresses for months.

His valedictory speech was entitled "To Be or Not to Be." The rigid tenth-grade teacher had helped him write it.

The weeks until graduation were filled with heady activities. A group of small children were to be presented in a play about buttercups and daisies and bunny rabbits. They could be heard throughout the building practicing their hops and their little songs that sounded like silver bells. The older girls (nongraduates, of course) were assigned the task of making refreshments for the night's festivities. A tangy scent of ginger, cinnamon, nutmeg and chocolate wafted around the home economics building as the budding cooks made samples for themselves and their teachers.

In every corner of the workshop, axes and saws split fresh timber as the woodshop boys made sets and stage scenery. Only the graduates were left out of the general bustle. We were free to sit in the library at the back of the building or look in quite detachedly, naturally, on the measures being taken for our event.

Even the minister preached on graduation the Sunday before. His subject was, "Let your light so shine that men will see your good works and praise your Father, Who is in Heaven." Although the sermon was purported to be addressed to us, he used the occasion to speak to backsliders, gamblers and general ne'er-do-wells. But since he had called our names at the beginning of the service we were **mollified**.

mollified
calmed; soothed

Among Negroes the tradition was to give presents to children going only from one grade to another. How much more important this was when the person was graduating at the top of the class. Uncle Willie and Momma had sent away for a Mickey Mouse watch like Bailey's. Louise gave me four embroidered handkerchiefs. (I gave her three crocheted doilies.) Mrs. Sneed, the minister's wife, made me an underskirt to wear for graduation, and nearly every customer gave me a nickel or maybe even a dime with the instruction "Keep on moving to higher ground," or some such encouragement.

Amazingly the great day finally dawned and I was out of bed before I knew it. I threw open the back door to see it more clearly, but Momma said, "Sister, come away from that door and put your robe on."

I hoped the memory of that morning would never leave me. Sunlight was itself still young, and the day had none of the insistence maturity would bring it in a few hours. In my robe and barefoot in the backyard . . . I gave myself up to the gentle warmth and thanked God that no matter what evil I had done in my life He had allowed me to live to see this day. Somewhere in my **fatalism** I had expected to die, accidentally, and never have the chance to walk up the stairs in the auditorium and gracefully receive my hard-earned diploma. Out of God's merciful bosom I had won reprieve.

fatalism
belief that events are predetermined and humans are powerless to change them

Bailey came out in his robe and gave me a box wrapped in Christmas paper. He said he had saved his money for months to pay for it. It felt like a box of chocolates, but I knew Bailey wouldn't save money to buy candy when we had all we could want under our noses.

He was as proud of the gift as I. It was a soft-leather-bound copy of a collection of poems by Edgar Allan Poe, or, as Bailey and I called him, "Eap."

I turned to "Annabel Lee" and we walked up and down the garden rows, the cool dirt between our toes, reciting the beautifully sad lines.

Momma made a Sunday breakfast although it was only Friday. After we finished the blessing, I opened my eyes to find the watch on my plate. It was a dream of a day. Everything went smoothly and to my credit. I didn't have to be reminded or scolded for anything. Near evening I was too jittery to attend to chores, so Bailey volunteered to do all before his bath.

Days before, we had made a sign for the Store, and as we turned out the lights Momma hung the cardboard over the doorknob. It read clearly: CLOSED. GRADUATION.

Momma made a Sunday breakfast although it was only Friday. After we finished the blessing, I opened my eyes to find the watch on my plate. It was a dream of a day.

My dress fitted perfectly and everyone said that I looked like a sunbeam in it. On the hill, going toward the school, Bailey walked behind with Uncle Willie, who muttered, "Go on, Ju." He wanted him to walk ahead with us because it embarrassed him to have to walk so slowly. Bailey said he'd let the ladies walk together, and the men would bring up the rear. We laughed, nicely.

Little children dashed by out of the dark like fireflies. Their crepe-paper dresses and butterfly wings were not made for running and we heard more than one rip, dryly, and the regretful "uh uh" that followed.

The school blazed without gaiety. The windows seemed cold and unfriendly from the lower hill. A sense of ill-fated timing crept over me, and if Momma hadn't reached for my hand I would have drifted back to Bailey and Uncle Willie, and possibly beyond. She made a few slow jokes about my feet getting cold, and tugged me along to the now-strange building.

Around the front steps, assurance came back. There were my fellow "greats," the graduating class. Hair brushed back, legs oiled, new dresses and pressed pleats, fresh pocket handkerchiefs and little handbags, all homesewn. Oh, we were up to snuff, all right. I joined my comrades and didn't even see my family go in to find seats in the crowded auditorium.

The school band struck up a march and all classes filed in as had been rehearsed. We stood in front of our seats, as assigned, and on a signal from the choir director, we sat. No sooner had this been accomplished than the band started to play the national anthem. We rose again and sang the song, after which we recited the pledge of allegiance. We remained standing for a brief minute before the choir director and the principal signaled to us, rather desperately I thought, to take our seats. The command was so unusual that our carefully rehearsed and smooth-running machine was thrown off. For a full minute we fumbled for our chairs and bumped into each other awkwardly. Habits change or solidify under pressure, so in our state of nervous tension we had been ready to follow our usual assembly pattern: the American national anthem, then the pledge of allegiance, then the song every Black person I knew called the Negro National Anthem. All done in the same key, with the same passion and most often standing on the same foot.

> *T*he command was so unusual that our carefully rehearsed and smooth-running machine was thrown off.

Finding my seat at least, I was overcome with a **presentiment** of worse things to come. Something unrehearsed, unplanned, was going to happen, and we were going to be made to look bad. I distinctly remember being explicit in the choice of pronoun. It was "we," the graduating class, the unit, that concerned me then.

presentiment
feeling that something is about to happen

The principal welcomed "parents and friends" and asked the Baptist minister to lead us in prayer. His **invocation** was brief and punchy, and for a second I thought we were getting back on the high road to right action. When the principal came back to the dais,[3] however, his voice had changed. Sounds always affected me profoundly and the principal's voice was one of my favorites. During assembly it melted and lowed weakly into the audience. It had not been in my plan to listen to him, but my curiosity was **piqued** and I straightened up to give him my attention.

invocation
a calling upon in prayer

piqued
stirred up; aroused

He was talking about Booker T. Washington, our "late great leader," who said we can be as close as the fingers on the hand, etc. . . . Then he said a few vague things about friendship and the friendship of kindly people to those less fortunate than themselves. With that his voice nearly faded, thin, away. Like a river diminishing to a steam and then to a trickle. But he cleared his throat and said, "Our speaker tonight, who is also our friend, came from Texarkana to deliver the commencement address, but due to the irregularity of

---

3 **dais:** a raised platform, especially for speakers

the train schedule, he's going to, as they say, 'speak and run.'" He said that we understood and wanted the man to know that we were most grateful for the time he was able to give us and then something about how we were willing always to adjust to another's program, and without more ado—"I give you Mr. Edward Donleavy."

Not one but two white men came though the door offstage. The shorter one walked to the speaker's platform, and the tall one moved over to the center seat and sat down. But that was our principal's seat, and already occupied. The dislodged gentleman bounced around for a long breath or two before the Baptist minister gave him his chair, then with more dignity than the situation deserved, the minister walked off the stage.

Donleavy looked at the audience once (on reflection, I'm sure that he wanted only to reassure himself that we were really there), adjusted his glasses and began to read from a sheaf of papers.

He was glad "to be here and to see the work going on just as it was in the other schools."

At the first "Amen" from the audience I willed the offender to immediate death by choking on the word. But Amen's and Yes sir's began to fall around the room like rain through a ragged umbrella.

He told us of the wonderful changes we children in Stamps had in store. The Central School (naturally, the white school was Central) had already been granted improvements that would be in use in the fall. A well-known artist was coming from Little Rock to teach art to them. They were going to have the newest microscopes and chemistry equipment for their laboratory. Mr. Donleavy didn't leave us long in the dark over who made these improvements available to Central High. Nor were we to be ignored in the general betterment scheme he had in mind.

He said that he had pointed out to people at a very high level that one of the first-line football tacklers at Arkansas Agricultural and Mechanical College had graduated from good old Lafayette County Training School. Here fewer Amen's were heard. Those few that did break through lay dully in the air with the heaviness of habit.

He went on to praise us. He went on to say how he had bragged that "one of the best basketball players at Fisk sank his first ball right here at Lafayette Training School."

The white kids were going to have a chance to become Galileos and Madame Curies and Edisons and Gauguins,[4] and our boys (the girls weren't even in on it) would try to be Jesse Owenses and Joe Louises.

Owens and the Brown Bomber were great heroes in our world, but what school official in the white-goddom of Little Rock had the right to decide that those two men must be our only heroes? Who decided that for Henry Reed to become a scientist he had to work like George Washington Carver, as a bootblack, to buy a lousy microscope? Bailey was obviously always going to be too small to be an athlete, so which concrete angel glued to what country seat had decided that if my brother wanted to become a lawyer he had to first pay penance for his skin by picking cotton and hoeing corn and studying correspondence books at night for twenty years?

Who decided that for Henry Reed to become a scientist he had to work like George Washington Carver, as a bootblack, to buy a lousy microscope?

The man's dead words fell like bricks around the auditorium and too many settled in my belly. Constrained by hard-learned manners I couldn't look behind me, but to my left and right the proud graduating class of 1940 had dropped their heads. Every girl in my row had found something new to do with her handkerchief. Some folded the tiny squares into love knots, some into triangles, but most were wadding them, then pressing them flat on their yellow laps.

On the dais, the ancient tragedy was being replayed. Professor Parsons sat, a sculptor's reject, rigid. His large, heavy body seemed devoid of will or willingness, and his eyes said he was no longer with us. The other teachers examined the flag (which was draped stage right) or their notes, or the windows which opened on our now-famous playing diamond.

---

4 **Galileos and Madame Curies and Edisons and Gauguins:** Galileo was an Italian astronomer whose observations in 1610 led him to believe that the sun, not the earth, was the center of the solar system. Madame Curie was a pioneer in the discovery of radioactive elements. Thomas Edison was a 19th-century American inventor of many electrical items, including the light bulb. Gauguin was an early 20th-century French painter who lived in the Polynesian islands. All are highly respected for their intellectual and creative accomplishments.

Graduation, the hush-hush magic time of frills and gifts and congratulations and diplomas, was finished for me before my name was called. The accomplishment was nothing. The meticulous maps, drawn in three colors of ink, learning and spelling decasyllabic[5] words, memorizing the whole of *The Rape of Lucrece*[6]—it was for nothing. Donleavy had exposed us.

We were maids and farmers, handymen and washerwomen, and anything higher that we aspired to was **farcical** and **presumptuous**.

Then I wished that Gabriel Prosser and Nat Turner[7] had killed all white folks in their beds and that Abraham Lincoln had been assassinated before the signing of the Emancipation Proclamation, and that Harriet Tubman[8] had been killed by that blow on her head and Christopher Columbus had drowned in the *Santa Mariá*.

It was awful to be Negro and have no control over my life. It was brutal to be young and already trained to sit quietly and listen to charges brought against my color with no chance of defense. We should all be dead. I thought I should like to see us all dead, one on top of the other. A pyramid of flesh with the white folks on the bottom, as the broad base, then the Indians with their silly tomahawks and teepees and wigwams and treaties, the Negroes with their mops and recipes and cotton sacks and spirituals sticking out of their mouths. The Dutch children should all stumble in their wooden shoes and break their necks. The French should choke to death on the Louisiana Purchase (1803) while silk worms ate all the Chinese with their stupid pigtails. As a species, we were an **abomination**. All of us.

Donleavy was running for election, and assured our parents that if he won we could count on having the only colored paved playing field in that part of Arkansas. Also—he never looked up to acknowledge the grunts of acceptance—also, we were bound to get some new equipment for the home economics building and the workshop.

He finished, and since there was no need to give any more than the most **perfunctory** thank-you's, he nodded to the men on the stage, and the tall white man who was never introduced joined him at the door. They left

farcical
silly; absurd

presumptuous
too bold; inappropriate

abomination
something worthy of disgust or hatred

perfunctory
superficial or routine

---

5 **decasyllabic:** made up of 10 syllables

6 *The Rape of Lucrece:* a long poem by William Shakespeare

7 **Gabriel Prosser and Nat Turner:** slaves who led rebellions

8 **Harriet Tubman:** an escaped slave who led over 70 other slaves to freedom in Canada

from *I Know Why the Caged Bird Sings*   25

Maya Angelou, 2005

with the attitude that now they were off to something really important. (The graduation ceremonies at Lafayette County Training School had been a mere preliminary.)

palpable
able to be felt

The ugliness they left was **palpable**. An uninvited guest who wouldn't leave. The choir was summoned and sang a modern arrangement of "Onward, Christian Soldiers," with new words pertaining to graduates seeking their place in the world. But it didn't work. Elouise, the daughter of the Baptist minister,

impertinence
irrelevance

recited "Invictus,"[9] and I could have cried at the **impertinence** of "I am the master of my fate, I am the captain of my soul."

My name had lost its ring of familiarity and I had to be nudged to go and receive my diploma. All my preparations had fled. I neither marched up to the stage like a conquering Amazon, nor did I look in the audience for Bailey's nod of approval. Marguerite Johnson, I heard the name again, my honors were read, there were noises in the audience of appreciation, and I took my place on the stage as rehearsed.

I thought about colors I hated: ecru, puce, lavender, beige and black. There was shuffling and rustling around me, then Henry Reed was giving the valedictory address, "To Be or Not to Be." Hadn't he heard the whitefolks? We couldn't *be*, so the question was a waste of time. Henry's voice came out clear

9 **Invictus:** a short poem, first published in 1875, by British poet William Ernest Henley. The title is Latin for "unconquered."

and strong. I feared to look at him. Hadn't he got the message? There was no "nobler in the mind" for Negroes because the world didn't think we had minds, and they let us know it. "Outrageous fortune"? Now, that was a joke. When the ceremony was over I had to tell Henry Reed some things. That is, if I still cared. Not "rub," Henry, "erase." "Ah, there's the erase."[10] Us.

Henry had been a good student in elocution. His voice rose on tides of promise and fell on waves of warnings. The English teacher had helped him to create a sermon winging through Hamlet's soliloquy. To be a man, a doer, a builder, a leader, or to be a tool, an unfunny joke, a crusher of funky toadstools. I marveled that Henry could go through with the speech as if we had a choice.

I had been listening and silently **rebutting** each sentence with my eyes closed; then there was a hush, which in an audience warns that something unplanned is happening. I looked up and saw Henry Reed, the conservative, the proper, the A student, turn his back to the audience and turn to us (the proud graduating class of 1940) and sing, nearly speaking,

rebutting
contradicting; furnishing a counterproof

> "Lift ev'ry voice and sing
> Till earth and heaven ring
> Ring with the harmonies of Liberty . . . "

It was the poem written by James Weldon Johnson. It was the music composed by J. Rosamond Johnson. It was the Negro National Anthem. Out of habit we were singing it.

Our mothers and fathers stood in the dark hall and joined the hymn of encouragement. A kindergarten teacher led the small children onto the stage and buttercups and daisies and bunny rabbits marked time and tried to follow:

> "Stony the road we trod
> Bitter the chastening rod
> Felt in the days when hope, unborn, had died.
> Yet with a steady beat
> Have not our weary feet
> Come to the place for which our fathers sighed?"

---

10 **"Ah, there's the erase":** The valedictory address is based on a speech from Shakespeare's play *Hamlet*, which includes the lines: "Whether 'tis nobler in the mind to suffer / The slings and arrows of outrageous fortune" and "To sleep: perchance to dream: ay, there the rub." The word *rub* in this context means "problem"; Maya Angelou takes it to be a synonym for *erase*.

Every child I knew had learned that song with his ABC's and along with "Jesus Loves Me This I Know." But I personally had never heard it before. Never heard the words, despite the thousands of times I had sung them. Never thought they had anything to do with me.

On the other hand, the words of Patrick Henry had made such an impression on me that I had been able to stretch myself tall and trembling and say, "I know not what course others may take, but as for me, give me liberty or give me death."

And now I heard, really for the first time:

> "We have come over a way that with tears
> has been watered,
> We have come treading our path through
> the blood of the slaughtered."

While echoes of the song shivered in the air, Henry Reed bowed his head, said "Thank you," and returned to his place in the line. The tears that slipped down many faces were not wiped away in shame.

We were on top again. As always, again. We survived. The depths had been icy and dark, but now a bright sun spoke to our souls. I was no longer simply a member of the proud graduating class of 1940, I was a proud member of the wonderful, beautiful Negro race.

Oh, Black known and unknown poets, how often have your auctioned pains sustained us? Who will compute the lonely nights made less lonely by your songs, or by the empty pots made less tragic by your tales?

If we were a people much given to revealing secrets, we might raise monuments and sacrifice to the memories of our poets, but slavery cured us of that weakness. It may be enough, however, to have it said that we survive in exact relationship to the dedication of our poets (include preachers, musicians and blues singers).

AFTER YOU READ

from *I Know Why the Caged Bird Sings*

Think and Discuss

1. Summarize the ups and downs of Marguerite Johnson's graduation day and explain what caused them.

2. How did Marguerite feel about her own identity and that of her fellow humans before, during, and after graduation?

3. How would you describe Marguerite's **character** and personality? Use details from the selection.

4. What role does the **setting** play in shaping Marguerite's personality? Give specific examples.

5. If a story is about *the* moment, not *a* moment (see page 13), what is *the* moment in this autobiographical story?

6. Graduation is a rite of passage. You graduated from eighth grade yourself not long ago. Copy the graphic organizer below into your Writer's Notebook. Then use it to compare Maya Angelou's rite of passage with your own.

Graduations	Maya Angelou's	Mine
Setting		
Traditions		
Speeches		
Feelings		

Write to Understand: Focused Freewriting

Review what you recorded in the graphic organizer about your graduation from eighth grade. Use that information to try to get yourself back in the moment of the experience—whether it was a formal ceremony or just the last day of eighth grade. Then, in your Writer's Notebook, start writing about the experience—what happened and what you were feeling. Write everything you can remember and keep writing for at least 10 minutes—longer if you have more to say.

BEFORE YOU READ
Through the Tunnel

Meet the Author: Doris Lessing

Doris Lessing was born in 1919 in Persia (now Iran), the daughter of British parents. When she was six, her family moved to Rhodesia (now Zimbabwe). Lessing once commented that unhappy childhoods tend to produce writers of fiction. Her own childhood was, in her words, "an uneven mix of some pleasure and much pain." She escaped through reading. Although she never finished high school, she made herself into a self-educated intellectual. In 1949, after two failed marriages, she moved to London with her young son and the manuscript of her first novel. Since then she has written fifty more books in a variety of styles and genres.

Build Background: Initiations

Coming of age is often marked by the completion of a task deemed challenging by one's culture, such as a vision quest to find a guardian animal spirit for some Native Americans and a Bar or Bat Mitzvah for some Jews. Sometimes, though, children set their own personal goals for making the passage out of childhood. Until their journey through the passage is complete, they may feel like strangers in both the world of children and the world of adults.

In "Through the Tunnel," a young boy on a seaside vacation in a foreign land pushes himself to his limit in order to accomplish a challenging task he sees older boys doing. As you read the story, think about these questions:

- What accomplishment might it take for you to feel like you have entered the adult world and become independent?

- At what times have you felt like a foreigner—uncomfortable and out of your element?

THE SEA URCHIN, Joseph Milner Kite

Through the Tunnel

DORIS LESSING

THROUGH THE TUNNEL

Doris Lessing

Going to the shore on the first morning of the vacation, the young English boy stopped at a turning of the path and looked down at a wild and rocky bay, and then over to the crowded beach he knew so well from other years. His mother walked on in front of him, carrying a bright striped bag in one hand. Her other arm, swinging loose, was very white in the sun. The boy watched that white, naked arm, and turned his eyes, which had a frown behind them, toward the bay and back again to his mother. When she felt he was not with her, she swung around. "Oh, there you are, Jerry!" she said. She looked impatient, then smiled. "Why, darling, would you rather not come with me? Would you rather—" She frowned, conscientiously worrying over what amusements he might secretly be longing for, which she had been too busy or too careless to imagine. He was very familiar with that anxious, apologetic smile. **Contrition** sent him running after her. And yet, as he ran, he looked back over his shoulder at the wild bay; and all morning, as he played on the safe beach, he was thinking of it.

Next morning, when it was time for the routine of swimming and sunbathing, his mother said, "Are you tired of the usual beach, Jerry? Would you like to go somewhere else?"

"Oh, no!" he said quickly, smiling at her out of that unfailing impulse of contrition—a sort of chivalry. Yet, walking down the path with her, he blurted out, "I'd like to go and have a look at those rocks down there."

She gave the idea her attention. It was a wild looking place, and there was no one there; but she said, "Of course, Jerry. When you've had enough, come to the big beach. Or just go straight back to the villa, if you like." She walked away, that bare arm, now slightly reddened from yesterday's sun, swinging. And he almost ran after her again, feeling it unbearable that she should go by herself, but he did not.

contrition
a feeling of sorrow or remorse

She was thinking, Of course he's old enough to be safe without me. Have I been keeping him too close? He mustn't feel he ought to be with me. I must be careful.

He was an only child, eleven years old. She was a widow. She was determined to be neither possessive nor lacking in devotion. She went worrying off to her beach.

As for Jerry, once he saw that his mother had gained her beach, he began the steep descent to the bay. From where he was, high up among red-brown rocks, it was a scoop of moving bluish green fringed with white. As he went lower, he saw that it spread among small **promontories** and inlets of rough, sharp rock, and the crisping, lapping surface showed stains of purple and darker blue. Finally, as he ran sliding and scraping down the last few yards, he saw an edge of white surf and the shallow, luminous movement of water over white sand, and, beyond that, a solid, heavy blue.

promontories high points of rock jutting into a body of water

He ran straight into the water and began swimming. He was a good swimmer. He went out fast over the gleaming sand, over a middle region where rocks lay like discolored monsters under the surface, and then he was in the real sea—a warm sea where irregular cold currents from the deep water shocked his limbs.

When he was so far out that he could look back not only on the little bay but past the promontory that was between it and the big beach, he floated on the buoyant surface and looked for his mother. There she was, a speck of yellow under an umbrella that looked like a slice of orange peel. He swam back to shore, relieved at being sure she was there, but all at once very lonely.

To be with them, of them, was a craving that filled his whole body.

On the edge of a small cape that marked the side of the bay away from the promontory was a loose scatter of rocks. Above them, some boys were stripping off their clothes. They came running, naked, down to the rocks. The English boy swam toward them, but kept his distance at a stone's throw. They were of that coast, all of them were burned smooth dark brown and speaking a language he did not understand. To be with them, of them, was a craving that filled his whole body. He swam a little closer; they turned and watched him with narrowed, alert dark eyes. Then one smiled and waved. It was enough. In

supplication
begging

a minute, he had swum in and was on the rocks beside them, smiling with a desperate, nervous **supplication**. They shouted cheerful greetings at him; and then, as he preserved his nervous, uncomprehending smile, they understood that he was a foreigner strayed from his own beach, and they proceeded to forget him. But he was happy. He was with them.

They began diving again and again from a high point into a well of blue sea between rough, pointed rocks. After they had dived and come up, they swam around, hauled themselves up, and waited their turn to dive again. They were big boys, men, to Jerry. He dived, and they watched him; and when he swam around to take his place, they made way for him. He felt he was accepted and he dived again, carefully, proud of himself.

Soon the biggest of the boys poised himself, shot down into the water, and did not come up. The others stood about, watching. Jerry, after waiting for the sleek brown head to appear, let out a yell of warning; they looked at him idly and turned their eyes back toward the water. After a long time, the boy came up on the other side of a dark rock, letting the air out of his lungs in a sputtering gasp and a shout of triumph. Immediately the rest of them dived in. One moment, the morning seemed full of chattering boys; the next, the air and the surface of the water were empty. But through the heavy blue, dark shapes could be seen moving and groping.

Jerry dived, shot past the school of underwater swimmers, saw a black wall of rock looming at him, touched it, and bobbed up at once to the surface, where there was a low barrier he could see across. There was no one visible; under him, in the water, the dim shapes of the swimmers had disappeared. Then one, and then another of the boys came up on the far side of the barrier of rock. And he understood that they had swum through some gap or hole in it. He plunged down again. He could see nothing through the stinging salt water but the blank rock. When he came up the boys were all on the diving rock, preparing to attempt the feat again. And now, in a panic of failure, he yelled up, in English, "Look at me! Look!" and he began splashing and kicking in the water like a foolish dog.

They looked down gravely, frowning. He knew the frown. At moments of failure, when he clowned to claim his mother's attention, it was with just this grave, embarrassed inspection that she rewarded him. Through his hot shame, feeling the pleading grin on his face like a scar that he could never remove, he looked up at the group of big brown boys on the rock and shouted, *"Bonjour! Merci! Au revoir! Monsieur, monsieur!"*[1] while he hooked his fingers round his ears and waggled them.

Water surged into his mouth; he choked, sank, came up. The rock, lately weighted with boys, seemed to rear up out of the water as their weight was removed. They were flying down past him, now, into the water; the air was full of falling bodies. Then the rock was empty in the hot sunlight. He counted one, two, three. . . .

At fifty, he was terrified. They must all be drowning beneath him, in the watery caves of the rock! At a hundred, he stared around him at the empty hillside, wondering if he should yell for help. He counted faster, faster, to hurry them up, to bring them to the surface quickly, to drown them quickly—anything rather than the terror of counting on and on into the blue emptiness of the morning. And then, at a hundred and sixty, the water beyond the rock was full of boys blowing like brown whales. They swam back to the shore without a look at him.

They must all be drowning beneath him, in the watery caves of the rock!

He climbed back to the diving rock and sat down, feeling the hot roughness of it under his thighs. The boys were gathering up their bits of clothing and running off along the shore to another promontory. They were leaving to get away from him. He cried openly, fists in his eyes. There was no one to see him, and he cried himself out.

It seemed to him that a long time had passed, and he swam out to where he could see his mother. Yes, she was still there, a yellow spot under an orange umbrella. He swam back to the big rock, climbed up, and dived into the blue pool among the fanged and angry boulders. Down he went, until he touched the wall of rock again. But the salt was so painful in his eyes that he could not see.

He came to the surface, swam to shore, and went back to the villa to wait for his mother. Soon she walked slowly up the path, swinging her

---

1 *"Bonjour! Merci! Au revoir! Monsieur, monsieur!":* "Good day! Thank you! Goodbye! Mister, mister!" These are probably the only words Jerry knew in French.

beseeching
pleading

striped bag, the flushed, naked arm dangling beside her. "I want some swimming goggles," he panted, defiant and **beseeching**.

She gave him a patient, inquisitive look as she said casually, "Well, of course, darling."

But now, now, now! He must have them this minute, and no other time. He nagged and pestered until she went with him to a shop. As soon as she had bought the goggles, he grabbed them from her hand, as if she were going to claim them for herself, and was off, running down the steep path to the bay.

*T*he impact of the water broke the rubber-enclosed vacuum, and the goggles came loose.

Jerry swam out to the big barrier rock, adjusted the goggles, and dived. The impact of the water broke the rubber-enclosed vacuum, and the goggles came loose. He understood that he must swim down to the base of the rock from the surface of the water. He fixed the goggles tight and firm, filled his lungs, and floated, face down, on the water. Now, he could see. It was as if he had eyes of a different kind—fish eyes that showed everything clear and delicate and wavering in the bright water.

Under him, six or seven feet down, was a floor of perfectly clean, shining white sand, rippled firm and hard by the tides. Two grayish shapes steered there, like long, rounded pieces of wood or slate. They were fish. He saw them nose toward each other, poise motionless, make a dart forward, swerve off, and come around again. It was like a water dance. A few inches above them the water sparkled as if sequins were dropping through it. Fish

myriads
great numbers

again—**myriads** of minute fish, the length of his fingernail, were drifting through the water, and in a moment he could feel the innumerable tiny touches of them against his limbs. It was like swimming in flaked silver. The great rock the boys had swum through rose sheer out of the white sand—black, tufted lightly with greenish weed. He could see no gap in it. He swam down to its base.

Again and again he rose, took a big chestful of air, and went down. Again and again he groped over the surface of the rock, feeling it, almost hugging it in the desperate need to find the entrance. And then, once, while he was clinging to the black wall, his knees came up and he shot his feet out forward and they met no obstacle. He had found the hole.

He gained the surface, **clambered** about the stones that littered the barrier rock until he found a big one, and, with this in his arms, let himself down over the side of the rock. He dropped, with the weight, straight to the sandy floor. Clinging tight to the anchor of stone, he lay on his side and looked in under the dark shelf at the place where his feet had gone. He could see the hole. It was an irregular, dark gap; but he could not see deep into it. He let go of his anchor, clung with his hands to the edges of the hole, and tried to push himself in.

clambered
climbed using hands and feet; scrambled

HIGH CLIFF, COAST OF MAINE. Winslow Homer, 1894

frond
large leaf or
something
resembling
a leaf

He got his head in, found his shoulders jammed, moved them in sidewise, and was inside as far as his waist. He could see nothing ahead. Something soft and clammy touched his mouth; he saw a dark **frond** moving against the grayish rock, and panic filled him. He thought of octopuses, of clinging weed. He pushed himself out backward and caught a glimpse, as he retreated, of a harmless tentacle of seaweed drifting in the mouth of the tunnel. But it was enough. He reached the sunlight, swam to shore, and lay on the diving rock. He looked down into the blue well of water. He knew he must find his way through that cave, or hole, or tunnel, and out the other side.

He knew he must find his way through that cave. . . .

First, he thought, he must learn to control his breathing. He let himself down into the water with another big stone in his arms, so that he could lie effortlessly on the bottom of the sea. He counted. One, two, three. He counted steadily. He could hear the movement of blood in his chest. Fifty-one, fifty-two. . . . His chest was hurting. He let go of the rock and went up into the air. He saw that the sun was low. He rushed to the villa and found his mother at her supper. She said only "Did you enjoy yourself?" and he said "Yes."

All night the boy dreamed of the water-filled cave in the rock, and as soon as breakfast was over he went to the bay.

That night, his nose bled badly. For hours he had been underwater, learning to hold his breath, and now he felt weak and dizzy. His mother said, "I shouldn't overdo things, darling, if I were you."

That day and the next, Jerry exercised his lungs as if everything, the whole of his life, all that he would become, depended upon it. Again his nose bled at night, and his mother insisted on his coming with her the next day. It was a torment to him to waste a day of his careful self-training, but he stayed with her on that other beach, which now seemed a place for small children, a place where his mother might lie safe in the sun. It was not his beach.

He did not ask for permission, on the following day, to go to his beach. He went, before his mother could consider the complicated rights and wrongs of the matter. A day's rest, he discovered, had improved his count by ten. The big boys had made the passage while he counted a hundred and sixty. He had been counting fast, in his fright. Probably now, if he tried, he could get through that long tunnel, but he was not going to try yet. A curious, most unchildlike persistence, a controlled impatience, made him wait. In the meantime, he lay under water on the white sand, littered now by stones he had brought down from the upper air, and studied the entrance to the tunnel. He knew every jut and corner of it, as far as it was possible to see. It was as if he already felt its sharpness about his shoulders.

He sat by the clock in the villa, when his mother was not near, and checked his time. He was incredulous and then proud to find he could hold his breath without strain for two minutes. The words "two minutes," authorized by the clock, brought close the adventure that was so necessary to him.

He was frightened. Supposing he turned dizzy in the tunnel? Supposing he died there, trapped?

In another four days, his mother said casually one morning, they must go home. On the day before they left, he would do it. He would do it if it killed him, he said defiantly to himself. But two days before they were to leave—a day of triumph when he increased his count by fifteen—his nose bled so badly that he turned dizzy and had to lie limply over the big rock like a bit of seaweed, watching the thick red blood flow on to the rock and trickle slowly down to the sea. He was frightened. Supposing he turned dizzy in the tunnel? Supposing he died there, trapped? Supposing—his head went around, in the hot sun, and he almost gave up. He thought he would return to the house, and lie down, and next summer, perhaps, when he had another year's growth in him—*then* he would go through the hole.

But even after he had made the decision, or thought he had, he found himself sitting up on the rock and looking down into the water; and he knew that now, this moment, when his nose had only just stopped bleeding, when his head was still sore and throbbing—this was the moment when he would try. If he did not do it now, he never would. He was trembling with fear that he would not go; and he was trembling with horror at that long, long tunnel under the rock, under the sea. Even in the open sunlight, the barrier rock seemed very wide and very heavy; tons of rock pressed down on where he would go. If he died there, he would lie until one day—perhaps not before the next year—those big boys would swim into it and find it blocked.

He put on his goggles, fitted them tight, tested the vacuum. His hands were shaking. Then he chose the biggest stone he could carry and slipped over the edge of the rock until half of him was in the cool, enclosing water and half in the hot sun. He looked up once at the empty sky, filled his lungs once, twice, and then sank fast to the bottom with the stone. He let it go and began to count. He took the edges of the hole in his hands and drew himself into it, wriggling his shoulders in sidewise as he remembered he must, kicking himself along with his feet.

> He put on his goggles, fitted them tight, tested the vacuum. His hands were shaking.

Soon he was clear inside. He was in a small rock-bound hole filled with yellowish gray water. The water was pushing him up against the roof. The roof was sharp and pained his back. He pulled himself along with his hands—fast, fast—and used his legs as levers. His head knocked against something; a sharp pain dizzied him. Fifty, fifty-one, fifty-two. . . . He was without light, and the water seemed to press upon him with the weight of rock. Seventy-one, seventy-two. . . . There was no strain on his lungs. He felt like an inflated balloon, his lungs were so light and easy, but his head was pulsing.

He was being continually pressed against the sharp roof, which felt slimy as well as sharp. Again he thought of octopuses, and wondered if the tunnel might be filled with weed that could tangle him. He gave himself a panicky, convulsive kick forward, ducked his head, and swam. His feet and hands moved freely, as if in open water. The hole must have widened out. He thought he must be swimming fast, and he was frightened of banging his head if the tunnel narrowed.

A hundred, a hundred and one. . . . The water paled. Victory filled him. His lungs were beginning to hurt. A few more strokes and he would be out. He was counting wildly; he said a hundred and fifteen, and then, a long time later, a hundred and fifteen again. The water was a clear jewel-green all around him. Then he saw, above his head, a crack running up through the rock. Sunlight was falling through it, showing the clean, dark rock of the tunnel, a single mussel shell, and darkness ahead.

He was at the end of what he could do. He looked up at the crack as if it were filled with air and not water, as if he could put his mouth to it to draw in air. A hundred and fifteen, he heard himself say inside his head—but he had said that long ago. He must go on into the blackness ahead, or he would drown. His head was swelling, his lungs cracking. A hundred and fifteen, a hundred and fifteen pounded through his head, and he feebly clutched at rocks in the dark, pulling himself forward, leaving the brief space of sunlit water behind. He felt he was dying. He was no longer quite conscious. He struggled on in the darkness between lapses into unconsciousness. An immense, swelling pain filled his head, and then the darkness cracked with an explosion of green light. His hands, groping forward, met nothing; and his feet, kicking back, propelled him out into the open sea.

He was at the end of what he could do. He looked up at the crack as if it were filled with air and not water, as if he could put his mouth to it to draw in air.

He drifted to the surface, his face turned up to the air. He was gasping like a fish. He felt he would sink now and drown; he could not swim the few feet back to the rock. Then he was clutching it and pulling himself up onto it. He lay face down, gasping. He could see nothing but a red-veined, clotted dark. His eyes must have burst, he thought; they were full of blood. He tore off his goggles and a **gout** of blood went into the sea. His nose was bleeding, and the blood had filled the goggles.

He scooped up handfuls of water from the cool, salty sea, to splash on his face, and did not know whether it was blood or salt water he tasted. After a time, his heart quieted, his eyes cleared, and he sat up. He could see the local boys diving and playing half a mile away. He did not want them. He wanted nothing but to get back home and lie down.

In a short while, Jerry swam to shore and climbed slowly up the path to the villa. He flung himself on his bed and slept, waking at the sound of feet on the path outside. His mother was coming back. He rushed to the bathroom, thinking she must not see his face with bloodstains, or tearstains, on it. He came out of the bathroom and met her as she walked into the villa, smiling, her eyes lighting up.

gout
mass of something fluid gushing or bursting out

"Have a nice morning?" she asked, laying her hand on his warm brown shoulder a moment.

"Oh, yes, thank you," he said.

"You look a bit pale." And then, sharp and anxious, "How did you bang your head?"

"Oh, just banged it," he told her.

She looked at him closely. He was strained; his eyes were glazed-looking. She was worried. And then she said to herself, Oh, don't fuss! Nothing can happen. He can swim like a fish.

They sat down to lunch together.

"Mummy," he said, "I can stay under water for two minutes—three minutes, at least." It came bursting out of him.

"Can you, darling?" she said. "Well, I shouldn't overdo it. I don't think you ought to swim any more today."

She was ready for a battle of wills, but he gave in at once. It was no longer of the least importance to go to the bay.

AFTER YOU READ
Through the Tunnel

Think and Discuss

1. Why was Jerry so determined to swim through the tunnel?

2. Does the story suggest Jerry is ready to undertake this personal challenge? Give examples from the story to explain your answer.

3. Which details of the **setting** are vital to the meaning of the story? Explain.

4. Doris Lessing uses many **similes** and other comparisons in her descriptions. The beach umbrella looked "like a slice of orange peel." When the boys surface, they blow "like brown whales." In your Writer's Notebook, create a simile chart like the one below. Scan the story for similes. On your chart, enter the similes you find and tell how each one helps you experience what is being described. (For a definition of **simile**, see the Glossary of Literary Terms.)

Simile	How It Helps You Experience What's Being Described

5. Think about a time you worked hard to achieve a goal. What was the goal and what did it mean to you?

6. Was Jerry's swim through the tunnel an initiation, a "rite of passage"? Give reasons for your answer.

Write to Understand: Description

Review your simile chart and think about how Doris Lessing uses similes in her descriptions. Then write your own paragraph to describe a place you have visited or an experience you have had. Try to make your description vivid, so that the reader can see the place in his or her mind or relive the experience with you. Use at least one simile in your description.

BEFORE YOU READ
Poems of Passage

Meet the Poets

Philip Booth was born in 1925 in New Hampshire . . . now lives in Maine. A poet and a professor, he is one of the most widely read 20th-century poets.

Billy Collins was born in New York in 1941. He was U.S. Poet Laureate from 2001 to 2003 and is in the center of a movement to introduce adolescents to poetry by having them read clear, meaningful contemporary poems.

Audre Lorde (1934–1992) was born in Harlem of Caribbean immigrants. As a child, she did not speak and began talking only when she started writing poetry. Her first poem was published when she was just fifteen.

Build Background: Going It Alone

If you can remember the first time you rode a two-wheeler on your own, you can probably easily bring to mind the mixture of fear and thrill you felt when the steadying hands you had relied on finally let go. Most young people approach "going it alone" with such mixed feelings. Fortunately, the lessons and guidance from adults usually stay with them and help them steady their course.

Poetry itself can help ease the passage out of childhood, as it did for Audre Lorde. Poems use super-charged words and images to express fears, hopes, and countless other feelings in ways that other writing cannot. And some poets, like Billy Collins, speak especially clearly to young people. Collins says that as he writes, he has "one reader in mind, someone who is in the room with me, and who I'm talking to, and I want to make sure I don't talk too fast, or too glibly."

- As you read the following poems, imagine yourself in the room with the poet. Pull up a chair and listen closely.

- What experiences have you had that have made you feel very much—maybe too much—as if you were going it alone?

First Lesson
PHILIP BOOTH

Lie back, daughter, let your head
be tipped back in the cup of my hand.
Gently, and I will hold you. Spread
your arms wide, lie out on the stream
and look high at the gulls. A dead- 5
man's-float is face down. You will dive
and swim soon enough where this tidewater
ebbs to the sea. Daughter, believe
me, when you tire on the long thrash
to your island, lie up, and survive. 10
As you float now, where I held you
and let go, remember when fear
cramps your heart what I told you:
lie gently and wide to the light-year
stars, lie back, and the sea will hold you. 15

On Turning Ten BILLY COLLINS

The whole idea of it makes me feel
like I'm coming down with something,
something worse than any stomach ache
or the headaches I get from reading in bad light—
a kind of measles of the spirit,   5
a mumps of the **psyche**,
a disfiguring chicken pox of the soul.

psyche
the soul or
spirit

You tell me it is too early to be looking back,
but that is because you have forgotten
the perfect simplicity of being one   10
and the beautiful complexity introduced by two.
But I can lie on my bed and remember every digit.
At four I was an Arabian wizard.
I could make myself invisible
by drinking a glass of milk a certain way.   15
At seven I was a soldier, at nine a prince.

But now I am mostly at the window
watching the late afternoon light.
Back then it never fell so solemnly
against the side of my tree house,   20
and my bicycle never leaned against the garage
as it does today,
all the dark blue speed drained out of it.

This is the beginning of sadness, I say to myself,
as I walk through the universe in my sneakers.   25
It is time to say good-bye to my imaginary friends,
time to turn the first big number.

It seems only yesterday I used to believe
there was nothing under my skin but light.
If you cut me I could shine.   30
But now when I fall upon the sidewalks of life,
I skin my knees. I bleed.

ON THE ARROWBACK, Ken Danby, 1975

Hanging Fire[1] AUDRE LORDE

I am fourteen
and my skin has betrayed me
the boy I cannot live without
still sucks his thumb
in secret   5
how come my knees are
always so ashy
what if I die
before morning
and momma's in the bedroom   10
with the door closed.

I have to learn how to dance
in time for the next party
my room is too small for me
suppose I die before graduation   15
they will sing sad melodies
but finally
tell the truth about me
There is nothing I want to do
and too much   20
that has to be done
and momma's in the bedroom
with the door closed.

Nobody even stops to think
about my side of it   25
I should have been on Math Team
my marks were better than his
why do I have to be
the one
wearing braces   30
I have nothing to wear tomorrow
will I live long enough
to grow up
and momma's in the bedroom
with the door closed.   35

Art © Vik Muniz/Licensed by VAGA, New York, NY

VALICIA BATHES IN SUNDAY CLOTHES,
Vik Muniz

I **Hanging Fire:** holding back or hesitating

AFTER YOU READ
Poems of Passage

Think and Discuss

1. In "First Lesson," the **speaker** (also called the *persona*) in the poem, is the father. What is his "first lesson" to his daughter?

2. The speaker in both "On Turning Ten" and "Hanging Fire" is a child. In your Writer's Notebook, create a comparison chart similar to the one below. In the center column, note ways in which the speakers in the two poems express similar feelings and ideas. In the left and right columns, note differences.

On Turning Ten	Both Poems	Hanging Fire

3. Each of these poems is an example of **free verse**—poetry that does not have regular meter or rhyme. One of the poems, however, does have rhyme, although it is used freely and not in the usual way. Identify the poem and explain how the poet has used rhyme.

4. Each verse paragraph in "Hanging Fire" ends with the same words: "and momma's in the bedroom / with the door closed." What does this repeated image contribute to the meaning of the poem?

5. Compare the attitudes about swimming and the sea in "Through the Tunnel" and "First Lesson." Use specific examples from the works.

6. In which of the three poems does the child seem most ready to make a passage out of childhood? Use words and images from the poems to explain your answer.

Write to Understand: Free Verse

Review what you wrote in the center column of your comparison chart. Which of these ideas and feelings can you relate to? Write your own free verse poem or a paragraph expressing one or several of these ideas and feelings. Express your thoughts in your own unique way. Like Billy Collins, write with one person in mind, as if that person is sitting in the room with you.

BEFORE YOU READ
Vegetarian Enough

Meet the Author: Annie Choi

Annie Choi was born and raised in the San Fernando Valley of Los Angeles. She now lives in New York City. She was working as a textbook editor when her boss suggested that she might improve her writing skills by taking a class. The one that fit into her work schedule was a class in memoir writing. That got her started, and seven years later, she published *Happy Birthday or Whatever: Track Suits, Kim Chee, and Other Family Disasters,* a collection of memoirs about growing up in the 1980s and 1990s an American-born kid in a very traditional Korean American family. "Vegetarian Enough" is one of the memoirs from this book.

Build Background: *Diet for a New America*

In 1987, John Robbins, the son of the co-founder of Baskin-Robbins ice cream, published his book *Diet for a New America.* The book advocates vegetarianism by showing how people's food choices affect not only their own health and well-being but also the health and well-being of the Earth. The book contains an abundance of facts and statistics, and many people were convinced by these to change their eating habits. Annie Choi was among those who became vegetarian, but she had other reasons than those offered in Robbins's book. As you read her memoir, think about these questions:

• How do your food choices reflect who you are and what you care about?

• What have you done to make a statement about your independence and who you are as an individual?

Art © The Educational Alliance, Inc/Estate of Peter Blume/Licensed by VAGA, New York, NY   VEGETABLE DINNER, Peter Blume, 1927

Vegetarian Enough

ANNIE CHOI

VEGETARIAN ENOUGH

Annie Choi

In my sophomore year high school, one of my best friends read *Diet for a New America* by John Robbins and decided to become vegetarian. Eating animals, Alyson explained to me, was bad for the Earth, bad for your health, and like totally bad for animals. Livestock was pumped full of antibiotics, hormones, appetite stimulants, and tranquilizers and they were debeaked, dehorned, and castrated[1] so they could wind up on our kitchen table and in our bodies where their flesh would slowly fester and poison us and cause heart disease, tumors, and a black soul. I did not want a black soul; I wanted to keep it fresh and yellow. Like a squash. So, I became vegetarian too. I didn't even bother reading the book. I figured if John Robbins could convince Alyson, then he could convince me. Done and done.

"WHAT?"

"No meat. I'm vegetarian." My mother and I were sitting on the living room floor, folding laundry. I crumpled Mike's shirt into a tight, wrinkled ball and tossed it aside. I figured if he wasn't going to help us, then I wasn't going to help him. "It's a better way of life."

"Better for who? You not eat meat, you get very sick. Then you die."

"Actually, you're wrong. Meat makes people sick. It's bad for you."

"What you mean bad for you?"

"It causes heart attacks and stuff."

"No, Anne, you cause heart attack. Who tell you this?"

"John Robbins."

"Who John Robbin? You friend at school? Teacher? I want have talk with him."

"No, no, his family started Baskin-Robbins."

"He ice cream man? What do ice cream man know? When you get so crazy? How can you be Korean without meat?"

I **debeaked, dehorned, and castrated:** having their beaks, horns, and reproductive organs removed

"Grandma is Korean, and she's Buddhist and vegetarian." Actually I knew my mother's mother wasn't really vegetarian, but I thought I'd try to slip that by my mother.

"Anne, Grandma eat meat!"

My grandmother is quite active at her small Korean Buddhist temple in Los Angeles. I used to accompany her to her temple, which is actually a two-story house converted into a temple, and play with my stuffed animals behind a large golden statue of the Buddha. I also used to take a burning stick of pine incense and run around with it, pretending to be an Olympic torchbearer.

"Yeah I know, I know, but she's not supposed to eat meat. She's gonna go to Buddhist hell, where everyone's vegetarian." I laughed at my own joke. Clever, clever girl.

"So that mean you go hell too because everyone in heaven eat meat."

OK, maybe not that clever. Mother 1, Annie 0. "Whatever."

"Grandma break rule because she know meat is good. She only vegetarian at temple. She say she vegetarian enough." My mother reached over and unfolded one of my shirts I had folded. "Fold this again. Why you fold like monkey?"

> "*G*randma break rule because she know meat is good. She only vegetarian at temple. She say she vegetarian enough."

"It doesn't matter—I'm still not eating meat. And I can fold my own shirts anyway I want."

"I not cook for you. You starve."

"I can cook for myself."

My mother laughed. "Like what?"

"I can make spaghetti."

"Everyday? Who eat spaghetti everyday?"

"Italians."

"Who are you? So-pia Loren?"[2]

---

2 **So-pia Loren:** Sophia Loren, an Italian movie star most popular in the 1950s to the 1970s

"I can get a cookbook. I can make us all vegetarian food. We can all be healthy together."

"No one eat it."

"More for me then."

My mother sighed and studied my face. Her eyes slowly moved over my eyes, nose, and cheeks. She seemed to be looking at me for the very first time; I was growing up and making my own bad decisions about my life, just like normal adults. "How long you be vegetarian? One year."

"Forever."

"Forever?"

"Forever."

"That long time, Anne. Forever is until you die."

"I know what forever means, and I mean it. Forever."

"You eat fish then."

"No, fish is meat, and I don't eat meat."

My mother smiled slyly as she folded a pair of my pants. "You remember when you little you want to be mailman. You want to drive little car. Then you want to be ballet dancer and you take one ballet class and you say, 'Mommy, my feet hurt so much,' and you cry *waah waah*."

"This is it. I'm a vegetarian. I'm never eating meat again."

"OK, we see."

The next week my mother prepared all my favorite dishes, which all happen to have meat: chicken stewed with potatoes and carrots, brisket slow-cooked in soy sauce, kim chee[3] stew with pork, soy bean stew with clams and shrimp. I knew what she was doing, trying to lure me back to the dark side, the side rich with protein and iron and low in carbohydrates, but I remained strong. This was not a war over meat, but like any teenage rebellion, it was a war over will, Annie and John Robbins vs. Mother and Pretty Much Everyone in the World, including America and Korea. Luckily, Korean food is pretty vegetarian-friendly. Each meal has several side dishes that consist of some kind of salted, pickled, or fried vegetable. I was perfectly content to forego the main dish, which once stood proudly on four legs or had wings.

---

3 **kim chee:** a Korean dish consisting of vegetables pickled in a solution of garlic salt and red chili peppers. The Korean government has named kim chee (sometimes spelled kimchi) a national treasure.

"What's wrong with Annie?" My father looked at my mother, confused. "She's not eating. Is she sick?"

"Very sick. Ask your daughter."

"What's wrong with you?"

"Nothing."

"Then why you not eat?"

"Because I don't eat meat."

"When did this happen?"

"Like forever ago. Last week. Where have you been?"

"I've been eating meat. Why are you vegetarian?"

"I already went through this. Meat is murder. It's bad for everyone. Even Earth." I wrapped a piece of dried seaweed around some rice and stuffed it in my mouth.

"You have to eat meat. How will you live without meat?"

"I've been living pretty awesome without meat."

> "I already went through this. Meat is murder. It's bad for everyone. Even Earth."

My father looked to my mother for reinforcement. She rolled her eyes. "Don't bother," she said in Korean, "your daughter does what she wants to do."

"You have to cook her something without meat."

"I'm not cooking anything special for her. She says she can take care of herself."

"She's lying. She's fifteen, what does she know?"

"Actually, I'm sixteen."

"Eat meat."

"No."

"I told you not to bother. Just leave her alone."

"I mean it Annie, eat meat."

"No."

"How could you let her do this?"

"I didn't let her do anything. She did this all on her own."

"Dad, it's not even an issue. It's just the way it is. Besides, I'm totally full and didn't even eat meat. How about that?"

Eyeing my bowl of plant matter, my father cringed. "Why do you do this to yourself? How will you eat my steakie?"

derivative
a word
formed from
another word

My father calls steak "steakie," which is a **derivative** of the Korean word for *steak, suh-tay-kuh*. My father prides himself on two things in the kitchen. The first is "steakie" for which he takes two slabs of London broil and sprinkles salt, pepper, garlic powder, and MSG on each side. After he's done broiling it, he uses scissors to cut the meat into perfect one-inch cubes that are tough and chewy enough to unhinge jaws. His second specialty is Rice Krispies treats, in which he uses margarine instead of butter, cuts the amount of marshmallow, and adds peanut butter, vanilla extract, peanuts, and raisins. The mixture is extremely crunchy, with the texture and flavor of drywall[4] with peanuts and raisins. He packs it into a pan so tightly that they turn into sandy bricks that shred the roof of my mouth into a bloody mess. Once my father caught me making normal light and fluffy Rice Krispies treats, using the traditional, unaltered recipe that the good people of Kellogg's developed, tested, and approved, and he looked so hurt that I never did it again. I used to plead for both of my father's specialties until I tried the real versions, but by then it was too late. My father had built his entire identity in the kitchen around chewy meat dice and drywall.

> *The mixture is extremely crunchy, with the texture and flavor of drywall with peanuts and raisins.*

"I guess steak is the one thing I'll miss." I smiled apologetically and helped myself to more sautéed bean sprouts.

Because I like to make my life as difficult as possible, I became vegetarian right before Thanksgiving. My family always hosts all the relatives for Thanksgiving and my mother spends the day cooking a traditional turkey dinner plus a large Korean meal. I told her once many years ago that Thanksgiving was too much work, that she should just stick to the turkey and skip the Korean food, and she scoffed and asked what kind of meal didn't have Korean food? When I explained that the pilgrims probably didn't eat Korean food, she laughed and said that they missed out—had they eaten Korean food they probably wouldn't have starved.

---

4 **drywall:** board used for covering walls; wallboard

Unit One   Rites of Passage

During the course of Thanksgiving dinner, my brother outed me and announced to the entire family that I had become vegetarian "like some kind of dirty hippie"[5] and soon all my aunts, uncles, and cousins were riding the express train to Nagsville.

"You're going to get **jaundice**, and if you're lucky, you'll die."

"Leave me alone, Mike."

"Do you eat anything that casts a shadow?" My cousin Andy is athletic and health-conscious, but even he decided that eating vegetarians was better than being one.

"Hey, isn't your belt made of leather?" my uncle asked me.

"Yes." I sighed and concentrated on my broccoli.

"What about yogurt, do you eat that?"

"Yes."

"What about eggs, do you eat that?"

I groaned. "Yes, Uncle, yes."

"Why not become a **vegan**? A Communist one. Start some kind of revolution against meat. Against everything delicious with lungs."

"I said leave me alone, Mike."

"But you're just skin and bones, if you don't eat meat, you'll start fainting," my aunt remarked in Korean. She tried to put the turkey on my plate but I moved it away.

"Please, no turkey. Really, I'm fine."

"OK try some of this," my uncle slopped a spoonful of stuffing on my plate.

"There's turkey in it!" I pushed the stuffing to the side.

"But you can't see the meat so it doesn't count. Stop being difficult."

"Meat tastes good, you should eat it," Tina said simply. She is the nice one in the family. "Just eat some turkey and everyone will leave you alone."

"Everyone, please, I'm fine, there's plenty of food here." The truth was there was a ton of vegetarian food: broccoli casserole, mashed potatoes, yams, beets, fried rice, three kinds of kim chee, scallion pancakes, fried tofu, and fruit salad. Clearly, there was enough food to feed an entire **kibbutz** of

jaundice
abnormal condition characterized by the skin turning yellow

vegan
a strict vegetarian who consumes no animal or dairy products

kibbutz
communal settlement, especially in Israel

---

5 **hippie:** a person with long hair, who dresses unconventionally, favors communal living, and advocates nonviolence. Hippies were the young rebels in the 1960s.

dirty vegetarian hippie revolutionaries prone to fainting, but without meat, I would starve to death, if jaundice didn't kill me first.

. . .

After my mother got cancer and then beat it into submission, she became more conscious of her health. She bought an enormous juicer that was powerful enough to squeeze juice from a rock, and proceeded to throw in everything she could get her hands on: apples, oranges, carrots, tomatoes, celery, beets, lettuce, persimmons, more or less everything in the produce aisle. She started making juices from strange combinations like apple-tomato-beet and celery-spinach-orange and offered me some, which I declined. I explained that I preferred to chew my vegetables. She talked to both her Western and Eastern doctors about dietary supplements and started taking vitamins, something I've never had the energy to research. She started eating a lot of oatmeal because it was better for her stomach, which was prone to ulcers, and drastically reduced her caffeine intake, another thing I've never been able to do but know I should.

"Anne, see? Now I eat like you. Vegetarian."

I had returned to college to start my second year and knew my mother had changed her eating habits, but I would never have thought my mother would actually become vegetarian. "What? Seriously? You don't eat any meat at all?"

"No, no meat. Only I eat fish, a lot of fish."

"That's not vegetarian. You eat fish."

"But I eat a lot of vegetable. So healthy! I think my skin feel better. How come you skin so dry? Maybe you not eat enough vegetable."

"I just have dry skin."

"Eat more vegetable."

"I do eat vegetables. That's all I eat. I'm vegetarian. A real one."

"Then maybe you need to eat fish."

I groaned. I can never win. "So you're not eating beef?" There is always some form of beef on the table.

"Doctor tell me I have to watch my cholesterol, so I eat very, very little beef. Better for me. See? I'm vegetarian, like you."

My mother gave me a few tofu recipes that were simple enough to prepare on my own and talked about the fruits and vegetables that were high in antioxidants and vitamins that could improve my skin. She told me to drink a lot of water and eat more beets. I imagined she sounded a lot like John Robbins, though I didn't really know since I hadn't read his books.

A few weeks later, my mother had fallen off the quasi-vegetarian wagon just as fast as she had gotten on it. She decided that life with very little mammal and poultry was not a life she wanted to live.

"Vegetarian so hard. What you eat?"

"I eat plenty."

"I get so hungry, I keep eat and eat and eat. I waste so much time."

"I thought you liked to eat. Everyone likes to eat. You know, people complain when they don't eat."

"Everything taste same."

"No they don't. Spinach and mushrooms do not taste the same, and tofu tastes different too."

"I miss beef and chicken and pork too much. They miss you too."

"That's ridiculous. They miss me because they know I won't eat them."

"Eat meat."

"No. Be vegetarian."

"No."

"I guess we're back where we started."

Sometimes I think that my mother and I are very close to finding a common ground, to finding an area of interest that we can explore together and bond over and discuss without bickering or nagging each other. But then I realize this is impossible, that if we didn't give each other a hard time, we probably wouldn't get along.

· · ·

I don't remember what chicken tastes like, nor do I recall the flavor or texture of pork and beef. I imagine them to be rubbery and grainy and maybe a little squishy. As of this moment, I've been vegetarian for thirteen years, four months, twelve days, and nine hours, plus or minus thirty minutes. I'm approaching the moment in my life when the number of years spent as an **omnivore** and as a vegetarian are equal, and yet, every time I talk to my mother, she asks me what I ate for dinner and if I'm still vegetarian, as if I'm still going through some kind of a phase. She'll leave messages on my voicemail: "Hi Anne, it Mommy. You still vegetarian? I get worry because you not eat meat. You have to eat meat again. Ok, it warm in L.A. Bye, bye." Why does she do this? Does she think that I'll suddenly stop and think, yes, you were right all along, please give me some beef, and then my mind will be blown and I'll start listening to everything she says? Could beef be the gateway drug[6] to pork, chicken, and ultimately, obedience?

To be honest, I'm not certain that I ever truly cared for the vegetarian cause. Sure it could be a healthier way of living, better for the environment and all of its creatures, but I'd be a big, fat liar with flaming, leather pants if I said that becoming vegetarian wasn't about rebellion and making decisions about my own life. As a teenager, vegetarianism fulfilled both these needs. Plus, I thought it was kind of cool. It made me feel unique, set me apart from other high-school kids—**albeit** in an inconvenient way—and annoyed my parents, and what adolescent wouldn't want that? I'm sure my parents know that the choice I made when I was sixteen was not the one I actually thought through, and my mother is laying in wait for the day when she can point and say, hah, it was all just a silly phase, one that lasted over thirteen years. But today, my being vegetarian is more about **inertia** than principle. I haven't eaten meat for so long, it's no longer part of my vocabulary. I'm set in my dietary ways, just the way meat-eaters are, and even if I wanted to give up being vegetarian, I couldn't. There's too much at steakie.

omnivore
one who eats both animals and vegetables

albeit
even though; even if; although

inertia
unwillingness to move or change

Annie Choi

---

6 **gateway drug:** a substance like tobacco, alcohol, or marijuana that is believed to lead to the abuse of "harder," more dangerous drugs

AFTER YOU READ
Vegetarian Enough

Think and Discuss

1. What do you think the title "Vegetarian Enough" means?

2. Annie Choi tells about a personal experience and shares her reflections on it thirteen years later. How does her understanding of why she became a vegetarian change during those years?

3. In this memoir, Annie Choi is at odds with her mother. They seem different in every possible way. Copy the graphic organizer below into your Writer's Notebook. Then use it to explore how Annie's **character** and her mother's are different. Use details from the selection to illustrate your observations.

Annie's Character	Her Mother's Character

4. Choi records exactly how her mother talks. What does the realistic **dialogue** add to Choi's memoir?

5. What effect do you think being Korean American had on the experiences Annie Choi shares in this memoir? Refer to specific details from the selection.

6. Do you think doing something your parents don't necessarily approve of is a necessary part of growing up and becoming an adult? Explain.

Write to Understand: Dialogue

Work with a partner to think of something, besides the importance of meat in a diet, that Annie Choi and her mother might disagree on. It could be something like tattoos, spiky hair, or becoming a doctor. Refer to your completed graphic organizer and with your partner write a dialogue between Choi and her mother. One of you will write what you think Annie might have to say on the subject; the other will write what her mother might say. When you have finished, act out the dialogue for your class.

BEFORE YOU READ
from *My Forbidden Face*

Meet the Author: Latifa

Latifa is not the real name of the young woman who wrote the following selection. She hides her identity to protect her family, who fled in 2001 from Afghanistan to Paris to escape the harsh rule of the Taliban. Until their escape, Latifa and her prosperous, well-educated family lived in Kabul, the capital of Afghanistan. Like so many teenagers the world over, Latifa attended school and went to parties and movies with friends. When the oppressive Taliban came to power, Latifa had just taken her exams to enter the university to study journalism. Suddenly, however, Latifa and all the women of Afghanistan became prisoners in their own homes. In defiance of the Taliban, Latifa founded a school, and she never gave up hope for her country.

Build Background: The Taliban

The Taliban are fundamentalist Muslims who controlled Afghanistan from 1996 to 2001. They imposed on the Afghan people the strictest interpretation of religious law ever experienced in the Muslim world. They were notorious for their harsh treatment of women. Women were not allowed to have jobs. They could not go to school after the age of eight. Women who wanted an education began to attend secret classes, and they and their teachers risked execution if they were found out. No woman could leave her house unless she was accompanied by a close male relative and wore a *chadri*—a long garment that covered her from head to foot with only a slit at the eyes to see through. Any woman who violated the law risked public flogging in the street or even execution.

As you read about Latifa's experience in the oppressive world ruled by the Taliban, think about these questions:

- What would you do if you were not allowed to get an education?

- If you lived in oppressive circumstances, where basic freedoms were denied you, what do you think you would miss most?

SAHARA, Firyal Al-Adhamy, 1992

FROM *My Forbidden Face*

Growing Up Under the Taliban: A Young Woman's Story

LATIFA

FROM *MY FORBIDDEN FACE*

Latifa

Eleven o'clock. Radio Sharia[1] comes back on to announce that the prime minister of the interim government, which is composed of six mullahs,[2] has issued the following statement.

"From now on the country will be ruled by a completely Islamic system. All foreign ambassadors are relieved of their duties. The new decrees in accordance with Sharia are as follows.

"Anyone in possession of a weapon must hand it in to the nearest mosque or military checkpoint.

"Women and girls are not permitted to work outside the home.

"All women who are obliged to leave their homes must be accompanied by a *mahram*:[3] their father, brother, or husband.

"Public transportation will provide buses reserved for men and buses reserved for women.

"Men must let their beards grow and trim their mustaches according to Sharia.

"Men must wear a white cap or turban on their heads.

"The wearing of suit and tie is forbidden. The wearing of traditional Afghan clothing is compulsory.

"Women and girls will wear the *chadri*.[4]

"Women and girls are forbidden to wear brightly colored clothes beneath the *chadri*.

"It is forbidden to wear nail polish or lipstick or makeup.

"All Muslims must offer ritual prayers at the appointed times wherever they may be."

---

1 **Sharia:** Islamic law; the word *Sharia* means "way" or "path"

2 **mullahs:** Muslim clerics

3 *mahram:* close male relative

4 *chadri:* a garment that covers a woman from head to foot, with a mesh-covered slit for the eyes

As the days go by, decrees rain down on us at the same hour from Radio Sharia, chanted with the same threatening voice in the name of Islamic law.

"It is forbidden to display photographs of animals and human beings.

"A woman is not allowed to take a taxi unless accompanied by a *mahram*.

"No male physician may touch the body of a woman under the pretext of a medical examination.

"A woman is not allowed to go to a tailor for men.

"A girl is not allowed to converse with a young man. Infraction of this law will lead to the immediate marriage of the offenders.

"Muslim families are not allowed to listen to music, even during a wedding.

> *"A girl is not allowed to converse with a young man. Infraction of this law will lead to the immediate marriage of the offenders.*

"Families are not allowed to photograph or videotape anything, even during a wedding.

"Women engaged to be married may not go to beauty salons, even in preparation for their weddings.

"Muslim families may not give non-Islamic names to their children.

"All non-Muslims, Hindus, and Jews must wear yellow clothing or a piece of yellow cloth. They must mark their homes with a yellow flag so that they may be recognizable.

"All merchants are forbidden to sell alcoholic beverages.

"Merchants are forbidden to sell female undergarments.

"When police punish an offender, no one is allowed to ask a question or complain.

"All those who break the laws of Sharia will be punished in the public square."

This time, they're really killing us, killing all girls and women. They're killing us **stealthily**, in silence. The worst **prohibitions**, which have already been established throughout the great majority of the country, **annihilate** us by locking us outside of society. All women are affected, from the youngest to the oldest. Women may no longer work: This means a collapse of medical services and government administration. No more school for girls, no more health care for women, no more fresh air for us anywhere. Women, go home!

stealthily
slowly and deliberately in secret

prohibitions
orders that forbid

annihilate
cause to cease to exist

from *My Forbidden Face*   65

Or disappear under the *chadri*, out of the sight of men. It's an absolute denial of individual liberty, a real sexual racism.

As a last insult to all Afghans, men and women, a new minister has been appointed. He bears the ridiculous title of Minister for the Promotion of Virtue and Prevention of Vice, or AMR *Bel Mahrouf* in Afghan.

I go to my room to look at all my things: my books, clothes, photos, comics, music tapes, videos, and posters. My nail polish, Soraya's[5] lipstick . . . We'll have to pack all this up in cardboard boxes and hide it in the closet. I'm crushed, at moments enraged, in tears a second later. My mother and sister and I find this petty tyranny over our personal lives intolerable. Mama has begun to wrap up forbidden items, family albums, baby pictures, photos of weddings—hers and Shakila's. Mama has taken down her lovely portrait painted by her brother, the picture of a woman in full bloom, an image of liberty the Taliban cannot stand. While Soraya and I pile our girlish treasures into the closet, our mother hides her own keepsakes from her years as a student, young woman, wife, and mother, concealing them in the back of a kitchen cupboard. I pack my prettiest dresses into a suitcase, keeping only pants and black running shoes. Soraya does the same thing. Her pretty Aryana Airlines[6] uniform, her short, colorful skirts, her spring blouses, her high heels and rainbow-hued sweaters, now "indecent." Then Soraya helps Mama go through the apartment to hunt down forbidden pictures, including calendars and the football and music posters in Daoud's room.

And I break down and cry, alone in the middle of our bedroom with the last books to be packed away. I feel faint. While I was busily filling boxes, I was acting as if I were just temporarily putting my things into storage. Now I feel as though I were coming apart. I happen to notice a cartoon I cut out of a newspaper last year. It shows two scientists bending over a microscope,

> *M*ama has begun to wrap up forbidden items, family albums, baby pictures, photos of weddings—hers and Shakila's.

---

5 **Soraya:** Latifa's 20-year-old sister. Their older sister, Shakila, lives in Pakistan with her husband. Daoud is their brother.

6 **Aryana Airlines:** the national airline of Afghanistan

studying some *talibs*[7] swarming on a specimen slide. The scientists seem perplexed and wonder what kind of germ they're looking at.

A nasty germ, a dangerously **virulent** microbe that **propagates** by spreading a serious disease **insidiously** fatal to the freedom of women. This microbe is highly infectious. The Taliban need only declare themselves through force the absolute masters of Sharia, the precepts of the Koran,[8] which they distort as they please without any respect for the holy book. In my family we are deeply religious; my parents know what the Sharia means for a good Muslim. And the injunctions of the Koran have nothing to do with what the Taliban want to impose on us.

The Taliban have already forbidden us to keep photos of animals; soon they will forbid us to keep the animals themselves, I'm sure of it. We have a canary in a cage on the living room balcony, which Papa converted into a glassed-in porch to protect us from the cold and from prying eyes. Our bird sings so sweetly at sunrise.

Retuning from the **mosque**, Papa finds me sobbing in my room.

"Calm down, Latifa! Nobody knows yet how things will turn out. You must be patient. This won't last, you'll see."

"Papa, we have to let the canary go. I want him, at least, to be free!"

Opening this cage is a vital symbolic gesture. I watch the canary hesitate before this unfamiliar freedom, take flight in a flurry of wings, and disappear into the distance in the cloudy September sky. It's my liberty he carries away with him. May God guide him safely to some peaceful valley!

• • •

In February 1997, I venture outside for the second time. Although they have forbidden women to work, the Taliban have promised to pay them their salaries for a few more months. Daoud and I accompany Soraya to the offices of Aryana Airlines, which are about a mile from our apartment. Since it's quite cold out, my sister and I are wearing long black dresses over dark sweaters and jogging pants. Our socks and running shoes are black, and

virulent
extremely dangerous

propagates
continues or increases

insidiously
having a gradual and cumulative effect

mosque
Islamic house of worship

---

7 *talibs*: members of the fundamentalist Sunni Muslim group, the Taliban

8 **Koran**: the holy book of Islam

from *My Forbidden Face*

our brown *chadris* are firmly anchored on our heads, so in theory there's no reason for the Taliban to be suspicious of us. The avenue has greatly changed since I last saw it. The television and airline company buildings are still closed and gloomy. Corrugated tin shacks have been set up a few yards from the entrances to the buildings, simple bins with doors cut out of them, doors reserved for women. That's where the *chadris* line up, going one at a time to have documents verified and to receive the appropriate compensation. I notice a small opening on one side, a sort of spy hole, and while we're waiting, I realize what it's for. A woman enters the container through the large opening and stands in front of the Judas hole,[9] through which she hands her papers to a *talib* on the other side, who checks them and returns them to her along with a stack of afghanis.[10]

The *chadri* isn't enough: They also have to have this shield of sheet metal between them and a woman. Just what is it they are afraid of? We are impure—but that doesn't stop them from slapping a woman with their bare hands and shoving her into barbed wire!

The women who have come today to get the money owed them begin to protest. Why are they being humiliated, refused entry into the building? Why are they being **relegated** to a tin shack?

One of the armed *talibs* sitting on the ground by the entrance to the container stands up to shoot a few rounds into the air and scare us. As far as I'm concerned, he succeeds. But Narguesse, a colleague of Soraya's and one of her best friends, is so **infuriated** that she rips off her *chadri* and screams, "It's disgraceful to treat us like this!"

Utter astonishment. She has dared signal her rebellion by showing in broad daylight the pretty face of an out-of-work flight attendant.

Then the other women become caught up in her fervor: Shouting angrily, they close in on the *talib,* who is quickly joined by other men who push us roughly inside the shack and drag away Narguesse, who struggles like a demon.

relegated
assigned to a place of insignificance

infuriated
extremely angry

---

9 **Judas hole:** a peephole or secret opening for spying; named for Judas, the disciple who betrayed Christ.

10 **afghanis:** the currency of Afghanistan

Once inside, we take off our *chadris*, shouting, "We won't leave here until you bring her back!"

There are only about twenty of us. I don't know if Daoud saw the disturbance—I don't think so. He probably thought the paperwork would take a long time and strolled off down the avenue. Everyone is talking at once inside the shack. We're all afraid for Narguesse and wondering what punishment she's suffering. Our sole means of exerting pressure is to stay here, with our faces uncovered, so that they hesitate to throw us out. It doesn't give us much leverage.

> Our sole means of exerting pressure is to stay here, with our faces uncovered, so that they hesitate to throw us out.

At last Narguesse reappears, extremely agitated; she is wearing her *chadri* again, but refuses to say anything. The *talibs* scream at us to get out.

Eight of us head back to Mikrorayan.[11] Along the way, Narguesse tells us what happened.

The *talibs* took her to the former personnel office on the ground floor of the building and made her put her *chadri* back on.

"Why did you remove your *chadri*? Why are you trying to defy and offend us?"

"Because you have no right to keep women from working. No right to receive us today like dogs in that shack. We helped make this company a success and we didn't wear *chadris* in the planes or in the offices!"

"You're nothing but a woman! You have no right to speak, no right to raise your voice. You have no right to take off your *chadri*. The days when you could travel and walk around without a *chadri* are over!"

Twice Narguesse tried to take off her *chadri* again, she tells us, and twice they stopped her.

"If you try that once more, we'll kill you."

Luckily for her, one of the *talibs* guarding the shack came to warn his superiors that we were refusing to leave until she returned. After hesitating a moment, they pushed her outside.

"Get out! And keep quiet!"

---

11 **Mikrorayan:** a town in which the Soviet rulers of Afghanistan built modern apartment complexes in the late 1970s

She escaped severe punishment, perhaps even death, for having rebelled like that, but why did they let her go? Because they were afraid of having to control a handful of women? True, there weren't a lot of them, either . . . Perhaps they'd received instructions? We'll never know.

seething
suffering violent internal feelings

Narguesse is still upset, **seething** with anger. She has always been willful and independent.

"We have to fight back. Today we couldn't do much because there weren't enough of us. But if tomorrow there are thousands of us, then we'll be able to overthrow these Taliban!"

We agree with her, but how can we rebel? Where can we meet? We risk endangering our families. We have no weapons, no freedom of expression, no press, no television. To whom can we appeal? How can we obtain outside help when we have no voices, no faces? We're ghosts.

This has been our first protest demonstration since the Taliban took over five months ago. I'm afraid. I'm still shaking inside when Daoud catches up with our little group on the way back to Mikrorayan.

This evening, in the apartment with its painted-over windows, in the gloom of the kerosene lamp, Soraya and I finally have something to tell our mother. But Mama, who used to be so defiant, places her tired hands sadly on her daughters' heads and sighs, "I'm sure you were very brave."

And with a sharp pain in my heart, I realize that she doesn't ever want to hear about war or rebellion again. Every night she swallows her sleeping pills to take refuge in a dreamless sleep . . . where the Taliban can't touch her.

AFTER YOU READ
from *My Forbidden Face*

Think and Discuss

1. Summarize what life was like for women in Afghanistan under Taliban rule.

2. Compare the way Latifa and Soraya react to the oppression of Taliban rule with the way their parents react. Give examples.

3. One writer has called the *chadri* a "mobile cage." What comparisons and **metaphors** does Latifa use in this selection? (For a definition of **metaphor** see the Glossary of Literary Terms.)

4. What **inferences** can you draw from the specific items the family packs away? What does this tell you about the kind of life they have had?

5. Think about the impact that the rule of the Taliban would have on your life. Create a chart like the one below in your Writer's Notebook. Then list the things you've done in the past twenty-four hours. Include things like watching TV, spending time with friends, and talking on the phone. For each thing you list, decide if you could have done this if you lived in Afghanistan when the Taliban were in power. For each item, write the number of the page where you found the evidence that helped you decide.

My Activities Today	Could It Have Happened There?

6. What "rite of passage" does Latifa go through in this selection? Explain.

Write to Understand: Focused Freewriting

Review your list of activities and consider how your life would change if you were subjected to the same kind of oppression the Afghani people were. Think about how the changes would make you feel and how you would react to them. Then start writing about your feelings and what you think you would do to survive. Keep writing for at least 10 minutes.

BEFORE YOU READ

Unfinished Business

"Good Night, Willie Lee, I'll See You in the Morning"

Meet the Authors

Elisabeth Kübler-Ross (1926–2004) spent most of her life working with the dying. She was born in Zurich, Switzerland, and graduated from medical school there in 1957. Beginning her medical career in New York City, she was appalled by the standard hospital treatment of dying patients. "They were shunned and abused, nobody was honest with them." She made a point of sitting with dying patients, comforting them and studying them. In 1969, she published the groundbreaking book *On Death and Dying,* which brought her international renown and influenced the way hospitals treat patients they cannot cure.

Alice Walker An award-winning poet and novelist, Alice Walker was born in 1944 to Willie Lee and Minnie Lou Grant Walker, poor Georgia sharecroppers. She won the Pulizer Prize in 1983. For more on Alice Walker, see page 700.

Build Background: Five Stages of Grief

In her book *On Death and Dying,* Elisabeth Kübler-Ross defined five stages that people who know they are dying pass through:

- Denial and isolation: Trying not to think or talk about what's happening.

- Anger: Raging against your bad fortune.

- Bargaining: Trying to figure out a way to avoid the inevitable.

- Depression: Realizing and mourning the inevitable.

- Acceptance: Finally making peace with what it is happening.

Kübler-Ross recognized that problems happen when people get stuck in one stage or when they don't complete a stage before moving on to the next. This emotional cycle also applies to the non-dying—to all who grieve a loss or who experience a negative life change.

- Why is understanding the stages of grief important for the people who are experiencing grief and for the people around them?

- What experience in your own life can you relate to this cycle of grief?

THE SICK CHILD, Oskar Kokoschka, 1917

Unfinished Business

ELISABETH KÜBLER-ROSS

Interview by Lynn Gilbert and Gaylen Moore

UNFINISHED BUSINESS

Elisabeth Kübler-Ross

I love to work with dying children. They're just so beautiful. Nobody knows what pearls they are. They have all the wisdom in the world. They know that they are dying. They know how and when they are dying. They teach you all about life if you can hear, if you can listen to them. They use an incredible symbolic language to convey to you how much they know. If people would only understand their symbolic language.

One of my girls, I took her home to die, but she couldn't die. She was just lying there week after week after week. And the father couldn't communicate with her. He was a very **nonverbal** man. The mother was very verbal and a practicing Catholic. Every family member was at a different stage and used his own coping mechanism. That's the time when you have to help always the ones who limp behind because they're going to hurt the most and they're going to have the most unfinished business. We try to help them finish the unfinished business *before* somebody dies, otherwise they have all the grief work afterward.

Grief is the most God-given gift to get in touch with your losses. You shed your tears and then stand up and start again like a child who falls and hurts his knees, cries for fifteen seconds and then jumps up and plays ball again. That's a natural thing. My work is preventive psychiatry, it's to finish as much as possible before death, like we bring flowers to our patients before they die so we don't have to pile them up on the casket afterward. If I love somebody, I tell them "I love you" now, so I can skip the **schmaltzy eulogies** afterward.

One day I asked the father of this twelve-year-old girl if he would give me permission to talk to the other children, six, ten and eleven years old. He said, "They don't know about it." I said, "Come, your child's arms and legs are like pieces of chalk, and her belly is like she's nine months pregnant, and she's lying there slowly dying in the living room. How can a six-, ten- and eleven-year-old not know?" I said, "All I want is for you to give your

nonverbal
unable to express feelings in words

schmaltzy
overly sentimental; the Yiddish word *schmaltz* means literally "rendered fat."

eulogies
words of praise honoring someone who has died, usually spoken at a funeral or memorial service

permission for me to sit with them without grownups, and I'll ask them to draw me a picture." We used the Susan Bach[1] method. She's a Jungian[2] analyst from London who worked in Zurich in my hospital there with children who had brain tumors. She saw that children who had brain tumors, little children, show in their pictures that they know they are going to die, and they share their concepts of life and death and unfinished business in their pictures.

I use this technique daily. In a few minutes I can evaluate the whole family and know who needs the most help and who's O.K. and who's in pain. You don't need hours and hours of psychiatric evaluation, which is just talking and just touches the surface. This is all **preconscious** material. It's the same material that you would get if you had ten consecutive dreams, but I can get it at a **morgue**, at a **wake**, in a church, in a school, in a motel, in a shack in Alaska in an Eskimo family, with Aborigines in Australia; it costs nothing, it takes five minutes, it **transcends** language, it's human. All human beings are the same anyway.

So the father finally gave me permission, and I went there at three-thirty when school was out so that the father wouldn't be back, you know, and have second thoughts and give in to his own anxiety. The children were absolutely gorgeous. I locked the dining room with a key so no grownup could interfere, and I said, "Let's have a competition. We're going to draw a picture and we have ten minutes." I limit the time so they don't start thinking, so it's as genuine and authentic and spontaneous as possible. In every picture these children revealed they knew that their sister was dying. I just said, "Use any color and draw a picture."

Anyway, the six-year-old was just gorgeous. His picture was so clear. I talked with him about it in the presence of the others. I said to him, "What your picture is telling is that your sister is dying." He said, "Yes." I said, "Well, if she's going to die tomorrow, is there anything you haven't done, because this is your last chance to say or do anything you want to do, so that you don't have to worry about it afterwards when it's too late. That's what grownups do,

preconscious
not present in consciousness but able to be recalled

morgue
a place where the bodies of dead people are kept temporarily

wake
a watch held over the body of a dead person before burial

transcends
rises above or goes beyond

---

1 **Susan Bach:** a psychoanalyst at the University of Zurich whose research was devoted to evaluating spontaneous paintings made by seriously ill patients, especially children suffering from leukemia and other cancers

2 **Jungian:** relating to the teachings of Swiss psychologist Carl Jung, who sought understanding of human emotions through the exploration of dreams, folklore, and mythology

but you don't have to do that." That challenged him. He said, "Yeah, I guess I'm supposed to tell her I love her." I said, "You're already a phoney-baloney at six years old." Children shouldn't be that contaminated. I said, "I've never seen a six-year-old who goes to a twelve-year-old and says, 'I love you.' There must have been a lot of things that she did that drove you up the wall, that she was unfair, you know, negative stuff." I said, "You can only really love her when you get rid of all the negative stuff, all the fights that you had, and when you get rid of that, then you love her so much that you don't need to say it, because she'll know it anyway and you'll know it."

He was fidgeting around at the table, and I said, "Come on, you're the youngest"—and the younger, the more honest they are—"get it out, what bugs you?" And he said, "Well, I really would like to tell her to get it over with already. I would like her to drop dead already." And I said, "Yes, naturally," as carefully as I could. And I said, "Why does it bug you that it takes so long?" He said, "I can't slam the doors ever, I can't bring my friends home, and I can't watch television anymore, and it's sickening how long it takes." You know, very natural, honest answers for a six-year-old.

I'm sitting there putting fuel on the fire and encouraging him to talk. The ten- and eleven-year-olds just sat there and stared at him. I said, "I wonder if you're honest enough and have the courage to share that with your sister." He said, "One ought not to do that." I said, "Who says? Do you think it's better to swallow this down, and then after she dies you have all these guilt trips and later on need counseling, or is it better to share it with your sister now and then you can love each other or forgive each other, whatever is necessary? And then you'll really feel super-duper. You will still miss her." They will have grief, you understand, but not grief *work*. He said, "Oh, I would love to be able to do that."

And you have to visualize . . . We go out into this living room where she lies there. And the six-year-old sits next to her, and I'm behind him, then the ten-year-old is behind me and the eleven-year-old behind her, then the mother came in and at the very end, the father behind her. And the arrangement was very symbolically beautiful. They came in the right chronological order in the courage they had to do that. Then the six-year-old starts **procrastinating** a little, and I give him a little nudge in the pants with my foot. Then he blurted it out and said to her, "You know, sometimes it takes so long, sometimes I pray to get it over with."

procrastinating intentionally putting off something that needs to be done

Unit One   Rites of Passage

He was just ready to explain, and something very beautiful happened with that symbolic language. His sister lifted her arms up with her last strength and fell over his shoulders, and hanging on to him she started to sob and sob and cry, not painful crying but tremendous relief. It was just like floodgates opening. In her sobbing she kept repeating, "Thank God, thank God, thank God. I prayed for the last three days for God to take me already because it really is getting too much now. And every time I finish my prayer, Mom comes in and stands in the doorway and said she spent the whole night sitting up, praying to God to keep me." And she said, "If you help me, then together we can outdo Mom."

Children take everything very concretely. And he was the proudest man in the world, he was just beaming, and they were holding onto each other, crying and laughing. It was one of the most moving moments of house calls, and I've made lots of them. The other siblings naturally were envious that they weren't the ones who had the courage to do that.

About three days later I went back to see not just how she was doing, but how the six-year-old was doing, if he had any second thoughts about it. He was in super shape, he was high. But the girl couldn't die and so I asked the mother, I said, "If you don't mind, I'm just going to ask her straightforward, not in symbolic language, why she can't die,

*I*t was one of the most moving moments of house calls, and I've made lots of them.

if that's O.K. with you. And I want you to come in and see how I'm doing that so you're never worried that I'm hurting anybody." She had great faith in me.

So I walked into the living room, and I looked at her and I said, "You just can't die, can you?" She said, "No." I said, "Why?" She said, "Because I can't get to heaven." I said, "Who told you that?" She said she was always taught for twelve years that nobody gets to heaven unless you have loved God more than anybody else in the whole world. Then she lifted her arms up and whispered in my ear as if she would try to prevent God from hearing her. She whispered very quietly, "You understand that I love my mommy and daddy better than anybody in the whole world."

punitive
inflicting or
involving
punishment

devastated
overwhelmed by
sadness

discrimination
treating people
differently, in
this case, based
on ability

That made me very sad that children have to apologize for that. What you then have to do is set aside your own anger at the people who teach this kind of **punitive** approach. I said, "We're not going to get into an argument about who is right and who is wrong, because each one believes what they need to believe. I can only work with you and talk with you the way I always have. You and I always talked about school, and the biggest dream of your life was to be a schoolteacher. The only time I ever saw you **devastated** was in September when the school buses rolled up and school started after the summer vacation, and your brothers and sisters boarded the school bus, and you looked through this window and you really looked devastated." I said, "I think what happened was that at that moment it began to dawn on you that you will never again go back to your beloved school and you will never become a teacher." I said, "I want to ask only one question. Sometimes your teacher gives very tough assignments to some students." It was in the back of my mind that she was an honor student. I said, "Does she give these assignments to lousy students? Does she give it to everybody in the class without **discrimination**, or does she give it to a very few of her hand-picked, chosen students?" Then her face lit up and she said, "Oh, she gives it to very few of us." I said, "Since God is also a teacher, do you think He gave you a tough assignment? Or an assignment He could give to any child?"

What she did then was symbolic language. At first she didn't answer me in words. Ever so slowly she looked down at her belly and her arms which were not thicker than my thumb, and her belly full of cancer. She very slowly looked down her body, and then looked up at me and said, "I don't think God could give a tougher assignment to any child."

She died about two and a half or three days later. My last communication with her was totally nonverbal and to me very beautiful because I knew that it helped her. I thought at that time she was in a coma, and I came then so as not to disturb the family in the last day or two. I stood in the doorway and took another look at her, and she suddenly opened her eyes. She couldn't speak anymore at that time. And she looked down at her belly and her legs, and she had a big smirk on her face. And I nodded. She knew what I talked about and I knew what she talked about. It was totally nonverbal. It was very beautiful.

I learn always from dying patients. Instead of always looking at the negative, what you see is the uniqueness and strength in every single human being. I have patients who never share, never communicate. They live a very bland life, and anybody who looked at them would say, Is this all there is to it? And then you really get to know those people. There is a beauty in them that very few see. And all you have to do is look.

Dying patients look back at their lives, and they review and evaluate what they would do over again if they had

BUTTERFLY, Michael Rothenstein

a second chance, and that's very instructive because dying patients throw overboard all the following: they don't have to impress you anymore, they do not have to pretend. They're not interested in material things. They have no secondary gains except to honestly share what life is all about and what lessons they have learned too late. And they pass it on to you, and I pass it on to others so they don't have to wait until they're on their deathbed and say the same thing. Dying patients literally teach you about life.

POETRY CONNECTION

"Good Night, Willie Lee, I'll See You in the Morning"

ALICE WALKER

Looking down into my father's
dead face
for the last time
my mother said without
tears, without smiles   5
but with *civility*
"Good night, Willie Lee, I'll see you
in the morning."
And it was then I knew that the healing
of all our wounds   10
is forgiveness
that permits a promise
of our return
at the end.

ANNA WASHINGTION DERRY,
Laura Wheeler Waring, 1927

AFTER YOU READ

Unfinished Business
"Good Night, Willie Lee, I'll See You in the Morning"

Think and Discuss

1. What does Elisabeth Kübler-Ross mean when she talks about "unfinished business"?

2. Discuss the two things that the girl thought were preventing her from dying. How does she manage to move beyond those things?

3. The selection is an interview with Elisabeth Kübler-Ross by Lynn Gilbert and Gaylen Moore. Give examples of how the **style** reveals that the language was originally spoken not written.

4. Kübler-Ross talks about the "incredible symbolic language" dying children use to convey how much they know. What did the dying girl express in **symbolic language** in her last communication with the author?

5. The author makes a distinction between *grief* and *grief work*. Use a graphic organizer like the following to illustrate the difference. Write examples of *grief* in one column and examples of *grief work* in the other. The examples can come from the selection, from your own experience, or from the experience of people you know.

Grief	Grief Work

6. In "Good Night Willie Lee, I'll See You in the Morning," does the widow seem to have made peace with her loss? Give reasons for your answer.

Write to Understand: Personal Narrative

Review the examples you listed in your graphic organizer under *Grief Work*. Select one of the examples and think hard about it. If the example comes from your own experience, recall how you felt and what you did. If the example comes from the selection or from the experience of someone you know, try to imagine yourself in that person's position. Imagine yourself telling someone about that grief work. Write what you would say just as you think you would say it, in your own natural voice.

Writers on Writing

Introduction to *Shelf Life*

Meet the Author: Gary Paulsen

Gary Paulsen (born 1939) is one of the best-known authors of books for young people. He lived for many years in the woods of northern Minnesota. A love of outdoor adventure led Paulsen to compete in two Iditarod dog sled races. He learned firsthand how to survive in the wilderness, a theme that plays out in many of his works. In his 175 books and more than 200 articles and short stories, Paulsen draws on a wide range of life experience for his material. He was at different times a carnival worker, an engineer, a ranch hand, and a sailor. But no work has meant more to him than his work as a writer, to which he often gives 18 to 20 hours a day.

Build Background: A "Write" of Passage

Gary Paulsen credits books with saving his life, of getting him through the passage from his difficult childhood into the world beyond his family. He is so grateful for the salvation he found in both reading and writing books that he has committed himself to promoting a love of the written word among adolescents. As part of that effort, Paulsen asked well-known authors to write a story for a new collection of short stories, with only one rule: the story had to include mention of a book. The selection that follows is the introduction to that collection, which is called *Shelf Life: Stories by the Book.*

- What books or stories have transported you from your everyday life into a world that you could lose yourself in as you read?

- How do you feel about yourself as a writer? Give examples.

Gary Paulsen and his dogs

INTRODUCTION TO *Shelf Life*

GARY PAULSEN

INTRODUCTION TO *SHELF LIFE*

Gary Paulsen

Books saved my life.

First reading them, then writing them.

As surely as my lead dog Cookie pulled me from the bottom of a lake after I fell through the ice, books are the reason I survived my miserable childhood. As certainly as my sloop[1] Scallywag has safely taken me through storms and huge seas, books have sustained me as an adult.

The awfulness of my childhood has been well covered. But I remember two women who took the time to help me when I was a boy and both women, not so coincidentally, helped me with books.

Because I lived from the age of seven to when I was nearly ten in the Philippine Islands and had a private military tutor, I had never been to a public school.

We came back to the States when I was just short of ten and moved to Washington, D.C., so my father, who was in the army, could work at the Pentagon. My mother promptly enrolled me in public school, took me there the first morning, handed me over to a teacher, and left.

I was painfully shy, terrified at the mob of kids and could not go into the room. It was an old school and at the back of the classroom, there was a cloakroom, a shallow closet the width of the room but closed in except for one door. I went in the closet and took my coat off with the rest of the children but then I could not leave, simply could not make my legs move to walk out into the classroom. I was too frightened.

There were many things the teacher could have done wrong. She could have forced me out, dragged me into the classroom, could have made me leave. Instead she did everything right.

She looked into the closet, saw me sitting back in the corner and disappeared for a moment and said something to the children. Then she

---

1 **sloop:** a sailboat with one mast

came back into the closet and sat down next to me in the corner and put her arm around me.

She had a book, a picture book. I cannot recall the contents of the book except that it had a horse's head on the cover and she sat next to me quietly for a time and read to me softly and let me turn the pages. I was lost in the quiet of the cloakroom, lost in the book so deeply that everything else fell away.

After a time, it could have been ten minutes or an hour or my whole life, she asked me if I thought I could come out into the room and take my seat at a desk. I nodded and she stood and took my hand and led me into the classroom.

A few years later, when I was thirteen, another woman, a librarian, gave me another book and I consider every good thing that has ever happened to me since then a result of that woman handing me that book.

. . . I consider every good thing that has happened to me since then a result of that woman handing me that book.

I'd been wandering the streets of the small Minnesota town we lived in one bitter winter evening, waiting for the drunks in the bars to get juiced. I sold newspapers, trying to scrape together a little money so that I could buy better clothes, believing, as kids do, that the right clothes might somehow lift me from my wretchedly unpopular social life. And if I waited for the men who hung around in the bars to get a few drinks in them, I could hustle them for extra change.

I stopped in the library to warm up. The librarian noticed me, called me over, and asked if I wanted a library card. Then she handed me a card with my name on it and gave me a book.

Later that night back at home, or what passed for home—a crummy apartment in the bad part of town—I took the book, a box of crackers, and a jar of grape jelly down to the basement, to a hideaway I'd created behind the furnace where someone had abandoned a creaky old armchair under a bare light bulb.

I sat in the corner, eating jelly-smeared crackers, plodding through the book. It took me forever to read. I was such a poor reader that, by the time I'd finished a page, I'd have forgotten what I'd read on the page before and I'd have to go back. That first book must have taken me over a month to finish, hunched over the pages late at night.

I wish I could remember the name of that first book—I can't even remember what it was about. What I do remember about that evening at the library was that it marked the first of many nights the librarian would give me a book. "Here," she'd say, handing me a few battered volumes. "I think you'll like these." She would hand select books that she thought would interest me—Westerns, mysteries, survival tales, science fiction, Edgar Rice Burroughs.[2] I would take them home to hide in the basement and read; I'd bring them back and we'd talk about them, and she'd give me more books.

But she wasn't just giving me books, she was giving me . . . everything. She gave me the first hint I'd ever had in my entire life that there was something other than my drunken parents screaming at each other in the kitchen. She handed me a world where I wasn't going to get beaten up by the school bullies. She showed me places where it didn't hurt all the time.

I read terribly at first but as I did more of it, the books became more a part of me and within a short time they gave me a life, a look at life outside myself that made me look forward instead of backward.

Years later, after I'd graduated from high school, joined the army, gotten married, had children, and made a career as an electronics engineer working in satellite tracking, books once again changed the course of my life. This time, though, I wrote them.

I was sitting in the satellite tracking station at about nine o'clock at night when suddenly I knew that I had to be a writer. In that instant, I gave up or lost everything that had made up my life until that point—my work, my family, certainly my earning potential.

Writing had suddenly become everything . . . everything . . . to me.

I stood up from the console, handed in my security badge, and headed for Hollywood. I had to go to a place where writers were; I had to

---

2 **Edgar Rice Burroughs:** American author best known for creating the jungle hero Tarzan

be near them, had to learn from them. I got a job as a proofreader of a men's magazine, going from earning $500 a week to $400 a month, and apprenticed myself to a couple of editors.

These two men gave me writing assignments, and in order to continue receiving their help, I had to write an article, a chapter of a book, or a short story every night, every single night, no exceptions, no excuses, for them to critique. If I missed a single day, they would no longer help me.

*W*e have decided to publish your book. Such words thunder, burn into your mind, your soul.

I have been writing for over thirty years, spent most of it starving, trying to make it work for me, in my mind; trying to make words come together in the right patterns, movements, what some have called the loops and whorls of the story dance, and it has always been hard. It is, sometimes, still difficult. But I love writing more now, I think, than I ever have. The way the words dance, the rhythms and movements of them, is grandly exciting to me.

I remember the first acceptance letter, the first time a publisher told me my writing was worthy of publication, the first after many, many rejections. There will never be another first like this one; not first love nor first hope nor first time never, no never like this.

Dear author: We have decided to publish your book.

Can you imagine? Your life, your work, your hopes and thoughts and songs and breath, we have decided to publish your book. We have decided to publish you. Such words thunder, burn into your mind, your soul.

Since then I have written every day and I have told many stories. Stories of love and death and cold and heat and ice and flame, stories sad and stories happy and stories of laughter and tears and places soft and hard, of dogs and the white blink of arctic ice, stories of great men and beautiful women and souls and devils and gods, stories of lost dreams and found joys and aches and torture and great rolling hills and towering storms and things quick and hot and slow and dull, stories of graves and horses, pigs and kings, war and the times between wars, stories of children's cheeks and the soft hair at a woman's temple when it is moist, stories of rage and spirit and spit and blood and bodies on fences and hay so sweet you could eat the grass.

I write from my life, from what I see and hear and smell and feel, from personal inspection at zero altitude and I write because it is, simply, all that I am, because in the end I do not want to do any other thing as much as I want to write. But the force behind it, the thing that pushes me to write, that wakes me at night with story ideas, that makes the hair on the back of my neck go up when a story works, that causes my breath to stop and hold with a sentence that comes right, and that makes coming to the computer or the pad of paper every morning with a cup of tea and a feeling of wonderful newness and expectations, the engine that drives me to write is, surely, love.

I personally want just two things. I want to write, and I want as many young readers as possible to see what I write. That's it. To write and to have readers.

I work all the time. I get up at four thirty in the morning, meditate for half an hour, then start working. Not always writing, but working. If I'm not writing, I read and study and write until I fall asleep at night.

I owe everything I am and everything that I will ever be to books.

AFTER YOU READ
Introduction to *Shelf Life*

Think and Discuss

1. Paulsen says that books saved his life. What do you think would have become of him without books? Explain, using details from the text.

2. What was it about books—those that were read to him, those he was given, and those he wrote—that helped Paulsen so much?

3. Suppose you are a magazine editor who wants to publish this piece as an essay. The **text features** of your magazine include headings to break up longer text. Where would you put the headings in this essay, and what would they be?

4. In most of this essay, Paulsen writes relatively short, concise sentences. Near the end, though, Paulsen's sentences go on and on and on when he is writing about *writing*. What feeling does this **style** of long sentences convey about the subject?

5. With your class, discuss books or stories you may have read by Gary Paulsen, such as *Hatchet*, *Brian's Winter*, or *Dogsong*. How would you describe Paulsen as a writer?

6. Scan this selection again. Then look back over the other autobiographical narratives in this unit (from *I Know Why the Caged Bird Sings*, page 15; "Vegetarian Enough" page 51; and from *My Forbidden Face*, page 63). Copy the graphic organizer below into your Writer's Notebook. Then use it to jot down the features these autobiographical narratives have in common.

Features of Autobiographical Narratives	
Subject Matter	
Point of View	
Structure and Organization	
Types of Details Used	

Write to Understand: Quickwrite

Review the features you noted in your graphic organizer. Then think of an experience in your life that would make a good subject for an autobiographical narrative. Quickwrite a draft of it—just get the ideas down on paper. Don't worry about mistakes, but try to give your quick draft the basic features you identified.

A *Writer's* WORKSHOP

AUTOBIOGRAPHICAL NARRATIVE

In this unit you have read about young people and their feelings as they approach adulthood. In the autobiographical narratives, *I Know Why the Caged Bird Sings*; page 15, "Vegetarian Enough," page 51; *My Forbidden Face*, page 63; and Shelf Life, page 83) you have had a chance to get to know about who the writer is deep inside. Now you have a chance to share a little of yourself with readers as you write your own autobiographical narrative.

Prewriting

REVIEWING IDEAS

The writing you've done so far in your Writer's Notebook includes possible ideas for an autobiographical narrative. Review what you have written to see which idea grabs you the most. A good subject for an autobiographical narrative is an incident:

- with a clear beginning, middle, and ending that shows how you made a passage of some kind and grew as a person or learned an important lesson

- that will allow readers to get a good sense of who you are.

If you don't find an incident in your Writer's Notebook that you want to write about, brainstorm other incidents from your life that might work well as the subject of an autobiographical narrative.

FREEWRITING TO DEVELOP DETAILS

Once you have chosen an incident for your narrative, write down everything you can remember about what happened. Include all of the people involved, the place, the time, and every other detail you can think of. Write freely without worrying about form or mistakes.

Sample Freewriting

I'm going to write about the time my sister and I went to the Bellwood Avenue shopping area by ourselves for the first time. It must have been spring because I remember my father's muddy boots when he came to pick us up. We went to the dimestore—I remember I bought a pencil case with my allowance money. I don't remember what Marsha bought. Marsha felt very grown up being in charge of me. I was wearing my favorite blue . . .

ORGANIZING IDEAS

Look over your freewriting. Circle each event in the story. Then copy and complete the framework below in your Writer's Notebook.

The passage you made or lesson learned	
Setting	
Event that begins narrative	
Next important event in narrative	
Next important event in narrative	
Event that ends the narrative	
What narrative shows about you	

Drafting

Use your chart to write a first draft. Also look back over the notes you made about other details you remember from this incident. Add these to your narrative to make it come alive and to show its importance to you. Use dialogue to reveal character.

COOPERATIVE LEARNING: PEER REVIEW

Pair up with a partner and exchange drafts. Discuss the strengths of your partner's draft as well as ways it can be improved. Be open to your partner's suggestions for improving your work.

Revising and Editing

Use your partner's comments to help you evaluate and revise your narrative. Keep revising until you are happy with your draft. Then check your work for errors in grammar, spelling, capitalization, and punctuation.

USING WORD PROCESSING

The most fundamental strategies for revising are *adding, deleting, substituting*, and *rearranging*. With a word processor, you can easily add, delete, substitute, or rearrange your ideas while revising by using the Cut and Paste functions. Highlight what you want to change. Then choose Cut (or Copy) from the Edit menu. If you choose Copy, position your cursor where you want to insert your highlighted text and choose Paste from the Edit menu. Save different versions of your work under different file names, such as autobiography1 and autobiography2. You can then compare them side by side as you continue to think of ways to improve your writing.

READING WITH AN EDITOR'S EYE

In narrative writing, transitional words and phrases help readers follow the passing of time. Here are some of the words and phrases Gary Paulsen uses as he recounts his early experience with books and reading (see page 85).

- After a time, it could have been ten minutes or an hour or my whole life, she asked me . . .

- A few years later, when I was thirteen . . .

- Later that night back at home . . .

As you are revising your autobiographical narrative, check to make sure you have clearly signaled to readers when time is passing so that they can follow the story easily. Use such words and phrases as *later, the next day, when I was eleven*, and *by the time I got home*.

USING A CHECKLIST

The Six-Trait checklist on the next page will help you evaluate and polish your narrative.

Six Traits of Writing: Autobiographical Narratives

Content and Ideas
- subject focuses on passage or lesson learned
- narrative reveals something about writer's personality or character
- vivid supporting details bring the experience to life

Organization
- narrative has clear beginning, middle, and ending
- events are presented in a clear time order

Voice or Style
- narrative uses first-person point of view
- writer's voice sounds natural, not forced
- dialogue is realistic and reveals character

Word Choice
- lively verbs and specific nouns give the writing energy
- such comparisons as similes and metaphors create memorable images

Sentence Fluency
- transitional words help the writing flow smoothly
- sentence length and sentence beginnings are varied and purposeful

Conventions
- sentences are complete and begin with a capital letter and end with a period
- grammar and usage are correct
- spelling and punctuation are correct

COOPERATIVE LEARNING: PEER EDITING
Exchange papers with your partner and check each other's editing. Fix any errors your partner points out. Make a neat final copy of your narrative.

Family Ties

I am seven; she is sixty something. We are cousins, very distant ones, and we have lived together— well, as long as I can remember.

Truman Capote, from "A Christmas Memory"

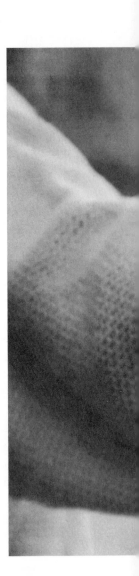

BEFORE YOU READ
The Scarlet Ibis

Meet the Author: James Hurst

James Hurst (born 1922) has been a farmer, soldier, engineering student, opera singer, banker, and celebrated writer. After his World War II service in the army, Hurst studied engineering but quit to pursue his true passion: singing. He attended the famous Juilliard School of Music, followed by four years of studying opera in Italy. Unable to turn his dream into a career, he instead became a banker who wrote fiction and drama in his spare time.

"The Scarlet Ibis" was published in *The Atlantic Monthly* in 1960 and has since become a modern classic. Hurst believes he wrote it in part to get over his failure as a professional singer.

Build Background: Birds of a Feather

A scarlet ibis is a beautifully plumed tropical bird, known for its bright red feathers. The bird's long neck and legs make it well-suited to wading in wet, marshy grounds—its normal habitat. Its long, curved beak helps to snare crabs, shrimp, and other food in the water.

As you read, watch for connections between people in the story and the natural world that surrounds them.

- What does the word *pride* mean to you? Do you think it is always a positive trait?

- The main character in the following story has a disabled brother. How do you think you would deal with that situation?

SCARLET IBIS, John James Audubon

The Scarlet Ibis

JAMES HURST

THE SCARLET IBIS

James Hurst

It was in the clove[1] of seasons, summer was dead, but autumn had not yet been born, that the ibis[2] lit in the bleeding tree.[3] The flower garden was stained with rotting brown magnolia petals and ironweeds grew **rank** amid the purple phlox. The five o'clocks by the chimney still marked time, but the oriole nest in the elm was untenanted and rocked back and forth like an empty cradle. The last graveyard flowers were blooming, and their smell drifted across the cotton field and through every room of our house, speaking softly the names of our dead.

rank
smelly or foul

It's strange that all this is still so clear to me, now that summer has long since fled and time has had its way. A grindstone[4] stands where the bleeding tree stood, just outside the kitchen door, and now if an oriole sings in the elm, its song seems to die up in the leaves, a silvery dust. The flower garden is prim, the house a gleaming white, and the pale fence across the yard stands straight and spruce.[5] But sometimes (like right now), as I sit in the cool green parlor, the grindstone begins to turn, and time with all its changes is ground away—and I remember Doodle.

Doodle was just about the craziest brother a boy ever had. Of course, he wasn't a crazy crazy like old Miss Leedie, who was in love with President Wilson and wrote him a letter every day, but was a nice crazy, like someone you meet in your dreams. He was born when I was six and was, from the outset, a disappointment. He seemed all head, with a tiny body which was red and shriveled like an old man's. Everybody thought he was going to die—everybody except Aunt Nicey, who had delivered him. She said he would live because he was born in a caul,[6] and cauls were made from Jesus' nightgown.

---

1 **clove:** the interval between two seasons

2 **ibis:** the scarlet ibis, a brilliant red tropical wading bird with a long bill, neck, and legs

3 **bleeding tree:** a kind of tropical tree that oozes dark red sappy resin when cut

4 **grindstone:** a flat circular stone used for shaping or sharpening

5 **spruce:** tidy, trim

6 **caul:** a filmy membrane that can cover or partly cover newborn mammals

Daddy had Mr. Heath, the carpenter, build a little mahogany coffin for him. But he didn't die, and when he was three months old, Mama and Daddy decided they might as well name him. They named him William Armstrong, which was like tying a big tail on a small kite. Such a name sounds good only on a tombstone.

I thought myself pretty smart at many things, like holding my breath, running, jumping, or climbing the vines in Old Woman Swamp, and I wanted more than anything else someone to race to Horsehead Landing, someone to box with, and someone to perch with in the top fork of the great pine behind the barn, where across the fields and swamps you could see the sea. I wanted a brother. But Mama, crying, told me that even if William Armstrong lived, he would never do these things with me. He might not, she sobbed, even be "all there." He might, as long as he lived, lie on the rubber sheet in the center of the bed in the front bedroom where the white marquisette curtains billowed out in the afternoon sea breeze, rustling like palmetto fronds.

They named him William Armstrong, which was like tying a big tail on a small kite. Such a name sounds good only on a tombstone.

It was bad enough having an invalid brother, but having one who possibly was not all there was unbearable, so I began to make plans to kill him by smothering him with a pillow. However, one afternoon as I watched him, my head poked between the iron posts of the foot of the bed, he looked straight at me and grinned. I skipped through the rooms, down the echoing halls, shouting, "Mama, he smiled. He's all there! He's all there!" and he was.

When he was two, if you laid him on his stomach, he began to move himself, straining terribly. The doctor said that with his weak heart this strain would probably kill him, but it didn't. Trembling, he'd push himself up, turning first red, then a soft purple, and finally collapse back onto the bed like an old worn-out doll. I can still see Mama watching him, her hand pressed tight across her mouth, her eyes wide and unblinking. But he learned to crawl (it was his third winter), and we brought him out of the front bedroom, putting him on the rug before the fireplace. For the first time he became one of us.

As long as he lay all the time in bed, we called him William Armstrong, even though it was formal and sounded as if we were referring to one of our ancestors, but with his creeping around on the deerskin rug and beginning to talk, something had to be done about his name. It was I who renamed him. When he crawled, he crawled backward, as if he were in reverse and couldn't change gears. If you called him, he'd turn around as if he were going in the other direction, then he'd back right up to you to be picked up. Crawling backward made him look like a doodlebug,[7] so I began to call him Doodle, and in time even Mama and Daddy thought it was a better name than William Armstrong. Only Aunt Nicey disagreed. She said caul babies should be treated with special respect since they might turn out to be saints. Renaming my brother was perhaps the kindest thing I ever did for him, because nobody expects much from someone called Doodle.

Although Doodle learned to crawl, he showed no signs of walking, but he wasn't idle. He talked so much that we all quit listening to what he said. It was about this time that Daddy built him a go-cart and I had to pull him around. At first I just paraded him up and down the piazza,[8] but then he started crying to be taken out in the yard, and it ended up by my having to lug him wherever I went. If I so much as picked up my cap, he'd start crying to go with me, and Mama would call from wherever she was, "Take Doodle with you."

He was a burden in many ways. The doctor had said that he mustn't get too excited, too hot, too cold, or too tired and that he must always be treated gently. A long list of don'ts went with him, all of which I ignored once we got out of the house. To discourage his coming with me, I'd run with him across the ends of the cotton rows and careen him around corners on two wheels. Sometimes I accidentally turned him over, but he never told Mama. His skin was very sensitive, and he had to wear a big straw hat whenever he went out. When the going got rough and he had to cling to the sides of the go-cart, the hat slipped all the way down over his ears. He was a sight. Finally, I could see I was licked. Doodle was my brother and he was going to cling to me forever, no matter what I did, so I dragged him across the burning cotton field to

---

7 **doodlebug:** a type of insect

8 **piazza:** a roofed open space outside of a house

share with him the only beauty I knew, Old Woman Swamp. I pulled the go-cart through the sawtooth fern, down into the green dimness where the palmetto fronds whispered by the stream. I lifted him out and sat him down in the soft rubber grass beside a tall pine. His eyes were round with wonder as he gazed about him, and his little hands began to stroke the rubber grass. Then he began to cry.

"For heaven's sake, what's the matter?" I asked, annoyed.

"It's so pretty," he said. "So pretty, pretty, pretty."

After that day, Doodle and I often went down into Old Woman Swamp. I would gather wildflowers, wild violets, honeysuckle, yellow jasmine, snakeflowers, and water lilies, and with wire grass we'd weave them into necklaces and crowns. We'd bedeck ourselves with our handiwork and loll about thus beautified, beyond the touch of the everyday world. Then when the slanted rays of the sun burned orange in the tops of the pines, we'd drop our jewels into the stream and watch them float away toward the sea.

There is within me (and with sadness I have watched it in others) a knot of cruelty borne by the stream of love, much as our blood sometimes bears the seed of our destruction, and at times I was mean to Doodle. One day I took him to the barn loft and showed him his casket, telling him how we all had believed he would die. It was covered with a film of Paris green[9] sprinkled to kill the rats, and screech owls had built a nest inside it.

Doodle studied the mahogany box for a long time, then said, "It's not mine."

"It is," I said. "And before I'll help you down from the loft, you're going to have to touch it."

"I won't touch it," he said **sullenly**.

"Then I'll leave you here by yourself," I threatened, and made as if I were going down. Doodle was frightened of being left.

"Don't go leave me, Brother," he cried, and he leaned toward the coffin. His hand, trembling, reached out, and when he touched the casket he screamed. A screech owl flapped out of the box into our faces, scaring us and covering us with Paris green. Doodle was paralyzed, so I put him on my

sullenly
resentfully; sulkily

---

9 **Paris green:** a poisonous insecticide

shoulder and carried him down the ladder, and even when we were outside in the bright sunshine, he clung to me, crying, "Don't leave me. Don't leave me."

When Doodle was five years old, I was embarrassed at having a brother of that age who couldn't walk, so I set out to teach him. We were down in Old Woman Swamp and it was spring and the sick-sweet smell of bay flowers hung everywhere like a mournful song. "I'm going to teach you to walk, Doodle," I said.

He was sitting comfortably on the soft grass, leaning back against the pine. "Why?" he asked.

I hadn't expected such an answer. "So I won't have to haul you around all the time."

"I can't walk, Brother," he said.

"Who says so?" I demanded.

"Mama, the doctor—everybody."

"Oh, you can walk," I said, and I took him by the arms and stood him up. He collapsed on to the grass like a half-empty flour sack. It was as if he had no bones in his little legs.

"Don't hurt me, Brother," he warned.

"Shut up. I'm not going to hurt you. I'm going to teach you to walk." I heaved him up again, and again he collapsed.

This time he did not lift his face up out of the rubber grass. "I just can't do it. Let's make honeysuckle wreaths."

"Oh yes you can, Doodle," I said. "All you got to do is try. Now come on," and I hauled him up once more.

It seemed so hopeless from the beginning that it's a miracle I didn't give up. But all of us must have something or someone to be proud of, and Doodle had become mine. I didn't know then that pride is a wonderful, terrible thing, a seed that bears two vines, life and death. Every day that summer we went to the pine beside the stream of Old Woman Swamp, and I put him on his feet at least a hundred times each afternoon. Occasionally I too became discouraged because it didn't seem as if he was trying and I would say, "Doodle, don't you want to learn to walk?"

He'd nod his head, and I'd say, "Well, if you don't keep trying, you'll never learn." Then I'd paint for him a picture of us as old men, white-haired, him with a long white beard and me still pulling him around in the go-cart. This never failed to make him try again.

Finally one day, after many weeks of practicing, he stood alone for a few seconds. When he fell, I grabbed him in my arms and hugged him, our laughter pealing through the swamp like a ringing bell. Now we knew it could be done. Hope no longer hid in the dark palmetto thicket but perched like a cardinal in the lacy toothbrush tree, brilliantly visible.

"Yes, yes," I cried, and he cried it too, and the grass beneath us was soft and the smell of the swamp was sweet.

With success so **imminent**, we decided not to tell anyone until he could actually walk. Each day, barring rain, we sneaked into Old Woman Swamp, and by cotton-picking time Doodle was ready to show what he could do. He still wasn't able to walk far, but we could wait no longer. Keeping a nice secret is very hard to do, like holding your breath. We chose to reveal all on October eighth, Doodle's sixth birthday, and for weeks ahead we mooned[10] around the house, promising everybody a most spectacular surprise. Aunt Nicey said that, after so much talk, if we produced anything less tremendous than the Resurrection,[11] she was going to be disappointed.

imminent about to happen

At breakfast on our chosen day, when Mama, Daddy, and Aunt Nicey were in the dinning room, I brought Doodle to the door in the go-cart just as usual and had them turn their backs, making them cross their hearts and hope to die if they peeked. I helped Doodle up, and when he was standing alone I let them look. There wasn't a sound as Doodle walked slowly across the room and sat down at his place at the table. Then Mama began to cry and ran over to him, hugging him and kissing him. Daddy hugged him too, so I went to Aunt Nicey, who was thanks praying in the doorway, and began to waltz her around. We danced together quite well until she came down on

Each day, barring rain, we sneaked into Old Woman Swamp, and by cotton-picking time Doodle was ready to show what he could do.

---

10 **mooned:** daydreamed

11 **the Resurrection:** the Christian belief that Jesus was crucified and rose from the dead three days later

my big toe with her brogans,[12] hurting me so badly I thought I was crippled for life.

Doodle told them it was I who had taught him to walk, so everyone wanted to hug me, and I began to cry.

"What are you crying for?" asked Daddy, but I couldn't answer. They didn't know that I did it for myself; that pride, whose slave I was, spoke to me louder than all their voices, and that Doodle walked only because I was ashamed of having a crippled brother.

Within a few months, Doodle had learned to walk well and his go-cart was put in the barn loft (it's still there) beside his little mahogany coffin. Now, when we roamed off together, resting often, we never turned back until our destination had been reached, and to help pass the time, we took up lying. From the beginning Doodle was a terrible liar and he got me in the habit. Had anyone stopped to listen to us, we would have been sent off to Dix Hill.[13]

My lies were scary, involved, and usually pointless, but Doodle's were twice as crazy. People in his stories all had wings and flew wherever they wanted to go. His favorite lie was about a boy named Peter who had a pet peacock with a ten-foot tail. Peter wore a golden robe that glittered so brightly that when he walked through the sunflowers they turned away from the sun to face him. When Peter was ready to go to sleep, the peacock spread his magnificent tail, enfolding the boy gently like a closing go-to-sleep flower, burying him in the gloriously **iridescent**, rustling **vortex**. Yes, I must admit it. Doodle could beat me lying.

iridescent
shimmering and rainbowlike

vortex
whirlpool; eddy

Doodle and I spent lots of time thinking about our future. We decided that when we were grown we'd live in Old Woman Swamp and pick dog-tongue for a living. Beside the stream, he planned, we'd build us a house of whispering leaves and the swamp birds would be our chickens. All day long (when we weren't gathering dog-tongue) we'd swing through the cypresses on the rope vines, and if it rained we'd huddle beneath an umbrella tree and play stickfrog. Mama and Daddy could come and live with us if they wanted

---

12 **brogans:** heavy leather shoes that reach to the ankle

13 **Dix Hill:** the location of a mental hospital in North Carolina

to. He even came up with the idea that he could marry Mama and I could marry Daddy. Of course, I was old enough to know this wouldn't work out, but the picture he painted was so beautiful and **serene** that all I could do was whisper Yes, yes.

serene
calm; peaceful

Once I had succeeded in teaching Doodle to walk, I began to believe in my own **infallibility**, and I prepared a terrific development program for him, unknown to Mama and Daddy, of course. I would teach him to run, to swim, to climb trees, and to fight. He, too, now believed in my infallibility, so we set the deadline for these accomplishments less than a year away, when, it had been decided, Doodle could start to school.

infallibility
inability to fail

That winter we didn't make much progress, for I was in school and Doodle suffered from one bad cold after another.

That winter we didn't make much progress, for I was in school and Doodle suffered from one bad cold after another. But when spring came, rich and warm, we raised our sights again. Success lay at the end of the summer like a pot of gold, and our campaign got off to a good start. On hot days, Doodle and I went down to Horsehead Landing, and I gave him swimming lessons or showed him how to row a boat. Sometimes we descended into the cool greenness of Old Woman Swamp and climbed the rope vines or boxed scientifically beneath the pine where he had learned to walk. Promise hung about us like the leaves, and wherever we looked, ferns **unfurled** and birds broke into song.

unfurled
unwound;
opened up

That summer, the summer of 1918, was **blighted**. In May and June there was no rain and the crops withered, curled up, and then died under the thirsty sun. One morning in July a hurricane came out of the east, tipping over the oaks in the yard and splitting the limbs of the elm trees. That afternoon it roared back out of the west, blew the fallen oaks around, snapping their roots and tearing them out of the earth like a hawk at the **entrails** of a chicken. Cotton bolls were wrenched from the stalks and lay like green walnuts in the valleys between the rows, while the cornfield leaned over uniformly so that the tassels touched the ground. Doodle and I followed Daddy out into the cotton field, where he stood, shoulders sagging, surveying the ruin. When his chin sank down onto his chest, we were frightened, and Doodle slipped his hand into mine. Suddenly Daddy straightened his shoulders, raised a

blighted
destroyed;
ruined

entrails
inner organs
of the body;
guts

giant knuckly fist, and with a voice that seemed to rumble out of the earth itself began cursing heaven, hell, the weather, and the Republican Party. Doodle and I, prodding each other and giggling, went back to the house knowing that everything would be all right.

And during that summer, strange names were heard through the house: Château-Thierry, Amiens, Soissons, and in her blessing at the supper table, Mama once said, "And bless the Pearsons, whose boy Joe was lost at Belleau Wood."[14]

So we came to that clove of seasons. School was only a few weeks away, and Doodle was far behind schedule. He could barely clear the ground when climbing up the rope vines, and his swimming was certainly not passable. We decided to double our efforts, to make the last drive and reach our pot of gold. I made him swim until he turned blue and row until he couldn't lift an oar. Wherever we went, I purposely walked fast, and although he kept up, his face turned red and his eyes became glazed. Once, he could go no further, so he collapsed on the ground and began to cry.

"Aw, come on, Doodle," I urged. "You can do it. Do you want to be different from everybody else when you start school?"

"Does it make any difference?"

"It certainly does," I said. "Now, come on," and I helped him up.

As we slipped through dog days, Doodle began to look feverish, and Mama felt his forehead, asking him if he felt ill. At night he didn't sleep well, and sometimes he had nightmares, crying out until I touched him and said, "Wake up, Doodle. Wake up."

It was Saturday noon, just a few days before school was to start. I should have already admitted defeat, but my pride wouldn't let me. The excitement of our program had now been gone for weeks, but still we kept on with a tired **doggedness**. It was too late to turn back, for we had both wandered too far into a net of expectations and had left no crumbs behind.

doggedness
stubbornness

Daddy, Mama, Doodle, and I were seated at the dining room table having lunch. It was a hot day, with all the windows and doors open in case a breeze should come. In the kitchen Aunt Nicey was humming softly. After a long silence, Daddy spoke. "It's so calm, I wouldn't be surprised if

---

14 **Château-Thierry . . . Belleau Wood:** all places in France where WWI battles were fought

we had a storm this afternoon."

"I haven't heard a rain frog," said Mama, who believed in signs, as she served the bread around the table.

"I did," declared Doodle. "Down in the swamp."

"He didn't," I said contrarily.

"You did, eh?" said Daddy, ignoring my denial.

"I certainly did," Doodle **reiterated**, scowling at me over the top of his iced-tea glass, and we were quiet again.

reiterated
repeated

Suddenly, from out in the yard, came a strange croaking noise. Doodle stopped eating, with a piece of bread poised ready for his mouth, his eyes popped round like two blue buttons. "What's that?" he whispered.

I jumped up, knocking over my chair, and had reached the door when Mama called, "Pick up the chair, sit down again, and say excuse me."

*S*uddenly, from out in the yard, came a strange croaking noise.

By the time I had done this, Doodle had excused himself and had slipped out into the yard. He was looking up into the bleeding tree. "It's a great big red bird!" he called.

The bird croaked loudly again, and Mama and Daddy came out into the yard. We shaded our eyes with our hands against the hazy glare of the sun and peered up through the still leaves. On the topmost branch a bird the size of a chicken, with scarlet feathers and long legs, was perched **precariously**. Its wings hung down loosely, and as we watched, a feather dropped away and floated slowly down through the green leaves.

precariously
insecurely;
perilously

"It's not even frightened of us," Mama said.

"It looks tired," Daddy added. "Or maybe sick."

Doodle's hands were clasped at his throat, and I had never seen him stand still for so long. "What is it?" he asked

Daddy shook his head. "I don't know, maybe it's—"

At that moment the bird began to flutter, but the wings were uncoordinated, and amid much flapping and a spray of flying feathers, it tumbled down, bumping though the limbs of the bleeding tree and landing at our feet with a thud. Its long, graceful neck jerked twice into an S, then straightened out, and the bird was still. A white veil came over the eyes and the long white beak unhinged. Its legs were crossed and its clawlike feet were delicately curved at rest. Even death did not mar its grace, for it lay on the earth like a broken vase of red flowers, and we stood around it, awed by its exotic beauty.

"It's dead," Mama said.

"What is it?" Doodle repeated.

"Go bring me the bird book," said Daddy.

I ran into the house and brought back the bird book. As we watched, Daddy thumbed through its pages. "It's a scarlet ibis," he said, pointing to a picture. "It lives in the tropics—South America to Florida. A storm must have brought it here."

Sadly, we all looked back at the bird. A scarlet ibis! How many miles it had traveled to die like this, in *our* yard, beneath the bleeding tree.

"Let's finish lunch," Mama said, nudging us back toward the dining room.

"I'm not hungry," said Doodle, and he knelt down beside the ibis.

"We've got peach cobbler for dessert," Mama tempted from the doorway.

Doodle remained kneeling. "I'm going to bury him."

"Don't you dare touch him," Mama warned. "There's no telling what disease he might have had."

"All right," said Doodle. "I won't."

Daddy, Mama, and I went back to the dining room table, but we watched Doodle through the open door. He took out a piece of string from his pocket and, without touching the ibis, looped one end around its neck.

Slowly, while singing softly "Shall We Gather at the River," he carried the bird around to the front yard and dug a hole in the flower garden, next to the petunia bed. Now we were watching him through the front window, but he didn't know it. His awkwardness at digging the hole with a shovel whose handle was twice as long as he was made us laugh, and we covered our mouths with our hands so he wouldn't hear.

When Doodle came into the dining room, he found us seriously eating our cobbler. He was pale and lingered just inside the screen door. "Did you get the scarlet ibis buried?" asked Daddy.

Doodle didn't speak but nodded his head.

"Go wash your hands, and then you can have some peach cobbler," said Mama.

"I'm not hungry," he said.

"Dead birds is bad luck," said Aunt Nicey, poking her head from the kitchen door. "Specially *red* dead birds!"

As soon as I had finished eating, Doodle and I hurried off to Horsehead Landing. Time was short, and Doodle still had a long way to go if he was going to keep up with the other boys when he started school. The sun, gilded with the yellow cast of autumn, still burned fiercely, but the dark green woods through which we passed were shady and cool. When we reached the landing, Doodle said he was too tired to swim, so we got into a skiff[15] and floated down the creek with the tide. Far off in the marsh a rail was scolding, and over on the beach locusts were singing in the myrtle trees. Doodle did not speak and kept his head turned away, letting one hand trail limply in the water.

After we had drifted a long way, I put the oars in place and made Doodle row back against the tide. Black clouds began to gather in the southwest, and he kept watching them, trying to pull the oars a little faster. When we reached Horsehead Landing, lightning was playing across half the sky and thunder roared out, hiding even the sound of the sea. The sun disappeared and darkness descended, almost like night. Flocks of marsh crows flew by, heading inland to their roosting trees; and two egrets, squawking, arose from the oyster-rock shallows and **careened** away.

> *B*lack clouds began to gather in the southwest, and he kept watching them, trying to pull the oars a little faster.

Doodle was both tired and frightened, and when he stepped from the skiff he collapsed onto the mud, sending an **armada** of fiddler crabs rustling off into the marsh grass. I helped him up, and as he wiped the mud off his trousers, he smiled at me ashamedly. He had failed and we both knew it, so we started back home, racing the storm. We never spoke (What are the words that can **solder** cracked pride?), but I knew he was watching me, watching for a sign of mercy. The lightning was near now, and from fear he walked so close behind me he kept stepping on my heels. The faster I walked, the

careened
swerved; moved at a tilt

armada
a line of moving things

solder
join; fuse

---

15 **skiff:** a small boat

faster he walked, so I began to run. The rain was coming, roaring through the pines, and then, like a bursting Roman candle,[16] a gum tree ahead of us was shattered by a bolt of lightening. When the deafening peal of thunder had died, and in the moment before the rain arrived, I heard Doodle, who had fallen behind, cry out, "Brother, Brother, don't leave me! Don't leave me!"

The knowledge that Doodle's and my plans had come to naught was bitter, and that streak of cruelty within me awakened. I ran as fast as I could, leaving him far behind with a wall of rain dividing us. The drops stung my face like nettles, and the wind flared the wet glistening leaves of the bordering trees. Soon I could hear his voice no more.

evanesced
faded;
vanished

I hadn't run too far before I became tired, and the flood of childish spite **evanesced** as well. I stopped and waited for Doodle. The sound of rain was everywhere, but the wind had died and it fell straight down in parallel paths like ropes hanging from the sky. As I waited, I peered through the downpour, but no one came. Finally I went back and found him huddled beneath a red nightshade bush beside the road. He was sitting on the ground, his face buried in his arms, which were resting on his drawn-up knees. "Let's go, Doodle," I said.

He didn't answer, so I placed my hand on his forehead and lifted his head. Limply, he fell backward onto the earth. He had been bleeding from the mouth, and his neck and the front of his shirt were stained a brilliant red.

"Doodle! Doodle!" I cried, shaking him, but there was no answer but the ropy rain. He lay very awkwardly, with his head thrown far back, making his **vermilion** neck appear unusually long and slim. His little legs, bent sharply at the knees, had never before seemed so fragile, so thin.

vermilion
a brilliant red

heresy
action at odds
with what
seems right

I began to weep, and the tear-blurred vision in red before me looked very familiar. "Doodle!" I screamed above the pounding storm and threw my body to the earth above his. For a long time, it seemed forever, I lay there crying, sheltering my fallen scarlet ibis from the **heresy** of rain.

---

16 **Roman candle:** a type of firework that discharges colored balls of fire

AFTER YOU READ
The Scarlet Ibis

Think and Discuss

1. The **narrator** says, "There is within me (and with sadness I have watched it in others) a knot of cruelty borne by the stream of love." How does this idea explain the narrator's treatment of Doodle?

2. Discuss the ways in which this story is about pride.

3. **Setting** refers to the time and place of the story. Copy the graphic organizer below into your Writer's Notebook. Use it to record the ways in which the setting provides a clue to the action, ideas, and the meaning of the story.

Elements of Setting	Supporting Details
Time/World Events	
Place (on a map/physical landscape)	
Plant/Animal Life	
Climate/Weather	
Cultural Attitudes and Practices	
Other	

4. A **symbol** is usually an object that stands for something more abstract. For example, a rose is often meant to symbolize love. How is the scarlet ibis used as a symbol in this story?

5. Review the story looking for words that refer to color. What does this color imagery add to the story?

6. In your opinion, what is the main lesson of "The Scarlet Ibis"?

Write to Understand: Using Imagery

Analyze how the writer of "The Scarlet Ibis" uses details about the setting to give readers the "feel of reality." Such precise information helps readers to believe they can see, feel, hear, and smell features of the setting. Look back at your graphic organizer. Use it to help you write a one-page essay analyzing Hurst's vivid setting. Which details do you find most important, striking, and/or memorable? Do visual or auditory sensory details dominate? How often is the setting referred to in the story? Why is the setting in this story so important to its success?

BEFORE YOU READ

from *Riding the Bus with My Sister*

Meet the Author: Rachel Simon

In her childhood, New Jersey native Rachel Simon (born 1959) experienced her parents' divorce and her sister Beth's mental disability. Frequent moves inspired Simon to write letter after letter to the friends she was forced to leave behind. For her, writing became a way to make sense of her unique childhood and reach out to others. Simon has authored a novel, *The Magic Touch;* a collection of stories, *Little Nightmares, Little Dreams*; and *The Writer's Survival Guide*. In 2002 she published *Riding the Bus with My Sister: A True Life Journey.* That book tells the story of the year she spent with Beth doing what Beth likes best: riding the buses of their city, making friends (and some foes) among the drivers and passengers. The book was made into a Hallmark Hall of Fame movie starring Rosie O'Donnell as Beth.

Build Background: Life with Beth

Family life can be intense when one of the children is mentally handicapped. Relationships between siblings can be complicated by misunderstanding, shame, resentment, and guilt. Outside friendships can also be difficult for both the disabled child and for other children in the family. Young people, especially, might despair at the sense that their family or a family member is perceived as different.

In the memoir from *Riding the Bus with My Sister*, Simon speaks candidly about what it was like when she and her "educable" sister Beth attended the same high school.

- What do you know about mental disabilities?

- Do you know anyone who is mentally disabled?

- What might a family gain by keeping a handicapped child at home? What might be lost?

CON ED/PARK AVENUE, Patti Mollica, 1996

from *Riding the Bus with My Sister*

A True Life Journey

RACHEL SIMON

from *RIDING THE BUS WITH MY SISTER*

Rachel Simon

Beth says, "Play it again."

I say, "You've already heard it fifty times. What's so special about Donny Osmond?"

"Play it."

"Which side?"

"One Bad Apple."

"That's not a side, it's a song. This is a forty-five, so there's an A-side and a B-side."

"Don't be mean. And do a puzzle with me, too."

"I don't want to do puzzles. I don't like puzzles."

"I like puzzles."

"I know. You're the Jimi Hendrix of puzzles."

"Who?"

"A famous guitarist."

"Donny. Play Donny."

I sigh and reach over to the portable record player sitting on her bed with us and pick dust off the needle. I know how to do things like pick dust off a needle now because I'm in junior high. I know how to roast a chicken so it's ready when Mom comes in from work because she says we're too old for babysitters. I know how to do a spitfire twirl with my baton (but I can't catch it as well as Laura catches hers). I know how to ride my bike to the five-and-ten with Max.[1] I know that Beth likes "Puppy Love" while I like "People Are Strange."

"Look," I say, "you want to see how to put the needle on the record? It's not hard."

I put the tone arm in her hand. She grabs it as if it were a banister railing.

I say "Lighter. Think of it like a tiny bird. You have to be gentle."

Her fingers do a little ripple, but her grip stays the same.

---

1 **Laura and Max:** other children in the family

"Lighter," I say.

"Iz lighter."

I sigh, and steer her rock of a hand to the vinyl. It'll start spinning when I make the tone arm cross a certain spot, and here we go, the record's cranking up into its regular revolutions. "Now we're going to set the needle down," I say.

Gradually, I lower our hands to the wheeling record. Beth's tongue is out in concentration.

"Now, let it touch down soft."

She jams the needle down like an ice pick, so hard the record stops spinning.

"*Beth*," I say in that edgy tone I've had with her lately. She is too slow for me, that's what this little whisper in my head keeps saying. Though sometimes I wonder if it's just that my patience with her is getting too short.

"I didn't *mean* to."

"I hope you didn't break it," I say, pulling our hands off.

But then a funny thing happens. As soon as the needle's free, the record starts moving again. The music comes on in that muddy way it does when the speed's wrong, but then it gets faster and faster until the record starts playing normally.

"See?" Beth says. "Iz all right." Donny Osmond comes on and she leans back on the bed and starts singing along, "One bad apple don't spoil the whole lunch, girl."

The music comes on in that muddy way it does when the speed's wrong, but then it gets faster and faster until the record starts playing normally.

I like it when she sings. She knows the tunes just fine but gets the words all wrong, and that makes us laugh, and then it makes her laugh.

I like helping her fix up her new room. We've moved again, to a two-story house on a lake in a farming part of New Jersey. Laura and I sleep in the attic bedrooms. Beth and Max and Mom sleep in the first-floor bedrooms. Beth's room is orange, thanks to me, because orange just became her favorite color, so I went to a store with Mom and got the most electric orange they had and painted Beth's walls for her. Then we pinned up posters of Donny Osmond—and David Cassidy, the Jackson 5, and Bobby Sherman. All her faves. She sees them in *Tiger Beat*. We got her a subscription for her birthday.

I like that she can read now. She reads picture books and *TV Guide*. She writes, too, and keeps notebooks listing every card, record, and knickknack she receives, all of it in orange marker, all in **chronological** order.

chronological
sequential; in time order

I like that Mom takes us to the library together. I pick up books like *A Wrinkle in Time* and *The Hobbit* and *War of the Worlds*. Beth gets *Make Way for Ducklings*. I sneak a look at hers when I've had enough of mine.

But I don't like it all. I don't like when we go to the lake across the street and she stays in the kids' swimming area. I don't like when she goes through my bookcase and finds the spelling book I've been saving since second grade, with stickers for all my 100s on every page, and she uses it like a coloring book. I cry when I find it. Mom says Beth didn't know it was important, I should be understanding, but now my prized book is ruined forever and I throw it away.

I don't like being bored by her puzzles. I don't like being bored by her music. I don't like telling her, No, I don't want to do that or that or that. I don't like that she doesn't get that I'm too old to play with her anymore.

But most of all, I don't like the way I feel when I'm walking down the hall at school around lunchtime, sticking to the walk-to-the-right rule along with a thousand other kids in their blue jeans and flannel shirts streaming to their next class, and the hall reeks of Herbal Essence shampoo and Clearasil and dirty bell-bottoms and Marlboros and pea coat wool, and all you hear is hollers and titters and grumbles echoing off the lockers, and everyone's secretly judging everyone else, and I'm staring straight ahead so no one picks on me, and ahead of me a wave of quiet starts rolling through the teenagers on my side of the hall and I know what this means. It means that when I get a few lockers closer I'll see the two special ed classes, the Trainable and Educable, ambling on the left side of the hall toward lunch. I know that if I were to stand on my toes to peer over all the varsity shoulders and shag haircuts, I'd see that the cheerleaders from my history class would be gazing at their feet, and the Black Sabbath fans from my home ec class would be looking over with curiosity and the chess club boys from English would be offering a quick look of pity, and the jocks from algebra would be **jostling** one another with **guffaws**. But I just let the flow take me forward and then the two special ed groups come into view on the left, nine or ten

jostling
pushing roughly

guffaws
bursts of loud laughter

people in each, walking out of step with us and one another. The Trainable students are in front. Led by their teacher, they grin and slouch, peering out at us with a kind of amazement in their eyes, as if they're surprised to see us. Then come the Educable students. I scan the bodies. There's Beth's school friend Billy in the striped shirt. She has milk and cookies with him. And there's Beth beside him, **lumbering** forward in her orange stretch pants and pink top, her frizzy hair almost the way Mom combed it this morning. We're a few feet from each other now, but she doesn't see me—no one in her class does. They're marching with their eyes on one another, but not giggling like my friends and I would. Instead, they look uncomfortable and walk in silence, as if they suspect they're being watched. And they are being watched: the teenagers around me are all quiet now, and walking stiffer and faster. To them, Beth's class is *different*. And they don't mean it in a nice way.

> **lumbering**
> moving slowly
> and heavily

Then Beth and I see each other. I give a low-key wave, and she gives me a faint smile back. I hate how I feel then. Like yelling, "Hi, Beth!" real loud, so everyone who knows me will spin around to see her and understand that these two separate worlds aren't two separate worlds at all. But once again, as we pass each other, our shoulders almost touching, I don't yell anything. Instead I let myself be pressed along with the herd. A burn rises up in my throat, but I don't speak. I go into class and swallow my disloyalty and just feel disgusted for us all.

> Beth's class is *different*. And they don't mean it in a nice way . . .

I hear the words people use.

I like words. At night I go up to my room, and after I've called my friends, I write lists of words as I hang out under this big blue clear plastic peace sign that I won at a county fair. It hangs from the sloped ceiling above my bed, and I put on the Who's *Tommy*, which Dad gave me during our last visit, and half lie down on my bed, and twirl the peace sign with my foot while the record sings, "Deaf, dumb, and blind boy, he's in a quiet vibration land." Then, on my bed, I write lists of words. I have pages of almost-synonyms in the back of my notebook:

PIG OUT, GORGE, WOLF, CHOW DOWN, CRAM IT IN,
STUFF YOUR FACE, LICK THE PLATTER CLEAN
WONDERLAND, NARNIA, LILLIPUT, OZ, SHANGRI-LA,
NEVER-NEVER LAND
BACKSIDE, BUM, BUTT, TUSHIE, TUFFET, DERRIERE, CAN, RUMP,
REAR END

But there's one kind of word I never write down. Kids in the halls at school use it, and teachers who talk about John Steinbeck's *Of Mice and Men*. I don't need to write it because it bangs around every day in my head:

DIMWIT, HALF-WIT, SIMPLETON, IDIOT, REJECT, SPAZZ,
IMBECILE, GALOOT, MORON, DEFECTIVE

And especially:

RETARD

They'll say these like it's nothing. Teachers will say, "Obviously in the childlike actions taken by the innocent half-wit Lennie,[2] you can see Steinbeck's extraordinary literary blah blah blah," and you're supposed to go along. I go along because what else can you do?

But I can't go along when kids bungle a book report and smack their heads and say, "I'm such a retard." Or when someone messes up on the parallel bars in gym, and on the mats below someone else calls out, "What a retard."

You're supposed to agree that, yes, that would be as bad as getting thrown out of the human race. You're supposed to laugh.

I never laugh. I just stare sharply and say, "My sister's retarded."

"Oh, sorry, I didn't mean it," they come back.

They look away from me in the classroom after that, sometimes with their noses up, sometimes with their heads down. Either way is fine with me.

SMACK, POW, PUNCH, SOCK, BELT, BONK, BASH, BOX, WHAM

Then I flip the notebook to the front and go back to writing. If [ethnic slurs[3]] are bad words, why not "retard"? What makes that one okay when all the rest get you sent to detention? I give my peace sign a good, hard kick.

We don't play together anymore, but Beth still wants to. I make excuses, which

---

2 **innocent half-wit Lennie:** a reference to a character in John Steinbeck's novel *Of Mice and Men*

3 **ethnic slurs:** insults directed against a particular race or culture

is easy because I have lots of friends. I can do headstands in Susan's yard. I can make is-your-refrigerator-running? prank phone calls with Marie. I can look at fashion magazines with David, or figure out the lyrics to "You Can't Always Get What You Want" with Keiko. Or I can just sit on the bed with any of them, and we can gossip and eat chips and laugh our heads off until their mothers call out, "Will you please keep it down?" and then we can laugh some more.

Sometimes when my friends aren't home, I boss Beth around. I know she wants to please me, so it's hard to fight the urge. "Get me a glass of water," I'll tell her when I'm in the living room watching *The 4:30 Movie* on Channel 7 and I'm in a bad mood that's come out of nowhere, as it does lately. "Get it!"

She'll slink off to the kitchen to do my bidding, but glare at me every step of the way.

Yet she keeps trying. She says hi to my friends when they come over. She gets the mail every day and delivers it to me, telling me I got a letter from Kim, or my new issue of *Rolling Stone.* She'll draw pictures and give them to me.

A winter day. We are watching TV, and *The 4:30 Movie* has just ended, and Beth wants to turn to *Gilligan's Island.*

"I want to see the news," I say.

"Don't want news."

"Just for a few minutes. We'll leave on Channel 7 until the weather."

But the real reason I want to see the news isn't the weather or the news, which is always about the war in Vietnam anyway. I want to see the great-looking reporter they have on Channel 7, this guy my friend Leslie has a crush on. His name is Geraldo Rivera, and all afternoon there were commercials saying he'd be doing some special report on Willowbrook at six o'clock. We go shopping at the Willowbrook Mall, and I want to watch him go shopping so I can tell Leslie about it the next day.

Beth sits next to me, and the news starts. Geraldo comes on, but he's not in a mall. He's in a big, dark place where people are crying and naked, and some of the people look beat-up, and the rooms are all bare, and the walls are covered with icky stuff—

"Thiz gross," Beth says.

I don't know what it is, but it gives me shivers. I get up quick to change the channel, and just as I reach for it, a man with Geraldo says, "This is the Willowbrook State School."

I flick that channel and sit back down. It's the Gilligan episode where astronauts land on the island, and Beth falls into it, glued, while I wonder what I just saw. It couldn't be about anyone I know, nothing on the news ever is. But one face had an expression that Beth sometimes wears, and I shoot a look at her and wonder: Was this one of those institutions? The places where we didn't send Beth, and thank God we never will, ever ever ever?

It can't be, I tell myself. It's just too . . . it's too *not human.* It's as far away from me and Beth as Vietnam. I won't think about it. I won't.

But mostly, Beth tries to spend time with me, and I say no.

"No, I don't want to watch *Adam-12.* I don't want to sing to your dolls."

She gets a hurt look. "Call your own friends," I say. But her few school friends live too far away for her to reach with her oversized tricycle, which sits rusting in the garage. Or they have physical disabilities and can't get to our house without their parents' help. Beth is stuck, because there are no trains or subways or buses around here. And, as she puts it, she's *bawd.*

"Dominoes?" she asks.

"No."

"Go Fish?"

"No."

"But we're twins!"

"Only one month in a year."

She slumps off to her orange room, and I climb upstairs to my peace sign.

She slumps off to her orange room, and I climb upstairs to my peace sign.

I guess she puts together a plan then. She will simply ambush me at the end of my school day. It's easy—she gets home before I do, and we have a park bench on the lawn looking out to the lake. She'll just sing to herself, sit there with Ringo,[4] and wait for my school bus.

The first time, I hear **snickering** in the seats behind me as the bus pulls up. Snickering about her, I know. So when I get off and she's standing at the bottom holding Ringo, grinning **ecstatically** at my arrival, I usher her into the house fast, before they laugh any more.

The next time, the snickering is bolder. I run off the bus, telling her, "Please wait inside."

But she does not wait inside the next day, or the next. I stop saying "please" and just blow past her to get in quickly.

Then one spring day, she can't stand it anymore. When she gets home, she finds her favorite water pistols. She slips on a pair of summer shorts and strips down to her undershirt. As my bus pulls up to our house, there she is at the curb in seminaked cowgirl glory, shooting off water double-handed, beaming up at my window.

The bus erupts. I seize my books and bolt down the aisle, my head down. The laughter slams against my ears. I have never heard anything so loud. I have never felt such humiliation.

"Get inside!" I blurt out in tears as I emerge from the bus.

And they laugh and laugh. And don't stop when we get inside and slam the door. Or when I run up to my room. I can hear it roll on and on until I blast Led Zeppelin. Until I beat my pillow in despair.

snickering
laughing in a mean or derogatory way

ecstatically
joyfully

---

4 **Ringo:** the family pet

Mom comes home late that night. She was out on a date. Not with a Clark Kent who wears a hat and shakes our hands, but with one of the **surly** types she sees now. They wear carpenter's belts or drive cement trucks, and they never shake hands. They don't bother to learn our names.

She tosses her pocketbook on her bureau. I tell her about that afternoon, and I can barely keep from crying. "So please," I beg her when I finish, "tell Beth not to come meet me at the bus! Tell her to wait for me inside!"

Mom pauses a minute. Then she says, "I will not tell her that. She has every right to wait for you on the lawn."

"But it was terrible!" I say. "I was so ashamed!"

Her face gets hard, as it does more and more these days. "You shouldn't be ashamed. They should be ashamed. I will not hide your sister from the world."

I storm out, furious at life. It's not fair! It's not fair that, on top of being a teenager, which is bad enough as it is, I have this extra worry! It's not fair that I know—and Laura and Max know—that we can never think of a future that doesn't include Beth!

It could have happened to any one of you.

When you're older, save money for her, so when we're gone you can take care of her.

We don't believe in the back room. She'll be in plain sight, as one of the family.

Never put her in an institution. Ever ever ever. Make room for her in your own house.

That night, I sob at the injustice of it all. I know it's true, and I know Mom's right. But I hate it all so much that I decide I'll walk home from school from now on. This clears my mind but not my temper and doesn't lighten my conscience at all.

AFTER YOU READ

from *Riding the Bus with My Sister*

Think and Discuss

1. How different would Rachel's life be without Beth? Explain.

2. What do you think Rachel has learned because Beth is part of her family?

3. Effective **dialogue** reveals what characters are like and how they relate to others. What does the dialogue in this memoir reveal about Beth and Rachel? Give examples to support your answer.

4. Explore the ways in which the exerpt from *Riding the Bus with My Sister* and "The Scarlet Ibis" are similar and different. Use a chart like the one below to compare things such as **genre**, **point of view**, **theme**, **action**, and **characterization**.

Points of Comparison	The Scarlet Ibis	from *Riding the Bus With My Sister*
Genre		
Point of View		
Characters		
Setting		
Theme		
Tone		

5. Rachel seems fascinated by the power of words. Review the lists of synonyms she writes in her notebook. Then use web organizers to create synonyms for the following words: *family, home, school, friends*. Share your ideas with the class (if they are not too personal).

Write to Understand: A Personal Response

What do you think of the way the author treats her sister? Write a letter to Rachel telling her how you responded to this selection. Include details about what you liked or disliked—what you learned and what, if anything, you found confusing. Share with her any experiences you may have had with disabled people and ask her any questions you have about her, Beth, or other family members. The graphic organizer you developed may help you pull together your thoughts. Also, like the writer, think carefully about the words you use. Make them specific so that they accurately reflect your true feelings.

BEFORE YOU READ

A Christmas Memory

Meet the Author: Truman Capote

Born in New Orleans in 1924 to a 16-year-old beauty queen, the young Truman Capote remained in the South with relatives after his mother divorced his father and moved away. Many believe that the most famous character Capote ever created was himself. Precocious as a child, witty and outrageous as an adult, he found quick success in New York City as a writer and bon vivant (man about town). He is best known for his book *In Cold Blood*, a vivid account of a Kansas farm family murdered by a pair of escaped convicts. Capote died at 60, a victim of alcoholism and drugs.

Build Background: Family and Fruitcakes

In this selection, Truman Capote paints a detailed picture of his unusual childhood in rural Alabama during the 1930s. His caretaker was an eccentric cousin nearly sixty years older than himself. Despite their lack of money, Buddy (as he was called then) and Miss Sook went all out to make Christmas as special as possible. They went to fantastic lengths to produce an abundance of fruitcakes, kites, and other homemade gifts. If a family is formed by its traditions and love, Buddy and Miss Sook had the most perfect family imaginable.

Critics disagree on whether to label this classic piece as fiction or nonfiction. While the main elements of the story are true, Capote may well have fabricated some details to enhance its telling.

- What holiday rituals do you and your family have that don't require money or outside help?

- Do you think it is possible for a child and an older person to have a relationship of equals? Why or why not?

The Breakfast, Pierre Bonnard

A Christmas Memory

TRUMAN CAPOTE

A CHRISTMAS MEMORY

Truman Capote

Imagine a morning in late November. A coming of winter morning more than twenty years ago. Consider the kitchen of a spreading old house in a country town. A great black stove is its main feature; but there is also a big round table and a fireplace with two rocking chairs placed in front of it. Just today the fireplace **commenced** its seasonal roar.

commenced
began; started

A woman with **shorn** white hair is standing at the kitchen window. She is wearing tennis shoes and a shapeless gray sweater over a summery calico dress. She is small and sprightly, like a bantam hen; but, due to a long youthful illness, her shoulders are pitifully hunched. Her face is remarkable—not unlike Lincoln's, **craggy** like that, and tinted by sun and wind; but it is delicate too, finely boned, and her eyes are sherry-colored and timid. "Oh my," she exclaims, her breath smoking the windowpane, "it's fruitcake weather!"

shorn
cut or sheared

craggy
rough or
rugged-looking

The person to whom she is speaking is myself. I am seven; she is sixty-something. We are cousins, very distant ones, and we have lived together—well, as long as I can remember. Other people inhabit the house, relatives; and though they have power over us, and frequently make us cry, we are not, on the whole, too much aware of them. We are each other's best friend. She calls me Buddy, in memory of a boy who was formerly her best friend. The other Buddy died in the 1880s, when she was still a child. She is still a child.

"I knew it before I got out of bed," she says, turning away from the window with a purposeful excitement in her eyes. "The courthouse bell sounded so cold and clear. And there were no birds singing; they've gone to warmer country, yes indeed. Oh, Buddy, stop stuffing biscuit and fetch our buggy. Help me find my hat. We've thirty cakes to bake."

inaugurating
making
a formal
beginning to

It's always the same: a morning arrives in November, and my friend, as though officially **inaugurating** the Christmas time of year that **exhilarates** her imagination and fuels the blaze of her heart, announces: "It's fruitcake weather! Fetch our buggy. Help me find my hat."

exhilarates
excites or
thrills

The hat is found, a straw cartwheel corsaged with velvet roses out-of-doors has faded: it once belonged to a more fashionable relative. Together, we guide our buggy, a dilapidated baby carriage, out to the garden and into a grove of pecan trees. The buggy is mine; that is, it was bought for me when I was born. It is made of wicker, rather unraveled, and the wheels wobble like a drunkard's legs. But it is a faithful object; springtimes, we take it to the woods and fill it with flowers, herbs, wild fern for our porch pots; in the summer, we pile it with picnic **paraphernalia** and sugar-cane fishing poles and roll it down to the edge of a creek; it has its winter uses, too: as a truck for hauling firewood from the yard to the kitchen, as a warm bed for Queenie, our tough little orange and white rat terrier who has survived distemper and two rattlesnake bites. Queenie is trotting beside it now.

paraphernalia
bits and pieces; stuff

Three hours later we are back in the kitchen hulling a heaping buggyload of windfall pecans. Our backs hurt from gathering them: how hard they were to find (the main crop having been shaken off the trees and sold by the orchard's owners, who are not us) among the concealing leaves, the frosted, deceiving grass. Caaarackle! A cheery crunch, scraps of miniature thunder sound as the shells collapse and the golden mound of sweet oily ivory meat mounts in the milk-glass bowl. Queenie begs to taste, and now and again my friend sneaks her a mite, though insisting we deprive ourselves. "We mustn't, Buddy. If we start, we won't stop. And there's scarcely enough as there is. For thirty cakes." The kitchen is growing dark. Dusk turns the window into a mirror: our reflections mingle with the rising moon as we work by the fireside in the firelight. At last, when the moon is quite high, we toss the final hull into the fire and, with joined sighs, watch it catch flame. The buggy is empty, the bowl is brimful.

> Together, we guide our buggy, a dilapidated baby carriage, out to the garden and into a grove of pecan trees.

We eat our supper (cold biscuits, bacon, blackberry jam) and discuss tomorrow. Tomorrow the kind of work I like best begins: buying. Cherries and citron,[1] ginger and vanilla and canned Hawaiian pineapple, rinds and raisins and walnuts and whiskey and oh, so much flour, butter, so many eggs, spices, flavorings: why, we'll need a pony to pull the buggy home.

---

1 **citron:** a lemon-like fruit

But before these purchases can be made, there is the question of money. Neither of us has any. Except for skinflint sums persons in the house occasionally provide (a dime is considered very big money); or what we earn ourselves from various activities: holding rummage sales, selling buckets of hand-picked blackberries, jars of home-made jam and apple jelly and peach preserves, rounding up flowers for funerals and weddings. Once we won seventy-ninth prize, five dollars, in a national football contest. Not that we know a fool thing about football. It's just that we enter any contest we hear about: at the moment our hopes are centered on the fifty-thousand-dollar Grand Prize being offered to name a new brand of coffee (we suggested "A.M."; and, after some hesitation, for my friend thought it perhaps sacrilegious,[2] the slogan "A.M.! Amen!"). To tell the truth, our only *really* profitable enterprise was the Fun and Freak Museum we conducted in a backyard woodshed two summers ago. The Fun was a stereopticon[3] with slide views of Washington and New York lent us by a relative who had been to those places (she was furious when she discovered why we'd borrowed it); the Freak was a three-legged biddy chicken hatched by one of our own hens. Everybody hereabouts wanted to see that biddy: we charged grownups a nickel, kids two cents. And took in a good twenty dollars before the museum shut down due to the decease of the main attraction.

But one way and another we do each year accumulate Christmas savings, a Fruitcake Fund. These moneys we keep hidden in an ancient bead purse under a loose board under the floor under a chamber pot[4] under my friend's bed. The purse is seldom removed from this safe location except to make a deposit or, as happens every Saturday, a withdrawal; for on Saturdays I am allowed ten cents to go to the picture show. My friend has never been to a picture show, nor does she intend to: "I'd rather hear you tell the story, Buddy. That way I can imagine it more. Besides, a person my age shouldn't **squander** their eyes. When the Lord comes, let me see Him clear." In addition to never having seen a movie, she has never: eaten in a restaurant, traveled more than five miles from home, received or sent a telegram, read

squander
waste; throw away

---

2 **sacrilegious:** insulting to sacred ideas or objects

3 **stereopticon:** a projector or "magic lantern"

4 **chamber pot:** before indoor plumbing, a pot kept under the bed for urine

anything except funny papers and the Bible, worn cosmetics, cursed, wished someone harm, told a lie on purpose, let a hungry dog go hungry. Here are a few things she has done, does do: killed with a hoe the biggest rattlesnake ever seen in this county (sixteen rattles), dip snuff [5] (secretly), tame hummingbirds (just try it) till they balance on her finger, tell ghost stories (we both believe in ghosts) so tingling they chill you in July, talk to herself, take walks in the rain, grow the prettiest japonicas [6] in town, know the recipe for every sort of oldtime Indian cure, including a magical wart-remover.

Now, with supper finished, we retire to the room in a faraway part of the house where my friend sleeps in a scrap-quilt-covered iron bed painted rose pink, her favorite color. Silently, **wallowing** in the pleasures of **conspiracy**, we take the bead purse from its secret place and spill its contents on the scrap quilt. Dollar bills, tightly rolled and green as May buds. **Somber** fifty-cent pieces, heavy enough to weight a dead man's eyes. [7] Lovely dimes, the liveliest coin, the one that really jingles. Nickels and quarters, worn smooth as creek pebbles. But mostly a hateful heap of bitter-odored pennies. Last summer others in the house contracted to pay us a penny for every twenty-five flies we killed. Oh, the carnage [8] of August: the flies that flew to heaven! Yet it was not work in which we took pride. And, as we sit counting pennies, it is as though we were back tabulating dead flies. Neither of us has a head for figures; we count slowly, lose track, start again. According to her calculations, we have $12.73. According to mine, exactly $13. "I do hope you're wrong, Buddy. We can't mess around with thirteen. The cakes will fall. Or put somebody in the cemetery. Why, I wouldn't dream of getting out of bed on the thirteenth." This is true: she always spends thirteenths in bed. So, to be on the safe side, we subtract a penny and toss it out the window.

> "We can't mess around with thirteen. The cakes will fall. Or put somebody in the cemetery."

---

5 **dip snuff:** rub chewing tobacco on the gums

6 **japonicas:** shrubs with red flowers

7 **weight a dead man's eyes:** a reference to the practice of putting coins on the eyes of a dead person to keep them closed

8 **carnage:** great slaughter

wallowing
rolling about; exulting in

conspiracy
plotting; scheming

somber
solemn; serious

Of the ingredients that go into our fruitcakes, whiskey is the most expensive, as well as the hardest to obtain: State laws forbid its sale. But everybody knows you can buy a bottle from Mr. Haha Jones. And the next day, having completed our more **prosaic** shopping, we set out for Mr. Haha's business address, a "sinful" (to quote public opinion) fish-fry and dancing café down by the river. We've been there before, and on the same errand; but in previous years our dealings have been with Haha's wife, an iodine-dark Indian woman with brassy peroxided hair and a dead-tired **disposition**. Actually, we've never laid eyes on her husband, though we've heard that he's an Indian too. A giant with razor scars across his cheeks. They call him Haha because he's so gloomy, a man who never laughs. As we approach his café (a large log cabin **festooned** inside and out with chains of garish-gay naked light bulbs and standing by the river's muddy edge under the shade of river trees where moss drifts through the branches like gray mist) our steps slow down. Even Queenie stops prancing and sticks close by. People have been murdered in Haha's cafe. Cut to pieces. Hit on the head. There's a case coming up in court next month. Naturally these goings-on happen at night when the colored lights cast crazy patterns and the Victrola[9] wails. In the daytime Haha's is shabby and deserted. I knock at the door, Queenie barks, my friend calls: "Mrs. Haha, ma'am? Anyone to home?"

Footsteps. The door opens. Our hearts overturn. It's Mr. Haha Jones himself!

Footsteps. The door opens. Our hearts overturn. It's Mr. Haha Jones himself! And he *is* a giant; he *does* have scars; he *doesn't* smile. No, he glowers at us through Satan-tilted eyes and demands to know: "What you want with Haha?"

For a moment we are too paralyzed to tell. Presently my friend half-finds her voice, a whispery voice at best: "If you please, Mr. Haha, we'd like a quart of your finest whiskey."

His eyes tilt more. Would you believe it? Haha is smiling! Laughing, too. "Which one of you is a drinkin' man?"

"It's for making fruitcakes, Mr. Haha. Cooking. "

This sobers him. He frowns. "That's no way to waste good whiskey."

---

9 **Victrola:** an old-fashioned record-player

Margin glossary:

prosaic
ordinary; dull

disposition
temperament; personality

festooned
decorated or adorned

Nevertheless, he retreats into the shadowed café and seconds later appears carrying a bottle of daisy-yellow unlabeled liquor. He demonstrates its sparkle in the sunlight and says: "Two dollars."

We pay him with nickels and dimes and pennies. Suddenly, jangling the coins in his hand like a fistful of dice, his face softens. "Tell you what," he proposes, pouring the money back into our bead purse, "just send me one of them fruitcakes instead."

"Well," my friend remarks on our way home, "there's a lovely man. We'll put an extra cup of raisins in *his* cake."

The black stove, stoked with coal and firewood, glows like a lighted pumpkin. Eggbeaters whirl, spoons spin round in bowls of butter and sugar, vanilla sweetens the air, ginger spices it; melting, nose-tingling odors saturate the kitchen, **suffuse** the house, drift out to the world on puffs of chimney smoke. In four days our work is done. Thirty-one cakes, dampened with whiskey, bask on windowsills and shelves.

Who are they for?

suffuse
spread
through

THE TABLE, Pierre Bonnard

A Christmas Memory   131

Friends. Not necessarily neighbor friends: indeed, the larger share is intended for persons we've met maybe once, perhaps not at all. People who've struck our fancy. Like President Roosevelt. Like the Reverend and Mrs. J. C. Lucey, Baptist missionaries to Borneo who lectured here last winter. Or the little knife grinder who comes through town twice a year. Or Abner Packer, the driver of the six o'clock bus from Mobile, who exchanges waves with us every day as he passes in a dust-cloud whoosh. Or the young Wistons, a California couple whose car one afternoon broke down outside the house and who spent a pleasant hour chatting with us on the porch (young Mr. Wiston snapped our picture, the only one we've ever had taken). Is it because my friend is shy with everyone except strangers that these strangers, and merest acquaintances, seem to us our truest friends? I think yes. Also, the scrapbooks we keep of thank-you's on White House stationery, time-to-time communications from California and Borneo, the knife grinder's penny post cards, make us feel connected to eventful worlds beyond the kitchen with its view of a sky that stops.

Is it because my friend is shy with everyone except strangers that these strangers, and merest acquaintances, seem to us our truest friends?

Now a nude December fig branch grates against the window. The kitchen is empty, the cakes are gone; yesterday we carted the last of them to the post office, where the cost of stamps turned our purse inside out. We're broke. That rather depresses me, but my friend insists on celebrating—with two inches of whiskey left in Haha's bottle. Queenie has a spoonful in a bowl of coffee (she likes her coffee chicory-flavored and strong). The rest we divide between a pair of jelly glasses. We're both quite awed at the prospect of drinking straight whiskey; the taste of it brings screwed-up expressions and sour shudders. But by and by we begin to sing, the two of us singing different songs simultaneously. I don't know the words to mine, just: *Come on along, come on along, to the dark-town strutters' ball.* But I can dance: that's what I mean to be, a tap-dancer in the movies. My dancing shadow rollicks on the walls; our voices rock the chinaware; we giggle: as if unseen hands were tickling us. Queenie rolls on her back, her paws plow the air, something like a grin stretches her black lips. Inside myself, I feel warm and sparky as those crumbling logs, carefree as the wind in the chimney. My friend waltzes round the stove, the hem of her poor calico skirt pinched between her fingers as though it were a party dress: *Show me the way to go home*, she sings, her tennis shoes squeaking on the floor. *Show me the way to go home.*

Enter: two relatives. Very angry. **Potent** with eyes that scold, tongues that scald. Listen to what they have to say, the words tumbling together into a wrathful tune: "A child of seven! whiskey on his breath! are you out of your mind? feeding a child of seven! must be loony! road to ruination! remember Cousin Kate? Uncle Charlie? Uncle Charlie's brother-in-law? shame! scandal! humiliation! kneel, pray, beg the Lord!"

Queenie sneaks under the stove. My friend gazes at her shoes, her chin quivers, she lifts her skirt and blows her nose and runs to her room. Long after the town has gone to sleep and the house is silent except for the chimings of clocks and the sputter of fading fires, she is weeping into a pillow already as wet as a widow's handkerchief.

"Don't cry," I say, sitting at the bottom of her bed and shivering despite my flannel nightgown that smells of last winter's cough syrup, "don't cry," I beg, teasing her toes, tickling her feet, "you're too old for that."

"It's because," she hiccups, "I *am* too old. Old and funny."

"Not funny. Fun. More fun than anybody. Listen. If you don't stop crying you'll be so tired tomorrow we can't go cut a tree."

She straightens up. Queenie jumps on the bed (where Queenie is not allowed) to lick her cheeks. "I know where we'll find real pretty trees, Buddy. And holly, too. With berries big as your eyes. It's way off in the woods. Farther than we've ever been. Papa used to bring us Christmas trees from there: carry them on his shoulder. That's fifty years ago. Well, now: I can't wait for morning."

Morning. Frozen rime[10] lusters the grass; the sun, round as an orange and orange as hot-weather moons, balances on the horizon, burnishes the silvered winter woods. A wild turkey calls. A renegade hog grunts in the undergrowth. Soon, by the edge of knee-deep, rapid-running water, we have to abandon the buggy. Queenie wades the stream first, paddles across barking complaints at the swiftness of the current, the pneumonia-making coldness

---

10 **rime:** a light covering of frost

chastising
punishing

of it. We follow, holding our shoes and equipment (a hatchet, a burlap sack) above our heads. A mile more: of **chastising** thorns, burrs and briers that catch at our clothes; of rusty pine needles brilliant with gaudy fungus and molted feathers. Here, there, a flash, a flutter, an ecstasy of shrillings remind us that not all the birds have flown south. Always, the path unwinds through lemony sun pools and pitchblack vine tunnels. Another creek to cross: a disturbed armada[11] of speckled trout froths the water round us, and frogs the size of plates practice belly flops; beaver workmen are building a dam. On the farther shore, Queenie shakes herself and trembles. My friend shivers, too: not with cold but enthusiasm. One of her hat's ragged roses sheds a petal as she lifts her head and inhales the pine-heavy air. "We're almost there; can you smell it, Buddy?" she says, as though we were approaching an ocean.

And, indeed, it is a kind of ocean. Scented acres of holiday trees, prickly-leafed holly. Red berries shiny as Chinese bells: black crows swoop upon them screaming. Having stuffed our burlap sacks with enough greenery and crimson to garland a dozen windows, we set about choosing a tree. "It should be," muses my friend, "twice as tall as a boy. So a boy can't steal the star." The one we pick is twice as tall as me. A brave handsome brute that survives thirty hatchet strokes before it keels with a creaking rending cry. Lugging it like a kill, we commence the long trek out. Every few yards we abandon the struggle, sit down and pant. But we have the strength of triumphant huntsmen; that and the tree's **virile**, icy perfume revive us, **goad** us on. Many compliments accompany our sunset return along the red clay road to town; but my friend is sly and **noncommittal** when passers-by praise the treasure perched in our buggy: what a fine tree and where did it come from? "Yonderways," she murmurs vaguely. Once a car stops, and the rich mill owner's lazy wife leans out and whines: "Giveya two-bits cash[12] for that ol tree." Ordinarily my friend is afraid of saying no; but on this occasion she promptly shakes her head: "We wouldn't take a dollar." The

virile
manly; powerful

goad
urge

noncommittal
vague;
unrevealing

---

11 **armada:** a fleet of warships

12 **two-bits cash:** twenty-five cents

Unit Two   Family Ties

mill owner's wife persists. "A dollar, my foot! Fifty cents. That's my last offer. Goodness, woman, you can get another one." In answer, my friend gently reflects: "I doubt it. There's never two of anything."

Home: Queenie slumps by the fire and sleeps till tomorrow, snoring loud as a human.

· · ·

A trunk in the attic contains: a shoebox of ermine[13] tails (off the opera cape of a curious lady who once rented a room in the house), coils of frazzled tinsel gone gold with age, one silver star, a brief rope of dilapidated, undoubtedly dangerous candy-like light bulbs. Excellent decorations, as far as they go, which isn't far enough: my friend wants our tree to blaze "like a Baptist window," droop with weighty snows of ornament. But we can't afford the made-in-Japan splendors at the five-and-dime. So we do what we've always done: sit for days at the kitchen table with scissors and crayons and stacks of colored paper. I make sketches and my friend cuts them out: lots of cats, fish too (because they're easy to draw), some apples, some watermelons, a few winged angels devised from saved-up sheets of Hershey-bar tin foil. We use safety pins to attach these creations to the tree; as a final touch, we sprinkle the branches with shredded cotton (picked in August for this purpose). My friend, surveying the effect, clasps her hands together. "Now honest, Buddy. Doesn't it look good enough to eat?" Queenie tries to eat an angel.

After weaving and ribboning holly wreaths for all the front windows, our next project is the fashioning of family gifts. Tie-dye scarves for the ladies, for the men a home-brewed lemon and licorice and aspirin syrup to be taken "at the first Symptoms of a Cold and after Hunting." But when it comes time for making each other's gift, my friend and I separate to work secretly. I would like to buy her a pearl-handled knife, a radio, a whole pound of chocolate-covered cherries (we tasted some once, and she always swears: "I could live on them, Buddy, Lord yes I could—and that's not taking His name in vain"). Instead, I am building her a kite. She would like to give me a bicycle (she's said so on several million occasions: "If only I could, Buddy. It's bad enough in life to do without something *you* want; but confound it, what gets my

---

13 **ermine:** a weasel-like animal that turns white in winter

goat is not being able to give somebody something you want *them* to have. Only one of these days I will, Buddy. Locate you a bike. Don't ask how. Steal it, maybe"). Instead, I'm fairly certain that she is building me a kite—the same as last year, and the year before: the year before that we exchanged slingshots. All of which is fine by me. For we are champion kite-fliers who study the wind like sailors; my friend, more accomplished than I, can get a kite aloft when there isn't enough breeze to carry clouds.

Christmas Eve afternoon we scrape together a nickel and go to the butcher's to buy Queenie's traditional gift, a good gnawable beef bone. The bone, wrapped in funny paper, is placed high in the tree near the silver star. Queenie knows it's there. She squats at the foot of the tree staring up in a trance of greed: when bedtime arrives she refuses to budge. Her excitement is equaled by my own. I kick the covers and turn my pillow as though it were a scorching summer's night. Somewhere a rooster crows: falsely, for the sun is still on the other side of the world.

"Buddy, are you awake!" It is my friend, calling from her room, which is next to mine; and an instant later she is sitting on my bed holding a candle. "Well, I can't sleep a hoot," she declares. "My mind's jumping like a jack rabbit. Buddy, do you think Mrs. Roosevelt will serve our cake at dinner?" We huddle in the bed, and she squeezes my hand I-love-you. "Seems like your hand used to be so much smaller. I guess I hate to see you grow up. When you're grown up, will we still be friends?" I say always. "But I feel so bad, Buddy. I wanted so bad to give you a bike. I tried to sell my cameo Papa gave me. Buddy"—she hesitates, as though embarrassed—"I made you another kite." Then I confess that I made her one, too; and we laugh. The candle burns too short to hold. Out it goes, exposing the starlight, the stars spinning at the window like a visible caroling that slowly, slowly daybreak silences. Possibly we doze; but the beginnings of dawn splash us like cold water: we're up, wide-eyed and wandering while we wait for others to waken. Quite deliberately my friend drops a kettle on the kitchen floor. I tap-dance in front of closed doors. One by one the household emerges, looking as though they'd like to kill us both; but it's Christmas, so they can't. First, a gorgeous breakfast: just everything you can imagine—from flapjacks and fried squirrel to hominy grits and honey-in-the-comb. Which puts everyone in a good humor except my friend and me. Frankly, we're so impatient to get at the presents we can't eat a mouthful.

Well, I'm disappointed. Who wouldn't be? With socks, a Sunday school shirt, some handkerchiefs, a hand-me-down sweater, and a year's subscription to a religious magazine for children. *The Little Shepherd*. It makes me boil. It really does.

My friend has a better haul. A sack of Satsumas,[14] that's her best present. She is proudest, however, of a white wool shawl knitted by her married sister. But she *says* her favorite gift is the kite I built her. And it *is* very beautiful; though not as beautiful as the one she made me, which is blue and scattered with gold and green Good Conduct stars; moreover, my name is painted on it, "Buddy."

"Buddy, the wind is blowing."

The wind is blowing, and nothing will do till we've run to a pasture below the house where Queenie has scooted to bury her bone (and where, a winter hence, Queenie will be buried, too). There, plunging through the healthy waist-high grass, we unreel our kites, feel them twitching at the string like sky fish as they swim into the wind. Satisfied, sun-warmed, we sprawl in the grass and peel Satsumas and watch our kites **cavort**. Soon I forget the socks and hand-me-down sweater. I'm as happy as if we'd already won the fifty-thousand-dollar Grand Prize in that coffee-naming contest.

cavort
play; frolic

"My, how foolish I am!" my friend cries, suddenly alert, like a woman remembering too late she has biscuits in the oven. "You know what I've always thought?" she asks in a tone of discovery and not smiling at me but a point beyond. "I've always thought a body would have to be sick and dying before they saw the Lord. And I imagined that when He came it would be like looking at the Baptist window: pretty as colored glass with the sun pouring through, such a shine you don't know it's getting dark. And it's been a comfort: to think of that shine taking away all the spooky feeling. But I'll wager it never happens. I'll wager at the very end a body realizes the Lord has already shown Himself. That things as they are"—her hand circles in a gesture that gathers clouds and kites and grass and Queenie pawing earth over her bone—" just what they've always seen, was seeing Him. As for me, I could leave the world with today in my eyes."

---

14 **Satsumas:** a fruit similar to tangerines or mandarin oranges

This is our last Christmas together.

Life separates us. Those who Know Best decide that I belong in a military school. And so follows a miserable succession of bugle-blowing prisons, grim reveille-ridden summer camps. I have a new home too. But it doesn't count. Home is where my friend is, and there I never go.

puttering
tinkering;
fiddling

And there she remains, **puttering** around the kitchen. Alone with Queenie. Then alone. ("Buddy dear," she writes in her wild hard-to-read script, "yesterday Jim Macy's horse kicked Queenie bad. Be thankful she didn't feel much. I wrapped her in a Fine Linen sheet and rode her in the buggy down to Simpson's pasture where she can be with all her Bones. . .") For a few Novembers she continues to bake her fruitcakes single-handed; not as many, but some: and, of course, she always sends me "the best of the batch." Also, in every letter she encloses a dime wadded in toilet paper: "See a picture show and write me the story." But gradually in her letters she tends to confuse me with her other friend, the Buddy who died in the 1880s; more and more, thirteenths are not the only days she stays in bed: a morning arrives in November, a leafless birdless coming of winter morning, when she cannot rouse herself to exclaim: "Oh my, it's fruitcake weather!"

And when that happens, I know it. A message saying so merely confirms a piece of news some secret vein had already received, severing from me an irreplaceable part of myself, letting it loose like a kite on a broken string. That is why, walking across a school campus on this particular December morning, I keep searching the sky. As if I expected to see, rather like hearts, a lost pair of kites hurrying toward heaven.

AFTER YOU READ

A Christmas Memory

Think and Discuss

1. Describe the relationship between the young narrator and his older companion. Why do you think they are so close?

2. What does "fruitcake weather" mean to Buddy and his friend?

3. Capote's story is rich with **sensory images**—details that appeal to the reader's sense of smell, taste, sight, touch, and sound. Use a chart like the one below to jot down some especially powerful images from the story.

Sight	Sound	Taste	Touch	Smell

4. An **anecdote** is a minor incident used to illustrate a point in the larger story. In this autobiographical fiction, Capote uses anecdotes in place of a highly structured plot. Cite an anecdote that you find especially moving or amusing.

5. What seasonal holidays does your family take special delight in? Share any interesting or unusual customs you look forward to every year.

Write to Understand: What a Character!

There are many ways in which an author creates a memorable character such as Buddy's friend. Review the story looking for details that describe her. Use a graphic organizer like the one below to list the details.

Buddy's Friend				
What She Says	What She Looks Like	What She Does	How Others Treat Her	Her Room

Now describe a character for a story of your own. Your creation can be realistic or as fantastic as you wish. Write a brief description of your character.

BEFORE YOU READ
Poems of Mothers and Grandmothers

Meet the Poets

Lucille Clifton A noted African American writer, Clifton (born 1936) is a former Poet Laureate of Maryland and member of the Academy of American Poets. In a National Public Radio interview, she said, "I write about being human. If you have ever been human, I invite you to that place that we share."

Edna St. Vincent Millay In the 1920s, Millay (1892–1950) was considered the voice of her generation: bold, humane, forward-thinking. She became the first woman to receive a Pulitzer Prize in poetry in 1923. Millay credited her mother, a single parent and a nurse, with encouraging her independent spirit and love for the arts.

Margaret Walker Walker (1915–1998) explores the African American experience in all her writing. She grew up in a South bitterly divided by race, where blacks were kept down by the so-called Jim Crow laws. She told one interviewer, "Before I was 10, I knew what it was to step off the sidewalk to let a white man pass; otherwise he might knock me off."

Build Background: Hard-headed Women

In these poems, three distinguished poets describe the strong and spirited women who were their ancestors. African American women especially needed courage and stamina to survive slavery and the racism that continued after the Civil War. St. Vincent Millay's mother was determined to raise her family alone in an era when few women were breadwinners.

Consider how all these women were shaped by the the times they lived in, and then think about your female relatives.

- Who would you write about if you were going to write a poem in her honor? Why?

- Maya Angelou, the Pulitzer Prize–winning poet, has said that courage is the most important virtue, for without it a person lacks the ability to stand up for her values and beliefs. What do you think is the most important virtue?

Memory

LUCILLE CLIFTON

ask me to tell how it feels
remembering your mother's face
turned to water under the white words
of the man at the shoe store. ask me,
though she tells it better than i do,   5
not because of her charm
but because it never happened
she says,
no bully salesman **swaggering**,
no rage, no shame, none of it   10
ever happened.
i only remember buying you
your first grown up shoes
she smiles. ask me
how it feels.   15

swaggering
acting
conceited or
smug

The Courage That My Mother Had

EDNA ST. VINCENT MILLAY

The courage that my mother had
Went with her, and is with her still:
quarried
excavated;
dug up
Rock from New England **quarried**;
Now granite in a granite hill.

The golden brooch my mother wore   5
She left behind for me to wear;
I have no thing I treasure more:
Yet, it is something I could spare.

Oh, if instead she'd left to me
The thing she took into the grave!—   10
That courage like a rock, which she
Has no more need of, and I have.

Lineage

MARGARET WALKER

My grandmothers were strong.
They followed plows and bent to toil.
They moved through fields sowing seed.
They touched earth and grain grew.
They were full of sturdiness and singing.   5
My grandmothers were strong.

My grandmothers are full of memories
Smelling of soap and onions and wet clay
With veins rolling roughly over quick hands
They have many clean words to say.   10
My grandmothers were strong.
Why am I not as they?

AFTER YOU READ
Poems of Mothers and Grandmothers

Think and Discuss

1. A complaint echoes through these three poems. What do you think it is?

2. Why do you believe these speakers feel such a marked difference between themselves and the older generation of women in their families?

3. Choose two of these poems to compare and contrast. Use a graphic organizer like the one below to show similarities and differences. The distinctive qualities of each poem go in the outer parts of the diagram and the things the poems have in common go in the middle.

As you work, consider the poets' word choice (called **diction**), the characters described in the poems, your personal response, and other elements of poetry such as rhyme, rhythm, and so forth.

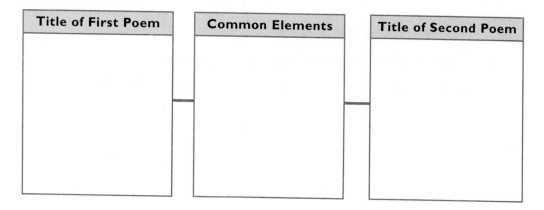

Title of First Poem	Common Elements	Title of Second Poem

4. Do any of these poems remind you of a person in your family? Explain.

Write to Understand: The Perfect Word in the Perfect Place

Write a poem about a family member whose values you admire, choosing one of the three you just studied as a model. Use specific details and diction that matches the tone and purpose of your poem. The work you did for item 3 above should help you develop ideas for the poem you want to create. Remember that poets must choose their words carefully, aiming for precision and the correct level of sophistication for their subject matter and audience.

BEFORE YOU READ

My Brother's Keeper

Meet the Author: Jay Bennett

Jay Bennett (born 1912) is the first person ever to receive back-to-back Edgar Allan Poe awards given by the Mystery Writers of America. He says that many of his writings are "cries against the violence" present in so much popular culture. Bennett's characters often wrestle with ethical dilemmas involving loved ones. His young adult titles include *The Long Black Coat, The Dangling Witness, Sing Me a Death Song, The Executioner,* and *Skinhead.* He is also the author of other novels, stage plays, and television scripts.

Build Background: Nothing But the Truth

According to Merriam-Webster's online dictionary, *truth* means to be in agreement with fact or actuality. A simple definition, and yet philosophers have argued for centuries about the nature of truth and whether or not it even exists. Realizing the complexity of the concept of "truth" may make it easier to identify with the dilemma at the heart of "My Brother's Keeper." It is easy enough to proclaim your belief that one should always be truthful—especially when asked to do so in a court of law. But what if your statements harm someone you love—perhaps irreparably?

- Would you ever ask someone to lie for you? Explain why or why not.

- Would you ever lie to save someone you love from serious trouble? Explain.

My Brother's Keeper

JAY BENNETT

MY BROTHER'S KEEPER

Jay Bennett

"*Do* you swear to tell the truth and nothing but the truth?"

The truth?

Nothing but the truth?

What is truth?

Jamie raised his hand, his right hand, in the hushed courtroom and as he did that, his senses began to reel, to reel back to the beginning.

The very beginning.

He had been sleeping, a restless sleep and then the clear ring of the telephone cut into him. His eyes slowly opened and he looked about the silent shadowy room, listening to the cold, **insistent** ring.

He was alone in the dark house.

Completely alone.

His uncle, with whom he lived, had gone off on a fishing trip near the state border.

"If the fishing is fine I'll stay awhile. If it's bad, real bad, I'll come on home. Anyway I'll be back before you go on to college."

Jamie nodded silently.

"I'll drive you up there. See you settled in."

"You don't have to, Harry. I'll manage."

"I know you can. But I want to do it."

Ted's away in his own fantasy world and I'm all you have left, Jamie thought.

"Okay," he said. "You'll take me up there."

The man smiled and started up the motor. Then he waved his lean, tanned hand and was gone.

Jamie was alone.

And now the phone was ringing.

He reached over to the night table and picked up the dark, gleaming receiver.

insistent
not giving up; unrelenting

The summer curtain rustled noiselessly.

Then he heard the voice.

"Jamie?"

A slight chill went through him and he was silent.

"Jamie?"

It was his brother.

His only brother.

"You alone?"

"Yes," Jamie said.

Outside in the distant night a dog began to bark.

A low mournful sound.

Jamie listened to it.

"Uncle Harry?"

"He's gone fishing."

"Where?"

"Upstate. Near the falls."

"Oh."

The barking had stopped and the silence of the long night flooded into the room.

And all the time Jamie waited.

Waited.

For his older brother to tell him.

Then he heard it.

"I'm in trouble, Jamie."

And you need me to bail you out, Jamie thought bitterly.

"Trouble."

This time the voice was almost a whisper.

But Jamie heard it clearly.

His lips thinned into a straight line.

I'm your kid brother. Five long years younger than you are and all the time, all through the years I had to act like I was the older brother.

All the time.

Jaime's hand tightened around the receiver.

"What have you done, Ted?"

"I want to come over and talk."

"I'm in trouble, Jamie."
And you need me to bail you out, Jamie thought bitterly.

"You slugged somebody in a bar? A guy came over to get your autograph and he got nasty and you were with a girl and you . . ."

"It's not that," Ted cut in.

"Then what?"

"It . . . it's hard to explain."

Jamie's voice grew harsh.

"Nothing's hard to explain. Tell me now."

"Let me see you. I have to."

Jamie breathed out and looked over at the clock on the night table. The clock Ted had given him as a birthday present along with a thousand-dollar check.

"It's three in the morning," he said. "Let it wait."

"It can't wait."

"What do you mean?"

"I'm coming over. Whether you want me or not. I need you."

There was a slight break in the voice.

And Jamie thought to himself bleakly, this time it must be bad.

Really bad.

"Okay," he said. "Come on over."

"Thanks, Jamie."

Jamie was silent.

"I'll never forget it."

You will, Ted. You will.

You always do.

Then he slowly put the receiver back onto its hook.

He sat there in the dark, narrow room a long time, thinking, ever thinking.

His hand clenched into a tight fist.

Then after a while, the hand unclenched.

And lay hopelessly against Jamie's side.

He let the doorbell ring three times, then he slowly went down the carpeted stairs and walked slowly through the dimly lit corridor to the front door.

His brother stood big and large against the night.

menacing
threatening

A **menacing** figure.

But the face was pale and gentle and the eyes haunting.

"Jamie."

And his brother reached out with his large, muscular arms and drew him close.

So very close.

Jamie was tall but his head barely reached Ted's shoulder.

He felt a deep tremor of love for the big man and then the tremor was gone.

The **bleak** feeling was back within him.

bleak
hopeless;
depressing

"I need you. Need you a lot," Ted murmured.

Jamie slowly drew away.

"Let's go into the kitchen and have a cup of coffee, Ted. You look like you could use one."

"Sure. Whatever you say."

Then Ted followed his smaller brother into the neat, yellow kitchen, lifted a heavy wooden chair, swung it about, set it down without a sound and slid into it gracefully.

It was all done in one smooth, flowing motion.

And watching him, Jamie thought of the times he had watched Ted weave and run and evade tacklers with an effortless grace.

The crowd in the packed stands roaring.

His teammates on the sidelines jumping with their hands raised high against a cold autumn sky.

And Jamie thought how on the football field Ted loomed large, so very large.

In full control of himself.

So very well put together.

So finely disciplined.

Rarely making a wrong move.

Every inch a grounded, mature man.

But once he stepped off the field and took off his uniform, he became a child.

A huge, gentle child.

Who got himself into scrapes and had to be bailed out.

Again and again.

Jamie lighted the jet under the coffeepot.

"What's it this time?"

Ted looked at his brother's trim, straight back and didn't speak.

Jamie was tall and slender, his fine-featured face with the ever-somber look on it always made him appear older than his eighteen years.

Ted fondly called him "Straight Arrow."

"Tell me, Ted."

"I . . . I hit a man."

Jamie stared at the blue jet on the gas range.

His voice was low when he spoke.

"Another bar fight? You're not a drinker. How do you get into these things?"

"No, Jamie," Ted murmured.

"Then what?"

"I was driving on Desmond Street and I . . . I hit a man."

Jamie didn't turn.

"He was drunk and he walked in front of the car. It was very dark and nobody was around. You know how deserted Desmond Street is. You know, Jamie. You know. Dark and deserted and . . . and . . ."

His voice tailed off into the silence.

Jamie's hands gripped the top of the white range.

The range was hot to the touch but he didn't feel it.

Then he heard his brother speak again.

"I was sober. Clean sober. It's the truth, Jamie. The truth."

"And?"

"I panicked and left him lying there."

Jamie swung about sharply.

His face white and tense.

His voice cold and harsh.

"What in the hell are you saying? What?"

The tears came into Ted's eyes.

His gentle blue eyes.

"I . . . I panicked."

Jamie came swiftly over to him.

"And you left him there?" he shouted.

His angry voice filled the narrow room.

Ted shivered.

His lips trembled.

"How? How could you do that?"

The big man looked up to him pleadingly.

When he spoke, his voice was low, very low.

As if he were talking to himself.

"I . . . I lost my head. . . . It wasn't my fault. He walked in front of the car. He was drunk. Drunk. Came out of the night. From nowhere. I wasn't going fast. I wasn't. I swear to you on Dad and Mom's graves that I . . ."

Jamie fiercely cut into him.

"You left him lying in the street? In the street?"

"There was nobody around. Nobody saw it. That's all that was in my mind."

"And you drove off?"

"All I was thinking of was my career and nobody saw it. I wasn't myself. You know I'm not like that. You know it. I help everybody. Everybody. I haven't a mean feeling in my . . . I wasn't myself."

He hit his knee with his big hand again and again.

"I got scared. Scared. I wasn't myself. I wasn't."

Jamie reached down and fiercely grabbed him by his shirt.

"But he was a human being. Not a dog. You don't even leave a dog lying in the street and run off."

"It all happened so fast. I couldn't handle it. Just couldn't."

Jamie slowly let go of the shirt and drew back.

"Was he dead?"

And he felt inside of him the heavy beating of his heart while he waited for the answer.

And also mixed within was an overwhelming pity for his lost brother.

Then he heard the words.

"No. Just hurt."

Jamie breathed out silently.

"Badly hurt?"

Ted shook his head and then ran his hand through his curly blond hair before answering.

"Just hurt."

> "Was he dead?"
> And he felt inside of him the heavy beating of his heart while he waited for the answer.

"How do you know that?"

"I went back. Walked. And there was an ambulance there. I stood where nobody could see me."

"And?"

"I could make out what was happening."

"He was hurt enough to be taken to a hospital," Jamie said sharply.

"He was."

Jamie's voice rose.

"In Christ's name, why didn't you come out of the dark and go over there and face it?"

"I . . . I just couldn't."

"The truth. All you needed was to tell them the truth. The truth."

"Couldn't do it. Just . . ."

And Jamie, looking at him, knew that he couldn't.

You're lost, Ted.

Lost.

Ever since Mom and Dad were killed in that crash.

You never got over it.

And you turned to me.

To me.

When Jamie spoke again, his voice was gentle.

"And then what did you do?"

"I went back to the car and drove away. Nobody saw me."

Jamie went over to the window and stared out into the night.

The dark, cloudless night.

He did it this time, Jamie thought.

He really did it.

Jamie heard his brother's voice drift over to him.

"I spoke to Carmody."

"Who is he?"

"The team's lawyer. He wants to talk to you."

"To me? Why?"

"He . . . he said he'd explain to you."

"Explain what to me?"

Ted looked at him and didn't answer.

"Tell me."

"I don't know. I really don't know."

"You do."

"I swear to you on Mom's . . ."

Jamie cut it savagely.

"Don't swear. Leave Mom and Dad out of this. Let them sleep in peace. Thank God, they're dead. Dead and away from you."

"Jamie, please don't talk to me that way. Please don't do it."

"You make me."

He came over to the table and sat down heavily and then looked across it at the big man.

"I'm tired of you, Ted," he said.

"Please, Jamie. Don't say that."

And the desperate lost look in his brother's eyes pierced through him.

"Jamie, don't leave me alone."

Jamie looked away from him and out to the night.

"I can't make it without you."

I know.

How well I know it.

"When does this Carmody want me to talk to him?"

"In the morning. Anytime you choose."

"Okay," Jamie murmured desolately. "I'll see him."

"Thanks."

That's all the big man said.

And Jamie knew that he was too full of emotion to say any more.

"Get upstairs," Jamie suddenly shouted.

Ted looked fearfully at him and didn't speak.

"Get to bed and try to get some rest. You look like a damned wreck."

Ted slowly rose.

"Sure, Jamie. Sure."

Then Jamie watched him turn and go to the stairs.

Watched him as he swung on the second step, swung around, with that smooth, graceful motion, and then stood stock-still and stared bewilderedly about him as if he didn't know where he was.

"I'm sorry, Jamie," he said. "I always bring you trouble. I'm sorry."

Then Jamie watched him go up the steps and out of sight.

Jamie was now alone in the night-filled room.

Thinking.
Ever thinking.

The truth.
  Nothing but the truth.

"Ted claims that nobody saw him. Nobody."
  "That's right," Ted murmured.
  The lawyer turned to him.
  "But soon somebody will come forward and say that he or she did see you in the car. It's happened before in my practice. And I've been a lawyer a long, long time."
  Jamie sat waiting.
  Carmody spoke again.
  "We must be ready."
  Ready for what? Jamie thought bleakly.
  They were sitting in the high-ceilinged, elaborately furnished office.
  The three of them.
  Carmody, Ted, and Jamie.
  The door of the room was closed.
  Tightly closed.

lithe
agile;
graceful

Carmody was a **lithe**, tanned man with dark alert eyes and a quiet, self-assured voice.
  "So far the police have no clues. Not a one."
  It's early, Jamie thought somberly.
  "I have some good friends there who will tell me if they come up with any. Such as a license-plate number."
  Carmody lit a cigarette and paused.
  Then he turned to Jamie.
  And quietly studied him.
  He spoke.
  "I understand that you were valedictorian[1] in your graduating class."
  "I was," Jamie said.

I **valedictorian:** student, usually with the best marks, who delivers the commencement speech

Unit Two   Family Ties

"And you've been accepted to a very **prestigious** college."

"Yale."

"He's getting a full scholarship. I told you that," Ted said proudly.

Carmody smiled.

"You did, Ted."

He puffed at his cigarette.

"There's not a blemish on your record, Jamie."

He pronounced the word "blemish" softly.

So very softly.

And Jamie knew instantly that he disliked the man.

Disliked him intensely.

Carmody spoke again.

"Your brother needs your help. Needs it badly."

"What does he need?"

"For you to say that he was with you on the night of the accident."

Jamie stared silently at the man.

The room had grown still.

Very still.

Ted had risen from his chair, a wild, anguished look on his face.

Carmody's voice cut through the stillness.

"Ted was with you all night long. Every minute of it. Never leaving you."

Ted walked over to the lawyer.

"You didn't tell me that Jamie would have to do that."

"We've no choice."

Ted loomed over the man.

"But it's against all he stands for. I know him. I don't want it."

Carmody snuffed out his cigarette, slowly and deliberately.

"You'll do as I tell you."

"No. I won't hold still for this."

"You'll have to."

Ted pounded the desk with his big fist.

"No. No."

His face was pale and sweat glistened on his forehead.

"Keep quiet and sit down."

Ted's big hands began to tremble.

"Sit," Carmody commanded.

The big man slowly turned and went back to his seat.

Carmody's voice when he spoke was precise and clean.

His eyes cold and **impassive**.

impassive
unemotional
or
inexpressive

"Listen to me. There's a real world out there. So listen. The two of you."

He paused and then went on.

"Ted, you are one of the young stars of pro football today. You made three million dollars your first year. You will make much, much more as you play on. You are sure to become the club's most valuable property."

The real world, Jamie thought bitterly.

The real world has its own truth.

But, dammit, I have my own.

My own.

Carmody was speaking.

". . . Ted, you did a damn fool thing. I believe you. It was not your fault. You panicked. But you drove away and left a man lying on the street, not knowing whether he was dead or alive."

"Lost my head. Lost it," Ted murmured.

"I know and understand. But you're going to be called into court. And when that happens I want to be there at your side with an airtight alibi. And no matter what they come up with, that alibi will pull us through. Do you hear me?"

Ted bowed his head and covered his face with his hands.

"I'll pull you through. I will."

Carmody turned to Jamie.

"You say you care for your brother."

"Yes."

"Then you must do this."

"Must?"

"Yes. I assure you that nothing will happen to you or him. Nothing."

"You know from experience?"

Carmody nodded.

"I know. Well, Jamie?"

Jamie looked away to Ted and and didn't answer.

He heard Carmody's voice.

"If you're thinking of the man who was injured . . . ?"

"I am."

Carmody smiled.

"He's going to fully recover. And then he's going to be quietly well taken care of. It will turn out to be the best thing that has ever happened to him."

He learned forward to Jamie.

"Well?"

"Let's wait and see what happens," Jamie said.

"But we can count on you?"

Jamie looked from Carmody over to his brother.

Ted still sat there, his head bowed, his face still covered by his big hands.

Jamie turned back to the lawyer.

"You can count on me."

*T*hen he said, "I can't tell you what to do, Jamie. It's your call."

"And you think it will work out like the lawyer says?"

"After the crash, when I came to get the two of you and take you home with me . . ."

Uncle Harry paused and looked out over the lake and didn't speak for a while.

His lean, lined face was tight and sad.

Jamie waited for him to speak again.

"It just tore my heart out. I reached over to get his hand but he turned away from me and went to you. And he stood there looking down into your face and then he reached out to you and held you and cried. And all the while you stood there, holding him, your face tight and silent. Like you were a big man, sheltering him."

The sun was still high and the lake rippled, ripples of gold.

Uncle Harry cast his line out again.

"He needs you. He'll always need you."

Then he said, "I can't tell you what to do, Jamie. It's your call."

"And you think it will work out like the lawyer says?"

Harry nodded.

"You'll end up in court in the witness chair. That's if you decide to go along with them."

"You can't help me decide?"

He shook his head.

"I'd give my right arm to help you decide. But I just can't. It's your call, Jamie. Yours alone."

He got up.

"I don't feel like fishing anymore. Let's pack up and go home."

He reeled in his line.

"It's getting cloudy anyway."

But the sun was shining.

Very brightly.

The voice pierced the dead silence of the courtroom.

"Do you swear to tell the truth and nothing but the truth?"

Jamie raised his right hand and looked over to where Ted sat.

The haunted, pleading look in Ted's eyes.

He knew that he would remember that look for the rest of his life.

But within he said:

I can't do it, Ted.

I just can't.

And Jamie knew that he could never again be his brother's keeper.

The tears came to his eyes.

And he bowed his head.

AFTER YOU READ
My Brother's Keeper

Think and Discuss

1. How would you describe the relationship between Jamie and Ted?

2. Why do you think his uncle refuses to give Jamie advice?

3. As you know, **characterization** refers to the ways in which a writer shapes the reader's understanding of a character. Some techniques include description, dialogue, showing how a character thinks and treats others, as well as how others in the story think about and treat him or her. How is Ted characterized in "My Brother's Keeper"?

4. An author's **style** is the way she or he writes, including word choice, level of difficulty, and preferences in subject matter and tone. How would you describe Jay Bennett's style in this short story? Create a chart like the one below in your Writer's Notebook. Use examples from the text to support your ideas.

Technique	Examples
Dialogue	
Choice of Specific Details	
Choice of Setting	
Choice of Characters	
Vocabulary	
Length of Sentence; Difficulty of Syntax	

5. What would you have done if you were in Jamie's place?

Write to Understand: Using Dialogue

One of the things you may have learned from working through the graphic organizer above is that Bennett has a distinctive and realistic way of using dialogue. Most sentences are short and staccato—a technique that keeps the reader racing through the story. Try your hand at creating a brief section of dialogue between two characters. Note that this is one instance in which sentence fragments can be used to add an authentic tone to your writing.

BEFORE YOU READ

from *Letters to a Young Brother*

Wild Geese

Meet the Authors

Hill Harper Actor Hill Harper (born 1966) wrote *Letters to a Young Brother* to dissuade young black men from making the same mistakes he made while growing up. He was fortunate to have two accomplished parents who encouraged him to succeed at school as well as on stage. He graduated from Harvard with degrees in both law and government, but could not pull himself away from acting. His lengthy screen credits include both television (*ER, The Sopranos*) and films, such as Spike Lee's *Get on the Bus* and *He Got Game*.

Mary Oliver Pulitzer Prize-winning poet Mary Oliver (born 1935) lived briefly in the home of Edna St. Vincent Millay, where she helped the poet's sister organize Millay's papers after her death. Oliver was influenced by Millay's poetry, but she is best known for the powerful themes of nature in her work and for her gentle, distinctive voice.

Build Background: When Quitting Isn't Giving Up

While this essay is aimed at young black men, its lessons should inspire anyone of any age. Harper believes in the value of role models. He describes his own experience as a successful law student and actor as well as those of more famous people, from Muhammad Ali to Lance Armstrong. In this selection, Harper explains the difference between quitting and changing your mind.

- How would you define the term "role model"?

- Why might Harper have decided to use a letter format rather than regular text to offer advice to young people?

from *Letters to a Young Brother*

HILL HARPER

FROM *LETTERS TO A YOUNG BROTHER*

Hill Harper

Quitting versus Changing Your Mind

I hated every minute of training, but I said, "Don't quit.
Suffer now and live the rest of your life as a champion."
MUHAMMAD ALI

August 22, 2005
New York

Dear Young Brotha,

Hey man, I'm in New York City shooting *CSI:NY*, and it is a scorching hot August day. You know what's interesting about the 22nd of August? It just so happens to be the anniversary date of the largest slave rebellion in U.S. history led by Nat Turner in 1831—look it up and learn more about it. Now, that was about 175 years ago; that's a while, isn't it? America has an incredible history of all types of people fighting for justice, equality, and positive change.

Today I want to talk to you about quitting, because there are many people in the history of this country who when faced with **adversity** never quit; people such as César Chavez, Martin Luther King, Jr., Muhammad Ali, John F. Kennedy, Rosa Parks, and the above-mentioned Nat Turner. As a matter of fact, anyone who is successful in life, who achieves his goals whether big or small, has done so with **perseverance**. And at different times *everyone* wants to quit or thinks about quitting, but the winners get past that thought and keep going. Now, I don't need you to lead thousands of people in a revolution. I want you to lead a revolution in your own mind, heart, and spirit. I want you to never quit, even when things get hard or doubt comes into your mind. Lance Armstrong, a gifted athlete, who had to quit cycling because of cancer but came back to win the Tour de France (the Super Bowl of bike racing) a record breaking seven times, believes: "Pain is temporary. It may last a minute, or an hour, or a day, or a year, but eventually it will subside and something else will take its place. If I quit, however, it lasts forever."

adversity
a difficult situation; hardship

perseverance
determination; resolve

In your last letter, you said you wanted to "quit" the track team. First of all, I don't like you or anyone in my crew using the word "quit." It is one of those four-letter words that I can't stand. I hate it almost as much as the word "try" (but more on that later). The most important thing for us is to really look at *why* you want to quit something. Before we decide whether you should or should not quit track, we need to analyze it and really know what quitting means. There is a difference between "quitting" something and "changing your mind" and deciding not to do it anymore. I'll explain.

First of all, words have power. By that I mean you could take the exact same action, but if you call it two different things, it will have an effect on the way you approach that action. After Michael Jordan had won numerous championships with the Chicago Bulls, he decided to leave basketball for baseball. After a season on a farm league baseball team, he changed his mind, returned to the Chicago Bulls, and won two more championships. Michael Jordan didn't quit baseball, he changed his mind. He followed his passion to pursue baseball, experienced it, then decided he loved playing in the NBA[1] more. In both cases, he followed his passion; he didn't "quit," he just replaced one passionate pursuit with another.

In your last letter, you said you wanted to "quit" the track team. First of all, I don't like you or anyone in my crew using the word "quit."

Let me tell you about my man Steve Jobs, a dude I respect a great deal. He's the guy who created Apple Computers, the iPod, and founded Pixar, the company that makes movies like *Toy Story* and *The Incredibles*. Well, his wealth is so huge he makes Michael Jordan look poor. For the past thirty-three years, every morning Steve Jobs gets up, looks in the mirror, and asks himself, "If today were the last day of my life, would I want to do what I'm about to do today?" If there were a bunch of mornings in a row where the answer was, "No," then he knew he had to change what he was doing. Now, there's nothing wrong with change if you decide to stop doing something that you are not passionate about or that you do not love. There is a poet who I love named Mary Oliver who says, "The only thing you have to do in your life is to let the soft animal of your body love what it loves."

I **NBA:** National Basketball Association

My point is, do what you love so you never have to quit. If you do change what you are doing for the right reasons, then we are not going to call it "quitting," we're going to call it "changing your mind," "doing something else," or "moving on." When you "change what you are doing," that means that you stop doing something that is holding you back from realizing your true destiny. Anything you spend your time doing day in and day out that you are not passionate about is okay to stop doing eventually. (Unless it is school or some other educational experience that is leading you toward a bigger, more passionate goal.)

As we discussed, it's important to be active and make decisions and choices. Right? But you can change your mind, and there's nothing wrong with that. Changing your mind is natural. It's okay. It's fine. It's supposed to change. As you learn and experience different things, as you walk though life, you will find you have a new "view" or perspective. This may lead you to want to change your mind. And that's cool. So given what I just said in this last paragraph, is there anything in your life right now that you want to change your mind about? Maybe you want to join the soccer team instead of the track team, or stop working part time at the fast-food restaurant in order to intern at a law firm, or you might want to pick a new major on your college applications. No, I'm serious; ask yourself that question right now. What in your life do you want to change your mind about? Write it down; then, let's make some changes in that area that you just wrote about, starting today. That's the new version of you, right now. In a week's or day's time, your mind may change about that, and that's cool too. Change is good. Know that!

When you say you are quitting something, it means you're stopping because it's hard, challenging, uncomfortable, or raises some kind of fear in you.

When you say you are quitting something, it means you're stopping because it's hard, challenging, uncomfortable, or raises some kind of fear in you. If something makes you a little scared, it usually means it's the exact thing you need to complete to go to the next level in your life's journey. Through working hard we develop new skill sets that make us stronger. That's why when someone lifts weights, their muscles become stronger; when you read books, the muscles in your brain become stronger; when speaking in front of a crowd, even though you are afraid, your public speaking muscles become stronger. Let's face it, we are all on life's journey, man, no matter how young or old you are. And the stronger all of our muscles are, the better. Some of us are moving forward, but unfortunately, most people who "quit" things are moving their feet, but getting nowhere or, worse still, moving their feet and going backward. Malcolm X talked about these people: "The treadmill is moving backwards faster than we're able to go forward in this direction. We're not even standing still, we're going backwards." If you quit track only to hang with a group of slackers who have no drive, then you are going backward. But, if you decide you want to give up track in order to spend that time doing something you are passionate about, like playing an instrument or another sport, or even taking a second language, then that is "changing your mind." That is moving forward. Standing still and going backward are no longer options for you and me, so you might as well get comfortable with being successful and unreasonably happy. You're part of my crew now, and all of my crew moves forward in their life's journey. Forward fast. Fast and furious, baby.

Hill Harper

I've definitely had my own experiences with "changing my mind" and "doing something else" versus "quitting." After graduating from Harvard Law School, people expected me to slide right into a high-paying job as a lawyer. I even expected to take a job in a law firm because I wanted to pay off my college loans and I knew the job would get me out of debt quickly. But here's what happened: I had already studied and fallen in love with acting. So instead of taking a job in a law firm, I moved to Los Angeles and began waiting tables and auditioning for acting jobs. Did I quit law? No, but I changed my mind about law as a career. Was law school a waste of time? Absolutely not. I learned so much and made some of my best friends whom I still have to this day; and, as a matter of fact, I still use my legal skills when I evaluate acting contracts. And since I changed my mind and pursued what I loved, the universe **conspired** to allow me to pay off my student loans much faster than I ever would have if I had continued to do something I was not passionate about. It works; I am a living testament.

conspired
plotted;
schemed

All that said, you asked, should you quit track? No, you shouldn't "quit," but it is okay for you to stop doing it if you clearly aren't passionate about it. I don't think the reason you want to stop running track is because you're afraid. I think the reason you want to end it is because you now know it doesn't fit into your life's journey and it doesn't contribute to your being unreasonably happy. So it's important that when you change your mind, about your A plan, you have a B plan ready. Is there another sport you'd enjoy more? Basketball, hockey, football (my personal favorite), tennis, wrestling, or another I didn't mention? Or do you want to join student government, or the debate team, or the yearbook staff? There are so many other sports and activities that may ignite your passion. The important thing right now is to find something you love and do it so that you can be unreasonably happy. So now, it's all about formulating an alternative plan. And that's cool. Feel me?

Man, I gotta get to the set and shoot a scene for *CSI:NY*, so we'll talk soon. E-mail or write me a letter when you can.

Peace.

Oh, and I've been writing you from this Chinese restaurant on Broadway, and it's not coincidental that I got a fortune cookie that speaks to exactly what we've been talking about. I'll throw it in the letter so you can check it out yourself.

Your friend,

Hill

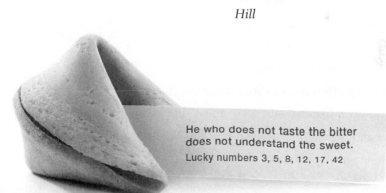

He who does not taste the bitter does not understand the sweet.
Lucky numbers 3, 5, 8, 12, 17, 42

POETRY CONNECTION

Wild Geese   MARY OLIVER

You do not have to be good.
You do not have to walk on your knees
for a hundred miles through the desert, repenting.
You only have to let the soft animal of your body
       love what it loves.   5
Tell me about despair, yours, and I will tell you mine.
Meanwhile the world goes on.
Meanwhile the sun and the clear pebbles of the rain
are moving across the landscapes,
over the prairies and the deep trees,   10
the mountains and the rivers.
Meanwhile the wild geese, high in the clean blue air,
are heading home again.
Whoever you are, no matter how lonely,
the world offers itself to your imagination,   15
calls to you like the wild geese, harsh and exciting—
over and over announcing your place
in the family of things.

AFTER YOU READ

from *Letters to a Young Brother*
Wild Geese

Think and Discuss

1. What is the difference between quitting and changing your mind, according to Hill Harper?

2. What is the connection between Harper's essay and Oliver's poem? Explain.

3. Harper uses many examples to support his argument. List some of them in a graphic organizer like the one below. The first example has been done for you.

Type	Example 1	Example 2	Example 3
Role Models	Muhammad Ali, Rosa Parks, Cesar Chavez, political activists	Lance Armstrong, Michael Jordan, sports stars	Steve Jobs, businessman
Personal Example	His own experiences as an African American who chose acting over career in law or government		
Quotations	Quote from Ali that opens the essay		
Literature	Mary Oliver's poem, Wild Geese		

4. Both Harper and Oliver use the **second-person perspective**, addressing the reader directly as "you." What are some of the benefits of this form?

5. Whom would you choose for a role model? What do you admire most about this person?

6. Apart from school, how do you spend your time? Is it what you love, or do you want to "change your mind"? Explain.

Write to Understand: An Advice Column

Almost every major newspaper has had an advice column in which writers such as Ann Landers answer questions and offer advice to readers who seek help with a personal problem. Pair off with another classmate. Each of you should write two or three questions that a character from this unit might ask. Then, exchange papers and answer each other's questions. Use what you have learned in this unit about families to help you formulate your answers. Back up your advice with examples such as the ones in the chart above. If possible, review some advice columns in papers or magazines and imitate their style.

Writers on Writing

BEFORE YOU READ
Grandfather's Blessing
I Remember My Father's Hands

Meet the Authors
Julia Alvarez Born in 1950 in New York City, Alvarez lived in her family's native country, the Dominican Republic, until she was ten. At that time, her family was forced to flee for political reasons, and they returned to New York. In high school, Alvarez fell in love with words and what she regarded as their ability to make people feel complete. The author of three prizewinning volumes of poetry and three novels, Alvarez currently teaches at Middlebury College in Vermont.

Lisa Suhair Majaj Born to an American mother and a Palestinian father, Majaj is a poet and scholar. She specializes in Arab American literature and lives in Cypress with her family.

Build Background: Generations
Julia Alvarez's story "Grandfather's Blessing" is from her book *Something to Declare*. The last half of the book is about her experiences as a writer. On the final page, she explains that writing matters to her because it "clarifies and intensifies, it deepens and connects me to others .... And because writing matters in this way to me, it does something else. It challenges me, not just to read and have that private enjoyment of clarity, but to pass it on."

"Passing it on" is something that both writers and family members from older generations do. As you read the following selections, think about these questions:

• What do younger generations learn from older ones, and what gifts do they receive?

• What do writers pass on to readers?

Grandfather's Blessing

JULIA ALVAREZ

GRANDFATHER'S BLESSING

Julia Alvarez

"**What** do you want to be when you grow up?" my grandfather asked, chuckling. It was a joke to think these little bits of Alvarez-Tavares, Tavares-Sánchez, Tavares-Kelner would grow up to drive jeepsters, run companies, nurse babies, and scold the maids.

Behind me the younger cousins were lined up, waiting for their moment of future at our grandfather's knee. This grandfather, my mother's Papi, was such a handsome gentleman, so slim, with such elegant long hands, such a fair complexion protected under his Panama hat, seersucker suit, and starched white shirt. He loved to recite bits of poetry, what he could remember. *Juventud, divino tesoro.*[1] *How do I love thee? Let me count the ways.*[2] *Out, out damned spot.*[3] He also had excellent manners. He ate his fruit with a knife and fork—which was unheard of in the Dominican Republic. But then my grandfather had traveled. He had been to Spain, London, Mexico, Rome and had brought back native costumes for all his grandchildren. At parties, we assembled, a **diminutive** guard from Buckingham Palace, seven señoritas with beauty marks on their upper lips, several cowboys from the Old West, a Dutch girl in clogs. He took good care of his family. Of course, we wanted to impress him.

diminutive
very small

"A bullfighter," I announced when it was my turn. I had never seen a bullfight, but on the coffee table at my grandfather's house lay a book on bullfighting. I had fallen in love with the trim men in their tight black pants and ruffly shirts, frozen in beautiful dance poses. Those pictures set me dreaming of the future.

"Bullfighter?!" my grandfather lifted his eyebrows and chuckled again. "I don't think there are any *girl* bullfighters," he noted, not exactly discouraging me but letting me know the odds.

---

1 *Juventud, divino tesoro:* Spanish for "Youth, divine treasure," a famous line of poetry by the Nicaraguan poet Rubén Darío

2 *How do I love thee? Let me count the ways:* from a sonnet by Elizabeth Barrett Browning

3 *Out, out damned spot:* from Shakespeare's drama *Macbeth*

I walked away from our brief interview and headed for the coffee table. I paged through the bullfighting book much as I would later page through my anthologies[4] looking for someone else with a Spanish-sounding name, someone else who had come to English when she was ten, someone else to prove that I could become what I dreamed of becoming. I learned early to turn to books, movies, music, paintings, rather than to the family to find out what was possible. The men in the bullfighting book all had little ponytails—they could have been girls. But when I looked at their chests, none of them had bosoms. Maybe my grandfather was right. You couldn't be female and fight the Furies,[5] you couldn't be an Alvarez-Tavares girl and enter the ring and take on the dangerous future.

> I learned early to turn to books, movies, music, paintings, rather than to the family to find out what was possible.

When I had my next chance to proclaim my future, I told my grandfather I wanted to be a cowboy. I suppose this was an Americanization of my bullfighting dream. I had seen a poorly dubbed[6] Western on a neighbor's new TV.

"You mean a cowgirl," my grandfather said, nodding as if this were much more reasonable than a bullfighter.

The next time he and Mamita came back from the United States of America, they brought me a cowgirl outfit. Somehow, the mock-leather skirt and vest and doodad tassels here and there didn't seem as serious as the cowboy outfits my boy cousins were wearing. Instead of a holster and gun, I got a little rawhide pocketbook with a mirror and a tiny brush and comb—nothing I could twirl, draw, aim, and shoot. All I could use my present for was to bribe the maids so they wouldn't tell on me when something broke or food was found floating in the water of the centerpiece orchids.

The cowboys, the wonderful, blond, and deeply tanned cowboys . . . They galloped across the screen, their horses' tails straight out behind them.

---

4 **anthologies:** collections of short stories, poems, and essays

5 **the Furies:** in Greek and Roman myth, the goddesses of vengeance

6 **dubbed:** translated from one language into another for broadcast

My heart soared, my chest tightened. Could it be possible, really possible, to get that far away from my mother and the aunts trying to teach me to hold my skirt down when the wind was blowing?

"I want to be a cowboy," I repeated to my grandfather when he corrected me. "I don't want to ride sidesaddle" was the best reason I could give him.

"Well, well," he said, chuckling, the way grown-ups always did when what they meant to say was, "You are going to get over this."

Meanwhile, the country was under tight rein. The dictatorship, twenty-five years old, was firmly in place. People were disappearing in the middle of the night. One evening the SIM, the military intelligence service, came for my grandfather and put him in jail for two days. He was not tortured but "persuaded" to sell a part of his land for the minimum price to the daughter of the dictator. It was property that my grandfather had been saving to give to his own children.

At parties, the handsome uncles were dancing flamenco on dining-room tables. My aunt Tití, who was not married at twenty-five because she knew Latin and read books and grew anthuriums in the garden instead of making herself pretty and positioning herself like a floral arrangement in the front parlor, designed an indoor pond in my grandparents' house. My grandfather stocked it with golden fish. When I thought no one was looking, I would lean over the tiled edge and try to catch them.

One day, I grabbed for one swirling bit of wonder and ended up falling into the pond. One of the maids found me.

After everyone had scolded me for almost getting myself killed, my grandfather took me aside. "Next time, call me. We'll catch the big gold one with the net. You'll be able to put your hand in and touch the scales."

"*I* want to be a cowboy," I repeated to my grandfather when he corrected me. "I don't want to ride sidesaddle" was the best reason I could give him.

My grandfather owned a ranch out in the country where our milk, eggs, and most of our víveres or starch vegetables came from. The cows all had the names of his granddaughters. Every morning when the milk was delivered, my grandfather would announce who gave the most milk. For the rest of the day the human namesake **preened** herself on her cow's accomplishment. What is peculiar is how each of the grown-up cousins now remembers that, on average, her cow gave the most milk.

On the way to the ranch, we sometimes stopped to visit the widow of one of my father's **illegitimate** brothers. My paternal grandfather, who was already dead by the time I was born, left twenty-five legitimate children and who knows how many illegitimate children behind. Many of the legitimates would have nothing to do with the illegitimates, which made it very difficult to draw up a guest list for a wedding or a noche buena[7] party. Burials, like my dead uncle's burial, were easier because in the face of death everybody was supposed to know better than carry on grudges.

My father was the only legitimate who kept up with all the illegitimates and their families. So, whenever my grandfather and father took us to the

preened
admired or congratulated

illegitimate
born outside a legal marriage

---

7 **noche buena:** Christmas Eve (translates to "Good Night")

ranch, we stopped to see my widowed aunt. She had three teenage sons whom I observed closely because I hoped that from them I might get a hint of things to come. One of the things I knew was coming to me was kissing.

My sisters and I had been practicing. We put a piece of paper between us because it wasn't really right for girls to kiss each other on the lips. We rubbed our mouths together until the paper between us was wet and shredded.

These young men were beginners as young men. Little bits of their younger selves still clung to them as if, like chicks, they had just crawled out of the cracked shells of their boyhood. Their voices did funny things, their hands and arms were too big for their bodies, their upper lips sported dark hairs and milk stains.

"They are good boys. They are studying hard," their widowed mother said in that weepy voice of mothers who secretly think their sons are depriving themselves if they aren't causing all the trouble their gender entitles them to enjoy.

One of the young men was going to be an engineer, like my grandfather. Another, a doctor. The third one wanted to be a poet. Actually, I met only the future engineer and the future doctor. The future poet will always be the sound of a shower running. Every time we stopped at their house, his mother said he was writing in the bathroom. He could only concentrate with the shower going to block out the noise of the rest of the world.

"But why?" I asked my grandfather when my father had taken his sister-in-law aside to give her some money. We had been left alone sipping our limonadas on the patio.

"¿Quién sabe?"[8] my grandfather said, chuckling. "'Juventud divino tesoro. If music be the food of love, play on.'" He went through his repertoire of memorized poetry. His voice was hushed as if he were awed by the mysterious workings of talent. As if one of these beautiful, terrifying, uncontrollable bullfighting bulls were locked in that bathroom.

"I tell him he has to be careful," the widow explained to my grandfather a little later, "que no se enferme." That he doesn't get sick.

---

8 **¿Quién sabe?:** Spanish for "Who knows?"

I had never in the world considered that books had that kind of power. They could make a person sick. They could make a young man lock himself in the bathroom with the shower going instead of coming out to say hello to visitors from the capital.

"He won't get sick," my grandfather reassured her. He himself had been one of three sons, raised by his two older brothers after their parents had died young. The older brothers had sent him to Cornell University where he studied engineering, though his passion for music and poetry might have tempted him in a different direction. But la familia and what it mandated were the order of his day. Finally, he came home to set up a business and raise his own family. Muy familial, everyone said of my grandfather, a family man. It was the best thing you could say about a person after you said he was kind and handsome, which you could also say about my grandfather.

I had never in the world considered that books had that kind of power. They could make a person sick.

While the adults sat on the patio, visiting, I snuck back inside, drawn by the sound of water. I listened at the door, holding my breath, my heart beating so loud that I thought the young poet would think there was somebody knocking. But all I heard was the shower, and every once in a while, the turning of pages. I touched my cheek to the wood and felt the vibration of pounding water. After a few minutes, I turned and pressed my lips hard on a knot in the grain of the door.

"A movie actress," I told my grandfather. "I want to wear all the costumes of the world and travel in airplanes and hot-air balloons." *Around the World in Eighty Days* had recently come to the Olympia movie theater.

My grandfather opened his eyes wide in a pantomime of surprise. "My, my," he said, "where does this little girl get such ideas?" My mother, who could never resist an opportunity to put in a plug for rules and regulations, noted, "If she wants to be an actress, she better learn to clean her plate."

That put a wrench in my dream. "Why?" I asked, disappointed. I had never heard that cleaning one's plate was one of the requirements of being an actress.

"You have to have legs and a fundillo," she said, slapping her bottom. "You have to put on some weight so you have something to show people."

"She could be a great dramatic actress," my grandfather intervened, "like Sarah Bernhardt. She could walk the boards of Covent Garden.[9] 'Out, out damned spot. The quality of mercy is not strained.[10] To be or not to be.'"[11] There was that far-off dreamy look in his eyes again, as if he could see the future, as if he had caught sight of me years and years from now standing where I wanted to be, waving back at him.

But for the moment, I didn't know who Sarah Bernhardt was or what the difference was between a dramatic and movie actress. The only walking of the boards I knew about was what pirates made prisoners do on the high seas. But I did know that actresses got to be all kinds of different people, not just second daughters to strict mothers, not just third granddaughters to elegant grandfathers, not just another girl cousin in a line-up of cousins, one of dozens of nieces to a multitude of uncles and aunts, half-uncles and half-aunts, who didn't even talk to one another—in other words, an actress got to be more than just a family person.

"She better learn how to sing," one of the aunts noted. "You've got to sing as an actress, you know? And dance," she added pointedly. This was the same aunt who had laughed with my mother when they overheard me singing, "Yo soy el aventurero,"[12] with Gladys. The aunt had told Mami that I sounded like a cow with a stomachache. The maid sounded, she added, like a cow without a stomachache. The two women had burst out laughing. As for my having to learn to dance, this was a sore point. Recently, I had

---

9 **Covent Garden:** A famous London theatre

10 **The quality of mercy is not strained:** from Shakespeare's drama *The Merchant of Venice*

11 **To be or not to be:** from Shakespeare's *Hamlet*

12 **"Yo soy el aventurero":** Spanish for "I am the adventurer."

been thrown out of ballet class for giving Madame Corbett a general's salute when she tapped my butt with her dancing cane.

So I couldn't be an actress either? Well, at least there were still lots of other things to be in this world. "I want to drive a red pickup," I said, amending my future. "I want to go to the moon in a rocket ship and under water in a submarine and work in an ice cream shop and be a guard at Buckingham Palace." I was stacking up all the exciting possibilities for the future, a big wall to keep everybody out. "And I want to be a pilot and go to Nueva York[13] and shop for toys, and I want to be a poet and write lots and lots of poems."

"A poet?" my grandfather said, smiling dreamily. The room went silent, aunts and uncles bracing themselves for one of his recitations. But he did not recite. Instead, he took my face in his hand, tilting it this way and that, as if he had caught the big gold fish in his net and wanted to see it up close. "A poet, yes. Now you are talking."

---

13 **Nueva York:** Spanish for "New York"

I Remember My Father's Hands

LISA SUHAIR MAJAJ

because they were large, and square,
fingers chunky, black hair like wire

because they fingered worry beads over and over
(that muted clicking, that constant motion, that **secular** prayer)

secular
not religious;
worldly

because they ripped bread with quiet purpose,   5
dipped fresh green oil like a birthright

because after his mother's funeral they raised a tea cup,
set it down untouched, uncontrollably trembling

because when they trimmed hedges, pruned roses,
their tenderness caught my breath with jealousy   10

because once when I was a child they cupped my face,
dry and warm, flesh full and calloused, for a long moment

because over his wife's still form they faltered
great mute helpless beasts

because when his own lungs filled and sank they reached out   15
for the first time pleading

because when I look at my hands
his own speak back

AFTER YOU READ

Grandfather's Blessing
I Remember My Father's Hands

Think and Discuss

1. Why do you think Alvarez's grandfather wanted her to become a poet?

2. Two people in this memoir show a special interest in poetry. What does it mean to each of those characters? Use details from the text to explain your answer.

3. How does the **setting** of this memoir relate to idea of poetry?

4. Alvarez repeatedly uses the **image** of the goldfish pond. What do you think the pond means to Alvarez and her grandfather?

5. What detail from the poem "I Remember My Father's Hands" calls to mind a similar detail in the memoir by Alvarez?

6. Scan the memoir again. Then look back over the other prose selections in this unit, both nonfiction and fiction. Copy the graphic organizer below into your Writer's Notebook. Then use it to compare the features of autobiographical narratives and short stories.

Comparison of Nonfiction and Fiction		
Feature	Nonfiction Narratives	Short Stories
Subject Matter		
Point of View		
Structure and Organization		
Writing Style		

Write to Understand: Double-Column Entries

Draw a vertical line down the middle of a page in your Writer's Notebook to create two columns. In the left-hand column, sketch out in writing a real-life event involving your family that you might develop into an autobiographical narrative. In the right-hand column, sketch out an idea for a fictional short story inspired by the real-life event. For example, change the setting, or imagine what the event would have been like if the characters were superheroes. Follow your imagination wherever it leads.

A Writer's WORKSHOP

SHORT STORY

Julia Alvarez wrote that people want to know "the secret heart of each other's lives." In everyday life, probing those secrets may be intrusive. In fiction, though, says Alvarez, "we can enter, without shame or without encountering defensiveness or embarrassment, the intimate lives of other people." In this unit, you have read about family ties in short stories that have invited you into a fictional world. Now you can invite readers into a world of your creation as you write a fictional short story related to family ties.

Prewriting

REVIEWING IDEAS

A glance back through your Writer's Notebook will show you that you already have ideas about family ties just waiting to be turned into a short story. Review what you have written to see which idea you can reshape with your imagination into a made-up story. A good subject for a short story is:

- a fictional incident in which a character faces a conflict that comes to a head at the high point of the story and then resolves one way or another

- an incident through which one or more characters learn something valuable.

You can also brainstorm for new ideas if nothing from your notebook grabs you.

BRAINSTORMING TO DEVELOP DETAILS

Once you have chosen a story idea, brainstorm a list of details. Include descriptions of characters, setting, and plot. Remember that this is fiction—let your imagination go!

Sample Brainstorming Notes

Setting - summer before high school starts, hot and humid, town in southern Illinois

Main character - Leeza. She's 14 years old, curly black hair, medium height, pale, likes to collect things

Other characters - Robyn, Leeza's cousin; Frank, wild boy who gets into trouble but has a good heart. He has black curly hair too.

ORGANIZING IDEAS

Copy the story frame below into your Writer's Notebook. Then complete it using your brainstorming notes and any new ideas that occur to you.

Characters	
Setting	
Conflict	
Event that starts the story in motion	
Other important events, in order	
High point where the conflict is greatest	
Resolution or outcome	

Drafting

Decide what point of view to use in telling your story. Then use your story frame to write a first draft. Also look back over your brainstorming notes to add details to your story. Use dialogue and inner thoughts to reveal character. Think of a zingy and meaningful title.

USING WORD PROCESSING

If you compose your draft on a word processor, you can feel free to write your first draft without worrying too much about mistakes. The word processor can help. In the Tools menu of your word processor, find AutoCorrect. From that menu you can choose to have the computer make some automatic corrections in capitalization and spelling. When you edit later, you still have to check everything by hand, but the AutoCorrect option will have caught many errors.

COOPERATIVE LEARNING: PEER REVIEW

Pair up with a partner and exchange drafts. Discuss the strengths of your partner's draft as well as ways it can be improved.

Revising and Editing

Use your partner's comments to help you evaluate and revise your short story. Keep revising until you are satisfied. Then check your work for errors in grammar, spelling, capitalization, and punctuation.

READING WITH AND EDITOR'S EYE

Check over the dialogue in your story to make sure it follows the conventions. Specifically, be sure that:

- Each time a speaker changes, a new paragraph begins.

- The speaker's words are surrounded by quotation marks.

- If they are interrupted by a speaker tag, such as *he said* or *she mumbled,* only the speaker's exact words are in quotation marks.

- The speaker tag is separated from the quote with a comma unless the quote ends with a question mark or exclamation point.

- If the quotation is a question or exclamation, the question mark or exclamation point goes inside the quotation marks.

The following example from "The Scarlet Ibis" shows these conventions.

He was sitting comfortably on the soft grass, leaning back against the pine. "Why?" he asked.

I hadn't expected such an answer. "So I won't have to haul you around all the time."

"I can't walk, Brother," he said.

"Who says so?" I demanded.

"Mama, the doctor—everybody."

"Oh, you can walk," I said, and I took him by the arms and stood him up. He collapsed on to the grass like a half-empty flour sack. . . .

USING A CHECKLIST

The Six-Trait checklist on the next page will help you evaluate and polish your short story.

Six Traits of Writing: Short Stories

Content and Ideas
- subject focuses on family ties
- story is fictional even if inspired by real-life events
- vivid details bring the setting and experience to life

Organization
- story has a clear "kick-off" event, rises to a high point of conflict, and then resolves
- events are presented in a clear time order

Voice or Style
- story uses an appropriate and consistent point of view
- writer's voice sounds natural, not forced
- dialogue and inner thoughts are realistic and reveal character

Word Choice
- lively verbs and specific nouns make the story easy to picture
- sensory images help readers "see" characters, settings, and events

Sentence Fluency
- transitional words help the writing flow smoothly
- sentence length and sentence beginnings are varied and purposeful

Conventions
- sentences are complete and begin with a capital letter and end with a period, unless fragments are used with a purpose
- grammar and usage are correct
- spelling and punctuation are correct

COOPERATIVE LEARNING: PEER EDITING

Exchange papers with your partner and check each other's editing. Fix any errors your partner points out. Pay special attention to the correct use of quotation marks. Make a neat final copy of your short story.

UNIT THREE

The Forces of Nature

I thrive on the crisp clean air and cold water here, the breath-sucking beauty of the creased and crenulated landscape and its abundant wildlife, the relative quiet and solitude and the personal joy it all adds up to. *These* are the things that I have come to value most in life.

David Petersen, from "Knee-Deep in Its Absence"

BEFORE YOU READ

The Interlopers

Meet the Author: Saki

Saki was the pen name of Hector Hugh Munro (1870–1916). He was born to English parents living in Burma, now known as Myanmar. He lived in both Burma and England, as well as other parts of Europe when he worked as a journalist. His experience gave him a sharp, insightful outlook on English culture at home and abroad. In his fiction he expressed his point of view in satires and short stories containing stark cruelty and sudden surprises.

The name Saki comes from a character in the famous poem *The Rubaiyat of Omar Khayyam* and is also the name of a South American monkey that looks gentle but is actually quite savage. Such a monkey is a character in one of Munro's stories.

Build Background: Edwardian England

H. H. Munro lived during England's Edwardian era, named for King Edward VII, who ruled from 1901 until his death in 1910. During this period, England was the world's most powerful nation, with colonies all over the globe. It was changing from a primarily rural society to a more urban and industrial economy in which newfound wealth could move people up the social ladder. These changes challenged long-held traditions. Hunting and other rural pursuits declined. Civil rights, women's rights, the responsibility of colonizing powers, and a new understanding of the human relationship with nature became important matters.

The following story tells about two men who see each other as interlopers, or intruders, in a disputed forestland. As you read, think about these questions:

- By what right do people own land or other natural resources?

- How have you settled disputes with your friends, neighbors, and rivals about what belongs to whom?

The Interlopers

SAKI

THE INTERLOPERS

Saki

In a forest of mixed growth somewhere on the eastern spurs of the Carpathians,[1] a man stood one winter night watching and listening, as though he waited for some beast of the woods to come within the range of his vision, and, later, of his rifle. But the game for whose presence he kept so keen an outlook was none that figured in the sportsman's calendar as lawful and proper for the chase; Ulrich von Gradwitz patrolled the dark forest in quest of a human enemy.

The forest lands of Gradwitz were of wide extent and well stocked with game; the narrow strip of **precipitous** woodland that lay on its outskirt was not remarkable for the game it harbored or the shooting it afforded, but it was the most jealously guarded of all its owner's territorial possessions. A famous lawsuit, in the days of his grandfather, had wrested it from the illegal possession of a neighboring family of petty landowners; the dispossessed party had never **acquiesced** in the judgment of the Courts, and a long series of **poaching** affrays[2] and similar scandals had embittered the relationships between the families for three generations. The neighbor feud had grown into a personal one since Ulrich had come to be head of his family; if there was a man in the world whom he detested and wished ill to it was Georg Znaeym, the inheritor of the quarrel and the tireless game-snatcher and raider of the disputed border-forest. The feud might, perhaps, have died down or been compromised if the personal ill-will of the two men had not stood in the way; as boys they had thirsted for one another's blood, as men each prayed that misfortune might fall on the other, and this wind-scourged winter night Ulrich had banded together his foresters to watch the dark forest, not in quest of four-footed quarry, but to keep a look-out for the prowling thieves whom he suspected of being afoot from across the land boundary. The roebuck,[3] which usually kept in the sheltered hollows during a storm-wind, were running like driven things tonight, and there was movement and unrest among the creatures that were

precipitous
very steep

acquiesced
accepted; went
along with

poaching
hunting illegally

---

1 **Carpathians**: a mountain range running through Eastern Europe, including Poland, Ukraine, Slovakia, and Romania

2 **affrays**: brawls

3 **roebuck**: a small male deer with forked antlers

wont to sleep through the dark hours. Assuredly there was a disturbing element in the forest, and Ulrich could guess the quarter from whence it came.

He strayed away by himself from the watchers whom he had placed in ambush on the crest of the hill, and wandered far down the steep slopes amid the wild tangle of undergrowth, peering through the tree-trunks and listening through the whistling and skirling[4] of the wind and the restless beating of the branches for sight or sound of the **marauders**. If only on this wild night, in this dark, lone spot, he might come across Georg Znaeym, man to man, with none to witness—that was the wish that was uppermost in his thoughts. And as he stepped round the trunk of a huge beech he came face to face with the man he sought.

The two enemies stood glaring at one another for a long silent moment. Each had a rifle in his hand, each had hate in his heart and murder uppermost in his mind. The chance had come to give full play to the passions of a lifetime. But a man who has been brought up under the code of a restraining civilization cannot easily nerve himself to shoot down his neighbor in cold blood and without word spoken, except for an offense against his hearth and honor. And before the moment of hesitation had given way to action, a deed of Nature's own violence overwhelmed them both. A fierce shriek of the storm had been answered by a splitting crash over their heads, and ere they could leap aside, a mass of falling beech tree had thundered down on them. Ulrich von Gradwitz found himself stretched on the ground, one arm numb beneath him and the other held almost as helplessly in a tight tangle of forked branches, while both legs were pinned beneath the fallen mass. His heavy shooting-boots had saved his feet from being crushed to pieces, but if his fractures were not as serious as they might have been, at least it was evident that he could not move from his present position till someone came to release him. The descending twigs had slashed the skin of his face, and he had to wink away some drops of blood from his eyelashes before he could take in a general view of the disaster. At his side, so near that under ordinary circumstances he could almost have touched him, lay Georg Znaeym, alive and struggling, but obviously as helplessly pinioned down as himself. All round them lay a thick strewn wreckage of splintered branches and broken twigs.

The two enemies stood glaring at one another for a long silent moment.

---

4 **skirling:** shrieking; screaming

Relief at being alive and **exasperation** at his captive plight brought a strange **medley** of **pious** thank-offerings and sharp curses to Ulrich's lips. Georg, who was nearly blinded with the blood which trickled across his eyes, stopped his struggling for a moment to listen, and then gave a short, snarling laugh.

"So you're not killed, as you ought to be, but you're caught, anyway," he cried; "caught fast. Ho, what a jest, Ulrich von Gradwitz snared in his stolen forest. There's real justice for you!"

And he laughed again, mockingly and savagely.

"I'm caught in my own forest-land," retorted Ulrich. "When my men come to release us you will wish, perhaps, that you were in a better plight than caught poaching on a neighbor's land, shame on you."

Georg was silent for a moment; then he answered quietly:

"Are you sure that your men will find much to release? I have men, too, in the forest tonight, close behind me, and *they* will be here first and do the releasing. When they drag me out from under these damned branches it won't need much clumsiness on their part to roll this mass of trunk right over on the top of you. Your men will find you dead under a fallen beech tree. For form's sake I shall send my **condolences** to your family."

"It is a useful hint," said Ulrich fiercely. "My men had orders to follow in ten minutes time, seven of which must have gone by already, and when they get me out—I will remember the hint. Only as you will have met your death poaching on my lands I don't think I can decently send any message of condolence to your family."

"Good," snarled Georg, "good. We fight this quarrel out to the death, you and I and our foresters, with no cursed **interlopers** to come between us. Death and damnation to you, Ulrich von Gradwitz."

"The same to you, Georg Znaeym, forest-thief, game-snatcher."

Both men spoke with the bitterness of possible defeat before them, for each knew that it might be long before his men would seek him out or find him; it was a bare matter of chance which party would arrive first on the scene.

Both had now given up the useless struggle to free themselves from the mass of wood that held them down; Ulrich limited his **endeavors** to an effort to bring his one partially free arm near enough to his outer coat pocket to draw out his wine flask. Even when he had accomplished that operation it was long before he could manage the unscrewing of the stopper or get any of the liquid down his throat. But what a Heaven-sent **draught** it seemed! It was an open winter, and little snow had fallen as yet, hence the captives suffered less from the cold than might have been the case at that season of the year; nevertheless, the wine was warming and reviving to the wounded man, and he looked across with something like a throb of pity to where his enemy lay, just keeping the groans of pain and weariness from crossing his lips.

"Could you reach this flask if I threw it over to you?" asked Ulrich suddenly; "there is good wine in it, and one may as well be as comfortable as one can. Let us drink, even if tonight one of us dies."

"No, I can scarcely see anything; there is so much blood caked round my eyes," said Georg, "and in any case I don't drink wine with an enemy."

Ulrich was silent for a few minutes, and lay listening to the weary screeching of the wind. An idea was slowly forming and growing in his brain, an idea that gained strength every time that he looked across at the man who was fighting so grimly against pain and exhaustion. In the pain and **languor** that Ulrich himself was feeling the old fierce hatred seemed to be dying down.

languor
lack of energy

"Neighbor," he said presently, "do as you please if your men come first. It was a fair **compact**. But as for me, I've changed my mind. If my men are the first to come you shall be the first to be helped, as though you were my guest. We have quarreled like devils all our lives over this stupid strip of forest, where the trees can't even stand upright in a breath of wind. Lying here tonight, thinking, I've come to think we've been rather fools; there are better things in life than getting the better of a boundary dispute. Neighbor, if you will help me to bury the old quarrel I—I will ask you to be my friend."

compact
agreement

Georg Znaeym was silent for so long that Ulrich thought, perhaps, he had fainted with the pain of his injuries. Then he spoke slowly and in jerks.

"How the whole region would stare and **gabble** if we rode into the market-square together. No one living can remember seeing a Znaeym and a von Gradwitz talking to one another in friendship. And what peace there would be among the forester folk if we ended our feud tonight. And if we choose to make peace among our people there is none other to interfere, no interlopers from outside. . . . You would come and keep the Sylvester night[5] beneath my roof, and I would come and feast on some high day at your castle. . . . I would never fire a shot on your land, save when you invited me as a guest; and you should come and shoot with me down in the marshes where the wildfowl are. In all the countryside there are none that could hinder if we willed to make peace. I never thought to have wanted to do other than hate you all my life, but I think I have changed my mind about

gabble
jabber; talk fast or foolishly

5 **Sylvester night:** New Year's Eve, a night of celebration in honor of Pope Sylvester I

things too, this last half-hour. And you offered me your wineflask. . . . Ulrich von Gradwitz, I will be your friend."

For a space both men were silent, turning over in their minds the wonderful changes that this dramatic **reconciliation** would bring about. In the cold, gloomy forest, with the wind tearing in fitful gusts through the naked branches and whistling round the tree trunks, they lay and waited for the help that would now bring release and **succor** to both parties. And each prayed a private prayer that his men might be the first to arrive, so that he might be the first to show honorable attention to the enemy that had become a friend.

Presently, as the wind dropped for a moment, Ulrich broke silence.

"Let's shout for help," he said; "in this lull our voices may carry a little way."

"They won't carry far through the trees and undergrowth," said Georg, "but we can try. Together, then."

The two raised their voices in a prolonged hunting call.

"Together again," said Ulrich a few minutes later, after listening in vain for an answering halloo.

"I heard something that time, I think," said Ulrich.

"I heard nothing but the **pestilential** wind," said Georg hoarsely.

There was silence again for some minutes, and then Ulrich gave a joyful cry.

"I can see figures coming through the wood. They are following in the way I came down the hillside."

Both men raised their voices in as loud a shout as they could muster.

"They hear us! They've stopped. Now they see us. They're running down the hill towards us," cried Ulrich.

"How many of them are there?" asked Georg.

"I can't see distinctly," said Ulrich; "nine or ten."

"Then they are yours," said Georg; "I had only seven out with me."

"They are making all the speed they can, brave lads," said Ulrich gladly.

"Are they your men?" asked Georg. "Are they your men?" he repeated impatiently as Ulrich did not answer.

"No," said Ulrich with a laugh, the idiotic chattering laugh of a man unstrung with hideous fear.

"Who are they?" asked Georg quickly, straining his eyes to see what the other would gladly not have seen.

"*Wolves.*"

reconciliation
establishment of friendship or harmony

succor
relief

pestilential
injurious or deadly

AFTER YOU READ
The Interlopers

Think and Discuss

1. At the beginning of the story, how do the two men feel about control of their lands? Use details from the story to explain your answer.

2. At the end of the story, how do the men feel about their control of the forest?

3. In what ways might the men's feelings at the end of the story reflect the changing views of the times in which the author lived (see p. 188)?

4. Georg and Ulrich's encounter in the forest is rife with **irony**. Irony occurs when things turn out differently than expected. For example, each man thinks he will kill or be killed by his neighbor, but both men are brought down by the same tree. Describe at least one other ironic event that unfolds in the forest.

5. Who are the interlopers in the story?

6. Copy the graphic organizer below into your Writer's Notebook. Quickly reread the story. As you scan, use the graphic organizer to note the events by which Ulrich's fate and Georg's fate are brought together. In one diagonal column, write the events Ulrich experiences. In the other, write the events Georg experiences.

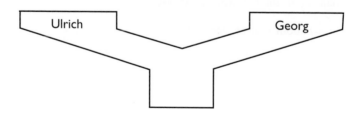

Write to Understand: Freewrite About Nature

Think of times when you might have felt like the men in this story—helpless against a force of nature. Maybe it was when a severe thunderstorm came rumbling by; maybe it was when you were swept up in a strong wave. Write freely to recall the specific details of the experience and how you felt. After about 5 or 10 minutes, look over what you wrote and try to generalize a main idea from your writing. Write that main idea in a sentence.

BEFORE YOU READ

from *Of Wolves and Men*

Meet the Author: Barry Holstun Lopez

Born in New York in 1945, Lopez studied engineering in college before changing to a major in English. After graduation, he worked as a nature photographer, but came to believe that this occupation caused him to think of nature as an object rather than a subject. So he turned to writing. In his work as a poet, naturalist, and short story writer, Lopez explores the deep ties between human culture and natural surroundings. His conversational style supports his goal to be a companion, rather than an authority, to his readers.

Build Background: "Other Nations"

Wolves are the villains of many fairy tales and have been feared and hunted throughout the centuries. In recent years, however, biologists have painted a somewhat different picture of wolves. The wolves' hunting of caribou, for example, helps keep the herd healthy by killing the sick and old and limiting the caribou population to a supportable level. Even that broader, more positive view of wolves, however, does not seem to tell the whole story about these fascinating creatures. Lopez begins his book *Of Wolves and Men* with a quote by naturalist Henry Beston:

"We need another and a wiser and perhaps a more mystical concept of animals. . . . They are not brethren [brothers], they are not underlings; they are other nations, caught with ourselves in the net of life and time, fellow prisoners of the splendor and travail of the earth."

As you read, think about the following questions:

- What do you know about wolves already?

- How do you feel about wolves?

from *Of Wolves and Men*

BARRY HOLSTUN LOPEZ

from *OF WOLVES AND MEN*

Barry Holstun Lopez

I imagine a wolf moving through the northern woods. The movement, over a trail he has traversed many times before, is distinctive, unlike that of a cougar or a bear, yet he appears, if you are watching, sometimes catlike or bearlike. It is purposeful, deliberate movement. Occasionally the rhythm is broken by the wolf's pause to inspect a scent mark, or a move off the trail to paw among stones where a year before he had **cached** meat.

cached
hidden in a
secure place

The movement down the trail would seem relentless if it did not appear so effortless. The wolf's body, from neck to hips, appears to float over the long, almost spindly legs and the flicker of wrists, a bicycling drift through the trees, **reminiscent** of the movement of water or of shadows.

reminiscent
reminding
one

The wolf is three years old. A male. He is of the subspecies *occidentalis*,[1] and the trees he is moving among are spruce and subalpine fir on the eastern slope of the Rockies in northern Canada. He is light gray; that is, there are more blond and white hairs mixed with gray in the saddle of fur that covers his shoulders and extends down his spine than there are black and brown. But there are silver and even red hairs mixed in, too.

It is early September, an easy time of year, and he has not seen the other wolves in his pack for three or four days. He has heard no howls, but he knows the others are about, in ones and twos like himself. It is not a time of year for much howling. It is an easy time. The weather is pleasant. Moose are fat. Suddenly the wolf stops in mid-stride. A moment, then his feet slowly come alongside each other. He is staring into the grass. His ears are rammed forward, stiff. His back arches and he rears up and pounces like a cat. A deer mouse is pinned between his forepaws. Eaten. The wolf drifts on. He approaches a trail crossing, an **undistinguished** crossroads. His movement is now slower and he sniffs the air as though aware of a possibility for scents. He sniffs a scent post,[2] a scrawny blueberry bush in use for years, and goes on.

undistinguished
not very noticable
or different from
surroundings

---

1 *occidentalis:* a species native to the western hemisphere

2 **scent post:** Wolves routinely mark particular objects with urine to establish their territory and its boundaries. Each item is known as a wolf's scent post.

The wolf weighs ninety-four pounds and stands thirty inches at the shoulder. His feet are enormous, leaving prints in the mud along a creek (where he pauses to hunt crayfish but not with much interest) more than five inches long by just over four wide. He has two fractured ribs, broken by a moose a year before. They are healed now, but a sharp eye would notice the irregularity. The skin on his right hip is scarred, from a fight with another wolf in a neighboring pack when he was a **yearling**. He has not had anything but a few mice and a piece of arctic char[3] in three days, but he is not hungry. He is traveling. The char was a day old, left on the rocks along the river by bears.

yearling
an animal one year old but not yet two

The wolf is tied by subtle threads to the woods he moves through. His fur carries seeds that will fall off, effectively **dispersed**, along the trail some miles from where they first caught in his fur. And miles distant is a raven perched on the ribs of a caribou the wolf helped kill ten days ago, pecking like a chicken at the decaying scraps of meat. A smart snowshoe hare that eluded the wolf and left him exhausted when he was a pup has been dead a year now, food for an owl. The den in which he was born one April evening was home to porcupines last winter.

dispersed
distributed or spread over a wide area

It is now late in the afternoon. The wolf has stopped traveling, has lain down to sleep on cool earth beneath a rock outcropping. Mosquitoes rest on his ears. His ears flicker. He begins to waken. He rolls on his back and lies motionless with his front legs pointed toward the sky but folded like wilted flowers, his back legs splayed, and his nose and tail curved toward each other on one side of his body. After a few moments he flops on his side, rises, stretches, and moves a few feet to inspect—**minutely**, delicately—a crevice in the rock outcropping and finds or doesn't find what draws him there. And then he ascends the rock face, bounding and balancing momentarily before bounding again, appearing slightly unsure of the process—but committed. A few minutes later he bolts suddenly into the woods, achieving full speed, almost forty miles per hour, for forty or fifty yards before he begins to skid, to lunge at a lodgepole pine cone. He trots away with it, his head erect, tail erect, his hips slightly to one side out of line with his shoulders, as though hindquarters were impatient with forequarters, the cone inert in his mouth. He carries it for a hundred feet before dropping it by the trail. He sniffs it. He goes on.

minutely
paying close attention to even the smallest details

The underfur next to his skin has begun to thicken with the coming of fall. In the months to follow it will become so dense between his shoulders it will be almost impossible to work a finger down to his skin. In seven months he will

---

3 **char:** a small trout native to Alaska and northern Canada

weigh less: eighty-nine pounds. He will have tried unsuccessfully to mate with another wolf in the pack. He will have helped kill four moose and thirteen caribou. He will have fallen through ice into a creek at twenty-two below zero but not frozen. He will have fought with other wolves.

He moves along now at the edge of a clearing. The wind coming down-valley surrounds him with a river of odors, as if he were a migrating salmon. He can smell ptarmigan[4] and deer droppings. He can smell willow and spruce and the fading sweetness of fireweed. Above, he sees a hawk circling, and farther south, lower on the horizon, a flock of sharp-tailed sparrows going east. He senses through his pads with each step the dryness of the moss beneath his feet, and the ridges of old tracks, some his own. He hears the sound his feet make. He hears the occasional movement of deer mice and voles. Summer food.

Toward dusk he is standing by a creek, lapping the cool water, when a wolf howls—a long wail that quickly reaches pitch and then tapers, with several harmonics, long moments to a tremolo.[5] He recognizes his sister. He waits a few moments, then, throwing his head back and closing his eyes, he howls. The howl is shorter and it changes pitch twice in the beginning, very quickly. There is no answer.

obliquely
on an angle;
indirectly

The female is a mile away and she trots off **obliquely** through the trees. The other wolf stands listening, laps water again, then he too departs, moving quickly, quietly through the trees, away from the trail he had been on. In a few minutes the two wolves meet. They approach each other briskly, almost formally, tails erect and moving somewhat as deer move. When they come together they make high squeaking noises and encircle each other, rubbing and pushing, poking their noses into each other's neck fur, backing away to stretch, chasing each other for a few steps, then standing quietly together, one putting a head over the other's back. And then they are gone, down a vague trail, the female first. After a few hundred yards they begin, simultaneously, to wag their tails.

In the days to follow, they will meet another wolf from the pack, a second female, younger by a year, and the three of them will kill a caribou. They will travel together ten or twenty miles a day, through the country where they live, eating and sleeping, birthing, playing with sticks, chasing ravens, growing old, barking at bears, scent-marking trails, killing moose, and staring at the way water in a creek breaks around their legs and flows on.

---

4 **ptarmigan:** small chicken-like birds

5 **tremolo:** a musical term from the Italian word for "a trembling" or "a shaking" describing a note that repeats or varies rapidly from tone to tone

AFTER YOU READ
from *Of Wolves and Men*

Think and Discuss

1. With what other living and nonliving things is the wolf's life intertwined? Describe the relationships.

2. Henry Beston wrote that animals are "gifted with extensions of the senses that we have lost or never attained, living by voices we shall never hear." How does the text suggest that Lopez believes this too? Refer to specific examples.

3. From whose **point of view** is this piece written?

4. Compare Lopez's image of wolves to that suggested in "The Interlopers."

5. How does the author's use of **details** affect your understanding of the wolf? Copy the chart below into your Writer's Notebook. Use it to note details that communicate the narrator's **point of view** as compared to the wolf's.

Points of View	
Lopez	Wolf

Write to Understand: Field Notes

Lopez creates an understanding of the wolf by observing and then writing a detailed study of the wolf's behavior. He observes its ways and tries to understand by imagining himself in the wolf's place. Choose an animal or something else from nature—a tree, a river, a weed—that you can observe over time. Observe your subject at different times of the day if possible, and write detailed and imaginative field notes to capture what you observe.

BEFORE YOU READ

Poems of Nature

Meet the Poets

Robert Frost Four-time winner of the Pulitzer Prize, Frost (1874–1963) remains one of the most respected and widely read American poets of the 20th century.

Kaga no Chiyo A master Haiku poet, Kaga no Chiyo (1701–1775) is also known as Chiyo-ni. His poems capture the art of everyday life.

Bashō Bashō was the pen name of Matsuo Munefusa (1644–1694). One of Japan's earliest and best known haiku masters, Bashō perfected a quiet, thoughtful style.

E. E. Cummings Cummings (1894–1962) experimented with unconventional capitalization and punctuation and even at times broke words into pieces. His poems are known for their stunning and playful images.

Build Background: Imagery

Imagery refers to the mental images readers form as they take in the details of a text. Using vivid language that appeals to the five senses is one way poets and writers create imagery. Using figurative language such as fresh, surprising similes, metaphors, and personification, or giving a nonhuman subject human qualities, is another tool for creating images and stirring strong feelings. To see the effect of imagery, compare the following statements.

No Imagery: Sometimes life is hard.

Imagery: Sometimes "life is too much like a pathless wood where your face burns and tickles with the cobwebs broken across it, and one eye is weeping from a twig's having lashed across it open." (from "Birches," by Robert Frost)

Think about these questions:

- What have you read that was so vividly written you could easily picture what was happening?

- What imagery is at the heart of each of the following poems?

Poems of Nature

Birches

ROBERT FROST

When I see birches bend to left and right
Across the line of straighter darker trees,
I like to think some boy's been swinging them.
But swinging doesn't bend them down to stay
As ice-storms do. Often you must have seen them   5
Loaded with ice a sunny winter morning
After a rain. They click upon themselves
As the breeze rises, and turn many-colored
As the stir cracks and crazes their enamel.
Soon the sun's warmth makes them shed crystal shells   10
Shattering and avalanching on the snow-crust—
Such heaps of broken glass to sweep away
You'd think the inner dome of heaven had fallen.
They are dragged to the withered **bracken** by the load,
And they seem not to break; though once they are bowed   15
So low for long, they never right themselves:
You may see their trunks arching in the woods
Years afterwards, trailing their leaves on the ground
Like girls on hands and knees that throw their hair
Before them over their heads to dry in the sun.   20
But I was going to say when Truth broke in
With all her matter-of-fact about the ice-storm
I should prefer to have some boy bend them
As he went out and in to fetch the cows—
Some boy too far from town to learn baseball,   25
Whose only play was what he found himself,
Summer or winter, and could play alone.
One by one he subdued his father's trees
By riding them down over and over again
Until he took the stiffness out of them,   30
And not one but hung limp, not one was left

bracken
a large, coarse
fern

For him to conquer. He learned all there was
To learn about not launching out too soon
And so not carrying the tree away
Clear to the ground. He always kept his poise   35
To the top branches, climbing carefully
With the same pains you use to fill a cup
Up to the brim, and even above the brim.
Then he flung outward, feet first, with a swish,
Kicking his way down through the air to the ground.   40

So was I once myself a swinger of birches.
And so I dream of going back to be.
It's when I'm weary of considerations,
And life is too much like a pathless wood
Where your face burns and tickles with the cobwebs   45
Broken across it, and one eye is weeping
From a twig's having lashed across it open.
I'd like to get away from earth awhile
And then come back to it and begin over.
May no fate willfully misunderstand me   50
And half grant what I wish and snatch me away
Not to return. Earth's the right place for love:
I don't know where it's likely to go better.
I'd like to go by climbing a birch tree,
And climb black branches up a snow-white trunk   55
Toward heaven, till the tree could bear no more,
But dipped its top and set me down again.
That would be good both going and coming back.
One could do worse than be a swinger of birches.

Haiku[1]   KAGA NO CHIYO

to tangle or untangle
the willow—
it's up to the wind

leaves like bird shadows
desolate—
the winter moon

---

[1] **Haiku:** an unrhymed verse form originating in Japan usually formed in three lines of five, seven, and five syllables

Haiku BASHŌ

Ah, summer grasses!
All that remains
Of the warriors' dreams.

Old dark sleepy pool
quick unexpected frog
goes plop! Watersplash

Spring is like a perhaps hand

E. E. CUMMINGS

Spring is like a perhaps hand
(which comes carefully
out of Nowhere)arranging
a window,into which people look(while
people stare   5
arranging and changing placing
carefully there a strange
thing and a known thing here)and

changing everything carefully

spring is like a perhaps   10
Hand in a window
(carefully to
and fro moving New and
Old things,while
people stare carefully   15
moving a perhaps
fraction of flower here placing
an inch of air there)and

without breaking anything.

FLOWERS, Pablo Picasso, 1958

AFTER YOU READ
Poems of Nature

Think and Discuss

1. Suppose you are putting together an anthology of nature poems grouped into three chapters: The Beauty of Nature, Nature's Power, and Conquering Nature. In which chapter would you place "Birches"? Why? If you think it does not belong in any of these chapters, create a new one for it and explain your choice.

2. What do you think the **speaker** in "Birches" means by the lines "Earth's the right place for love"?

3. Reread the haiku by Kaga no Chiyo about the willow and the wind. Does it express a view of nature similar to or different from that in "Birches"? Explain your answer using details from the poems.

4. What relationship between humans and nature does the poem "Spring is like a perhaps hand" convey? Explain.

5. Each of the poems in this lesson includes **imagery**. Use the graphic organizer below to identify the types of imagery you find in each poem. (For a definition of *imagery*, see the Glossary of Literary Terms.)

Kind of Imagery	Frost	Kaga no Chiyoi	Bashō	Cummings
Vivid Words				
Similes (comparisons that use *like* or *as*)				
Metaphors				
Personification				

Write to Understand: Poetic Images

Many poems describe in detail an image the poet sees or imagines, one that affects him or her emotionally or seems especially meaningful. Choose a subject you encounter daily and describe it in detail in your Writer's Notebook. Use imagery. You may use line breaks as in poetry to heighten awareness of particular details, or you may write your description in prose.

BEFORE YOU READ

from *An Inconvenient Truth*

Meet the Author: Al Gore

Al Gore (born 1948) graduated with a degree in government from Harvard, where he was first introduced to the science of global warming. Like his father before him, Gore served in the United States Congress. He was also Bill Clinton's vice president. Throughout his years of service, he raised awareness of the environment. In 2000, Gore ran for president. His loss gave him an opportunity to devote even more time to spreading the word about global warming and what people can do to combat it. He traveled around the world with a slideshow explaining the urgency of taking action. In 2007, the film version of this slideshow, *An Inconvenient Truth,* won an Academy Award. In the same year he also won a Nobel Prize.

Build Background: Global Warming

Every severe storm, flood, earthquake, or volcano is a reminder of the unstoppable force of nature and its effect on humans. But what about the power of humans to affect nature? Scientists and naturalists have long documented ways in which pollution from human activity poisons the planet's air, water, and land. In recent decades, most of them have determined that carbon dioxide (CO_2) from burning fossil fuels such as coal, oil, and natural gas causes even more profound changes. It traps heat within Earth's atmosphere and has been a significant factor in global warming.

Think about these questions before and during your reading of the following excerpts from Gore's book.

- What do you already know about global warming?

- In what ways do your everyday activities affect the natural environment?

- What actions, if any, have you taken to reduce any harmful effect you may have on the environment?

Al Gore speaks on global warming

from *An Inconvenient Truth*

The Crisis of Global Warming

AL GORE

from *AN INCONVENIENT TRUTH*
The Crisis of Global Warming

Al Gore

A SILENT ALARM

Mark Twain once said, "It ain't what you don't know that gets you into trouble, it's what you know for sure that just ain't so." His words are especially true in relation to the climate crisis. Many people are convinced, mistakenly, that the Earth is so big, human beings can't do serious damage to it.

Maybe that was true at one time. But not now. There are so many people on Earth (6.5 billion) and technologies have become so powerful that we are capable of causing serious harm to the environment.

What is the most vulnerable part?

The atmosphere surrounding the Earth, because it's such a thin layer.

My friend, the late Carl Sagan, used to say, "If you had a globe covered with a coat of varnish, the thickness of that varnish would be about the same as the thickness of the Earth's atmosphere compared to the Earth itself."

The Earth's atmosphere is so thin that we are capable of dramatically changing its composition. Indeed, we have already dangerously increased the amount of greenhouse gases in the atmosphere.

What Exactly Are Greenhouse Gases?

They are gases in our atmosphere that hold in heat, such as carbon dioxide, methane, and nitrous oxide. They maintain an average temperature on Earth of 59°F. Without greenhouse gases, the Earth's surface temperature would drop to around 0°F.

But trouble has arisen because industry, technology, and our modern lifestyle release too much of these greenhouse gases. And that's not good.

Of all the greenhouse gases, carbon dioxide (CO_2) usually gets top billing because it accounts for 80 percent of total greenhouse gas emissions. We release

CO_2 in the atmosphere when we burn fossil fuels—oil, natural gas, and coal used in cars, homes, factories, and power plants. Cutting down forests and producing cement also release CO_2.

In a pre-industrial world,[1] just the right amount of the sun's energy was soaked up by greenhouse gases in the atmosphere. It was a wonderfully balanced system and accounts for why Earth is sometimes called the Goldilocks planet—neither too hot like Venus with its thick poisonous atmosphere nor too cold like Mars, which has practically no atmosphere at all.

But when too much of the atmosphere is made up of greenhouse gases, it leads to global warming. This image shows how it happens. The sun's energy enters the atmosphere. Some of that energy warms up the Earth and its atmosphere and then is re-radiated back into space in the form of **infrared** radiation. But greenhouse gases soak up some of the infrared, preventing it from escaping into space.

infrared
outside
the visible
spectrum

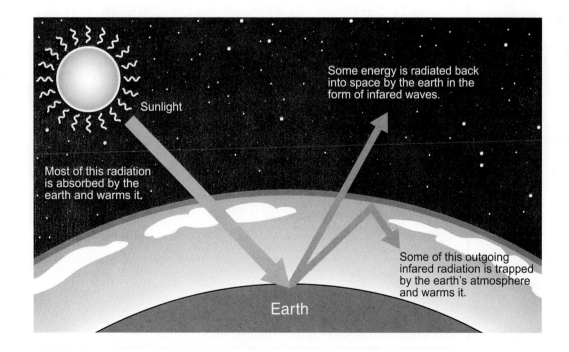

I **pre-industrial world:** the era before the advent of heavy machinery and factories

The problem we now face is that the atmosphere is being filled by huge quantities of human-caused carbon dioxide and other greenhouse gases. This traps a lot of the infrared radiation that would otherwise escape. As a result, the temperature of the Earth's atmosphere and oceans is getting dangerously warmer.

This is what the climate crisis is all about.

The amount of CO_2 in the atmosphere can be measured. It was my wonderful teacher, Dr. Roger Revelle, who first proposed doing this in 1958. A pattern of steadily increasing CO_2 was visible after the first several years of Revelle's measurements, as seen in this graph. The pattern has continued year by year for almost a half-century. This remarkable and patiently collected daily record now stands as one of the most important series of measurements in the history of science.

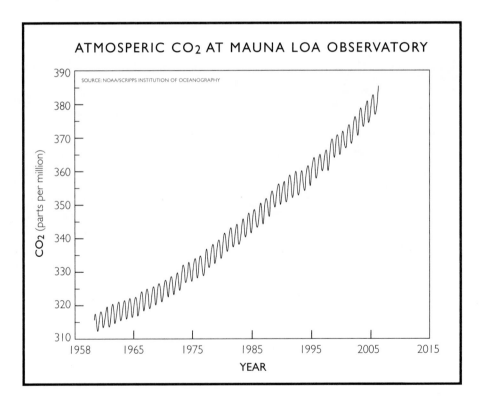

I asked Revelle why the line marking CO_2 concentration goes up sharply and then down once each year. He explained that the vast majority of the Earth's land mass—as illustrated in this picture—is north of the equator. This means the vast majority of the Earth's vegetation is also north of the equator.

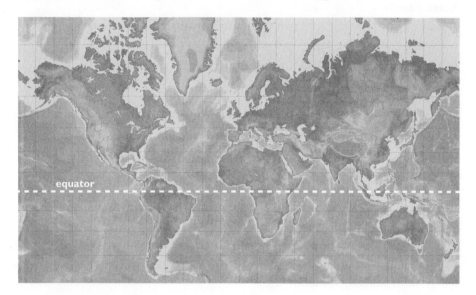

equator

When the Northern Hemisphere is tilted toward the sun during the spring and summer, the leaves come out. They breathe in CO_2, thus decreasing the amount of it worldwide.

However, when the Northern Hemisphere is tilted away from the sun in autumn and winter, the leaves fall and release CO_2. The amount of this gas in the atmosphere goes back up again.

It's as if the entire Earth takes a big breath in and out once each year.

The "inhale" accounts for the yearly dip in CO_2.

. . .

CRISIS = OPPORTUNITY

Another big problem with global warming is that an astonishing number of people go straight from denial to despair, without pausing at the step in between. Yes, there's a crisis . . . But we can do something about it.

Luckily, more and more businesses are going in the right direction. Individual families are, too. We are constantly developing new technology that can help fight global warming.

Solar Panels
On a bright sunny day, the sun shines approximately 1,000 watts of energy per square yard. Solar panels can collect that energy and turn it into electricity to power homes and offices.

Geothermal Power Stations
The heat stored in the earth can produce electricity. Geothermal power stations are now generating electricity this way. They can be built wherever there is high-temperature groundwater near the surface.

Fluorescent Lightbulbs

incandescent producing light by radiating hot, visible light

A "normal" lightbulb (also known as an **incandescent** lightbulb) produces a lot of heat in addition to light. The heat is a waste of energy. A **fluorescent** bulb uses a different, much more efficient method to produce light. You can buy a 15-watt fluorescent bulb that will produce the same amount of light as a 60-watt incandescent bulb.

fluorescent producing light by bombarding a glowing material with electrons

Green Roofs
A green roof is one that is built to support plant life. Green roofs not only filter pollutants such as CO_2 from the air, they can also provide food, reduce heat in densely populated areas of cities, insulate buildings—and they are beautiful.

Hybrid Cars
Hybrid cars don't depend on gas alone to move. They also use batteries. Most commonly, hybrids use electric batteries to power the engine.

Hydrogen Fuel-Cell Buses
Depending only partially on gas, fuel-cell hybrid buses offer mass transportation that is better for the environment. For example, buses that use hydrogen cells emit exhaust that is water vapor instead of CO_2. Certain cities in California have had successful trial runs of these vehicles.

Wind Power

Without wind power, some pioneers might never have settled in the Great Plains. It was the windmill that for generations tirelessly pumped underground water to the surface, helping settlers cook, wash, and tend their livestock.

Today, utility companies are investing in gigantic wind farms. A 100-megawatt wind farm (fifty 300-foot towers carrying mammoth turbines) can power 24,000 homes. You would have to burn 50,000 tons of coal—releasing vast amounts of CO_2—to provide the same amount of electricity.

The problem of global warming is harder to solve. It demands more of us.

The climate crisis presents us with an inconvenient truth. It means we are going to have to change the way we live our lives. Whether these changes involve something as minor as using different lightbulbs, or as major as switching from oil and coal to other fuels, they will require effort and cost money. But many of these needed changes will actually save money and make us more efficient and productive. We all must take action so that our democracy creates laws to protect our planet, because we simply can't afford not to act.

> The climate crisis presents us with an inconvenient truth. It means we are going to have to change the way we live our lives.

The twenty-first century is your century—and you can make it a time of renewal by seizing the opportunities that are bound up in this crisis. You can preserve the health of our planet so that it will remain beautiful for generations and centuries to come.

TAKE ACTION

We have everything we need to begin solving the climate crisis.

Each one of us is a cause of global warming, but each of us can become part of the solution: in the decisions we make on what we buy, the amount of electricity we use, the car our family drives, and how we live our lives.

We can make choices so that no unnecessary carbon is released because of our own individual actions.

Here are a few examples of actions you can take to make a difference:

—Avoid overpackaged food and other products with extra wrappers and layers of unnecessary plastic. For instance, use a refillable water bottle instead of buying single-use plastic bottles.

—Ride your bike or walk instead of riding in a car.

—When you're at home, remember to turn off any lights that you aren't using. And don't stand in front of an open refrigerator door—leaving it open for just a few seconds wastes a lot of energy.

—Talk to your parents, teachers, and friends about the impact they might be having on the environment. Explain what they can do to help solve the climate crisis.

For additional information, you can go to www.climatecrisis.net.

Al Gore during one of his slideshows

AFTER YOU READ

from *An Inconvenient Truth*

Think and Discuss

1. Why does Gore call information about climate change "an inconvenient truth"?

2. What evidence does Gore offer that humans are contributing to global warming?

3. Gore refers to several graphics—a **diagram**, a **chart**, an **illustration**, and a **photo**. In each case, compare the written explanation with the graphic. Explain what the graphics add to the text.

4. The facts and statistics in these excerpts, on their own, could be tedious to read. What techniques does Gore use to keep readers interested? Find at least three examples.

5. Gore's book outlines problems and solutions related to global warming. The following graphic organizer identifies some of the problems highlighted in the article. Come up with some suggestions of your own for solving these problems and complete the table below.

Problem	Possible Solution(s)
Wasteful Home Heating Systems	
Energy-wasting Lightbulbs	
Pollution from Vehicles	
Industrial Pollution	
Excess Carbon Dioxide	
Rising Sea Levels	
Violent Weather	

Write to Understand: Zooming In

Writers often supplement their factual writing with a close-up look at how their subject relates to real, specific people. Choose an aspect of this excerpt on global warming and write a brief example that explains it further by focusing on how it affects real people. Base it on your own knowledge and experience. For example, you might write about someone you know who rides a bike instead of driving, a family that's "greening" its house, or a school or community center that is raising public awareness of global warming.

BEFORE YOU READ
Tsunami 2004

Meet the Authors
National Geographic Society The first article in his collection was written by the writers and editors of the National Geographic Society. For years, the Society has sponsored explorers and has published a magazine—and now a Web site—in which outstanding writers and photographers bring each subject to vivid life.

Shaikh Azizur Rahman The second article is by Shaikh Azizur Rahman, a reporter from Mumbai, India, who works for the British Broadcasting Corporation.

Dale Wisely The poem is by Dale Wisely, a psychologist and school administrator in Birmingham, Alabama, where he also writes poetry. He is the editor of the online poetry journal *Right Hand Pointing*.

Build Background: Tsunamis
A tsunami is a series of waves resulting from undersea or shoreline earthquakes, volcanoes, landslides, explosions, or meteorite impacts. Some tsunamis are small, but others are enormous, causing damage to both land and people. Offshore tsunamis usually have a small wave height and a large wave length. They are relatively easy to navigate. Tsunamis that crest upon steep shorelines, however, can crash upon and destroy whole villages.

The first selection that follows gives information on the tragic tsunami that rocked the Indian Ocean in December of 2004. Next is a newspaper article published on December 31, 2005, telling how the tsunami affected one family. As you read, think about these questions:

• What are the environmental risks and benefits of the place where you live?

• What do you do to increase your safety in case of such disasters?

Nagapattinam beach, south of the Indian city of Madras, 2004

The Deadliest Tsunami in History?

NATIONAL GEOGRAPHIC NEWS
UPDATED JANUARY 7, 2005

THE DEADLIEST TSUNAMI IN HISTORY?

National Geographic News
Updated January 7, 2005

The earthquake that generated the great Indian Ocean tsunami of 2004 is estimated to have released the energy of 23,000 Hiroshima-type atomic bombs,[1] according to the U.S. Geological Survey (USGS).

Giant forces that had been building up deep in the Earth for hundreds of years were released suddenly on December 26, shaking the ground violently and unleashing a series of killer waves that sped across the Indian Ocean at the speed of a jet airliner.

By the end of the day more than 150,000 people were dead or missing and millions more were homeless in 11 countries, making it perhaps the most destructive tsunami in history.

epicenter
the point of the Earth's surface directly above something, usually the point directly above an earthquake

The **epicenter** of the 9.0 magnitude quake[2] was under the Indian Ocean near the west coast of the Indonesian island of Sumatra, according to the USGS, which monitors earthquakes worldwide. The violent movement of sections of the Earth's crust, known as tectonic plates, displaced an enormous amount of water, sending powerful shock waves in every direction.

millennia
thousands of years

The earthquake was the result of the sliding of the portion of the Earth's crust known as the India plate under the section called the Burma plate. The process has been going on for **millennia**, one plate pushing against the other until something has to give. The result on December 26 was a rupture the USGS estimates was more than 600 miles (1,000 kilometers) long, displacing the seafloor above the rupture by perhaps 10 yards (about 10 meters) horizontally and several yards vertically. That doesn't sound like much, but the trillions of tons of rock that were moved along hundreds of miles caused the planet to shudder with the largest magnitude earthquake in 40 years.

---

1 **Hiroshima-type atomic bombs:** The atomic bomb the United States dropped on Hiroshima in 1945 directly killed about 70,000 people and destroyed about 70 percent of the city's buildings.

2 **9.0 magnitude quake:** the power of an earthquake on the Richter scale, from 1 to 10, with each number representing ten times more power than the last

Above the disturbed seafloor the great volume of the ocean was displaced along the line of the rupture, creating one of nature's most deadly phenomena: a tsunami. Within hours killer waves radiating from the earthquake zone slammed into the coastline of 11 Indian Ocean countries, snatching people out to sea, drowning others in their homes or on beaches, and demolishing property from Africa to Thailand.

Tsunamis have been relatively rare in the Indian Ocean, at least in human memory. They are most **prevalent** in the Pacific. But every ocean has generated the **scourges**. Many countries are at risk.

prevalent
commonly occurring

scourges
causes of great pain or punishment

The Indian Ocean tsunami traveled as much as 3,000 miles (nearly 5,000 kilometers) to Africa, arriving with sufficient force to kill people and destroy property.

A tsunami may be less than a foot (30 centimeters) in height on the surface of the open ocean, which is why they are not noticed by sailors. But the powerful pulse of energy travels rapidly through the ocean at hundreds of miles per hour. Once a tsunami reaches shallow water near the coast it is slowed down. The top of the wave moves faster than the bottom, causing the sea to rise dramatically.

The Indian Ocean tsunami caused waves as high as 50 feet (15 meters) in some places, according to news reports. But in many other places witnesses described a rapid surging of the ocean, more like an extremely powerful river or a flood than the advance and retreat of giant waves.

*W*ithin hours killer waves radiating from the earthquake zone slammed into the coastline of 11 Indian Ocean countries, snatching people out to sea, drowning others in their homes or on beaches, and demolishing property from Africa to Thailand.

Tsunamis can extend inland by a thousand feet (300 meters) or more. The enormous force and weight of so much water sweeps away almost everything in its path. As many as a third of the people who died in the Indian Ocean tsunami were children; many of them would not have been strong enough to resist the force of the water. Many people were crushed by **debris** or when the sea hurled them against structures.

debris
scattered remains; rubble

Witnesses said the approaching tsunami sounded like three freight trains or the roar of a jet. In some places the tsunami advanced as a torrent of foaming water.

In several places the tsunami announced itself in the form of a rapidly receding ocean. Many reports quoted survivors saying how they had never seen the sea withdraw such a distance, exposing seafloor never seen before, stranding fish and boats on the sand. Tragically the novelty of the sight apparently stoked the curiosity of the people who ran out onto the exposed seafloor. Tourists in Thailand were seen wandering around photographing the scene.

Geographic Knowledge Saved Lives

People who knew geography knew what the receding ocean meant. Survivors who knew it meant trouble reported how they ran for high ground, rounded up family and friends, and tried to warn people who were drawn to the water's edge. Experts say that a receding ocean may give people as much as five minutes' warning to escape to high ground. That may have been enough time for many of the people who were killed by the 2004 tsunami to save themselves, if only they knew what to do.

A British newspaper reported that a school student, on vacation in Thailand, recalled a geography lesson about tsunamis and what the withdrawal of the ocean meant. She warned her family and they saved themselves.

In India a man told the Associated Press how he saved his village of some 1,500 people because he recalled watching a National Geographic television documentary about tsunamis [Killer Wave], and remembered that when the ocean receded it was a sign of danger. He sounded the alarm and led the people to high ground, saving almost the entire village.

Somehow the animals also seemed to know that disaster was imminent. Many people reported that they saw animals fleeing for high ground minutes before the tsunami arrived. Very few animal bodies were found afterwards.

When the ocean started to return on December 26 it was in the form of the tsunami—a series of crashing waves in some places and a sudden flood hundreds of yards inland in others. Reports quoted survivors saying they could not run away fast enough, although many people did manage to escape.

Death struck randomly. People who were together when the tsunami struck were separated in the torrent. Some survived; others succumbed or disappeared. A baby was found floating safely on a mattress.

Survivors of the Indian Ocean tsunami reported that the sea surged out as fast and as powerfully as it came ashore. Many people who had survived the wall of water rushing inland were seen being swept out to sea when the ocean retreated.

A tsunami is a series of waves, and the first wave may not be the most dangerous. A tsunami "wave train" may come as surges five minutes to an hour apart. The cycle may be marked by repeated retreat and advance of the ocean. Some people did not know this on December 26. Once the first wave had gone, they thought it was safe to go down to the beach.

The Indian Ocean tsunami destroyed thousands of miles of coastline and even submerged entire islands permanently. The island country Maldives rises only a few feet above sea level, but it is largely protected by outlying coral reefs. Even so, the tsunami swept across the reefs and was reported to have washed over some islands entirely. The capital and many tourist resorts in the Maldives were flooded. Astonishingly, relatively few people were killed. The country was likely protected from the full force of the tsunami by its reefs.

The Human Toll			
Country	**Fatalities**	**Missing**	**Total**
Indonesia	130,736	37,000	167,736
Sri Lanka	35,322		35,322
India	12,405	5,640	18,045
Maldives	82	26	108
Thailand	8,212		8,212
Myanmar	61		61
Malaysia	69	6	75
Somalia	78	211	289
Tanzania	13		13
Seychelles	2		2
Bangladesh	2		2
Kenya	1		1
Total	**186,983**	**42,883**	**229,866**

Source: UN Office of the Special Envoy for Tsunami Recovery

Rotting Corpses

As the day of horror drew to a close the ocean calmed. But where at the start of the day people were going about their normal lives or relaxing at exotic beach resorts now millions of people were struggling with the reality of tens of thousands of dead or missing relatives, destroyed homes, and shattered lives. The thousands of corpses, many hanging in trees or washed up on beaches, immediately started to rot in the tropical heat. With no food or clean water and open wounds, the risk of famine and epidemic diseases was high. Health authorities feared that the death toll might double to 300,000.

magnitude
size; greatness

Across the world the **magnitude** of the disaster and the scale of the suffering prompted a new wave—one of sympathy, support, and assistance for the people affected by the tsunami.

Children line up to receive food in India

pent-up
shut up;
contained

Deep beneath the ocean, at the source of the great earthquake and tsunami, the Earth's tectonic plates continued their relentless pressing against one another. Pressure was already building for the day when **pent-up** energy will once again be released violently—but hopefully not for hundreds of years.

ORPHANS GIVE INDIAN COUPLE WILL TO LIVE; 2004 TSUNAMI KILLED THEIR SON, TWO DAUGHTERS

Shaikh Azizur Rahman, *The Washington Times*
Nagapattinam, India

Sitting on the lawn in front of his seaside villa, Karibeeran Paramesvaran caught hold of 3-year-old Priya and gestured with a stick that he would beat her.

"You are joking. You can never hurt me . . . I know you love me, Appa," said the child, staring into her stepfather's eyes.

As he kissed Priya on the cheek and the child gave him a happy smile, Mr. Paramesvaran, 41, held the little girl in a hug.

"She is right. Had she and 15 other children not been with me, survival would have been difficult for me and my wife after losing all three of our children to the tsunami," he said, tears welling in his eyes.

It was hard to tell whether the tears were of sadness at remembering the three children he lost to last year's Dec. 26 earthquake-generated sea wave, or of joy at the sight of the tsunami orphans he had taken into his home.

Last year when he turned 40 and his three children were preparing to celebrate his Dec. 26 birthday, the undersea earthquake struck and turned the day into the most horrible of his life.

"I vividly remember how my son Kirubasan pulled me from bed and wished me a happy birthday. My two daughters brought me tea, wished me many happy returns, and kissed me," Mr. Paramesvaran said.

"I still remember how my daughters' shrill cries for help were buried by surging water, and how I vainly tried to save my son by holding him to my chest." Tears rolled down his cheeks and his voice trailed off as he held a framed picture of himself and the three children. The photograph of Rakshanya, 12, Karunya, 9, and Kirubasan, 5, was taken days before the tragedy last year.

On the morning of the day after Christmas, Mr. Paramesvaran had taken his three children and seven relatives of his wife to the nearby beach for a stroll. They were tossing a Frisbee on the beach when the sea turned hostile.

wrested
pulled

Mr. Paramesvaran had no chance to reach his daughters. He caught hold of his son for a few seconds before the killer waves **wrested** the little boy away. The man saved himself by clinging to a palm tree.

When the water receded, Mr. Paramesvaran and his wife, Choodamani, found the bodies of their three children and those of his wife's seven relatives lying among hundreds of others on the beach.

"I washed and dressed my children's bodies, and then dug a grave in the burial ground with my own hands. The whole town being shut down, I could not buy flowers or coffins for them. Before placing all three of them in that [one] grave, I kissed them and begged forgiveness for not being able to get them a proper burial," Mr. Paramesvaran said in a tear-choked voice.

I washed and dressed my children's bodies, and then dug a grave in the burial ground with my own hands.

The distraught couple was contemplating suicide when "God asked" them to stop grieving and start a new life with some other children orphaned by the tsunami.

consolation
comfort

"We were terribly depressed and felt life without our children was meaningless on this Earth. Then we saw the miseries of some just-orphaned children in our neighborhood and heard a voice from God offering us **consolation**, we found hope of a new life," said Mrs. Paramesvaran.

A month after the tragedy, the couple brought four orphans into their home. Soon, other children followed from other fishing villages of Nagapattinam, where the tsunami took about 8,000 lives. More than 250 children lost both parents, and about 900 more lost a mother or father.

Mr. Paramesvaran, an oil technician in a state-owned company, turned the ground floor of his large villa into a home for 16 tsunami orphans and named it "Nambikkai," meaning "hands of hope."

Because of strict government rules, he has not been able to formally adopt the children, but Mr. Paramesvaran has taken full responsibility for their welfare, including their schooling.

"We shall give them the best housing, clothing, food and education that we can, we have pledged to God. In our first life, we had three children. In this second life now, we have 16. When some people call them ' tsunami orphans' and call Nambikkai an orphanage, I feel offended because we [he and his wife] are their parents and we are still alive," said Mr. Paramesvaran.

The children of Nambikkai—ranging in age from 3 to 15 years—are from poor fishing families. Social workers are now urging the couple to take in more tsunami orphans.

"I don't want to bite off more than I can chew. If I take more children into this home, I shall not be able to provide them as much support as I want," said Mr. Paramesvaran.

"However, there are many other poor tsunami victim children who need our help, and we are planning to build one or two separate homes for them."

The Nambikkai children from poorer families either did not attend school before the tsunami struck or studied in government-run schools. But now Mr. Paramesvaran has placed some of them in English-teaching convent schools.

"My birth parents were very poor and they could never pay for my studies," said tsunami orphan Theboral, 9, whose parents were fishing laborers. "But here Appa and Amma [Father and Mother, meaning Mr. and Mrs. Paramesvaran] have put me in a very good school and I dream of becoming a teacher."

During a visit last May to Nagapattinam, former President Bill Clinton was deeply moved by the Nambikkai project.

"I will never forget your story as long as I live. It reflects the best in humanity, as you try to honor your children by helping orphans," Mr. Clinton said in a personal meeting with the Paramesvaran couple.

But Mr. Paramesvaran said it is not he who is helping the Nambikkai children. "After we lost our three children, we lost

Mr. Paramesvaran and some of his adopted children

interest in life and this house was taken over by a ghostly silence. But that painful void has been filled by these 16 children now," said Mr. Paramesvaran.

"These children have helped us get back to life. We are not helping them. In fact they are helping us to stay alive."

Wave

DALE WISELY

My child
Born to me by water
And by water
Swept away.

12/2004

AFTER YOU READ
Tsunami 2004

Think and Discuss

1. Compare and contrast the main idea of the *National Geographic* article with that of *The Washington Times* article about the orphans. Explain their similarities and differences.

2. Which details in each article linger in your memory? Try to explain why they do.

3. What does Wisely's poem communicate about the power of water?

4. Rahman wrote a **feature article** in which news serves as a platform for a human interest story. What information does this article focus on?

5. Contrast the **text features** of Rahman's article, which first appeared in a newspaper, with those of other nonfiction selections in this book. Text features include headings, captions, "point of view", and length of paragraphs. Explain the differences.

6. The *National Geographic* article is a **news article** which is intended to answer the questions: *Who? What? Where? When? Why?* and *How?* Copy the following graphic organizer in your Writer's Notebook. Skim back over the text to record the ways in which the article answers those questions. Use the information in the charts and graphs to help clarify the information in the articles.

Who	
What	
When	
Where	
Why	
How	

7. Which of these two articles more closely resembles the excerpts from *An Inconvenient Truth*? Explain the similarities.

Write to Understand: Summarize

Use your graphic organizer to write a factual summary of the key events in the tragic tsunami that struck in December of 2004. Decide which are the most important points to include and which details to leave out, and use your own words. Write a second summary of the story about Mr. Paramesvaran.

BEFORE YOU READ

The Birds
"Hope" is the thing with feathers

Meet the Authors

Daphne du Maurier A British author who lived between 1907 and 1989, du Maurier grew up in a wealthy, artistic family. Her creative parents allowed her to spend her childhood traveling, sailing, and writing stories. When she was in her early twenties, she began publishing novels, many of which became bestsellers. "The Birds" became a famous film directed by Alfred Hitchcock, a master of suspense.

Emily Dickinson Born in Amhurst, Massachusetts, in 1830, where she died in 1886, Dickinson wrote more than 1,700 poems. After what appeared to be a normal childhood, she became increasingly withdrawn. She published only a few poems during her lifetime and was not known for her poetry until years after her death. She is now recognized as one of the most important and beloved American poets.

Build Background: Animals as Symbols

Are you as sly as a fox or as courageous as a lion? As quick as a bunny? As quiet as a mouse? Expressions like these show the qualities people think are most prominent in certain animals. Sometimes animals are used symbolically to suggest that the people associated with them have those same qualities. England's King Richard, for example, became known as "the Lionhearted" because of his courage.

The story you are about to read is called "The Birds." As you read, think about these questions:

- What qualities do humans associate with birds? For example, when birds are used as symbols, what do they stand for? (Think of the American eagle, for example, or the dove.)

- What human activity has been inspired by the abilities of birds?

- What would you expect a story called "The Birds" to be about?

The Birds

DAPHNE DU MAURIER

THE BIRDS

Daphne du Maurier

On December the third the wind changed overnight and it was winter. Until then the autumn had been mellow, soft. The leaves had lingered on the trees, golden-red, and the hedgerows were still green. The earth was rich where the plow had turned it.

Nat Hocken, because of a wartime disability, had a pension and didn't work full-time at the farm. He worked three days a week, and they gave him the lighter jobs: hedging, thatching, repairs to the farm buildings.

disposition
personality

Although he was married, with children, his was a solitary **disposition**; he liked best to work alone. It pleased him when he was given a bank to build up or a gate to mend at the far end of the peninsula, where the sea surrounded the farmland on either side. Then, at midday, he would pause and eat the pasty[1] that his wife had baked for him and, sitting on the cliff's edge, would watch the birds. Autumn was best for this, better than spring. In spring the birds flew inland, purposeful, intent; they knew where they were bound, the rhythm and

brooked
tolerated

ritual of their life **brooked** no delay. In autumn those that had not migrated overseas but remained to pass each winter were caught up in the same driving urge, but because migration was denied them, followed a pattern of their own. Great flocks of them came to the peninsula, restless, uneasy, spending them-

wheeling
turning sharply

selves in motions; now **wheeling**, circling in the sky, now settling to feed on the rich, new-turned soil, but even when they fed, it was as though they did so without hunger, without desire. Restlessness drove them to the skies again.

Black and white, jackdaw and gull, mingled in strange partnership, seeking some sort of liberation, never satisfied, never still. Flocks of starlings, rustling like silk, flew to fresh pasture, driven by the same necessity of movement, and the small birds, the finches and the larks, scattered from tree to hedge as if compelled.

Nat watched them, and he watched the sea birds too. Down in the bay they waited for the tide. They had more patience. Oystercatchers, redshank,

---

I **pasty:** a turnover, usually containing meat

sanderling, and curlew watched by the water's edge; as the slow sea sucked at the shore and then withdrew, leaving the strip of seaweed bare and the shingle[2] churned, the sea birds raced and ran upon the beaches. Then that same impulse to flight seized upon them too. Crying, whistling, calling, they skimmed the **placid** sea and left the shore. Make haste, make speed, hurry and begone; yet where, and to what purpose? The restless urge of autumn unsatisfying, sad, had put a spell upon them and they must flock, and wheel, and cry; they must spill themselves of motion before winter came.

placid
still; tranquil

"Perhaps," thought Nat, munching his pasty by the cliff's edge, "a message comes to the birds in autumn, like a warning. Winter is coming. Many of them perish. And like people who, **apprehensive** of death before their time, drive themselves to work or folly, the birds do likewise."

apprehensive
anxious;
concerned about

The birds had been more restless than ever this fall of the year, the agitation more marked because the days were still. As the tractor traced its path up and down the western hills, the figure of the farmer silhouetted on the driving seat, the whole machine and the man upon it, would be lost momentarily in the great cloud of wheeling, crying birds. There were many more than usual, Nat was sure of this. Always, in autumn, they followed the plow, but not in great flocks like these, nor with such **clamor**.

clamor
insistence and
noise

Nat remarked upon it when hedging was finished for the day. "Yes," said the farmer, "there are more birds about than usual; I've noticed it too. And daring, some of them, taking no notice of the tractor. One or two gulls came so close to my head this afternoon I thought they'd knock my cap off! As it was, I could scarcely see what I was doing when they were overhead and I had the sun in my eyes. I have a notion the weather will change. It will be a hard winter. That's why the birds are restless."

Nat, tramping home across the fields and down the lane to his cottage, saw the birds still flocking over the west hills in the last glow of the sun. No wind, and the gray sea calm and full. Campion in bloom yet in the hedges, and the air mild. The farmer was right, though, and it was that night the weather turned. Nat's bedroom faced east. He woke just after two and heard the wind

> The birds had been more restless than ever this fall of the year, the agitation more marked because the days were still.

---

2 **shingle:** stone-covered beach

in the chimney. Not the storm and bluster of a sou'westerly gale, bringing the rain, but east wind, cold and dry. It sounded hollow in the chimney, and a loose slate rattled on the roof. Nat listened, and he could hear the sea roaring in the bay. Even the air in the small bedroom had turned chill: A draft came under the skirting of the door, blowing upon the bed. Nat drew the blanket round him, leaned closer to the back of his sleeping wife, and stayed wakeful, watchful, aware of misgiving without cause.

Then he heard the tapping on the window. There was no creeper on the

cottage walls to break loose and scratch upon the pane. He listened, and the tapping continued until, irritated by the sound, Nat got out of bed and went to the window. He opened it, and as he did so something brushed his hand, jabbing at his knuckles, grazing the skin. Then he saw the flutter of the wings and it was gone, over the roof, behind the cottage.

It was a bird, what kind of bird he could not tell. The wind must have driven it to shelter on the sill.

He shut the window and went back to bed, but feeling his knuckles wet, put his mouth to the scratch. The bird had drawn blood. Frightened, he supposed, and bewildered, the bird, seeking shelter, had stabbed at him in the darkness. Once more he settled himself to sleep.

Presently the tapping came again, this time more forceful, more insistent, and now his wife woke at the sound and, turning in the bed, said to him, "See to the window, Nat, it's rattling."

"I've already seen to it," he told her, "there's some bird there, trying to get in. Can't you hear the wind? It's blowing from the east, driving the birds to shelter."

"Send them away," she said, "I can't sleep with that noise."

He went to the window for the second time, and now when he opened it there was not one bird upon the sill but half a dozen; they flew straight into his face, attacking him.

He shouted, striking out at them with his arms, scattering them; like the first one, they flew over the roof and disappeared. Quickly he let the window fall and latched it.

"Did you hear that?" he said. "They went for me. Tried to peck my eyes." He stood by the window, peering into the darkness, and could see nothing. His wife, heavy with sleep, murmured from the bed.

"I'm not making it up," he said, angry at her suggestion. "I tell you the birds were on the sill, trying to get into the room."

Suddenly a frightened cry came from the room across the passage where the children slept.

"It's Jill," said his wife, roused at the sound, sitting up in bed. "Go to her, see what's the matter."

Nat lit the candle, but when he opened the bedroom door to cross the passage the draft blew out the flame.

There came a second cry of terror, this time from both children, and stumbling into their room, he felt the beating of wings about him in the darkness. The window was wide open. Through it came the birds, hitting first the ceiling and the walls, then swerving in mid-flight, turning to the children in their beds.

"It's all right, I'm here," shouted Nat, and the children flung themselves, screaming, upon him, while in the darkness the birds rose and dived and came for him again.

"What is it, Nat, what's happened?" his wife called from the further bedroom, and swiftly he pushed the children through the door to the passage and shut it upon them, so that he was alone now in their bedroom with the birds.

He seized a blanket from the nearest bed and, using it as a weapon, flung it to right and left about him in the air. He felt the thud of bodies, heard the fluttering of wings, but they were not yet defeated, for again and again they turned to the assault, jabbing his hands, his head, the little stabbing beaks sharp as a pointed fork. The blanket became a weapon of defense; he wound it about his head, and then in greater darkness beat at the birds with his bare hands. He dared not stumble to the door and open it, lest in doing so the birds should follow him.

How long he fought with them in the darkness he could not tell, but at last the beating of the wings about him lessened and then withdrew, and through the density of the blanket he was aware of light. He waited, listened; there was no sound except the fretful crying of one of the children from the bedroom beyond. The fluttering, the whirring of the wings had ceased.

He took the blanket from his head and stared about him. The cold gray morning light exposed the room. Dawn and the open window had called the living birds; the dead lay on the floor. Nat gazed at the little corpses, shocked and horrified. They were all small birds, none of any size; there must have been fifty of them lying there upon the floor. There were robins, finches, sparrows, blue tits, larks, and bramblings, birds that by nature's law kept to their own flock and their own territory, and now, joining one with another in their urge for battle, had destroyed themselves against the bedroom walls or in the strife had been destroyed by him. Some had lost feathers in the fight, others had blood, his blood, upon their beaks.

Sickened, Nat went to the window and stared out across his patch of garden to the fields.

It was bitter cold, and the ground had all the hard, black look of frost. Not white frost, to shine in the morning sun, but the black frost that the east wind brings. The sea, fiercer now with the turning tide, white-capped and steep, broke harshly in the bay. Of the birds there was no sign. Not a sparrow chattered in the hedge beyond the garden gate, no early missel-thrush or blackbird pecked on the grass for worms. There was no sound at all but the east wind and the sea.

Nat shut the window and the door of the small bedroom and went back across the passage to his own. His wife sat up in bed, one child asleep beside her, the smaller in her arms, his face bandaged. The curtains were tightly drawn across the window, the candles lit. Her face looked **garish** in the yellow light. She shook her head for silence.

garish
strangely
or brightly
colored

"He's sleeping now," she whispered, "but only just. Something must have cut him, there was blood at the corner of his eyes. Jill said it was the birds. She said she woke up, and the birds were in the room."

His wife looked up at Nat, searching his face for **confirmation**. She looked terrified, bewildered, and he did not want her to know that he was also shaken, dazed almost, by the events of the past few hours.

confirmation
agreement

"There are birds in there," he said, "dead birds, nearly fifty of them. Robins, wrens, all the little birds from hereabouts. It's as though madness seized them, with the east wind." He sat down on the bed beside his wife, and held her hand. "It's the weather," he said, "it must be that, it's the hard weather. They aren't the birds, maybe, from here around. They've been driven down from upcountry."

"But Nat," whispered his wife, "it's only this night that the weather turned. There's been no snow to drive them. And they can't be hungry."

"It's the weather," repeated Nat. "I tell you, it's the weather."

His face too was drawn and tired, like hers. They stared at one another for a while without speaking.

"I'll go downstairs and make a cup of tea," he said.

The sight of the kitchen reassured him. The cups and saucers, neatly stacked upon the dresser, the table and chairs, his wife's roll of knitting on her basket chair, the children's toys in a corner cupboard.

He knelt down, raked out the old embers, and relit the fire. The glowing sticks brought normality, the steaming kettle and the brown teapot, comfort and security. He drank his tea, carried a cup up to his wife. Then he washed in the scullery[3] and, putting on his boots, opened the back door.

The sky was hard and leaden, and the brown hills that had gleamed in the sun the day before looked dark and bare. The east wind, like a razor, stripped the trees, and the leaves, crackling and dry, shivered and scattered with the wind's blast. Nat stubbed the earth with his boot. It was frozen hard. He had never known a change so swift and sudden. Black winter had descended in a single night.

The children were awake now. Jill was chattering upstairs and young Johnny crying once again. Nat heard his wife's voice, soothing, comforting. Presently they came down. He had breakfast ready for them and the routine of the day began.

"Did you drive away the birds?" asked Jill, restored to calm because of the kitchen fire, because of day, because of breakfast.

"Yes, they've all gone now," said Nat. "It was the east wind brought them in. They were frightened and lost. They wanted shelter."

"They tried to peck us," said Jill. "They went for Johnny's eyes."

"Fright made them do that," said Nat. "They didn't know where they were in the dark bedroom."

---

3 **scullery:** small room off the kitchen, for dishwashing and other chores

"I hope they won't come again," said Jill. "Perhaps if we put bread for them outside the window they will eat that and fly away."

She finished her breakfast and then went for her coat and hood, her school books and her satchel. Nat said nothing, but his wife looked at him across the table. A silent message passed between them.

"I'll walk with her to the bus," he said. "I don't go to the farm today."

And while the child was washing in the scullery he said to his wife, "Keep all the windows closed, and the doors too. Just to be on the safe side, I'll go to the farm. Find out if they heard anything in the night." Then he walked with his small daughter up the lane. She seemed to have forgotten her experience of the night before. She danced ahead of him, chasing the leaves, her face whipped with the cold and rosy under the pixie hood.

"Is it going to snow, Dad?" she said. "It's cold enough."

He glanced up at the bleak sky, felt the wind tear at his shoulders.

"No," he said, "it's not going to snow. This is a black winter, not a white one."

All the while he searched the hedgerows for the birds, glanced over the top of them to the fields beyond, looked to the small wood above the farm where the rooks and jackdaws gathered. He saw none.

The other children waited by the bus stop, muffled, hooded like Jill, the faces white and pinched with cold.

Jill ran to them, waving. "My dad says it won't snow," she called, "it's going to be a black winter."

She said nothing of the birds. She began to push and struggle with another little girl. The bus came ambling up the hill. Nat saw her onto it, then turned and walked back toward the farm. It was not his day for work, but he wanted to satisfy himself that all was well. Jim, the cowman, was clattering in the yard.

"Boss around?" asked Nat.

"Gone to market," said Jim. "It's Tuesday, isn't it?"

He clumped off round the corner of a shed. He had no time for Nat. Nat was said to be superior. Read books and the like. Nat had forgotten it was Tuesday. This showed how the events of the preceding night had shaken him. He went to the back door of the farmhouse and heard Mrs. Trigg singing in the kitchen, the wireless[4] making a background to her song.

"Are you there, missus?" called out Nat.

---

4 **wireless:** battery operated radio

She came to the door, beaming, broad, a good-tempered woman.

"Hullo, Mr. Hocken," she said. "Can you tell me where this cold is coming from? Is it Russia? I've never seen such a change. And it's going on, the wireless says. Something to do with the Arctic Circle."

"We didn't turn on the wireless this morning," said Nat. "Fact is, we had trouble in the night."

"Kiddies poorly?"

"No . . ." He hardly knew how to explain it. Now, in daylight, the battle of the birds would sound absurd.

He tried to tell Mrs. Trigg what had happened, but he could see from her eyes that she thought his story was the result of a nightmare.

"Sure they were real birds," she said, smiling, "with proper feathers and all? Not the funny-shaped kind that the men see after closing hours on a Saturday night?"

"Mrs. Trigg," he said, "there are fifty dead birds, robins, wrens, and such, lying low on the floor of the children's bedroom. They went for me; they tried to go for young Johnny's eyes."

Mrs. Trigg stared at him doubtfully.

"Well there, now," she answered. "I suppose the weather brought them. Once in the bedroom, they wouldn't know where they were to. Foreign birds maybe, from that Arctic Circle."

"No," said Nat, "they were the birds you see about here every day."

"Funny thing," said Ms. Trigg, "no explaining it, really. You ought to write up and ask the *Guardian*. They'd have some answer for it. Well, I must be getting on."

She nodded, smiled, and went back into the kitchen.

Nat, dissatisfied, turned to the farm gate. Had it not been for those corpses on the bedroom floor, which he must now collect and bury somewhere, he would have considered the tale exaggeration too.

Jim was standing by the gate.

"Had any trouble with the birds?" asked Nat.

"Birds? What birds?"

"We got them up our place last night. Scores of them, came in the children's bedroom. Quite savage they were."

"Oh?" It took time for anything to penetrate Jim's head. "Never heard of birds acting savage," he said at length. "They get tame, like, sometimes. I've seen them come to the windows for crumbs."

"These birds last night weren't tame."

"No? Cold, maybe. Hungry. You put out some crumbs."

Jim was no more interested than Mrs. Trigg had been. It was, Nat thought, like air raids in the war. No one down this end of the country knew what the Plymouth folk had seen and suffered. You had to endure something yourself before it touched you. He walked back along the lane and crossed the **stile** to his cottage. He found his wife in the kitchen with young Johnny.

stile
steps set up for crossing a fence

"See anyone?" she asked.

"Mrs. Trigg and Jim," he answered. "I don't think they believed me. Anyway, nothing wrong up there."

"You might take the birds away," she said. "I daren't go into the room to make the beds until you do. I'm scared."

"Nothing to scare you now," said Nat. "They're dead, aren't they?"

He went up with a sack and dropped the stiff bodies into it, one by one. Yes, there were fifty of them, all told. Just the ordinary, common birds of the hedgerow, nothing as large even as a thrush. It must have been fright that made them act the way they did. Blue tits, wrens, it was incredible to think of the power of their small beaks jabbing at his face and hands the night before. He took the sack out into the garden and was faced now with a fresh problem. The ground was too hard to dig. It was frozen solid, yet no snow had fallen, nothing had happened in the past hours but the coming of the east wind. It was unnatural, queer. The weather prophets must be right. The change was something connected with the Arctic Circle.

The wind seemed to cut him to the bone as he stood there uncertainly, holding the sack. He could see the whitecapped seas breaking down under in the bay. He decided to take the birds to the shore and bury them.

headland
a high cliff that juts out over the sea

When he reached the beach below the **headland** he could scarcely stand, the force of the east wind was so strong. It hurt to draw breath, and his bare hands were blue. Never had he known such cold, not in all the bad winters he could remember. It was low tide. He crunched his way over the shingle to the softer sand and then, his back to the wind, ground a pit in the sand with his heel. He meant to drop the birds in it, but as he opened up the sack the force of the wind carried them, lifted them, as though in flight again, and they were blown away from him along the beach, tossed like feathers, spread and scattered, the bodies of the fifty frozen birds. There was something ugly in the sight. He did not like it. The dead birds were swept away from him by the wind.

"The tide will take them when it turns," he said to himself.

He looked out to sea and watched the crested **breakers**, combing green. They rose swiftly, curled, and broke again, and because it was ebb tide the roar was distant, more remote, lacking the sound and thunder of the flood.

**breakers** waves that break on the shore

Then he saw them. The gulls. Out there, riding the seas.

What he had thought at first to be the whitecaps of the waves were gulls. Hundreds, thousands, tens of thousands . . . They rose and fell in the trough of the seas, heads to the wind, like a mighty fleet at anchor, waiting on the tide. To eastward and to the west, the gulls were there. They stretched as far as his eye could reach. In close formation, line upon line. Had the sea been still they would have covered the bay like a white cloud, head to head, body packed to body. Only the east wind, whipping the sea to breakers, hid them from the shore.

> *What he had thought at first to be the whitecaps of the waves were gulls. Hundreds, thousands, tens of thousands . . . They rose and fell in the trough of the seas, heads to the wind, like a mighty fleet at anchor, waiting on the tide.*

Nat turned, and leaving the beach climbed the steep path home. Someone should know of this. Someone should be told. Something was happening, because of the east wind and the weather, that he did not understand. He wondered if he should go to the call box[5] by the bus stop and ring up the police. Yet what could they do? What could anyone do? Tens of thousands of gulls riding the sea there, in the bay, because of storm, because of hunger. The police would think him mad, or drunk, or take the statement from him with great calm. "Thank you. Yes, the matter has already been reported. The hard weather is driving the birds inland in great numbers." Nat looked about him. Still no sign of any other bird. Perhaps the cold had sent them all from upcountry? As he drew near to the cottage his wife came to meet him at the door. She called to him, excited. "Nat," she said, "it's on the wireless. They've just read out a special news bulletin. I've written it down."

"What's on the wireless?" he said.

---

5 **call box:** telephone booth

"About the birds," she said. "It's not only here, it's everywhere. In London, all over the country. Something has happened to the birds."

Together they went into the kitchen. He read the piece of paper lying on the table.

"Statement from the Home Office at 11 A.M. today. Reports from all over the country are coming in hourly about the vast quantity of birds flocking above towns, villages, and outlying districts, causing obstruction and damage and even attacking individuals. It is thought that the Arctic air stream, at present covering the British Isles, is causing birds to migrate south in immense numbers and that intense hunger may drive these birds to attack human beings. Householders are warned to see to their windows, doors, and chimneys, and to take reasonable precautions for the safety of their children. A further statement will be issued later."

A kind of excitement seized Nat; he looked at his wife in triumph.

"There you are," he said. "Let's hope they'll hear that at the farm. Mrs. Trigg will know it wasn't any story. It's true. All over the country. I've been telling myself all morning there's something wrong. And just now, down on the beach, I looked out to sea and there are gulls, thousands of them, tens of thousands, you couldn't put a pin between their heads, and they're all out there, riding on the sea, waiting."

"What are they waiting for, Nat?" she asked.

He stared at her, then looked down again at the piece of paper.

"I don't know," he said slowly. "It says here the birds are hungry."

He went over to the drawer where he kept his hammer and tools.

"What are you going to do, Nat?"

"See to the windows and the chimneys too, like they tell you."

"You think they would break in, with the windows shut? Those sparrows and robins and such? Why, how could they?"

He did not answer. He was not thinking of the robins and the sparrows. He was thinking of the gulls. . . .

He went upstairs and worked there the rest of the morning, boarding the windows of the bedrooms, filling up the chimney bases. Good job it was his free day and he was not working at the farm. It reminded him of the old days, at the beginning of the war. He was not married then, and he had made all the blackout boards for his mother's house in Plymouth. Made the shelter too. Not that it had been of any use when the moment came. He wondered if they would take the precautions up at the farm. He doubted it. Too easygoing. Harry Trigg and his missus. Maybe they'd laugh at the whole thing. Go off to a dance or a whist drive.[6]

"Dinner's ready." She called him, from the kitchen.

"All right. Coming down."

He was pleased with his handiwork. The frames fitted nicely over the little panes and at the base of the chimneys.

When dinner was over and his wife was washing up, Nat switched on the one o'clock news. The same announcement was repeated, the one which she had taken down during the morning, but the news bulletin enlarged upon it. "The flocks of birds have caused dislocation in all areas," read the announcer, "and in London the sky was so dense at ten o'clock this morning that it seemed as if the city was covered by a vast black cloud.

---

6 **whist drive:** party or tournament at which the card game whist is played

"The birds settled on rooftops, on window ledges, and on chimneys. The species include blackbird, thrush, the common house sparrow, and, as might be expected in the metropolis, a vast quantity of pigeons and starlings and that frequenter of the London river, the black-headed gull. The sight has been so unusual that traffic came to a standstill in many thoroughfares, work was abandoned in shops and offices, and the streets and pavements were crowded with people standing about to watch the birds."

Various incidents were **recounted**, the suspected reason of cold and hunger stated again, and warnings to householders repeated. The announcer's voice was smooth and suave. Nat had the impression that this man, in particular, treated the whole business as he would an elaborate joke. There would be others like him, hundreds of them, who did not know what it was to struggle in darkness with a flock of birds. There would be parties tonight in London, like the ones they gave on election nights. People standing about, shouting and laughing, getting drunk. "Come and watch the birds!"

Nat switched off the wireless. He got up and started work on the kitchen windows. His wife watched him, young Johnny at her heels.

"What, boards for down here too?" she said. "Why, I'll have to light up before three o'clock. I see no call for boards down here."

"Better be sure than sorry," answered Nat. "I'm not going to take any chances."

"What they ought to do," she said, "is to call the Army out and shoot the birds. That would soon scare them off."

"Let them try," said Nat. "How'd they set about it?"

"They have the Army to the docks," she answered, "when the dockers[7] strike. The soldiers go down and unload the ships."

"Yes," said Nat, "and the population of London is eight million or more. Think of all the buildings, all the flats and houses. Do you think they've enough soldiers to go around shooting birds from every roof?"

"I don't know. But something should be done. They ought to do something."

Nat thought to himself that "they" were no doubt considering the problem at that very moment, but whatever "they" decided to do in London and the big cities would not help the people here, three hundred miles away. Each householder must look after his own.

---

7 dockers: dock workers

Unit Three   The Forces of Nature

"How are we off for food?" he said.

"Now, Nat, whatever next?"

"Never mind. What have you got in the larder?"

"It's shopping day tomorrow. You know that I don't keep uncooked food hanging about; it goes off. Butcher doesn't call till the day after. But I can bring back something when I go tomorrow."

Nat did not want to scare her. He thought it possible that she might not go to town tomorrow. He looked in the larder for himself and in the cupboard where she kept her tins. They would do for a couple of days. Bread was low.

"What about the baker?"

"He comes tomorrow too."

He saw she had flour. If the baker did not call she had enough to bake one loaf.

"We'd be better off in the old days," he said, "when the women baked twice a week, and had pilchards[8] salted, and there was food for a family to last a siege, if need be."

"I've tried the children with tinned fish; they don't like it," she said.

Nat went on hammering the boards across the kitchen windows. Candles. They were low in candles too. That must be another thing she meant to buy tomorrow. Well, it could not be helped. They must go early to bed tonight. That was if . . .

He got up and went out of the back door and stood in the garden, looking down toward the sea. There had been no sun all day, and now, at barely three o'clock, a kind of darkness had already come, the sky sullen, heavy, colorless like salt. He could hear the vicious sea drumming on the rocks. He walked down the path, halfway to the beach, and then he stopped. He could see the tide had turned. The rock that had shown in midmorning was now covered, but it was not the sea that held his eyes. The gulls had risen. They were circling, hundreds of them, thousands of them, lifting their wings against the wind. It was the gulls that made the darkening of the sky. And they were silent. They made not a sound. They just went on soaring and circling, rising, falling, trying their strength against the wind.

Nat turned. He ran up the path, back to the cottage.

"I'm going for Jill," he said. "I'll wait for her, at the bus stop."

"What's the matter?" asked his wife. "You've gone quite white."

---

8 **pilchards:** sardines

"Keep Johnny inside," he said. "Keep the door shut. Light up now, and draw the curtains."

"It's only just gone three," she said.

"Never mind. Do what I tell you."

He looked inside the toolshed outside the back door. Nothing here of much use. A spade was too heavy, and a fork no good. He took the hoe. It was the only possible tool, and light enough to carry.

He started walking up the lane to the bus stop and now and again glanced back over his shoulder.

The gulls had risen higher now, their circles were broader, wider; they were spreading out in huge formation across the sky.

He hurried on; although he knew the bus would not come to the top of the hill before four o'clock, he had to hurry. He passed no one on the way. He was glad of this. No time to stop and chatter.

At the top of the hill he waited. He was much too soon. There was half an hour still to go. The east wind came whipping across the fields from the higher ground. He stamped his feet and blew upon his hands. In the distance he could see the clay hills, white and clean, against the heavy **pallor** of the sky. Something black rose from behind them, like a smudge at first, then widening, becoming deeper, and the smudge became a cloud, and the cloud divided again into five other clouds, spreading north, east, south, and west, and they were not clouds at all; they were birds. He watched them travel across the sky, and as one section passed overhead, within two or three hundred feet of him, he knew, from their speed, they were bound inland, upcountry; they had no business with the people here on the peninsula. They were rooks, crows, jackdaws, magpies, jays, all birds that usually preyed upon the smaller species; but this afternoon they were bound on some other mission.

pallor
paleness

"They've been given the towns," thought Nat, "they know what they have to do. We don't matter so much here. The gulls will serve for us. The others go to the towns. . . ."

He went to the call box, stepped inside, and lifted the receiver. The exchange would do. They would pass the message on.

"I'm speaking from the highway," he said, "by the bus stop. I want to report large formations of birds traveling upcountry. The gulls are also forming in the bay."

laconic
using so few
words as to
appear rude

"All right," answered the voice, **laconic**, weary.

"You'll be sure and pass this message on to the proper quarter?"

"Yes . . . Yes . . ." Impatient now, fed up. The buzzing note resumed.

"She's another," thought Nat, "she doesn't care. Maybe she's had to answer calls all day. She hopes to go to the pictures tonight. She'll squeeze some fellow's hand and point at the sky and say 'Look at all them birds!' She doesn't care . . . ."

The bus came **lumbering** up the hill. Jill climbed out and three or four other children. The bus went on toward the town.

"What's the hoe for, Dad?"

They crowded around him, laughing, pointing.

"I just brought it along," he said. "Come on now, let's get home. It's cold, no hanging about. Here, you. I'll watch you across the fields, see how fast you can run."

He was speaking to Jill's companions, who came from different families living in the council houses.[9] A shortcut would take them to the cottages.

"We want to play a bit in the lane," said one of them.

"No, you don't. You go off home or I'll tell your mammy."

They whispered to one another, round-eyed, then scuttled off across the fields. Jill stared at her father, her mouth sullen.

"We always play in the lane," she said.

"Not tonight, you don't," he said. "Come on now, no **dawdling**."

He could see the gulls now, circling the fields, coming in toward the land. Still silent. Still no sound.

"Look, Dad, look over there, look at all the gulls."

"Yes. Hurry, now."

"Where are they flying to? Where are they going?"

"Upcountry, I dare say. Where it's warmer."

He seized her hand and dragged her after him along the lane.

"Don't go so fast. I can't keep up."

The gulls were copying the rooks and crows. They were spreading out in formation across the sky. They headed, in bands of thousands, to the four compass points.

"Dad, what is it? What are the gulls doing?"

They were not intent upon their flight, as the crows, as the jackdaws had been. They still circled overhead. Nor did they fly so high. It was as though they waited upon some signal. As though some decision had yet to be given. The order was not clear.

lumbering
moving slowly and heavily

dawdling
wasting time

---

9 **council houses:** government housing

"Do you want me to carry you, Jill? Here, come pickaback."[10]

This way he might put on speed; but he was wrong. Jill was heavy. She kept slipping. And she was crying too. His sense of urgency, of fear, had communicated itself to the child.

"I wish the gulls would go away. I don't like them. They're coming closer to the lane."

He put her down again. He started running, swinging Jill after him. As they went past the farm turning, he saw the farmer backing his car out of the garage. Nat called to him.

"Can you give us a lift?" he said.

"What's that?"

rubicund
healthy and reddish; ruddy

Mr. Trigg turned in the driving seat and stared at them. Then a smile came to his cheerful, **rubicund** face.

"It looks as though we're in for some fun," he said. "Have you seen the gulls? Jim and I are going to take a crack at them. Everyone's gone bird crazy, talking of nothing else. I hear you were troubled in the night. Want a gun?"

Nat shook his head.

The small car was packed. There was just room for Jill, if she crouched on top of petrol[11] tins on the back seat.

"I don't want a gun," said Nat, "but I'd be obliged if you'd run Jill home. She's scared of the birds."

He spoke briefly. He did not want to talk in front of Jill.

"OK," said the farmer. "I'll take her home. Why don't you stop behind and join the shooting match? We'll make the feathers fly."

Jill climbed in, and turning the car, the driver sped up the lane. Nat followed after. Trigg must be crazy. What use was a gun against a sky of birds?"

Now Nat was not responsible for Jill, he had time to look about him. The birds were circling still above the fields. Mostly herring gull, but the black-backed gull amongst them. Usually they kept apart. Now they were united. Some bond had brought them together. It was the black-backed gull that attacked the smaller birds, and even newborn lambs, so he'd heard. He'd never seen it done. He remembered this now, though, looking above him in the sky. They were coming in toward the farm. They were circling

---

10 **pickaback:** piggy back

11 **petrol:** gasoline

lower in the sky, and the black-backed gulls were to the front, the black-backed gulls were leading. The farm, then, was their target. They were making for the farm.

Nat increased his pace toward his own cottage. He saw the farmer's car turn and come back along the lane. It drew up beside him with a jerk.

"The kid has run inside," said the farmer. "Your wife was watching for her. Well, what do you make of it? They're saying in town the Russians have done it. The Russians have poisoned the birds."

"How could they do that?" asked Nat.

"Don't ask me. You know how stories get around. Will you join my shooting match?"

"No, I'll get along home. The wife will be worried else."

"My missus says if you could eat gull, there'd be some sense in it," said Trigg. "We'd have roast gull, baked gull, and pickle 'em into the bargain. You wait until I let off a few barrels[12] into the brutes. That'll scare 'em."

"Have you boarded your windows?" asked Nat.

"No. Lot of nonsense. They like to scare you on the wireless. I've had more to do today than to go round boarding up my windows."

"I'd board them now, if I were you."

"Garn. You're windy.[13] Like to come to our place to sleep?"

"No, thanks all the same."

"All right. See you in the morning. Give you a gull breakfast."

The farmer grinned and turned his car to the farm entrance.

Nat hurried on. Past the little wood, past the old barn, and then across the stile to the remaining field.

As he jumped the stile he heard the whir of wings. A black-backed gull dived down at him from the sky, missed, swerved in flight, and rose to dive again. In a moment it was joined by others, six, seven, a dozen, black-backed and herring mixed. Nat dropped his hoe. The hoe was useless. Covering his head with his arms, he ran toward the cottage. They kept coming at him from the air, silent save for the beating wings. The terrible, fluttering wings. He could feel the blood on his hands, his wrist, his neck. Each stab of a swooping beak

---

12 **let off a few barrels:** a barrel is the discharging tube of a gun. Letting off a few barrels is British slang for emptying one's gun a few times.

13 **windy:** British slang for scared, often used in the military

tore his flesh. If only he could keep them from his eyes. Nothing else mattered. He must keep them from his eyes. They had not learned yet how to cling to a shoulder, how to rip clothing, how to dive in mass upon the head, upon the body. But with each dive, with each attack, they became bolder. And they had no thought for themselves. When they dived low and missed, they crashed, bruised and broken, on the ground. As Nat ran he stumbled, kicking their spent bodies in front of him.

He found the door; he hammered upon it with his bleeding hands. Because of the boarded windows no light shone. Everything was dark.

"Let me in," he shouted, "it's Nat. Let me in."

He shouted loud to make himself heard above the whirr of the gulls' wings.

Then he saw the gannet,[14] poised for the dive, above him in the sky. The gulls circled, retired, soared, one after another, against the wind. Only the gannet

---

14 **gannet:** a fast-diving bird with pointed wings and a long bill, known for how much it can eat

remained. One single gannet above him in the sky. The wings folded suddenly to its body. It dropped like a stone. Nat screamed, and the door opened. He stumbled across the threshold, and his wife threw her weight against the door.

They heard the thud of the gannet as it fell.

His wife dressed his wounds. They were not deep. The backs of his hands had suffered most, and his wrists. Had he not worn a cap they would have reached his head. As to the gannet . . . The gannet could have split his skull.

The children were crying, of course. They had seen the blood on their father's hands.

"It's all right now," he told them. "I'm not hurt. Just a few scratches. You play with Johnny, Jill. Mammy will wash these cuts."

He half shut the door to the scullery so that they could not see. His wife was ashen. She began running water from the sink.

"I saw them overhead," she whispered. "They began collecting just as Jill ran in with Mr. Trigg. I shut the door fast, and it jammed. That's why I couldn't open it at once when you came."

"Thank God they waited for me," he said. Jill would have fallen at once. One bird alone would have done it."

Furtively, so as not to alarm the children, they whispered together as she bandaged his hands and the back of his neck.

furtively secretly; sneakily

"They're flying inland," he said, "thousands of them. Rooks, crows, all the bigger birds. I saw them from the bus stop. They're making for the towns."

"But what can they do, Nat?"

"They'll attack. Go for everyone out in the streets. Then they'll try the windows, the chimneys."

"Why don't the authorities do something? Why don't they get the Army, get machine guns, anything?"

"There's been no time. Nobody's prepared. We'll hear what they have to say on the six o'clock news."

Nat went back into the kitchen, followed by his wife. Johnny was playing quietly on the floor. Only Jill looked anxious.

"I can hear the birds," she said. "Listen, Dad."

Nat listened. Muffled sounds came from the windows, from the door. Wings brushing the surface, sliding, scraping, seeking a way of entry. The sound of many bodies, pressed together, shuffling on the sills. Now and again came a thud, a crash, as some bird dived and fell. "Some of them will kill themselves that way," he thought, "but not enough. Never enough."

"All right," he said aloud. "I've got boards over the windows, Jill. The birds can't get in."

He went and examined all the windows. His work had been thorough. Every gap was closed. He would make extra certain, however. He found wedges, pieces of old tin, strips of wood and metal, and fastened them at the sides to reinforce the boards. His hammering helped to deafen the sound of the birds, the shuffling, the tapping, and more ominous—he did not want his wife or the children to hear it—the splinter of cracked glass.

"Turn on the wireless," he said, "let's have the wireless."

This would drown the sound also. He went upstairs to the bedrooms and reinforced the windows there. Now he could hear the birds on the roof, the scraping of claws, a sliding, jostling sound.

He decided they must sleep in the kitchen, keep up the fire, bring down the mattresses, and lay them out on the floor. He was afraid of the bedroom chimneys. The boards he had placed at the chimney bases might give way. In the kitchen they would be safe because of the fire. He would have to make a joke of it. Pretend to the children they were playing at camp. If the worst happened, and the birds forced an entry down the bedroom chimneys, it would be hours, days perhaps, before they could break down the doors. The birds would be imprisoned in the bedrooms. They could do no harm there. Crowded together, they would stifle and die.

He began to bring the mattresses downstairs. At sight of them his wife's eyes widened in apprehension. She thought the birds had already broken in upstairs.

"All right," he said cheerfully, "we'll all sleep together in the kitchen tonight. More cozy here by the fire. Then we shan't be worried by those silly old birds tapping at the windows."

He made the children help him rearrange the furniture, and he took the precaution of moving the dresser, with his wife's help, across the window. It fitted well. It was an added safeguard. The mattresses could now be lain, one beside the other, against the wall where the dresser had stood.

"We're safe enough now," he thought. "We're snug and tight, like an air-raid shelter. We can hold out. It's just the food that worries me. Food and coal for the fire. We've enough for two or three days, not more. By that time . . . ."

No use thinking ahead as far as that. And they'd be giving directions on the wireless. People would be told what to do. And now, in the midst of many problems, he realized that it was dance music only, coming over the air. Not Children's Hour, as it should have been. He glanced at the dial. Yes, they were on the Home Service all right. Dance records. He switched to the Light program. He knew the reason. The usual programs had been abandoned. This only happened at exceptional times. Elections and such. He tried to remember if it had happened in the war, during the heavy raids on London. But of course. The B.B.C.[15] was not stationed in London during the war. The programs were broadcast from other, temporary quarters. "We're better off here," he thought, "we're better off here in the kitchen, with the windows and the doors boarded, than they are up in the towns. Thank God we're not in the towns."

At six o'clock the records ceased. The time signal was given. No matter if it scared the children, he must hear the news. There was a pause after the pips.[16] Then the announcer spoke. His voice was solemn, grave. Quite different from midday.

"This is London," he said. "A National Emergency was proclaimed at four o'clock this afternoon. Measures are being taken to safeguard the lives and property of the population, but it must be understood that these are not easy to effect immediately, owing to the unforeseen and unparalleled nature of the present crisis. Every householder must take precautions to his own building, and where several people live together, as in flats and apartments, they must unite to do the utmost they can to prevent entry. It is absolutely **imperative** that every individual stay indoors tonight and that no one at all remain on the streets or roads or anywhere outdoors. The birds, in vast numbers, are attacking anyone on sight and have already begun an assault upon buildings; but these, with due care, should be impenetrable. The population is asked to remain calm and not to panic. Owing to the exceptional nature of the emergency, there will be no further transmission from any broadcasting station until 7 A.M. tomorrow."

imperative necessary, not to be avoided or put off

They played the National Anthem. Nothing more happened. Nat switched off the set. He looked at his wife. She stared back at him.

"What's it mean?" said Jill. "What did the news say?"

---

15 **B.B.C.:** British Broadcasting Company

16 **pips:** high-pitched tones

"There won't be any more programs tonight," said Nat. "There's been a breakdown at the B.B.C."

"Is it the birds?" asked Jill. "Have the birds done it?"

"No," said Nat, "it's just that everyone's very busy, and then of course they have to get rid of the birds, messing everything up, in the towns. Well, we can manage without the wireless for one evening."

"I wish we had a gramophone,"[17] said Jill. "That would be better than nothing."

She had her face turned to the dresser backed against the windows. Try as they did to ignore it, they were all aware of the shuffling, the stabbing, the persistent beating and sweeping of wings.

"We'll have supper early," suggested Nat, "something for a treat. Ask Mammy. Toasted cheese, eh? Something we all like?"

He winked and nodded at his wife. He wanted the look of dread, of apprehension, to go from Jill's face.

He helped with the supper, whistling, singing, making as much clatter as he could, and it seemed to him that the shuffling and the tapping were not so intense as they had been at first. Presently he went up to the bedrooms and listened, and he no longer heard the jostling for place upon the roof.

"They've got reasoning powers," he thought, "they know it's hard to break in here. They'll try elsewhere. They won't waste their time with us."

Supper passed without incident, and then, when they were clearing away, they heard a new sound, droning, familiar, a sound they all knew and understood.

His wife looked up at him, her face alight. "It's planes," she said, "they're sending out planes after the birds. That's what I said they ought to do all along. That will get them. Isn't that gunfire? Can't you hear guns?"

It might be gunfire out at sea. Nat could not tell. Big naval guns might have an effect upon the gulls out at sea, but the gulls were inland now. The guns couldn't shell the shore because of the population.

"It's good, isn't it," said his wife, "to hear the planes?" And Jill, catching her enthusiasm, jumped up and down with Johnny. "The planes will get the birds. The planes will shoot them."

Just then they heard a crash about two miles distant, followed by a second, then a third. The droning became more distant, passed away out to sea.

---

17 **gramophone:** record player

"What was that?" asked his wife. "Were they dropping bombs on the birds?"

"I don't know," answered Nat. "I don't think so."

He did not want to tell her that the sound they had heard was the crashing of aircraft. It was, he had no doubt, a venture on the part of the authorities to send out reconnaissance forces, but they might have known the venture was suicidal. What could aircraft do against birds that flung themselves to death against propeller and **fuselage** but hurtle to the ground themselves? This was being tried now, he supposed, over the whole country. And at a cost. Someone high up had lost his head.

fuselage body of a plane

"Where have the planes gone, Dad?" asked Jill.

"Back to base," he said. "Come on, now, time to tuck down for bed."

It kept his wife occupied, undressing the children before the fire, seeing to the bedding, one thing and another, while he went round the cottage again, making sure that nothing had worked loose. There was no further drone of aircraft, and the naval guns had ceased. "Waste of life and effort," Nat said to himself. "We can't destroy enough of them that way. Cost heavy. There's always gas. Maybe they'll try spraying with gas, mustard gas.[18] We'll be warned first, of course, if they do. There's one thing, the best brains of the country will be on to it tonight."

Somehow the thought reassured him. He had a picture of scientists, naturalists, technicians, and all those chaps they called the back-room boys, summoned to a council; they'd be working on the problem now. This was not a job for the government, for the chiefs of staff—they would merely carry out the orders of the scientists.

"They'll have to be ruthless," he thought. "Where the trouble's worst they'll have to risk more lives if they use gas. All the livestock, too, and the soil—all contaminated. As long as everyone doesn't panic. That's the trouble. People panicking, losing their heads. The B.B.C. was right to warn us of that."

Upstairs in the bedrooms all was quiet. No further scraping and stabbing at the windows. A lull in battle. Forces regrouping. Wasn't that what they called it in the old wartime bulletins? The wind hadn't dropped, though. He could still hear it roaring in the chimneys. And the sea breaking down on the shore. Then he remembered the tide. The tide would be on the turn. Maybe the lull in battle was because of the tide. There was some law the birds obeyed, and it was all to do with the east wind and the tide.

---

18 **mustard gas:** a poisonous gas used as a weapon in World War I

He glanced at his watch. Nearly eight o'clock. It must have gone high water an hour ago. That explained the lull: The birds attacked with the flood tide. It might not work that way inland, upcountry, but it seemed as if it was so this way on the coast. He reckoned the time limit in his head. They had six hours to go without attack. When the tide turned again, around one-twenty in the morning, the birds would come back . . . .

There were two things he could do. The first to rest, with his wife and children, and all of them snatch what sleep they could, until the small hours. The second to go out, see how they were faring at the farm, see if the telephone was still working there, so that they might get news from the exchange.

He called softly to his wife, who had just settled the children. She came halfway up the stairs and he whispered to her.

"You're not to go," she said at once, "you're not to go and leave me alone with the children. I can't stand it."

Her voice rose hysterically. He hushed her, calmed her.

It was pitch dark. The wind was blowing harder than ever, coming in steady gusts, icy, from the sea. He kicked at the step outside the door. It was heaped with birds.

"All right," he said, "all right. I'll wait till morning. And we'll get the wireless bulletin then too, at seven. But in the morning, when the tide ebbs again, I'll try for the farm, and they may let us have bread and potatoes, and milk too."

His mind was busy again, planning against emergency. They would not have milked, of course, this evening. The cows would be standing by the gate, waiting in the yard, with the household inside, battened behind boards, as they were here at the cottage. That is, if they had time to take precautions. He thought of the farmer, Trigg, smiling at him from the car. There would have been no shooting party, not tonight.

The children were asleep. His wife, still clothed, was sitting on her mattress. She watched him, her eyes nervous.

"What are you going to do?" she whispered.

He shook his head for silence. Softly, stealthily, he opened the back door and looked outside.

It was pitch dark. The wind was blowing harder than ever, coming in steady gusts, icy, from the sea. He kicked at the step outside the door. It was heaped with birds. There were dead birds everywhere. Under the windows, against the walls. These were the suicides, the divers, the ones with broken necks. Wherever he looked he saw dead birds. No trace of the living. The living had flown seaward with the turn of the tide. The gulls would be riding the seas now, as they had done in the forenoon.

In the far distance, on the hill where the tractor had been two days before, something was burning. One of the aircraft had crashed; the fire, fanned by the wind, had set light to a stack.

He looked at the bodies of the birds, and he had a notion that if he heaped them, one upon the other, on the window sills they would make added protection for the next attack. Not much, perhaps, but something. The bodies would have to be clawed at, pecked, and dragged aside before the living birds gained purchase[19] on the sills and attacked the panes. He set to work in the darkness. It was queer; he hated touching them. The bodies were still warm and bloody. The blood matted their feathers. He felt his stomach turn, but he went on with his work. He noticed grimly that every windowpane was shattered. Only the boards had kept the birds from breaking in. He stuffed the cracked panes with the bleeding bodies of the birds.

When he had finished he went back into the cottage. He barricaded the kitchen door, made it doubly secure. He took off his bandages, sticky with the birds' blood, not with his own cuts, and put on fresh plaster.[20]

His wife had made him cocoa and he drank it thirstily. He was very tired. "All right," he said, smiling, "don't worry. We'll get through."

He lay down on his mattress and closed his eyes. He slept at once. He dreamt uneasily because through his dreams there ran a thread of something forgotten. Some piece of work, neglected, that he should have done. Some precaution that he had known well but had not taken, and he could not put a name to it in his dreams. It was connected in some way with the burning aircraft and the stack upon the hill. He went on sleeping, though; he did not awake. It was his wife shaking his shoulder that awoke him finally.

"They've begun," she sobbed. "They've started this last hour. I can't listen to it any longer alone. There's something smelling bad too, something burning."

Then he remembered. He had forgotten to make up the fire. It was smoldering, nearly out. He got up swiftly and lit the lamp. The hammering had started

---

19 **gained purchase:** took hold

20 **plaster:** tape for dressing a wound

at the windows and the doors, but it was not that he minded now. It was the smell of singed feathers. The smell filled the kitchen. He knew at once what it was. The birds were coming down the chimney, squeezing their way down to the kitchen range.

He got sticks and paper and put them on the embers, then reached for the can of **paraffin**.

"Stand back," he shouted to his wife, "we've got to risk this."

He threw the paraffin onto the fire. The flame roared up the pipe, and down upon the fire fell the scorched, blackened bodies of the birds.

The children woke, crying. "What is it?" said Jill. "What's happened?"

Nat had no time to answer. He was raking the bodies from the chimney, clawing them out onto the floor. The flames still roared, and the danger of the chimney catching fire was one he had to take. The flames would send away the living birds from the chimney top. The lower joint was the difficulty, though. This was choked with the smoldering, helpless bodies of the birds caught by fire. He scarcely heeded the attack on the windows and the door: let them beat their wings, break their beaks, lose their lives in the attempt to force an entry into his home. They would not break in. He thanked God he had one of the old cottages, with small windows, stout walls. Not like the new council houses. Heaven help them up the lane in the new council houses.

"Stop crying," he called to the children. "There's nothing to be afraid of, stop crying."

He went on raking at the burning, smoldering bodies as they fell into the fire.

"This'll fetch them," he said to himself, "the draft and the flames together. We're all right, as long as the chimney doesn't catch. I ought to be shot for this. It's all my fault. Last thing I should have made up the fire. I knew there was something."

Amid the scratching and tearing at the window boards came the sudden homely striking of the kitchen clock. Three A.M. A little more than four hours yet to go. He could not be sure of the exact time of high water. He reckoned it would not turn much before half-past seven, twenty to eight.

"Light up the Primus,"[21] he said to his wife. "Make us some tea, and the kids some cocoa. No use sitting around doing nothing."

---

21 **Primus:** portable stove used by campers

That was the line. Keep her busy, and the children too. Move about, eat, drink; always best to be on the go.

He waited by the range. The flames were dying. But no more blackened bodies fell from the chimney. He thrust his poker up as far as it could go and found nothing. It was clear. The chimney was clear. He wiped the sweat from his forehead.

"Come on now, Jill," he said, "bring me some more sticks. We'll have a good fire going directly." She wouldn't come near him, though. She was staring at the heaped singed bodies of the birds.

"Never mind them," he said, "we'll put those in the passage when I've got the fire steady."

The danger of the chimney was over. It could not happen again, not if the fire was kept burning day and night.

"I'll have to get more fuel from the farm tomorrow," he thought. "This will never last. I'll manage, though. I can do all that with the ebb tide. It can be worked, fetching what we need, when the tide's turned. We've just got to adapt ourselves, that's all."

They drank tea and cocoa and ate slices of bread and Bovril.[22] Only half a loaf left, Nat noticed. Never mind, though, they'd get by.

"Stop it," said young Johnny, pointing to the windows with his spoon, "stop it, you old birds."

"That's right," said Nat, smiling, "we don't want the old beggars, do we? Had enough of 'em."

They began to cheer when they heard the thud of the suicide birds.

"There's another, Dad," cried Jill, "he's done for."

"He's had it," said Nat, "there he goes, the blighter."[23]

This was the way to face up to it. This was the spirit. If they could keep this up, hang on like this until seven, when the first news bulletin came through, they would not have done too badly.

"Give us a cigarette," he said to his wife. "A bit of a smoke will clear away the smell of the scorched feathers."

"There's only two left in the packet," she said. "I was going to buy you some from the Co-op."

---

22 **Bovril:** a salty British spread made of beef extract

23 **blighter:** British slang for a pest or annoyance

"I'll have one," he said. "T'other will keep for a rainy day."

No sense trying to make the children rest. There was no rest to be got while the tapping and the scratching went on at the windows. He sat with one arm round his wife and the other round Jill, with Johnny on his mother's lap and the blankets heaped about them on the mattress.

persistence
the quality of
not giving up

"You can't help admiring the beggars," he said, "they've got **persistence.** You'd think they'd tire of the game, but not a bit of it."

Admiration was hard to sustain. The tapping went on and on and a new rasping note struck Nat's ear, as though a sharper beak than any hitherto had come to take over from its fellows. He tried to remember the names of birds, he tried to think which species would go for this particular job. It was not the tap of the woodpecker. That would be light and frequent. This was more serious because if it continued long the wood would splinter, as the glass had done. Then he remembered the hawks. Could the hawks have taken over from the gulls? Were there buzzards now upon the sills, using talons as well as beaks? Hawks, buzzards, kestrels, falcons—he had forgotten the birds of prey. He had forgotten the gripping power of the birds of prey. Three hours to go, and while they waited, the sound of the splintering wood, the talons tearing at the wood.

Nat looked about him, seeing what furniture he could destroy to fortify the door. The windows were safe because of the dresser. He was not certain of the door. He went upstairs, but when he reached the landing he paused and listened. There was a soft patter on the floor of the children's bedroom. The birds had broken through . . . . He put his ear to the door. No mistake. He could hear the rustle of wings and the light patter as they searched the floor. The other bedroom was still clear. He went into it and began bringing out the furniture, to pile at the head of the stairs should the door of the children's bedroom go. It was a preparation. It might never be needed. He could not stack the furniture against the door, because it opened inward. The only possible thing was to have it at the top of the stairs.

"Come down, Nat, what are you doing?" called his wife.

"I won't be long," he shouted. "Just making everything shipshape up here."

He did not want her to come; he did not want her to hear the pattering of the feet in the children's bedroom, the brushing of those wings against the door.

At five-thirty he suggested breakfast, bacon and fried bread, if only to stop the growing look of panic in his wife's eyes and to calm the fretful children.

She did not know about the birds upstairs. The bedroom, luckily, was not over the kitchen. Had it been so she could not have failed to hear the sound of them up there, tapping the boards. And the silly, senseless thud of the suicide birds, the death and glory boys, who flew into the bedroom, smashing their heads against the walls. He knew them of old, the herring gulls. They had no brains. The black-backs were different; they knew what they were doing. So did the buzzards, the hawks . . . .

He found himself watching the clock, gazing at the hands that went so slowly round the dial. If his theory was not correct, if the attack did not cease with the turn of the tide, he knew they were beaten. They could not continue through the long day without air, without rest, without more fuel, without . . . his mind raced. He knew there were so many things they needed to withstand siege. They were not fully prepared. They were not ready. It might be that it would be safer in the towns, after all. If he could get a message through on the farm telephone to his cousin, only a short journey by train up country, they might be able to hire a car. That would be quicker—hire a car between tides . . . .

His wife's voice, calling his name, drove away the sudden, desperate desire for sleep.

"What is it? What now?" he said sharply.

"The wireless," said his wife. "I've been watching the clock. It's nearly seven."

"Don't twist the knob," he said, impatient for the first time, "it's on the Home where it is. They'll speak from the Home."

They waited. The kitchen clock struck seven. There was no sound. No chimes, no music. They waited until a quarter past, switching to the Light. The result was the same. No news bulletin came through.

"We've heard wrong," he said. "They won't be broadcasting until eight o'clock."

They left it switched on, and Nat thought of the battery, wondered how much power was left in it. It was generally recharged when his wife went shopping in the town. If the battery failed, they would not hear the instructions.

"It's getting light," whispered his wife. "I can't see it, but I can feel it. And the birds aren't hammering so loud."

She was right. The rasping, tearing sound grew fainter every moment. So did the shuffling, the jostling for place upon the step, upon the sills. The tide was on the turn. By eight there was no sound at all. Only the wind. The children, lulled at last by the stillness, fell asleep. At half-past eight Nat switched the wireless off.

"What are you doing? We'll miss the news," said his wife.

"There isn't going to be any news," said Nat. "We've got to depend upon ourselves."

He went to the door and slowly pulled away the barricades. He drew the bolts, and kicking the bodies from the step outside the door, breathed the cold air. He had six working hours before him, and he knew he must reserve his strength for the right things, not waste it in any way. Food and light and fuel; these were the necessary things. If he could get them in sufficiency, they could endure another night.

He stepped into the garden, and as he did so he saw the living birds. The gulls had gone to ride the sea, as they had done before; they sought sea food and the buoyancy of the tide, before they returned to the attack. Not so the land birds. They waited and watched. Nat saw them, on the hedgerows, on the soil, crowded in the trees, outside in the field, line upon line of birds, all still, doing nothing.

He went to the end of his small garden. The birds did not move. They went on watching him.

"I've got to get food," said Nat to himself. "I've got to go to the farm to find food."

He went back to the cottage. He saw to the windows and the doors. He went upstairs and opened the children's bedroom. It was empty, except for the dead birds on the floor. The living were out there, in the garden, in the fields. He went downstairs.

"I'm going to the farm," he said

His wife clung to him. She had seen the living birds from the open door.

"Take us with you," she begged. "We can't stay here alone. I'd rather die than stay here alone."

He considered the matter. He nodded.

"Come on, then," he said. "Bring baskets, and Johnny's pram.[24] We can load up the pram."

They dressed against the biting wind, wore gloves and scarves. His wife put Johnny in the pram. Nat took Jill's hand.

"The birds," she whimpered, "they're all out there in the fields."

---

24 **pram:** short for perambulator, the British word for *stroller*

"They won't hurt us," he said, "not in the light."

They started walking across the field toward the stile, and the birds did not move. They waited, their heads turned to the wind.

When they reached the turning to the farm, Nat stopped and told his wife to wait in the shelter of the hedge with the two children.

"But I want to see Mrs. Trigg," she protested. "There are lots of things we can borrow if they went to market yesterday, not only bread, and . . . ."

"Wait here," Nat interrupted. "I'll be back in a moment."

The cows were lowing, moving restlessly in the yard, and he could see a gap in the fence where the sheep had knocked their way through, to roam unchecked in the front garden before the farmhouse. No smoke came from the chimneys. He was filled with misgiving. He did not want his wife or the children to go down to the farm.

"Don't gib²⁵ now," said Nat, harshly, "do what I say."

She withdrew with the pram into the hedge, screening herself and the children from the wind.

He went down alone to the farm. He pushed his way through the herd of bellowing cows, which turned this way and that, distressed, their udders full. He saw the car standing by the gate, not put away in the garage. The windows of the farmhouse were smashed. There were many dead gulls lying in the yard and around the house. The living birds perched on the group of trees behind the farm and on the roof of the house. They were quite still. They watched him.

Jim's body lay in the yard . . . what was left of it. When the birds had finished, the cows had trampled him. His gun was beside him. The door of the house was shut and bolted, but as the windows were smashed it was easy to lift them and climb through. Trigg's body was close to the telephone. He must have been trying to get through to the exchange when the birds came for him. The receiver was hanging loose, the instrument torn from the wall. No sign of Mrs. Trigg. She would be upstairs. Was it any use going up? Sickened, Nat knew what he would find.

"Thank God," he said to himself, "there were no children."

He forced himself to climb the stairs, but halfway he turned and descended again. He could see her legs, protruding from the open bedroom door. Beside her were the bodies of the black-backed gulls and an umbrella, broken.

---

25 **gib:** lose courage

"It's no use," thought Nat, "doing anything. I've only got five hours, less than that. The Triggs would understand. I must load up with what I can find."

He tramped back to his wife and children.

"I'm going to fill up the car with stuff," he said. "I'll put coal in it, and paraffin for the Primus. We'll take it home and return for a fresh load."

"What about the Triggs?" asked his wife.

"They must have gone to friends," he said.

"Shall I come and help you, then?"

"No; there's a mess down there. Cows and sheep all over the place. Wait, I'll get the car. You can sit in it."

Clumsily he backed the car out of the yard and into the lane. His wife and the children could not see Jim's body from there.

"Stay here," he said, "never mind the pram. The pram can be fetched later. I'm going to load the car."

Her eyes watched his all the time. He believed she understood, otherwise she would have suggested helping him to find the bread and groceries.

They made three journeys altogether, backward and forward between their cottage and the farm, before he was satisfied they had everything they needed. It was surprising, once he started thinking, how many things were necessary. Almost the most important of all was planking for the windows. He had to go round searching for timber. He wanted to renew the boards on all the windows at the cottage. Candles, paraffin, nails, tinned stuff; the list was endless. Besides all that, he milked three of the cows. The rest, poor brutes, would have to go on bellowing.

On the final journey he drove the car to the bus stop, got out, and went to the telephone box. He waited a few minutes, jangling the receiver. No good, though. The line was dead. He climbed onto a bank and looked over the countryside, but there was no sign of life at all, nothing in the fields but the waiting, watching birds. Some of them slept—he could see the beaks tucked into the feathers.

"You'd think they'd be feeding," he said to himself, "not just standing in that way."

Then he remembered. They were gorged with food. They had eaten their fill during the night. That was why they did not move this morning . . . .

No smoke came from the chimneys of the council houses. He thought of the children who had run across the fields the night before.

"I should have known," he thought. "I ought to have taken them home with me."

He lifted his face to the sky. It was colorless and gray. The bare trees on the landscape looked bent and blackened by the east wind. The cold did not affect the living birds, waiting out there in the fields.

"This is the time they ought to get them," said Nat, "they're a sitting target now. They must be doing this all over the country. Why don't our aircraft take off now and spray them with mustard gas? What are all our chaps doing? They must know, they must see for themselves."

He went back to the car and got into the driver's seat.

"Go quickly past that second gate," whispered his wife. "The postman's lying there. I don't want Jill to see."

He accelerated. The little Morris[26] bumped and rattled along the lane. The children shrieked with laughter.

"Up-a-down, up-a-down," shouted young Johnny.

It was a quarter to one by the time they reached the cottage. Only an hour to go.

---

26 **Morris:** popular British car

"Better have cold dinner," said Nat. "Hot up something for yourself and the children, some of that soup. I've no time to eat now. I've got to unload all this stuff."

He got everything inside the cottage. It could be sorted later. Give them all something to do during the long hours ahead. First he must see to the windows and the doors.

He went round the cottage methodically, testing every window, every door. He climbed onto the roof also, and fixed boards across every chimney except the kitchen. The cold was so intense he could hardly bear it, but the job had to be done. Now and again he would look up, searching the sky for aircraft. None came. As he worked he cursed the inefficiency of the authorities.

"It's always the same," he muttered. "They always let us down. Muddle, muddle, from the start. No plan, no real organization. And we don't matter down here. That's what it is. The people upcountry have priority. They're using gas up there, no doubt, and all the aircraft. We've got to wait and take what comes."

He paused, his work on the bedroom chimney finished, and looked out to sea. Something was moving out there. Something gray and white amongst the breakers.

"Good old Navy," he said, "they never let us down. They're coming down-channel; they're turning in the bay."

He waited, straining his eyes, watering in the wind, toward the sea. He was wrong, though. It was not ships. The Navy was not there. The gulls were rising from the sea. The massed flocks in the fields, with ruffled feathers, rose in formation from the ground and, wing to wing, soared upward to the sky.

The tide had turned again.

Nat climbed down the ladder and went inside the kitchen. The family were at dinner. It was a little after two. He bolted the door, put up the barricade, and lit the lamp.

"It's nighttime," said young Johnny.

His wife had switched the wireless once again, but no sound came from it.

"I've been all round the dial," she said, "foreign stations, and that lot. I can't get anything."

"Maybe they have the same trouble," he said. "Maybe it's the same right through Europe."

She poured out a plateful of the Triggs' soup, cut him a large slice of the Triggs' bread, and spread their dripping upon it.

They ate in silence. A piece of the dripping ran down young Johnny's chin and fell onto the table.

"Manners, Johnny," said Jill, "you should learn to wipe your mouth."

The tapping began at the windows, at the door. The rustling, the jostling, the pushing for position on the sills. The first thud of the suicide gulls upon the step.

"Won't America do something?" said his wife. "They've always been our allies, haven't they? Surely America will do something?"

Nat did not answer. The boards were strong against the windows and on the chimneys too. The cottage was filled with stores, with fuel, with all they needed for the next few days. When he had finished dinner he would put the stuff away, stack it neatly, get everything shipshape, handy-like. His wife could help him, and the children too. They'd tire themselves out, between now and a quarter to nine, when the tide would ebb; then he'd tuck them down on their mattresses, see that they slept good and sound until three in the morning.

He had a new scheme for the windows, which was to fix barbed wire in front of the boards. He had brought a great roll of it from the farm. The nuisance was, he'd have to work at this in the dark, when the lull came between nine and three. Pity he had not thought of it before. Still, as long as the wife slept, and the kids, that was the main thing.

The smaller birds were at the window now. He recognized the light tap-tapping of their beaks and the soft brush of their wings. The hawks ignored the windows. They concentrated their attack upon the door. Nat listened to the tearing sound of splintering wood and wondered how many million years of memory were stored in those little brains, behind the stabbing beaks, the piercing eyes, now giving them this instinct to destroy mankind with all the **deft** precision of machines.

deft
skillful

"I'll smoke that last cigarette," he said to his wife. "Stupid of me—it was the one thing I forgot to bring back from the farm."

He reached for it, switched on the silent wireless. He threw the empty packet on the fire, and watched it burn.

POETRY CONNECTION

"Hope" is the thing with feathers

EMILY DICKINSON

"Hope" is the thing with feathers—
That perches in the soul—
And sings the tune without the words—
And never stops—at all—

And sweetest—in the **Gale** is heard—   5
And sore must be the storm—
That could **abash** the little Bird
That kept so many warm—

I've heard it in the chillest land—
And on the strangest Sea—   10
Yet, never, in **Extremity**,
It asked a crumb—of Me.

gale
a strong
current of wind

abash
embarrass

extremity
extreme
circumstances,
usually hardship

AFTER YOU READ

The Birds
"Hope" is the thing with feathers

Think and Discuss

1. The story centers on an ominous and unrelenting attack by birds. What other kind of attack does the text mention repeatedly?

2. Some of the solutions suggested in the story to fight off the birds were used to respond to the other kind of attack mentioned. How effective do you think those solutions would be against the attack of the birds? Explain.

3. Both du Maurier and Dickinson treat birds as a **metaphor** for something else. To what is each writer comparing birds? Use examples from the texts in your answer. (For a definition of *metaphor*, see the Glossary of Literary Terms.)

4. How does du Maurier use **word choice** to create suspense and an expectation of violence? Give examples from the story of suspenseful words and expressions.

5. In terms of ideas and **themes**, which other selection in this unit is "The Birds" most like? Give convincing reasons for your answer.

6. The story is left unresolved at the end. How do you think the story might end? Copy the graphic organizer below into your Writer's Notebook. In the left column, write a possible course of action that Nat Hocken or someone else in the story might follow. Use actions that are suggested in the text. Then write a few sentences explaining the outcome of that course of action.

If this happens.....	....then this will be the outcome.

Write to Understand: Ending the Story

Choose one of the options you sketched out in your graphic organizer. Write an extended ending for "The Birds" based on the option you chose. Try to use suspenseful language and keep the characters consistent with the rest of the story. Share your ending with the rest of the class.

Writers on Writing

BEFORE YOU READ
Knee-Deep in Its Absence

Meet the Author: David Petersen

For decades naturalist David Petersen (born 1946) and his wife Caroline lived in comfort in southern California. However, Petersen himself might be the first to tell you that his real life began in 1981, when he left all of that behind. He and Caroline packed up a Volkswagen bus and headed for southwest Colorado to live a simpler life, close to nature. They built a modest cabin on the side of a mountain and began the daily adventures of living in the wild. Petersen relates his experiences and insights in a recently published book called *On the Wild Edge: In Search of Natural Life*.

Build Background: Nature Writing

In one way or another, nature is the subject of all the selections in this unit. Some of the writers weave nature into fictional stories; some report the news of all-too-real natural disasters; some distill nature in lines of poetry. Still other writers work in a very specific nonfiction genre known as "nature writing." They blend close and sometimes scientific observation with often poetic language in an attempt to re-create their subjects for readers. And readers crave nature writing. Such nature books as *The Sea Around Us* by Rachel Carson and *Pilgrim at Tinker's Creek* by Annie Dillard were national bestsellers. The question the following selection asks is, "Why?" What is it about nature writing that attracts both readers and writers?

- What nature writing have you read?

- Why do you think people are drawn to nature writing?

Knee-Deep in Its Absence

DAVID PETERSEN

KNEE-DEEP IN[1] ITS ABSENCE

David Petersen

Occasionally, I'm asked why I've chosen to make my career (so-called) writing about nature. The answer is easy: I *have* no choice; it's in my genes, and in my heart. As it just may be in yours . . . .

Naturally, the character of the place in which a nature writer lives and works (or longs to return to) colors his or her work. My own place is the San Juan Mountains of southwestern Colorado. I thrive on the crisp clean air and cold clear water here, the breath-sucking beauty of the creased and crenulated[2] landscape and its abundant wildlife, the relative quiet and solitude and the personal joy it all adds up to. *These* are the things I have come to value most in life. It follows that these are also the things I am **compelled** to write about. In my case at least, the nature of the place has become the nature of the man, of the writer.

During the first few years that Caroline and I lived here, high in the southern Rockies, we had a most pleasant habit of walking or snow-shoeing a mile down the mountain to spend Sunday mornings lazing around an antique woodstove drinking coffee and chatting with an **octogenarian** rancher friend named Helen. Having spent her entire long life on the **verdant** riverside spread where she was born in 1905, Helen is living local history and a captivating storyteller. Among my favorites is her tale of the naked fat man.

In the summer of 1913, when Helen had just turned eight, her father went hunting up the tight little creek valley where my hillside cabin now squats. There, in "blowdown timber so thick you couldn't ride a horse through," Helen's father killed an exceptionally large, brown-colored bear that could have been the dead-last grizzly in these parts. With helping hands

compelled
forced

octogenarian
someone
between 80 and
90 years old

verdant
green

---

1 **knee-deep in:** standing in something that reaches the knees; used as an idiom it means "too much of something."

2 **crenulated:** indented and notched; Petersen refers to the mountainous, irregular terrain.

and horses, the hunter hauled the bruin[3] home and hoisted it by the hind legs into a sturdy tree, then skinned it in preparation for butchering. (Few country folk in those lean and **pragmatic** days wasted fresh meat of any kind, and "woods pork" was widely considered a delicacy.)

pragmatic
practical

It was then, with the bare bear hanging there and her father standing beside it, bloody knife in hand, that young Helen wandered into the scene. Horrified at what she saw, she burst into tears and fled. Eighty years later, Helen laughs when she recalls how that poor flayed bear "looked like a naked fat man hanging there. I thought Dad had killed somebody and was fixing to cut him up and feed him to us. I haven't been able to stomach bear meat since."

> It was then, with the bare bear hanging there and her father standing beside it, bloody knife in hand, that young Helen wandered into the scene.

Story **spawns** story.

spawns
gives rise to

Some years ago, while exploring a secluded aspen grove some miles up the mountain from my cabin, I stumbled upon a hidden spring. Abundant spoor[4] announced that deer, elk, bears, turkeys and other wildlife visited the place regularly to drink from the little pool, to browse the lush vegetation watered by the pool's brief overflow and, I like to think, just to be there.

Shadowy and quiet and just a bit spooky at twilight, the place exudes a preternatural ambience.[5] Since that day I've visited this sylvan[6] shrine often; it has become my local refuge from Babylon.[7] And among the most significant elements of the spirit of the place are its bear trees: across the decades, the soft white skins of several of the larger aspens ringing the spring have collected hundreds of blackened bear-claw scars. This in itself is hardly unique. I've seen scores of bruin-scarred aspens near dozens of secluded spring pools throughout the Rockies. Most often, it's black bear cubs that do the climbing

---

3 **bruin:** bear

4 **spoor:** signs of a creature that animal trackers look for

5 **exudes a preternatural ambience:** gives off an other-worldly feeling

6 **sylvan:** of the woodlands

7 **Babylon:** an ancient and highly developed city in Mesopotamia; Petersen uses it here to stand for city life in general.

Aspen trees in the Rocky Mountains

and whose needle-sharp claws scratch and gouge the impressionable bark, leaving distinctively curved, parallel signatures. As the aspens grow, these modest tracks harden, blacken, stretch and swell, eventually coming to look as if they were made by the most monstrous of bruins.

But two special aspens near my spring wear a different sort of signature entirely: heavy, widely spaced vertical claw marks more than a foot long and at just the right height, allowing for decades of subsequent growth, to suggest that a very large bear once stood upright, stretched as high as possible and raked heavily downward—exactly as grizzlies are wont[8] to do.

In parallel with my old friend Helen, those storybook aspens have survived nearly a century rooted firmly in this **cloistered** San Juan pocket. I find it a deeply **poignant** experience to sit quietly in that enchanted refugium[9] and study those crude autographs and imagine them being inscribed by Helen's "naked fat man" himself. Not likely, of course. But possible nonetheless.

On one of the last occasions Caroline and I went to visit Helen, I found myself admitting to her that I was terribly envious of the simple, self-sufficient, quietly satisfying life she'd known while growing up and living on a working ranch in the good old days of a still-wild West. "I'd give anything," I confessed, "to have lived your life."

"Hell," Helen snorted, "you can *have* my life. I wish I'd been born fifty years sooner." Surprised, I asked why.

"So I wouldn't be around today to see what the [land developers] are doing to this place."

What the Buddha Might Say, Were She Here Today

> In the forest
> walk, sit, see.
> Inhale . . . silence.
> Exhale . . . solace.
> At the forest's edge
> live
> gently
> without pretense or harm.

As another old friend, A. B. Guthrie Jr., was quick to warn: "The thing you've got to watch out for with 'progress' is, there's no turning back."

Helen is pushing one hundred now and no longer guides hunters and fly fishers on wilderness horse-packing trips or plants a big garden or keeps chickens by the score or hauls hay out to feed snow-stranded cattle or drives

cloistered
secluded, like a place of religious devotion

poignant
touching

---

8 **wont:** accustomed

9 **refugium:** an area that has escaped the ecological changes of other nearby areas and so can support life from an earlier time

a horse-drawn sleigh fourteen miles to town for medicine in winter blizzards. No more grizzlies in the neighborhood either.

Instead, we have ever more care-less destroyers. Ever more new roads slicing like daggers into the shrinking heart of wildness. Ever more urban refugees arriving to build ever more **pretentious**, wasteful houses along those new roads. My magical bear trees are in mortal danger of being "harvested" for the polluting pulp mill that makes the waferboard[10] used to build those houses. Wal-Mart is upon us.

pretentious
showy and overdone

"The thought of what was here once and is gone forever will not leave me as long as I live. It is as though I walk knee-deep in its absence."

Wendell Berry said that, and I live it with him daily.

Standard advice to aspiring writers is: "Write about what you know about." For aspiring nature writers, I'd refine that to: Write about what you know about and *love*.

---

10 **waferboard:** a board made from wood flakes bonded with resin; particleboard

AFTER YOU READ
Knee-Deep in Its Absence

Think and Discuss

1. What does Petersen value most about his "place"?

2. How are Helen's story about the bear and Petersen's secluded aspen grove related?

3. Give some examples of the **specialized vocabulary** in this selection and explain why it may be needed in nature writing in general.

4. How would you describe the **structure** of this essay?

5. Think of things from the natural world whose absence you have experienced—a pet that died, or a tree that had to be cut down, for example. In your Writer's Notebook, create a cluster diagram like the one below. Use it to think of as many different experiences of "nature loss" as you can. Some categories are provided. Feel free to add more.

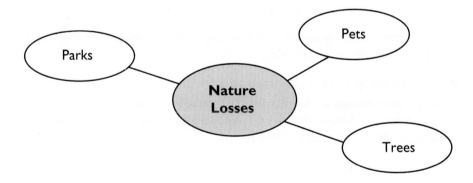

Write to Understand: Preserving Nature in Writing

Write a memorial tribute for one of the subjects on your cluster diagram. Recall what you loved about the subject and tell what you miss most. Then reflect on the experience: What effect did writing about your subject have on you? Jot down some thoughts and feelings about that in your Writer's Notebook.

A Writer's WORKSHOP

NATURE POETRY

The selections in this unit have presented a variety of ideas, attitudes, and feelings about the forces of nature and their interplay with humans. Each writer or poet has invited you into a re-created world, sometimes based on fact, sometimes on fiction. As a reader, you have been invited to stand "knee-deep" in the natural world of the story or poem. Now create your own natural world—or a very small part of one—in a nature poem.

Prewriting

REVIEWING IDEAS

Look through your Writer's Notebook for possible subjects for a nature poem. The writing you have done in this unit's activities should provide lots of ideas. Follow Petersen's advice and "write about what you know about and love." A good subject for a nature poem is:

- something in nature that you know well and have strong feelings for

- something in nature that has a special meaning to you

You are always free to brainstorm for new subject ideas if you do not connect strongly with any in your Writer's Notebook.

FREEWRITING TO DEVELOP DETAILS

When you have chosen a subject, avoid the temptation to just sit down and begin writing your poem. Instead, freewrite. Put down everything you know or can think of about your subject and what it means to you.

OBSERVING FROM DIFFERENT ANGLES

Next, observe (or imagine) your subject from different angles or at different times of the day or year. Create written "snapshots" taken from these angles. For example, what does the squirrel you see in the park during the day do at night? What does it look like when it sleeps?

COOPERATIVE LEARNING: PEER EXCHANGE

Share your snapshots with a partner. As you read each other's writing, lightly circle the images that seem especially vivid.

CRYSTALIZING IMAGES

Look back over your freewriting and your partner's circles. Then copy and complete the graphic organizer below in your Writer's Notebook.

The single most important aspect of your subject—the feature that means the most to you	
Imagery you might use to describe this feature and other aspects of your subject (for example, what might you compare it to?)	
Why this subject matters to you—why you love it	

Drafting

Decide what kind of poem you want to write. Do you want it to rhyme and have a regular meter? Do you want to write a poem in free verse? When you have decided, use your freewriting notes and chart to help you draft your poem. Make your imagery as sharp and vivid as you can. Suggest (without coming right out and saying) why your subject means so much to you.

COOPERATIVE LEARNING: PEER EXCHANGE

Share your poem with a small group of students. Read it aloud—or have someone else read it aloud—so that readers can get a good feel for the sound of the words and the rhythms. Ask for feedback, and offer it to others in your group on their poems.

Revising and Editing

Use the comments from your group to help you revise your poem. Keep at it until you feel the poem expresses exactly what you want it to.

READING WITH AN EDITOR'S EYE

If you look at any of the poems in this book, or any other book, you can see that the conventions of capitalization and punctuation do not necessarily apply to poetry. Take another look at the second stanza of the poem "Spring is like a perhaps hand" by E.E. Cummings. Where do you see lowercase letters where you might expect uppercase, and no commas where you might expect commas? Why do you think the last line is separated from the rest of the stanza?

spring is like a perhaps
Hand in a window
(carefully to
and fro moving New and
Old things,while
people stare carefully
moving a perhaps
fraction of flower here placing
an inch of air there)and

without breaking anything.

You'll never know for sure why E. E. Cummings laid out his poem as he did, but you can figure out the effect of the unusual capitalization and punctuation on you, the reader. Chances are you really take notice of the unexpected things—they may help emphasize certain words and ideas.

As you edit the final draft of your poem, pay attention to what you regard as your most important ideas and consider bending the rules of capitalization and punctuation if doing so enhances your poem.

USING A CHECKLIST

Use the Six-Trait checklist on the next page to go over your poem again to make it the best it can be.

Six Traits of Writing: Nature Poetry

Content and Ideas
- subject is from the natural world
- poem conveys a central idea about the subject

Organization
- the movement from line to line or verse to verse makes sense
- the rhythm and rhyme scheme of the poem are consistent if you intend them to be and are well suited to the subject of the poem

Voice or Style
- the speaker has a distinctive voice
- the voice sounds natural, not forced

Word Choice
- words that appeal to the senses create strong imagery
- such devices as similes, metaphors, and personification provide insights

Sentence Fluency
- sentences—or fragments if you prefer to use them—are effective in conveying the ideas of the poem
- sentence length and sentence beginnings are varied and purposeful

Conventions
- the style of punctuation and capitalization is intentional—chosen to reflect the poem's meaning
- the poem has a title

USING WORD PROCESSING

With the students in your small group, create a mini-anthology of your poems. As a group, discuss the order in which to present the poems, and give good reasons for your order. Design each page carefully using a word processor and add graphics where appropriate. Print out your anthology to share with the other groups.

Other Worlds

It felt warm and dark and primitive, as though Jeremy knew this place, as though he'd been here long ago, when he was a baby waiting to be born.

Gloria Skurzynski, from "Nethergrave"

BEFORE YOU READ
A Sound of Thunder

Meet the Author: Ray Bradbury

Ray Bradbury was born in 1920 in Waukegan, Illinois. For almost sixty years, he has been a leading writer of science fiction. His works have been so widely read that they have influenced popular culture. For example, *Apollo* astronauts named a moon crater Dandelion Crater, for Bradbury's book *Dandelion Wine*. Elton John based his song "Rocket Man" on Bradbury's story of the same name. Bradbury's book *Fahrenheit 451* inspired the title of Michael Moore's film *Fahrenheit 9/11*. Bradbury's book is set in a future society where reading is forbidden and fire fighters burn books. (Paper burns at 451° F.) On the subject, Bradbury has said: "There are worse crimes than burning books. One of them is not reading them."

Build Background: Time Travel

Time travel has been a theme of science fiction since 1895 when H. G. Wells first published *The Time Machine*. In that work, an amateur inventor, known only as "The Time Traveler," builds a time machine that takes him far into the future, to the year 802,701 a.d. Since Wells wrote his now-famous book, the idea of time travel—to both the past and future—has captured the popular imagination.

Time travel into the past introduces the mind-boggling possibility of interfering with the past in a way that would alter the present—and in so doing creating an entirely different world.

- If you could travel through time, would you do it? Why or why not?

- Which do you think is more intriguing—time travel to the future or time travel to the past? Why?

A Sound of Thunder

RAY BRADBURY

A SOUND OF THUNDER

Ray Bradbury

The sign on the wall seemed to quaver under a film of sliding warm water. Eckels felt his eyelids blink over his stare, and the sign burned in this momentary darkness:

> TIME SAFARI, INC.
> SAFARIS TO ANY YEAR IN THE PAST.
> YOU NAME THE ANIMAL.
> WE TAKE YOU THERE.
> YOU SHOOT IT.

A warm **phlegm** gathered in Eckels' throat; he swallowed and pushed it down. The muscles around his mouth formed a smile as he put his hand slowly out upon the air, and in that hand waved a check for ten thousand dollars to the man behind the desk.

"Does this safari guarantee I come back alive?"

"We guarantee nothing," said the official, "except the dinosaurs." He turned. "This is Mr. Travis, your Safari Guide in the Past. He'll tell you what and where to shoot. If he says no shooting, no shooting. If you disobey instructions, there's a stiff penalty of another ten thousand dollars, plus possible government action, on your return."

Eckels glanced across the vast office at a mass and tangle, a snaking and humming of wires and steel boxes, at an **aurora** that flickered now orange, now silver, now blue. There was a sound like a gigantic bonfire burning all of Time, all the years and all the parchment calendars, all the hours piled high and set aflame.

A touch of the hand and this burning would, on the instant, beautifully reverse itself. Eckels remembered the wording in the advertisements to the letter. Out of **chars** and ashes, out of dust and coals, like golden salamanders, the old years, the green years, might leap; roses sweeten the air, white hair turn Irish-black, wrinkles vanish; all, everything fly back to seed, flee death, rush down to their beginnings, suns rise in western skies and set in glorious easts, moons eat themselves opposite to the custom, all and everything cupping one

phlegm
mucus in breathing passages

aurora
a glow or display of light

chars
matter blackened by burning

in another like Chinese boxes, rabbits into hats, all and everything returning to the fresh death, the seed death, the green death, to the time before the beginning. A touch of a hand might do it, the merest touch of a hand.

"Unbelievable." Eckels breathed, the light of the Machine on his thin face. "A real Time Machine." He shook his head. "Makes you think. If the election had gone badly yesterday, I might be here now running away from the results. Thank God Keith won. He'll make a fine President of the United States."

"Yes," said the man behind the desk. "We're lucky. If Deutscher had gotten in, we'd have the worst kind of dictatorship. There's an anti-everything man for you, a militarist, anti-Christ, anti-human, anti-intellectual. People called us up, you know, joking but not joking. Said if Deutscher became President, they wanted to go live in 1492. Of course it's not our business to conduct escapes, but to form safaris. Anyway, Keith's President now. All you got to worry about is—"

"Shooting my dinosaur," Eckels finished it for him.

"A *Tyrannosaurus rex*. The Tyrant Lizard, the most incredible monster in history. Sign this release. Anything happens to you, we're not responsible. Those dinosaurs are hungry."

Eckels flushed angrily. "Trying to scare me!"

"*W*e're here to give you the severest thrill a *real* hunter ever asked for. Traveling you back sixty million years to bag the biggest game ever in all of Time . . . ."

"Frankly, yes. We don't want anyone going who'll panic at the first shot. Six Safari leaders were killed last year, and a dozen hunters. We're here to give you the severest thrill a *real* hunter ever asked for. Traveling you back sixty million years to bag the biggest game in all of Time. Your personal check's still there. Tear it up."

Mr. Eckels looked at the check. His fingers twitched.

"Good luck," said the man behind the desk. "Mr. Travis, he's all yours."

They moved silently across the room, taking their guns with them, toward the Machine, toward the silver metal and the roaring light.

First a day and then a night and then a day and then a night, then it was day-night-day-night-day. A week, a month, a year, a decade! A.D. 2055. A.D. 2019. 1999! 1957! Gone! The Machine roared.

They put on their oxygen helmets and tested the intercoms.

Eckels swayed on the padded seat, his face pale, his jaw stiff. He felt the trembling in his arms, and he looked down and found his hands tight on the new rifle. There were four other men in the Machine. Travis, the Safari Leader; his assistant, Lesperance; and two other hunters, Billings and Kramer. They sat looking at each other, and the years blazed around them.

"Can these guns get a dinosaur cold?" Eckels felt his mouth saying.

"If you hit them right," said Travis on the helmet radio. "Some dinosaurs have two brains, one in the head, another far down the spinal column. We stay away from those. That's stretching luck. Put your first two shots into the eyes, if you can, blind them, and go back into the brain."

The Machine howled. Time was a film run backwards. Suns fled and ten million moons fled after them. "Think," said Eckels. "Every hunter that ever lived would envy us today. This makes Africa seem like Illinois."

The Machine slowed; its scream fell to a murmur. The Machine stopped.

The sun stopped in the sky.

The fog that had enveloped the Machine blew away, and they were in an old time, a very old time indeed, three hunters and two Safari Heads with their blue metal guns across their knees.

"Christ isn't born yet," said Travis. "Moses has not gone to the mountain to talk with God. The Pyramids are still in the earth, waiting to be cut out and put up. *Remember* that. Alexander, Caesar, Napoleon, Hitler—none of them exists."

The man nodded.

"That"—Mr. Travis pointed— "is the jungle of sixty million, two thousand and fifty-five years before President Keith."

He indicated a metal path that struck off into green wilderness, over streaming swamp, among giant ferns and palms.

"And that," he said, "is the Path, laid by Time Safari for your use. It floats six inches above the earth. Doesn't touch so much as one grass blade, flower, or tree. It's an anti-gravity metal. Its purpose is to keep you from touching this world of the past in any way. Stay on the Path. Don't go off it. I repeat. *Don't go off.* For *any* reason! If you fall off, there's a penalty. And don't shoot any animal we don't okay."

> "Stay on the Path. Don't go off it. I repeat. *Don't go off.* For *any* reason! If you fall off, there's a penalty. And don't shoot any animal we don't okay."

"Why?" asked Eckels.

They sat in the ancient wilderness. Far birds' cries blew on a wind, and the smell of tar and old salt sea, moist grasses, and flowers the color of blood.

"We don't want to change the Future. We don't belong here in the Past. The government doesn't *like* us here. We have to pay big **graft** to keep our **franchise**. A Time Machine is finicky business. Not knowing it, we might kill an important animal, a small bird, a roach, a flower even, thus destroying an important link in a growing species."

graft
illegal or questionable contributions; bribes

franchise
a special right or priviledge

"That's not clear," said Eckels.

"All right," Travis continued, "say we accidentally kill one mouse here. That means all the future families of this one particular mouse are destroyed, right?"

"Right."

"And all the families of the families of the families of that one mouse! With a stamp of your foot, you annihilate first one, then a dozen, then a thousand, a million, a *billion* possible mice!"

"So they're dead," said Eckels. "So what?"

"So what?" Travis snorted quietly. "Well, what about the foxes that'll need those mice to survive? For want of ten mice, a fox dies. For want of ten foxes, a lion starves. For want of a lion, all manner of insects, vultures, infinite billions of life forms are thrown into chaos and destruction. Eventually it all boils down to this: fifty-nine million years later, a caveman, one of a dozen in the *entire world*, goes hunting wild boar or saber-toothed tiger for food. But you, friend, have *stepped* on all the tigers in that region. By stepping on *one* single mouse. So the caveman starves. And the caveman, please note, is not just *any* expendable man, no! He is an *entire future nation.* From his loins would have sprung ten sons. From *their* loins one hundred sons, and thus onward to a civilization. Destroy this one man, and you destroy a race, a people, an entire history of life. It is comparable to slaying some of Adam's grandchildren. The stomp of your foot, on one mouse, could start an earthquake, the effects of which could shake our earth and destinies down through Time to their very foundations. With the death of that one caveman, a billion others unborn are throttled in the womb. Perhaps Rome never rises on its seven hills. Perhaps Europe is forever a dark forest, and only Asia waxes healthy and teeming. Step on a mouse, and you crush the pyramids. Step on a mouse, and you leave your print, like a Grand Canyon, across Eternity. Queen Elizabeth might never be born, Washington might not cross the Delaware, there might never be a United States at all. So be careful. Stay on the Path. *Never* step off!"

"I see," said Eckels. "Then it wouldn't pay for us even to touch the *grass*?"

infinitesimally
in an extremely small way

"Correct. Crushing certain plants could add up **infinitesimally**. A little error here could multiply in sixty million years, all out of proportion. Of course, maybe our theory is wrong. Maybe time *can't* be changed by us. Or maybe it can be changed only in little, subtle ways. A dead mouse here makes an insect imbalance there, a population disproportion later, a bad harvest further on, a depression, mass starvation, and, finally, a change in *social*

temperament
one's nature or personality

temperament in far-flung countries. Something much more subtle, like that. Perhaps only a soft breath, a whisper, a hair, pollen on the air, such a slight, *slight* change that unless you looked close you wouldn't see it. Who knows? Who really can say he knows? We don't know. We're guessing. But until we do know for certain whether our messing around in Time *can* make a big roar or a little rustle in history, we're being careful. This Machine, this Path, our clothing and bodies, were sterilized, as you know, before the journey. We wear these oxygen helmets so we can't introduce our bacteria into an ancient atmosphere."

"How do we know which animals to shoot?"

"They're marked with red paint," said Travis. "Today, before our journey, we sent Lesperance here back with the Machine. He came to this particular era and followed certain animals."

"Studying them?"

"Right," said Lesperance. "I track them through their entire existence, noting which of them lives longest. Very few. How many times they mate. Not often. Life's short. When I find one that's going to die when a tree falls on him, or one that drowns in a tar pit, I note the exact hour, minute, and second. I shoot a paint bomb. It leaves a red patch on his side. We can't miss it. Then I correlate our arrival in the Past so that we meet the Monster not more than two minutes before he would have died anyway. This way, we kill only animals with no future, that are never going to mate again. You see how *careful* we are?"

"But if you came back this morning in Time," said Eckels eagerly, "you must've bumped into *us*, our Safari! How did it turn out? Was it successful? Did all of us get through—alive?"

Travis and Lesperance gave each other a look.

"That'd be a **paradox**," said the latter. "Time doesn't permit that sort of mess—a man meeting himself. When such occasions threaten, Time steps aside. Like an airplane hitting an air pocket. You felt the Machine jump just before we stopped? That was us passing ourselves on the way back to the Future. We saw nothing. There's no way of telling *if* this expedition was a success, *if* we got our monster, or whether all of us—meaning *you*, Mr. Eckels—got out alive."

Eckels smiled palely.

"Cut that," said Travis sharply. "Everyone on his feet!"

They were ready to leave the Machine.

The jungle was high and the jungle was broad and the jungle was the entire world forever and forever. Sounds like music and sounds like flying tents filled the sky, and those were pterodactyls soaring with **cavernous** gray wings, gigantic bats of **delirium** and night fever. Eckels, balanced on the narrow Path, aimed his rifle playfully.

"Stop that!" said Travis. "Don't even aim for fun, blast you! If your gun should go off—"

Eckels flushed. "Where's our *Tyrannosaurus*?"

paradox
a statement that contradicts itself

cavernous
cave-like

delirium
crazed thoughts or mental confusion

Lesperance checked his wrist watch. "Up ahead. We'll bisect his trail in sixty seconds. Look for the red paint! Don't shoot till we give the word. Stay on the Path. *Stay on the Path!*"

They moved forward in the wind of morning.

"Strange," murmured Eckels. "Up ahead, sixty million years, Election Day over. Keith made President. Everyone celebrating. And here we are, a million years lost, and they don't exist. The things we worried about for months, a lifetime, not even born or thought of yet."

"Safety catches off, everyone!" ordered Travis. "You, first shot, Eckels. Second, Billings. Third, Kramer."

"I've hunted tiger, wild boar, buffalo, elephant, but now, this is *it*," said Eckels. "I'm shaking like a kid."

"Ah," said Travis.

Everyone stopped.

Travis raised his hand. "Ahead," he whispered. "In the mist. There he is. There's His Royal Majesty now."

The jungle was wide and full of twitterings, rustlings, murmurs, and sighs.

Suddenly it all ceased, as if someone had shut a door.

Silence.

A sound of thunder.

Out of the mist, one hundred yards away, came *Tyrannosaurus rex.*

"It," whispered Eckels. "It . . . "

"Sh!"

resilient
capable of withstanding shock

piston
a machine part that moves up and down

mail
armor made of metal links or plates

It came on great oiled, **resilient**, striding legs. It towered thirty feet above half of the trees, a great evil god, folding its delicate watchmaker's claws close to its oily, reptilian chest. Each lower leg was a **piston**, a thousand pounds of white bone, sunk in thick ropes of muscle, sheathed over in a gleam of pebbled skin like the **mail** of a terrible warrior. Each thigh was a ton of meat, ivory, and steel mesh. And from the great breathing cage of the upper body those two delicate arms dangled out front, arms with hands which might pick up and examine men like toys, while the snake neck coiled. And the head itself, a ton of sculptured stone, lifted easily upon the sky. Its mouth gaped, exposing a fence of teeth like daggers. Its eyes rolled, ostrich eggs, empty of all expression save hunger. It closed its mouth in a death grin. It ran, its pelvic bones crushing aside trees and bushes, its taloned feet clawing damp earth, leaving prints six inches deep wherever it settled its weight. It ran with a gliding ballet step, far too poised and balanced for its ten tons. It moved into a sunlit arena warily, its beautifully reptilian hands feeling the air.

"Why, why," Eckels twitched his mouth. "It could reach up and grab the moon."

"Sh!" Travis jerked angrily. "He hasn't seen us yet."

"It can't be killed." Eckels pronounced this verdict quietly, as if there could be no argument. He had weighed the evidence and this was his considered opinion. The rifle in his hands seemed a cap gun. "We were fools to come. This is impossible."

"Shut up!" hissed Travis.

"Nightmare."

"Turn around," commanded Travis. "Walk quietly to the Machine. We'll remit one half your fee."

"I didn't realize it would be this *big*," said Eckels. "I miscalculated, that's all. And now I want out."

"It *sees* us!"

"There's the red paint on its chest!"

The Tyrant Lizard raised itself. Its armored flesh glittered like a thousand green coins. The coins, crusted with slime, steamed. In the slime, tiny insects wriggled, so that the entire body seemed to twitch and **undulate,** even while the monster itself did not move. It exhaled. The stink of raw flesh blew down the wilderness.

undulate
move in waves

"Get me out of here," said Eckels. "It was never like this before. I was always sure I'd come through alive. I had good guides, good safaris, and safety. This time, I figured wrong. I've met my match and admit it. This is too much for me to get hold of."

"Don't run," said Lesperance. "Turn around. Hide in the Machine."

"Yes." Eckels seemed to be numb. He looked at his feet as if trying to make them move. He gave a grunt of helplessness.

"Eckels!"

He took a few steps, blinking, shuffling.

"Not *that* way!"

The Monster, at the first motion, lunged forward with a terrible scream. It covered one hundred yards in six seconds. The rifles jerked up and blazed fire. A windstorm from the beast's mouth engulfed them in the stench of slime and old blood. The Monster roared, teeth glittering with sun.

A Sound of Thunder

Eckels, not looking back, walked blindly to the edge of the Path, his gun limp in his arms, stepped off the Path and walked, not knowing it, in the jungle. His feet sank into green moss. His legs moved him, and he felt alone and remote from the events behind.

The rifles cracked again. Their sound was lost in shriek and lizard thunder. The great level of the reptile's tail swung up, lashed sideways. Trees exploded in clouds of leaf and branch. The Monster twitched its jeweler's hands down to fondle at the men, to twist them in half, to crush them like berries, to cram them into its teeth and its screaming throat. Its boulder-stone eyes leveled with the men. They saw themselves mirrored. They fired at the metallic eyelids and blazing black iris.

Like a stone idol, like a mountain avalanche, *Tyrannosaurus* fell. Thundering, it clutched trees, pulled them with it. It wrenched and tore the metal Path. The men flung themselves back and away. The body hit, ten tons of cold flesh and stone. The guns fired. The Monster lashed its armored tail, twitched its snake jaws and lay still. A fount of blood spurted from its throat. Somewhere inside, a sac of fluid burst. Sickening gushes drenched the hunters. They stood, red and glistening.

The thunder faded.

The jungle was silent. After the avalanche, a green peace. After the nightmare, morning.

Billings and Kramer sat on the pathway and threw up. Travis and Lesperance stood with smoking rifles, cursing steadily.

In the Time Machine, on his face, Eckels lay shivering. He had found his way back to the Path, climbed into the Machine.

Travis came walking, glanced at Eckels, took cotton gauze from a metal box and returned to the others, who were sitting on the Path.

"Clean up."

They wiped the blood from their helmets. They began to curse too. The Monster lay, a hill of solid flesh. Within, you could hear the sighs and murmurs as the farthest chambers of it died, the organs malfunctioning, liquids running a final instant from pocket to sac to spleen, everything shutting off, closing up forever. It was like standing by a wrecked locomotive or a steam shovel at quitting time, all valves being released or levered tight. Bones cracked; the tonnage of its own flesh, off balance, dead weight, snapped the delicate forearms, caught underneath. The meat settled, quivering.

Another cracking sound. Overhead, a gigantic tree branch broke from its heavy mooring, fell. It crashed upon the dead beast with finality.

"There." Lesperance checked his watch. "Right on time. That's the giant tree that was scheduled to fall and kill this animal originally." He glanced at the two hunters. "You want the trophy picture?"

"What?"

"We can't take a trophy back to the Future. The body has to stay right where it would have died originally, so the insects, birds, and bacteria can get at it, as they were intended to. Everything in balance. The body stays. But we *can* take a picture of you standing near it."

"*This fool nearly killed us. But it isn't *that* so much, no. It's his *shoes*! Look at them! He ran off the Path. That *ruins* us!"*

The two men tried to think, but gave up, shaking their heads.

They let themselves be led along the metal Path. They sank wearily into the Machine cushions. They gazed back at the ruined Monster, the stagnating mound, where already strange reptilian birds and golden insects were busy at the steaming armor.

A sound on the floor of the Time Machine stiffened them. Eckels sat there, shivering.

"I'm sorry," he said at last.

"Get up!" cried Travis.

Eckels got up.

"Go out on that Path alone," said Travis. He had his rifle pointed. "You're not coming back in the Machine. We're leaving you here!"

Lesperance seized Travis's arm. "Wait—"

"Stay out of this!" Travis shook his hand away. "This fool nearly killed us. But it isn't *that* so much, no. It's his *shoes*! Look at them! He ran off the Path. That *ruins* us! We'll forfeit! Thousands of dollars of insurance! We guarantee no one leaves the Path. He left it. Oh, the fool! I'll have to report to the government. They might revoke our license to travel. Who know *what* he's done to Time, to History!"

"Take it easy, all he did was kick up some dirt."

"How do we *know*?" cried Travis. "We don't know anything! It's all a mystery! Get out here, Eckels!"

Eckels fumbled his shirt. "I'll pay anything. A hundred thousand dollars!"

Travis glared at Eckels's checkbook and spat. "Go out there. The Monster's next to the Path. Stick your arms up to your elbows in his mouth. Then you can come back with us."

"That's unreasonable!"

"The Monster's dead, you idiot. The bullets! The bullets can't be left behind. They don't belong in the Past; they might change anything. Here's my knife. Dig them out!"

The jungle was alive again, full of the old tremorings and bird cries. Eckels turned slowly to regard the primeval garbage dump, that hill of nightmares and terror. After a long time, like a sleepwalker he shuffled out along the Path.

He returned, shuddering, five minutes later, his arms soaked and red to the elbow. He held out his hands. Each held a number of steel bullets. Then he fell. He lay where he fell, not moving.

"You didn't have to make him do that," said Lesperance.

"Didn't I? It's too early to tell." Travis nudged the still body. "He'll live. Next time he won't go hunting game like this. Okay." He jerked his thumb wearily at Lesperance. "Switch on. Let's go home."

1492. 1776. 1812.

They cleaned their hands and faces. They changed their caking shirts and pants. Eckels was up and around again, not speaking. Travis glared at him for a full ten minutes.

"Don't look at me," cried Eckels. "I haven't done anything."

"Who can tell?"

"Just ran off the Path, that's all, a little mud on my shoes—what do you want me to do, get down and pray?"

"We might need it. I'm warning you, Eckels, I might kill you yet. I've got my gun ready."

"I'm innocent. I've done nothing."

1999. 2000. 2055.

The Machine stopped.

"Get out," said Travis.

The room was there as they had left it. But not the same as they had left it. The same man sat behind the same desk. But the same man did not quite sit behind the same desk.

Travis looked around swiftly. "Everything okay here?" he snapped.

"Fine. Welcome home!"

Travis did not relax. He seemed to be looking at the very atoms of the air itself, at the way the sun poured through the one high window.

"Okay, Eckels, get out. Don't ever come back."

Eckels could not move.

"You heard me," said Travis. "What're you *staring* at?"

Eckels stood smelling the air, and there was a thing to the air, a chemical **taint** so subtle, so slight, that only a faint cry of his **subliminal** senses warned him it was there. The colors, white, gray, blue, orange, in the wall, in the furniture, in the sky beyond the window, were . . . were . . . And there was a *feel*. His flesh twitched. His hands twitched. He stood drinking the oddness with the pores of his body. Somewhere, someone must have been screaming one of those whistles that only a dog can hear. His body screamed silence in return. Beyond this room, beyond this wall, beyond this man who was not quite the same man seated at this desk . . . lay an entire world of streets and people. What sort of world it was now, there was no telling. He could feel them moving there, beyond the walls, almost, like so many chess pieces blown in a dry wind. . . .

But the immediate thing was the sign painted on the office wall, the same sign he had read earlier today on first entering.

Somehow, the sign had changed:

> TYME SEFARI INC.
> SEFARIS TU ANY YEER EN THE PAST.
> YU NAIM THE ANIMALL.
> WEE TAEKYUTHAIR.
> YU SHOOT ITT.

Eckels felt himself fall into the chair. He fumbled crazily at the thick slime on his boots. He held up a clod of dirt, trembling. "No, it *can't* be. Not a *little* thing like that. No!"

Embedded in the mud, glistening green and gold and black, was a butterfly, very beautiful and very dead.

"Not a little thing like *that*! Not a butterfly!" cried Eckels.

It fell to the floor, an exquisite thing, a small thing that could upset balances and knock down a line of small dominoes and then big dominoes and then gigantic dominoes, all down the years across Time. Eckels' mind whirled. It *couldn't* change things. Killing one butterfly couldn't be *that* important! Could it?

taint
contaminating mark or influence

subliminal
below the threshold of consciousness

A Sound of Thunder   299

His face was cold. His mouth trembled, asking: "Who—Who won the presidential election yesterday?"

The man behind the desk laughed. "You joking? You know very well. Deutscher, of course! Who else? Not that fool weakling Keith. We got an iron man now, a man with guts!" The official stopped. "What's wrong?"

Eckels moaned. He dropped onto his knees. He **scrabbled** at the golden butterfly with shaking fingers. "Can't we," he pleaded to the world, to himself, to the officials, to the Machine, "can't we take it *back*, can't we *make* it alive again? Can't we start over? Can't we—"

He did not move. Eyes shut, he waited, shivering. He heard Travis breathe loud in the room; he heard Travis shift his rifle, click the safety catch and raise the weapon.

There was a sound of thunder.

BUTTERFLY: *Papilio Ulysses*, Edward Donovank, 1800

AFTER YOU READ
A Sound of Thunder

Think and Discuss

1. Is the sound of thunder at the end of the story caused by the same thing as the sound of thunder earlier? Explain.

2. Use a chart like the one below to analyze how things in the office are different when the Time Safari returns to the present. Think about the changes. How would you characterize the differences caused by the death of the butterfly?

Before the Safari	After the Safari

3. Think about the **character** of Eckels. Does Bradbury present him in a sympathetic way or an unsympathetic way? Support your answer with evidence from the text.

4. Bradbury uses both **similes** and **metaphors** in his description of time travel, of the prehistoric jungle, and of *Tyrannosaurus rex*. Review the text and select a simile or metaphor that you find particularly effective. Tell why. (For a definition of *simile* and *metaphor*, see the Glossary of Literary Terms.)

5. "A Sound of Thunder" was written in 1952, just seven years after the end of World War II. In that war the United States and its allies fought against Japan and Germany, which was ruled by the dictator Adolf Hitler. What details does Ray Bradbury include in the story—for example, the name Deutscher, which means "German"—that might be a reference to the war and its causes?

6. In today's world, loss of habitat and climate change are causing species to die out faster than the natural rate. If "a little error here could multiply in sixty million years, all out of proportion," what impact might the loss of species have on the future? Use a specific example, such as the polar bear, to explain your answer.

Write to Understand: Focused Freewriting

Review the chart you created to compare the Time Safari office at the beginning of the story and at the end—before and after Eckels' ill-fated trip back in time. Think about the nature of the changes in that place. Then imagine what the characters might discover when they left the Time Safari office and returned to their homes. Start writing your ideas about what might be different because of the "butterfly effect." Write everything you can think of and keep writing for at least 10 minutes—longer if you keep getting more ideas.

BEFORE YOU READ

Nolan Bushnell

All Watched Over by Machines of Loving Grace

Meet the Authors

David E. Brown   A freelance writer and editor, David E. Brown lives and works in Brooklyn, New York. His writing concentrates on the fields of design, architecture, and science, and he is especially interested in situations where these fields intersect. This selection about Nolan Bushnell comes from his book *Inventing Modern America: From the Microwave to the Mouse*, which profiles thirty-five inventors and tells the sometimes surprising stories of how familiar objects and technologies came to be.

Richard Brautigan   Born in 1935, Richard Brautigan wrote a number of novels, including the best-selling *Trout Fishing in America*. He began writing poetry when he was a teenager and once said he wrote poetry for seven years to learn how to write a sentence. Brautigan died in 1984.

Build Background: Video Games

Most children have had some experience with video games and the virtual worlds they create. But what is the effect on the real world of spending time in these virtual worlds? Proponents say video games stimulate the brain, promote learning and problem solving, and help develop fine motor skills and coordination. Opponents warn that too much video playing can lead to poor social skills; time away from family, school work, and hobbies; lower grades and less reading; weight problems resulting from lack of exercise; and aggressive thoughts and behavior.

The selection that follows is about the man who started the video game phenomenon more than thirty years ago. As you read, think about these questions:

- In your opinion, why are video games so popular?

- What do *you* get out of them?

Atari founder, Nolan Bushnell

Nolan Bushnell

DAVID E. BROWN

NOLAN BUSHNELL

David E. Brown

In just three decades, video games have taken a prominent and permanent place in American culture. They have more than a hundred million fans, have **spawned** dozens of magazines, and have even captured the attention (and disapproval) of the U.S. Senate. The demands made by games have been responsible for many improvements in computer technology, advances that have led to higher graphics and speed capabilities in today's personal computers.

The more than $6 billion Americans now spend on video games every year started with the first quarter dropped into Computer Space in 1971. That game—a small computer hooked up to a black-and-white TV, housed in a futuristic-looking plastic case—was the creation of Nolan Bushnell, a young engineer from Utah. Bushnell went on to found Atari, whose products, from Pong to Football to the Atari 2600, brought video games into every arcade and millions of homes. And while Computer Space was based on the already-classic spaceship battle game called Spacewar, it was Bushnell's genius to see the potential games had beyond the computer lab.

"I've always been a tinkerer," Bushnell says. As a teenager, he was one of the youngest ham radio operators in the country, and he did science experiments in his garage. At least one of those went awry: A liquid-fuel rocket attached to a roller skate crashed into the back of his garage, igniting a bright but short-lived fireball. Rockets were a side interest, though. "I loved electronics from an early age," Bushnell remembers. "But I was also always a game player." He was a tournament chess player, and a fan of the Chinese board game Go. (Atari is a Japanese word announced when a Go player has almost captured an opponent.) He also learned about business when he was young. After his father died, Bushnell took over the family's concrete business. He was just 15.

Bushnell discovered computer games in the early 1960s while studying electrical engineering at the University of Utah. The school's computer had a copy of Spacewar, the **seminal** game created at MIT[1] by Steve Russell. Two starships circling a sun battled each other and the star's gravity, firing "torpedoes" and occasionally resorting to "hyperspace" to jump out of, and sometimes into, trouble. (Hyperspace would reappear in 1978 in Atari's Asteroids game.) Spacewar was immensely popular among computer scientists and students, and was soon being played on computers around the world. The visionary computer designer Alan Kay once declared, "The game of Spacewar blossoms spontaneously wherever there is a graphics display connected to a computer." Bushnell was hooked and he would sneak into the computer lab late at night to play.

seminal
strongly influencing later developments

During his college summers Bushnell managed the arcade at a local amusement park, where he saw how eager people were to play games. It was this experience that gave Bushnell his big idea. "It was very easy for me to see that if I could put a quarter slot on [Spacewar] and put it in the amusement park, I'd make money. It wasn't really a huge Aha!"

> "It was very easy for me to see that if I could put a quarter slot on [Spacewar] and put it in the amusement park, I'd make money."

he says. But Spacewar ran on huge, expensive computers. "You'd divide 25 cents into a $7 million computer, and you'd see, gee, this doesn't work," he continues. "But in the back of your mind, you'd say, If I can build it cheap enough it will work. And one day the costs came in such that I thought that it was possible."

By 1971, Bushnell had moved to Silicon Valley and had begun to work on his game. He took over one of his daughters' rooms and built from scratch the circuits that would run his own version of Spacewar, which he called Computer Space. The biggest technical challenge was the display. The computers that ran Spacewar used what were essentially adapted radar screens, each of which cost about $30,000. So Bushnell made circuits that would display graphics on an ordinary black-and-white television set. At his kitchen table he sculpted a scale model of Computer Space's curvy, futuristic case out of clay. (The game looked so distinctive that it was used as a prop in the 1973 sci-fi movie *Soylent Green*.)

I **MIT:** Massachusett's Institute of Technology

Computer Space was licensed to a company called Nutting Associates, which built about 1,500 of the machines. The game was a moderate success, but not a runaway hit; many people thought it was too complicated. Bushnell had a different complaint about its manufacturer. "Nutting Associates was an extremely incompetent company," he says. "I've often thought that that was a huge blessing because it was clear that these guys were succeeding in spite of being really stupid. There's nothing like being around that to embolden yourself."

> *P*eople lined up to feed quarters into Pong, and played it nonstop.

Bushnell began designing other games and he hired a staff of engineers. In 1972, Bally, a company that made pinball and slot machines, contracted him to make a video driving game. He gave the task to one of his new hires, Al Alcorn. But Alcorn didn't yet know the tricks of making a video game, so Bushnell gave him a smaller task to make a game with a ball bouncing back and forth on the screen. (Bushnell had seen a similar game demonstrated that year as part of the Odyssey home video game, designed by Ralph Baer and marketed by Magnavox.) "I defined this very simple game for Alcorn as a learning project," he explains. "I thought it was going to be a throwaway. It took him less than a week to get it partially running. And the thing was just incredibly fun."

Bushnell took a copy of Alcorn's game, named Pong after one of its noises, to Bally's headquarters in Chicago, hoping that they would buy it instead of the driving game. At the same time, Alcorn built a case for their other copy of Pong, complete with a 13-inch TV set and a slot for quarters. There was one sentence of instruction on the cabinet. "Avoid Missing Ball for High Score." Alcorn set Pong up at a bar in Sunnyvale, California.

In Chicago, Bally's turned Pong down. Back in California, the reaction was different. People lined up to feed quarters into Pong, and played it nonstop. The next day, the machine suddenly stopped working; Alcorn went to see what was wrong and discovered that the machine was too full of quarters—they'd spilled out of their container and shorted the game out. Pong, released by Atari rather than Bally's, became a hit and ushered in the first golden age of video games. Rich from Pong's success, the company designed dozens of successful games: first, variations on Pong and later, hits like Atari Football, the driving games Night Driver and Sprint, and, in 1978, the best-selling Asteroids. Bushnell also helped usher in a new era in Silicon Valley. Although the area (which extends from Palo Alto to San Jose) had long been a center for the electronics industry, most of the companies there were large and

In 1975, Atari introduced a version of Pong for the home, which quickly sold hundreds of thousands of copies and spawned dozens of imitators.

corporate. Atari was different. Bushnell always wore jeans, and encouraged his engineers and technicians to do the same. His management style was not very rigid or **hierarchical**; as long as someone got his or her job done, almost anything went. These principles were proved in 1976, when Bushnell hired a young technician named Steve Jobs. The long-haired Jobs would often work barefoot, talked of going to India, and was **abrasive** to some of the other engineers. Bushnell gave Jobs the task of designing a game he had thought of, a new variation on Pong called Breakout. Jobs worked the night shift, and with lots of technical help from his friend Steve Wozniak, built Breakout on a very short schedule. The two would continue their collaboration that year by building and marketing the Apple computer.

hierarchical arranged by rank

abrasive rough; harsh

In 1975, Atari introduced a version of Pong for the home, which quickly sold hundreds of thousands of copies and spawned dozens of imitators. Two years later the company introduced the Video Computer System, also known as the Atari 2600. This was the first successful home system that used interchangeable cartridges, so players could enjoy dozens (and eventually hundreds) of different games. More than 25 million systems were sold, and the system-and-cartridge idea has been adapted by Nintendo, Sega, and Sony. "That's something I'm really proud of," Bushnell says. "I set up the economic model, the software/hardware link that's been the pattern ever since. There wasn't anything out there like it."

Bushnell sold Atari in 1978 and left the company soon after that. He has launched several businesses since then, including the Chuck E. Cheese chain of video pizza parlors and, in the 1980s, Axlon, which made small robots for the home. He has now returned to his video game roots, running a company called uWink that is introducing a line of arcade games that will be linked up over the Internet. Bushnell envisions game tournaments with thousands of participants linked up around the country or the world.

Almost thirty years after that first arcade game, Bushnell remains excited about the promise of video games, as much for their effects on players as for their business opportunities. Just as Spacewar attracted him to the computer lab as a youth in Utah, today's games excite kids about technology, and even make them smarter. "I call them the training wheels of computer literacy," he says. "It's very clear that game playing grows **dendrites**. So people are smarter. The brain is something that if you exercise it you can be smarter. It turns out that games are that exercise."

dendrites
brain cells that serve as connectors and receive messages

PREHISTORY OF VIDEO GAMES

Late eighteenth century—Bagatelle, a miniature tabletop game related to billiards, becomes popular.

1871 A small version of bagatelle with a spring-loaded plunger becomes popular; it is the ancestor of the pinball machine.

1905 The first nickelodeon opens, in Pittsburgh. Customers can see a short movie by dropping a nickel in a machine's slot.

1931 The first coin-operated pinball machine is built.

1947 The pinball flipper is invented, ushering in the Golden Age of Pinball. The game is banned in New York City the following year.

1958 Willy Higinbotham, an engineer at Brookhaven National Laboratory on Long Island, New York, uses an analog computer to make a "ball" bounce back and forth across the screen of a small oscilloscope. He adds a "net," and the first computer tennis game is born. Visitors to the lab's open house line up for hours to play.

1961–1962 At MIT, Steve Russell and others create Spacewar on the university's PDP-1 computer. Copies of Spacewar wind up at universities around the country, draining countless hours of expensive computer time and inspiring a generation of programmers. The first gaming controls, the ancestors of the joystick, are built by Spacewar-playing MIT students.

Mid-1960s More games are written for the PDP-1 and other computers, including Lunar Lander, which simulates a moon landing; Hunt the Wumpus, a search-and-destroy mission; and ADVENT, the world's first adventure game.

1966–1967 Ralph Baer, a defense company engineer, builds a small computer and hooks it up to a TV set and makes two electronic dots chase each other across the screen. Within a year, he and some colleagues turn it into a system that plays Ping-Pong, football, and shooting games. When it's released as the Magnavox Odyssey in 1972, Baer's invention becomes the first home video game system.

POETRY CONNECTION

All Watched Over by Machines of Loving Grace

RICHARD BRAUTIGAN

I like to think (and
the sooner the better!)
of a **cybernetic** meadow
where mammals and computers
live together in mutually   5
programming harmony
like pure water
touching clear sky.

I like to think
(right now, please!)   10
of a cybernetic forest
filled with pines and electronics
where deer stroll peacefully
past computers
as if they were flowers   15
with spinning blossoms.

I like to think
(it has to be!)
of a cybernetic ecology
where we are free of our labors   20
and joined back to nature,
returned to our mammal
brothers and sisters,
and all watched over
by machines of loving grace.   25

cybernetic
having the
quality of
humans and
machines
combined

AFTER YOU READ

Nolan Bushnell
All Watched Over by Machines of Loving Grace

Think and Discuss

1. What did Nolan Bushnell see in the 1960s and early 1970s that others—even experts in the field—did not see?

2. In what ways might the computer game business be like a game itself?

3. Think of three or four words that describe Bushnell's personality. Find the **details** in the text that support each of those qualities.

4. Like most works of biography, this selection about Nolan Bushnell is told in **chronological order**. Use the facts from the selection to create a timeline to trace Bushnell's life from the time he discovered computer games in the 1960s until the end of the selection. In your Writer's Notebook, make a graphic organizer like the following as the basis for your timeline.

1960s	1970s	1980s	1990s	Since 2000

5. In the world Richard Brautigan creates in "All Watched Over by Machines of Loving Grace," what is the relationship between humans and machines?

6. Why are the graphics such an important part of video games? Explain how they affect the experience of playing the game.

Write to Understand: A Chronological Summary

The timeline you made organizes important events in Nolan Bushnell's career. Look back at the timeline called Prehistory of Video Games (page 309). It outlines inventions that led up to and set the stage for Bushnell's Computer Space. Study the timeline. Then use the information in it to write a few paragraphs summarizing what led up to Bushnell's efforts. Use your own words, and use smooth transitions so readers can follow the chronology.

BEFORE YOU READ
Nethergrave

Meet the Author: Gloria Skurzynski
Some authors spend their childhoods reading and know from a young age that they want
to be writers. For Gloria Skurzynski, who was born in 1930, things were different. She
grew up in a home where there were very few books, and she didn't know she wanted to
be a writer until she was a grown woman with five children. Once she got started, nothing
could stop her. So far, she has written more than forty books, both fiction and nonfiction.
She has written about the past, but what fascinates her most is imagining the future. "I only
wish I could live forever, so I could see how the future turns out."

Build Background: Science Fiction
Science fiction is sometimes thought of as fantasy set in the future. The difference between
fantasy and science fiction is what brings about the fantastic elements in the story. In
fantasy, the cause is magic. In science fiction, the role of magic is replaced by advanced
technology. One test of whether or not something is science fiction or fantasy is the role
science or technology plays in the story. Some think a work shouldn't be called science
fiction unless science or technology is critical to the plot.

   The story that follows is set in the present. It involves virtual reality—something we
can experience now with a personal computer and a mouse. The story is very realistic, yet
it is a work of science fiction.

- How can a realistic story set in the present be science fiction?

- Think about your own experiences with virtual reality. What is the appeal of
  experiencing things in a simulated environment?

Nethergrave

GLORIA SKURZYNSKI

NETHERGRAVE

Gloria Skurzynski

"*Beacon* Heights Academy Lets Boys Excel!"

What a dumb motto. Did it ever occur to the school administrators, when they collected the thousand-dollar-a-month tuition fee per student, that maybe a boy didn't *want* to excel? Jeremy wished the motto was "Beacon Heights Academy Lets Boys Alone."

Each term every student in the academy had to participate in at least one after-school activity: drama, debate, the science fair, or a sport. Even if the student didn't board at the expensive, exclusive boys' school, but lived in town and went home every day after classes. Like Jeremy.

Jeremy had chosen soccer. Not because he liked it; not because he was any good at it; but because the coach was so determined to field a winning team that Jeremy knew he'd never get played—never in a real game, and rarely even in practice.

Until today. It was the last week of the spring term, which meant that to fulfill the school's requirement, Jeremy would have to play for at least one minute. And this would be a real game: the Beacon Heights Bulldogs against a tough team from across the valley, the Midvale Marauders. All day long Jeremy had been wondering if he could fake stomach cramps or appendicitis, but the coach would never believe him. Jeremy might be a scared, skinny eighth-grade wimp, but he was a healthy one.

Didn't matter that he'd deliberately forgotten to bring his jersey and his shin guards to school. "Dig some out of the box," Coach barked. From the bottom of the smelly equipment box Jeremy pulled ratty shin guards and a sagging, much too large red jersey. When he ran out of the field house, a couple of his fellow eighth graders elbowed each other and snickered—maybe because of what Jeremy was wearing, but more likely because that was the way they usually reacted to him.

He sat on the bench so long his bony rump started to hurt. As the score seesawed—first the Beacon Heights Bulldogs were ahead, then the Midvale Marauders—Jeremy kept praying that the coach had forgotten about him. Not a chance. Coach was checking the list of boys from Beacon Heights, frowning at it, crossing off names with a pencil.

"Jeremy! You!" Coach barked. "Get out there. Replace the forward."

Shoulders hunched, Jeremy ran onto the field. Inside his head he was great at sports and games. On a computer he was unbeatable. He understood the geometry of basketball, baseball, football, and soccer, and he knew all the rules because he memorized things so easily. If only he'd had a reasonable amount of coordination, plus a little bit of muscle, he might have played soccer passably. But when Jeremy ran, his head and neck, arms and hands, legs and feet looked like a bunch of paper clips that had been shaken up in a bag: Hooked together haphazardly, they stuck out at all kinds of weird angles.

The coach blew his whistle. Jeremy stumbled forward, trying to get into the open so one of his teammates could pass him the ball. As if they would. All of them knew that a pass to Jeremy would mean losing the ball to the Midvale Marauders. Yet, there it was—the soccer ball—and it looked like it was coming right at him! He got a foot on it, lost it, and in the **mayhem** of other boys' arms and legs, noticed the ball rolling loose. Running after it, he started dribbling toward the goal.

mayhem
confusion; violence

Unbelievable! He was moving that soccer ball down the field and it appeared he might even kick a goal, his first in his whole two years at Beacon Heights. Concentrating, pumped with adrenaline, he didn't notice that his teammates weren't anywhere near him. No one was helping him, he had no protection, no chance to pass, but it didn't matter, because Jeremy was going to do it! Make a goal! He pulled his eyes off the ball just for a second, barely in time to notice that the goalie was—a Beacon Heights Bulldog! Frantically, the goalie waved his arms and shook his head, but not in time to stop Jeremy's foot, which had already begun its **trajectory** to kick the ball into the net. A perfect kick! Jeremy scored!—for the Midvale Marauders. He'd kicked a goal at the wrong end of the field, scoring a point for the opposing team.

trajectory
curved path through space

Coach looked ready to burst a blood vessel as he screamed at Jeremy to get off the field. The Marauders looked ready to bust a gut, punching one another in hilarity while they laughed themselves stupid. The Bulldogs—well, Jeremy knew what would be coming later from his teammates. He was used to it.

At school he was constantly getting tripped in the halls, in the aisles, on the gym floor, in the locker room. The other guys had raised tripping Jeremy to an art form. He figured that today, since he'd blown the game, he'd be

choreographed
arranged
or directed
movements, as in
a dance

in for a world-class tripping. He was right. In the locker room three of his teammates **choreographed** it perfectly: As one tripped him, another bumped Jeremy's left shoulder from behind, while a third boy, in front of him, shoved Jeremy's right shoulder, whipping him around to be pitched face down onto a bench.

"Jeremy, grab a towel and hold it under your nose," the coach bellowed in disgust. "You're getting blood all over the floor."

The bleeding stopped, but the swelling didn't. Afterward, walking home, Jeremy hung inside the late afternoon shadows so no one could notice him. He hoped his mother wouldn't get home until the swelling had gone down at least a bit. If she saw it, she'd just sigh and shake her head in that pitying way, wondering how she'd ever produced such an incompetent son. But his mother rarely got home before eight or nine at night. Usually she had dinner with a client.

Jeremy didn't have to worry about his father seeing his swollen nose, since his father never saw him at all. Once in a while Jeremy would find his father's picture in *Forbes* magazine[1] or in the business section of *U.S. News and World Report*,[2] which listed him as one of the computer industry's rich, triumphant successes. He owned a corporation that designed printed circuit boards. With Bill Gates[3] and Steve Wozniak and Steve Jobs,[4] Jeremy's father had been in the right place at the right time when the computer revolution took off.

Not once since his parents' divorce twelve years ago had Jeremy and his father come face-to-face. Like clockwork, though, every year on Jeremy's birthday a van would back up to the front door of his house. Two techno-brains would carry in a brand-new computer with the most powerful chip produced that particular year, with the greatest amount of memory, the fastest modem, and the biggest monitor screen. They'd install the new computer and transfer all Jeremy's previous programs onto its hard drive, then pack up last year's computer to haul it away.

---

1 *Forbes* **magazine:** a business magazine known for publishing lists of the biggest or most successful companies and the richest people

2 *U.S. News and World Report:* a weekly news magazine that covers national and world affairs and business trends

3 **Bill Gates:** the founder of Microsoft

4 **Steve Wozniak and Steve Jobs:** the founders of Apple Computers

Did his father actually *order* the world's best PC each year for Jeremy's birthday? Did he speak the words "I want a top-of-the-line personal computer system delivered to my son"? Or was it just a digital instruction, programmed to come up automatically on the screens of the two techno-brains? It didn't matter. Equipment like that would have made Jeremy the envy of his friends, if he'd had any.

He unlocked the front door. Even though he was hungry, he didn't open the refrigerator, because the clock showed 4:05. He was fifteen minutes late. He'd wasted too much time skulking in the shadows on the way home. Hurrying to his room, he threw his books onto his bed, dropped his jacket on the floor, and turned on his computer.

On the screen, he checked his contact list. The others were already online, their names highlighted in blue:

Hangman
PrincessDie[5]
Dr.Ded

When he clicked on his own online name, Xtermin8r, the screen split from three to four boxes in the chat module he shared with his online friends.

Hurrying to his room, he threw his books onto his bed, dropped his jacket on the floor, and turned on his computer.

"*You're late, X,*" Hangman typed, the words flowing into the right-hand box on top of the screen. *X* was what they called Jeremy, because *Xtermin8r* took too long to type.

"*Sorry,*" Jeremy typed back in his own box; he automatically got the one at top left.

"*We didn't do the jokes yet. We waited,*" PrincessDie typed.

"*So begin now.*" The words from Dr.Ded marched slowly across his quarter of the screen. He wasn't a very fast typist.

The four of them met online every day after school. They'd first come across one another in a music chat room dedicated to the Grateful Dead.[6] Eventually, after a couple of weeks of meeting in that much larger chat

---

5 **PrincessDie:** a play on Princess Di, a familiar name used for Diana, Princess of Wales, mother to Prince William and Prince Harry of Britain

6 **Grateful Dead:** a rock band formed in San Francisco in 1965, known for a style that fused elements of rock, folk music, bluegrass, country, blues, jazz, gospel, and psychedelic music

group, they'd decided to form their own module, limited to the four of them. Calling themselves the DeadHeads, they chose online names that had to do with death, and began every afternoon's chat session with "dead" jokes.

PrincessDie: *Okay, here goes. Question: What does a songwriter do after he dies? Answer: He de-composes.*

Hangman: *Good one. Here's mine. Question: What does a walking corpse call his parents? Answer: Mummy and Dead-y.*

Dr.Ded: *Ha ha. Q: How do you kill a vegetarian vampire? A: Put a steak through his heart.*

Hangman: *All right!!! Your turn, X.*

With all that had happened that day, Jeremy hadn't thought up a dead joke. He hesitated, then typed, "Q: What kind of pants do ghosts wear? A: Boo jeans."

Hangman: *Bad one, X.*

Dr. Ded: *Your joke stinks, X. It's from preschool. You better do better than that.*

PrincessDie: *Yeah—you better—do better—the Grateful Dead could have made a song out of that.*

Hangman: *Your penalty, X—find two excellent dead jokes for tomorrow. I mean excellent.*

Jeremy was the fastest typist in the group. His fingers flew across the keys as he entered, "*I apologize, guys. Today was a busy day for me. I played in a soccer tournament at school, and I kicked the winning goal. Everyone in the stands jumped up, and they were yelling my name and cheering—so cool! Then my mom and dad took me out for burgers and fries to celebrate. That's why I logged on late today. Even this morning I was too busy to look up dead jokes. In gym they announced I'm gonna be the captain of the wrestling team.*"

If his online friends only knew it, that was the biggest joke Jeremy could have possibly told them.

Now he typed even faster, trying to get it all in before the three other DeadHeads started up again. "*After they made me captain, the wrestling team guys poured a bottle of Evian water over my head. They said it should have been champagne, except we'd all get kicked out of school if they did that. So I was wet all over and I had to borrow a hair dryer from Miss Jepson—she's my French teacher and she's a real babe and she likes me—like more than just a regular student. I think she'd go out with me if I asked her.*"

He'd told his online friends he was a high school junior. They thought he was a star athlete and a student-body officer and a lot of other things Jeremy was careful to keep track of so he wouldn't forget what he'd told them. To keep his lies straight, he printed out each day's online chat and saved the hard copies in a three-ring binder.

Hangman: *Gotta go now.*

Jeremy typed, *"Already? I just got here."*

Hangman: *Gotta write a heavy-duty report for earth science.*

PrincessDie: *Me, too, gotta go. To meet a guy. Don't freak, Xtermin8r. I know you want to be my guy, but you're in Ohio and I'm in Oregon.*

In real life—IRL—Jeremy lived in Pasadena, California, but his father had been born in Ohio, so that's where he told his online friends he was from.

Dr.Ded: *I'm outta here too, guys. Gonna do some major surfing—the ocean kind. Surf's up too great to waste. Find you all tomorrow. Don't forget, X, you owe us two "good" jokes.*

On the screen, the names of his three friends turned green: The color change meant they'd gone offline. Then their boxes disappeared, leaving Jeremy's words alone on the screen.

It wasn't that they'd deserted him, he told himself. He'd been late—they'd probably chatted for quite a while before he got there. At least they hadn't done the dead jokes until he logged on. Why hadn't he come up with a better dead joke? Maybe they didn't like him today because he'd typed such a rotten joke. He felt himself sinking into his expensive padded office chair, weighed down as if he'd swallowed a heavy paving brick. His last words, "Already? I just got here," vibrated on the screen.

*M*ore words followed: *Click your middle mouse button, Jeremy. And turn on your microphone.*

He sighed. Might as well print out the day's chat and file it in his binder. His cursor was on its way to the "Print" command when his name appeared on the screen.

Jeremy, followed by a question mark. One of his online buddies must be back.

He typed, *"I'm here."*

More words followed: *Click your middle mouse button, Jeremy. And turn on your microphone.*

When he clicked the mouse, the screen exploded with color—swirling waves of such brilliant hue he raised his hand to shade his eyes. "Hey, what is this?" he asked out loud into the mike.

A man's voice, deep and mellow, answered through the audio system, "Welcome to Nethergrave, Jeremy."

On Jeremy's twenty-one-inch monitor screen, with its sixteen million colors, a whirling **vortex** appeared, so three-dimensional he felt he could dive into it. Never had he seen color this intense, or screen resolution so high. It was more vivid than an Imax theater movie.

He stared, unblinking, until it seemed he was being sucked inside the vortex. Wow! What fantastic imaging, he thought, but then he quit thinking so he could give himself entirely to the illusion of flying through the **whorls**. They rotated around him; he was a weightless body caught in a fast-spinning, kaleidoscopic tunnel. As he neared the end of the vortex he saw the face of a man growing larger and larger until it filled the screen.

A real face? Probably not. It looked more like a mask. The black eyebrows angled upward, too symmetrical to be natural. Beneath the cheekbones, green-tinged shadows formed triangles with the apex at the bottom, just touching the corners of the too-red, too-smiling mouth. Black hair peaked in the center of the man's forehead, then swept back as sleekly as if it were molded plastic.

"Who are you?" Jeremy asked.

His lips moving in not quite perfect **synchronization**, the man answered, "I'm NetherMagus. You've entered my **domain**."

Jeremy glanced at the Internet address on the top of his screen—http://nethergrave.xx/. He'd never heard of a domain extender called "dot xx," but then, new ones got added to the Internet every day.

The man—or the mask—continued, "Before you come any further into Nethergrave, Jeremy, select a **persona** for yourself. Your very own **avatar**. You can choose whoever you would most like to be. Or I should say, *whatever* you would most like to be."

One by one, images emerged on the screen, not simply masks like NetherMagus's, but full-body images: a unicorn; a princess wearing a tall, peaked cap with a filmy scarf wafting from it; a Roman soldier with a bronze breastplate; a falcon; a Medusa who had hair of writhing

---

vortex
something that resembles a whirlpool

whorls
things that whirl, coil, or spiral

synchronization
having sound happen at the same time as action

domain
territory

persona
the personality one projects in public

avatar
an electronic image that represents the computer user

snakes; a Japanese warrior, his samurai sword raised as if to strike; a hood shadowing his face so that no feature showed, only glowing eyes; a sinewy jaguar that loped gracefully, its muscles bunching beneath a sleek, tawny coat that gave off shimmers of light like ripples of sheet lightning on a hot midnight—

"That one," Jeremy said, pointing. "The jaguar."

Immediately he saw clawed feet running just ahead of his line of vision. They were his feet, because he was the jaguar, looking out through gleaming, molten jaguar eyes. Shifting his glance from side to side he saw whiskers projecting outward from the edges of his face, and a moist black nose—he had to almost cross his eyes to see the nose in front of his face, but there it was: a jaguar nose. When he tried wrinkling it, the muzzle curled as if in a snarl. And it didn't hurt like his real nose did. But wait! His real nose had stopped hurting; had it actually become the animal nose? It didn't matter—this was a fantastic role-playing game, with a great first-person point of view. He felt as if he were inside the jaguar, looking out through its eyes.

"It's so cool!" he exclaimed. "I never knew a game existed with graphics and special effects like these. Can I download it so I can have it on my hard drive?"

Still smiling, NetherMagus merely answered, "There's much more to see. Come forward."

Jeremy no longer needed the mouse; he just willed himself to move. Mental control, wow! He'd read about it, but this was a first for him. On his monitor screen the **terrain** spread out before him, and then surrounded him. He saw thick, densely leaved trees with strange faces and bodies—animal and human—entwined in their branches. How could colors be

terrain
landscape;
territory

dark and at the same time so vibrant? And the sounds! Frogs croaked, waves splashed, water dripped; he heard dim growls, subdued roars, the soft moaning of wind, but none of it was scary. It felt warm and dark and primitive, as though Jeremy knew this place, as though he'd been here long ago, when he was a baby waiting to be born.

"Move around, Jeremy the Jaguar," NetherMagus told him. "Explore my domain."

With his shoulders and haunches swiveling powerfully, Jeremy stalked the rain forest, feeling every muscle as it contracted in his perfectly coordinated body. He was passing cleanly through odd, swaying creatures: a clown head on a seal's body; a mermaid on a swing made of moss; a pool with dozens of **submerged** birds, their feathers changing colors as they fluttered beneath the water. "I gotta E-mail your URL address to my friends," he cried. "They'll freak over this!"

submerged
under water

"Your friends, the DeadHeads," NetherMagus said, not as a question but as a statement.

"How'd you know?"

"I'm a **Magus**; I know things," the mask answered. "I know about PrincessDie—the only one of your group who is what she says she is: a pretty girl, an excellent student. But she's growing bored with the rest of you, Jeremy. Tomorrow she'll leave you, because she has outgrown your little chat quartet."

Magus
magician or
sorcerer

Figures swam past Jeremy—exotic **gargoyles** and pale spheres as transparent as air. "Then I guess it'll just be us three guys," he answered, shrugging, surprised at how mighty his shoulders felt in the shrug. "Just Dr.Ded and Hangman and me."

gargoyles
grotesque
human or
animal figures

NetherMagus murmured, "Hangman will be lost to you too, Jeremy, although not because he wants to be. His school grades are so bad that tonight his parents will remove the computer from his room. He will be—as you young people say—grounded. From the Internet. Until his grades improve, which they will not, because very soon he will join a street gang."

"You couldn't possibly know all that stuff," Jeremy said scornfully as his claws—no, his fingernails—dug into soft turf. No! Dug into the keyboard. This was a game, the most incredible game he'd ever played, but still a game.

His father's people must have programmed it into the computer's hard drive months ago, as a surprise for Jeremy, just before they delivered the new computer on his birthday. They probably figured Jeremy would stumble onto the game right away. Long before this.

Maybe, during all these months, his dad had been hoping to hear from him. Waiting for Jeremy to thank him. What if he'd had the game designed especially for Jeremy and was right now sitting expectantly in that big office Jeremy had once seen in a picture in *Newsweek*, just waiting for a phone call from the son he'd abandoned twelve years earlier—

Or maybe—not.

"Come back, Jeremy," NetherMagus urged gently. "Don't you want to know about Dr.Ded?"

"No!" When Jeremy shook his head violently, his ears moved in an odd way, as though they were flexible and had grown higher on his head. "Wait, I guess I do. Yes."

NetherMagus told him, "Dr.Ded has deceived you far more than you've deceived any of the others."

"Me? Deceive? Oh, I guess you mean those stories I make up online. You know about them?"

"I know everything about you, Jeremy. I know that today you disgraced yourself on the soccer field—a truly humiliating experience! But back to Dr.Ded. He isn't a boy like you. He isn't a boy at all. He's a fifty-two-year-old stroke victim. He can't walk."

"Wrong! He said he was going surfing this afternoon."

The deep voice remained gentle. "He's confined to his bed, Jeremy. Soon he'll be moved to a nursing home that doesn't have an Internet connection. And you'll be all alone, Jeremy, abandoned by each of your online friends."

Jeremy swallowed, but his throat made an animal sound like a whimper. "What'll I do?"

The red smile on the face, or mask, grew even wider, as though it had been sliced by the samurai warrior's sword. "Stay with us, Jeremy. Live forever in Nethergrave. Here no one will ever abandon you, I promise."

"How do I get to Nethergrave?"

"You're already there!"

• • •

"Jeremy?" The call came from outside his bedroom door.

After a moment the door opened and his mother called again, "Jeremy? Sorry I'm so late—I was with a really important client. I just checked the refrigerator and you didn't eat your dinner. Why not?"

Entering the room, she peered around for her son. His schoolbooks had been flung on the bed, and his computer monitor glowed, but Jeremy wasn't there.

She bent down to pick up his jacket from the floor. As she straightened she caught sight of the computer screen. On it a jaguar raced through a clearing in a rain forest, its lean, sinewy body stretching and compressing as it ran, its tail soaring proudly. Struck by the animal's power and the incredible gracefulness of its movements, she stood quiet for a minute, staring, pressing Jeremy's jacket against her chest. The image of the jaguar moved her in a way she didn't understand. The animal was more than beautiful; it looked—triumphant!

She wondered if Jeremy had seen it.

Struck by the animal's power and the incredible gracefulness of its movements, she stood quiet for a minute, staring, pressing Jeremy's jacket against her chest.

AFTER YOU READ
Nethergrave

Think and Discuss

1. How does what Jeremy and the other DeadHeads—Hangman, PrincessDie, and Dr.Ded—say about themselves relate to what's actually true about them? Give specific examples.

2. At what point in the **plot** does Jeremy realize that Nethergrave is not just a computer game?

3. At what point in the story did *you* figure this out?

4. Relate the disappearance of Jeremy's father to Jeremy's **motivation** to play games and enter the world of Nethergrave.

5. Jeremy chooses the jaguar as his avatar. Use a chart like the one below to explore the significance of this choice by comparing the real Jeremy with Jeremy the Jaguar. Use descriptive details from the text.

Jeremy in Reality	Jeremy in Virtual Reality

6. Science fiction stories are often set in the future. This story is set in the present. What makes it an example of science fiction?

7. The obvious "Other World" in this story is Nethergrave, but before he discovers it, Jeremy has another "alternative reality"—the one he shares with his online buddies. Explain how his chats with the DeadHeads function as an "Other World" for Jeremy.

Write to Understand: Invent an Avatar

Review the chart you created to compare the real Jeremy and the avatar he selects—the jaguar. What did you discover about Jeremy's choice? Now think about the avatar you would choose if you had the chance. It might be something that embodies all your best qualities. Or it might, like Jeremy's avatar, possess qualities that are the opposite of what you consider your worst qualities. Write a description of the avatar you would create for yourself. Tell about the qualities and abilities it would possess.

BEFORE YOU READ
The Secret Life of Walter Mitty

Meet the Author: James Thurber

James Thurber (1894–1961) was born in Columbus, Ohio. He was partially blinded as a child when his brother accidentally shot him with an arrow. This injury kept him from playing games. Being often alone, he developed a rich fantasy life. He started his career as a reporter for the *Columbus Dispatch*. In 1926, he went to New York, where his friend E. B. White (author of *Charlotte's Web*), helped him get a job at *The New Yorker*. His career as a cartoonist began in 1930, when White rescued some of Thurber's drawings from the trash and submitted them to be printed in the magazine. Thurber's works include essays, short stories, and a popular play called *A Thurber Carnival*.

Build Background: Walter Mitty

The story you are about to read is James Thurber's best known and most beloved story. It appeared for the first time in *The New Yorker* in 1939. Seventy years later, it's still being read. The character of Walter Mitty has become part of American culture. He even has his own entry in the dictionary. The Merriam-Webster dictionary gives this definition: "a commonplace unadventurous person who seeks escape from reality through daydreaming." Walter Mitty is so much a part of our popular culture that, on the official *Peanuts* Web site, Charlie Brown's dog, Snoopy, is described as "an extroverted beagle with a Walter Mitty complex."

Walter Mitty lives in two worlds—the real world and his fantasy world—and he moves back and forth between them.

- What are the benefits of daydreaming and having a rich fantasy life?

- How could someone bring the two worlds—the real world and the fantasy world—together?

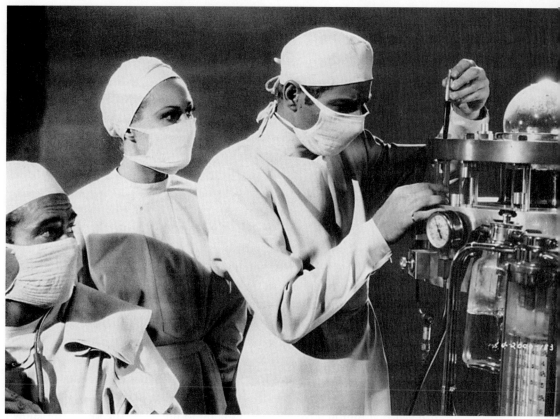

Actor Danny Kaye in the title role of the film *The Secret Life of Walter Mitty*

The Secret Life of Walter Mitty

JAMES THURBER

THE SECRET LIFE OF WALTER MITTY

James Thurber

"We're going through!" The Commander's voice was like thin ice breaking. He wore his full-dress uniform, with the heavily braided white cap pulled down **rakishly** over one cold gray eye. "We can't make it, sir. It's spoiling for a hurricane, if you ask me." "I'm not asking you, Lieutenant Berg," said the Commander. "Throw on the power lights! Rev her up to 8500! We're going through!" The pounding of the cylinders increased: ta-pocketa-pocketa-pocketa-pocketa-pocketa. The Commander stared at the ice forming on the pilot window. He walked over and twisted a row of complicated dials. "Switch on No. 8 **auxiliary**!" he shouted. "Switch on No. 8 auxiliary!" repeated Lieutenant Berg. "Full strength in No. 3 turret!" shouted the Commander. "Full strength in No. 3 turret!" The crew, bending to their various tasks in the huge, hurtling eight-engined Navy hydroplane, looked at each other and grinned. "The Old Man'll get us through," they said to one another. "The Old Man ain't afraid of hell!" . . .

"Not so fast! You're driving too fast!" said Mrs. Mitty. "What are you driving so fast for?"

"Hmm?" said Walter Mitty. He looked at his wife, in the seat beside him, with shocked astonishment. She seemed grossly unfamiliar, like a strange woman who had yelled at him in a crowd. "You were up to fifty-five," she said. "You know I don't like to go more than forty. You were up to fifty-five." Walter Mitty drove on toward Waterbury in silence, the roaring of the SN202 through the worst storm in twenty years of Navy flying fading in the remote, intimate airways of his mind. "You're tensed up again," said Mrs. Mitty. "It's one of your days. I wish you'd let Dr. Renshaw look you over."

Walter Mitty stopped the car in front of the building where his wife went to have her hair done. "Remember to get those overshoes while I'm having my hair done," she said. "I don't need overshoes," said Mitty. She put her mirror back into her bag. "We've been all through that," she said, getting out of the car. "You're not a young man any longer." He raced the engine a little. "Why don't you wear your gloves? Have you lost your gloves?" Walter Mitty reached in a pocket and brought out the gloves. He put them on, but after she had turned and gone into the building and he had driven on to a red light, he took them off again. "Pick it up, brother!" snapped a cop as the light changed, and Mitty hastily pulled on his gloves and lurched ahead. He drove around the streets aimlessly for a time, and then he drove past the hospital on his way to the parking lot.

. . . "It's the millionaire banker, Wellington McMillan," said the pretty nurse. "Yes?" said Walter Mitty, removing his gloves slowly. "Who has the case?" "Dr. Renshaw and Mr. Benbow, but there are two specialists here, Dr. Remington from New York and Mr. Pritchard-Mitford from London. He flew over." A door opened down a long, cool corridor and Dr. Renshaw came out. He looked distraught and **haggard**. "Hello, Mitty," he said. "We're having the devil's own time with McMillan, the millionaire banker and close personal friend of Roosevelt.[1] Obstreosis of the ductal tract. Tertiary.[2] Wish you'd take a look at him." "Glad to," said Mitty.

In the operating room there were whispered introductions: "Dr. Remington, Dr. Mitty. Mr. Pritchard-Mitford, Dr. Mitty." "I've read your book on streptothricosis," [3] said Pritchard-Mitford, shaking hands. "A brilliant performance, sir." "Thank you," said Walter Mitty. "Didn't know you were in the States, Mitty," grumbled Remington. "Coals to Newcastle, bringing Mitford and me up here for a tertiary." "You are very kind," said Mitty. A huge, complicated machine, connected to the operating table, with many tubes and wires, began at this moment to go pocketa-pocketa-pocketa. "The new anesthetizer is giving way!" shouted an intern. "There is no one in the East who knows how to fix it!" "Quiet, man!" said Mitty, in a low, cool voice. He sprang to the machine, which was now going pocketa-pocketa-queep-pocketa-queep. He began fingering delicately a row of glistening dials. "Give me a fountain pen!" he snapped. Someone handed him a fountain pen. He pulled a faulty piston out of the machine and inserted the pen in its place. "That will hold for ten minutes," he said. "Get on with the operation. A nurse hurried over and whispered to Renshaw, and Mitty saw the man turn pale. "Coreopsis[4] has set in," said Renshaw nervously. "If you would take over, Mitty?" Mitty looked at him and at the **craven** figure of Benbow, who drank, and at the grave, uncertain faces of the two great specialists. "If you wish,"

haggard
having
a worn
appearance

craven
lacking the
least bit of
courage

---

1 **Roosevelt:** Franklin Delano Roosevelt, then the President of the United States

2 **Obstreosis of the ductal tract. Tertiary:** pseudo-medical jargon

3 **streptothricosis:** another pseudo-medical term, related to a Latin word for bacteria

4 **Coreopsis:** another pseudo-medical term—*coreopsis* is the Latin name for a common yellow flower

he said. They slipped a white gown on him; he adjusted a mask and drew on thin gloves; nurses handed him shining . . .

"Back it up, Mac!! Look out for that Buick!" Walter Mitty jammed on the brakes. "Wrong lane, Mac," said the parking-lot attendant, looking at Mitty closely. "Gee. Yeh," muttered Mitty. He began cautiously to back out of the lane marked "Exit Only." "Leave her sit there," said the attendant. "I'll put her away." Mitty got out of the car. "Hey, better leave the key." "Oh," said Mitty, handing the man the ignition key. The attendant **vaulted** into the car, backed it up with **insolent** skill, and put it where it belonged.

They're so damn cocky, thought Walter Mitty, walking along Main Street; they think they know everything. Once he had tried to take his chains[5] off, outside New Milford, and he had got them wound around the axles. A man had had to come out in a wrecking car and unwind them, a young, grinning garageman. Since then Mrs. Mitty always made him drive to a garage to have the chains taken off. The next time, he thought, I'll wear my right arm in a sling; they won't grin at me then. I'll have my right arm in a sling and they'll see I couldn't possibly take the chains off myself. He kicked at the slush on the sidewalk. "Overshoes," he said to himself, and he began looking for a shoe store.

When he came out into the street again, with the overshoes in a box under his arm, Walter Mitty began to wonder what the other thing was his wife had told him to get. She had told him twice before they set out from their house for Waterbury. In a way he hated these weekly trips to town—he was always getting something wrong. Kleenex, he thought, Squibb's,[6] razor blades? No. Toothpaste, toothbrush, bicarbonate, Carborundum,[7] initiative and referendum? He gave it up. But she would remember it. "Where's the what's-its-name?" she would ask. "Don't tell me you forgot the what's-its-name." A newsboy went by shouting something about the Waterbury trial.

. . . "Perhaps this will refresh your memory." The District Attorney suddenly thrust a heavy automatic at the quiet figure on the witness stand. "Have you ever seen this before?" Walter Mitty took the gun and examined it expertly. "This is my Webley-Vickers 50.80," he said calmly. An excited buzz ran around the courtroom. The judge rapped for order. "You are a crack shot with any sort of firearms, I

---

5 **chains:** short for *snow chains*, which are chains put on tires to give traction in snow

6 **Squibb's:** a popular pharmaceutical product made by the Squibb Corporation

7 **Carborundum:** a brand of sandpaper

vaulted
jumped

insolent
insultingly
disrespectful

believe?" said the District Attorney, insinuatingly. "Objection!" shouted Mitty's attorney. "We have shown that the defendant could not have fired the shot. We have shown that he wore his right arm in a sling on the night of the fourteenth of July." Walter Mitty raised his hand briefly and the bickering attorneys were stilled. "With any known make of gun," he said evenly, "I could have killed Gregory Fitzhurst at three hundred feet *with my left hand.*"

Pandemonium broke loose in the courtroom. A woman's scream rose above the **bedlam** and suddenly a lovely, dark-haired girl was in Walter Mitty's arms. The District Attorney struck at her savagely. Without rising from his chair, Mitty let the man have it on the point of the chin. "You miserable **cur**!". . .

bedlam
uproar;
confusion

cur
surly,
cowardly
fellow; also
mutt or
mixed breed
dog

"Puppy biscuit," said Walter Mitty. He stopped walking and the buildings of Waterbury rose up out of the misty courtroom and surrounded him again. A woman who was passing laughed. "He said 'Puppy biscuit,'" she said to her companion. "That man said 'Puppy biscuit' to himself." Walter Mitty hurried on. He went into an A. & P.,[8] not the first one he came to but a smaller one farther up the street. "I want some biscuit for small, young dogs," he said to the clerk. "Any special brand, sir?" The greatest pistol shot in the world thought a moment. "It says 'Puppies Bark for It' on the box," said Walter Mitty.

His wife would be through at the hairdresser's in fifteen minutes Mitty saw in looking at his watch, unless they had trouble drying it; sometimes they had trouble drying it. She didn't like to get to the hotel first; she would want him to be there waiting for her as usual. He found a big leather chair in the lobby, facing a window, and he put the overshoes and the puppy biscuit on the floor beside it. He picked up an old copy of *Liberty* and sank down into the chair. "Can Germany Conquer the World Through the Air?" Walter Mitty looked at the pictures of bombing planes and of ruined streets.

. . . "The cannonading[9] has got the wind up in[10] young Raleigh, sir," said the sergeant. Captain Mitty looked up at him through tousled hair. "Get him to bed," he said wearily. "With the others. I'll fly alone." "But you can't, sir," said the sergeant anxiously. "It takes two men to handle that bomber and the Archies[11] are

---

8 **A. & P.:** short for Atlantic & Pacific Tea Company, which operated food stores mainly along the eastern seaboard from Connecticut to Maryland

9 **cannonading:** attacking with artillery

10 **got the wind up in:** excited; upset

11 **Archies:** a term from the First World War for anti-aircraft fire

pounding hell out of the air. Von Richtman's circus is between here and Saulier."[12] "Somebody's got to get that ammunition dump," said Mitty. "I'm going over. Spot of brandy?" He poured a drink for the sergeant and one for himself. War thundered and whined around the dugout and battered at the door. There was a **rending** of wood and splinters flew through the room. "A bit of a near thing," said Captain Mitty carelessly. "The box barrage[13] is closing in," said the sergeant. "We only live once, Sergeant," said Mitty, with his faint, fleeting smile. "Or do we?" He poured another brandy and tossed it off. "I never see a man could hold his brandy like you, sir," said the sergeant. "Begging your pardon, sir." Captain Mitty stood up and strapped on his huge Webley-Vickers automatic. "It's forty kilometers through hell, sir," said the sergeant. Mitty finished one last brandy. "After all," he said softly, "what isn't?" The pounding of the cannon increased; there was the rat-tat-tatting of machine guns, and from somewhere came the menacing pocketa-pocketa-pocketa of the new flame-throwers. Walter Mitty walked to the door of the dugout humming "Aupres de Ma Blonde."[14] He turned and waved to the sergeant. "Cheerio!" he said. . . .

Something struck his shoulder. "I've been looking all over this hotel for you," said Mrs. Mitty. "Why do you have to hide in this old chair? How did you expect me to find you?" "Things close in," said Walter Mitty vaguely. "What?" Mrs. Mitty said. "Did you get the what's-its-name? The puppy biscuit? What's in that box?" "Overshoes," said Mitty. "Couldn't you have put them on in the store?" "I was thinking," said Walter Mitty. "Does it ever occur to you that I am sometimes thinking?" She looked at him. "I'm going to take your temperature when I get you home," she said.

They went out through the revolving doors that made a faintly **derisive** whistling sound when you pushed them. It was two blocks to the parking lot. At the drugstore on the corner she said, "Wait here for me. I forgot something. I won't be a minute." She was more than a minute. Walter Mitty lighted a cigarette. It began to rain, rain with sleet in it. He stood up against the wall of the drugstore, smoking. . . . He put his shoulders back and his heels together. "To hell with the handkerchief," said Walter Mitty scornfully. He took one last drag on his cigarette and snapped it away. Then, with that faint, fleeting smile playing about his lips, he faced the firing squad; erect and motionless, proud and **disdainful**, Walter Mitty the Undefeated, **inscrutable** to the last.

rending
splitting

derisive
expressing
scorn or
contempt

disdainful
full of
contempt

inscrutable
mysterious;
not readily
understood

---

12 **Von Richtman's circus is between here and Saulier:** military-sounding jargon

13 **box barrage:** an anti-aircraft barrage delivered in a box-shape pattern by guns

14 **"Aupres de Ma Blonde":** French for "Next to My Girlfriend," the title of a song whose lively melody is used for military marches

AFTER YOU READ
The Secret Life of Walter Mitty

Think and Discuss

1. What is alike about all the fantasies that Walter Mitty has? Refer in your answer to each of the five times Walter Mitty slips into his fantasy world.

2. Walter Mitty moves back and forth between his fantasy world and the real world, but sometimes there is an overlap. Something from one world makes its way into the other and triggers the transition. With a partner, talk about how Mitty's worlds sometimes blend together.

3. What details of **setting** and **character** might explain Mitty's interest in entering his fantasy life?

4. Thurber is sometimes criticized by female readers for portraying women in a bad light. Think about the **character** of Mrs. Mitty. Which are given more emphasis, her positive traits or her negative traits? Use details from the story to back up your answer.

5. How do you feel about the character of Walter Mitty? What in the story led you to feel that way?

6. Jeremy, the main character in "Nethergrave," and Walter Mitty have a lot in common. Use a chart like this one to explore their similarities.

	Jeremy	Walter Mitty
Personality in Reality		
Personality in Fantasy		
Embarrassing Moment		
Family Ties		
How they Relate to Others		

Write to Understand: Compare Characters

Use your comparison chart to help you write a paragraph or two comparing Jeremy and Walter Mitty. Explore how the two characters are alike, including the way they deal with situations in the real world, how they escape to a fantasy world, and how their fantasy lives and their real lives differ.

BEFORE YOU READ

The Mystery of China's Celtic Mummies

Meet the Author: Clifford Coonan

Clifford Coonan is an Irish foreign correspondent based in Beijing. He writes for *The Irish Times* and *The Independent* and is a regular contributor to *Variety*, the magazine of the entertainment industry in the United States. He writes about all areas of political, social, and economic life in China, and his work takes him to many of China's most remote places. "China is one of the world's truly amazing stories," says Coonan, "and I love my front-row seat to observe histories unfold that will affect the whole world." Coonan holds a B.A. in English and German from Trinity College in Dublin and an M.A. in journalism from Dublin City University.

Build Background: The Celts

The Celts are the ancient ancestors of the people of Ireland, Scotland, Wales, Cornwall, the Isle of Mann, and the French region of Brittany. When the Romans invaded the British Isles in 55 b.c., a Celtic culture had already existed there for more than 500 years. The Celts were not a structured, centrally governed civilization. They were fiercely barbaric warriors, but they also brought ironworking to the British Isles.

Much of what we know about the ancient Celts comes from the writings of the Romans, who conquered them. It is possible that their reports were not entirely objective and that they exaggerated the Celts' barbaric qualities in order to promote themselves as the great civilizing force.

- What are the ways that we learn about people who lived more than 2,500 years ago?

- Why is it important to today's world to study the world of ancient peoples?

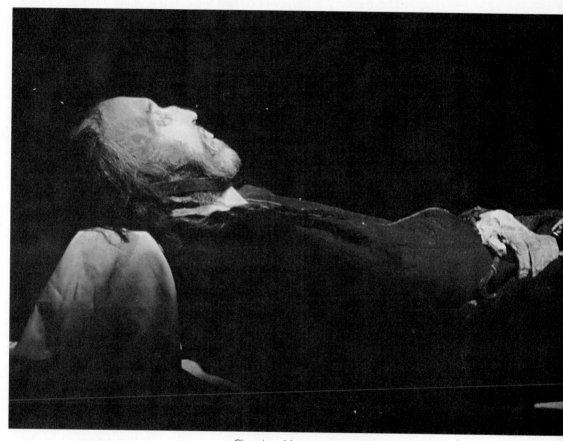

Cherchen Man, a mummy found in April 1994

The Mystery of China's Celtic Mummies

CLIFFORD COONAN

THE MYSTERY OF CHINA'S CELTIC MUMMIES

*The discovery of European corpses thousands of miles away
suggests a hitherto unknown connection between East and West
in the Bronze Age.*

Clifford Coonan

Solid as a warrior of the Caledonii tribe,[1] the man's hair is reddish brown flecked with grey, framing high cheekbones, a long nose, full lips and a ginger beard. When he lived three thousand years ago, he stood six feet tall, and was buried wearing a red twill tunic and tartan[2] leggings. He looks like a Bronze Age European. In fact, he's every inch a Celt. Even his DNA says so.

But this is no early Celt from central Scotland. This is the mummified corpse of Cherchen Man, unearthed from the scorched sands of the Taklamakan Desert in the far-flung region of Xinjiang in western China, and now housed in a new museum in the provincial capital of Urumqi. In the language spoken by the local Uighur people in Xinjiang, "Taklamakan" means: "You come in and never come out."

The extraordinary thing is that Cherchen Man was found—with the mummies of three women and a baby—in a burial site thousands of miles to the east of where the Celts established their biggest settlements in France and the British Isles.

DNA testing confirms that he and hundreds of other mummies found in Xinjiang's Tarim Basin are of European origin. We don't know how he got there, what brought him there, or how long he and his kind lived there for. But, as the desert's name suggests, it is certain that he never came out. His discovery provides an unexpected connection between east and west and some valuable clues to early European history.

One of the women who shared a tomb with Cherchen Man has light brown hair which looks as if it was brushed and braided for her funeral only

---

1 **Caledonii tribe:** a Celtic tribe in northern Britain. The Romans called the area that would become Scotland "Caledonia."

2 **tartan:** plaid

yesterday. Her face is painted with curling designs, and her striking red burial gown has lost none of its luster during the three millenniums that this tall, fine-featured woman has been lying beneath the sand of the Northern Silk Road.[3]

The bodies are far better preserved than the Egyptian mummies, and it is sad to see the infants on display; to see how the baby was wrapped in a beautiful brown cloth tied with red and blue cord, then a blue stone placed on each eye. Beside it was a baby's milk bottle with a teat, made from a sheep's udder.

Based on the mummy, the museum has reconstructed what Cherchen Man would have looked like and how he lived. The similarities to the traditional Bronze Age Celts are uncanny, and analysis has shown that the weave of the cloth is the same as that of those found on the bodies of salt miners in Austria from 1300 B.C..

The burial sites of Cherchen Man and his fellow people were marked with stone structures that look like dolmens[4] from Britain, ringed by round-faced, Celtic figures, or standing stones. Among their icons were figures reminiscent of the sheela-na-gigs, wild females who flaunted their bodies and can still be found in mediaeval churches in Britain. A female mummy wears a long, conical hat which has to be a witch or a wizard's hat. Or a druid's,[5] perhaps? The wooden combs they used to fan their tresses are familiar to students of ancient Celtic art.

The bodies are far better preserved than the Egyptian mummies, and it is sad to see the infants on display . . .

At their peak, around 300 B.C., the influence of the Celts stretched from Ireland in the west to the south of Spain and across to Italy's Po Valley, and probably extended to parts of Poland and Ukraine and the central plain of

---

3 **Northern Silk Road:** The Silk Road is a series of interconnected ancient trade routes connecting China with Asia Minor and the Mediterranean. At the Tibetan Plateau, the Silk Road divides into two routes: one going north of the mountains, and one going south.

4 **dolmens:** tombs consisting of three or more upright stones supporting a large flat horizontal capstone

5 **druids:** member of an ancient Celtic religion, Druidism

Turkey in the east. These mummies seem to suggest, however, that the Celts penetrated well into central Asia, nearly making it as far as Tibet.

The Celts gradually infiltrated Britain between about 500 and 100 B.C.. There was probably never anything like an organized Celtic invasion: they arrived at different times, and are considered a group of peoples loosely connected by similar language, religion, and cultural expression.

The eastern Celts spoke a now-dead language called Tocharian, which is related to Celtic languages and part of the Indo-European group. They seem to have been a peaceful folk, as there are few weapons among the Cherchen find and there is little evidence of a caste system.[6]

Even older than the Cherchen find is that of the 4,000-year-old Loulan Beauty, who has long flowing fair hair and is one of a number of mummies discovered near the town of Loulan. One of these mummies was an eight-year-old child wrapped in a piece of patterned wool cloth, closed with bone pegs.

The Loulan Beauty's features are Nordic. She was 45 when she died, and was buried with a basket of food for the next life, including domesticated wheat, combs and a feather.

desiccated
preserved by drying

The Taklamakan desert has given up hundreds of **desiccated** corpses in the past 25 years, and archaeologists say the discoveries in the Tarim Basin are some of the most significant finds in the past quarter of a century.

"From around 1800 B.C., the earliest mummies in the Tarim Basin were exclusively Caucasoid, or Europoid,"[7] says Professor Victor Mair of Pennsylvania University, who has been captivated by the mummies since he spotted them partially obscured in a back room in the old museum in 1988. "He looked like my brother Dave sleeping there, and that's what really got me. Lying there with his eyes closed," Professor Mair said.

exercises
engages the attention and effort of

It's a subject that **exercises** him and he has gone to extraordinary lengths, dodging difficult political issues, to gain further knowledge of these remarkable people.

East Asian migrants arrived in the eastern portions of the Tarim Basin

---

6 **caste system:** a system that divides people into groups by social class

7 **Caucausoid, or Europoid:** characteristic of a race of humankind native to Europe and having light skin color

about 3,000 years ago, Professor Mair says, while the Uighur peoples arrived after the collapse of the Orkon Uighur Kingdom,[8] based in modern-day Mongolia, around the year 842.

A believer in the "inter-relatedness of all human communities," Professor Mair resists attempts to impose a theory of a single people arriving in Xinjiang, and believes rather that the early Europeans headed in different directions, some traveling west to become the Celts in Britain and Ireland, others taking a northern route to become the Germanic tribes, and then another offshoot heading east and ending up in Xinjiang.

This section of the ancient Silk Road is one of the world's most barren **precincts**. You are further away from the sea here than at any other place, and you can feel it. This is where China tests its nuclear weapons. Labor camps are scattered all around—who would try to escape? But the remoteness has worked to the archaeologists' advantage. The ancient corpses have avoided decay because the Tarim Basin is so dry, with alkaline soils. Scientists have been able to glean information about many aspects of our Bronze Age forebears from the mummies, from their physical make-up to information about how they buried their dead, what tools they used and what clothes they wore.

precincts
places;
locales

In her book *The Mummies of Urumchi*, the textile expert Elizabeth Wayland Barber examines the tartan-style cloth, and reckons it can be traced back to Anatolia[9] and the Caucasus, the steppe area north of the Black Sea. Her theory is that this group divided, starting in the Caucasus and then splitting, one group going west and another east.

> The ancient corpses have avoided decay because the Tarim Basin is so dry, with alkaline soils.

Even though they have been dead for thousands of years, every perfectly preserved fiber of the mummies' make-up has been relentlessly politicized.

---

8 **Orkon Uighur Kingdom:** an empire established about 744 when the Uighurs, a federation of nomadic tribes, seized power from the Gok Turks

9 **Anatolia:** a peninsula in southwestern Asia that forms the Asian part of Turkey; also known as Asia Minor

The received[10] wisdom in China says that two hundred years before the birth of Christ, China's emperor Wu Di sent an ambassador to the west to establish an alliance against the marauding Huns, then based in Mongolia. The route across Asia that the emissary, Zhang Qian, took eventually became the Silk Road to Europe. Hundreds of years later Marco Polo[11] came, and the opening up of China began.

The very thought that Caucasians were settled in a part of China thousands of years before Wu Di's early contacts with the west and Marco Polo's travels has enormous political ramifications. And that these Europeans should have been in **restive** Xinjiang hundreds of years before East Asians is explosive.

The Chinese historian Ji Xianlin, writing a preface to *Ancient Corpses of Xinjiang* by the Chinese archaeologist Wang Binghua, translated by Professor Mair, says China "supported and admired" research by foreign experts into the mummies. "However, within China a small group of ethnic **separatists** have taken advantage of this opportunity to stir up trouble and are acting like buffoons. Some of them have even styled themselves the descendants of these ancient 'white people' with the aim of dividing the motherland. But these **perverse** acts will not succeed," Ji wrote.

Many Uighurs consider the Han Chinese as invaders. The territory was annexed by China in 1955, and the Xinjiang Uighur Autonomous Region established, and there have been numerous incidents of unrest over the years. In 1997 in the northern city of Yining there were riots by Muslim separatists and Chinese security forces cracked down, with nine deaths. There are occasional outbursts, and the region remains very heavily policed.

Not surprisingly, the government has been slow to publicize these valuable historical finds for fear of fuelling separatist currents in Xinjiang.

The Loulan Beauty, for example, was claimed by the Uighurs as their symbol in song and image, although genetic testing now shows that she was in fact European.

restive
stubbornly resisting control

separatists
those who want to break away for racial, cultural, or ethnic reasons

perverse
wrongheaded; stubbornly opposing what is right, reasonable, or accepted

---

10 **received:** widely accepted to be true

11 **Marco Polo:** a trader and explorer from Venice who was one of the first Westerners to travel the Silk Road to China

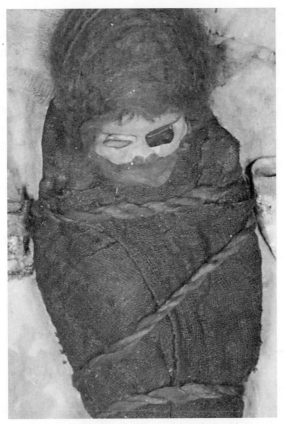
Xinjiang mummy of an infant with stones covering the eyes found in April 1994

Professor Mair acknowledges that the political dimension to all this has made his work difficult, but says that the research shows that the people of Xinjiang are a dizzying mixture. "They tend to mix as you enter the Han Dynasty. By that time the East Asian component is very noticeable," he says. "Modern DNA and ancient DNA show that Uighurs, Kazaks, Kyrgyzs, the peoples of central Asia are all mixed Caucasian and East Asian. The modern and ancient DNA tell the same story," he says.

Altogether there are 400 mummies in various degrees of desiccation and decomposition, including the prominent Han Chinese warrior Zhang Xiong and other Uighur mummies, and thousands of skulls. The mummies will keep the scientists busy for a long time. Only a handful of the better-preserved ones are on display in the impressive new Xinjiang museum. Work began in 1999, but was stopped in 2002 after a corruption scandal and the jailing of a former director for involvement in the theft of antiques.

The museum finally opened on the 50th anniversary of China's annexation of the restive region, and the mummies are housed in glass display cases (which were sealed with what looked like Sellotape[12]) in a multi-media wing.

In the same room are the much more recent Han mummies—equally interesting, but rendering the display confusing, as it groups all the mummies closely together. Which makes sound political sense.

This political correctness continues in another section of the museum dedicated to the achievements of the Chinese revolution, and boasts artifacts from the Anti-Japanese War (1931–1945).

Best preserved of all the corpses is Yingpan Man, known as the Handsome Man, a 2,000-year-old Caucasian mummy discovered in 1995. He had a gold foil death mask—a Greek tradition—covering his blond, bearded face, and wore elaborate golden embroidered red and maroon wool garments with images of fighting Greeks or Romans. The hemp mask is painted with a soft smile and the thin moustache of a dandy.[13] Currently on display at a museum in Tokyo, the handsome Yingpan man was two meters tall (six feet six inches), and pushing 30 when he died. His head rests on a pillow in the shape of a crowing cockerel.[14]

12 **Sellotape:** British brand name for cellophane tape similar to Scotch® tape

13 **dandy:** a man with elegant dress and appearance

14 **cockeral:** rooster

AFTER YOU READ
The Mystery of China's Celtic Mummies

Think and Discuss

1. What is so extraordinary about the discovery of mummified bodies of Celts in the Xinjiang Province of western China?

2. What is Professor Victor Mair's theory about how the Caucasoid, or Europoid, peoples settled in a part of China more than a thousand years before Marco Polo traveled the Silk Road?

3. Based on the **descriptive details** about the clothing and other items found with the mummies, imagine and describe what an ordinary day in the lives of these people might have been like. Consider how they dressed, took care of their young, obtained food, and dealt with their physical environment.

4. What "Other Worlds" are represented in this article?

5. Create a timeline to understand how some of the significant dates in the article fit together. Include the dates for each of the following in your timeline: Yingpan Man, the Loulan Beauty, Cherchen Man, the Celts' infiltration of the British Isles, and the peak of Celtic influence in Europe. As you create your timeline, remember that 2000 B.C. is now 4,000 years ago.

2000 B.C.	1500 B.C.	1000 B.C.	500 B.C.	Birth of Christ

Write to Understand: Draw Conclusions

Sciences like archaeology and anthropology involve drawing conclusions based on available evidence. When new evidence is discovered, it either confirms the conclusions or forces scientists to change their theories. Think about the evidence you recorded in your timeline. Then write an explanation of how Celtic people may have come to be in western China that is supported by that evidence.

BEFORE YOU READ

The Handsomest Drowned Man in the World

Meet the Author: Gabriel García Márquez

Gabriel García Márquez was born in 1928 in the small Colombian village of Aracataca. Raised by his grandparents, he grew up listening to the fantastic tales of Colombian history and myth that his grandmother told him. Her stories and the superstitions and myths that abounded in the village nurtured his imagination. It is from this rich background that García Márquez creates his fiction. A journalist, novelist, and writer of short stories, García Márquez was awarded the Nobel Prize for Literature in 1982. His most famous work is the novel *One Hundred Years of Solitude*, which was first published in 1967.

Build Background: Magical Realism

Gabriel García Márquez is a central figure in a literary movement known as "magical realism." The term was first coined in 1949 to describe the combination of the fantastic and the everyday in Latin American fiction. In works of magical realism, everything about the story is realistic—the setting, the characters, the events—but there are mysterious elements to the story, and everyday occurrences can have a kind of mystical effect on the characters' lives. García Márquez himself once said that he tries to tap "the magic in commonplace events."

In the story you are about to read, the residents of a small fishing village discover the body of a drowned man washed ashore. What is for them a fairly commonplace event has an unanticipated effect on the entire village.

- What story or book have you read that you would describe as containing elements of magical realism?

- How do you think the fantastic and mysterious might reveal itself in everyday life?

THE DEATH OF LEANDER, Frederic Leighton, 1887

The Handsomest Drowned Man in the World

GABRIEL GARCÍA MÁRQUEZ

THE HANDSOMEST DROWNED MAN IN THE WORLD

Gabriel García Márquez

The first children who saw the dark and slinky bulge approaching through the sea let themselves think it was an enemy ship. Then they saw it had no flags or masts and they thought it was a whale. But when it washed up on the beach, they removed the clumps of seaweed, the jellyfish tentacles, and the remains of fish and **flotsam**, and only then did they see that it was a drowned man.

flotsam
floating refuse

They had been playing with him all afternoon, burying him in the sand and digging him up again, when someone chanced to see them and spread the alarm in the village. The men who carried him to the nearest house noticed that he weighed more than any dead man they had ever known, almost as much as a horse, and they said to each other that maybe he'd been floating too long and the water had got into his bones. When they laid him on the floor they said he'd been taller than all other men because there was barely enough room for him in the house, but they thought that maybe the ability to keep on growing after death was part of the nature of certain drowned men. He had the smell of the sea about him and only his shape gave one to suppose that it was the corpse of a human being, because the skin was covered with a crust of mud and scales.

They did not even have to clean off his face to know that the dead man was a stranger. The village was made up of only twenty-odd wooden houses that had stone courtyards with no flowers and which were spread about on the end of a desertlike **cape**. There was so little land that mothers always went about with the fear that the wind would carry off their children and the few dead that the years had caused among them had to be thrown off the cliffs. But the sea was calm and bountiful and all the men fitted into seven boats. So when they found the drowned man they simply had to look at one another to see that they were all there.

cape
point of land jutting into the sea

That night they did not go out to work at sea. While the men went to find out if anyone was missing in neighboring villages, the women stayed behind to care for the drowned man. They took the mud off with grass swabs, they removed the underwater stones entangled in his hair, and they scraped the crust off with tools used for scaling fish. As they were doing that they noticed that the vegetation on him came from faraway oceans and deep water

Not only was he the tallest, strongest, most virile, and best built man they had ever seen, but even though they were looking at him there was no room for him in their imagination.

and that his clothes were in tatters, as if he had sailed through **labyrinths** of coral. They noticed too that he bore his death with pride, for he did not have the lonely look of other drowned men who came out of the sea or that haggard, needy look of men who drowned in rivers. But only when they finished cleaning him off did they become aware of the kind of man he was and it left them breathless. Not only was he the tallest, strongest, most **virile**, and best built man they had ever seen, but even though they were looking at him there was no room for him in their imagination.

labyrinths
places full of intricate passageways and blind alleys

virile
manly; masterful

They could not find a bed in the village large enough to lay him on nor was there a table solid enough to use for his wake. The tallest men's holiday pants would not fit him, not the fattest ones' Sunday shirts, nor the shoes of the one with the biggest feet. Fascinated by his huge size and his beauty, the women then decided to make him some pants from a large piece of sail and a shirt from some bridal linen so that he could continue through his death with dignity. As they sewed, sitting in a circle and gazing at the corpse between stitches, it seemed to them that the wind had never been so steady nor the sea so restless as on that night and they supposed that the change had something to do with the dead man. They thought that if that magnificent man had lived in the village, his house would have had the widest doors, the highest ceiling, and the strongest floor, his bedstead would have been made from a midship frame held together by iron bolts, and his wife would have been the happiest woman. They thought that he would have had so much authority that he could have drawn fish out of the sea simply by calling their names and that he would have put so much work into his land that springs would have burst forth from among the rocks so that he would have been able to plant flowers on the cliffs. They secretly compared him to their own men, thinking that for all their lives theirs were incapable of doing what he could do in one night, and they ended up dismissing them deep in their hearts as the weakest, meanest, and most useless creatures on earth. They were wandering through that maze of fantasy when the oldest woman, who as the oldest had looked upon the drowned man with more compassion than passion, sighed:

"He has the face of someone called Esteban."

It was true. Most of them had only to take another look at him to see that he could not have any other name. The more stubborn among them, who were the youngest, still lived for a few hours with the illusion that when they put his clothes on and he lay among the flowers in patent leather shoes his name might be Lautaro.[1] But it was a vain illusion. There had not been enough canvas, the poorly cut and worse sewn pants were too tight, and the hidden strength of his heart popped the buttons on his shirt. After midnight the whistling of the wind died down and the sea fell into its Wednesday drowsiness. The silence put an end to any last doubts: he was Esteban. The women who had dressed him, who had combed his hair, had cut his nails and shaved him were unable to hold back a shudder of pity when they had to resign themselves to his being dragged along the ground. It was then that they understood how unhappy he must have been with that huge body since it bothered him even after death. They could see him in life, condemned to going through doors sideways, cracking his head on crossbeams, remaining on his feet during visits, not knowing what to do with his soft, pink, sea lion hands while the lady of the house looked for her most resistant chair and begged him, frightened to death, sit here, Esteban, please, and he, leaning against the wall, smiling, don't bother, ma'am, I'm fine where I am, his heels raw and his back roasted from having done the same thing so many times whenever he paid a visit, don't bother, ma'am, I'm fine where I am, just to avoid the embarrassment of breaking up the chair, and never knowing

---

1 **Lautaro:** The name suggests heroism and romance. Lautaro was a Chilean military icon for his revolutionary strategy and his innovative tactics. Lautaro is also a significant character in the epic poem *La Araucana* by Alonso de Ercilla, which is about the Spanish conquest of Chile.

perhaps that the ones who said don't go, Esteban, at least wait till the coffee's ready, were the ones who later on would whisper the big boob finally left, how nice, the handsome fool has gone. That was what the women were thinking beside the body a little before dawn. Later, when they covered his face with a handkerchief so that the light would not bother him, he looked so forever dead, so defenseless, so much like their men that the first **furrows** of tears opened in their hearts. It was one of the younger ones who began the weeping. The others, coming to, went from sighs to wails, and the more they sobbed the more they felt like weeping, because the drowned man was becoming all the more Esteban for them, and so they wept so much, for he was the most destitute, most peaceful, and most obliging man on earth, poor Esteban. So when the men returned with the news that the drowned man was not from the neighboring villages either, the women felt an opening of **jubilation** in the midst of their tears.

"Praise the Lord," they sighed, "he's ours!"

The men thought the fuss was only womanish **frivolity**. Fatigued because of the difficult nighttime inquiries, all they wanted was to get rid of the bother of the newcomer once and for all before the sun grew strong on that arid, windless day. They improvised a litter[2] with the remains of foremasts and gaffs,[3] tying it together with rigging so that it would bear the weight of the body until they reached the cliffs. They wanted to tie the anchor from a cargo ship to him so that he would sink easily into the deepest waves, where fish are blind and divers die of nostalgia, and bad currents would not bring him back to shore, as had happened with other bodies. But the more they hurried, the more the women thought of ways to waste time. They walked about like startled hens, pecking with the sea charms on their breasts, some interfering on one side to put a scapular[4] of the good wind on the drowned

furrows
grooves;
channels

jubilation
joyfulness

frivolity
foolishness

It was one of the younger ones who began the weeping. The others, coming to, went from sighs to wails . . .

---

2 **litter:** stretcher

3 **gaffs:** spars or poles used to extend some fore-and-aft sails

4 **scapular:** a garment worn over the shoulders to signify membership in a religious group

man, some on the other side to put a wrist compass on him, and after a great deal of *get away from there, woman, stay out of the way, look, you almost made me fall on top of the dead man*, the men began to feel mistrust in their livers and started grumbling about why so many main-altar decorations for a stranger, because no matter how many nails and holy-water jars he had on him, the sharks would chew him all the same, but the women kept piling on their junk relics, running back and forth, stumbling, while they released in sighs what they did not in tears, so that the men finally exploded with *since when has there ever been such a fuss over a drifting corpse, a drowned nobody, a piece of cold Wednesday meat.* One of the women, mortified by so much lack of care, then removed the handkerchief from the dead man's face and the men were left breathless too.

He was Esteban. It was not necessary to repeat it for them to recognize him. If they had been told Sir Walter Raleigh,[5] even they might have been impressed with his gringo accent, the macaw on his shoulder, his cannibal-killing blunderbuss,[6] but there could be only one Esteban in the world and there he was, stretched out like a sperm whale, shoeless, wearing the pants of an undersized child, and with those stony nails that had to be cut with a knife. They only had to take the handkerchief off his face to see that he was ashamed, that it was not his fault that he was so big or so heavy or so handsome, and if he had known that this was going to happen, he would have looked for a more discreet place to drown in, seriously, I even would have tied the anchor of a galleon around my neck and staggered off a cliff like someone who doesn't like things in order not to be upsetting people now with this Wednesday dead body, as you people say, in order not to be bothering anyone with this filthy piece of cold meat that doesn't have anything to do with me. There was so much

> One of the women, mortified by so much lack of care, then removed the handkerchief from the dead man's face and the men were left breathless too.

---

5 **Sir Walter Raleigh:** English adventurer and explorer who made several voyages to the New World

6 **blunderbuss:** an old-fashioned rifle with a flared barrel

truth in his manner that even the most mistrustful men, the ones who felt the bitterness of endless nights at sea fearing that their women would tire of dreaming about them and begin to dream of drowned men, even they and others who were harder still shuddered in the marrow of their bones at Esteban's sincerity.

That was how they came to hold the most splendid funeral they could ever conceive of for an abandoned drowned man. Some women who had gone to get flowers in the neighboring villages returned with other women who could not believe what they had been told, and those women went back for more flowers when they saw the dead man, and they brought more and more until there were so many flowers and so many people that it was hard to walk about. At the final moment it pained them to return him to the waters as an orphan and they chose a father and mother from among the best people, and aunts and uncles and cousins, so that through him all the inhabitants of the village became kinsmen. Some sailors who heard the weeping from a distance went off course and people heard of one who had himself tied to the mainmast, remembering ancient fables about sirens.[7] While they fought for the privilege of carrying him on their shoulders along the steep **escarpment** by the cliffs, men and women became aware for the first time of the desolation of their streets, the dryness of their courtyards, the narrowness of their dreams as they faced the splendor and beauty of their drowned man. They let him go without an anchor so that he could come back if he wished and whenever he wished, and they all held their breath for the fraction of centuries the body took to fall into the abyss. They did not need to look at one another to realize that they were no longer all present, that they would never be. But they also knew that everything would be different from then on, that their

> *They let him go without an anchor so that he could come back if he wished and whenever he wished . . .*

escarpment
long cliff or
steep slope

---

7 **one who had himself tied to the mainmast, remembering ancient fables about sirens:** a reference to Ulysses, the hero of the *Odyssey*, who stopped the ears of his crew with wax and had himself tied to the mast when their ship passed the Sirens' island because the Sirens' song was so alluring it caused sailors to throw themselves into the sea. (This section of the *Odyssey* can be found on pages 497–499.)

houses would have wider doors, higher ceilings, and stronger floors so that Esteban's memory could go everywhere without bumping into beams and so that no one in the future would dare whisper the big boob finally died, too bad, the handsome fool has finally died, because they were going to paint their house fronts gay colors to make Esteban's memory eternal and they were going to break their backs digging for springs among the stones and planting flowers on the cliffs so that in future years at dawn the passengers on great liners would awaken, suffocated by the smell of gardens on the high seas, and the captain would have to come down from the bridge in his dress uniform, with his astrolabe,[8] his pole star,[9] and his row of war medals and, pointing to the **promontory** of roses on the horizon, he would say in fourteen languages, look there, where the wind is so peaceful now that it's gone to sleep beneath the beds, over there, where the sun's so bright that the sunflowers don't know which way to turn, yes, over there, that's Esteban's village.

promontory
a high point of land

---

8 **astrolabe:** instrument used to measure the stars for navigation

9 **pole star:** star lined up with the axis of the Earth and pointing to a pole

AFTER YOU READ

The Handsomest Drowned Man in the World

Think and Discuss

1. García Márquez gave this story the subtitle, "A Tale for Children." If, like many children's stories, it has a lesson or moral in it, what might that be? Explain.

2. Why are the women so happy to learn that the stranger is not from a neighboring village?

3. What effect does the **point of view** García Márquez chose for this story have on the reader's understanding of the story? (For a definition of *point of view*, see the Glossary of Literary Terms.)

4. Explore how the story is an example of **magical realism**. Copy the chart below into your Writer's Notebook. In the left column, list the story events. In the center column, indicate whether or not that event was realistic—could it happen in real life? In the right column, describe the element of magic surrounding or associated with that event. If there is nothing magical about the particular event, leave this column blank. A few are done for you.

Story Event	Realistic?	Element of Magic
Drowned man washes up on the beach.	Yes.	
Men go to see if anyone is missing in nearby villages.	Yes.	
Women stay behind to lay out the drowned man and get ready for burial.	Yes.	While they work, the wind is steady and the sea restless, as it has never been before.

5. How does this story relate to the theme "Other Worlds"?

Write to Understand: Magical Realism and the Effect of Esteban

Review the graphic organizer you completed and think about how in this story Gabriel García Márquez interweaves a realistic story with fantastic elements. As you are thinking, begin writing about the effect the drowned man has on the village and the neighboring villages. Explore your thoughts about why he has this effect.

Writers on Writing

BEFORE YOU READ
The World of Poetry

Meet the Authors

Ishmael Reed Born in 1938, Reed has written novels, essays, and poems that have earned him a place among the most important writers of modern America. An African-American, he is a strong promoter of multiculturalism. He co-founded the Before Columbus Foundation, an organization dedicated to a cross-cultural view of America.

Martin Espada An award-winning American poet, Espada (born 1957) draws on his Puerto Rican heritage and his diverse work experiences as subjects and inspiration for his poetry and other writings. Espada is also a renowned scholar on the works of the great Chilean poet Pablo Neruda.

Denise Levertov Denise Levertov (1923–1997) was born in England but became an American citizen in 1955. She was influenced by American experimental poets and she wrote anti-war poetry in the 1960s and 1970s. Raised as Jew, she converted to Catholicism in the last decade of her life, and religious themes dominate her later poetry.

Build Background: A World Run by Poetry

In this unit you have read about other worlds run by forces beyond the normal world. "Nethergrave," for example, imagines a world in which virtual reality overtakes reality. "The Sound of Thunder" creates a world in which time travel unleashes frightening possibilities. "The Secret Life of Walter Mitty" explores a fantasy world governed by an overactive imagination.

What would a world governed by poetry look like? The poems that follow imagine a world in which poetry is in charge, one way or another.

- Have you ever read a poem that really got to you when you read it and that stuck with you long afterwards? Think about why.

- What kinds of power does poetry have?

Beware: Do Not Read This Poem

ISHMAEL REED

tonite, *thriller* was
abt an ol woman, so vain she
surrounded her self w/
    many mirrors

It got so bad that finally she   5
locked herself indoors & her
whole life became the
    mirrors

one day the villagers broke
into her house, but she was too   10
swift for them. she disappeared
    into a mirror
each tenant who bought the house
after that, lost a loved one to
    the ol woman in the mirror: 15
    first a little girl
    then a young woman
    then the young woman/s husband

the hunger of this poem is legendary
it has taken in many victims   20
back off from this poem
it has drawn in yr feet
back off from this poem
it has drawn in yr legs
back off from this poem   25
it is a greedy mirror
you are into this poem. from
    the waist down
nobody can hear you can they?

this poem has had you up to here   30
    belch

this poem aint got no manners
you cant call out frm this poem
relax now & go w/ this poem
move & roll on to this poem   35

    do not resist this poem
    this poem has yr eyes
    this poem has his head
    this poem has his arms
    this poem has his fingers   40
    this poem has his fingertips

this poem is the reader & the
    reader this poem

statistic: the us bureau of missing persons reports
    that in 1968 over 100,000 people disappeared   45
  leaving no solid clues
    nor trace   only
a space   in the lives of their friends

The Republic of Poetry

For Chile[1]

MARTIN ESPADA

In the republic of poetry,
a train full of poets
rolls south in the rain
as plum trees rock
and horses kick the air,   5
and village bands
parade down the aisle
with trumpets, with bowler hats,[2]
followed by the president
of the republic,   10
shaking every hand.

In the republic of poetry,
monks print verses about the night
on boxes of monastery chocolate,
kitchens in restaurants   15
use odes for recipes
from eel to artichoke,
and poets eat for free.

---

1 **Chile:** In 2004, Espada was one of many poets who went to Chile to honor the memory of Pablo Neruda, Chile's foremost poet. Some of the events mentioned in this poem refer to actual events, including the leafleting with poetry of the National Palace in 2001.

2 **bowler hats:** rounded hats, also known as Derby hats, sometimes associated in the 1930s and 1940s with people who had lifted themselves out of the working class

In the republic of poetry,
poets read to the baboons   20
at the zoo, and all the primates,
poets and baboons alike, scream for joy.

In the republic of poetry,
poets rent a helicopter
to bombard the national palace   25
with poems on bookmarks,
and everyone in the courtyard
rushes to grab a poem
fluttering from the sky,
blinded by weeping.   30

In the republic of poetry,
the guard at the airport
will not allow you to leave the country
until you declaim[3] a poem for her
and she says *Ah! Beautiful.*   35

THE FLOWER PARADE, Marc Chagall

---

3 **declaim:** recite in public

PORTRAIT OF TWO GIRLS, John Stanton Ward, 1993

The Secret   DENISE LEVERTOV

Two girls discover
the secret of life
in a sudden line of
poetry.

I who don't know the   5
secret wrote
the line. They
told me

(through a third person)
they had found it   10
but not what it was
not even

what line it was. No doubt
by now, more than a week
later, they have forgotten   15
the secret,

the line, the name of
the poem. I love them
for finding what
I can't find,   20

and for loving me
for the line I wrote,
and for forgetting it
so that

a thousand times, till death   25
finds them, they may
discover it again, in other
lines

in other
happenings. And for   30
wanting to know it,
for

assuming there is
such a secret, yes,
for that   35
most of all.

AFTER YOU READ
The World of Poetry

Think and Discuss

1. What is the title "Beware: Do Not Read This Poem" warning against?

2. That poem has two main parts: the first is about the woman and the mirrors; the second is about poetry. What does one part have to do with the other?

3. Explain verse by verse what a "real world" republic would be like compared to the republic of poetry. For example, in the first verse, who might be riding the train instead of poets, and in the second verse, who might eat for free?

4. According to the poem by Levertov, are poets or the poems themselves in charge in the world of poetry? Explain your answer.

5. Choose one of the **images** or ideas in one of the poems. Tell what it brings to mind from your own experience.

6. Copy the following graphic organizer three times in your Writer's Notebook. Then complete the organizer based on your response to each of the three poems.

Response Notes	
Did I like the poem? Explain.	
Did I "get" it? Explain.	
What does the poem say to me?	
How would I describe the language and presentation of the poem?	
What images stand out?	
How would I rank this poem in relation to the other two? Explain.	

Write to Understand: Developing Personal Responses

Using your response notes in your graphic organizer, write a rough draft of a personal response essay. Choose two of the three poems. Focus on one poem at a time. When you write about the second poem, however, relate your ideas back to what you have written about the first poem, so that you are clearly comparing and contrasting. When you have finished writing about the second poem, read over your draft. Sum up your key thoughts about each poem, and their relation to each other, by writing a thesis, or main idea, statement.

A Writer's WORKSHOP

Critical Essay: Science Fiction

Experiencing other worlds is one reason people enjoy reading science fiction stories or seeing science fiction movies. What makes one science fiction story better or more effective than another? You can find answers to that question by writing a critical essay.

Prewriting

REVIEWING IDEAS

Skim back over the two science fiction stories in this unit, "The Sound of Thunder" (page 287), and "Nethergrave" (page 313). Look over any notes you made in your Writer's Notebook on these stories. Jot down any new ideas you have.

RECORDING RESPONSES

Use a Response Notes graphic organizer similar to the one on page 361 to summarize and record your responses to the two stories.

Response Notes: The Sound of Thunder

Did I like the story? Explain. I liked The Sound of Thunder because it really made me think about how connected everything is. Plus the writing is good.

Did I "get" it? I followed the story fine, and I think I get the main idea.

What does the story say to me? It says that in small ways, everything we do has an effect on our surroundings. I actually thought about all the species that have become extinct and how one thing can set a lot of other effects in motion.

How would I describe the language and presentation of the story? There are parts that are very realistic, like the dialogue, very natural sounding. Then there are parts that are very descriptive, like when he describes the machine. He doesn't go into detail about the mechanics but paints a picture of it with colors and lights.

FREEWRITING: THUMBS UP, THUMBS DOWN

Imagine you are a reviewer of stories for a TV show based on the popular movie review shows. Freewrite a mini-review of each story using the ideas in your Response Notes. If readers could read only one story, which would you recommend, and why?

COOPERATIVE LEARNING:
IDENTIFYING TRAITS OF STRONG SCIENCE FICTION

In a small group, compare your reviews. Then discuss what makes a good science fiction story. Make a list of the traits you come up with. This list of traits will serve as the rubric you use for evaluating the stories in your critical essay.

EVALUATING WITH A RUBRIC

Copy the following graphic organizer into your Writer's Notebook. Fill in the first column with the traits you and your group came up with. In the second and third columns, decide whether or not, or to what degree, each story measures up to each trait. Give examples from the text and write down quotes that support your assessment.

Traits	The Sound of Thunder	Nethergrave
Trait #1	Rating: Evidence:	Rating: Evidence
Trait #2	Rating: Evidence:	Rating: Evidence:
Trait #3	Rating: Evidence:	Rating: Evidence:

Drafting

Look over your graphic organizer. Which story seems to rank higher? Write up your assessments in the first draft of a critical essay. Begin with an introduction that catches the readers' attention and states your main idea. Follow with a well-organized evaluation of the two stories. Wrap up with a strong ending.

COOPERATIVE LEARNING: PEER REVIEW

Share your draft with a partner. Ask for feedback, and offer it on your partner's work.

USING A WORD PROCESSOR

You can add comments or notes to your partner's essay using a word processor. Place your cursor at the spot where you want to make a comment. Then go to the Insert menu and click on Comment or Notes. You will see a space in the margin made for you to add your thoughts. After comments or notes have been reviewed, you can delete or hide them. Check the Help menu of your word processor for directions on creating, hiding, and deleting comments or notes.

Revising and Editing

Use your partner's comments to help you revise your critical essay. Make it the best it can be.

READING WITH AN EDITOR'S EYE

When referring to short works such as articles, stories, short poems, and songs, use quotation marks before and after the titles and correct capitalization. Longer works as well as the names of newspapers and magazines are italicized or underlined.

Short Story	Bradbury's story "The Sound of Thunder" was published most recently in 2005 in a book called *The Sound of Thunder and Other Stories*.
Poem	"The Secret" is a poem by Denise Levertov that was published in a collection of her poetry called *Selected Poems*.
Article	"Nolan Bushnell" is one of the biographies included in the book <u>Inventing Modern America: From the Microwave to the Mouse</u>.
Newspaper	Clifford Coonan, author of "The Mysteries of China's Celtic Mummies," writes regularly for the newspaper *The Independent*.

Check to make sure you have enclosed the titles of short stories in quotation marks and capitalized the first word and other important words, but not the small words in the middle.

USING A CHECKLIST

Use the Six-Trait checklist on the following page to polish your critical essay.

Six Traits of Writing: Critical Essays

Content and Ideas
- a main idea is clearly stated
- the body of the essay evaluates a work of literature according to a rubric or some other expressed standards
- the ideas in the body are supported by details from the text(s)

Organization
- the essay has a clear introduction with main idea, body in which the evaluation is developed, and conclusion that effectively ties ideas together
- the ideas in the body are presented in a logical order

Voice or Style
- the voice sounds natural, not forced
- the voice is more formal than speech

Word Choice
- the writer uses specific and vivid nouns and adjectives
- the writer avoids the passive voice

Sentence Fluency
- sentences are complete
- sentence length and sentence beginnings are varied and purposeful
- transitions between ideas are clear and smooth

Conventions
- the essay is free of errors in usage, spelling, capitalization, and punctuation
- works referred to are presented according to the style required by the school (for example, titles of short stories are in quotes)

Crossing Borders

The boy wasn't happy with his line of work, and in his short life he had never imagined that it was work he'd do. But by taking people illegally into the United States, he'd seen Ohio, Kentucky, and snakes in the desert, and he was proud of that.

Sam Quinones, from "Delfino II: Diez in the Desert"

BEFORE YOU READ
Bridge of the Gods

Meet the Author: Ancient Ancestors

Software specialist Glenn Welker maintains a number of Web sites devoted to the indigenous, or native, people of North America. He says that he hopes he is educating non-native people about the "beautiful literature, stories, [and] fables that not many people know about." In so doing, he also hopes he is building a bridge for better understanding between indigenous and non-native peoples. He explains that the stories he has compiled on his Web sites "belong to the people." These stories were passed from generation to generation—they are "owned" by everyone.

Build Background: Legends of the Gods

Before the age of science, people relied on legends and myths to understand and give meaning to the forces of nature that amazed or frightened them. Stories helped explain the origin of the landscape as well as such natural disasters as earthquakes and volcanic eruptions. The Wasco Indians in the Pacific Northwest, for example, believed mountain thunderstorms were the work of the god Thunderbird. This supernatural bird could flap its wings to cause thunder or flash its eye to cause lightning. It was greatly respected by all who had experienced the incredible force of mountain thunderstorms.

The Wasco and other tribes have vivid legends to explain the origin and ultimate collapse of a natural bridge across the Columbia River. Scientists note that in the place where the "Bridge of the Gods" stood, a landslide took place about 300 years ago, diverting the Columbia River. Over time, the force of the river carved through the landslide, leaving only the rocky bridge on top. In time the bridge crumbled too. Later, a suspension bridge was built on this site.

As you read, think about the following questions:

- Why do people yearn to understand their natural environments?

- What do you know about the environment and ways of living of Indians of the Pacific Northwest?

This bridge spans the river where the Bridge of the Gods once stood.
POSTCARD COURTESY, Lyn Topinka.

Bridge of the Gods

BRIDGE OF THE GODS

In the days of the animal people, a great bird lived in the land of the setting sun. It was Thunderbird. All of the animal people were afraid of it. Thunderbird created five high mountains and then said to the animal people, "I made a law that no one is to pass over these five high mountains. If anyone does, I will kill him. No one is to come where I live."

Wolf did not believe the law. "I will go," declared Wolf. "I will be the first to see what Thunderbird will do to me."

"I will go with you," said Wolf's four brothers.

So the five Wolf brothers went to the first mountain. They stood in a row, and each stepped with his right foot at the same time. Immediately the five wolf brothers were dead.

When the animal people heard that the five Wolf brothers were dead, Grizzly Bear, the strongest of the animals, decided that he would go.

"I will cross over the mountains," announced Grizzly Bear. "I will not die as the Wolf brothers have died."

"We will go with you," said Grizzly Bear's four brothers.

So the five Grizzly Bear brothers went to the first mountain. They stood in a row, and each stepped with his right foot, all at the same time. Then each stepped with his left foot, all at the same time. Immediately the five Grizzly Bears were dead.

"I will go now," said Cougar. "I will take a long step and leap over the mountain."

Cougar's four brothers went with him. They made one leap together, and then all were dead.

> Wolf did not believe the law. "I will go," declared Wolf. "I will be the first to see what Thunderbird will do to me."

"We will go next," said the five Beaver brothers. "We will go under the mountain. We will not be killed. We will not be like the Wolf brothers, the Grizzly brothers, and the Cougar brothers."

But as they tried to cross under the mountains, all five Beaver brothers were killed.

Then Coyote's oldest son said, "I will talk to the mountains. I will break down the law so that people may live and pass to the sunset."

His four brothers went with him, and two of them talked to the five mountains. They made the mountains move up and down; they made the mountains dance and shake. But the five sons of Coyote were killed. The five mountains still stood. No one could pass over or under them to the sunset.

Coyote's sons had not told their father their plans. He had told them that they must never stay away from home overnight. When they did not return, he knew that they had been killed by Thunderbird. Coyote was wiser than the others. He had been instructed in wisdom by the Spirit Chief.

"*Y*ou cannot break the law of the Thunderbird. You cannot go over the five mountains. Thunderbird has made the law."

After his sons had been gone five nights, Coyote was sure that they were dead. He cried loud and long. He went to a lonely place in the mountains and rolled on the ground, wailing and howling with grief.

Then he prayed to the Spirit Chief for strength to bring his five sons back to life.

After Coyote had cried and prayed for a long time, he heard a voice. "You cannot break the law of the Thunderbird. You cannot go over the five mountains. Thunderbird has made the law."

Coyote continued crying and praying, rolling on the ground in a lonely place in the mountains. After a time he heard the voice again.

"The only thing you can do is to go up to the Above-World. It will take you five days and five nights. There you will be told how you can bring your five sons to life again."

So for five days and five nights Coyote traveled to the Above-World. There he told his troubles to the Spirit Chief. "Give me strength," he ended. "Give me so much strength that I can fight Thunderbird. Then the people can cross over the mountains to the sunset."

At last the Spirit Chief promised to help.

"I will blind the eyes of Thunderbird," he promised. "Then you can go over the five mountains and kill him."

"I will tell you what you must do," continued the Spirit Chief. "When you get back to the earth, find the big bird called Eagle. He has great strength. Ask him for a feather from his youngest son. Ask for a feather, a small feather from under his wing. This feather is downy and has great strength. It has power running out from the heart because it grows near the heart. Return now to the earth."

After five days and five nights, Coyote reached the earth again. He found Eagle and told him all that the Great Spirit had said. Then he asked, "Will you give me the feather that grows nearest the heart of your youngest son?"

"*W*ill you give me the feather that grows nearest the heart of your youngest son?"

"I will do as the Spirit Chief bids," replied Eagle. "If he told you to come to me, then I will give you my power to fight Thunderbird."

So Eagle picked a feather from under the wing of his youngest son. It was such a small downy feather that it could not be seen when it floated through the air. The coyote followed the next commandment the Spirit Chief had given him.

"Fast for ten days and ten nights," he had said. "If you will go without food and drink for ten days and nights, you will be changed to a feather. You will then be able to go anywhere."

So Coyote fasted. After ten days and ten nights, he was turned into a feather, like the one Eagle had given him. He floated through the air toward the five mountains. At a distance from them, he made a noise like thunder, as the Spirit Chief had told him to do. Three times he made a slow, deep rumbling, off toward the sunrise.

Thunderbird heard the rumble and asked, "Who is making this noise? I alone was given the power to make that rumbling sound. This noise must be coming from the Above-World. I am dead! I am dead! I am dead!"

A fourth time Coyote rumbled, this time closer to Thunderbird. Thunderbird became angry. "I will kill whoever this is that is making the noise. I will kill him! I will kill him!" he repeated angrily.

Thunderbird made a mighty noise, a greater thunder than Coyote had made. Coyote, in the form of a feather, went into the air, higher and higher and ever higher. He darted and whirled, but could not be seen.

Thunderbird was afraid. He knew that if a fifth rumble of thunder came he would be dead. He sought the deep water of Great River, to hide himself there. He heard Coyote far above him.

Coyote prayed to the Spirit Chief. "Help me one more time, just one more time. Help me kill Thunderbird so that the people may live, so that my sons will come to life again."

The Spirit Chief heard Coyote and helped him. Thunderbird sank deeper into the water, terrified. Coyote, still invisible above him, made a greater noise than ever, a noise like the bursting of the world. The five mountains crumbled and fell. Pieces of the mountain, floating down the Great River, formed islands along its course.

Thunderbird died, and his giant body formed a great bridge above the river. The five sons of Coyote and all the other animal people who had been killed by Thunderbird came back to life.

Though many hundreds of snows had passed, the great bridge formed from the rocks that had been made out of Thunderbird's body still stood above the river. It was there long after the first Indians came to the earth. The Indians always called it "the Bridge of the Gods." No one must look at the rocks of the bridge. People knew that some day it would fall. They must not anger the Spirit Chief by looking at it, their wise men told them.

Coyote prayed to the Spirit Chief. "Help me one more time, just one more time. Help me kill Thunderbird . . ."

The Klickitat Indians[1] had a different law. Only a few men necessary to paddle the canoes would pass under the bridge. All the others would land when they approached the Bridge of the Gods, walk around to the opposite side of it, and there reenter the canoes. The oarsmen always bade their friends good-bye, fearing that the bridge would fall while they were passing under it.

After many snows, no one knows how many, the prophecy of the wise men came true. The Bridge of the Gods fell. The rocks that had once been the body of Thunderbird formed the rapids in the river that were long known as Cascades of the Columbia.

---

1 **Klickitat Indians:** another tribe of the Pacific Northwest, since the 1970s no longer existing as a separate tribe

AFTER YOU READ
Bridge of the Gods

Think and Discuss

1. Often, the characters in myths and legends exhibit traits or values that the people in that culture admire or need to survive. What values are enacted in this story?

2. Why do you think the Indians knew that someday the rocks would fall?

3. **Myths** and **legends** are traditional stories that try to explain the origins of the universe, of a specific people, or of things in the natural world. Find all the things that "Bridge of the Gods" tries to explain.

4. **Personification** means giving human traits to non-human things such as supernatural figures or animals. Copy the following chart in your Writer's Notebook and fill it in to show how the animals in this story express certain ideas.

Supernatural Figure/Animal	Human Characteristics	Idea or Concept Expressed
Thunderbird, a great bird	Speaks; threatens with violence	Immense, frightening power
Wolves		
Grizzly Bears		
Cougars, Beavers, Coyotes		
Coyote's father		
Spirit Chief		

Write to Understand: Myth-making

Is there a place or a thing in your surroundings that a myth could explain—for example, unusual geologic structures, plants, or animal behavior? Write a myth that explains how it came to be, using any of the following mythical elements.

- an anonymous narrator

- a specific setting: a real or imaginary time and place

- characters that are either human, animal, or supernatural

- a conflict, probably one that is caused by nature

- language that is simple and clear, as befits a myth or legend

BEFORE YOU READ

Borders

Meet the Author: Thomas King

Thomas King (born 1943)—a Canadian with U.S. roots, who is part Blackfoot, part Cherokee—may have personal reasons for his interest in borders. He explores that interest in witty, insightful fiction about Native Americans. In addition to writing award-winning novels for adults and young readers, King teaches at the University of Guelph, Ontario, Canada. He is also a fine arts photographer and broadcasts a weekly radio show called "The Dead Dog Café Comedy Hour."

Build Background: Mapping the Borders

In order to make way for the trans-Canadian railroad, in 1877 the Canadian government signed a treaty confining certain Indians to small reserves. After that, natives who shared ethnic roots with U.S. tribes were divided from their tribespeople by two borders: international and reserve.

The First Nations of Canada have a highly visible cultural and political presence in Canada though they represent only one percent of the Canadian population. More than 50 native languages and many dialects display the cultural vitality of the First Nation.

- Many students face borders in their own lives—boundaries that may be social, geographic, religious, or cultural. Think of a border passing you have to make, or resist making, in your family, school, city, or other part of your life.

- Why are countries so watchful about people crossing their borders?

Borders

THOMAS KING

BORDERS

Thomas King

When I was twelve, maybe thirteen, my mother announced that we were going to go to Salt Lake City to visit my sister who had left the reserve, moved across the line, and found a job. Laetitia had not left home with my mother's blessing, but over time my mother had come to be proud of the fact that Laetitia had done all of this on her own.

"She did real good," my mother would say.

Then there were the fine points to Laetitia's going. She had not, as my mother liked to tell Mrs. Manyfingers, gone floating after some man like a balloon on a string. She hadn't snuck out of the house, either, and gone to Vancouver or Edmonton or Toronto to chase rainbows down alleys. And she hadn't been pregnant.

"She did real good."

I was seven or eight when Laetitia left home. She was seventeen. Our father was from Rocky Bay on the American side.

"Dad's American," Laetitia told my mother," so I can go and come as I please."

"Send us a postcard."

Laetitia packed her things, and we headed for the border. Just outside of Milk River, Laetitia told us to watch for the water tower.

"Over the next rise. It's the first thing you see."

"We got a water tower on the reserve," my mother said. "There's a big one in Lethbridge, too."

"You'll be able to see the tops of the flagpoles, too. That's where the border is."

When we got to Coutts, my mother stopped at the convenience store and bought her and Laetitia a cup of coffee. I got an Orange Crush.

"This is real lousy coffee."

"You're just angry because I want to see the world."

"It's the water. From here on down, they got lousy water."

"I can catch the bus from Sweetgrass. You don't have to lift a finger."

"You're going to have to buy your water in bottles if you want good coffee."

There was an old wooden building about a block away, with a tall sign in the yard that said "Museum." Most of the roof had been blown away. Mom told me to go and see when the place was open. There were boards over the windows and doors. You could tell that the place was closed, and I told Mom so, but she said to go and check anyway. Mom and Laetitia stayed by the car. Neither one of them moved. I sat down on the steps of the museum and watched them, and I don't know that they ever said anything to each other. Finally, Laetitia got her bag out of the trunk and gave Mom a hug.

I wandered back to the car. The wind had come up, and it blew Laetitia's hair across her face. Mom reached out and pulled the strands out of Laetitia's eyes, and Laetitia let her.

"You can still see the mountain from here," my mother told Laetitia in Blackfoot.

"Lots of mountains in Salt Lake," Laetitia told her in English.

"The place is closed," I said. "Just like I told you."

Laetitia tucked her hair into her jacket and dragged her bag down the road to the brick building with the American flag flapping on a pole. When she got to where the guards were waiting, she turned, put the bag down, and waved to us. We waved back. Then my mother turned the car around, and we came home.

We got postcards from Laetitia regular, and, if she wasn't spreading jelly on the truth, she was happy. She found a good job and rented an apartment with a pool.

"And she can't even swim," my mother told Mrs. Manyfingers.

Most of the postcards said we should come down and see the city, but whenever I mentioned this, my mother would stiffen up.

So I was surprised when she bought two new tires for the car and put on her blue dress with the green and yellow flowers. I had to dress up, too, for my mother did not want us crossing the border looking like Americans. We made sandwiches and put them in a big box with pop and potato chips and some apples and bananas and a big jar of water.

"But we can stop at one of those restaurants, too, right?"

"We maybe should take some blankets in case you get sleepy."

"But we can stop at one of those restaurants, too, right?"

The border was actually two towns, though neither one was big enough to amount to anything. Coutts was on the Canadian side and consisted of the convenience store and gas station, the museum that was closed and boarded up, and a motel. Sweetgrass was on the American side, but all you could see was an overpass that arched across the highway and disappeared into the prairies. Just hearing the names of these towns, you would expect that Sweetgrass, which is a nice name and sounds like it is related to other places such as Medicine Hat and Moose Jaw and Kicking Horse Pass, would be on the Canadian side, and that Coutts, which sounds abrupt and rude, would be on the American side. But this was not the case.

Between the two borders was a duty-free shop where you could buy cigarettes and liquor and flags. Stuff like that.

We left the reserve in the morning and drove until we got to Coutts.

"Last time we stopped here," my mother said, "you had an Orange Crush. You remember that?"

"Sure," I said. "That was when Laetitia took off."

"You want another Orange Crush?"

"That means we're not going to stop at a restaurant, right?"

My mother got a coffee at the convenience store, and we stood around and watched the prairies move in the sunlight. Then we climbed back in the car. My mother straightened the dress across her thighs, leaned against the wheel, and drove all the way to the border in first gear, slowing, as if she were trying to see through a bad storm or riding high on black ice.

The border guard was an old guy. As he walked to the car, he swayed from side to side, his feet set wide apart, the holster on his hip pitching up and down. He leaned into the window, looked into the backseat, and looked at my mother and me.

"Morning, ma'am."

"Good morning."

"Where you heading?"

"Salt Lake City."

"Purpose of your visit?"

"Visit my daughter."

"Citizenship?"

"Blackfoot," my mother told him.

"Ma'am?"

"Blackfoot," my mother repeated.

"Canadian?"

"Blackfoot."

It would have been easier if my mother had just said "Canadian" and been done with it, but I could see she wasn't going to do that. The guard wasn't angry or anything. He smiled and looked towards the building. Then he turned back and nodded.

"Morning, ma'am."

"Good morning."

"Any firearms or tobacco?"

"No."

"Citizenship?"

"Blackfoot."

He told us to sit in the car and wait, and we did. In about five minutes, another guard came out with the first man. They were talking as they came, both men swaying back and forth like two cowboys headed for a bar or a gunfight.

"Morning, ma'am."

"Good morning."

"Cecil tells me you and the boy are Blackfoot."

"That's right."

"Now, I know that we got Blackfeet on the American side and the Canadian got Blackfeet on their side. Just so we can keep our records straight, what side do you come from?"

I knew exactly what my mother was going to say, and I could have told them if they had asked me.

"Canadian side or American side?" asked the guard.

"Blackfoot side," she said.

It didn't take them long to lose their sense of humor. I can tell you that. The one guard stopped smiling altogether and told us to park our car at the side of the building and come in.

We sat on a wood bench for about an hour before anyone came over to talk to us. This time it was a woman. She had a gun, too.

"Hi," she said. "I'm Inspector Pratt. I understand there is a little misunderstanding."

"I'm going to visit my daughter in Salt Lake City," my mother told her. "We

> "Canadian side or American side?" asked the guard.
> "Blackfoot side," she said.

don't have any guns or beer."

"It's a legal technicality, that's all."

"My daughter's Blackfoot, too."

The woman opened a briefcase and took out a couple forms and began to write on one of them. "Everyone who crosses our border has to declare their citizenship. Even Americans. It helps us keep track of the visitors we get from various countries."

She went on like that for maybe fifteen minutes, and a lot of the stuff she told us was interesting.

"I can understand how you feel about having to tell us your citizenship, and here's what I'll do. You tell me, and I won't put it down on the form. No one will know but you and me."

Her gun was silver. There were several chips in the wood handle and the name "Stella" was scratched into the metal butt.

We were in the border office for about four hours, and we talked to almost everyone there. One of the men bought me a Coke. My mother brought a couple of sandwiches in from the car. I offered part of mine to Stella, but she said she wasn't hungry.

I told Stella that we were Blackfoot and Canadian, but she said that that didn't count because I was a minor. In the end, she told us that if my mother didn't declare her citizenship, we would have to go back to where we came from. My mother stood up and thanked Stella for her time. Then we got back in the car and drove to the Canadian border, which was only about a hundred yards away.

I was disappointed. I hadn't seen Laetitia for a long time, and I had never been to Salt Lake City. When she was still at home, Laetitia would go on and on about Salt Lake City. She had never been there, but her boyfriend Lester Tallbull had spent a year in Salt Lake at a technical school.

"It's a great place," Lester would say. "Nothing but blondes in the whole state."

When he said that, Laetitia would slug him on his shoulder hard enough to make him flinch. He had some brochures on Salt Lake and some maps, and every so often the two of them would spread them out on the table.

"That's the temple. It's right downtown. You got to have a pass to get in."

"Charlotte says anyone can go in and look around."

"When was Charlotte in Salt Lake? Just when the hell was Charlotte in Salt

Lake?"

"Last year."

"This is Liberty Park. It's got a zoo. There's good skiing in the mountains."

"Got all the skiing we can use," my mother would say. "People come from all over the world to ski at Banff. Cardston's got a temple, if you like those kinds of things."

"Oh, this one is real big," Lester would say. "They got armed guards and everything."

"Not what Charlotte says."

"What does she know?"

Lester and Laetitia broke up, but I guess the idea of Salt Lake stuck in her mind.

The Canadian border guard was a young woman, and she seemed happy to see us. "Hi," she said. "You folks sure have a great day for a trip. Where are you coming from?"

"Standoff."

"Is that in Montana?'

"No."

"Where are you going?"

"Standoff."

The woman's name was Carol and I don't guess she was any older than Laetitia. "Wow, you both Canadians?"

"Blackfoot."

"Really? I have a friend I went to school with who is Blackfoot. Do you know Mike Harley?"

"No."

He went to school in Lethbridge, but he's really from Browning."

It was a nice conversation and there were no cars behind us, so there was no rush.

"You're not bringing any liquor back, are you?"

"No."

"Any cigarettes or plants or stuff like that?"

"No."

"Citizenship?"

"Blackfoot."

"I know," said the woman, "and I'd be proud of being Blackfoot if I were Blackfoot. But you have to be American or Canadian."

When Laetitia and Lester broke up, Lester took his brochures and maps with him, so Laetitia wrote to someone in Salt Lake City, and, about a month later, she got a big envelope of stuff. We sat at the table and opened up all the brochures, and Laetitia read each one out loud.

"Salt Lake City is the gateway to some of the world's most magnificent skiing.

"Salt Lake City is the home of one of the newest professional basketball franchises, the Utah Jazz.

"The Great Salt Lake is one of the natural wonders of the world."

It was kind of exciting seeing all those color brochures on the table and listening to Laetitia read all about how Salt Lake City was one of the best places in the entire world.

"That Salt Lake City place sounds too good to be true," my mother told her.

"It has everything."

"We got everything right here."

"It's boring here."

People in Salt Lake City are probably sending away for brochures of Calgary and Lethbridge and Pincher Creek right now."

In the end, my mother would say that maybe Laetitia should go to Salt Lake City, and Laetitia would say that maybe she would.

We parked the car to the side of the building and Carol led us into a small room on the second floor. I found a comfortable spot on the couch and flipped through some back issues of *Saturday Night* and *Alberta Report*.

When I woke up, my mother was just coming out of another office. She didn't say a word to me. I followed her down the stairs and out to the car. I thought we were going home, but she turned the car around and drove back towards the American border, which made me think we were going to visit Laetitia in Salt Lake City after all. Instead she pulled into the parking lot of the duty-free store and stopped.

"We going to see Laetitia?"

"No."

"We going home?"

Pride is a good thing to have, you know. Laetitia had a lot of pride, and so did my mother. I figured that someday, I'd have it too.

"So where are we going?"

Most of that day, we wandered around the duty-free store, which wasn't very large. The manager had a name tag with a tiny American flag on one side and a tiny Canadian flag on the other. His name was Mel. Towards evening he began suggesting that we should be on our way. I told him we had nowhere to go, that neither the Americans nor the Canadians would let us in. He laughed at that and told us that we should buy something or leave.

Towards evening he began suggesting that we should be on our way. I told him we had nowhere to go, that neither the Americans nor the Canadians would let us in.

The car was not very comfortable, but we did have all that food and it was April, so even if it did snow as it sometimes does on the prairies, we wouldn't freeze. The next morning my mother drove to the American border.

It was a different guard this time, but the questions were the same. We didn't spend as much time in the office as we had the day before. By noon, we were back at the Canadian border. By two we were back in the duty-free shop parking lot.

The second night in the car was not as much fun as the first, but my mother seemed in good spirits, and, all in all, it was as much an adventure as an inconvenience. There wasn't much food left and that was a problem, but we had lots of water as there was a faucet at the side of the duty-free shop.

One Sunday, Laetitia and I were watching television. Mom was over at Mrs. Manyfingers's. Right in the middle of the program, Laetitia tuned off the set and said she was going to Salt Lake City, that life around here was too boring. I had wanted to see the rest of the program and really didn't care if Laetitia went to Salt Lake City or not. When Mom got home, I told her what Laetitia had said.

What surprised me was how angry Laetitia got when she found out that I had told Mom.

"You got a big mouth."

"That's what you said."

"What I said is none of your business."

"I didn't say anything."

"Well, I'm going for sure, now."

That weekend, Laetitia packed her bags, and we drove her to the border.

Mel turned out to be friendly. When he closed up for the night and found us still parked in the lot, he came over and asked us if our car was broken down or something. My mother thanked him for his concern and told him that we were fine, that things would get straightened out in the morning.

"You're kidding," said Mel. "You'd think they could handle the simple things."

"We got some apples and a banana," I said, "but we're all out of ham sandwiches."

"You know, you read about these things, but you just don't believe it. You just don't believe it."

"Hamburgers would be even better because they got more stuff for energy."

My mother slept in the backseat. I slept in the front because I was smaller and could lie under the steering wheel. Late that night, I heard my mother open the car door. I found her sitting on her blanket leaning against the bumper of the car.

"You see all those stars," she said. "When I was a little girl, my grandmother used to take me and my sisters out on the prairies and tell us stories about all the stars."

"Do you think Mel is going to bring us any hamburgers?"

"Every one of those stars has a story. You see that bunch of stars over there that look like a fish?"

"He didn't say no."

"Coyote went fishing, one day. That's how it all started." We sat out under the stars that night, and my mother told me all sorts of stories. She was serious about it, too. She'd tell them slow, repeating parts as she went, as if she expected me to remember each one.

Early the next morning, the television vans began to arrive, and guys in suits and women in dresses came trotting over to us, dragging microphones and cameras and lights behind them. One of the vans had a table set up with orange juice and sandwiches and fruit. It was for the crew, but when I told them we hadn't eaten for a while, a really skinny blonde woman told us we could eat as much as we wanted.

They mostly talked to my mother. Every so often one of the reporters would come over and ask me questions about how it felt to be an Indian without a country. I told them we had a nice house on the reserve and that my cousins had a couple of horses we rode when we went fishing. Some of the television people went over to the American border, and then they went to the Canadian border.

Around noon, a good-looking guy in a dark blue suit and an orange tie with little ducks on it drove up in a fancy car. He talked to my mother for a while, and, after they were done talking, my mother called me over, and we got into our car. Just as my mother started the engine, Mel came over and gave us a bag of peanut brittle and told us that justice was a damn hard thing to get, but that we shouldn't give up.

*E*very so often one of the reporters would come over and ask me questions about how it felt to be an Indian without a country.

I would have preferred lemon drops, but it was nice of Mel anyway.

"Where are we going now?"

"Going to visit Laetitia."

The guard who came out to our car was all smiles. The television lights were so bright they hurt my eyes and, if you tried to look through the windshield in certain directions, you couldn't see a thing.

"Morning, ma'am."

"Good morning."

"Where you heading?"

"Salt Lake City."

"Purpose of your visit?"

"Visit my daughter."

"Any tobacco, liquor, or firearms?"

"Don't smoke."

"Any plants or fruit?"

"Not any more."

"Citizenship?"

"Blackfoot."

The guard rocked back on his heels and jammed his thumbs into his gun belt. "Thank you," he said, his fingers patting the butt of the revolver. "Have a pleasant trip."

My mother rolled the car forward, and the television people had to scramble out of the way. They ran alongside the car as we pulled away from the border, and, when they couldn't run any farther, they stood in the middle of the highway and waved and waved and waved.

We got to Salt Lake City the next day. Laetitia was happy to see us, and, that first night, she took us out to a restaurant that made really good soups. The list of pies took up a whole page. I had cherry. Mom had chocolate. Laetitia said that she saw us on television the night before and, during the meal, she had us tell her the story over and over again.

Laetitia took us everywhere. We went to a fancy ski resort. We went to the temple. We got to go shopping in a couple of large malls, but they weren't as large as the one in Edmonton, and Mom said so.

After a week or so, I got bored and wasn't at all sad when my mother said we should be heading back home. Laetitia wanted us to stay longer, but Mom said no, that she had things to do back home and that, next time, Laetitia should come up and visit. Laetitia said she was thinking about moving back, and Mom told her to do as she pleased, and Laetitia said that she would.

On the way home, we stopped at the duty-free shop, and my mother gave Mel a green hat that said "Salt Lake" across the front. Mel was a funny guy. He took the hat and blew his nose and told my mother that she was an inspiration to us all. He gave us some more peanut brittle and came out into the parking lot and waved at us all the way to the Canadian border.

It was almost evening when we left Coutts. I watched the border through the rear window until all you could see were the tops of the flagpoles and the blue water tower, and then they rolled over a hill and disappeared.

AFTER YOU READ
Borders

Think and Discuss

1. Why doesn't the mother just say "Canadian" in answer to the border guards' queries about her citizenship?

2. How does this story convey the importance of the mother's native heritage to her?

3. **Point of view** means the perspective from which an author presents the characters and events of a story. Why do you think the author chooses to tell this story from the **first-person point of view** through eyes of a young boy?

4. In fiction, **motivation** refers to a moving force that causes a character to act in a certain way. What is the mother's motivation for telling the boy her stories at a time when the two of them are an "international incident"?

5. The story as the boy tells it actually takes place in several different times. Copy the graphic organizer below into your Writer's Notebook. Use it to separate out the different times represented in the story. In each column, list the events in **chronological order**, or time order. A few examples are done to show you how.

Events in the story that happen when the boy is 12 or 13	Events that happened at an earlier time
• mother announces to boy they are going to see sister	• Laetitia's boyfriend Lester talks about Salt Lake City
• mother buys new tires and makes sandwiches for the trip	• Laetitia and Lester break up

6. Why is this short story a good selection for a unit on "Crossing Borders"?

Write to Understand: The Use of Flashbacks

Look over your graphic organizer and note how the story moves back and forth in time. The parts of the story that take place in the past are called **flashbacks**. Think about why the author might have told the story that way. For example, what if he had started the story where the flashback story begins, and then told the whole rest of the story in chronological order? Write a paragraph explaining what you think the effect of that way of presenting the story would have been, and compare that to the effect the flashbacks helped create.

BEFORE YOU READ

Delfino II: Diez in the Desert
Mexicans Begin Jogging

Meet the Authors

Sam Quinones Quinones is drawn to stories about drug smugglers, tomato pickers, popsicle entrepreneurs and other immigrants. On his Web site, he says, "I suppose my books try to tell the stories of unnoticed people. My favorite stories to do are those where the people I'm interviewing have never met a reporter."

Gary Soto Born in 1952, Soto was five years old when his father died in a factory accident. Like many Mexican Americans in California's Central Valley, the Soto family worked as migrant laborers and had little time to encourage their children's reading. Soto, however, became an avid reader. His writing draws heavily on his Chicano heritage and the vivid street life of his youth. His goal: to inspire the next generation of Mexican American writers.

Build Background: Faces of Immigration

Quinones and Soto write about the Mexicans who pursue the American Dream. Some enter the United States illegally, preferring a dangerous border crossing to living poor in their villages or urban slums. Once here, they can work at pay rates that average ten times more per day than in Mexico.

To Quinones, these immigrants are neither heroes nor villains. They are simply people caught up in a vast migration that is changing both Mexico and the United States. Soto, a child of immigrants, writes about the complex variety of the Mexican American experience. The true-life essay and the autobiographical poem that follow put a human face on the complicated subject of Mexican immigration. Trace your own feelings about them as you read.

- What is your own family's experience of immigration?

- What does the word *border* mean to you? Think about what it means to those in the following essay and poem.

original velvet painting by Daneil Marquez

Delfino II: Diez in the Desert

SAM QUINONES

DELFINO II: DIEZ IN THE DESERT

Sam Quinones

The boy wasn't happy with his line of work, and in his short life he had never imagined that it was work he'd do. But by taking people illegally into the United States, he'd seen Ohio, Kentucky, and snakes in the desert, and he was proud of that. He was sure that he'd seen more of the world than men in his village who were twice his age. He had shepherded his first crew of people across the desert and into the United States before he could have legally driven in that country. Fear accompanied him always, but he'd seen that he could control it. One night, driving a group of illegals into Birmingham, Alabama, his car broke down; he calmly walked them all night along the highway into town. This kind of accomplishment was liberating and left him trusting his own abilities. Almost eighty people were in the United States because of him. . . .

His mother had named him Daniel, but everyone called him Diez— Ten—a nickname that was for his having been born on May 10, this in 1987. So he'd been sixteen for less than a month when, on June 7, 2003, he led a raggedy group of ten folks from Veracruz[1] through the Arizona desert.

protruded
stuck out

physique
body type;
build

Diez was short and slight, but he had a confidence that **protruded** like a muscle beyond his thin **physique** and convinced many people who met him that he was bigger and more in control than he was. He had high cheekbones, with hair cut in a fade. His voice crackled. He punctuated it often with a dry laugh and spoke fast, slurring his speech, filling it with the slang of Mexican youth. He often ended sentences in, "you understand?" He hadn't known his father, who'd deserted the family for another woman when he was young. His mother, grandmother, and uncle had raised him. To them and to his siblings, whom he supported, he was an object of admiration.

Though he was a small-town boy, Diez had hip-hop tastes. He liked baggy shorts, baseball caps, and he had a barbed-wire tattoo engraved

---

I **Veracruz:** a city and state in Mexico

around his right bicep. Occupying the place of honor in the front room of his family's concrete-block house was a silver Panasonic stereo, which he obtained as partial payment from a client. On this he played CDs of Spanish rap, Eminem, and Mexican *ranchera* music.[2] His dream was to have the nicest truck in his town. A few more trips north and he'd have enough money for a black 1994 Ram pickup that a friend was going to bring down from the United States. . . .

He had left school in junior high, **ostensibly** because his mother was ill. At times he regretted having dropped out, particularly when he saw kids his age wearing backpacks. But he had felt nothing for school and viewed it as drudgery. So he'd stopped going and, at fifteen, went to the United States with a coyote[3] from a nearby town. With that coyote, he walked through the desert for the first time.

Eventually, he arrived in Phoenix, at the home of some friends. He stayed in Phoenix for eight months, but never could find work. However, the coyote who took him across had noticed something in him—a daring, a boldness, Diez figured, for this is what Diez

*C*oyote was a term he disliked. He thought it sounded bad. In Mexico the word had sleazy, cowardly associations. Instead, he referred to smuggling humans as "the work."

saw in himself. The coyote offered to take him on as a partner, to help out in future trips. Every few weeks after that, Diez would head down from Phoenix to Sonoyta, a small Mexican border town. There he and his new partner would take north ten or twelve people at a time. This is how Diez, who first went to the United States looking for work, learned to smuggle illegal immigrants when he was not yet sixteen years old, and came to lead much older men through the Arizona desert.

Coyote was a term he disliked. He thought it sounded bad. In Mexico the word had sleazy, cowardly associations. Instead, he referred to smuggling humans as "the work." He didn't like the work any more than the job title, but he had nothing else. He wasn't afraid of the Border Patrol, for they hadn't

---

2 *ranchera* **music:** a type of traditional music in Mexico, often featuring romantic and patriotic themes

3 **coyote:** term used for someone who smuggles people across the Mexico-U.S. border

caught him yet. Although he felt responsible for breaking up families, the people were desperate to go north. How else, he reasoned, could a junior high dropout like himself support his family and be in line to have the hippest truck in all of [his home town] of Chocamán? So, to cover his moral bases, he made frequent references to God. "God first," he said often. "God willing." It sounded hollow, but he knew that it pleased his mother to hear him talk like this. He spoke more believably of the necessity of faith, particularly when crossing the desert, and how it was essential to inspire his charges with the belief that they could make it through even as their bodies began to break down.

The city of Córdoba . . . serves as the hub of western Veracruz. The group Diez was to take on his second trip as leader met for the first time in Córdoba's bus station, on the afternoon of Wednesday, June 4.

There was Tavo, a boy he was training to help out on the trip. Diez brought two young men from a nearby village named Xocotla. . . . One of these young men was Guadalupe Cocotle. He was eighteen and two of his brothers were already in a suburb of Los Angeles called Bell, where they had work installing carpeting and wood floors. Guadalupe was short and thin, the son of a retired teacher.

Shorter and thinner was the friend accompanying him. Delfino Juárez had worked construction in Mexico City since he was twelve. Since that age he'd been his family's lone source of support. . . .

Eight months before Delfino left for the United States, his wife had given birth to a boy. They named him Axel. Now Delfino knew construction work in Mexico City wasn't going to be enough. . . .

From a village named Tijan came two men and a teenage boy. There were also three women from the village of Cosaltepec—a friend and two sisters-in-law. Finally, there was a man from Guatemala, and he came to be known to all as simply Guatemala. Diez never knew the names of anyone on the trip. He preferred not to ask. It was business. He didn't want to know their personal lives. Each person would pay him fourteen thousand pesos—thirteen hundred dollars—to have him cross the border and get them to Los Angeles.

That afternoon, they took a bus from Córdoba to Mexico City. There they boarded a bus for Sonoyta in the northern state of Sonora, abutting

Arizona. For the next thirty-four hours, they cut west across Mexico to the Pacific coast and then north to the border. On the way, Diez imparted what wisdom his seventeen trips across the desert had taught him. He told them not to wear bright clothing that would stand out to a helicopter. They were to bring only one change of clothes.

. . . As they settled in to the trip, the new acquaintances talked. The conversation naturally drifted to what each hoped from the United States and how long each would spend up north: a year, two years, three years, enough time to build a house back home. As many immigrants do, they spoke of the United States in terms of a fishing trip. How would they do and what stories would they have to tell when they returned? Visions of ten-dollars-an-hour wages danced before them.

. . . *They took a taxi east several miles, to an isolated spot, got out, and began walking north . . .*

One of the women was short and heavy. She was older than the two women—her sister-in-law and a friend—who accompanied her. She was determined, saying she was going to work really hard and hoped to earn a lot of money in Los Angeles, where her brother lived. Her husband had beat her and left her penniless with two children. She left the kids with her mother; one day she would send for them. Guadalupe noticed a couple times on the bus that she bled from her nose.

As they talked and the dreams animated the conversation, Diez watched and thought to himself, "God willing, it'll happen."

By the time the bus trip ended, these strangers were a **cohesive** group, and though they never knew each other's names, they were friendly and getting along. They arrived Friday in Sonoyta, directly across the border from the Tohono O'odham Indian reservation. Diez found them a motel where they slept that night. Before dawn the next morning, they took a taxi east several miles, to an isolated spot, got out, and began walking north and into the reservation.

cohesive
close

A few miles outside Tucson, the Tohono O'odham Indian reservation is a silent land of two million acres **splayed** across southwest Arizona down to the Sonora border. . . . Just across the border is Papago Farms, a farm run by the Tohono O'odham tribe. Running north from the farm is a paved two-lane

splayed
spread out in a clumsy way

highway, Federal Route 21. The road has few travelers apart from Border Patrol jeeps. The first population along this road is twelve miles north of the border—the Indian settlement of Santa Cruz, known for a large salt cedar tree with flowing branches giving lots of shade.

North of the farm, the desert is patches of low scrub brush and beige silt. This area is silent. It is so heavily trafficked by smugglers of drugs and people that the Tohono O'odham Indians say the animals and birds have been scared off.

A few miles later, large bushes and a stand of majestic saguaro cactus gradually emerge. Rising thirty and forty feet above the brush with their arms outstretched, the saguaros appear like mannequins[4] caught forever in surprise, triumph, or joy. A saguaro cactus lives to two hundred yeas old, and must be fifty before it can grow arms. Saguaros are also 95 percent water— each one amounting to a living water-storage tank that is all but impossible for humans to get at.

After a few more miles, the saguaros disappear and give way to paloverde and mesquite—small trees of green and dark bark. Lower to the ground are ironwood, creosote, greasewood, and ocotillo, a bony, leafless plant whose many branches rise from the ground like electrified hair.

unnerving
frightening;
scary

Most **unnerving** of all this desert's plant life is the cholla cactus. Its dark trunk is topped by a hydra-head[5] of tubes covered with blond needles and spines. From a distance these spines appear soft and furry, which is why the species common to the area is called the Teddy Bear cholla. Up close, though, the spines loom more like sharp clenched teeth ready to bite. Desert wanderers dying of thirst have been known to imagine the cholla is a container of water and stick their faces in it.

ample
plentiful;
abundant

gaunt
scrawny; thin

Like the cholla cactus, this desert, from a distance, appears almost lush and inviting. Rainfall averages about seven inches a year, which is enough to cover much of the land in vegetation. But the flora, on closer look, is menacing and turns the desert into an endless obstacle course for those walking through it. Each plant is a potential abrasion or a needle imbedded in the skin. Though the plant life is **ample**, it is so **gaunt** that it provides

---

4 **mannequins:** dummies used to display clothes in a store window

5 **hydra-head:** a head like the Hydra, a monster in Greek mythology that has many serpent-like heads

little shelter from the sun. . . . Many people grow **disoriented** in the desert heat and wander until they die, with a house or road only a hundred yards away.

June is the desert's hottest month. In July, the summer rains begin. The saguaros produce their fruit, the ocotillo's bare branches grow a green fur and red berry, and the Tohono O'odham calendar begins. But the desert's **denizens** can only hunker down and endure June. Moisture vanishes from the air. The sun is at its highest point. In June, the National Weather Service often reports temperatures well over 100 degrees. But even when they are only 98 to 101 degrees, as they were on June 7, 2003, temperatures on the unprotected desert floor can rise to 130 degrees or more.

As it happened, Diez was aware of none of this. This was only the second group he'd led, though he had walked the desert with his partner many times and felt he knew the routine. Walking steadily, they would need ten to twelve hours to arrive at the Indian village of Santa Cruz, where Diez had a contact who would take them to Tucson. From there they would connect with the **legion** of private drivers that has emerged in Tucson and Phoenix. Diez could hire them to take each immigrant where he wanted to go in the United States.

Together, his group carried six limes, cans of corn and sardines, a sheet, a blanket, and twenty-two five-liter bottles of water. He'd told his charges to wear dark clothing—nothing white or red or yellow that might stand out. He wore tennis shoes, black jeans, a gray basketball jersey, and his lucky black baseball cap **emblazoned** with the letters *SA*. He had no idea what they referred to. He'd been given the cap about the time he took his first trip. It was tattered, and his friends had told him to get rid of it, but he always used it when he was taking people across. No one had sunglasses, and, other than Diez, no one had a hat. . . .

During the first few hours, the trek proceeded as planned. The group walked single file behind Diez. Guadalupe thought they were almost done when they crossed the border an hour after dawn. Delfino was filled with **bravado**. Walking a couple of hours in the early morning, he felt nothing and didn't know what all the fuss was about, this desert and its heat. He figured he was just tough.

disoriented
confused;
mixed-up

denizens
citizens

legion
a crowd or
multitude

emblazoned
decorated

bravado
daring;
boldness

Within a few hours, though, the sun was high in the sky, and its intensity unnerved the **tenderfoots.** Diez kept walking and walking. Each walker quickly learned to concentrate on what was before him. The rocks could twist an ankle. Cactus spines pierced shoe soles, and even slightly grazing a cholla could **lacerate** skin. Talking ceased. All their mental energy focused on avoiding the dangers the desert presented with every step.

Four hours into the walk, they passed Federal Route 21. And a half hour after that, things began to fall apart. The heavyset woman had been doing poorly. The group was walking fast, and she couldn't keep up. Guadalupe saw the blood again coming from her nose. She asked how far they had to go. They weren't even a quarter of the way, Diez told her. He tried to encourage her, but she had to stop.

They made her a shade hut by placing the sheet over some plants, while the rest of the group stood around her in the sun. She was scared and bleeding, and they joked with her to cheer her up. After a while, they asked if she could go on. She said she could. They began walking with her, pulling her along at times. But as she walked, she grew **delirious**. She **hallucinated**. She recognized no one, and finally she foamed at the mouth. She collapsed. The group stopped. Guadalupe saw she was going to die. He kept this to himself. The flow of blood from her nose increased and drenched her shirt. It terrified him.

Diez said they should turn back, put a quick end to the trip, and give up to the Border Patrol. The highway wasn't that far away. So they laid her on the blanket and began to carry her back the way they'd come. After a few dozen agonizing yards, they stopped to rest. The woman lurched her head to her side, threw up, and died.

"I don't think she's breathing anymore," said her sister-in-law.

Diez stood over her, stunned and panicked. The gravity of what had occurred set in. He began to cry. The others gathered around. Looking down at her, the sun above, their shadows fell over her corpse. They were terrified in the silent desert. She'd been talking, hoping. Now she lay dead. No matter what they'd seen on television about people dying in this desert, they were too flush with the dreams of dollars to believe they'd see it.

They looked at each other and stared down at her body. Quickly, what to do? Pulling himself together Diez said they should reach the highway and give up. But now that the woman was dead, no one wanted to do that.

Maybe we should bury her, suggested Delfino. Diez thought he should stay with the body, but realized that no one else knew the way to the Indian settlement ahead, and he didn't want to answer police questions about how they got where they were.

Finally, the woman's friends and Tavo, the coyote trainee, decided to stay with the body. Diez and the others would head on. Wait till we've been gone for three hours, he told the three who stayed with the corpse. Then go back to the highway and wave down the Border Patrol.

Diez's group was now down to six men. They would have to make time. To lighten their load, he buried the cans of sardines and corn near where the woman died.

One of the first things Diez had learned about being a coyote was to remain positive and never show confusion or fear. His charges weren't used to the desert, and terror could easily infect them. Every group usually had at least one person who wasn't physically fit. As the sun rose, these people needed encouragement, a pat on the back. If they began to straggle or stop, it would slow the group and throw off the trek's timing. . . . Diez had developed a whole pep talk that he'd start giving about five hours into the trip. It had to do with how people in worse shape than they had made it. Think of the dollars you'll make. Keep on going. You can do it. Sometimes it included little lies, usually regarding how much farther they had to go.

The speech now deserted Diez as the diminished group he led continued beyond where the woman's body lay. Her death beat on him like the sun's rays. It drained him. He hadn't eaten since the day before. He **salved** his conscience thinking she must have had some physical condition he wasn't aware of. Still, he imagined the years he'd spend in prison. He tried not to let this show, fearing the others would lose heart. . . . He trudged on through the brush and cactus. At times, **compelled** onward, rushing to get to the Indian settlement, he tried to run. He found he could only run a few yards in this heat. He was too weak.

Just twenty-four hours earlier they were . . . imagining their new lives in

salved
soothed;
comforted

compelled
forced;
pushed

the United States. Now the trek had become a grim march. The woman's ordeal had slowed them **irreparably**. This terrified Diez. He calculated that they had spent two or three hours with her. Another seven or eight hours of walking remained. He didn't like walking at night. It was too easy to break a leg or walk face first into a cactus. They would have to spend the night in the desert.

irreparably
without being able to be repaired

All this **coursed** through his mind as he and his group walked on, each man alone with his thoughts. After three hours, shadows lengthened across the desert floor. They found a **ravine** and the six of them crumpled into its shade. Diez told them that the Indian's house was a couple hours away and they could do it easily in the morning. It was a lie, but he didn't want to upset them. It was ten miles to Santa Cruz. In their condition, that distance would take at least five hours of walking.

coursed
ran or flowed

ravine
a steep and narrow valley

The others were quickly asleep. For Diez, though, the night seemed endless. He tried to sleep but could not. He smoked cigarettes and tried to drink, but he threw up whatever went down. His mind churned over the day's events. The death of the woman whose name he didn't know weighed upon him. Out there alone, through the night, he thought of her dying on the desert floor. He'd go to jail. His mother would die of **anguish**. What would people say of him? Several times during the night, he closed his eyes. But the wind made a high cooing sound that Diez, in his panic, took for police radios. He'd start awake with a charge of adrenaline.[6]

anguish
suffering; torment

Through the night, he thought of what lay ahead. They had packed only enough water for a ten-hour trip. They were down to a few gulps of water apiece and the six limes. He didn't know if they'd make it.

None of this did he tell his charges as he woke them at first light. They trudged off into the desert again. They walked for one hour, then another, and another. They found nothing. The sun was high in the sky, and its rays drenched them in inescapable heat.

By 8:00 A.M., they were out of water. They turned to the limes and sucked them ferociously. Diez's skin burned and was stuck with cactus spines. His face was lacerated from the brush. It was so hot, he felt, that if you had put a plate of beans on his head, it would have cooked. He wilted quickly, and now knew he wouldn't make it.

---

6 **adrenaline:** a hormone the body releases in response to stress

His charges, who had slept well, carried him on. They were terrified. He alone knew the trail to the Indian settlement. It was now they who gave him the pep talk. Come on, Diez, they told him, you can do it. How many times have you made this trip before? His arms slung around their shoulders, Diez slipped in and out of consciousness.

By midmorning, the limes were gone. They were oblivious to the tanks of water standing in the mighty saguaros around them. Only one source of liquid remained. To survive, Diez told them, they would now have to drink their own urine. They began to urinate in plastic baggies, but the liquid was too hot to drink. So they dug down beneath the topsoil and found cool earth and mixed this with the liquid. Diez was so dehydrated that his body could produce no urine at all. He drank the urine of one of the men from Tijan.

This, however, was not enough to sustain him. He sagged as they carried him along, his arms draped across their shoulders. Finally, he told them, "I can't go on." Far off in the distance, he knew, was a white water tank and the Indians' houses. They couldn't see it, but he knew it was there.

"Go that way," he told them.

Some of the men wanted to stay and wait for the temperature to drop. Privately, Guadalupe said to Delfino, "Let's go. If we stay here, we're going to die." So the group left Diez lying there and walked on in the direction he had pointed them.

. . . . From his pocket, Diez took a wad of three thousand dollars and threw it in the air. What good was money to him now? The bills fluttered and settled around him. Diez wanted the people who found his corpse to put the money to good use. He lay down and placed his cap over his face and passed out. He lay there for a long time.

The six men, meanwhile, stumbled on. They'd been on the desert floor now for a day and a half of sun. The woman was dead. Diez, with whom they trusted their lives, was dying. They were out of water and had drunk their own urine. Their skin boiled, and they were near tears. Waves of chills swept over them and made them shudder. Their lips were torn and no one could talk. No one cared anymore about the dollars he was going to make.

Delfino fainted once, or maybe twice. There was no escape from the heat. He felt like screaming. In a frenzy, he ripped off his shirt and pants.

The men began to separate. Delfino and Guadalupe walked on with the man from Guatemala. Guadalupe fell. He imagined that they would die and no one would know what had become of them. He wanted to be buried in his village. He wondered why he'd ever come.

Somehow, he pulled himself to his feet. As he did, he saw that Guatemala had kept walking and now veered away from the direction Diez had pointed them. Guadalupe stood and whistled at him.

"Come back, Guatemala," he called. "Come back."

"No," Guatemala said. "I'm heading on."

They never saw Guatemala again.

animated
brought to life

Their whistles, though, **animated** the three men from Tijan, who were now scattered about the desert floor. Believing someone had seen something, one of them scaled a paloverde and, finally, spotted a house in the distance.

"*Casa*,"[7] he yelled and pointed.

They made for it.

The house belonged to an Indian couple, who were startled to see five ragged Mexicans stumble out of the desert.

"*Agua*,"[8] they said. "*Agua*."

Then they collapsed in the shade under the enormous salt cedar tree in front of the couple's house. For one hundred dollars, the Indian couple filled their jugs with water and gave them bread and a few sodas. The kid who'd spotted the house broke down and sobbed.

As this was going on, Diez lay under the sun a couple hundred yards back. At one point he picked himself up and tried to walk but could not go far and collapsed again, face down in the dirt. He passed out.

He woke to voices calling, "Diez, Diez." He raised his lucky *SA* hat and waved it listlessly, then his arm fell to the ground. The next thing he knew, they were over him, pouring water on him and plying him with soda. His skin was green, and his eyes were deep in their sockets. He had soiled himself and he was crying and couldn't talk.

. . . Diez survived. The soda and water gave him cramps, but the cramps shot him full of life. Thus revived, he was able to walk under his own power to the

---

7 *casa*: Spanish for *house*

8 *agua*: Spanish for *water*

Indian houses. He paid a Tohono O'odham Indian to take what remained of his group to Tucson in a pickup truck, stacked on top of each other. From there Diez had them driven to Phoenix, where a woman named Maria Elena ran a fleet of cars and an underground travel business for illegal immigrants. She brought them to a house, gave them food and toothbrushes. A few hours later, one of her drivers took the group to Los Angeles.

Diez stayed in Phoenix for a month working landscaping, fearing that police would be looking for him back home in Chocamán. One night, he saw on the news that 248 people had died crossing the border already that year. A month later, he bought a DVD player and went home to Chocamán.

For Guadalupe Cocotle and Delfino Juárez, the trip ended on a garage floor in Bell, a small working-class suburb of Los Angeles that is now almost all Mexican. They found work alongside Guadalupe's brother installing carpets and wooden floors in suburban homes for weekly cash payments that amounted to something near minimum wage. The business owner, Porfirio Quiñónez, once an undocumented immigrant[9] himself, gave them his garage floor on which to sleep. After a while he began charging them for the privilege. Without a car, or a license, illegally in the country and not speaking English, they were more or less captive workers of Mr. Quiñónez and his carpet business.

> *O*ne night, he saw on the news that 248 people had died crossing the border already that year.

. . . .Two months later, on the Tohono O'odham reservation in the dead heat of August, a thin boy with a black baseball cap sat on a rock not far from where the woman died. He dug up the cans of corn and sardines he had buried and discovered they hadn't spoiled. Around him sat another group of seven would-be immigrants, heading to Los Angeles and counting the dollars they would make. This time none were women. As they ate, in his crackly voice and dry laugh, he told them the story of how the heavyset woman he'd known only as "Señora" had died, and how he'd had to drink another man's urine, thrown his money in the air, and almost expired himself.

"She died," he said, "right over there," pointing to the spot.

---

9 **undocumented immigrant:** an individual lacking legal papers, such as a passport, visa, or Social Security card, that allow him or her to work in a country

Mexicans Begin Jogging

GARY SOTO

At the factory I worked
In the fleck of rubber, under the press
Of an oven yellow with flame,
Until the border patrol opened

Their vans and my boss waved for us to run.   5
"Over the fence, Soto," he shouted,
And I shouted that I was American.
"No time for lies," he said, and pressed
A dollar in my palm, hurrying me

Through the back door.   10
Since I was on his time, I ran
And became the wag to a short tail of Mexicans—
Ran past the amazed crowds that lined
The street and blurred like photographs, in rain.

I ran from that industrial road to the soft   15
Houses where people paled at the turn of an autumn sky.
What could I do but yell *vivas*[1]
to baseballs, milkshakes, and those sociologists
who would clock me

as I jog into the next century   20
On the power of a great, silly grin.

---

1 *vivas:* Spanish for "you live." In this context, he means "Long may you live!"

AFTER YOU READ

Delfino II: Diez in the Desert
Mexicans Begin Jogging

Think and Discuss

1. Describe and compare the characters of Diez and the speaker in "Mexicans Begin Jogging." Cite details from the essay and poem that support your description.

2. **Nonfiction** uses many of the tools of fiction—vivid storytelling, characters, and settings—to write about true things. Like fiction, it relies on specific details, colorful images, and sometimes dialogue to make the writing come to life. Copy the following organizer into your Writer's Notebook. Use it to chart how some of the elements of "Delfino II: Diez in the Desert" tell the story of Diez's life. One example is done for you.

Category of Fact	Example	What It Contributes to the Story
Specific Detail	Diez "had a confidence that protruded like a muscle beyond his thin physique"	Adds to image of Diez as being an impressive person despite his youth and size
Vivid Imagery		
Made-up Dialogue		
Other Facts		

3. The overall **mood**, or atmosphere, of a piece of writing communicates a certain feeling to the reader. Many elements can work together to create a mood, such as descriptive details, dialogue, and setting. Name some of the elements of the essay and poem that contribute to their respective moods.

4. After reading these two selections, explain whether your opinion of illegal immigration has changed. Why or why not?

Write to Understand: Who Are They?

Write a summary (two or more paragraphs) of the events related in "Delfino II: Diez in the Desert." Skim the selection again before you begin to write. Write as clearly and directly as possible. Imagine you are writing this for someone who has not read these selections. You are trying to answer the questions Who? What? Where? and When? in a short, general summary. Compare your summary to the graphic organizer you created and draw a conclusion about the relationship of a summary to the original text.

BEFORE YOU READ
Poems Across the Divide

Meet the Authors

Robert Frost A four-time Pulitzer Prize winner, Robert Frost (1874–1963) took as much pride in his farm as in his writing. Many of his poems revolve around country life and his deep appreciation of nature.

Marina de Bellagente Born in Italy in the late 1940s, de Bellagente calls herself a performance poet, arts critic, and sound collagist. She says she has always been interested in "operating at a boundary—between pop song and classical/avant-garde tradition, music and poetry, speaking and singing."

Georgia Douglas Johnson Johnson (1877–1966) was one of the most famous women poets of the Harlem Renaissance, the period after World War I when African American artists, jazz musicians, dramatists, and painters flourished. Prominent writers of the day traveled regularly between Harlem and Johnson's celebrated literary salon at her home in Washington, D.C.

Build Background: Breaking the Barriers

Walls can limit and deny freedom. They can also give people a sense of comfort and security. In the following poems, the speakers address the human impulse to build walls and fences. They speak of actual walls, built of stone and chain link, and of barriers that exist mostly in the mind.

- In Robert Frost's poem "Mending Wall," the speaker's neighbor believes strongly in the saying "good fences make good neighbors." What do you think that means?

- We all have borders and restrictions in our lives—both real and imagined. They function both to keep us in as well as to keep others out. What fences and chains would you like to escape, or see others escape?

Mending Wall

ROBERT FROST

Something there is that doesn't love a wall,
That sends the frozen-ground-swell under it,
And spills the upper boulders in the sun;
And makes gaps even two can pass abreast.
The work of hunters is another thing: 5
I have come after them and made repair
Where they have left not one stone on stone,
But they would have the rabbit out of hiding,
To please the yelping dogs. The gaps I mean,
No one has seen them made or heard them made,   10
But at spring mending-time we find them there.
I let my neighbor know beyond the hill;
And on a day we meet to walk the line
And set the wall between us once again.
We keep the wall between us as we go.   15
To each the boulders that have fallen to each.
And some are loaves and some so nearly balls
We have to use a spell to make them balance:
'Stay where you are until our backs are turned!'
We wear our fingers rough with handling them.   20
Oh, just another kind of outdoor game,
One on a side. It comes to little more:
There where it is we do not need a wall:
He is all pine and I am apple orchard.
My apple trees will never get across   25

And eat the cones under his pines, I tell him.

He only says, 'Good fences make good neighbors.'

Spring is the mischief in me, and I wonder

If I could put a notion in his head:

'*Why* do they make good neighbors? Isn't it 30

Where there are cows? But here there are no cows.

Before I built a wall I'd ask to know

What I was walling in or walling out,

And to whom I was like to give offense.

Something there is that doesn't love a wall, 35

That wants it down.' I could say 'Elves' to him,

But it's not elves exactly, and I'd rather

He said it for himself. I see him there,

Bringing a stone grasped firmly by the top

In each hand, like an old-stone savage armed. 40

He moves in darkness as it seems to me,

Not of woods only and the shade of trees.

He will not go behind his father's saying,

And he likes having thought of it so well

He says again, 'Good fences make good neighbors.' 45

I Am the Land. I Wait.　MARINA DE BELLAGENTE

I am the land. I wait.
You say you own me.
I wait.

You shout. I lie patient.
You buy me. I wait.　　　　　5
With muddy holes and
car lot eyes I stare . . .
　　Then someone
tickles me, plants life—fruit
grass—trees/ children dance/ someone　　　10
　　　Sings

You come with guns
A chainlink necklace
chokes me now

I wait.　　　　　15
YOU CANNOT PUT A FENCE
AROUND THE PLANET EARTH.
I am the land. I wait.

Your World   GEORGIA DOUGLAS JOHNSON

Your world is as big as you make it
I know, for I used to abide
In the narrowest nest in a corner
My wings pressing close to my side.

But I sighted the distant horizon   5
Where the sky-line encircled the sea
And I throbbed with a burning desire
To travel this **immensity**.

immensity
hugeness or
vastness

I battered the cordons[1] around me
And cradled my wings on the breeze   10
Then soared to the **uttermost** reaches
with rapture, with power, with ease!

uttermost
farthest or
outermost

I **cordons:** barriers or other protective enclosures

AFTER YOU READ
Poems Across the Divide

Think and Discuss

1. Why do you think a wall or chain is such a powerful **symbol** for a poet? Explain.

2. A poem is written by an author, but it is spoken by an invented **speaker**. Describe the speaker in each of these poems based on clues in the texts

3. What is the **theme**, or underlying meaning, of each poem?

4. The **tone** of a poem refers to the poet's attitude toward his or her subject or toward the reader. Copy the graphic organizer below into your Writer's Notebook. Fill in the chart with words and phrases that point to the tone each poet is trying to achieve. The first one already has some ideas added.

	Example 1	Example 2	Example 2	Tone?
"Mending Wall"	Boulders are compared to "loaves" and "balls."	"He is all pine and I am apple orchard."	"I could say Elves to him"	Simple, bemused, gently ironic, philosophical in a mischievous way
"I Am the Land. I Wait."				
"Your World"				

5. How can you relate each of these poems to your own life?

Write to Understand: Using Supporting Details in a Comparison

Though each poem uses a symbolic image such as a wall or chains, each one is different in tone, or attitude. Using details from the chart you filled out for item 4 above, compare how each writer achieves a different tone. Which tone do you find most appealing?

BEFORE YOU READ

Hip-Hop Planet
Ka'Ba
Harlem II

Meet the Authors

James McBride Born in 1957, James McBride wrote a celebrated memoir, *The Color of Water*, in which he describes being raised by his white, Jewish mother in a very large, poor black family. She refused to be labeled, claiming, "God is the color of water." McBride is also a talented musical composer, his songs performed by world-famous jazz artists.

Amiri Baraka Controversial activist and writer Amiri Baraka was born Leroi Jones in 1934. One of the foremost black writers, jazz critics, and poets of the 20th century, Baraka believes that "Poetry is music and nothing but music. Words with musical emphasis."

Langston Hughes Often called the "Poet Laureate of Harlem," Langston Hughes (1902–1967) is beloved for capturing the vivid rhythms of the streets and for his lifelong commitment to justice and equality. In his own words, he wrote for "People up today and down tomorrow, working this week and fired the next, beaten and baffled, but determined not to be wholly beaten."

Build Background: Purpose and Audience in Informational Nonfiction

In "Hip-Hop Planet," the African-American writer James McBride explains how hip-hop music, also known as rap, came to be and why it has become a worldwide cultural movement. The article was published in *National Geographic* in April 2007. McBride's *purpose*, then was to explain how a popular music has crossed many borders. His *audience* was the readers of *National Geographic*. Like all writers of informational articles, McBride focuses his writing so that it achieves his purpose and reaches his audience.

- Think about what you already know about hip-hop—the artists, songs, dances, and movies that have been inspired by it. What more would you like to learn about hip-hop?

- Knowing that this selection was an article in *National Geographic*, what do you expect it to be like?

Hip-Hop Planet

JAMES MCBRIDE

HIP-HOP PLANET

James McBride

Burning Man

Imagine a burning man. He is on fire. He runs into the room. You put out the flames. Then another burning man arrives. You put him out and go about your business. Then two, three, four, five, ten appear. You **extinguish** them all, send them to the hospital. Then imagine no one bothers to examine why the men caught fire in the first place. That is the story of hip-hop.

It is a music dipped in the boiling cauldron[1] of race and class, and for that reason it is clouded with mystics, snake oil salesmen, two-bit scholars, race-baiters,[2] and sneaker salesmen, all **professing** to know the facts, to be "real," when the reality of race is like shifting sand, dependent on time, place, circumstance, and who's telling the history. Here's the real story: In the mid-1970s, New York City was nearly broke. The public school system cut funding for the arts drastically. Gone were the days when you could wander into the band room, rent a clarinet for a minimal fee, and march it home to squeal on it and drive your parents nuts.

The kids of the South Bronx and Harlem came up with something else. In the summer of 1973, at 1595 East 174th Street in the Bronx River Houses, a black teenager named Afrika Bambaataa stuck a speaker in his mother's first-floor living room window, ran a wire to the turntable in his bedroom, and set the housing project of 3,000 people alight with party music. At the same time, a Jamaican teenager named Kool DJ Herc was starting up the scene in the East Bronx, while a technical whiz named Grandmaster Flash was rising to **prominence** a couple of miles south. The Bronx became a music magnet for Puerto Ricans, Jamaicans, Dominicans, and black Americans from the surrounding areas. Fab 5 Freddy, Kurtis Blow, and

extinguish
douse or quench

professing
claiming or purporting

prominence
fame; importance

---

1 **cauldron:** kettle or cooking vessel

2 **snake oil salesmen, two-bit scholars, race-baiters:** people who try to sell things with no value; second-rate scholars; people who claim that everything bad that happened to them is a result of the effects of racism

Melle Mel were only a few of the pioneers. Grand Wizard Theodore, Kool DJ AJ, the Cold Crush Brothers, Spoony Gee, and the Rock Steady Crew of B-boys showed up to "battle"—dance, trade quips and rhymes, check out each other's records and equipment—not knowing as they strolled through the doors of the community center near Bambaataa's mother's apartment that they were writing musical history. Among them was an MC named Lovebug Starski, who was said to utter the phrase "hip-hop" between breaks to keep time.

This is how it worked: One guy, the DJ, played records on two turntables. One guy—or girl—served as master of ceremonies, or MC. The DJs learned to move the record back and forth under the needle to create a "scratch," or to drop the needle on the record where the beat was the hottest, playing "the break" over and over to keep the folks dancing. The MCs "rapped" over the music to keep the party going. One MC sought to outchat the other. Dance styles were created —"locking" and "popping" and "breaking." Graffiti artists spread the word of the "I" because the music was all about identity: I am the best. I spread the most love in the Bronx, in Harlem, in Queens. The focus initially was not on the MCs, but on the dancers, or B-boys. Commercial radio ignored it. DJs sold mix tapes out of the back of station wagons. "Rapper's Delight" by the Sugarhill Gang—the song I first heard at that face-slapping party in Harlem—broke the music onto radio in 1979.

That is the short history.

The long history is that spoken-word music made its way here on slave ships from West Africa centuries ago: Ethnomusicologists[3] trace hip-hop's roots to the dance, drum, and song of West African griots, or storytellers, its pairing of word and music the **manifestation** of the painful journey of slaves who survived the middle passage.[4] The ring shouts, field hollers, and spirituals of early slaves drew on common elements of African music, such

> *T*he DJs learned to move the record back and forth under the needle to create a "scratch . . ."

manifestation
expression

---

3 **Ethnomusicologists:** people who study music from different cultures

4 **the middle passage:** the passage of slave ships across the Atlantic Ocean from Africa to the so-called New World

improvisation
making up or inventing on-the-spot

self-deprecating
putting down or belittling one's self

foreshadowing
prediction or foretelling

as call and response and **improvisation**. "Speech-song has been part of black culture for a long, long time," says Samuel A. Floyd, director of the Center for Black Music Research at Columbia College in Chicago. The "dozens," "toasts," and "signifying" of black Americans—verbal dueling, rhyming, **self-deprecating** tales, and stories of blacks outsmarting whites—were defensive, empowering strategies.

You can point to jazz musicians such as Oscar Brown, Jr., Edgar "Eddie" Jefferson, and Louis Armstrong, and blues greats such as John Lee Hooker, and easily find the **foreshadowing** of rap music in the verbal play of their work. Black performers such as poet Nikki Giovanni and Gil Scott-Heron, a pianist and vocalist who put spoken political lyrics to music (most famously in "The Revolution Will Not Be Televised"), elevated spoken word to a new level.

But the artist whose work arguably laid the groundwork for rap as we know it was Amiri Baraka, a beat poet out of Allen Ginsberg's Greenwich Village scene. In the late 1950s and '60s, Baraka performed with shrieks, howls, cries, stomps, verse floating ahead of or behind the rhythm, sometimes in staccato syncopation.[5] It was performance art, delivered in a dashiki and Afro,[6] in step with the anger of a bold and sometimes frightening nationalistic black movement, and it inspired what might be considered the first rap group, the Last Poets.

reverberated
echoed; rang

embodied
personified

demise
death or end of something

I was 13 when I first heard the Last Poets in 1970. They scared me. . . . In a world where blacks were evolving from "Negroes" to "blacks," and the assassinations of civil rights leaders Malcolm X and Martin Luther King, Jr., still **reverberated** in the air like a shotgun blast, the Last Poets **embodied** black power. Their records consisted of percussion and spoken-word rhyme. They were wildly popular in my neighborhood. Their debut recording sold 400,000 records in three months, says Last Poet member Umar Bin Hassan. "No videos, no radio play, strictly word of mouth." The group's **demise** coincided with hip-hop's birth in the 1970s.

---

5 **staccato syncopation:** a musical rhythm with a pronounced offbeat

6 **dashiki and Afro:** colorful West African upper garment and natural hairstyle in which curly hair extends out from the head

Grand Master Flash in 2006

It's unlikely that the Last Poets ever dreamed the revolution they sang of would take the form it has. "We were about the movement," Abiodun Oyewole, a founder of the group, says. "A lot of today's rappers have talent. But a lot of them are driving the car in the wrong direction."

The Crossover

Highways wrap around the city of Dayton, Ohio, like a ribbon bow-tied on a box of chocolates from the local Esther Price candy factory. They have six ladies at the plant who do just that: Tie ribbons around boxes all day. Henry Rosenkranz can tell you about it. "I love candy," says Henry, a slim white teenager in glasses and a hairnet, as he strolls the factory, bucket in hand. His full-time after-school job is mopping the floors.

prototypical
classic; typical

purview
the range of expertise or authority

affluent
rich; wealthy

rationale
reason

unabashedly
without embarrassment

Henry is a model American teenager—and the **prototypical** consumer at which the hip-hop industry is squarely aimed, which has his parents sitting up in their seats. The music that was once the **purview** of black America has gone white and gone commercial all at once. A sea of white faces now rises up to greet rap groups as they perform, many of them teenagers like Henry. . . .

Obviously, it's not just working-class whites, but also **affluent**, suburban kids who identify with this music with African-American roots. A white 16-year-old hollering rap lyrics at the top of his lungs from the driver's seat of his dad's late-model Lexus may not have the same **rationale** to howl at the moon as a working-class kid whose parents can't pay for college, yet his own anguish is as real to him as it gets. . . .

Hip-hop has continually changed form, evolving from party music to social commentary with the 1982 release of Grandmaster Flash and the Furious Five's "The Message." Today, alternative hip-hop artists continue to produce socially conscious songs, but . . . most rap songs **unabashedly** function as walking advertisements for luxury cars, designer clothes, and liquor. Agenda Inc., a "pop culture brand strategy agency," listed Mercedes-Benz as the number one brand mentioned in *Billboard*'s top 20 singles in 2005. . . .

*L*ike teenagers across the world, he fantasizes about working in the hip-hop business and making millions himself. . . .

In many ways, the music represents an old dream. It's the pot of gold to millions of kids like Henry, who quietly agonizes over how his father slaves 14 hours a day at two tool-and-die machine jobs to make ends meet. Like teenagers across the world, he fantasizes about working in the hip-hop business and making millions himself. . . .

Full Circle

You breathe in and breathe out a few times and you are there. Eight hours and a wake-up shake on the flight from New York, and you are on the tarmac in Dakar, Senegal. Welcome to Africa. The assignment: Find the roots of hip-hop. The music goes full circle. The music comes home to

Africa. That whole bit. Instead it was the old reporter's joke: You go out to cover a story and the story covers you. The stench of poverty in my nostrils was so strong it pulled me to earth like a hundred-pound ring in my nose. Dakar's Sandaga market is full of "local color"—unless you live there. It was packed and filthy, stalls full of new merchandise surrounded by shattered pieces of life everywhere, broken pipes, bicycle handlebars, fruit flies, soda bottles, beggars, dogs, cell phones. A teenage beggar, his body malformed by polio, crawled by on hands and feet, like a spider. He said, "Hey brother, help me." When I looked into his eyes, they were a bottomless ocean.

Around the globe, rap music has become a universal expression of outrage, its macho pose borrowed from commercial hip-hop in the U.S.

The Hotel Teranga is a fortress, packed behind a concrete wall where beggars gather at the front gate. The French tourists march past them, the women in high heels and stonewashed jeans. They **sidle** through downtown Dakar like royalty, **haggling** in the market, swimming in the hotel pool with their children, a scene that resembles Birmingham, Alabama, in the 1950s—the blacks serving, the whites partying. Five hundred yards (460 meters) away, Africans eat off the sidewalk and sell peanuts for a **pittance**. There is a restlessness, a deep sense of something gone wrong in the air.

The French can't smell it, even though they've had a mouthful back home. A good amount of the torching of Paris suburbs in October 2005 was courtesy of the children of immigrants from former French African colonies, exhausted from being bottled up in housing projects for generations with no job prospects. They telegraphed the punch in their music—France is the second largest hip-hop market in the world—but the message was ignored. Around the globe, rap music has become a universal expression of outrage, its macho pose borrowed from commercial hip-hop in the U.S.

In Dakar, where every kid is a microphone and turntable away from **squalor**, and American rapper Tupac Shakur's picture hangs in market stalls of folks who don't understand English, rap is king. There are

sidle
walk sideways; edge

haggling
bargaining

pittance
tiny or meager amount

squalor
dirt and filth

hundreds of rap groups in Senegal today. French television crews troop in and out of Dakar's nightclubs filming the kora harp lute and *tama* talking drum[7] with regularity. But beneath the drumming and the dance lessons and the jingling sound of tourist change, there is a quiet rage, a desperate fury among the Senegalese, some of whom seem to bear an intense dislike of their former colonial rulers.

"We know all about French history," says Abdou Ba, a Senegalese producer and musician. "We know about their kings, their castles, their art, their music. We know everything about them. But they don't know much about us."

Assane N'Diaye, 19, loves hip-hop music. Before he left his Senegalese village to work as a DJ in Dakar, he was a fisherman, just like his father, like his father's father before him. Tall, lean, with a muscular build and a handsome chocolate face, Assane became a popular DJ, but the equipment he used was borrowed, and when his friend took it back, success **eluded** him. He has returned home to Toubab Dialaw, about 25 miles (40 kilometers) south of Dakar, a village marked by a huge boulder, perhaps 40 feet (12 meters) high, facing the Atlantic Ocean.

About a century and a half ago, a local ruler led a group of people fleeing slave traders to this place. He was told by a white trader to come here, to Toubab Dialaw. When he arrived, the slavers followed. A battle **ensued**. The ruler fought bravely but was killed. The villagers buried him by the sea and marked his grave with a small stone, and over the years it is said to have sprouted like a tree planted by God. It became a huge, arching boulder that stares out to sea, protecting the village behind it. When the fishermen went deep out to sea, the boulder was like a lighthouse that marked the way home. The Great Rock of Toubab Dialaw is said to hold a magic spirit, a spirit that Assane N'Diaye believes in.

In the shadow of the Great Rock, Assane has built a small restaurant, Chez Las, decorated with hundreds of seashells. It is where he lives his hip-hop dream. At night, he and his brother and cousin stand by the Great Rock and face the sea. They meditate. They pray. Then they write rap lyrics that are worlds away from the bling-bling culture[8] of today's commercial

eluded
escaped; got away from

ensued
began; started

---

7 **kora harp lute and *tama* talking drum:** instruments common to West Africa

8 **bling-bling culture:** any rich western society that values extravagant jewelry and clothing

hip-hoppers. They write about their lives as village fishermen, the scarcity of catch forcing them to fish in deeper and deeper waters, the hardship of fishing for 8, 10, 14 days at a time in an open pirogue[9] in rainy season, the high fee they pay to rent the boat, and the **paltry** price their catches fetch on the market. They write about the humiliation of poverty, watching their town sprout up around them with rich Dakarians and richer French. And they write about the relatives who leave in the morning and never return, surrendered to the sea, sharks, and God.

paltry
measly;
insignificant

The dream, of course, is to make a record. They have their own demo, their own logo, and their own name, Salam T. D. (for Toubab Dialaw). But rap music represents a deeper dream: a better life. "We want money to help our parents," Assane says over dinner. "We watch our mothers boil water to cook and have nothing to put in the pot."

He fingers his food lightly. "Rap doesn't belong to American culture," he says. "It belongs here. It has always existed here, because of our pain and our hardships and our suffering."

On this cool evening in a restaurant above their village, these young men, clad in baseball caps and T-shirts, appear no

"Rap doesn't belong to American culture," he says. "It belongs here. It has always existed here . . ."

different from their African-American counterparts, with one exception. After a dinner of chicken and rice, Assane says something in Wolof to the others. Silently and without ceremony, they take every bit of the leftover dinner—the half-eaten bread, rice, pieces of chicken, the chicken bones—and dump them into a plastic bag to give to the children in the village. They silently rise from the table and proceed outside. The last I see of them, their regal figures are outlined in the dim light of the doorway, heading out to the darkened village, holding on to that bag as though it held money.

The City of Gods

Some call the Bronx River Houses the City of Gods. . . . The 10 drab, red-brick buildings spread out across 14 acres (5.7 hectares), coming into

9 **pirogue:** small, flat-bottomed boat used for fishing in West Africa and the caribbean

view as you drive east across the East 174th Street Bridge. The Bronx is the hallowed holy ground of hip-hop, the place where it all began. Visitors take tours through this neighborhood now, care of a handful of fortyish "old-timers," who point out the high and low spots of hip-hop's birthplace. . . .

The rap artists come and go, but the conditions that produced them linger. Forty percent of New York City's black males are jobless. One in three black males born in 2001 will end up in prison. The life expectancy of black men in the U.S. ranks below that of men in Sri Lanka and Colombia. . . .

Hip-hop culture is not mine. Yet I own it. Much of it I hate. Yet I love it, the good of it. To confess a love for a music that, at least in part, embraces violence is no easy matter, but then again our national anthem talks about bombs bursting in air, and I love that song, too. At its best, hip-hop lays bare the empty moral cupboard that is our generation's legacy. This music that once made visible the inner culture of America's greatest social problem, its legacy of slavery, has taken the dream deferred to a global scale. Today, 2 percent of the Earth's adult population owns more than 50 percent of its household wealth, and indigenous cultures[10] are swallowed with the rapidity of a teenager gobbling a bag of potato chips. The music is calling. Over the years, the instruments change, but the message is the same. The drums are pounding out a warning. They are telling us something. Our children can hear it.

The question is: Can we?

---

10 **indigenous cultures:** native peoples

POETRY CONNECTION

Ka'Ba

AMIRI BARAKA

A closed window looks down
on a dirty courtyard, and black people
call across or scream across or walk across
defying physics[1] in the stream of their will

Our world is full of sound   5
Our world is more lovely than anyone's
tho we suffer, and kill each other
and sometimes fail to walk the air

We are beautiful people
with african imaginations   10
full of masks and dances and swelling chants
with african eyes, and noses, and arms,
though we sprawl in gray chains in a place
full of winters, when what we want is sun.

We have been captured,   15
brothers. And we labor
to make our getaway, into
the ancient image, into a new

correspondence with ourselves   **correspondence**
and our black family. We read magic   20   way of speaking;
now we need the spells, to raise up   communication
return, destroy, and create. What will be

the sacred words?

---

l **physics:** science dealing with the interaction of matter and energy

Harlem II   LANGSTON HUGHES

deferred
delayed;
postponed

What happens to a dream **deferred**?

Does it dry up
Like a raisin in the sun?

fester
cause
continuing
pain; rankle

Or **fester** like a sore—
And then run?   5
Does it stink like rotten meat?
Or crust and sugar over—
like a syrupy sweet?

Maybe it just sags
like a heavy load.   10

Or does it explode?

AFTER YOU READ
Hip-Hop Planet / Ka'Ba / Harlem II

Think and Discuss

1. What new information about hip-hop music did you learn from "Hip-Hop Planet"? Be specific in your answers.

2. Most writers write for a specific **purpose**, such as to **persuade**, to offer an **opinion**, to **inform**, or to **entertain**. McBride's overriding purpose was to explain hip-hop music. However, he may have had other purposes within that larger purpose. In small groups, try to determine some of the possible reasons that McBride wrote the essay "Hip-Hop Planet." Consider such matters as tone, language, and literary techniques.

3. A **simile** is a comparison of one thing to another that uses the words *like* or *as*. Find the similes in "Hip-Hop Planet" and "Harlem II." Then, in a graphic organizer like the one below, record these similes, and say what they compare and why.

Hip-Hop Planet			Harlem II		
Simile	Items Being Compared	Meaning	Simile	Items Being Compared	Meaning

4. What do you think Georgia Douglas Johnson, Amiri Baraka, and Langston Hughes would have to say to each other about the experience of black Americans today? Discuss this in small groups, using what you know from reading their work as well as other knowledge and experience you may have.

Write to Understand: Develop a Simile

Some people are bothered by the hip-hop lyrics, while fans like James McBride find them powerful. What do you think? Develop a simile to express how you feel about hip-hop. Refer to your graphic organizer to help you.

BEFORE YOU READ

Blues Ain't No Mockin Bird

Meet the Author: Toni Cade Bambara

Raised in Harlem, Toni Cade Bambara (1939–1995) went on to become a highly respected teacher, social activist, documentary filmmaker, and writer. Impatient with the lack of black women's writing in the 1960s and early 1970s, she began writing short stories and putting together anthologies of African-American writing. Her fiction often features characters who might be stand-ins for herself: sharp, smart-mouthed, but good-hearted city girls. Bambara's short stories and novels are praised for their humor, warmth, and sheer verbal energy. Bambara claimed that her prose rhythms were inspired by her love of bop jazz.

Build Background: A Great Society?

Bambara's story "Blues Ain't No Mockin Bird" is set in the rural South around the 1960s. In fact, Bambara wrote most of her work in the 1960s and 1970s, a time of dramatic changes in U.S. cultural and political life. The Civil Rights movement was gaining momentum, and in 1964 the landmark Civil Rights Act became law. In that same year, President Johnson announced a governmental "War on Poverty" as part of his plan to create a "Great Society." Some of the programs, including food stamps (a government voucher given to poor people that can be exchanged for food) and free medical care for the elderly and needy, are still in place today. However, real change—and the dropping of racial barriers—was a long time coming to many places, especially the South.

- Given the title of the story and its setting, what do you think this story might be about?

- What do you think the title means?

WOMAN IRONING, William H. Johnson, 1944

Blues Ain't No Mockin Bird

TONI CADE BAMBARA

BLUES AIN'T NO MOCKIN BIRD

Toni Cade Bambara

The puddle had frozen over, and me and Cathy went stompin in it. The twins from next door, Tyrone and Terry, were swingin so high out of sight we forgot we were waitin our turn on the tire. Cathy jumped up and came down hard on her heels and started tap dancin. And the frozen patch splinterin every which way underneath kinda spooky.

"Looks like a plastic spider web," she said. "A sort of weird spider, I guess, with many mental problems." But really it looked like the crystal paperweight Granny kept in the parlor. She was on the back porch, Granny was, making the cakes drunk. The old ladle drippin rum into the Christmas tins, like it used to drip maple syrup into the pails when we lived in the Judson's woods, like it poured cider into the vats when we were on the Cooper place, like it used to scoop buttermilk and soft cheese when we lived at the dairy.

"Go tell that man we ain't a bunch of trees."

"Ma'am?"

"I said to tell that man to get away from here with that camera." Me and Cathy look over toward the meadow where the men with the station wagon'd been roamin around all mornin. The tall man with a huge camera lassoed to his shoulder was buzzin our way.

"They're makin movie pictures," yelled Tyrone, stiffenin his legs and twistin so the tire'd come down slow so they could see.

"They're makin movie pictures," sang out Terry.

"That boy don't never have anything original to say," say Cathy grownup.

By the time the man with the camera had cut across our neighbor's yard, the twins were out of the trees swingin low and Granny was onto the steps, the screen door bammin soft and scratchy against her palms. "We thought we'd get a shot or two of the house and everything and then—"

"Good mornin," Granny cut him off. And smiled that smile.

"Good mornin," he said, head all down the way Bingo does when you yell at him about the bones on the kitchen floor. "Nice place you got here, aunty. We thought we'd take a—"

"Did you?" said Granny with her eyebrows. Cathy pulled up her socks and giggled.

"Nice things here," said the man, buzzin his camera over the yard. The pecan barrels, the sled, me and Cathy, the flowers, the printed stones along the driveway, the trees, the twins, the toolshed.

"I don't know about the thing, the it, and the stuff," said Granny, still talkin with her eyebrows. "Just people here is what I tend to consider."

Camera man stopped buzzin. Cathy giggled into her collar.

"Mornin, ladies," a new man said. He had come up behind us when we weren't lookin. "And gents," discoverin the twins givin him a nasty look. "We're filmin for the county," he said with a smile. "Mind if we shoot a bit around here?"

"I do indeed," said Granny with no smile. Smilin man was smilin up a storm. So was Cathy. But he didn't seem to have another word to say, so he and the camera man backed on out the yard, but you could hear the camera buzzin still.

"Suppose you just shut that machine off," said Granny real low through her teeth, and took a step down off the porch and then another.

"Now, aunty," Camera said, pointin the thing straight at her.

"Your mama and I are not related."

Smilin man got his notebook out and a chewed-up pencil. "Listen," he said movin back into our yard, "we'd like to have a statement from you . . . for the film. We're filmin for the county, see. Part of the food stamp campaign. You know about the food stamps?"

Granny said nuthin.

"Maybe there's somethin you want to say for the film. I see you grow your own vegetables," he smiled real nice. "If more folks did that, see, there'd be no need—"

> "**S**uppose you just shut that machine off," said Granny real low through her teeth . . .

Granny wasn't sayin nuthin. So they backed on out, buzzin at our clothesline and the twins' bicycles, then back on down to the meadow. The twins were danglin in the tire, lookin at Granny. Me and Cathy were waitin, too, cause Granny always got somethin to say. She teaches steady with no letup. "I was on this bridge one time," she started off. "Was a crowd cause this man was goin to jump, you understand. And a minister was there and the police and some other folks. His woman was there, too."

"What was they doin?" asked Tyrone.

"Tryin to talk him out of it was what they was doin. The minister talkin about how it was a mortal sin, suicide. His woman takin bites out of her own hand and not even knowin it, so nervous and cryin and talkin fast."

"So what happened?" asked Tyrone.

"So here comes . . . this person . . . with a camera, takin pictures of the man and the minister and the woman. Takin pictures of the man in his misery about to jump, cause life so bad and people been messin with him so bad. This person takin up the whole roll of film practically. But savin a few, of course."

"Of course," said Cathy, hatin the person. Me standin there wonderin how Cathy knew it was "of course" when I didn't and it was *my* grandmother.

After a while Tyrone say, "Did he jump?"

"Yeh, did he jump?" say Terry all eager.

And Granny just stared at the twins till their faces swallow up the eager and they don't even care any more about the man jumpin. Then she goes back onto the porch and lets the screen door go for itself. I'm lookin to Cathy to finish the story cause she knows Granny's whole story before me even. Like she knew how come we move so much and Cathy ain't but a third cousin we picked up on the way last Thanksgivin visitin. But she knew it was on account of people drivin Granny crazy till she'd get up in the night and start packin. Mumblin and packin and wakin everybody up sayin, "Let's get on away from here before I kill me somebody." Like people wouldn't pay her for things like they said they would. Or Mr. Judson bringin us boxes of old clothes and raggedy magazines. Or Mrs. Cooper comin in our kitchen and touchin everything and sayin how clean it all was. Granny goin crazy, and Granddaddy Cain pullin her off the people, sayin, "Now, now, Cora." But next day loadin up the truck, with rocks all in his jaw, madder than Granny in the first place.

"I read a story once," said Cathy soundin like Granny teacher. "About this lady Goldilocks who barged into a house that wasn't even hers. And not invited, you understand. Messed over the people's groceries and broke up the people's furniture. Had the nerve to sleep in the folks' bed."

"Then what happened?" asked Tyrone. "What they do, the folks, when they come in to all this mess?"

"Did they make her pay for it?" asked Terry, makin a fist. "I'd've made her pay me."

I didn't even ask. I could see Cathy actress was very likely to just walk away and leave us in mystery about this story which I heard was about some bears.

"Did they throw her out?" asked Tyrone, like his father sounds when he's bein extra nasty-plus to the washin-machine man.

"Woulda," said Terry. "I woulda gone upside her head with my fist and—"

"You woulda done whatcha always do—go cry to Mama, you big baby," said Tyrone. So naturally Terry starts hittin on Tyrone, and next thing you know they tumblin out the tire and rollin on the ground. But Granny didn't say a thing or send the twins home or step out on the steps to tell us about how we can't afford to be fightin amongst ourselves. She didn't say nuthin. So I get into the tire to take my turn. And I could see her leanin up against the pantry table, starin at the cakes she was puttin up for the Christmas sale, mumblin real low and grumpy and holdin her forehead like it wanted to fall off and mess up the rum cakes.

Behind me I hear before I can see Granddaddy Cain comin through the woods in his field boots. Then I twist around to see the shiny black oilskin[1] cuttin through what little left there was of yellows, reds, and oranges. His great white head not quite round cause of this bloody thing high on his shoulder, like he was wearin a cap on sideways. He takes the shortcut through the pecan grove, and the sound of twigs snappin overhead and

---

1 **oilskin:** heavy cloth waterproofed with oil; here a coat made of this cloth

underfoot travels clear and cold all the way up to us. And here comes Smilin and Camera up behind him like they was goin to do somethin. Folks like to go for him sometimes. Cathy say it's because he's so tall and quiet and like a king. And people just can't stand it. But Smilin and Camera don't hit him in the head or nuthin. They just buzz on him as he stalks by with the chicken hawk slung over his shoulder, squawkin, drippin red down the back of the oilskin. He passes the porch and stops a second for Granny to see he's caught the hawk at last, but she's just starin and mumblin, and not at the hawk. So he nails the bird to the toolshed door, the hammerin crackin through the eardrums. And the bird flappin himself to death and droolin down the door to paint the gravel in the driveway red, then brown, then black. And the two men movin up on tiptoe like they was invisible or we were blind, one.

"Get them persons out of my flower bed, Mister Cain," say Granny moanin real low like at a funeral.

"How come your grandmother calls her husband 'Mister Cain' all the time?" Tyrone whispers all loud and noisy and from the city and don't know no better. Like his mama, Miss Myrtle, tell us never mind the formality as if we had no better breeding than to call her Myrtle, plain. And then this awful thing—a giant hawk—come wailin up over the meadow, flyin low and tilted and screamin, zigzaggin through the pecan grove, breakin branches and hollerin, snappin past the clothesline, flyin every which way, flyin into things reckless with crazy.

"He's come to claim his mate," say Cathy fast, and ducks down. We all fall quick and flat into the gravel driveway, stones scrapin my face. I squinch my eyes open again at the hawk on the door, tryin to fly up out of her death like it was just a sack flown into by mistake. Her body holdin her there on that nail, though. The mate beatin the air overhead and clutchin for hair, for heads, for landing space.

The camera man duckin and bendin and runnin and fallin, jigglin the camera and scared. And Smilin jumpin up and down swipin at the huge bird, tryin to bring the hawk down with just his raggedy ole cap. Granddaddy Cain straight up and silent, watchin the circles of the hawk, then aimin the hammer off his wrist. The giant bird fallin, silent and slow. Then here comes Camera and Smilin all big and bad now that the awful screechin thing is on its back and broken, here they come. And Granddaddy

Cain looks up at them like it was the first time noticin, but not payin them too much mind cause he's listenin, we all listenin, to that low groanin music comin from the porch. And we figure any minute, something in my back tells me any minute now, Granny gonna bust through that screen with somethin in her hand and murder on her mind. So Granddaddy say above the buzzin, but quiet, "Good day, gentlemen." Just like that. Like he'd invited them in to play cards and they'd stayed too long and all the sandwiches were gone and Reverend Webb was droppin by and it was time to go.

But like Cathy say, folks can't stand Granddaddy tall and silent and like a king.

They didn't know what to do. But like Cathy say, folks can't stand Granddaddy tall and silent and like a king. They can't neither. The smile the men smilin is pullin the mouth back and showin the teeth. Lookin like the wolf man, both of them. Then Granddaddy holds his hand out—this huge hand I used to sit in when I was a baby and he'd carry me through the house to my mother like I was a gift on a tray. Like he used to on the trains. They called the other men just waiters. But they spoke of Granddaddy separate and said, The Waiter. And said he had engines in his feet and motors in his hands and couldn't no train throw him off and couldn't nobody turn him round. They were big enough for motors, his hands were. He held that one hand out all still and it gettin to be not at all a hand but a person in itself.

"He wants you to hand him the camera," Smilin whispers to Camera, tiltin his head to talk secret like they was in the jungle or somethin and come upon a native that don't speak the language. The men start untyin the straps, and they put the camera into that great hand speckled with the hawk's blood all black and crackly now. And the hand don't even drop with the weight, just the fingers move, curl up around the machine. But Granddaddy lookin straight at the men. They lookin at each other and everywhere but at Granddaddy's face.

"We filmin for the county, see," say Smilin. "We putting together a movie for the food stamp program . . . filmin all around these parts. Uhh, filmin for the county."

"Can I have my camera back?" say the tall man with no machine on his shoulder, but still keepin it high like the camera was still there or needed to be. "Please, sir."

Then Granddaddy's other hand flies up like a sudden and gentle bird, slaps down fast on top of the camera and lifts off half like it was a calabash[2] cut for sharing.

"Hey," Camera jumps forward. He gathers up the parts into his chest and everything unrollin and fallin all over. "Whatcha tryin to do? You'll ruin the film." He looks down into his chest of metal reels and things like he's protectin a kitten from the cold.

"You standin in the misses' flower bed," say Granddaddy. "This is our own place."

The two men look at him, then at each other, then back at the mess in the camera man's chest, and they just back off. One sayin over and over all the way down to the meadow, "Watch it, Bruno. Keep ya fingers off the film." Then Granddaddy picks up the hammer and jams it into the oilskin pocket, scrapes his boots, and goes into the house. And you can hear the squish of his boots headin through the house. And you can see the funny shadow he throws from the parlor window onto the ground by the stringbean patch. The hammer draggin the pocket of the oilskin out so Granddaddy looked even wider. Granny was hummin now—high, not low and grumbly. And she was doin the cakes again, you could smell the molasses from the rum.

"There's this story I'm goin to write one day," say Cathy dreamer. "About the proper use of the hammer."

"Can I be in it?" Tyrone say with his hand up like it was a matter of first come, first served.

"Perhaps," say Cathy, climbin onto the tire to pump us up. "If you there and ready."

---

2 **calabash:** a type of gourd often used as a container

AFTER YOU READ
Blues Ain't No Mockin Bird

Think and Discuss

1. What borders are being trespassed in this story?

2. Describe the grandmother's attitude toward the photographers. What is their attitude toward her? Explain the contrast.

3. Why has the family moved often? Refer to specific details in the story.

4. **Titles** are used to attract readers' attention as well as to hint at a story's **tone** and/or **meaning**. What do you think is the writer's purpose for this unusual title: "Blues Ain't No Mockin Bird"?

5. **Dialect** is a form of language particular to a specific group or region. Copy the following graphic organizer into your Writer's Notebook. Use it to record additional examples of each type of dialect and the standard usage it replaces.

Type of Dialect	Examples	Standard Usage, If Any
Word Choice	Extra nasty-plus	Especially nasty
Word Order	And the frozen patch splinterin every which way underneath kinda spooky	Underneath, the frozen patch splintered in several directions, which was spooky-looking.
Pronunciation	Stompin	Stomping
Idioms (word pictures/ sayings)	He held that one hand out all still and it gettin to be not at all a hand but a person in itself.	His hand was starting to appear larger and more ominous, as large as a person itself.

6. How do you feel about Mister Cain? What in the story makes you feel that way?

Write to Understand: The Power of Dialect

To better understand the power of the dialect that Toni Cade Bambara gives her characters, try rewriting a passage of it in Standard English. For a starting point, look at the examples in your chart. After you have rewritten a passage, write a sentence or two comparing the effect of each version.

BEFORE YOU READ

Rules of the Game

Meet the Author: Amy Tan

Amy Tan was born in California in 1952 to Chinese parents who kept up Chinese traditions in their home. Tan wrestled with the identity problems she felt as a "hyphenated American," a Chinese-American. She also often found herself in conflict with her mother, who wanted her to grow up to be a neurosurgeon. Tan, however, wanted to write. She began her writing career as a technical writer, but a novel she wrote as a form of therapy, *The Joy Luck Club*, became a national bestseller. Tan followed that with other best-selling novels, drawing on her personal struggles and family life to animate her characters and plots.

Build Background: Chess and Life

The 64-square chessboard looks simple enough. Over its surface, however, pass many distinctive pieces—queens, kings, knights, bishops, rooks, and pawns—each moving according to its own rules. Some have vast powers to destroy; some are lowly, often sacrificed for a better position. Chess players move their pieces to take advantage of opponents' weaknesses and to increase their own strength until they can trap the opposing king in checkmate.

The story that follows makes a connection between life and chess. It follows the progress of Meimei as she tries to achieve her dream of becoming a chess champion. Confronting her are many barriers: her youth, her gender, and her background as a Chinese-American from San Francisco's Chinatown. But her biggest hurdle is her mother, whose Old World ways make it difficult for Meimei to enjoy her success while remaining a typical girl.

- What might be some of the barriers that hold back immigrants in the United States?

- At what times in your own life have you faced barriers to reaching your goals?

Rules of the Game

AMY TAN

RULES OF THE GAME

Amy Tan

I was six when my mother taught me the art of invisible strength. It was a strategy for winning arguments, respect from others, and eventually, though neither of us knew it at the time, chess games.

"Bite back your tongue," scolded my mother when I cried loudly, yanking her hand toward the store that sold bags of salted plums. At home, she said, "Wise guy, he not go against wind. In Chinese we say, "Come from South, blow with wind—poom!—North will follow. Strongest wind cannot be seen."

The next week I bit back my tongue as we entered the store with the forbidden candies. When my mother finished her shopping, she quietly plucked a small bag of plums from the rack and put it on the counter with the rest of the items.

imparted
passed along

My mother **imparted** her daily truths so she could help my older brothers and me rise above our circumstances. We lived in San Francisco's Chinatown.[1] Like most of the other Chinese children who played in the back alleys of restaurants and curio shops, I didn't think we were poor. My bowl was always full, three five-course meals every day, beginning with a soup of mysterious things I didn't want to know the names of.

We lived on Waverly Place, in a warm, clean, two-bedroom flat that sat above a small Chinese bakery specializing in steamed pastries and dim sum.[2] In the early morning, when the alley was still quiet, I could smell fragrant red beans as they were cooked down to a pasty sweetness. By daybreak, our flat was heavy with the odor of fried sesame balls and sweet curried chicken crescents. From my bed, I would listen as my father got ready for work, then locked the door behind him, one-two-three clicks.

---

1 **Chinatown:** a large, mainly Chinese neighborhood in San Francisco first settled by Chinese immigrants in the mid-1800s

2 **dim sum:** light Chinese snacks often including dumplings

At the end of our two-block alley was a small sandlot playground with swings and slides well-shined down the middle with use. The play area was bordered by wood-slat benches where old-country people sat cracking roasted watermelon seeds with their golden teeth and scattering the husks to an impatient gathering of gurgling pigeons. The best playground, however, was the dark alley itself. It was crammed with daily mysteries and adventures. My brothers and I would peer into the medicinal herb shop, watching old Li dole out onto a stiff sheet of white paper the right amount of insect shells, saffron-colored[3] seeds, and **pungent** leaves for his ailing customers. It was said that he once cured a woman dying of an ancestral curse that had eluded the best of American doctors. Next to the pharmacy was a printer who specialized in gold-embossed wedding invitations and festive red banners.

> *T*he best playground, however, was the dark alley itself. It was crammed with daily mysteries and adventures.

pungent
sharp tasting

Farther down the street was Ping Yuen Fish Market. The front window displayed a tank crowded with doomed fish and turtles struggling to gain footing on the slimy green-tiled sides. A hand-written sign informed tourists, "Within this store, is all for food, not for pet." Inside, the butchers with their bloodstained white smocks **deftly** gutted the fish while customers cried out their orders and shouted, "Give me your freshest," to which the butchers always protested, "All are freshest." On less crowded market days, we would inspect the crates of live frogs and crabs which we were warned not to poke, boxes of dried cuttlefish,[4] and row upon row of iced prawns, squid, and slippery fish. The sand dabs[5] made me shiver each time; their eyes lay on one flattened side and reminded me of my mother's story of a careless girl who ran into a crowded street and was crushed by a cab. "Was smash flat," reported my mother.

deftly
nimbly, with good control of hands

---

3 **saffron-colored:** yellow, like the saffron spice

4 **cuttlefish:** members of the octopus family

5 **sand dabs:** small flatfish native to western North America

At the corner of the alley was Hong Sing's, a four-table café with a **recessed** stairwell in front that led to a door marked "Tradesmen." My brothers and I believed the bad people emerged from this door at night. Tourists never went to Hong Sing's, since the menu was printed only in Chinese. A Caucasian man with a big camera once posed me and my playmates in front of the restaurant. He had us move to the side of the picture window so the photo would capture the roasted duck with its head dangling from a juice-covered rope. After he took the picture, I told him he should go into Hong Sing's and eat dinner. When he smiled and asked me what they served, I shouted, "Guts and duck's feet and octopus gizzards!" Then I ran off with my friends, shrieking with laughter as we scampered across the alley and hid in the entryway grotto of the China Gem Company, my heart pounding with hope that he would chase us.

> *...My* family called me Meimei, "Little Sister." I was the youngest, the only daughter.

My mother named me after the street that we lived on: Waverly Place Jong, my official name for important American documents. But my family called me Meimei, "Little Sister." I was the youngest, the only daughter. Each morning before school, my mother would twist and yank on my thick black hair until she had formed two tightly wound pigtails. One day, as she struggled to weave a hard-toothed comb through my disobedient hair, I had a sly thought.

I asked her, "Ma, what is Chinese torture?" My mother shook her head. A bobby pin was wedged between her lips. She wetted her palm and smoothed the hair above my ear, then pushed the pin in so that it nicked sharply against my scalp.

"Who say this word?" she asked without a trace of knowing how wicked I was being. I shrugged my shoulders and said, "Some boy in my class said Chinese people do Chinese torture."

"Chinese people do many things," she said simply. "Chinese people do business, do medicine, do painting. Not lazy like American people. We do torture. Best torture."

My older brother Vincent was the one who actually got the chess set. We had gone to the annual Christmas party held at the First Chinese Baptist Church at the end of the alley. The missionary ladies had put together a Santa bag of gifts donated by members of another church. None of the gifts had names on them. There were separate sacks for boys and girls of different ages.

One of the Chinese parishioners had donned a Santa Claus costume and a stiff paper beard with cotton balls glued to it. I think the only children who thought he was the real thing were too young to know that Santa Claus was not Chinese. When my turn came up, the Santa man asked me how old I was. I thought it was a trick question; I was seven according to the American formula and eight by the Chinese calendar. I said I was born on March 17, 1951. That seemed to satisfy him. He then solemnly asked if I had been a very, very good girl this year and did I believe in Jesus Christ and obey my parents. I knew the only answer to that. I nodded back with equal **solemnity**.

My older brother Vincent was the one who actually got the chess set.

solemnity
seriousness

Having watched the older children opening their gifts, I already knew that the big gifts were not necessarily the nicest ones. One girl my age got a large coloring book of biblical characters, while a less greedy girl who selected a smaller box received a glass vial of lavender toilet water. The sound of the box was also important. A ten-year-old boy had chosen a box that jangled when he shook it. It was a tin globe of the world with a slit for inserting money. He must have thought it was full of dimes and nickels, because when he saw that it had just ten pennies, his face fell with such undisguised disappointment that his mother slapped the side of his head and led him out of the church hall, apologizing to the crowd for her son who had such bad manners he couldn't appreciate such a fine gift.

As I peered into the sack, I quickly fingered the remaining presents, testing their weight, imagining what they contained. I chose a heavy, compact one that was wrapped in shiny silver foil and a red satin ribbon. It was a twelve-pack of Life Savers and I spent the rest of the party arranging and rearranging the candy tubes in the order of my favorites.

My bother Winston chose wisely as well. His present turned out to be a box of intricate plastic parts; the instructions on the box proclaimed that when they were properly assembled he would have an authentic miniature replica of a World War II submarine.

Vincent got the chess set, which would have been a very decent present to get at a church Christmas party, except it was obviously used and, as we discovered later, it was missing a black pawn and a white knight. My mother graciously thanked the unknown benefactor, saying, "Too good. Cost too much." At which point, an old lady with fine white, wispy hair nodded toward our family and said with a whistling whisper, "Merry, merry Christmas."

When we got home, my mother told Vincent to throw the chess set away. "She not want it. We not want it," she said, tossing her head stiffly to the side with a tight, proud smile. My brothers had deaf ears. They were already lining up the chess pieces and reading from the dog-eared instruction book.

I watched Vincent and Winston play during Christmas week. The chess board seemed to hold elaborate secrets waiting to be untangled. The chessmen were more powerful than Old Li's magic herbs that cured ancestral curses. And my brothers wore such serious faces that I was sure something was at stake that was greater than avoiding the tradesmen's door to Hong Sing's.

"Let me! Let me!" I begged between games when one brother or the other would sit back with a deep sigh of relief and victory, the other annoyed, unable to let go of the outcome. Vincent at first refused to let me play, but when I offered my Life Savers as replacements for the buttons that filled in for the missing pieces, he relented. He chose the flavors: wild cherry for the black pawn and peppermint for the white knight. Winner could eat both.

As our mother sprinkled flour and rolled out small doughy circles for the steamed dumplings that would be our dinner that night, Vincent explained the rules, pointing to each piece. "You have sixteen pieces and so do I. One king and queen, two bishops, two knights, two castles, and eight pawns. The pawns can only move forward one step, except on the first move. Then they can move two. But they can only take men by moving crossways like this, except in the beginning, when you can move ahead and take another pawn."

"Why?" I asked as I moved my pawn. "Why can't they move more steps?"

"Because they're pawns," he said.

"But why do they go crossways to take other men? Why aren't there any women and children?"

"Why is the sky blue? Why must you always ask stupid questions?" asked Vincent. "This is a game. These are the rules. I didn't make them up. See. Here. In the book." He jabbed a page with a pawn in his hand. "Pawn. P-A-W-N. Pawn. Read it yourself."

My mother patted the flour off her hands. "Let me see book," she said quietly. She scanned the pages quickly, not reading the foreign English symbols, seeming to search deliberately for nothing in particular.

> "*W*hy must you always ask stupid questions?" asked Vincent. "This is a game. These are the rules."

"This American rules," she concluded at last. "Every time people come out from foreign country, must know rules. You not know, judge say, Too bad, go back. They not telling you why so you can use their way go forward. They say, Don't know why, you find out yourself. But they knowing all the time. Better you take it, find out why yourself." She tossed her head back with a satisfied smile.

I found out about all the whys later. I read the rules and looked up all the big words in a dictionary. I borrowed books from the Chinatown library. I studied each chess piece, trying to absorb the power each contained.

I learned about opening moves and why it's important to control the center early on; the shortest distance between two points is straight down the middle. I learned about the middle game and why tactics between two **adversaries** are like clashing ideas; the one who plays better has the clearest plans for both attacking and getting out of traps. I learned why it is essential in the endgame to have foresight, a mathematical understanding of all possible moves, and patience; all weaknesses and advantages become evident to a strong adversary and are **obscured** to a tiring opponent. I discovered that for the whole game one must gather invisible strengths and see the endgame before the game begins.

adversaries
opponents;
enemies

obscured
hidden

I also found out why I should never reveal "why" to others. A little knowledge withheld is a great advantage one should store for future use. That is the power of chess. It is a game of secrets in which one must show and never tell.

I loved the secrets I found within the sixty-four black and white squares. I carefully drew a handmade chessboard and pinned it to the wall next to my bed, where I would stare for hours at imaginary battles. Soon I no longer lost any games or Life Savers, but I lost my adversaries. Winston and Vincent decided they were more interested in roaming the streets after school in their Hopalong Cassidy[6] cowboy hats.

On a cold spring afternoon, while walking home from school, I detoured through the playground at the end of our alley. I saw a group of old men, two seated across a folding table playing a game of chess, others smoking pipes, eating peanuts, and watching. I ran home and grabbed Vincent's chess set, which was bound in a cardboard box with rubber bands. I also carefully selected two prized rolls of Life Savers. I came back to the park and approached a man who was observing the game.

"Want to play?" I asked him. His face widened with surprise and he grinned as he looked at the box under my arm.

"Little sister, been a long time since I play with dolls," he said, smiling **benevolently**. I quickly put the box down next to him on the bench and displayed my **retort**.

benevolently
with good will

retort
sharp or strong reply

Lau Po, as he allowed me to call him, turned out to be a much better player than my brothers. I lost many games and many Life Savers. But over the weeks, with each diminishing roll of candies, I added new secrets. Lau Po gave me the names. The Double Attack from the East and West Shores. Throwing Stones on the Drowning Man. The Sudden Meeting of the Clan. The Surprise from the Sleeping Guard. The Humble Servant Who Kills the King. Sand in the Eyes of Advancing Forces. A Double Killing Without Blood.

There were also the fine points of chess etiquette. Keep captured men in neat rows, as well-tended prisoners. Never announce "Check" with

---

6 **Hopalong Cassidy:** a radio, movie, and TV cowboy who became famous in the 1950s

vanity, lest someone with an unseen sword slit your throat. Never hurl pieces into the sandbox after you have lost a game, because then you must find them again, by yourself, after apologizing to all around you. By the end of the summer, Lau Po had taught me all he knew, and I had become a better chess player.

A small weekend crowd of Chinese people and tourists would gather as I played and defeated my opponents one by one. My mother would join the crowds during these outdoor exhibition games. She sat proudly on the bench, telling my admirers with proper Chinese humility, "Is luck."

A man who watched me play in the park suggested that my mother allow me to play in local chess tournaments. My mother smiled graciously, an answer that meant nothing. I desperately wanted to go, but I bit back my tongue. I knew she would not let me play among strangers. So as we walked home I said in a small voice that I didn't want to play in the local tournament. They would have American rules. If I lost, I would bring shame on my family.

A man who watched me play in the park suggested that my mother allow me to play in local chess tournaments.

"Is shame you fall down nobody push you," said my mother.

During my first tournament, my mother sat with me in the front row as I waited for my turn. I frequently bounced my legs to unstick them from the cold metal seat of the folding chair. When my name was called, I leapt up. My mother unwrapped something in her lap. It was her *chang,* a small tablet of red jade which held the sun's fire. "Is luck," she whispered, and tucked it into my dress pocket. I turned to my opponent, a fifteen-year-old boy from Oakland. He looked at me, wrinkling his nose.

As I began to play, the boy disappeared, the color ran out of the room, and I saw only my white pieces and his black ones waiting on the other side. A light wind began blowing past my ears. It whispered secrets only I could hear.

"Blow from the South," it murmured. "The wind leaves no trail." I saw a clear path, the traps to avoid. The crowd rustled. "Shhh! Shhh!" said the corners of the room. The wind blew stronger. "Throw sand from the East to distract him." The knight came forward ready for the sacrifice. The wind hissed, louder and louder. "Blow, blow, blow. He cannot see. He is blind now. Make him lean away from the wind so he is easier to knock down."

"Check," I said, as the wind roared with laughter. The wind died down to little puffs, my own breath.

My mother placed my first trophy next to a new plastic chess set that the neighborhood Tao society had given to me. As she wiped each piece with a soft cloth, she said, "Next time win more, lose less."

"Ma, it's not how many pieces you lose," I said. "Sometimes you need to lose pieces to get ahead."

"Better to lose less, see if you really need."

At the next tournament, I won again, but it was my mother who wore the triumphant grin.

"Lost eight piece this time. Last time was eleven. What I tell you? Better off lose less!" I was annoyed, but I couldn't say anything.

I attended more tournaments, each one farther away from home. I won all games, in all divisions. The Chinese bakery downstairs from our flat displayed my growing collection of trophies in its window, amidst the dust-covered cakes that were never picked up. The day after I won an important regional tournament, the window encased a fresh sheet cake with whipped-cream frosting and red script saying "Congratulations, Waverly Jong, Chinatown Chess Champion." Soon after that, a flower shop, headstone engraver, and funeral parlor offered to sponsor me in national tournaments. That's when my mother decided I no longer had to do the dishes. Winston and Vincent had to do my chores.

"Why does she get to play and we do all the work," complained Vincent.

"Is new American rules," said my mother. "Meimei play, squeeze all her brains out for win chess. You play, worth squeeze towel."

By my ninth birthday, I was a national chess champion. I was still some 429 points away from grand-master status, but I was touted as the Great American Hope, a child **prodigy** and a girl to boot. They ran a

prodigy
an unusually talented child

photo of me in *Life* magazine next to a quote in which Bobby Fischer[7] said, "There will never be a woman grand master." "Your move, Bobby," said the caption.

The day they took the magazine picture I wore neatly plaited braids clipped with plastic barrettes trimmed with rhinestones. I was playing in a large high school auditorium that echoed with phlegmy coughs and the squeaky rubber knobs of chair legs sliding across freshly waxed wooden floors. Seated across from me was an American man, about the same age as Lau Po, maybe fifty. I remember that his sweaty brow seemed to weep at my every move. He wore a dark, **malodorous** suit. One of his pockets was stuffed with a great white kerchief on which he wiped his palm before sweeping his hand over the chosen chess piece with great flourish.

malodorous bad smelling

In my crisp pink-and-white dress with scratchy lace at the neck, one of two my mother had sewn for these special occasions, I would clasp my hands under my chin, the delicate points of my elbows poised lightly on the table in the manner my mother had shown me for posing for

I went to school, then directly home to learn new chess secrets, cleverly concealed advantages, more escape routes.

the press. I would swing my patent leather shoes back and forth like an impatient child riding on a school bus. Then I would pause, suck in my lips, twirl my chosen piece in midair as if undecided, and then firmly plant it in its new threatening place, with a triumphant smile thrown back at my opponent for good measure.

I no longer played in the alley of Waverly Place. I never visited the playground where the pigeons and old men gathered. I went to school, then directly home to learn new chess secrets, cleverly concealed advantages, more escape routes.

But I found it difficult to concentrate at home. My mother had a habit of standing over me while I plotted out my games. I think she thought of

---

7 **Bobby Fischer:** the first and only American to win the World Chess Championship (1972)

herself as my protective ally. Her lips would be sealed tight, and after each move I made, a soft "Hmmmmph" would escape from her nose.

"Ma, I can't practice when you stand there like that," I said one day. She retreated to the kitchen and made loud noises with the pots and pans. When the crashing stopped, I could see out of the corner of my eye that she was standing in the doorway. "Hmmmph!" Only this one came out of her tight throat.

My parents made many concessions to allow me to practice. One time I complained that the bedroom I shared was so noisy that I couldn't think. Thereafter, my brothers slept in a bed in the living room facing the street. I said I couldn't finish my rice; my head didn't work right when my stomach was too full. I left the table with half-finished bowls and nobody complained. But there was one duty I couldn't avoid. I had to accompany my mother on Saturday market days when I had no tournament to play. My mother would proudly walk with me, visiting many shops, buying very little. "This my daughter Wave-ly Jong," she said to whoever looked her way.

> "Why do you have to use me to show off? If you want to show off, then why don't you learn to play chess?"

One day after we left a shop I said under my breath, "I wish you wouldn't do that, telling everybody I'm your daughter." My mother stopped walking. Crowds of people with heavy bags pushed past us on the sidewalk, bumping into first one shoulder, than another.

"Aii-ya. So shame be with mother?" She grasped my hand even tighter as she glared at me.

I looked down. "It's not that, it's just so obvious. It's just so embarrassing."

"Embarrass you be my daughter?" Her voice was cracking with anger.

"That's not what I meant. That's not what I said."

"What you say?"

I knew it was a mistake to say anything more, but I heard my voice speaking. "Why do you have to use me to show off? If you want to show off, then why don't you learn to play chess?"

My mother's eyes turned into dangerous black slits. She had no words for me, just sharp silence.

I felt the wind rushing around my hot ears. I jerked my hand out of my mother's tight grasp and spun around, knocking into an old woman. Her bag of groceries spilled to the ground.

"Aii-ya! Stupid girl!" my mother and the woman cried. Oranges and tin cans careened down the sidewalk. As my mother stooped to help the old woman pick up the escaping food, I took off.

I raced down the street, dashing between people, not looking back as my mother screamed shrilly, "Meimei! Meimei!" I fled down an alley, past dark, curtained shops and merchants washing the grime off their windows. I sped into the sunlight, into a large street crowded with tourists examining trinkets and souvenirs. I ducked into another dark alley, down another street, up another alley. I ran until it hurt and I realized I had nowhere to go, that I was not running from anything. The alleys contained no escape routes.

My breath came out like angry smoke. It was cold. I sat down on an upturned plastic pail next to a stack of empty boxes, cupping my chin with my hands, thinking hard. I imagined my mother, first walking briskly down one street or another looking for me, then giving up and returning home to await my arrival. After two hours, I stood up on creaking legs and slowly walked home. The alley was quiet and I could see the yellow lights shining from our flat like two tiger's eyes in the night. I climbed the sixteen steps to the door, advancing quietly up each so as not to make any warning sounds. I turned the knob; the door was locked. I heard a chair moving, quick steps, the locks turning-click! click! click!—and then the door opened.

"About time you got home," said Vincent. "Boy, are you in trouble."

He slid back to the dinner table. On a platter were the remains of a large fish, its fleshy head still connected to bones swimming upstream in vain escape. Standing there waiting for my punishment, I heard my mother speak in a dry voice.

"About time you got home," said Vincent. "Boy, are you in trouble." He slid back to the dinner table.

"We not concerning this girl. This girl not have concerning for us."

Nobody looked at me. Bone chopsticks clinked against the inside of bowls being emptied into hungry mouths.

I walked into my room, closed the door, and lay down on my bed. The room was dark, the ceiling filled with shadows from the dinnertime lights of neighboring flats.

In my head, I saw a chessboard with sixty-four black and white squares. Opposite me was my opponent, two angry black slits. She wore a triumphant smile. "Strongest wind cannot be seen," she said.

Her black men advanced across the plane, slowly marching to each successive level as a single unit. My white pieces screamed as they scurried and fell off the board one by one. As her men drew closer to my edge, I felt myself growing light. I rose up into the air and flew out the window. Higher and higher, above the alley, over the tops of tiled roofs, where I was gathered up by the wind and pushed up toward the night sky until everything below me disappeared and I was alone.

I closed my eyes and pondered my next move.

AFTER YOU READ
Rules of the Game

Think and Discuss

1. What are some of the barriers Meimei faces as she pursues her dream of becoming a chess champion?

2. Whose side of the **conflict** between Meimei and her mother were you on? Why?

3. **Conflicts** can be both **internal** and **external**. Find some of each type of conflict in this story.

4. What **images** in the story show how Meimei approaches her own life as if it were a chess game? Give specific examples.

5. What borders must Mrs. Jong contend with?

6. Copy the graphic organizer below into your Writer's Notebook. As you scan the story, use the graphic organizer to note ways in which the barriers in Meimei's life remind you of obstacles you have faced as you try to reach your goals.

Meimei's Barriers	Remind me Of→	My Barriers

Write to Understand: Focused Freewriting

Explore through focused freewriting how the barriers you face are like and unlike Meimei's. Look over the graphic organizer you completed. In your Writer's Notebook, begin writing freely about what you jotted down in your organizer. Try to answer the question: "How are the barriers in my path to success like and unlike Meimei's?" Use the experiences you noted in the organizer to help answer that question. Keep your pen moving. If you can't think of anything, write, "I can't think of anything to write" until more ideas occur to you.

Writers on Writing

BEFORE YOU READ
In the Canon, for All the Wrong Reasons

Meet the Author: Amy Tan

Once a year, Amy Tan and a number of other highly successful writers—including humorist Dave Barry, horror writer Stephen King, and Simpsons creator Matt Groening—get together and put on a rock concert to raise money for charity. Their band is called the Rock Bottom Remainders (remainders are books that haven't sold well and have their prices slashed). Amy Tan sings in the band, and all the charitable organizations they contribute to are related to books. A recent tour, for example, raised money for Get Caught Reading, a national program to remind people how much fun reading is. Since reading and writing have been so important in her life, Tan enjoys the opportunity to support programs that promote them.

Build Background: A Voice for Hyphenated Americans?

Though Amy Tan appreciated the many readers who turned to her books for pleasure and inspiration, she soon found that she was regarded as an authority in matters beyond her expertise. For example, she was often asked to give advice to young people growing up in bi-cultural families. She said, "I have a lot of young people coming up to me and saying . . . 'I feel like I don't know if I'm Chinese.' 'Am I American? Am I Korean? What should I be? How should I feel about this?'" One way she has answered is to say "that this whole question of who you are is a very, very interesting question and having two cultures to add to the mix of it makes it even more interesting."

However, she does not feel comfortable offering anything like expert advice. In the essay that follows, she explains why.

- What obligation, if any, do writers have to present their culture in a positive way?

- What progress have you made in answering the "whole question of who you are" and in understanding the role of your ethnic heritage in that answer?

In the Canon, for All the Wrong Reasons

AMY TAN

IN THE CANON,[1]
FOR ALL THE WRONG REASONS

Amy Tan

Several years ago I learned that I had passed a new literary

milestone. I had made it to the Halls of Education under the rubric[2] of "Multicultural Literature," also known in many schools as "Required Reading."

Thanks to this development, I now meet students who proudly tell me they're doing their essays, term papers, or master's theses on me. By that they mean that they are analyzing not just my books but me—my grade-school achievements, youthful **indiscretions**, marital status, as

well as the movies I watched as a child, the slings and arrows[3] I suffered as a minority, and so forth—all of which, with the hindsight of classroom literary investigation, prove to contain many Chinese omens that made it inevitable that I would become a writer.

Once I read a master's thesis on feminist writings, which included examples from *The Joy Luck Club*. The student noted that I had often used the number four, something on the order of thirty-two or thirty-six times—in any case, a number divisible by four. She pointed out that there were four mothers, four daughters, four sections of the book, four stories per section. Furthermore, there were four sides to a mah jong[4] table, four

---

1 **canon:** works of writing that are considered to be representative of the best of literature

2 **rubric:** a category or class

3 **slings and arrows:** misfortunes; an allusion to the play *Hamlet*, by William Shakespeare.
The character of Hamlet has a famous soliloquy which begins,
To be, or not to be: that is the question:
Whether 'tis nobler in the mind to suffer
The slings and arrows of outrageous fortune,
Or to take arms against a sea of troubles,
And by opposing end them?

4 **mah jong:** a game of Chinese origin, in which players complete sets of tiles

directions of the wind, four players. More important, she **postulated** my use of the number four was a symbol for the four stages of psychological development, which corresponded in **uncanny** ways to the four stages of some type of Buddhist philosophy I had never heard of before. The student recalled that the story contained a character called fourth wife, symbolizing death, and a four-year-old girl with a feisty spirit, symbolizing regeneration.

In short, her literary **sleuthing** went on to reveal a mystical and rather Byzantine[5] puzzle, which, once explained, proved to be completely brilliant and precisely logical. She wrote me a letter and asked if her analysis had been correct. How I longed to say "absolutely."

The truth is, if there are symbols in my work they exist largely by accident or through someone else's interpretive design. If I wrote of an "orange moon rising on a dark night," I would more likely ask myself later if the image was a cliché, not whether it was a symbol for the feminine force rising in anger, as one master's thesis postulated. To plant symbols like that, you need a plan, good organizational skills, and a **prescient** understanding of the story you are about to write. Sadly, I lack those traits.

All this is by way of saying that I don't claim my use of the number four to be a brilliant symbolic device. In fact, now that it's been pointed out to me in rather astonishing ways, I consider my overuse of the number to be a flaw.

Reviewers and students have enlightened me about not only how I write but why I write. Apparently, I am driven to capture the immigrant experience, to **demystify** Chinese culture, to point out the difference between Chinese and American culture, even to pave the way for other Asian American writers.

If only I were that noble. Contrary to what is assumed by some students, reporters, and community organizations wishing to bestow honors on me, I am not an expert on China. Chinese culture, mah jong, the psychology of mothers and daughters, generation gaps, immigration, illegal aliens, **assimilation**, **acculturation**, racial tension, Tiananmen Square,[6] the Most

postulated
suggested; proposed

uncanny
eerie; mysterious

sleuthing
detecting

prescient
farsighted; visionary

demystify
to remove the mystery from

assimilation
absorption into another country or culture

acculturation
adopting the social traits and patterns of another group

---

5 **Byzantine:** highly complicated, a common allusion to the 5th century AD Byzantine Empire, noted for its ornate decorative and architectural style

6 **Tiananmen Square:** a large plaza in central Beijing, China, famous as the site of major student demonstrations in 1989 suppressed by the government

Favored Nation trade agreements,[7] human rights, Pacific Rim[8] economics, the purported one million missing baby girls of China, the future of Hong Kong after 1997,[9] or, I am sorry to say, Chinese cooking. Certainly I have personal opinions on many of these topics, but by no means do my **sentiments** and my world of make-believe make me an expert.

sentiments
feelings;
emotions

So I am alarmed when reviewers and educators assume that my very personal, specific, and fictional stories are meant to be representative down to the nth[10] detail not just of Chinese Americans but, sometimes, of all Asian culture. Is Jane Smiley's *A Thousand Acres* supposed to be taken as representative of all of American culture? If so, in what ways? Are all American fathers tyrannical? Do all American sisters betray one another? Are all American conscientious objectors[11] flaky in love relationships?

Over the years my editor has received hundreds of permissions requests from publishers of college textbooks and multicultural anthologies, all of them wishing to reprint my work for "educational purposes." One publisher wanted to include an excerpt from *The Joy Luck Club*, a scene in which a Chinese woman invites her non-Chinese boyfriend to her parents' house for dinner. The boyfriend brings a bottle of wine as a gift and commits a number of social gaffes[12] at the dinner table. Students were supposed to read this excerpt, then answer the following question: "If you are invited to a Chinese family's house for dinner, should you bring a bottle of wine?"

In many respects, I am proud to be on the reading lists for courses such as Ethnic Studies and Asian American Studies, Asian American Literature, Asian American History, Women's Literature, Feminist Studies, Feminist Writers of Color, and so forth. What writer wouldn't want her work to be read? I also

---

7 **Most Favored Nation trade agreements:** advantageous trade relations between the United States and other countries. Because of various controversies, China did not receive this designation until 2000.

8 **Pacific Rim:** the cities and countries located next to the Pacific Ocean

9 **Hong Kong after 1997:** Hong Kong lost its British sovereignty after 1997 and returned to the rule of the People's Republic of China.

10 **nth:** the last or greatest number in an indefinitely large series of numbers; the most extreme

11 **conscientious objectors:** individuals who resist serving in the military because of their moral and ethical beliefs

12 **gaffes:** mistakes or blunders

take a certain **perverse** glee in imagining countless students, sleepless at three in the morning, trying to read *The Joy Luck Club* for the next day's midterm. Yet I'm also not altogether comfortable about my book's status as required reading.

Let me relate a conversation I had with a professor at a school in southern California. He told me he uses my books in his literature class but he makes it a point to **lambast** those passages that depict China as backward or unattractive. He objects to any descriptions that have to do with spitting, filth, poverty, or superstitions. I asked him if China in the 1930s and 1940s was free of these elements. He said, No, such descriptions are true; but he still believes it is "the obligation of the writer of ethnic literature to create positive, progressive images."

I secretly shuddered and thought, Oh well, that's southern California for you. But then, a short time later, I met a student from UC Berkeley, a school that I myself attended. The student was standing in line at a book signing. When his turn came, he swaggered up to me, then took two steps back and said in a loud voice, "Don't you think you have a responsibility to write about Chinese men as positive role models?"

In the past, I've tried to ignore the potshots. . . .

"Well," I said, "You can't please everyone can you?" I pointed out that readers are free to interpret a book as they please, and that they are free to appreciate or not appreciate the result. Besides, reacting to your critics makes a writer look defensive, **petulant**, and like an all-around bad sport.

But lately I've started thinking it's wrong to take such a laissez-faire[13] attitude. Lately I've come to think that I must say something, not so much to defend myself and my work but to express my hopes for American literature for what it has the potential to become in the twenty-first century—that is, a truly American literature, democratic in the way it includes many colorful voices.

Until recently, I didn't think it was important for writers to express their private intentions in order for their work to be appreciated; I believed that my analysis of my intentions belonged behind the closed doors of literature classes. But I've come to realize that the study of literature does have its effect on how books are being read, and thus on what might be read, published,

---

13 **laissez-faire:** in the spirit of noninterference

antidote
counteraction;
cure

and written in the future. For that reason, I do believe writers today must talk about their intentions—if for no other reason than to serve as an **antidote** to what others say our intentions should be.

For the record, I don't write to dig a hole and fill it with symbols. I don't write stories as ethnic themes. I don't write to represent life in general. And I certainly don't write because I have answers. If I knew everything there is to know about mothers and daughters, Chinese and Americans, I wouldn't have any stories left to imagine. If I had to write about only positive role models, I wouldn't have enough imagination left to finish the first story. If I knew what to do about immigration, I would be a sociologist or a politician and not a long-winded storyteller.

So why do I write?

obsessions
fixations;
persistent
ideas

Because my childhood disturbed me, pained me, made me ask foolish questions. And the questions still echo. Why does my mother always talk about killing herself? Why did my father and brother have to die? If I die, can I be reborn into a happy family? Those early **obsessions** led to a belief that writing could be my salvation, providing me with the sort of freedom and danger, satisfaction and discomfort, truth and contradiction I can't find in anything else in life.

I write to discover the past for myself. I don't write to change the future for others. And if others are moved by my work—if they love their mothers more, scold their daughters less, or divorce their husbands who were not positive role models—I'm often surprised, usually grateful to hear from kind readers. But I don't take either credit or blame for changing their lives for better or for worse.

Writing, for me, is an act of faith, a hope that I will discover what I mean by "truth." I also think of reading as an act of faith, a hope that I will discover something remarkable about ordinary life, about myself. And if the writer and the reader discover the same thing, if they have that connection, the act of faith has resulted in an act of magic. To me, that's the mystery and the wonder of both life and fiction—the connection between two individuals who discover in the end that they are more the same than they are different.

And if that doesn't happen, it's nobody's fault. There are still plenty of other books on the shelf. Choose what you like.

AFTER YOU READ

In the Canon, for All the Wrong Reasons

Think and Discuss

1. According to Tan, what reasons have people given for why she writes?

2. What reasons does Tan give for why she writes?

3. What is the **main idea** in each section of this essay?

4. Tan writes that "readers are free to interpret a book as they please," and that they are "free to appreciate or not appreciate the result." Do you feel that as a student you are free to interpret a book as you please?

5. Look back over the following selections, all by writers on the subject of writing: "Shelf Life" by Gary Paulsen (pages 83–88), "Grandfather's Blessing" by Julia Alvarez (pages 171–179), and "Knee-Deep In Its Absence" by David Petersen (pages 273–278). Copy the graphic organizer below into your Writer's Notebook. Then use it to summarize the reasons each writer gives for why he or she writes.

Author	Reasons for Writing
Amy Tan	
Gary Paulsen	
Julia Alvarez	
David Petersen	

Write to Understand: Synthesizing Ideas

Using your graphic organizer, write two or three paragraphs comparing and contrasting the reasons these four authors have given to explain why they write. What do the writers have in common? What makes each distinctive? After you have examined the reasons these authors write, think about what *you* get out of writing, and write about it.

A Writer's WORKSHOP

INFORMATIONAL ESSAY

In this unit you read an informational article on the growth and meaning of hip-hop music (see pages 413–422), a style of music that has crossed many borders. In previous units there were informational articles on global warming (pages 211–218), the tsunami of 2004 (pages 221–230), and mysterious mummies found in China (pages 335–342). Your history and science textbooks contain informational writing, as do the manuals that come with your cell phones or computers. Writing an informational essay will not only allow you to share your knowledge with others but also help make you a better reader of the informational texts you will encounter all your life.

Prewriting

FINDING IDEAS

Throughout this unit you have been reading and thinking about the theme of crossing borders. Most people in the United States—or their ancestors—have arrived here by crossing borders, though they often brought the customs and traditions of the land of their birth along with them. Brainstorm or freewrite to discover customs or traditions in your family that have their origins in some other land or culture. From these, you can choose a topic for an informational essay. A good subject for an informational essay is one that you

- know well

- can find some source materials on

- have some ideas about and personal experience with

- think readers might not know about and would enjoy learning.

After a good brainstorming session, look over your ideas and choose the topic that you think will make the best informational essay.

DEVELOPING A MAIN IDEA

What have you learned about your custom or tradition that you have found especially interesting? What aspect of your subject would you most like to share with an interested reader? One way to answer these questions is to conduct interviews.

COOPERATIVE LEARNING: INTERVIEWING

Pair up with a partner. Tell your topic to your partner and then ask him or her to interview you about it, asking questions that they find genuinely interesting. During the interview, notice the ideas that seem to repeat or that you seem to emphasize. Your main idea might be found among those. When you have finished, write your main idea in a sentence. Then switch roles and interview your partner.

DEVELOPING SUPPORTING DETAILS

Copy the graphic organizer below into your Writer's Notebook. Use it to develop the three key points that will support your main idea. In informational writing, supporting details include:

- facts, examples, statistics, reasons

- views of experts in the field

- your own experiences and other stories that illustrate a point.

Try to find a book, article, or Web site on your subject, or interview people in your family who know a lot about it, so that you can include some expert comments.

Main Idea:	
Key supporting point:	Details for that supporting point:
Key supporting point:	Details for that supporting point:
Key supporting point:	Details for that supporting point:

ORGANIZING YOUR ESSAY

Decide in which order to present the key supporting points and the details for each one. Make an outline or a graphic sketch of the organization of your essay.

Drafting

Think of an engaging way to begin your essay, a way that will capture the readers' attention. You might want to start with a story or with a personal statement about what the custom or tradition means to you. You may also want to make a connection to the theme of crossing borders. Use your outline or graphic sketch to draft the body of your essay. Then spend some time writing a strong conclusion. You might want to refer back to an idea in the introduction and to the theme.

COOPERATIVE LEARNING: PEER REVIEW

Pair up with a partner and exchange drafts. Discuss both strengths and areas for improvement.

Revising and Editing

Consider your partner's comments. Also, stand back from your essay and read it with fresh eyes. Is there anything out of order? Is there anything that is not needed? Is there anything that you could replace with a graphic, such as an illustration or timeline, which would convey the information more effectively? Make any changes you see fit.

READING WITH AN EDITOR'S EYE

Pay special attention to the use of capital letters and italics (or underlines). Remember to capitalize all nationalities, races, languages, religions, religious holidays, and religious references. If you use a foreign word or phrase, put it in italics or underline it.

> EXAMPLE: For Mexican Christians, the holiday *Las Posadas* begins on December 16th and ends on Christmas.

USING A WORD PROCESSOR

Your word processor is likely to make automatic capitalization corrections as you type. It will also place a red squiggly line under words that do not appear in the program's dictionary. Read over your keyboarded essay looking for those red squiggly lines. They may help you identify words that you need to underline or put in italics.

USING A CHECKLIST

Use the Six-Trait checklist on the following page to further polish your informational essay. When you have revised and edited until the essay is the best it can be, make a neat final copy.

Six Traits of Writing: Informational Essays

Content and Ideas
- subject is nonfiction
- essay conveys information about a custom or tradition
- strong supporting details, including facts, statistics, examples, and expert opinions, provide clarity

Organization
- the introduction draws readers in
- the body contains at least three key points and the supporting details needed to back them up
- the conclusion provides a strong sense of ending

Voice or Style
- writer's voice sounds natural, not forced
- writer's personality comes through without detracting from the focus on information

Word Choice
- specific words and verbs in the active voice make the writing come alive
- any specialized terms are defined for the reader

Sentence Fluency
- transitional words show how ideas are related to one another
- sentence length and sentence beginnings are varied and purposeful

Conventions
- sentences are complete and begin with a capital letter and end with a period, unless fragments are used with a purpose
- grammar and usage are correct
- spelling and punctuation are correct

Echoes from the Past

And I thought, as I wiped my eyes on the corner
of my apron:

This is an ancient gesture, authentic, antique . . .

Edna St. Vincent Millay,
from "An Ancient Gesture"

Temple of Poseidon, Sounion, Greece

BEFORE YOU READ

from the *Odyssey*, Part I

Meet the Authors
Homer Credited with writing two of the greatest epics of all time, the *Iliad* and the *Odyssey*, Homer's work has influenced William Shakespeare, James Joyce, and many other writers. Yet, great as his achievements are, not much is known about him. According to tradition, Homer is the "blind bard of the Archaic Age of Greece." He was born in the 8th century B.C., and since his poems are in predominantly Ionic dialect, he is believed to have been a native of Ionia. He traveled from place to place reciting his poems. Most of the other early biographical information about Homer, however, is fictitious.

Constantine Cavafy Cavafy (1863–1933) was a major Greek poet who also worked as a journalist and civil servant. He had a vast knowledge of ancient Greek history and culture.

Build Background: The Epic Poems of Homer
Few works of ancient times have echoed more profoundly through centuries of Western literature than two works attributed to Homer, the *Iliad* and the *Odyssey*. Both are *epic poems*—long narrative poems, highly stylized, that tell a story of heroic events. Homer's two epics were the basis of Greek education and culture throughout the Classical Age and continued to be the foundation of a humane education into the time of the Roman Empire. Even today, well-educated people are expected to be familiar with these two works.

Both poems are about events related to the Trojan War, a legendary conflict between the early Greeks and the people of Troy, or Ilium. The *Iliad* tells the story of the war itself, which lasted ten years, and of the wrath of Achilles, the greatest warrior on the Greek side. The *Odyssey* tells the story of the journey of one of the Greek warriors, Odysseus, back to his home in Ithaca after the war was over and the Greeks were victorious. At the point in the story where the following selection begins, Odysseus has been away from home for 18 years.

- What do you already know about ancient Greece, the Trojan War, and the *Odyssey*?

- What message do you think the *Odyssey* can have for someone reading it today?

THE HEAD OF ULYSSES (ODYSSEUS), fragment of a marble statue, 1st Century B.C.

from the Odyssey, Part 1

HOMER

from the *ODYSSEY*

Homer

translated by Robert Fitzgerald

PART I
ODYSSEUS AND THE CYCLOPES

"*What* shall I
say first? What shall I keep until the end?
The gods have tried me in a thousand ways.
But first my name: let that be known to you,
and if I pull away from pitiless death,   5
friendship will bind us, though my land lies far.

I am Laertes' son, Odysseus.

                            Men hold me

formidable for **guile** in peace and war:
this fame has gone abroad to the sky's rim.   10
My home is on the peaked sea-mark of Ithaca
under Mount Neion's wind-blown robe of leaves,
in sight of other islands—Dulichium,
Same, wooded Zacynthus—Ithaca
being most lofty in that coastal sea,   15
and northwest, while the rest lie east and south.
A rocky isle but good for a boy's training;
I shall not see on earth a place more dear,
though I have been detained long by Calypso,[1]

formidable
tending to
inspire awe
or wonder

guile
skill in
strategy and
outwitting an
opponent

---

1 **Calypso:** a sea nymph who lived alone on a lush, mythical island in the Ionian Sea. Calypso fell in love with Odysseus when he was shipwrecked on her island and promised him eternal youth and immortality if he would stay with her. Although he stayed in Calypso's island paradise for seven years, nothing could overcome his desire to return home. Eventually, Zeus asked Calypso to release Odysseus. She gave Odysseus provisions and materials to build a raft and died of grief when Odysseus left.

loveliest among goddesses, who held me   20
in her smooth caves, to be her heart's delight,
as Circe of Aeaea,[2] the enchantress,
desired me, and detained me in her hall.
But in my heart I never gave consent.
Where shall a man find sweetness to surpass   25
his own home and his parents? In far lands
he shall not, though he find a house of gold.

What of my sailing, then from Troy?
                              What of those years
of rough adventure, weathered under Zeus?"   30

       . . .

"I might have made it safely home, that time,
but as I came round Malea the current
took me out to sea, and from the north
a fresh gale drove me on, past Cythera.
Nine days I drifted on the teeming sea   35
before dangerous high winds. Upon the tenth
we came to the coastline of the Lotus Eaters,
who live upon that flower. We landed there
to take on water. All ships' companies
mustered alongside for the mid-day meal.   40   **mustered**
Then I sent out two picked men and a runner   gathered
to learn what race of men that land sustained.
They fell in, soon enough, with Lotus Eaters,
who showed no will to do us harm, only
offering the sweet Lotus to our friends—   45
but those who ate this honeyed plant, the Lotus,
never cared to report, nor to return:

---

2 **Circe of Aeaea:** a sorceress known for her ability to turn men into animals. Although
Odysseus makes reference to Circe here, he hasn't met her yet in the course of the journey.
His encounter with Circe is told in Part II of the *Odyssey*.

they longed to stay forever, browsing on
that native bloom, forgetful of their homeland.
I drove them, all three wailing, to the ships,   50
tied them down under their rowing benches,
called the rest: 'All hands aboard;
come, clear the beach and no one taste
the Lotus, or you lose your hope of home'.
Filing in to their places by the rowlocks   55
my oarsmen dipped their long oars in the surf,
and we moved out again on our sea faring.

In the next land we found were Cyclopes,
giants, louts, without a law to bless them.
In ignorance leaving the fruitage of the earth in mystery   60
to the immortal gods, they neither plow
nor sow by hand, nor till the ground, though grain—
wild wheat and barley—grows untended, and
wine-grapes, in clusters, ripen in heaven's rain.
Cyclopes have no muster and no meeting,   65
no consultation or old tribal ways,
but each one dwells in his own mountain cave
dealing out rough justice to wife and child,
indifferent to what the others do."

*Odysseus and his crew land in a dense fog, on an island across the bay from
the land of the Cyclopes, one-eyed giants. The island is lush and unoccupied,
and they spend their time there feasting on wild goat and wine, all the while
observing the mainland where the Cyclopes live. On the third day, Odysseus
and his crew decide to sail across to the mainland to find out more about the
creatures called Cyclopes.*

"When the young Dawn with fingertips of rose[3]   70
came in the east, I called my men together
and made a speech to them:

            'Old shipmates, friends,
the rest of you stand by; I'll make the crossing
in my own ship, with my own company,   75
and find out what the mainland natives are—
for they may be wild savages and lawless,
or hospitable and god-fearing men.'
At this I went aboard, and gave the word
to cast off by the stern. My oarsmen followed,   80
filing in to their benches by the rowlocks,
and all in line dipped oars in the gray sea.

As we rowed on, and nearer to the mainland,
at one end of the bay, we saw a cavern
yawning above the water, screened with laurel,   85
and many rams and goats about the place
inside a sheepfold—made from slabs of stone
earthfast between tall trunks of pine and rugged
towering oak trees.

            A **prodigious** man   90
slept in this cave alone, and took his flocks
to graze afield—remote from all companions,
knowing none but savage ways, a brute
so huge, he seemed no man at all of those
who eat good wheaten bread; but he seemed rather   95
a shaggy mountain reared in solitude.
We beached there, and I told the crew
to stand by and keep watch over the ship;

prodigious
enormous;
monstrous

---

3 **the young Dawn with fingertips of rose:** This personification of dawn has become part
of our culture. You may have heard people make reference to "rosy-fingered Dawn." The
original source for this is the *Odyssey*.

as for myself I took my twelve best fighters
and went ahead. I had a goatskin full   100
of that sweet liquor that Euanthes' son,
Maron,[4] had given me.

                                          . . .

                                          A wineskin full
victuals   I brought along, and **victuals** in a bag,
food   for in my bones I knew some towering brute   105
               would be upon us soon—all outward power,
               a wild man, ignorant of civility.

               We climbed, then, briskly to the cave. But Cyclops
               had gone afield, to pasture his fat sheep,
               so we looked round at everything inside: 110
               a drying rack that sagged with cheeses, pens
               crowded with lambs and kids, each in its class:
               firstlings apart from middlings, and the 'dewdrops,'
               or newborn lambkins, penned apart from both.
whey   And vessels full of **whey** were brimming there—   115
the watery   bowls of earthenware and pails for milking.
part of   My men came pressing round me, pleading:
milk that is
separated
from the   'Why not
curds in the   Take these cheeses, get them stowed, come back,
process of   throw open all the pens, and make a run for it?   120
making cheese We'll drive the kids and lambs aboard. We say
               put out again on good salt water!'

4 **Euanthes' son, Maron:** Odysseus had met Maron earlier on in his journey. Maron's father
was one of Apollo's priests, and Maron gave Odysseus gifts—including wine that was so
good no one could refuse to drink it—to thank Odysseus for protecting him, his wife, and
his child.

Ah,
how sound that was! Yet I refused. I wished
to see the caveman, what he had to offer—   125
no pretty sight, it turned out, for my friends.
We lit a fire, burnt an offering,
and took some cheese to eat; then sat in silence
around the embers, waiting. When he came
he had a load of dry boughs on his shoulder   130
to **stoke** his fire at suppertime. He dumped it
with a great crash into that hollow cave,
and we all scattered fast to the far wall.
Then over the broad cavern floor he ushered
the ewes he meant to milk. He left his rams   135
and he-goats in the yard outside, and swung
high overhead a slab of solid rock
to close the cave. Two dozen four-wheeled wagons,
with heaving wagon teams, could not have stirred
the tonnage of that rock from where he wedged it   140
over the doorsill. Next he took his seat
and milked his bleating ewes. A practiced job
he made of it, giving each ewe her suckling;
thickened his milk, then, into curds and whey,
sieved out the curds to drip in withy baskets,[5]   145
and poured the whey to stand in bowls
cooling until he drank it for his supper.
When all these chores were done, he poked the fire,
heaping on brushwood. In the glare he saw us.

'Strangers,' he said, 'who are you? And where from?   150
What brings you here by sea ways—a fair traffic?[6]
Or are you wandering rogues, who cast your lives
like dice, and ravage other folk by sea?'

stoke
supply with
fuel

---

5 **withy baskets:** willow baskets

6 **fair traffic:** honest commerce and trading

We felt a pressure on our hearts, in dread
of that deep rumble and that mighty man.   155
But all the same I spoke up in reply:

'We are from Troy, Achaeans,[7] blown off course
by shifting gales on the Great South Sea;
homeward bound, but taking routes and ways
uncommon; so the will of Zeus would have it.   160
We served under Agamemnon, son of Atreus[8]—
the whole world knows what city
he laid waste, what armies he destroyed.
It was our luck to come out here; here we stand,
beholden for your help, or any gifts   165
you give—as custom is to honor strangers.
We would entreat you, great Sir, have a care
for the gods' courtesy; Zeus will avenge
the unoffending guest.'

                      He answered this   170
from his brute chest, unmoved:
                        'You are a ninny,
or else you come from the other end of nowhere,
telling me, mind the gods! We Cyclopes
care not a whistle for your thundering Zeus   175
or all the gods in bliss; we have more force by far.
I would not let you go for fear of Zeus—
you or your friends—unless I had a whim to.
Tell me, where was it, now, you left your ship—
around the point, or down the shore, I wonder?'   180

He thought he'd find out, but I saw through this,
and answered with ready lie:

---

7 **Achaeans:** Greeks

8 **Agamemnon, son of Atreus:** the Greek king who led the war against the Trojans

'My ship?
Poseidon Lord,[9] who sets the earth a-tremble,
broke it up on the rocks at your land's end.   185
A wind from seaward served him, drove us there.
We are survivors, these good men and I.'

Neither reply nor pity came from him,
but in one stride he clutched at my companions
and caught two in his hands like squirming puppies   190
to beat their brains out, spattering the floor.
Then he dismembered them and made his meal,
gaping and crunching like a mountain lion—
everything: innards, flesh, and marrow bones.
We cried aloud, lifting our hands to Zeus,   195
powerless, looking on at this, appalled;
but Cyclops went on filling up his belly
with manflesh and great gulps of whey,
then lay down like a mast among his sheep.
My heart beat high now at the chance of action,   200
and drawing the sharp sword from my hip I went
along his flank to stab him where the midriff
holds the liver. I had touched the spot
when sudden fear stayed me: if I killed him
we perished there as well, for we could never   205
move his ponderous doorway slab aside.
So we were left to groan and wait for morning.

When the young Dawn with fingertips of rose
lit up the world, the Cyclops built a fire
and milked his handsome ewes, all in due order,   210
putting the sucklings to the mothers. Then,
his chores being all dispatched, he caught
another **brace** of men to make his breakfast,

brace
pair

---

9 **Poseidon Lord:** the god of the sea, earthquakes, and horses. Odysseus is making up this story about a shipwreck, but it is actually prophetic. Polyphemus, the Cyclops Odysseus is speaking with, is Poseidon's son.

and whisked away his great door slab
to let his sheep go through—but he, behind,   215
reset the stone as one would cap a quiver.[10]
There was a din of whistling as the Cyclops
rounded his flock to higher ground, then stillness.
And now I pondered how to hurt him worst,
if but Athena[11] granted what I prayed for.   220
Here are the means I thought would serve my turn:

fold
sheepfold; i.e.,
the cavern
where the
Cyclops lives

a club, or staff, lay there along the **fold**—
an olive tree, felled green and left to season
for Cyclops' hand. And it was like a mast
a lugger of twenty oars,[12] broad in the beam—   225
a deep-sea-going craft—might carry:
so long, so big around, it seemed. Now I
chopped out a six-foot section of this pole
and set it down before my men, who scraped it;

hewed
cut

and when they had it smooth, I **hewed** again   230
to make a stake with pointed end. I held this
in the fire's heart and turned it, toughening it,
then hid it, well back in the cavern, under
one of the dung piles in **profusion** there.

profusion
great quantity

Now came the time to toss for it: who ventured   235
along with me? whose hand could bear to thrust
and grind that spike in Cyclops' eye, when mild
sleep had mastered him? As luck would have it,
the men I would have chosen won the toss—
four strong men, and I made five as captain.   240

---

10 **cap a quiver:** put a lid on a case for carrying arrows

11 **Athena:** the goddess of wisdom and strength and Odysseus's special protector
throughout the *Odyssey*

12 **a lugger of twenty oars:** a small, wide sailing ship propelled by twenty oars

At evening came the shepherd with his flock,
his woolly flock. The rams as well, this time,
entered the cave: by some sheep-herding whim—
or a god's bidding—none were left outside.
He hefted his great boulder into place   245
and sat him down to milk the bleating ewes
in proper order, put the lambs to suck,
and swiftly ran through all his evening chores.
Then he caught two more men and feasted on them.
My moment was at hand, and I went forward   250
holding an ivy bowl of my dark drink,
looking up, saying:

                      'Cyclops, try some wine.
Here's liquor to wash down your scraps of men.
Taste it, and see the kind of drink we carried   255
under our planks. I meant it for an offering
if you would help us home. But you are mad,
unbearable, a bloody monster! After this,
will any other traveler come to see you?'

He seized and drained the bowl, and it went down   260
so fiery and smooth he called for more:
'Give me another, thank you kindly. Tell me,
how are you called? I'll make a gift will please you.
Even Cyclopes know the wine-grapes grow
out of grassland and loam in heaven's rain,   265
but here's a bit of nectar and **ambrosia**!'

ambrosia
food for the
gods

Three bowls I brought him, and he poured them down.
I saw the fuddle and flush come over him,
then I sang out in cordial tones:

POLYPHEMUS, Giulio Romano

          'Cyclops,   270
you ask my honorable name? Remember
the gift you promised me, and I shall tell you.
My name is Nohbdy: mother, father, and friends,
everyone calls me Nohbdy.'

         And he said: 275
'Nohbdy's my meat, then, after I eat his friends.
Others come first. There's a noble gift, now.'

Even as he spoke, he reeled and tumbled backward,
his great head lolling to one side; and sleep
took him like any creature. Drunk, hiccupping,   280
he dribbled streams of liquor and bits of men.

Now, by the gods, I drove my big hand spike
deep in the embers, charring it again,
and cheered my men along with battle talk
to keep their courage up: no quitting now.   285
The pike of olive, green though it had been,
reddened and glowed as if about to catch.
I drew it from the coals and my four fellows
gave me a hand, lugging it near the Cyclops
as more than natural force nerved them; straight   290
forward they sprinted, lifted it, and rammed it
deep in his crater eye, and I leaned on it
turning it as a shipwright turns a drill
in planking,[13] having men below to swing
the two-handled strap that spins it in the groove.   295
So with our band we bored that great eye socket
while blood ran out around the red hot bar.
Eyelid and lash were seared; the pierced ball
hissed broiling, and the roots popped.

                       In a smithy[14]   300
one sees a white-hot axe head or an **adze**
plunged and wrung in a cold tub, screeching stream—
the way they made soft iron **hale** and hard—:
just so that eyeball hissed around the spike.
The Cyclops bellowed and the rock roared round him,   305
and we fell back in fear. Clawing his face
he tugged the bloody spike out of his eye,
threw it away, and his wild hands went groping;
then he set up a howl for Cyclopes
who lived in caves on windy peaks nearby.   310
Some heard him; and they came by **divers** ways
to clump around outside and call:

adze
a cutting tool
with an arched
blade set at
right angles to
a handle

hale
sound; free
from defect

divers
diverse;
various

---

13 **as a shipwright turns a drill in planking:** in the same way a shipbuilder turns the drill
to make a hole in wood

14 **smithy:** blacksmith's metalworking shop

                                              'What ails you,
Polyphemus?[15] Why do you cry so sore
in the starry night? You will not let us sleep.   315
Sure no man's driving off your flock? No man
has tricked you, ruined you?'

                                        Out of the cave
the mammoth Polyphemus roared in answer:

'Nohbdy, Nohbdy's tricked me. Nohbdy's ruined me!'   320

sage
wise
To this rough shout they made a **sage** reply:

'Ah well, if nobody has played you foul
there in your lonely bed, we are no use in pain
given by great Zeus. Let it be your father,
Poseidon Lord, to whom you pray.'   325

                                        So saying
they trailed away. And I was filled with laughter
to see how like a charm the name deceived them.
Now Cyclops, wheezing as the pain came on him,
fumbled to wrench away the great doorstone   330

breach
opening
and squatted in the **breach** with arms thrown wide
for any silly beast or man who bolted—
hoping somehow I might be such fool.
But I kept thinking how to win the game:
death sat there huge; how could we slip away?   335
I drew on all my wits, and ran through tactics,
reasoning as a man will for dear life,
until a trick came—and it pleased me well.
The Cyclops' rams were handsome, fat, with heavy
fleeces, a dark violet.   340

---

15 **Polyphemus:** the Cyclops' name

Three abreast

I tied them silently together, twining
cords of willow from the ogre's bed;
then slung a man under each middle one
to ride there safely, shielded left and right.   345
So three sheep could convey each man. I took
the woolliest ram, the choicest of the flock,
and hung myself under his kinky belly,
pulled up tight, with fingers twisted deep
in the sheepskin ringlets for an iron grip.   350
So, breathing hard, we waited until morning.

When Dawn spread out her fingertips of rose
the rams began to stir, moving for pasture,
and peals of bleating echoed round the pens
where dams with udders full called for a milking.   355

ULYSSES ESCAPING POLYPHEMUS, THE CYCLOPS, Greco-Roman stone sculpture

from the *Odyssey*, Part I   481

Blinded, and sick with pain from his head wound,
the master stroked each ram, then let it pass,
but my men riding on the pectoral fleece[16]
the giant's blind hands blundering never found.
Last of them all my ram, the leader, came,   360
weighted by wool and me with my meditations.
The Cyclops patted him, and then he said:

'Sweet cousin ram, why lag behind the rest
in the night cave? You never linger so,
but graze before them all, and go afar   365
to crop sweet grass, and take your stately way
leading along the streams, until at evening
you run to be the first one in the fold.
Why, now, so far behind? Can you be grieving
over your Master's eye? That carrion rogue[17]   370
and his accurst companions burnt it out
when he had conquered all my wits with wine.
Nohbdy will not get out alive, I swear.
Oh, had you brain and voice to tell
where he may be now, dodging all my fury!   375
Bashed by this hand and bashed on this rock wall
his brains would strew the floor, and I should have
rest from the outrage Nohbdy worked upon me.'

He sent us into the open, then. Close by,
I dropped and rolled clear of the ram's belly,   380
going this way and that to untie the men.
With many glances back, we rounded up
his fat, stiff-legged sheep to take aboard,
and drove them down to where the good ship lay.
We saw, as we came near, our fellows' faces   385
shining; then we saw them turn to grief

---

16 **pectoral fleece:** the wool on the sheep's chest
17 **carrion rogue:** vile scoundrel

tallying those who had not fled from death.
I hushed them, jerking head and eyebrows up,
and in a low voice told them: 'Load this herd;
move fast, and put the ship's head toward the breakers.'[18]   390
They all pitched in at loading, then embarked
and struck their oars into the sea. Far out,
as far off shore as shouted words would carry,
I sent a few back to the adversary:

'O Cyclops! Would you feast on my companions?   395
Puny, am I, in a Caveman's hands?
How do you like the beating that we gave you,
you damned cannibal? Eater of guests
under your roof! Zeus and the gods have paid you!'

The blind thing in his doubled fury broke   400
a hilltop in his hands and heaved it after us.
Ahead of our black prow it struck and sank
whelmed in a spuming geyser, a giant wave
that washed the ship stern foremost back to shore.[19]
I got the longest boathook out and stood   405
fending us off, with furious nods to all
to put their backs into a racing stroke—
row, row, or perish. So the long oars bent
kicking the foam sternward, making head
until we drew away, and twice as far.   410
Now when I cupped my hands I heard the crew
in low voices protesting:

                              'Godsake, Captain!
Why bait the beast again? Let him alone!'

---

18 **put the ship's head toward the breakers:** turn the ship around so that it is heading
out to sea

19 **whelmed in a spuming geyser, a giant wave that washed the ship stern foremost
back to shore:** The top of the mountain that Polyphemus hurls into the sea causes a giant
wave that pushes Odysseus's ship backward to the shore.

'That tidal wave he made on the first throw   415
all but beached us.'

                          'All but stove us in!'[20]

'Give him our bearing with your trumpeting,
he'll get the range and lob a boulder.'[21]

                                        'Aye   420
he'll smash our timbers and our heads together!'

I would not heed them in my glorying spirit,
but let my anger flare and yelled:

                              'Cyclops,
if ever mortal man inquire   425
how you were put to shame and blinded, tell him
Odysseus, raider of cities, took your eye:
Laertes' son, whose home's on Ithaca!'

                    ▪ ▪ ▪

When the young Dawn with fingertips of rose
touched the world, I roused the men, gave orders   430
to man the ships, cast off the mooring lines;
and filing in to sit beside the rowlocks
oarsmen in line dipped oars in the gray sea.
So we moved out, sad in the vast offing,
having our precious lives, but not our friends.   435

---

20 **stove us in:** smashed a hole in the boat

21 **"Give him our bearing with your trumpeting, he'll get the range and lob a
boulder":** Odysseus's men are warning him that if he keeps shouting at Polyphemus, the
Cyclops, even though he cannot see, will be able to use the sound to figure out where the
ship is and where he needs to direct a rock to hit it.

POETRY CONNECTION

Ithaka   C. P. CAVAFY

As you set out for Ithaka
hope the voyage is a long one,
full of adventure, full of discovery.
Laistrygonians[1] and Cyclops,
angry Poseidon—don't be afraid of them: 5
you'll never find things like that on your way
as long as you keep your thoughts raised high,
as long as a rare excitement
stirs your spirit and your body.
Laistrygonians and Cyclops,   10
wild Poseidon—you won't encounter them
unless you bring them along inside your soul,
unless your soul sets them up in front of you.

Hope the voyage is a long one.
May there be many summer mornings when,   15
with what pleasure, what joy,
you come into the harbors seen for the first time;
may you stop at Phoenician trading stations
to buy fine things,
mother of pearl and coral, amber and ebony,   20
sensual perfume of every kind—
as many sensual perfumes as you can;
and may you visit many Egyptian cities
to gather stores of knowledge from their scholars.

---

1 **Laistrygonians:** hostile giants who treat Odysseus in a way that is not unlike his treatment at the hand of Polyphemus. They hurl rocks at Odysseus's ships, destroying all but Odysseus's own ship. Then they massacre the crews of the ships they have wrecked.

Keep Ithaka always in your mind. 25
Arriving there is what you are destined for.
But do not hurry the journey at all.
Better if it lasts for years,
so you are old by the time you reach the island,
wealthy with all you have gained on the way, 30
not expecting Ithaka to make you rich.

Ithaka gave you the marvelous journey.
Without her you would not have set out.
She has nothing left to give you now.

And if you find her poor, Ithaka won't have fooled you. 35
Wise as you will have become, so full of experience,
you will have understood by then what these Ithakas mean.

The Greek island of Ithaca

AFTER YOU READ
from the *Odyssey*, Part I
Ithaka

Think and Discuss

1. At the beginning of this part of the poem, what does Odysseus tell us about himself and his journey? Summarize the background information he offers.

2. Odysseus tells us that people consider him to be "formidable for guile." How does he show in his encounter with the Cyclops that this reputation is deserved? Make an organizer like this in your Writer's Notebook and list the tricks Odysseus plays on the Cyclops and the effect each one has.

Tricks Odysseus Plays on the Cyclops	The Effect the Trick Has

3. The description of Odysseus's experience with the Cyclops includes a number of memorable **similes**. Recall one that you found especially vivid. Explain the effect the simile has on the reader. (For a definition of *simile*, see the Glossary of Literary Terms.)

4. Odysseus is clever, but he also reveals other **character traits** in this part of the poem. Tell what they are and explain their influence—positive or negative—on his quest to reach his home in Ithaca.

5. In the poem "Ithaka," do you think Cavafy is referring to a literal journey to Ithaca or to something else? Explain.

6. The word *odyssey* has become a part of our language. It can mean "a long wandering or voyage" or "an intellectual or spiritual wandering or quest." The word has been used to name books, movies, video games, problem-solving competitions—even a car! With a partner, brainstorm all the things you know about that have *odyssey* in their title. Then think about what they have in common.

Write to Understand: Summarize

Review your graphic organizer. Then use it to help you summarize Odysseus's encounter with Polyphemus. In your summary, tell what happens from the time Odysseus enters the cave of Polyphemus until he and his men finally sail away from the land of the Cyclopes. Decide which ideas are important to include and which details can be left out. Use your own words, and use the present tense.

BEFORE YOU READ
from the *Odyssey*, Part II

Meet the Authors

Homer The identity of Homer has caused controversy among scholars. The differences between the *Iliad* and the *Odyssey* have led some people to believe that the two epics were written by two different people. The *Iliad* is about war and heroes. The *Odyssey* is full of adventure tales and the fantastic. Aristotle, a prominent ancient Greek philosopher, explained the differences in the works by suggesting that the *Iliad* is the early work and the *Odyssey* was written late in the poet's life. The English critic and novelist Aldous Huxley, weary of the controversy, dismissed it all with this joke: "The author of the *Iliad* [and the *Odyssey*] is either Homer or, if not Homer, somebody else of the same name."

Margaret Atwood Born in 1939, Atwood is a Canadian poet who is known for her feminist outlook and for exploring social myths about women.

Build Background: The Geography of the *Odyssey*

Odysseus seems to have wandered around for ten years in a geographical area that by modern standards was very small: the western Mediterranean. Many scholars and travelers have tried to map Odysseus's journey, connecting the places mentioned in Odysseus's narrative with actual places. The home of Calypso, for example, was on Malta, or maybe at the Straits of Gibraltar. The land of the Cyclopes was somewhere near Marsala in western Sicily. The interest in connecting the story to reality even led one German scientist to suggest the Sirens, whom you will meet in this part of the *Odyssey*, were really monk seals that Odysseus encountered on the Li Galli Islands, off Sorrento on Italy's Amalfi coast. Most classical scholars today, however, take the view that the places Odysseus visits are imaginary places. They may have been inspired by real places, but it is useless to try to locate them on a map. The *Odyssey* is not a travel book but a work of imagination and poetry. It takes place not in the sphere of real-world geography but in a mythical wonderland.

- Before you read, remind yourself of what happened in the *Odyssey*, Part I.

- Based on the title of the next section ("Odysseus Meets Circe and the Sirens") and what you remember from Part I, what do you think might happen in Part II?

CIRCE OFFERING THE CUP TO ULYSSES, John William Waterhouse, 1891

from the Odyssey, Part II

HOMER

from the ODYSSEY

Homer
translated by Robert Fitzgerald

PART II
ODYSSEUS MEETS CIRCE AND THE SIRENS

After *escaping from the Cyclops, Odysseus and his men sail to the island of Aeolus, the keeper of the wind. There they are shown the hospitality befitting strangers in the classical world. When they are ready to leave, Aeolus gives Odysseus two parting gifts: a fair west wind that will blow his ships toward Ithaca and a big bag that holds all the unfavorable, stormy winds.*

The bag makes the men curious. No one but Odysseus knows what the bag contains. The men think it might contain gold and silver, so when Odysseus is asleep, they open it and release the bad winds. They are in sight of Ithaca, but the stormy winds that escape from the bag blow them right back to Aeolus's island. Unfortunately, he is not willing to help them again. He is now convinced that their voyage is cursed by the gods.

Discouraged, Odysseus and his men sail on. Their next stop is the land of the Laestrygones (or Laistrygonians)—a race of giant cannibals. The Laestrygones hurl boulders at Odysseus's ships, destroying all but one. Then they massacre the ships' crews. Only Odysseus, his ship, and its crew of forty-five survive the gruesome assault.

The lone ship then sails to Aeaea, the home of Circe. There Odysseus decides to divide his men into two groups. Eurylochus will lead one group to explore the island. Odysseus will stay behind with the second group to guard the ship.

"In the wild wood they found an open glade,
around a smooth stone house—the hall of Circe—
and wolves and mountain lions lay there, mild
in her soft spell, fed on her drug of evil.
None would attack—oh, it was strange, I tell you—   5
but switching their long tails they faced our men
like hounds, who look up when their master comes
with tidbits for them—as he will—from table.
Humbly those wolves and lions with mighty paws
fawned on[1] our men—who met their yellow eyes   10
and feared them.

                              In the entrance way they stayed
to listen there: inside her quiet house
they heard the goddess Circe.

                                          Low she sang   15
in her **beguiling** voice, while on her loom
she wove ambrosial[2] fabric sheer and bright,
by that craft known to the goddesses of heaven.
No one would speak, until Polites—most
faithful and likeable of my officers, said: 20

'Dear friends, no need for **stealth**: here's a young weaver
singing a pretty song to set the air
a-tingle on these lawns and paven courts.
Goddess she is, or lady. Shall we greet her?' .

So reassured, they all cried out together,   25
and she came swiftly to the shining doors
to call them in. All but Eurylochus—
who feared a **snare**—the innocents went after her.
On thrones she seated them, and lounging chairs,
while she prepared a meal of cheese and barley   30
and amber honey mixed with Pramnian wine,

beguiling
charmingly
deceiving

stealth
being
secretive
or hidden

snare
trap

---

1 **fawned on:** flattered and sought favor

2 **ambrosial:** extremely pleasing; fit for the gods

vile
evil

adding her own **vile** pinch, to make them lose
desire or thought of our dear father land.
Scarce had they drunk when she flew after them
with her long stick and shut them in a pigsty—   35
bodies, voices, heads, and bristles, all
swinish now, though minds were still unchanged.
So, squealing, in they went. And Circe tossed them
acorns, mast,³ and cornel berries⁴—fodder
for hogs who rut and slumber on the earth.   40

Down to the ship Eurylochus came running
to cry alarm, foul magic doomed his men!
But working with dry lips to speak a word
he could not, being so shaken; blinding tears
foreboding   welled in his eyes; **foreboding** filled his heart.   45
sense of   When we were frantic questioning him, at last
coming evil   we heard the tale: our friends were gone."

*Eurylochus reports that Circe has turned Odysseus's men into swine and begs
him to leave her island. Instead, Odysseus rushes to rescue his men. He meets the
god Hermes along the way. Hermes gives him a plant called* moly *with magical
powers to protect him from Circe. Hermes also tells Odysseus that he must make
Circe swear not to play any "witches' tricks." With these protections, Odysseus
arrives at Circe's hall, where the enchantress welcomes him and offers him a chair
studded with silver.*

"The lady Circe
mixed me a golden cup of honeyed wine,
adding in mischief her unholy drug.   50
I drank, and the drink failed. But she came forward
aiming a stroke with her long stick, and whispered:

'Down in the sty and snore among the rest!'

3 **mast:** nuts accumulated on the forest floor
4 **cornel berries:** berries from the dogwood tree

Without a word, I drew my sharpened sword
and in one bound held it against her throat.   55
She cried out, then slid under to take my knees,
catching her breath to say, in her distress:

'What champion, of what country, can you be?
Where are your kinsmen and your city?
Are you not sluggish with my wine? Ah, wonder!   60
Never a mortal man that drank this cup
but when it passed his lips he had **succumbed**.
Hale must your heart be and your **tempered** will.
Odysseus then you are, O great **contender**,
of whom the glittering god with golden wand   65
spoke to me ever, and foretold
the black swift ship would carry you from Troy.
Put up your weapon in the sheath. We two
shall mingle and make love upon our bed.
So mutual trust may come of play and love.'   70

To this I said:
                              'Circe, am I a boy,
that you should make me soft and **doting** now?
Here in this house you turned my men to swine;
now it is I myself you hold, **enticing**,   75
into your chamber, to your dangerous bed,
to take my manhood when you have me stripped.
I mount no bed of love with you upon it.
Or swear me first a great oath, if I do,
you'll work no more enchantment to my harm.'   80

She swore at once, outright, as I demanded,
and after she had sworn, and bound herself,
I entered Circe's flawless bed of love."

*Circe's maids prepare a bath for Odysseus and offer him a tempting meal, but
all Odysseus can think of is the fate of his men.*

succumbed
given in;
surrendered

tempered
hardened and
strengthened

contender
competitor

doting
excessively
fond

enticing
luring;
seducing

disconsolate
dejected;
in low spirits

chided
gently scolded

"Circe regarded me, as there I sat
disconsolate, and never touched a crust.   85
Then she stood over me and **chided** me:

'Why sit at table mute, Odysseus?
Are you mistrustful of my bread and drink?
Can it be treachery that you fear again,
after the gods' great oath I swore for you?'   90

I turned to her at once, and said:

                                                            'Circe,

where is the captain who could bear to touch
this banquet, in my place? A decent man
would see his company before him first.   95
Put heart in me to eat and drink—you may,
by freeing my companions. I must see them.'

But Circe had already turned away.
Her long staff in her hand, she left the hall
and opened up the sty. I saw her enter,   100
driving those men turned swine to stand before me.
She stroked them, each in turn, with some new chrism;[5]
and then, behold! their bristles fell away,
the coarse pelt grown upon them by her drug
melted away, and they were men again,   105
younger, more handsome, taller than before.
Their eyes upon me, each one took my hands,
and wild regret and longing pierced them through,
so the room rang with sobs, and even Circe
pitied that transformation. Exquisite   110
the goddess looked as she stood near me, saying:

'Son of Laertes and the gods of old,
Odysseus, master mariner and soldier,

---

5 **chrism:** ointment

go to the sea beach and sea-breasting ship;
drag it ashore, full-length upon the land;   115
stow gear and stores in rock-holes under cover;
return; be quick; bring all your dear companions.'

Now, being a man, I could not help consenting.
So I went down to the sea beach and the ship,
where I found all my other men on board,   120
weeping, in despair along the benches.
Sometimes in farmyards when the cows return
well-fed from pasture to the barn, one sees
the pens give way before the calves in **tumult**,   **tumult**
breaking through to cluster about their mothers,   125   confusion;
bumping together, bawling. Just that way   agitation
my crew poured round me when they saw me come—
their faces wet with tears as if they saw
their homeland, and the crags of Ithaca,
even the very town where they were born.   130
And weeping still they all cried out in greeting:

'Prince, what joy this is, your safe return!
Now Ithaca seems here, and we in Ithaca!
But tell us now, what death befell our friends?'

And, speaking gently, I replied: 135

'First we must get the ship high on the shingle,⁶
and stow our gear and stores in clefts of rock
for cover. Then come follow me, to see
your shipmates in the magic house of Circe
eating and drinking, endlessly **regaled**.'   140   **regaled**
                                                              entertained
                                                              grandly

. . .

---

6 shingle: pebbly beach

As we were men we could not help consenting,
So day by day we lingered, feasting long
on roasts and wine, until a year grew fat.
But when the passing months and wheeling seasons
brought the long summery days, the pause of summer,   145
my shipmates one day summoned me and said:

'Captain, shake off this trance, and think of home—
if home indeed awaits us,
                          if we shall ever see
your own well-timbered[7] hall on Ithaca.'   150

They made me feel a pang, and I agreed.
That day, and all day long, from dawn to sundown,
we feasted on roast meat and ruddy wine,
and after sunset when the dusk came on
my men slept in the shadowy hall, but I   155
went through the dark to Circe's flawless bed

supplication
earnest and
humble request

and took the goddess' knees in **supplication,**
urging, as she bent to hear:
                         'O Circe,
now you must keep your promise; it is time.   160
Help me make sail for home. Day after day
my longing quickens, and my company
give me no peace, but wear my heart away
pleading when you are not at hand to hear.'

The loveliest of goddesses replied: 165

'Son of Laertes and gods of old,
Odysseus, master mariner and soldier,
you shall not stay here longer against your will;
but home you may not go
unless you take a strange way round and come   170

---

7 well-timbered: strongly built with timbers

to the cold homes of Death and pale Persephone.[8]
You shall hear prophecy from the rapt shade
of blind Tiresias of Thebes,[9] forever
charged with reason even among the dead;
to him alone, of all the flitting ghosts,   175
Persephone has given a mind undarkened.'[10]

At this I felt a weight like stone within me,
and, moaning, pressed my length against the bed,
with no desire to see the daylight more."

*Odysseus and his men visit the Underworld where the spirits of the dead reside.
There Odysseus speaks with the spirit of the prophet Tiresias, who warns him that
unless he and his crew act with control and restraint, death and destruction will
follow. He also encounters the spirit of his mother, who died of grief over Odysseus's
long absence.*

*When they leave the Underworld, Odysseus and his men return to Circe's
island. As his men sleep, Circe gives Odysseus valuable advice.*

              "Then said the Lady Circe: 180
'So: all those trials are over.
                      Listen with care
to this, now, and a god will arm your mind.
Square in your ship's path are Sirens, crying
beauty to bewitch men coasting by;   185
woe to the innocent who hears that sound!
He will not see his lady nor his children
in joy, crowding about him, home from sea;
the Sirens will sing his mind away

lolling
idling;

on their sweet meadow **lolling**. There are bones   190

lounging

---

8 **and come to the cold homes of Death and pale Persephone:** Circe tells Odysseus
that he must go home by way of the Underworld.

9 **the rapt shade of blind Tiresias of Thebes:** Tiresias, the blind prophet, whose spirit
now dwells in the Underworld

10 **Persephone has given a mind undarkened:** Persephone, the goddess of the
Underworld, has allowed Tiresias to keep his mental powers

flayed
stripped off

of dead men rotting in a pile beside them
and **flayed** skins shrivel around the spot.
                                        Steer wide;
keep well to seaward, plug your oarsmen's ears
with beeswax kneaded soft; none of the rest   195
should hear that song.
                              But if you wish to listen,
let the men tie you in the lugger, hand
and foot, back to the mast, lashed to the mast,
so you may hear those harpies' thrilling voices;[11]   200
shout as you will, begging to be untied,
your crew must only twist more line around you
and keep their stroke up, till the singers fade.

· · ·

Odysseus and his men set off at dawn. As they sail, he tells them what Circe
warned him about the Sirens. Then suddenly the wind stops.

                              "The crew were on their feet
briskly, to furl the sail, and stow it; then,   205
each in place, they poised the smooth oar blades

scudding
moving swiftly

and sent the white foam **scudding** by. I carved
a massive cake of beeswax into bits
and rolled them in my hands until they softened—
no long task, for a burning heat came down   210
from Helios, lord of high noon. Going forward
I carried wax along the line, and laid it
thick on their ears. They tied me up, then, plumb
amidships,[12] back to the mast, lashed to the mast,
and took themselves again to rowing. Soon,   215

---

11 **those harpies' thrilling voices:** Harpies are foul and evil creatures in Greek mythology
that are part woman and part bird.

12 **plumb amidships:** exactly in the middle of the ship

ULYSSES AND THE SIRENS, John William Waterhouse, 1891

as we came smartly within hailing distance,
the two Sirens, noting our fast ship
off their point, made ready, and they sang.

.   .   .

The lovely voices in **ardor** appealing over the water
made me crave to listen, and I tried to say   220
'Untie me!' to the crew, jerking my brows;
but they bent steady to the oars. Then Perimedes
got to his feet, he and Eurylochus,
and passed more line about, to hold me still.
So all rowed on, until the Sirens   225
dropped under the sea rim, and their singing
dwindled away.
    My faithful company
rested on their oars now, peeling off
the wax that I had laid thick on their ears;   230
then set me free.

ardor
passion

dwindled away
became steadily less

But scarcely had that island
faded in blue air than I saw smoke
and white water, with sound of waves in tumult—
a sound the men heard, and it terrified them.   235
Oars flew from their hands, the blades went knocking
wild alongside till the ship lost way,
with no oarblades to drive her through the water.

Well, I walked up and down from bow to stern,
trying to put heart into them, standing over   240
every oarsman, saying gently,

                            'Friends,
have we never been in danger before this?
More fearsome, is it now, than when the Cyclops
penned us in his cave? What power he had!   245
Did I not keep my nerve, and use my wits
to find a way out for us?

                         Now I say
by hook or crook this peril too shall be
something that we remember.   250
    Heads up, lads!
We must obey the orders as I give them.
Get the oarshafts in your hands, and lay back
hard on your benches; hit these breaking seas.
Zeus help us pull away before we **founder**.   255
You at the tiller, listen, and take in
all that I say—the rudders are your duty;
keep her out of the **combers** and the smoke;
steer for that headland; watch the drift, or we
fetch up in the smother, and you drown us.'[13]   260

        . . .

founder
sink

combers
long curling
waves of
the sea

---

13 **watch the drift, or we fetch up in the smother, and you drown us:** Odysseus is
telling the man at the tiller to keep the ship on course, or it could be crushed by the waves
and rough water.

POETRY CONNECTION

Siren Song   MARGARET ATWOOD

This is the one song everyone
would like to learn: the song
that is irresistible:

the song that forces men
to leap overboard in **squadrons**   5   **squadrons**
even though they see beached skulls   large groups

the song nobody knows
because anyone who had heard it
is dead, and the others can't remember.

Shall I tell you the secret   10
and if I do, will you get me
out of this bird suit?[1]

I don't enjoy it here
squatting on this island
looking picturesque and mythical   15
with these two feathery maniacs,
I don't enjoy singing
this trio, fatal and valuable.

---

1 **this bird suit:** Although the Sirens are mentioned for the first time in the *Odyssey*, their
appearance is not described there. Other works tell us that the Sirens have women's heads
and birds' bodies. In the *Odyssey*, there are only two Sirens. In later works, there are three.

I will tell the secret to you,
to you, only to you.   20
Come closer. This song

is a cry for help: Help me!
Only you, only you can,
you are unique

at last. Alas   25
it is a boring song
but it works every time.

Greek vase showing Ulysses bound to the mast
as the Sirens call, 5th century B.C.

AFTER YOU READ
from the *Odyssey*, Part II
Siren Song

Think and Discuss

1. Circe is unable to turn Odysseus into a swine, because Hermes has told him how to protect himself from her power. Still, he is not completely unaffected by her. In what way does Circe influence Odysseus and interfere with his quest?

2. Why does Odysseus have to protect his men and himself from the Sirens?

3. An **epic simile** is an extended simile that elaborates on a comparison in great detail. Such a simile often goes on for several lines. The description of how Odysseus's men greet him when he returns from Circe's palace is an example of an epic simile. How does the simile help you visualize the scene that Odysseus is describing?

4. The Sirens' song is irresistible. Circe warns Odysseus that the Sirens "will sing [a man's] mind away." In spite of the risk, Odysseus wants to hear their song. What does this choice reveal about the **character** of Odysseus?

5. Some of what we learn about Odysseus in Part II is consistent with what we learned about him in Part I, but some new aspects of his personality are revealed as well. Use a Venn diagram to help you analyze Odysseus's character. In the left circle, list the qualities of Odysseus's personality that are revealed only in Part I. In the right circle, list the qualities that he shows in Part II. In the overlapping section, list the qualities that have so far been consistent.

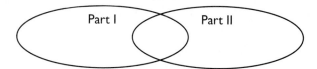

6. Margaret Atwood's poem "Siren Song" provides insight into why the song of the Sirens is irresistible. What does the poem suggest is the true nature of the song's appeal?

Write to Understand: Define a Hero

Review the Venn diagram you used to analyze and compare the qualities of Odysseus that are revealed in Part I and Part II of the poem. Use the information you assembled in the diagram to write a description of the kind of person Odysseus is. As you write your description, bear in mind that Odysseus is the model Greek hero. Think about how the qualities exhibited by Odysseus have defined a hero in Western culture.

BEFORE YOU READ
from the *Odyssey*, Part III
An Ancient Gesture

Meet the Authors

Homer According to the earliest theories, Homer must have lived not much later than the Trojan War he wrote about. The assumption was that he was writing about something of which he had historic knowledge. Modern scholars, however, agree that Homer was working with a body of knowledge that existed in oral tradition. Homer, who was very likely an *aoidos,* or "singer," inherited a repertoire of heroic songs about the Trojan War that could be performed at feasts and gatherings. Homer's accomplishment was to shape these songs together into a monumental poem that could achieve new and more complex effects and to write the poems down.

Edna St. Vincent Millay Born in 1892, Millay was an American poet and playwright. She died in 1950. (See page 140 for more information.)

Build Background: Helen of Troy

In this part of the *Odyssey,* Odysseus finally makes it back to Ithaca and, after twenty years, is reunited with his wife, Penelope. The Trojan War is the reason Odysseus left home in the first place, and to appreciate the account of the end of his long adventure, it is helpful to understand how that war began.

Paris, the son of King Priam of Troy, was invited to be a judge in a beauty contest of Olympian importance. The contestants were Athena, the goddess of wisdom; Hera, the goddess of marriage; and Aphrodite, the goddess of love. Aphrodite bribed Paris to pick her by promising him the most beautiful woman in the world. The problem was, the most beautiful woman in the world, Helen, was already married to Menelaus, the king of Sparta. Paris chose Aphrodite; then he went to Greece, seduced Helen, and took her back with him to Troy. In retaliation, the Greeks launched a great expedition of warriors and ships to go to Troy and take Helen back.

- The gods took sides in the Trojan War. Whose side do you suppose Athena and Hera were on—the Greeks' or the Trojans'?

- What do you expect might happen when Odysseus returns to Ithaca in Part III?

PENELOPE, Violet Brunton

from the Odyssey, Part III

HOMER

from the ODYSSEY

Homer

translated by Robert Fitzgerald

PART III
THE RETURN TO ITHACA

Odysseus's goal throughout the epic Odyssey has been
to return to his home in Ithaca. He's been gone for twenty years. He left to fight the
Trojan War, which lasted ten years, and he spent another ten years sailing about,
encountering perils and monsters and trying to get home. Now finally, Odysseus has
reached the shores of Ithaca, where his wife and son have been waiting for him for
two decades.

The wait has been almost as eventful for Penelope as the journey was for
Odysseus. She has been pestered by suitors—more than a hundred of them—who
have concluded from Odysseus's long absence that he is dead and Penelope is free
to remarry. Penelope has used trickery to put them off. At one point she promised to
choose a suitor as soon as she finished weaving a burial shroud for Odysseus's elderly
father, Laertes. Every day, she would work at her loom, and every night, she would
undo the day's work. She kept this up for three years and might have done it longer
if her maidens hadn't discovered her trickery and told the suitors.

When Odysseus arrives at Ithaca, he is met by the goddess Athena. She warns
him that his palace is overrun by suitors who are interested in not only his wife but
also his fortune. She advises him to return home disguised as a beggar, which he
does so successfully that only his old dog recognizes him.

Part III begins with Penelope bringing a heavy bow that Odysseus left behind.
She proposes to the suitors an archery contest using this weapon. The winner
will get Penelope as his wife.

Now Penelope
sank down, holding the weapon on her knees,
and drew her husband's great bow out, and sobbed
and bit her lip and let the salt tears flow.
Then back she went to face the crowded hall,   5
tremendous bow in hand, and on her shoulder hung
the quiver spiked with coughing death. Behind her
maids bore a basket full of axeheads, bronze
and iron implements for the master's game.
Thus in her beauty she approached the suitors,   10
and near a pillar of the solid roof
she paused, her shining veil across her cheeks,
her maids on either hand and still,
then spoke to the banqueters:

                                   "My lords, hear me: 15
suitors indeed, you **commandeered** this house   **commandeered**
to feast and drink in, day and night, my husband   took by force
being long gone, long out of mind. You found
no **justification** for yourselves—none   **justification**
except your lust to marry me. Stand up, then: 20   reason or
we now declare a contest for that prize.   excuse
Here is my lord Odysseus' hunting bow.
Bend and string it if you can. Who sends an arrow
through iron axe-helve sockets, twelve in line?[1]
I join my life with his, and leave this place, my home,   25
my rich and beautiful bridal house, forever
to be remembered, though I dream it only."

Then to Eumaeus:[2]

        "Carry the bow forward.

---

1 **Who sends an arrow . . . twelve in a line?:** Penelope proposes a contest that has two
parts. First, the contestants must bend and string Odysseus's heavy bow. Then they must
shoot an arrow through the holes of twelve ax heads that are lined up one behind the other.

2 **Eumaeus:** a swineherd who, along with the cowherd, was a servant of Odysseus

Carry the blades."   30
    Tears came to the swineherd's eyes
as he reached out for the big bow. He laid it
down at the suitors' feet. Across the room
the cowherd sobbed, knowing the master's weapon.
Antinous[3] growled, with a glance at both: 35

                                  "Clods.
They go to pieces over nothing.
                          You two, there,
why are you sniveling? To upset the woman
even more? Has she not pain enough   40
over her lost husband? *Sit down.*
Get on with dinner quietly, or cry about it
outside if you must. Leave us the bow.
A clean-cut game, it looks to me.
Nobody bends that bowstave easily   45
in this company. Is there a man here
made like Odysseus? I remember him
from childhood: I can see him even now."

That was the way he played it, hoping inwardly
to span the great horn bow with corded gut   50
and drill the iron with his shot—he, Antinous,
destined to be the first of all to savor
blood from a biting arrow at his throat,
a shaft drawn by the fingers of Odysseus
whom he had mocked and **plundered**, leading on   55
the rest, his boon companions.[4]

*The suitors try to string the bow, going through the effort of heating it and
greasing it to try to make the task easier. When all but Antinous have tried and
failed, Odysseus, disguised as an old beggar steps forward and asks permission to
try the challenge.*

plundered
taken
wealth or
possessions
from
wrongfully

---

3 **Antinous:** one of the front-running suitors

4 **boon companions:** good company for feasting and drinking

Then spoke Odysseus, all craft and **gall**:
"My lords, contenders for the queen, permit me:
a passion in me moves me to speak out.
I put it to Eurymachus[5] above all   60
and to that brilliant prince, Antinous. . .
But let me try my hand at the smooth bow!
Let me test my fingers and my pull
to see if any of the oldtime kick is there,
or if thin fare and roving[6] took it out of me."   65

Now irritation beyond reason swept them all,
since they were nagged by fear that he could string it.
Antinous answered, coldly and at length:

"You bleary vagabond, no rag of sense is left you.
Are you not coddled here enough, at table   70
taking meat with gentlemen, your betters,
denied nothing, and listening to our talk?
When have we let a tramp hear all our talk?
The sweet **goad** of wine has made you **rave**!"

· · ·

At this the watchful queen Penelope   75
interposed:

                              "Antinous, discourtesy
to a guest of Telemachus[7]—whatever guest—
that is not handsome. What are you afraid of?
Suppose this exile put his back into it   80
and drew the great bow of Odysseus—

---

gall
a combination
of boldness
and attitude;
nerve

goad
something
that urges
or prods

rave
speak
irrationally

interposed
put a
remark into
a conversation

5 **Eurymachus:** another "frontrunner" in the suitor competition. Eurymachus was the last
  suitor to try and fail. Antinous has not taken his turn yet.

6 **thin fare and roving:** poor food and wandering about

7 **Telemachus:** the son of Odysseus

could he then take me home to be his bride?
You know he does not imagine that! No one
need let that prospect weigh upon his dinner!
How very, very improbable it seems." 85

*Telemachus, who knows that the old beggar is his father in disguise, asks
Penelope to leave and let the men settle the matter. Before asking to be part of
the competition, Odysseus spoke with Eumaeus, the swineherd, and Philoetius, the
cowherd—the two men who wept when they saw the bow and were reminded of
their master. Odysseus revealed himself to them and enlisted their help.*

The swineherd had the horned bow in his hands
moving toward Odysseus, when the crowd
in the banquet hall broke into an ugly din,
shouts rising from the flushed young men:

                        "Ho! Where 90
do you think you are taking that, you smutty slave?"

dithering
acting
nervously or
indecisively

"What is this **dithering**?"

                  "We'll toss you back alone
among the pigs, for your own dogs to eat,
if bright Apollo nods and the gods are kind!" 95

He faltered, all at once put down the bow, and stood
in panic, buffeted by waves of cries,
hearing Telemachus from another quarter
shout:

"Go on, take him the bow! 100
                  Do you obey this pack?
You will be stoned back to your hills! Young as I am
my power is over you! I wish to God
I had as much the upper hand of these!
There would be suitors pitched like dead rats 105
through our gate, for the evil plotted here!"

Telemachus' **frenzy** struck someone as funny,
and soon the whole room roared with laughter at him,
so that all tension passed. Eumaeus picked up
bow and quiver, making for the door,   110
and there he placed them in Odysseus' hands.
Calling Eurycleia[8] to his side he said:

       "Telemachus
trusts you to take care of the women's doorway.
Lock it tight. If anyone inside   115
should hear the shock of arms or groans of men
in hall or court, not one must show her face,
but go on with her weaving."

      The old woman
nodded and kept still. She disappeared   120
into the women's hall, bolting the door behind her.
Philoetius left the house now at one bound,
catlike, running to bolt the courtyard gate.
A coil of deck-rope of papyrus fiber
lay in the gateway; this he used for lashing,   125
and ran back to the same stool as before,
fastening his eyes upon Odysseus.

    And Odysseus took his time,
turning the bow, tapping it, every inch,
for borings that termites might have made   130
while the master of the weapon was abroad.
The suitors were now watching him, and some
jested among themselves:

      "A bow lover!"
"Dealer in old bows"!   135

frenzy
agitation

---

8 **Eurycleia:** Penelope's aged servant, who also cared for Odysseus and Telemachus when
they were babies

. . . .

"Maybe he has one like it
at home!"

"Or has an itch to make one for himself."

"See how he handles it; the sly old buzzard!"

And one disdainful suitor added this: 140

"May his fortune grow an inch for every inch he bends it!"

contending
competing;
vying in a
contest

heft
heaviness

But the man skilled in all ways of **contending,**
satisfied by the great bow's look and **heft,**
like a musician, like a harper, when
with quiet hand upon his instrument   145
he draws between his thumb and forefinger
a sweet new string upon a peg: so effortlessly
Odysseus in one motion strung the bow.
Then slid his right hand down the cord and plucked it,
so the taut gut vibrating hummed and sang   150
a swallow's note.

smote
struck

In the hushed hall it **smote** the suitors
and all their faces changed. Then Zeus thundered
overhead, one loud crack for a sign.[9]
And Odysseus laughed within him that the son   155
of crooked-minded Cronus[10] had flung that omen down.
He picked one ready arrow from his table
where it lay bare; the rest were waiting still
in the quiver for the young men's turn to come.
He nocked it,[11] let it rest across the handgrip,   160

---

9 **one loud crack for a sign:** The thunder, sent by Zeus, is sign that the gods are on
Odysseus's side.

10 **the son of crooked-minded Cronus:** Zeus. His father, Cronus, may be called
"crooked-minded" because he castrated his father and tried to swallow his own children.

11 **nocked it:** placed the notched end of the arrow against the string

ULYSSES AT ITHACA, Francesco Primaticcio

and drew the string and grooved butt of the arrow,
aiming from where he sat upon the stool.

                  Now flashed
arrow from twanging bow clean as a whistle
through every socket ring, and grazed not one,   165
to thud with heavy **brazen** head beyond.

               Then quietly
Odysseus said:

          "Telemachus, the stranger
you welcomed in your hall has not disgraced you.   170
I did not miss, neither did I take all day
stringing the bow. My hand and eye are sound,

brazen
made of
brass

contemptible
worthy of
contempt

not so **contemptible** as the young men say.
The hour has come to cook their lordships' mutton—
supper by daylight. Other amusements later,   175
with song and harping that adorn a feast."

He dropped his eyes and nodded, and the prince
Telemachus, true son of King Odysseus,
belted his sword on, clapped hand to his spear,
and with a clink and glitter of keen bronze   180
stood by his chair, in the forefront near his father.

• • •

wiliest
cleverest

Now shrugging off his rags the **wiliest** fighter of the islands
leapt and stood on the broad door sill, his own bow in his hand.
He poured out at his feet a rain of arrows from the quiver
and spoke to the crowd: 185

"So much for that. Your clean-cut game is over.
Now watch me hit a target that no man has hit before,
if I can make this shot. Help me, Apollo."

He drew to his fist the cruel head of an arrow for Antinous
just as the young man leaned to lift his beautiful drinking cup,   190
embossed, two-handled, golden: the cup was in his fingers:
the wine was even at his lips: and did he dream of death?

revelry
merrymaking

How could he? In that **revelry** amid his throng of friends
who would imagine a single foe—though a strong foe
indeed—   195
could dare to bring death's pain on him and darkness on
his eyes?
Odysseus' arrow hit him under the chin
and punched up to the feathers through his throat.
Backward and down he went, letting the winecup fall   200
from his shocked hand. Like pipes his nostrils jetted

crimson **runnels**, a river of mortal red,
and one last kick upset his table
knocking the bread and meat to soak in dusty blood.

Now as they craned to see their champion where he lay 205
the suitors jostled in uproar down the hall,
everyone on his feet. Wildly they turned and scanned
the walls in the long room for arms; but not a shield,
not a good ashen spear was there for a man to take and throw.
All they could do was yell in outrage at Odysseus: 210

. . .

"Buzzards will tear your eyes out!"

*The suitors hope that the killing of Antinous was unintended, but Odysseus sets
them straight by telling them that for the plunder of his household and the bid for
his wife they will pay in blood. The men desperately look for escape but find none.
Eurymachus tells Odysseus that Antinous was the ringleader, and since he is already
dead, Eurymachus asks Odysseus to spare the others. They offer to make up to him
by providing wine, meat, oxen, and gifts of bronze and gold. Odysseus thunders back
that nothing will satisfy him until the score is paid, and he challenges them all to fight
or run. They decide to fight. Odysseus and Telemachus kill the first two contenders.
Telemachus offers to get shields and spears and to arm Eumaeus and the cowherd.*

Said Odysseus:

"Run then, while I hold them off with arrows.

                         While he had arrows
he aimed and shot, and every shot brought down 215
one of his huddling enemies.
But when all barbs had flown from the bowman's fist,
he leaned his bow in the bright entry way
beside the door, and armed: a four-ply shield
hard on his shoulder, and a crested **helm**, 220
horsetailed, nodding stormy upon his head,
then took his tough and bonze-shod spears.

runnels
streams

helm
helmet

Athena urges Odysseus on to battle—to drive out the suitors and reclaim his home and his wealth. At first, she holds back her full support while she waits for Odysseus and Telemachus to prove themselves. When six suitors attack Odysseus, Athena turns their arrows away. Odysseus and his men now move to attack, and more suitors are killed. During the fighting, Athena reveals her presence by making the shape of her shield visible above the hall. The suitors realize that Odysseus has the gods on his side and they try desperately to escape, with no success. Odysseus and his men fight like falcons that show no mercy to a flock of birds they pursue and capture.

When the brutal fight is over, Odysseus at long last can ready himself to meet Penelope.

Greathearted Odysseus, home at last,	
was being bathed now by Eurynome[12]	
and rubbed with golden oil, and clothed again	225
in a fresh tunic and a cloak. Athena	
lent him beauty, head to foot. She made him	
taller, and massive, too, with crisping hair	
in curls like petals of wild hyacinth	
but all red-golden. Think of gold infused	230
on silver by a craftsman, whose fine art	
Hephaestus[13] taught him, or Athena: one	
whose work moves to delight: just so she **lavished**	
beauty over Odysseus' head and shoulders.	
He sat then in the same chair by the pillar,	235
facing his silent wife, and said:	

lavished
gave
generously

> "Strange woman,

the immortals of Olympus[14] made you hard,	
harder than any. Who else in the world	
would keep aloof as you do from her husband	240
if he returned to her from years of trouble,	
cast on his own land in the twentieth year?	
Nurse, make up a bed for me to sleep on.	

---

12 **Eurynome:** a female servant

13 **Hephaestus:** the god of metalworking

14 **the immortals of Olympus:** the gods, who live on Mount Olympus

Unit Six   Echoes from the Past

THE RETURN OF ULYSSES, Edward Armitage

Her heart is iron in her breast."

Penelope   245
spoke to Odysseus now. She said:

"Strange man,
if man you are . . . This is no pride on my part
nor scorn for you—not even wonder, merely.
I know so well how you—how he—appeared   250
boarding the ship for Troy. But all the same . . .

Make up his bed for him, Eurycleia.
Place it outside the bedchamber my lord
built with his own hands. Pile the big bed
with fleeces, rugs, and sheets of purest linen."   255

With this she tried him to the breaking point,
and he turned on her in a flash raging:

"Woman, by heaven you've stung me now!
Who dared to move my bed? No builder had the skill for that—unless
a god came down to turn the trick. No mortal   260
in his best days could budge it with a crowbar.
There is our pact and pledge, our secret sign,
built into that bed—my handiwork
and no one else's!

　　　　　　　　　　An old trunk of olive   265
grew like a pillar on the building plot,
and I laid out our bedroom round that tree,
lined up the stone walls, built the walls and roof,
gave it a doorway and smooth-fitting doors.
Then I lopped off the silvery leaves and branches,   270
hewed and shaped that stump from the roots up
into a bedpost, drilled it, let it serve
as model for the rest. I planed them all,
inlaid them all with silver, gold and ivory,
and stretched a bed between—a **pliant** web   275
of oxhide **thongs** dyed crimson.

pliant
flexible;
yielding

thongs
strips of
leather or
hide

　　　　　　　　　　　　There's our sign!
I know no more. Could someone else's hand
have sawn that trunk and dragged the frame away?"
Their secret! as she heard it told, her knees   280

tremulous
shaky

grew **tremulous** and weak, her heart failed her.
With eyes brimming tears she ran to him,
throwing her arms around his neck and kissed him,
murmuring:

　　　　　　　　　　"Do not rage at me, Odysseus!   285
No one ever matched your caution! Think
what difficulty the gods gave: they denied us
life together in our prime and flowering years,
kept us from crossing into age together.
Forgive me, don't be angry. I could not   290

welcome you with love on sight! I armed myself
long ago against the frauds of men,
imposters who might come—and all those many
whose underhanded ways bring evil on!
Helen of Argos, daughter of Zeus and Leda,[15]   295
would she have joined the stranger, lain with him,
if she had known her destiny? known the Achaeans
in arms would bring her back to her own country?
Surely a goddess moved her to adultery,
her blood unchilled by war and evil coming,   300
the years, the **desolation**; ours, too.
But here and now, what sign could be so clear
as this of our own bed?
No other man has ever laid eyes on it—
only my own slave, Actoris, that my father   305
sent with me as a gift—she kept our door.
You make my stiff heart know that I am yours."

Now from his breast into his eyes the ache
of longing mounted, and he wept at last,
his dear wife, clear and faithful, in his arms,   310
longed for
        as the sunwarmed earth is longed for by a swimmer
spent in rough water where his ship went down
under Poseidon's blows, gale winds and tons of sea.
Few men can keep alive through a big surf   315
to crawl, clotted with brine,[16] on kindly beaches
in joy, in joy, knowing the abyss behind:
and so she too rejoiced, her gaze upon her husband,
her white arms round him pressed as though forever.

desolation
loneliness

---

15 **Helen of Argos, daughter of Zeus and Leda:** Helen of Troy. It was her adultery that
caused the Trojan War, which was the reason Odysseus left Ithaca twenty years earlier.

16 **clotted with brine:** covered with sea salt

from the *Odyssey*, Part III   519

An Ancient Gesture

EDNA ST. VINCENT MILLAY

I thought, as I wiped my eyes on the corner of my apron:
Penelope did this too.
And more than once: you can't keep weaving all day
And undoing it all through the night;
Your arms get tired, and the back of your neck gets tight;   5
And along towards morning, when you think it will never be light,
And your husband has been gone, and you don't know where, for years.
Suddenly you burst into tears;
There is simply nothing else to do.

And I thought, as I wiped my eyes on the corner of my apron: 10
This is an ancient gesture, authentic, antique,
In the very best tradition, classic, Greek;
Ulysses did this too.
But only as a gesture,—a gesture which implied
To the assembled throng that he was much too moved to speak.   15
He learned it from Penelope . . .

Penelope, who really cried.

AFTER YOU READ
from the *Odyssey*, Part III
An Ancient Gesture

Think and Discuss

1. When Odysseus finally reaches Ithaca, Athena advises him to disguise himself as a beggar. What might have happened to Odysseus if he had not followed Athena's advice? Why?

2. For years, Penelope has been coming up with ways to deceive her suitors and put them off. Why is her idea for an archery contest just another way for her to avoid choosing a suitor and becoming his wife?

3. How does Penelope test Odysseus before she acknowledges him as her long-lost husband and welcomes him home?

4. Choose a passage from this section that you especially like. Explain what makes it **poetry** and how it is different from narrative prose.

5. If Odysseus is the **classic hero**, Penelope is the **classic wife**. In many ways, they define what was perceived as the perfect man and woman in the classical world. They share some characteristics, but in others they are opposite. Use a chart like the one below to analyze them. In the center box, write the qualities that the two share. In the box at the left, write the qualities that are Odysseus's alone. In the box at the right, write the qualities that are Penelope's alone. Are any of the qualities for one character the opposite of a quality you wrote for the other?

Odysseus's Qualities	Qualities They Share	Penelope's Qualities

6. Edna St. Vincent Millay's poem "An Ancient Gesture" implies a comparison between Penelope and Odysseus. How would you explain and expand on that comparison? Make reference to events in the *Odyssey* in your response.

Write to Understand: Focused Freewriting

Review the chart you created to compare the qualities of Odysseus and Penelope. Then think about the personal qualities that we value in our society today. Have those qualities changed since classical times? Are the qualities we value different for men and for women? Write your ideas and keep writing for at least 10 minutes.

BEFORE YOU READ
from *The Penelopiad*

Meet the Author: Margaret Atwood

You have already met Margaret Atwood, the Canadian poet who wrote "Siren Song" (page 488). In addition to poetry, Atwood has written a number of best-selling novels, including *The Handmaid's Tale*, which won the Arthur C. Clarke Award for science fiction in 1987. The book paints a picture of a negative Utopia in which women are repressed by force. She has also written works of "space opera." Space opera is a kind of science fiction that focuses on romantic stories—like those in soap operas—set in exotic imaginary settings. Atwood is known for exploring gender-related themes in her work.

Build Background: The Untold Stories

The spotlight in the *Odyssey* always shines most brightly on Odysseus himself, the great hero—brave and strong, with the appealing personality of a born leader. What if the focus shifted, however, and the patient Penelope became the object of greatest attention? Margaret Atwood answers that question in *The Penelopiad,* a retelling of parts of the *Odyssey* from Penelope's point of view.

Atwood became interested in this retelling as a way to highlight a little-explained event in the *Odyssey* that had bothered her ever since she first read about it as a girl. That untold story involves Penelope's twelve young maids, or servants, some of whom Penelope adored as if they were her own daughters. When Penelope asked them to spy among the suitors, they did so obediently. However, when Odysseus returned and slew the suitors, he also had the twelve maids killed for having mingled with the suitors, his enemies. Telemachus strung them up by a single rope and hanged them from a ship's bow.

Atwood begins *The Penelopiad* in the Underworld, where Penelope at long last has a chance to tell her side of the story and deal with the guilt she feels about the death of her maids. The maids themselves appear in the work as a Greek chorus, commenting and singing between the chapters of Penelope's story.

Three selections from *The Penelopiad* follow. The first is Penelope's opening speech. The second is one of several commentaries by the chorus of twelve maids. The final selection tells Penelope's version of the return of Odysseus.

As you read these selections, think about these questions:

- How is Penelope's version of the story different from Homer's?

- What value is there in looking at a myth or classic story from another point of view?

PENELOPE, Anthony Frederick Augustus Sandys, 1878

from *The Penelopiad*

MARGARET ATWOOD

FROM *THE PENELOPIAD*

Margaret Atwood

A LOW ART

*N**ow** that I'm dead I know everything.* This is what I wished would happen, but like so many of my wishes it failed to come true. I know only a few **factoids** that I didn't know before. It's much too high a price to pay for the satisfaction of curiosity, needless to say.

Since being dead—since achieving this state of bonelessness, liplessness, breastlessness—I've learned some things I would rather not know, as one does when listening at windows or opening other people's letters. You think you'd like to read minds? Think again.

Down here everyone arrives with a sack, like the sacks used to keep the winds in, but each of these sacks is full of words—words you've spoken, words you've heard, words that have been said about you. Some sacks are very small, others large; my own is of a reasonable size, though a lot of the words in it concern my **eminent** husband. What a fool he made of me, some say. It was a specialty of his: making fools. He got away with everything, which was another of his specialties: getting away.

He was always so **plausible**. Many people have believed that his version of events was the true one, give or take a few murders, a few beautiful seductresses,[1] a few one-eyed monsters. Even I believed him, from time to time. I knew he was tricky and a liar, I just didn't think he would play his tricks and try out his lies on me. Hadn't I been faithful? Hadn't I waited, and waited, and waited, despite the temptation—almost the **compulsion**—to do otherwise? And what did I amount to, once the official version gained ground? An **edifying** legend. A stick used to beat other women with. Why couldn't they be as considerate, as trustworthy, as all-suffering as I had been? That was the line they took, the singers, the yarn-spinners. *Don't follow my example,* I want to scream in your ears—yes, yours! But when I try to scream, I sound like an owl.

> **factoid**
> trivial facts or questionable statements that have the appearance of fact

> **eminent**
> important; well-known and respected

> **plausible**
> believable

> **compulsion**
> uncontrollable impulse or drive

> **edifying**
> morally instructive, enlightening

---

1 **seductresses:** women who lure men

Of course I had inklings, about his slipperiness, his wiliness, his foxiness, his—how can I put this?—his **unscrupulousness**, but I turned a blind eye. I kept my mouth shut; or, if I opened it, I sang his praises. I didn't contradict, I didn't ask awkward questions, I didn't dig deep. I wanted happy endings in those days, and happy endings are best achieved by keeping the right doors locked and going to sleep during the rampages.

But after the main events were over and things had become less legendary, I realized how many people were laughing at me behind my back—how they were jeering, making jokes about me, jokes both clean and dirty; how they were turning me into a story, or into several stories, though not the kind of stories I'd prefer to hear about myself. What can a woman do when **scandalous** gossip travels the world? If she defends herself she sounds guilty. So I waited some more.

Now that all the others have run out of air, it's my turn to do a little story-making. I owe it to myself. I've had to work myself up to it; it's a low art, tale-telling. Old women go in for it, strolling beggars, blind singers, maidservants, children—folks with time on their hands. Once, people would have laughed if I'd tried to play the minstrel[2]—there's nothing more **preposterous** than an aristocrat fumbling around with the arts—but who cares about public opinion now? The opinion of the people down here: the opinion of shadows, of echoes. So I'll spin a thread of my own.

The difficulty is that I have no mouth through which I can speak. I can't make myself understood, not in your world, the world of bodies, of tongues and fingers; and most of the time I have no listeners, not on your side of the river.[3] Those of you who may catch the odd whisper, the odd squeak, so easily mistake my words for breezes rustling the dry reeds, for bats at twilight, for bad dreams.

But I've always been of a determined nature. Patient, they used to call me. I like to see a thing through to the end.

■ ■ ■

unscrupulousness the quality of being without integrity or honesty

scandalous shameful

preposterous absurd; ridiculous

---

2 **minstrel:** a singer of verses accompanied by music

3 **your side of the river:** the land of the living, separated from the Underworld by the River Styx

THE CHORUS LINE:
IF I WAS A PRINCESS, A POPULAR TUNE

As Performed by the Maids, with a Fiddle, an Accordion, and a Penny Whistle

First Maid:
If I was a princess, with silver and gold,
And loved by a hero, I'd never grow old:
Oh, if a young hero came a-marrying me,
I'd always be beautiful, happy, and free!

Chorus:
Then sail, my fine lady, on the billowing wave—
The water below is as dark as the grave,
And maybe you'll sink in your little blue boat—
It's hope, and hope only, that keeps us afloat.

Second Maid:
I fetch and I carry, I hear and obey,
It's Yes sir and No ma'am the whole bleeding day;
I smile and I nod with a tear in my eye,
I make the soft beds in which others do lie.

Third Maid:
Oh gods and oh prophets, please alter my life,
And let a young hero take me for his wife!
But no hero comes to me, early or late—
Hard work is my destiny, death is my fate!

Chorus:
Then sail, my fine lady, on the billowing wave—
The water below is as dark as the grave,
And maybe you'll sink in your little blue boat—
It's hope, and hope only, that keeps us afloat.

The Maids all cursty.

Melantho of the Pretty Cheeks, passing the hat:
Thank you, sir. Thank you. Thank you.
Thank you. Thank you.

• • •

HEART OF FLINT[4]

I descended the staircase, considering my choices. I'd pretended not to believe Eurycleia when she told me that it was Odysseus who'd killed the Suitors. Perhaps this man was an imposter, I'd told her—how would I know what Odysseus looked like now, after twenty years? I was also wondering how I must seem to him. I'd been very young when he'd sailed away; now I was a **matron**. How could he fail to be disappointed?

matron
older married woman with children

I decided to make him wait: I myself had waited long enough. Also I would need time in order to fully disguise my true feelings about the unfortunate hanging of my twelve young maids.

So when I entered the hall and saw him sitting there, I didn't say a thing. Telemachus wasted no time: almost immediately he was scolding me for not giving a warmer welcome to his father. Flinty-hearted, he called me scornfully. I could see he had a rosy little picture in his mind: the two of them siding against me, grown men together, two roosters in charge of the henhouse. Of course I wanted the best for him—he was my son, I hoped he would succeed, as a political leader or a warrior or whatever he wanted to be—but at that moment I wished there would be another Trojan War so I could send him off to it and get him out of my hair. Boys with their first beards can be a thorough pain in the neck.

The hardness of my heart was a notion I was glad to **foster**, however, as it would reassure Odysseus to know that I hadn't been throwing myself into the arms of every man who'd turned up claiming to be him. So I looked at him blankly, and said it was too much for me to swallow, the idea that this dirty, blood-smeared **vagabond** was the same as my fine husband who had sailed away, so beautifully dressed, twenty years before.

foster
promote; help grow

vagabond
person who wanders aimlessly from place to place

Odysseus grinned—he was looking forward to the big revelation scene, the part where I would say, 'It was you all along! What a terrific disguise!' and throw my arms around his neck. Then he went off to take a much-needed bath. When he came back in clean clothes, smelling a good deal better than when he'd gone, I couldn't resist teasing him one last time. I ordered Eurycleia to move the bed outside the bedroom of Odysseus, and to make it up for the stranger.

You'll recall that one post of this bed was carved from a tree still rooted in the ground. Nobody knew about it except Odysseus, myself, and my maid Actoris, from Sparta, who by that time was long dead.

Assuming that someone had cut through his cherished bedpost, Odysseus lost his temper at once. Only then did I relent, and go through the business of recognizing him. I shed a satisfactory number of tears, and embraced him, and

---

4 **flint:** hard stone

claimed that he'd passed the bedpost test, and that I was now convinced.

And so we climbed into the very same bed where we'd spent a great many happy hours when we were first married, before Helen took it into her head to run off with Paris, lighting the fires of war and bringing desolation to my house. I was glad it was dark by then, as in the shadows we both appeared less **wizened** than we were.

> **wizened**
> shriveled;
> wrinkled

'We're not spring chickens any more,' I said.

'That which we are, we are,' said Odysseus.

After a little time had passed and we were feeling pleased with each other, we took up our old habits of story-telling. Odysseus told me of all his travels and difficulties. . . . He recounted the many lies he'd invented, the false names he'd given himself—telling the Cyclops his name was No One was the cleverest of such tricks, though he'd spoiled it by boasting—and the **fraudulant** life histories he'd concocted for himself, the better to conceal his identity and his intentions. In my turn, I related the tale of the Suitors, and my trick with the shroud of Laertes,[5] and my deceitful encouraging of the Suitors, and the skillful ways in which I'd misdirected them and led them on and played them off against one another.

> **fraudulant**
> untrue

Then he told me how much he'd missed me, and how he'd been filled with longing for me even when enfolded in the white arms of goddesses; and I told him how very many tears I'd shed while waiting twenty years for his return, and how tediously faithful I'd been, and how I would never have even so much as thought of betraying his gigantic bed with its wondrous bedpost by sleeping in it with any other man.

The two of us were—by our own admission—**proficient** and shameless liars of long standing. It's a wonder either of us believed a word the other said.

> **proficient**
> accomplished,
> competent

But we did.

Or so we told each other.

No sooner had Odysseus returned than he left again. He said that, much as he hated to tear himself away from me, he'd have to go adventuring again. He'd been told by the spirit of the **seer** Teiresias that he would have to purify himself by carrying an oar so far inland that the people there would mistake it for a winnowing fan.[6] Only in that way could he rinse the blood of the Suitors from himself, avoid their vengeful ghosts and their vengeful relatives, and **pacify** the anger of the sea-god Poseidon, who was still furious with him for blinding his son the Cyclops.

> **seer**
> someone
> who can see
> the future

> **pacify**
> calm

It was a likely story. But then, all of his stories were likely.

---

5 **shroud of Laertes:** the burial garment of Odysseus's aged father (see page 506)

6 **winnowing fan:** a device used to separate the lightweight chaff, or waste, from the heavier wheat seeds after harvesting

AFTER YOU READ
from *The Penelopiad*

Think and Discuss

1. How does Penelope in this work compare to the character of Penelope in Homer's work? Give two or three points of comparison or contrast.

2. According to Penelope, what two things is Odysseus especially good at?

3. How would you describe the **tone** Penelope takes in telling her story?

4. What qualities does the **character** of Telemachus have in this version? Give specific examples.

5. Copy the following graphic organizer into your Writer's Notebook. Use it to compare and contrast the feelings of the characters in the different versions.

Odyssey	The Penelopiad
How Odysseus feels: Evidence of his feelings:	How Odysseus feels: Evidence of his feelings:
How Penelope feels: Evidence of her feelings:	How Penelope feels: Evidence of her feelings:

6. Do you agree with Penelope on her views about Odysseus or do you disagree? Give reasons for your answer.

Write to Understand: The "Telemachus-iad"

Review your graphic organizer and reflect on how the different versions portray different emotions in the characters. With that in mind, choose a part of the *Odyssey* and write the events from the point of view of Telemachus. Be sure to show his feelings about both his mother and his father.

BEFORE YOU READ
Orpheus and Eurydice

Meet the Author: Betty Bonham Lies

Betty Bonham Lies was born in 1935. She wrote poetry all through her childhood, but she gave it up when she reached college. "In the dark ages of the fifties," she said, "we read only dead, white European and American male poets. We were told, in effect, you can't write poetry unless you're a man."

Thirty years later, Betty Lies, who is a teacher, rediscovered her own muse. Today she writes poetry and retells classical myths, especially those that feature women. She has also written a book for teachers of creative writing called *The Poet's Pen: Writing Poetry with Middle and High School Students.*

Build Background: The World of Myth

Greek mythology is a huge body of stories about the gods and heroes of ancient Greece. The myths involve a big cast of characters—both mortal and immortal—who star in their own stories and reappear in the stories of others. They also cover a vast mythical landscape that extends from Mount Olympus, the home of the gods, to the Underworld, where the god Hades and his wife Persephone preside over the spirits of the dead.

Many characters from Greek myth are mentioned in the story of Orpheus and Eurydice that you're about to read. Some you've already met in the *Odyssey*. Some will be new to you, and their mention here may inspire you to read more about them.

- Over the centuries, people have read Greek myths and interpreted them in different ways. What do you think accounts for the enduring appeal of myth?

- Do you enjoy reading myths? Why or why not?

ORPHEUS AND EURYDICE, Sir Edward John Poynter, 1862

Orpheus and Eurydice

BETTY BONHAM LIES

ORPHEUS AND EURYDICE

Betty Bonham Lies

In the very early time of the world, gods mingled more freely with mortals than they do in these later days. So it was not surprising that the Muse Calliope, she who inspires epic poetry, gave birth to a son whose father was a mortal man. He was the king of Thrace, the most musical of all the people of Greece. Calliope named her son Orpheus, and from his infancy, she and her sister Muses were his teachers. Even before he reached manhood, he was accomplished in all the arts, but especially in poetry and music.

When Orpheus made music, all the world stopped to listen. Wild beasts drew near him, so entranced they put aside their fierceness. Trees gathered around to hear his beautiful notes. Rivers stopped flowing along the banks so that they could hear Orpheus, whose music was more harmonious than theirs. The very rocks softened when he touched his lyre.[1]

Orpheus drew the most wonderful music from his instrument. With his gift he could embolden people to do deeds they didn't dream they had in them. When he sailed on the Argo with Jason to search for the Golden Fleece,[2] it was his lyre that heartened the men on those nights when they lost courage and despaired of reaching their goal. It was his lyre that soothed and calmed them when quarrels threatened to sow disharmony. It was his lyre, singing louder than the sultry song of the Sirens, that saved the Argonauts,[3] who might have left their bones on that dangerous island as so many other sailors had.

But music was not enough. Something was missing in Orpheus's life. He knew what it was when he met the wood nymph Eurydice and for the first time felt the joy of love. She returned his feelings, and happily agreed to become his wife.

---

1 **lyre:** a stringed instrument of the harp family

2 **Jason to search for the Golden Fleece:** Jason's quest for the Golden Fleece is one of the hero quest tales of Greek mythology. Finding the Golden Fleece was considered an impossible task. Jason was sent on this quest by Pelias, the son of Poseidon and a mortal woman, because Pelias thought that Jason was the man the oracle warned would be his downfall.

3 **Argonauts:** the heroes who sail with Jason in the great ship *Argo*

Orpheus invited Hymen, the god of marriage, to bless the wedding with his presence. Hymen came, but his words were not **auspicious**, and the omens he brought with him were not happy ones. The torch smoked,[4] bringing tears to the eyes of the wedding party. When it was swung, it would not blaze into flame.

auspicious
favorable

And the omens proved true. The loving couple's happiness was all too brief. Their marriage was not an hour old when Eurydice, walking across the meadow with her bridesmaids, innocently trod upon a viper, who struck out at her and stung her on the foot. At once, she was carried away to the Underworld, the dark region of the dead.

Orpheus was **distraught**. Grieving, he bore the young body of his beloved Eurydice to the grave, and the music he played tore at the hearts of everyone who followed. It was whispered among their friends that the gods were jealous and would not let a mortal man and woman live together in immortal happiness. Whether that is true or not, the **bereft** husband was inconsolable. How could he live without his wife, the other half of his soul? Orpheus determined to perform an unthinkable act, an act no mortal man had ever attempted. He would do this for his love: he would follow her into the Underworld, and there he would beg the dark powers to give her back to him.

distraught
agitated
with pain

bereft
bereaved;
deprived of a
loved one

So Orpheus set out, taking with him only his songs and the lyre with which he would accompany his plea. He found the crack in the dark cave that leads to Hades, the realm of death, and he followed it down, deeper and deeper. Soon he saw the River Styx, which separates the Underworld from the world of the living. As he approached, he played on his lyre, and hearing his sweet song, the boatman Charon could not resist it. He agreed to ferry Orpheus to the other side of the river, even though the living should not be allowed to cross.

Then, at the mouth of Hades, Orpheus played and sang to Cerberus, the three-headed dog who guards the entryway to keep away those who have not died. Cerberus dropped his three heads low, ceased snarling for a moment, and let him pass. Once inside, Orpheus searched through the long dark passageways, calling for Eurydice and plucking the strings of his lyre. The **shades** of the dead, among whom he searched for his wife, drew just out of sight as he went by.

shades
spirits

---

4 **The torch smoked:** Torches were part of casting omens to predict the success of a marriage. Hymen is often depicted with a marriage feast torch in his hand.

Frightened but determined, Orpheus continued, winning his way by the beauty of his music. As the dark passages opened up for him, his music gave a moment of relief to many of the souls who suffer eternally to pay for the sins they have committed in the upper world.

Over there was Sisyphus, who for a lifetime's deeds struggles endlessly to push an enormous boulder up a hill. When he reaches the top, it rolls back down again. Orpheus passed and he played, and for a moment Sisyphus was able to sit upon his rock to rest.

And a little farther along, there was Tantalus, whose unspeakable offense against the gods dooms him to torture by burning thirst and stabbing hunger, while he stands neck-deep in a pool of water that recedes from his lips every time he stoops to drink, and just within reach of luscious grapes that wither away when he stretches to pick them. Orpheus passed and he played, and Tantalus too was given a moment of rest.

So were the Danaides,[5] who stabbed their husbands on their wedding night, and for that deed must try eternally to scoop up water in a sieve. Next he saw the fiery winged wheel, on which Ixion spins in torment forever because he committed mankind's first murder, the murder of his brother. At Orpheus's song, for a moment the wheel ceased its spinning.

Even the Furies—the terrible goddesses who inflict these punishments and who keep the dead from escaping Hades to return to the upper world—even they were moved. Orpheus passed and he played, and for the first time ever, the faces of these dread powers grew wet with tears.

At last, Orpheus stood before the thrones of Hades, the dark-browed king of the Underworld, and his queen, Persephone, her fair face veiled by the shadows of that terrible place. What could he say to the god and goddess of death that would persuade them to give Eurydice back to him? He plucked the strings of his lyre, and put his whole heart into the song that would plead his cause:

> *You who rule this dark and silent world*
> *are masters of all who walk on the Earth.*
> *Every one of us will come to you,*
> *even the most beautiful and best loved belong to you at last.*

---

5 **Danaides:** These are the fifty daughters of King Danaus of Argos. They were married in one ceremony to fifty suitors, and they acted on their father's instruction when all but one of them murdered their husbands on their wedding night.

You are the creditor who must always be paid.
We only belong to the upper world for a short time,
and then we are yours forever and ever.
But there is one who came to you too soon,
a bud that died before it ever grew into a flower.
I tried to bear the loss, but it was too great.
O king, I could not bear it. Love was too strong.
Hear me and weave again the web of life,
put together the threads cut from the loom too soon for my Eurydice.
I ask you only for a loan, and not a gift to me,
for she'll be given back to you when her years are full.

Orpheus's music was so compelling that even the ice-hard heart of Hades melted. Persephone whispered a plea in his ear, and tears flowed from his eyes. Just this once he had to yield before the force of love.

Hades called for Eurydice, and she came forth from among the newest shades, still limping from her wound. Orpheus's wish was granted. But there was one condition: she must follow in his shadow and he must not pause, or speak, or turn to look on her until they reached the upper world.

Of course, Orpheus agreed, and at once the couple turned away from the throne of death to begin their difficult journey. Through dark and **tortuous** passageways, through the chill of death, they made their way in terrible silence. Orpheus listened with all his being to hear the footsteps of Eurydice in the shadows behind him. At each step he desperately wanted to turn, to make sure she was still there, and even more, he longed to look upon her face. But he controlled his yearning and kept going, up and up, until utter darkness began to change to only black, then gray, and then lighter gray, and at last he could see the light of day ahead.

tortuous
marked by repeated twists and turns; winding

Some people say that what happened next was just a moment of forgetfulness. Others maintain that Orpheus had reached the sunlight and turned to help Eurydice, believing she was out, too. There are those who think he didn't trust Hades, and had to see that she was really there, or that he couldn't hear her steps and was overcome by a terror that she was no longer following him. But you might believe—and I believe it too—that his great love for her overwhelmed him. He could not keep himself from turning around, just to see her beloved face at last.

Orpheus and Eurydice   535

At the very instant he turned, Eurydice was snatched away for the second time, this time forever. He heard a faint cry—"Farewell!"—and knew that it held no tone of reproach. How could she blame him when his only fault was loving her too much?

Desperately, Orpheus stretched out his arms and called her name: "Eurydice!" But it was too late. His arms clasped the cold air, and a long deep sigh echoed from the darkness. He would never see her again while he lived.

broached
broke into or
opened up

In vain, Orpheus tried to follow his bride. But this time the Underworld was firmly closed to him. No other mortal had **broached** it once, and certainly he was not going to get a second chance. The power of his music failed him at last. Charon turned a deaf ear to his pleas, and all the gods agreed that a living mortal could not enter the world of the dead again.

For seven days and seven nights, Orpheus remained at the entryway, unable to sing or even speak, taking no food or drink, wishing for death. But even death refused him. Finally, he had no choice but to get up and go back into the world. Once there, he avoided every scene of joy, and turned his back on women, although there were many maidens who would have liked to make him forget Eurydice.

Orpheus traveled into the mountain forests, seeking solitude or the companionship of beasts rather than men. Although he still played his lyre, he played only to melt the hearts of tigers, to move the mountains and the oak trees. His songs were so sad that no human could bear to listen to them.

One day, as Orpheus slept in a clearing, a band of Maenads,[6] women driven to madness by their worship of Dionysus, came upon him and demanded that he join their revels. Horrified, he refused them. In their fury, they closed in on him like hunters on a deer. First they stoned him, then smashed his precious lyre. Finally, in a frenzy they tore his body to pieces and threw him into a stream. From there he floated out to sea, and people say that as he floated he still sang the name of Eurydice. His body was washed ashore on the island of Lesbos.[7] There it was buried by the Muses, who lamented for their beloved Orpheus.

And to this day, the nightingales sing more sweetly on that island than anywhere else in the world.

---

6 **Maenades:** What these female devotees of Dionysus do to Orpheus is characteristic for them. In their wild frenzy, they typically tear animals apart and devour their flesh.

7 **the island of Lesbos:** This island is the birthplace of the poet Sappho, who is sometimes called the "Tenth Muse" or the "mortal Muse."

AFTER YOU READ
Orpheus and Eurydice

Think and Discuss

1. Hades grants Orpheus's request to give Eurydice back to him, but there is one condition. What it that condition?

2. **Hyperbole** is a figure of speech. It is an extravagantly exaggerated description or statement. Lies uses hyperbole when she describes the beauty of Orpheus's music. With a partner, look back at the text and find examples of hyperbole. Discuss the effect of hyperbole on the story.

3. The song Orpheus composes to plead his cause employs an **extended metaphor**. Identify the two things compared by the metaphor. Then tell if you think the metaphor is an effective one, and why or why not. (For a definition of *metaphor*, see the Glossary of Literary Terms.)

4. In preparation for retelling a myth, Lies reads every version of the story she can find. Her explanation of why Orpheus turned to look back at Eurydice is evidence of that. Of all the reasons that have been given, do you think Lies chose the right one? Explain.

5. A myth like "Orpheus and Eurydice" has been retold many times. Each retelling may use different words and include different details, but the basic events of the story remain the same. Create a story map like the one below to record the events that are critical to the story of Orpheus and Eurydice and would appear in every version.

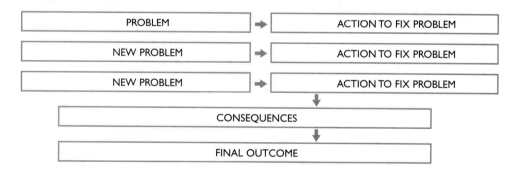

Write to Understand: Retelling the Myth

Review the critical events of the Orpheus and Eurydice story you recorded on your story map. Then use these events to help you retell the story in your own words.

BEFORE YOU READ

Eurydice

Meet the Author: Sarah Ruhl

Born in 1974, Sarah Ruhl is one of the brightest new stars in American playwriting. Her plays have been produced throughout the United States and Europe. *The Clean House* was a Pulitzer Prize finalist in 2005. In 2006, she received a MacArthur Fellowship—also known as a "genius" grant.

Ruhl wrote *Eurydice* when she was a graduate student at Brown University. In her "re-imagining" of the classic myth, she invents a father with whom Eurydice is reunited in the Underworld. Ruhl's own father died of cancer when she was 20. "In a way, I think I was trying to have more conversations with my own father by writing his story," says Ruhl.

Build Background: Orpheus and Eurydice

The tale of Orpheus and Eurydice has inspired at least three significant operas, two classic movies, a Stravinsky-Balanchine ballet, and two plays which preceded Ruhl's work: Jean Anouilh's *Eurydice* (1941), which sets the story among a troupe of performers in 1930s France, and Tennessee Williams's *Orpheus Descending* (1957), which sets the story in 1950s America.

Sarah Ruhl's play has been called a "quirky contemporary meditation" on the popular myth. Written in contemporary language, the story is told from the perspective of Eurydice. Orpheus is a classical musician, who thinks only about music. Eurydice is into words and loves books. She can't remember a melody or clap out a rhythm.

- Remind yourself of the myth of Orpheus and Eurydice to set your mind for reading this play. What are the main events in the plot?

- Sarah Ruhl introduces a new character into the myth: Eurydice's father, with whom she is reunited in the Underworld. What effect do you think this will have on the story?

ORPHEUS, Marc Chagall, 1969

Eurydice

SARAH RUHL

EURYDICE

Sarah Ruhl

CHARACTERS:

EURYDICE
HER FATHER
ORPHEUS
A NASTY INTERESTING MAN/THE LORD OF THE UNDERWORLD
A CHORUS OF STONES:
    BIG STONE
    LITTLE STONE
    LOUD STONE

SETTING:

The set contains a raining elevator,[1] a water pump, some rusty exposed pipes, an abstracted River of Forgetfulness, an old-fashioned glow-in-the-dark globe.

NOTES:

Eurydice and Orpheus should be played as though they are a little too young and a little too in love. They should resist the temptation to be "classical."

The underworld should resemble the world of Alice in Wonderland *more than it resembles Hades.*

The Stones might be played as though they are nasty children at a birthday party.

When people compose letters in this play they needn't actually scribble them—they can speak directly to the audience.

The set should allow for fluid transitions from moment to moment—from underworld to overworld and back again.

The play should be performed without an intermission.

---

1 **raining elevator:** an elevator in which it is raining. This is one of the stage effects specified by the playwright that helps to place the play in the realm of fantasy.

FIRST MOVEMENT
Scene I

A young man—ORPHEUS—and a young woman—EURYDICE.
They wear swimming outfits from the 1950s.
ORPHEUS makes a sweeping gesture with his arm, indicating the sky.

EURYDICE. All those birds? Thank you.

(He nods. They make a quarter turn and he makes a sweeping gesture,
indicating an invisible sea.)
   And—the sea! For me? When?
(ORPHEUS opens his hands.)
   Now? It's mine already?
(ORPHEUS nods.)
   Wow.
(They kiss. He indicates the sky.)
   Surely not—surely not the sky and the stars too?!
(ORPHEUS nods.)
   That's very generous.
(ORPHEUS nods.)
   Perhaps too generous?
(ORPHEUS shakes his head no.)
   Thank you.
   Now—walk over there.
(ORPHEUS walks in a straight line on an unseen boardwalk.)
   Don't look at me.
(He turns his face away from hers and walks.)
   Now—stop.
(He stops.)
(She runs and jumps into his arms.
He doesn't quite catch her and they fall down together.
She crawls on top of him and kisses his eyes.)
   What are you thinking about?
ORPHEUS. Music.
EURYDICE. How can you think about music? You either hear it or you
   don't.

ORPHEUS. I'm hearing it then.

EURYDICE. Oh.

(Pause)

I read a book today.

ORPHEUS. Did you?

EURYDICE. Yes. It was very interesting.

ORPHEUS. That's good.

EURYDICE. Don't you want to know what it was about?

ORPHEUS. Of course.

EURYDICE. There were—stories—about people's lives—how some come out well—and others come out badly.

ORPHEUS. Do you love the book?

EURYDICE. Yes—I think so.

ORPHEUS. Why?

EURYDICE. It can be interesting to see if other people—like dead people who wrote books—agree or disagree with what you think.

ORPHEUS. Why?

EURYDICE. Because it makes you—a larger part of the human community. It had very interesting arguments.

ORPHEUS. Oh. And arguments that are interesting are good arguments?

EURYDICE. Well—yes.

ORPHEUS. I didn't know an argument should be interesting. I thought it should be right or wrong.

EURYDICE. Well, these particular arguments were very interesting.

ORPHEUS. Maybe you should make up your own thoughts. Instead of reading them in a book.

EURYDICE. I do. I do think up my own thoughts.

ORPHEUS. I know you do. I love how you love books. Don't be mad.

(Pause)

I made up a song for you today.

EURYDICE. Did you?!

ORPHEUS. Yup. It's not *interesting* or *not interesting.* It just—is.

EURYDICE. Will you sing it for me?

ORPHEUS. It has too many parts.

EURYDICE. Let's go in the water.

(They start walking, arm in arm,
on extensive unseen boardwalks, toward the water.)

ORPHEUS. Wait—remember this melody.

(He hums a bar of melody.)

EURYDICE. I'm bad at remembering melodies. Why don't you remember it?

ORPHEUS. I have eleven other ones in my head, making for a total of twelve. You have it?

EURYDICE. Yes. I think so.

ORPHEUS. Let's hear it.

(She sings the melody.
She misses a few notes.
She's not the best singer in the world.)

Pretty good. The rhythm's a little off. Here—clap it out.

(She claps.)
(He claps the rhythmic sequence for her.
She tries to imitate.
She is still off.)

EURYDICE. Is that right?

ORPHEUS. We'll practice.

EURYDICE. I don't need to know about rhythm. I have my books.

ORPHEUS. Don't books have rhythm?

EURYDICE. Kind of. Let's go in the water.

ORPHEUS. Will you remember my melody under the water?

EURYDICE. Yes! I WILL ALWAYS REMEMBER YOUR MELODY! It will be imprinted on my heart like wax.

ORPHEUS. Thank you.

EURYDICE. You're welcome. When are you going to play me the whole song?

ORPHEUS. When I get twelve instruments.

EURYDICE. Where are you going to get twelve instruments?

ORPHEUS. I'm going to make each strand of your hair into an instrument. Your hair will stand on end as it plays my music and become a hair orchestra. It will fly you up into the sky.

EURYDICE. I don't know if I want to be an instrument.

ORPHEUS. Why?

EURYDICE. Won't I fall down when the song ends?

ORPHEUS. That's true. But the clouds will be so moved by your music that they will fill up with water until they become heavy and you'll sit on one and fall gently down to earth. How about that?

EURYDICE. Okay.

(They stop walking for a moment.
They gaze at each other.)

ORPHEUS. It's settled then.

EURYDICE. What is?

ORPHEUS. Your hair will be my orchestra and—I love you.

(Pause)

EURYDICE. I love you, too.

ORPHEUS. How will you remember?

EURYDICE. That I love you?

ORPHEUS. Yes.

EURYDICE. That's easy. I can't help it.

ORPHEUS. You never know. I'd better tie a string around your finger to remind you.

EURYDICE. Is there string at the ocean?

ORPHEUS. I always have string. In case I come upon a broken instrument.

(He takes out a string from his pocket.
He takes her left hand.)

This hand.

(He wraps string deliberately around her fourth finger.)

Is this too tight?

EURYDICE. No—it's fine.

ORPHEUS. There—now you'll remember.

EURYDICE. That's a very particular finger.

ORPHEUS. Yes.

EURYDICE. You're aware of that?

ORPHEUS. Yes.

EURYDICE. How aware?

ORPHEUS. Very aware.

EURYDICE. Orpheus—are we?

ORPHEUS. You tell me.

EURYDICE. Yes. I *think* so.

ORPHEUS. You think so?

EURYDICE. I wasn't thinking.
I mean—yes. Just: Yes.

ORPHEUS. Yes?

EURYDICE. Yes.

ORPHEUS. Yes!

EURYDICE. Yes!

ORPHEUS. May our lives be full of music!

(Music.
He picks her up and throws her into the sky.)

EURYDICE. Maybe you could also get me another ring—a gold one—to put over the string one. You know?

ORPHEUS. Whatever makes you happy. Do you still have my melody?

EURYDICE. It's right here.

(She points to her temple.
They look at each other. A silence.)

What are you thinking about?

ORPHEUS. Music.

(Her face falls.)

Just kidding. I was thinking about you. And music.

EURYDICE. Let's go in the water. I'll race you!

(She puts on her swimming goggles.)

ORPHEUS. I'll race *you*!

EURYDICE. I'll race *you*!

ORPHEUS. I'll race *you*!

EURYDICE. I'll race *you*!

(They race toward the water.)

Scene 2

(The FATHER, dressed in a gray suit, reads from a letter.)

FATHER. Dear Eurydice,

A letter for you on your wedding day.

There is no choice of any importance in life but the choosing of a beloved. I haven't met Orpheus, but he seems like a serious young man. I understand he's a musician.

If I were to give a speech at your wedding I would start with one or two funny jokes, and then I might offer some words of advice. I would say:

Cultivate the arts of dancing and small talk.

Everything in moderation.

Court the companionship and respect of dogs.

Grilling a fish or toasting bread without burning requires singleness of purpose, vigilance and steadfast watching.

Keep quiet about politics, but vote for the right man.

Take care to change the light bulbs.

Continue to give yourself to others because that's the ultimate satisfaction in life—to love, accept, honor and help others.

As for me, this is what it's like being dead: the atmosphere smells. And there are strange high-pitched noises—like a tea kettle always boiling over. But it doesn't seem to bother anyone. And, for the most part, there is a pleasant atmosphere and you can work and socialize, much like at home. I'm working in the business world and it seems that, here, you can better see the far-reaching consequences of your actions. Also, I am one of the few dead people who still remembers how to read and write. That's a secret. If anyone finds out, they might dip me in the River again.[2]

I write you letters. I don't know how to get them to you.

Love,
Your Father

(He drops the letter as though into a mail slot.
It falls on the ground.
Wedding music.
In the underworld, the FATHER walks in a straight line as though he is walking his daughter down the aisle. He is affectionate, then solemn, then glad, then solemn, then amused, then solemn.
He looks at his imaginary daughter; he looks straight ahead; he acknowledges the guests at the wedding; he gets choked-up; he looks at his daughter and smiles an embarrassed smile for getting choked-up.
He looks straight ahead, calm.
He walks.
Suddenly, he checks his watch. He exits, in a hurry.)

Scene 3

(EURYDICE, by a water pump.
The noise of a party, from far off.)

EURYDICE. I hate parties.

---

2 **If anyone finds out, they might dip me in the River again:** The River is the River of Forgetfulness. In the *Odyssey*, when Odysseus visits the Underworld, he speaks with Tiresias the blind prophet who, unlike the other spirits, has been allowed to keep his mental powers.

And a wedding party is the biggest party of all. All the guests arrived and Orpheus is taking a shower. He's always taking a shower when the guests arrive so he doesn't have to greet them. Then I have to greet them.

A wedding is for daughters and fathers. The mothers all dress up, trying to look like young women. But a wedding is for a father and a daughter. They stop being married to each other on that day.

I always thought there would be more interesting people at my wedding.

(She drinks a cup of water from the water pump.
A NASTY INTERESTING MAN, *wearing a trench coat, appears.)*

MAN. Are you a homeless person?

EURYDICE. No.

MAN. Oh. I'm on my way to a party where there are really very interesting people. Would you like to join me?

EURYDICE. No. I just left my own party.

MAN. You were giving a party and you just—left?

EURYDICE. I was thirsty.

MAN. You must be a very interesting person, to leave your own party like that.

EURYDICE. Thank you.

MAN. You mustn't care at all what other people think of you. I always say that's a mark of a really interesting person, don't you?

EURYDICE. I guess.

MAN. So would you like to accompany me to this interesting affair?

EURYDICE. No, thank you. I just got married, you see.

MAN. Oh—lots of people do that.

EURYDICE. That's true—lots of people do.

MAN. What's your name?

EURYDICE. Eurydice.

(He looks at her, hungry.)

MAN. Eurydice.

EURYDICE. Good-bye, then.

MAN. Good-bye.

(She exits. He sits by the water pump.
He notices a letter on the ground.
He picks it up and reads it.
To himself:)

 Dear Eurydice . . .

(Musty dripping sounds.)

Scene 4

(The FATHER *tries to remember how to do the jitterbug in the underworld. He does the jitterbug with an imaginary partner.*
He has fun.)
*(*ORPHEUS *and* EURYDICE *dance together at their wedding.*
They are happy. They have had some champagne. They sing together:)

ORPHEUS AND EURYDICE.
Don't sit under the apple tree
With anyone else but me
Anyone else but me
Anyone else but me
No no no.
Don't sit under the apple tree
With anyone else but me
Till I come marching home . . . [3]

(On the other side of the stage,
the FATHER *checks his watch.*
He stops doing the jitterbug.
He exits, in a hurry.)
Don't go walking down lover's lane
With anyone else but me
Anyone else but me
Anyone else but me
No no no.
Don't go walking down lover's lane
With anyone else but me
Till I come marching home . . .

EURYDICE. I'm warm. Are you warm?

ORPHEUS. Yes!

EURYDICE. I'm going to get a drink of water.

ORPHEUS. Don't go.

EURYDICE. I'll be right back.

ORPHEUS. Promise?

EURYDICE. Yes.

ORPHEUS. I can't stand to let you out of my sight today.

EURYDICE. Silly goose.

(They kiss.)

---

3 **Don't sit under the apple tree . . . :** lyrics of a World War II era song introduced by the Andrews Sisters in 1942

Scene 5

(EURYDICE *at the water pump,*
getting a glass of water.
The NASTY INTERESTING MAN *appears.*)

EURYDICE. Oh—you're still here.

MAN. Yes. I forgot to tell you something. I have a letter. Addressed to Eurydice—that's you— from your father.

EURYDICE. That's not possible.

MAN. He wrote down some thoughts—for your wedding day.

EURYDICE. Let me see.

MAN. I left it at home. It got delivered to my elegant high-rise apartment by mistake.

EURYDICE. Why didn't you say so before?

MAN. You left in such a hurry.

EURYDICE. From my father?

MAN. Yes.

EURYDICE. You're sure?

MAN. Yes.

EURYDICE. I knew he'd send something!

MAN. It'll just take a moment. I live around the block. What an interesting dress you're wearing.

EURYDICE. Thank you.

Scene 6

(ORPHEUS, *from the water pump.*)

ORPHEUS. Eurydice?

Eurydice!

Scene 7

(*The sound of a door closing.*
The Interesting Apartment—a giant loft space with no furniture.
EURYDICE *and the* MAN *enter, panting.*)

MAN. Voilà.

EURYDICE. You're very high up.

MAN. Yes. I am.

EURYDICE. I feel a little faint.

MAN. It'll pass.

EURYDICE. Have you ever thought about installing an elevator?

MAN. No. I prefer stairs.

I think architecture is so interesting, don't you?

EURYDICE. Oh, yes. So, where's the letter?

MAN. But isn't this an interesting building?

EURYDICE. It's so—high up.

MAN. Yes.

EURYDICE. There's no one here. I thought you were having a party.

MAN. I like to celebrate things quietly. With a few other interesting people. Don't you?

(She tilts her head to the side and stares at him.)

Would you like some champagne?

EURYDICE. Maybe some water.

MAN. Water it is! Make yourself comfortable.

(He switches on Brazilian mood music. He exits. EURYDICE looks around.)

EURYDICE. I can't stay long!

(She looks out the window. She is very high up.)

I can see my wedding from here!
The people are all so small—they're dancing!
There's Orpheus!
He's not dancing.

MAN *(shouting from offstage).* So, who's this guy you're marrying?

EURYDICE. *(shouting).* His name is Orpheus.

(As he attempts to open champagne offstage:)

MAN. Orpheus. Not a very interesting name. I've heard it before.

EURYDICE. Maybe you've heard of him. He's kind of famous. He plays the most beautiful music in the world, actually.

MAN. I can't hear you!

EURYDICE. So the letter was delivered—here—today?

MAN. That's right.

EURYDICE. Through the post?

MAN. It was—mysterious.

(The sound of champagne popping.
He enters with one glass of champagne.)

Voilà.

(He drinks the champagne.)

So. Eurydice. Tell me one thing. Name me one person you find interesting.

EURYDICE. Why?

MAN. Just making conversation.

(He sways a little to the music.)

EURYDICE. Right. Um—all the interesting people I know are dead or speak French.

MAN. Well, I don't speak French, Eurydice.

(He takes one step toward her.
She takes one step back.)

EURYDICE. I'm sorry. I have to go. There's no letter, is there?

MAN. Of course there's a letter. It's right here. *(He pats his breast pocket.)* Eurydice. I'm not interesting, but I'm strong. You could teach me to be interesting. I would listen. Orpheus is too busy listening to his own thoughts. There's music in his head. Try to pluck the music out and it bites you. I'll bet you had an interesting thought today, for instance.

*(She tilts her head to the side, **quizzical**.)*

I bet you're always having them, the way you tilt your head to the side and stare . . .

(She jerks her head back up.
Musty dripping sounds.)

EURYDICE. I feel dizzy all of a sudden. I want my husband. I think I'd better go now.

MAN. You're free to go, whenever you like.

EURYDICE. I know. I think I'll go now, in fact. I'll just take my letter first, if you don't mind.

(She holds out her hand for the letter.
He takes her hand.)

MAN. Relax.

(She takes her hand away.)

EURYDICE. Good-bye.

quizzical
skeptical;
questioning

(She turns to exit.
He blocks the doorway.)

MAN. Wait. Eurydice. Don't go. I love you.

EURYDICE. Oh no.

MAN. You need to get yourself a real man. A man with broad shoulders like me. Orpheus has long fingers that would tremble to pet a bull or pluck a bee from a hive—

EURYDICE. How do you know about my husband's fingers?

MAN. A man who can put his big arm around your little shoulders as he leads you through the crowd, a man who answers the door at parties . . . A man with big hands, with big stupid hands like potatoes, a man who can carry a cow in labor.

(The MAN backs EURYDICE against the wall.)

My lips were meant to kiss your eyelids, that's obvious!

EURYDICE. Close your eyes, then!

(He closes his eyes, expecting a kiss.
She takes the letter from his breast pocket.
She slips by him and opens the door to the stairwell.
He opens his eyes.
She looks at the letter.)

It's his handwriting!

MAN. Of course it is!

(He reaches for her.)

EURYDICE. Good-bye.

(She runs for the stairs.
She wavers, off-balance, at the top of the stairwell.)

MAN. Don't do that, you'll trip! There are six hundred stairs!

EURYDICE. Orpheus!

(From the water pump:)

ORPHEUS. Eurydice!

She runs, trips and pitches down the stairs, holding her letter.
She follows the letter down, down down . . .
Blackout.

vertigo
a disordered
state;
dizzyness

A clatter. Strange sounds—xylophones, brass bands, sounds of falling, sounds of ***vertigo.***
Sounds of breathing.)

SECOND MOVEMENT
Scene 1

(The underworld. There is no set change. Strange watery noises. Drip, drip, drip. The movement to the underworld is marked by the entrance of stones.)

THE STONES.   We are a chorus of stones.

LITTLE STONE.   I'm a little stone.

BIG STONE.   I'm a big stone.

LOUD STONE.   I'm a loud stone.

THE STONES.   We are all three stones.

LITTLE STONES.   We live with the dead people in the land of the dead.

BIG STONE.   Eurydice was a great musician. Orpheus was his wife.

LITTLE STONE (*correcting* BIG STONE).   Orpheus was a great musician. Eurydice was his wife. She died.

LITTLE STONE.   Then he played the saddest music. Even we—

THE STONES.   the stones—

LITTLE STONE.   cried when we heard it.

(The sound of three drops of water hitting the pond.)

Oh, look, she is coming into the land of the dead now.

BIG STONE.   Oh!

LOUD STONE.   Oh!

LITTLE STONE.   Oh! We might say: "Poor Eurydice"—

LOUD STONE.   but stones don't feel bad for dead people.

(The sound of an elevator ding.
An elevator door opens.
Inside the elevator, it is raining.
EURYDICE gets rained on inside the elevator.
She carries a suitcase and an umbrella.
She is dressed in the kind of 1930s suit that women wore when they eloped.
She looks bewildered.
The sound of an elevator ding. EURYDICE steps out of the elevator.
The elevator door closes.
She walks toward the audience and opens her mouth, trying to speak.
There is a great humming noise.
She closes her mouth.
The humming noise stops.
She opens her mouth for the second time, attempting to tell her story to the audience.

There is a great humming noise.
She closes her mouth—the humming noise stops.
*She has a **tantrum** of despair.*
The STONES, to the audience:)

tantrum
outburst of
bad behavior

THE STONES. Eurydice wants to speak to you.
  But she can't speak your language anymore.
  She talks in the language of dead people now.

LITTLE STONE. It's a very quiet language.

LOUD STONE. Like if the pores in your face
  opened up and talked.

BIG STONE. Like potatoes sleeping in the dirt.

*(LITTLE STONE and LOUD STONE look at BIG STONE as though that were a
dumb thing to say.)*

LITTLE STONE. Pretend that you understand her or she'll be embarrassed.

BIG STONE. Yes—pretend for a moment that you understand the language of stones.

LOUD STONE. Listen to her the way you would listen
  to your own daughter
  if she died too young
  and tried to speak to you
  across long distances.

(EURYDICE *shakes out her umbrella.*
She approaches the audience.
This time, she can speak.)

EURYDICE. There was a roar, and a coldness—
  I think my husband was with me.
  What was my husband's name?

(EURYDICE *turns to the* STONES.)

  My husband's name. Do you know it?

(*The* STONES *shrug their shoulders.*)

  How strange. I don't remember.
  It was horrible to see his face
  when I died. His eyes were
  two black birds
  and they flew to me.
  I said: no—stay where you are—
  he needs you in order to see!
  When I got through the cold
  they made me swim in a river
  and I forgot his name.
  I forgot all the names.
  I know his name starts with my mouth
  shaped like a ball of twine—
  Oar—oar.
  I forget.
  They took me to a tiny boat.
  I only just fit inside.
  I looked at the oars
  and I wanted to cry.
  I tried to cry but I just drooled a little.
  I'll try now.

(*She tries to cry but finds that she can't.*)

  What happiness it would be to cry.

(She takes a breath.)

> I was not lonely
> only alone with myself
> begging myself not to leave my own body
> but I was leaving.
> Good-bye, head—I said—
> it inclined itself a little, as though to nod to me
> in a solemn kind of way.

(She turns to the STONES. *)*

> How do you say good-bye to yourself?

(They shake their heads.
A train whistle.
EURYDICE *steps onto a platform, surveying a large crowd.)*

> A train!

LITTLE STONE. The station is like a train but
there is no train.

BIG STONE. The train has wheels that are not wheels.

LOUD STONE. There is the opposite of a wheel and the
opposite of smoke and the opposite of a train.

(A train pulls away.)

EURYDICE. Oh! I'm waiting for someone to meet me, I think.

(EURYDICE's FATHER approaches and takes her baggage.)

FATHER. Eurydice.

EURYDICE *(to the* STONES*)*. At last, a porter to meet me! *(To the*
FATHER.*)* Do you happen to know where the bank is? I need money.
I've just arrived. I need to exchange my money at the Bureau de
Change. I didn't bring traveler's checks because I left in such a hurry.
They didn't even let me pack my suitcase. There's nothing in it! That's
funny, right? Funny—ha ha! I suppose I can buy new clothes here. I
would *really* love a bath.

FATHER. Eurydice!

EURYDICE. What is that language you're speaking? It gives me tingles.
Say it again.

FATHER. Eurydice!

EURYDICE. Oooh—it's like a fruit! Again!

FATHER. Eurydice—I'm your father.

EURYDICE *(strangely imitating)*. Eurydice—I'm your father! How funny!
You remind me of something but I can't understand a word you're
saying. Say it again!

FATHER. Your father.

THE STONES *(to the* FATHER*).* Shut up, shut up!
She doesn't understand you.
She's dead now, too.
You have to speak in the language of stones.

FATHER *(to* EURYDICE*).* You're dead now. I'm dead, too.

EURYDICE. Yes, that's right. I need a reservation. For the fancy hotel.

FATHER. When you were alive, I was your father.

THE STONES. Father is not a word that dead people understand.

BIG STONE. He is what we call **subversive**.

FATHER. When you were alive, I was your tree.

EURYDICE. My tree! Yes, the tall one in the backyard! I used to sit all
day in its shade!

(She sits at the feet of her FATHER.*)*
Ah—there—shade!

LITTLE STONE. There is a problem here.

EURYDICE. Is there any entertainment at the hotel? Any dancing ladies?
Like with the great big fans?

FATHER. I named you Eurydice. Your mother named all the other
children. But Eurydice I chose for you.

BIG STONE. Be careful, sir.

FATHER. Eurydice. I wanted to remember your name. I asked the stones.
They said: forget the names—the names make you remember.

LOUD STONE. We told you how it works!

FATHER. One day it would not stop raining.
I heard your name inside the rain—somewhere between the drops—I
saw falling letters. Each letter of your name—I began to translate.
E—I remembered elephants. U—I remembered ulcers and under.
R—I remembered reindeers. I saw them putting their black noses into
snow. Y—youth and yellow. D—dog, dig, daughter, day. Time poured
into my head. The days of the week. Hours, months . . .

EURYDICE. The tree talks so beautifully.

THE STONES. Don't listen!

EURYDICE. I feel suddenly hungry! Where is the porter who met me at
the station?

FATHER. Here I am.

EURYDICE. I would like a continental breakfast, please. Maybe some
rolls and butter. Oh—and jam. Please take my suitcase to my room, if
you would.

subversive
working to
undermine
the established
rules and order
of things

FATHER. I'm sorry, miss, but there are no rooms here.

EURYDICE. What? No rooms? Where do people sleep?

FATHER. People don't sleep here.

EURYDICE. I have to say I'm very disappointed. It's been such a tiring day. I've been traveling all day—first on a river, then on an elevator that rained, then on a train . . . I thought someone would meet me at the station . . .

(EURYDICE *is on the **verge** of tears.*)

verge
edge

THE STONES. Don't cry! Don't cry!

EURYDICE. I don't know where I am and there are all these stones and I hate them! They're horrible! I want a bath! I thought someone would meet me at the station!

FATHER. Don't be sad. I'll take your luggage to your room.

THE STONES. THERE ARE NO ROOMS!

(*He picks up her luggage.*
He gives the STONES *a dirty look.*
The sound of water in rusty pipes.)

Scene 2

(ORPHEUS *writes a letter to* EURYDICE.)

ORPHEUS. Dear Eurydice,

I miss you.
No—that's not enough.

(*He crumples up the letter.*
He writes a new letter.
He thinks. He writes:)

Dear Eurydice,

Symphony for twelve instruments.

(*A pause.*
He hears the music in his head.
He conducts.)

Love,
Orpheus

(*He drops the letter as though into a mail slot.*)

Scene 3

(The FATHER creates a room out of string for EURYDICE.
He makes four walls and a door out of string.
Time passes.
It takes time to build a room out of string.
EURYDICE observes the underworld.
There isn't much to observe.
She plays hop-scotch without chalk.
Every so often, the FATHER looks at her, happy to see her,
while he makes her room out of string.
She looks back at him, polite.)

Scene 4

(The FATHER has completed the string room.
He gestures for EURYDICE to enter.
She enters with her suitcase.)

EURYDICE. Thank you. That will do.

(She nods to her FATHER.
He doesn't leave.)

 Oh.

 I suppose you want a tip.

(He shakes his head no.)

 Would you run a bath for me?

FATHER. Yes, miss.

(He exits the string room.
EURYDICE opens her suitcase.
She is surprised to find nothing inside.
She sits down inside her suitcase.)

Scene 5

ORPHEUS. Dear Eurydice,

 I love you. I'm going to find you. I play the saddest music now that you're gone. You know I hate writing letters. I'll give this letter to a worm. I hope he finds you.

 Love,
 Orpheus

(He drops the letter as though into a mail slot.)

Scene 6

(The FATHER *enters the string room with a letter on a silver tray.)*

FATHER. There is a letter for you, miss.

EURYDICE. A letter?

(He nods.)

FATHER. A letter.

(He hands her the letter.)

   It's addressed to you.

EURYDICE. There's dirt on it.

*(*EURYDICE *wipes the dirt off the letter.*
She opens it.

scrutinizes
examines
closely

She ***scrutinizes*** *it.*
She does not know how to read it.
She puts it on the ground, takes off her shoes, stands on the letter, and
shuts her eyes.
She thinks, without language for the thought,
the melody: There's no place like home . . .)

FATHER. Miss.

EURYDICE. What is it?

FATHER. Would you like me to *read* you the letter?

EURYDICE. Read me the letter?

FATHER. You can't do it with your feet.

(The FATHER *guides her off the letter, picks it up and begins to read.)*

It's addressed to Eurydice. That's you.

EURYDICE. That's you.

FATHER. You.

It says: I love you.

EURYDICE. I love you?

FATHER. It's like your tree.

EURYDICE. Tall?

(The FATHER *considers.)*

Green?

FATHER. It's like sitting in the shade.

EURYDICE. Oh.

FATHER. It's like sitting in the shade with no clothes on.

EURYDICE. Oh!—yes.

FATHER *(reading).* I'm going to find you. I play the saddest music—

EURYDICE. Music?

(He whistles a note.)

FATHER. It's like that.

(She smiles.)

EURYDICE. Go on.

FATHER. You know I hate writing letters. I'll give this letter to a worm.
I hope he finds you.
Love,
Orpheus

EURYDICE. Orpheus?

FATHER. Orpheus.

(A pause)

EURYDICE. That word!
It's like—I can't breathe.
Orpheus! My husband.

Scene 7

ORPHEUS.

Dear Eurydice,
Last night I dreamed that we climbed Mount Olympus and we started
to make love and all the strands of your hair were little faucets and
water was streaming out of your head and I said, why is water coming
out of your hair? And you said, gravity is very **compelling**.

And then we jumped off Mount Olympus and flew through the clouds
and you held your knee to your chest because you skinned it on a
sharp cloud and then we fell into a salty lake. Then I woke up and
the window frightened me and I thought: Eurydice is dead. Then I
thought—who is Eurydice? Then the whole room started to float and
I thought: what are people? Then my bed clothes smiled at me with a
crooked green mouth and I thought: who am I? It scares me, Eurydice.

Please come back.

Love,
Orpheus

Scene 8

(EURYDICE and her FATHER in the string room.)

FATHER. Did you get my letters?

EURYDICE. No! You wrote me letters?

FATHER. Every day.

EURYDICE. What did they say?

FATHER. Oh—nothing much. The usual stuff.

EURYDICE. Tell me the names of my mother and brothers and sisters.

FATHER. I don't think that's a good idea. It will make you sad.

EURYDICE. I want to know.

FATHER. It's a long time to be sad.

EURYDICE. I'd rather be sad.

THE STONES. Being sad is not allowed! Act like a stone.

compelling
forceful

Scene 9

(Time shifts. EURYDICE *and her* FATHER *in the string room.)*

EURYDICE. Teach me another.

FATHER. Ostracize.

EURYDICE. What does it mean?

FATHER. To exclude. The Greeks decided who to banish. They wrote the name of the banished person on a white piece of pottery called ostrakon.

EURYDICE. Ostrakon. Another.

FATHER. Peripatetic. From the Greek. It means to walk slowly, speaking of weighty matters, in bare feet.

EURYDICE. Peripatetic: a learned fruit, wandering through the snow. Another.

FATHER. Defunct.

EURYDICE. Defunct.

FATHER. It means dead in a very abrupt way. Not the way I died, which was slowly. But all at once, in cowboy boots.

EURYDICE. Tell me a story of when you were little.

FATHER. Well, there was the time your uncle shot at me with a BB gun and I was mad at him so I swallowed a nail.

Then there was the time I went to a dude ranch and I was riding a horse and I lassoed a car. The lady driving the car got out and spanked me. And your grandmother spanked me, too.

EURYDICE. Remember the Christmas when she gave me a doll and I said, "If I see one more doll I'm going to throw up"?

FATHER. I think Grammy was a little surprised when you said that.

EURYDICE. Tell me a story about your mother.

FATHER. The most vivid recollection I have of Mother was seeing her at parties and in the house playing piano. When she was younger she was extremely animated. She could really play the piano. She could play everything by ear. They called her Flaming Sally.

EURYDICE. I never saw Grammy play the piano.

FATHER. She was never the same after my father died. My father was a very gentle man.

EURYDICE. Tell me a story about your father.

FATHER. My father and I used to duck hunt. He would call up old Frank the night before and ask, "Where are the ducks moving tonight?" Frank was a guide and a farmer. Old Frank, he could really call the ducks. It was hard for me to kill the poor little ducks, but you get caught up in the **fervor** of it. You'd get as many as ten ducks.

If you went over the limit—there were only so many ducks per person—Father would throw the ducks to the side of the creek we were paddling on and make sure there was no game warden. If the warden was gone, he'd run back and get the extra ducks and throw them in the back of the car. My father was never a great **conversationalist**, but he loved to **rhapsodize** about hunting. He would always say, if I ever have to die, it's in a duck pond. And he did.

EURYDICE. There was something I always wanted to ask you. It was—how to do something—or—a story—or someone's name—I forget.

FATHER. Don't worry. You'll remember. There's plenty of time.

Scene 10

(ORPHEUS *writes a letter.*)

ORPHEUS.
   Dear Eurydice,
   I wonder if you miss reading books in the underworld.

(ORPHEUS *holds the* Collected Works of Shakespeare *with a long string attached.*
He drops it slowly to the ground.)

Scene 11

(EURYDICE *holds the* Collected Works of Shakespeare.)

EURYDICE. What is this?
(*She opens it.*
She doesn't understand it.
She throws the book on the ground.)
   What are you?
(*She is wary of it, as though it might bite her.*
She tries to understand the book.
She tries to make the book do something.
To the book:)

What do you do?
What do you DO?!
Are you a thing or a person?
Say something!
I hate you!

(She stands on the book, trying to read it.)

Damn you!

(She throws the book at the STONES.
They duck.)

THE STONES. That is not allowed!

(Drops of water.
Time passes.
The FATHER picks up the book.
He brushes it off.
The FATHER teaches EURYDICE how to read.
She looks over his shoulder as he reads out loud from King Lear.*)*

FATHER. We two alone will sing like birds in the cage.
When thou dost ask my blessing, I'll kneel down
And ask of thee forgiveness; so we'll live,
And pray and sing . . .⁴

Scene 12

(ORPHEUS, with a telephone)

ORPHEUS. For Eurydice—E, U, R, Y—that's right. No, there's no last name.
It's not like that. What? No, I don't know the country. I don't know the
city either. I don't know the street. I don't know—it probably starts with a
vowel. Could you just—would you mind checking please—I would really
appreciate it. You can't enter a name without a city? Why not? Well, thank
you for trying. Wait—miss—it's a special case. She's dead. Well, thank you
for trying. You have a nice day, too.

(He hangs up.)

I'll find you. Don't move!

(He fingers a glow-in-the-dark globe, looking for EURYDICE.)

---

4 **We two alone will . . . pray and sing:** Eurydice's father reads from Act V, Scene iii, the
final scene of *King Lear*. Lear and Cordelia, his youngest daughter and the only one of his three
daughters who has remained loyal to him, are led on stage as prisoners. Lear, now blind and
drifting in and out of madness, fantasizes about how he and Cordelia will live in love together.

Scene 13

(EURYDICE and her FATHER in the string room.)

EURYDICE. Tell me another story of when you were little.

FATHER. Let's see.
There was my first piano recital. I was playing "I Got Rhythm." I played the first few chords and I couldn't remember the rest. I ran out of the room and locked myself in the bathroom.

EURYDICE. Then what happened?

FATHER. Your grandmother pulled me out of the bathroom and made me apologize to everyone in the auditorium. I never played piano after that. But I still know the first four chords—let's see—

(He plays the chords in the air with his hands.)
Da Da *Dee* Da
Da Da *Dee* Da
Da Da *Dee* Da . . .

EURYDICE. What are the words?

FATHER. I can't remember.
Let's see . . .
Da Da *Dee* Da
Da Da *Dee* da . . .

(They both start singing to the tune of "I Got Rhythm":)

FATHER AND EURYDICE
Da da *Dee* Da
Da da *Dee* Da
Da da *Dee* Da
Da dee da da doo dee dee da.

Da da Da da
Da da Da da
Da Da da Da
Da da da . . .

Da da *Dee* Da
Da da *dee* da . . .

THE STONES. WHAT IS THAT NOISE?

LITTLE STONE. Stop singing!

LOUD STONE. STOP SINGING!

BIG STONE. Neither of you can carry a tune.

LITTLE STONE. It's awful.

THE STONES. DEAD PEOPLE CAN'T SING!

EURYDICE. I'm not a very good singer.

FATHER. Neither am I.

THE STONES *(to the* FATHER*)*. Stop singing and go to work!

Scene 14

(The FATHER *leaves for work.*
He takes his briefcase.
He waves to EURYDICE.
She waves back.
She is alone in the string room.
She touches the string.
A child, the Lord of the Underworld, enters on his red tricycle.
Music from a heavy metal band accompanies his entrance.
His clothes and his hat are too small for him.
He stops pedaling at the entrance to the string room.)

CHILD. Knock, knock.

EURYDICE. Who's there?

CHILD. I am Lord of the Underworld.

EURYDICE. Very funny.

CHILD. I am.

EURYDICE. Prove it.

CHILD. I can do chin-ups inside your bones. Close your eyes.

(She closes her eyes.)

EURYDICE. Ow.

CHILD. See?

EURYDICE. What do you want?

CHILD. You're pretty.

EURYDICE. I'm dead.

CHILD. You're pretty.

EURYDICE. You're little.

CHILD. I grow downward like a turnip.

EURYDICE. What do you want?

CHILD. I wanted to see if you were comfortable.

EURYDICE. Comfortable?

CHILD. You're not itchy?

EURYDICE. No.

CHILD. That's good. Sometimes our residents get itchy. Then I scratch them.

EURYDICE. I'm not itchy.

CHILD. What's all this string?

EURYDICE. It's my room.

CHILD. Rooms are not allowed! (*To the* STONES) Tell her.

THE STONES. Rooms are not allowed!

CHILD. Who made your room?

EURYDICE. My father.

CHILD. Fathers are not allowed! Where is he?

EURYDICE. He's at work.

CHILD. We'll have to dip you in the river again and make sure you're good and dunked.

EURYDICE. Please, don't.

CHILD. Oooh—say that again. It's nice.

EURYDICE. Please don't.

CHILD. Say it in my ear.

EURYDICE (*toward his ear*). Please, don't.

CHILD. I like that.

(*A seduction*)

I'll huff and I'll puff and I'll blow your house down!

(*He blows on her face.*)

I mean that in the nicest possible way.

EURYDICE. I have a husband.

CHILD. Husbands are for children. You need a lover. I'll be back.

(*To the* STONES)

See that she's . . . comfortable.

THE STONES. We will!

CHILD. Good-bye.

EURYDICE. Good-bye.

THE STONES. Good-bye.

CHILD. I'm growing. Can you tell? I'm growing!

(*He laughs his hysterical laugh and speeds away on his red tricycle.*)

Scene 15

(A big storm. The sound of rain on a roof.
ORPHEUS *in a rain slicker.*
Shouting above the storm:)

ORPHEUS. If a drop of water enters the soil
at a particular angle, with a particular pitch,
what's to say a man can't ride one note
into the earth like a fireman's pole?

(He puts a bucket on the ground to catch rain falling.
He looks at the rain falling into the bucket.
He tunes his guitar,
trying to make the pitch of each note correspond with the pitch of each water drop.
ORPHEUS *wonders if one particular pitch might lead him to the underworld.*
ORPHEUS *wonders if the pitch he is searching for might correspond to the pitch*
of a drop of rain, as it enters the soil.
A pitch.)

Eurydice—did you hear that?

(Another pitch)

Eurydice? That's the note. That one, right there.

Scene 16

(EURYDICE and her FATHER in the string room.)

EURYDICE. Orpheus never liked words. He had his music. He would get a
funny look on his face and I would say what are you thinking about and
he would always be thinking about music.

If we were in a restaurant, sometimes I would get embarrassed because
Orpheus looked sullen and wouldn't talk to me and I thought people
felt sorry for me. I should have realized that women envied me. Their
husbands talked too much.

But I wanted to talk to him about my notions. I was working on a new
philosophical system. It involved hats.

This is what it is to love an artist: The moon is always rising above your
house. The houses of your neighbors look dull and lacking in moonlight.
But he is always going away from you. Inside his head there is always
something more beautiful.

Orpheus said the mind is a slide ruler. It can fit around anything. Words
can mean anything. Show me your body, he said. It only means one thing.

(She looks at her father, embarrassed for revealing too much.)

Or maybe two or three things. But only one thing at a time.

Scene 17

ORPHEUS.

Eurydice!

Before I go down there, I won't practice my music. Some say practice. But practice is a word invented by cowards. The animals don't have a word for practice. A gazelle does not run for practice. He runs because he is scared or he is hungry. A bird doesn't sing for practice. She sings because she's happy or sad. So I say: store it up. The music sounds better in my head than it does in the world. When songs are pressing against my throat, then, only then, I will go down and sing for the devils and they will cry through their parched throats.

Eurydice, don't kiss a dead man. Their lips look red and tempting but put your tongue in their mouths and it tastes like oatmeal. I know how much you hate oatmeal.

I'm going the way of death.

Here is my plan: tonight, when I go to bed, I will turn off the light and put a straw in my mouth. When I fall asleep, I will crawl through the straw and my breath will push me like a great wind into the darkness and I will sing your name and I will arrive. I have consulted the almanacs, the footstools, and the architects, and everyone agrees. Wait for me.

Love,
Orpheus

Scene 18

EURYDICE. I got a letter. From Orpheus.

FATHER. You sound serious. Nothing wrong I hope.

EURYDICE. No.

FATHER. What did he say?

EURYDICE. He says he's going to come find me.

FATHER. How?

EURYDICE. He's going to sing.

Scene 19

(Darkness.
An unearthly light surrounds ORPHEUS.
He holds a straw up to his lips in slow motion.
He blows into the straw.
The sound of breath.
He disappears.)

Scene 20

(The sound of a knock)

LITTLE STONE. Someone is knocking!

BIG STONE. Who is it?

LOUD STONE. Who is it?

(The sound of three loud knocks, insistent)

THE STONES. NO ONE KNOCKS AT THE DOOR OF THE DEAD!

THIRD MOVEMENT
Scene 1

(ORPHEUS stands at the gates of hell.
He opens his mouth.
He looks like he's singing, but he's silent.
Music surrounds him.
The melody ORPHEUS hummed in the first scene, repeated over and over again.
Raspberries, peaches and plums drop from the ceiling into the River.
ORPHEUS keeps singing.
The STONES weep. They look at their tears, bewildered.
ORPHEUS keeps singing. The child comes out of a trapdoor.)

CHILD. Who are you?

ORHPEUS. I am Orpheus.

CHILD. I am Lord of the Underworld.

ORHPEUS. But you're so young!

CHILD. Don't be rude.

ORHPEUS. Sorry.
   Did you like my music?

CHILD. No. I prefer happy music with a nice beat.

ORHPEUS. Oh.

CHILD. You've come for Eurydice.

ORHPEUS. Yes!

CHILD. And you thought singing would get you through the gates of hell.

ORHPEUS. See here. I want my wife. What do I have to do?

CHILD. You'll have to do more than sing.

ORHPEUS. I'm not sure what you mean, sir.

CHILD. Start walking home. Your wife just might be on the road behind you. We make it real nice here. So people want to stick around. As you walk, keep your eyes facing front. If you look back at her—poof! She's gone.

ORHPEUS. I can't look at her?

CHILD. No.

ORHPEUS. Why?

CHILD. Because.

ORHPEUS. Because?

CHILD. Because. Do you understand me?

ORHPEUS. I look straight ahead. That's all?

CHILD. Yes.

ORHPEUS. That's easy.

CHILD. Good.

(The CHILD smiles. He exits.)

Scene 2

(EURYDICE and her FATHER)

EURYDICE. I hear him at the gates! That's his music!

He's come to save me!

FATHER. Do you want to go with him?

EURYDICE. Yes, of course!

Oh—you'll be lonely, won't you?

FATHER. No, no. You should go to your husband. You should have grandchildren. You'll all come down and meet me one day.

EURYDICE. Are you sure?

FATHER. You should love your family until the grapes grow dust on their purple faces.

I'll take you to him.

EURYDICE. Now?

FATHER. It's for the best.

(He takes her arm.
They progress, arm in arm, as at a wedding.
Wedding music.
They are solemn and glad.
They walk.
They see ORPHEUS *up ahead.)*

Is that him?

EURYDICE. Yes—I think so—

FATHER. His shoulders aren't very broad. Can he take care of you?

(EURYDICE nods.)

Are you sure?

EURYDICE. Yes.

FATHER. There's one thing you need to know. If he turns around and sees you, you'll die a second death. Those are the rules. So step quietly. And don't cry out.

EURYDICE. I won't.

FATHER. Good-bye.

(They embrace.)

EURYDICE. I'll come back to you. I seem to keep dying.

FATHER. Don't let them dip you in the River too long, the second time. Hold your breath.

EURYDICE. I'll look for a tree.

FATHER. I'll write you letters.

EURYDICE. Where will I find them?

FATHER. I don't know yet. I'll think of something. Good-bye, Eurydice.

EURYDICE. Good-bye.

(They move away.
The FATHER waves.
She waves back,
as though on an old steamer ship.
The FATHER exits.
EURYDICE takes a deep breath.
She takes a big step forward toward the audience, on an unseen gangplank.

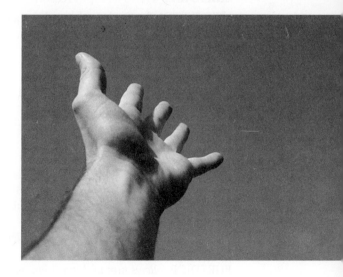

She is brave.
She takes another step forward.
She hesitates.
She is all of a sudden not so brave.
She is afraid.
She looks back.
She turns in the direction of her father,
her back to the audience.
He's out of sight.)

    Wait, come back!

LITTLE STONE. You can't go back now, Eurydice.

LOUD STONE. Face forward!

BIG STONE. Keep walking.

EURYDICE. I'm afraid!

LOUD STONE. Your husband is waiting for you, Eurydice.

EURYDICE. I don't recognize him! That's a stranger!

LITTLE STONE. Go on. It's him.

EURYDICE. I want to go home! I want my father!

LOUD STONE. You're all grown-up now. You have a husband.

THE STONES. TURN AROUND!

EURYDICE. Why?

THE STONES. BECAUSE!

EURYDICE. That's a stupid reason.

LITTLE STONE. Orpheus braved the gates of hell to find you.

LOUD STONE. He played the saddest music.

BIG STONE. Even we—

THE STONES. The stones—

LITTLE STONE. cried when we heard it.

(EURYDICE turns slowly, facing front.)

EURYDICE. That's Orpheus?

THE STONES. Yes, that's him!

EURYDICE. Where's his music?

THE STONES. It's in your head.

(ORPHEUS walks slowly, in a straight line, with the focus of a tightrope walker.
EURYDICE moves to follow him. She follows him, several steps behind.
THEY WALK.
EURYDICE follows him with precision, one step for every step he takes.
She makes a decision.

She increases her pace.
She takes two steps for every step that ORPHEUS takes.
She catches up to him.)

EURYDICE. Orpheus?
(He turns toward her, startled.
ORPHEUS *looks at* EURYDICE.
EURYDICE *looks at* ORPHEUS.
The world falls away.)

ORPHEUS. You startled me.

(A small sound—ping.
They turn their faces away from each other, matter-of-fact, compelled.
The lights turn blue.)

EURYDICE. I'm sorry.

ORPHEUS. Why?

EURYDICE. I don't know.

(Syncopated:)

ORPHEUS.

  You always clapped your hands
  on the third beat
  you couldn't wait for the fourth.
  Remember—
  I tried to teach you—

  you were always one step ahead
  of the music
  your sense of rhythm—
  it was—off—

EURYDICE.

  I could never spell the word
  rhythm—
  it is such a difficult
  word to spell—
  r—y—no—there's an H in
  it—
  somewhere—a breath—
  rhy—rhy—
  rhy—

ORPHEUS. I would say clap on the downbeat—
  no, the downbeat—
  It's dangerous not
  to have a sense of rhythm.
  You *lose* things when you can't
  keep a simple beat—
  why'd you have to say my name—
  Eurydice—

EURYDICE. I'm sorry.

ORPHEUS. I know we used to fight—
  it seems so silly now—if—

EURYDICE. If ifs and ands were pots and pans
  there'd be no need for tinkers—[5]

---

5 **If ifs and ands . . . tinkers:** from an old nursery rhyme meaning: Just wishing for
  something doesn't make it happen

ORPHEUS. Why?

(They begin walking away from each other on extensive unseen boardwalks, their figures long shadows, looking straight ahead.)

EURYDICE. If ifs and ands were pots and pans
  there'd be no need for tinkers—

ORPHEUS. Eurydice—

EURYDICE. I think I see the gates.
  The stones—the boat—
  it looks familiar—the stones look happy to see me—

ORPHEUS. Don't look—

EURYDICE. Wow! That's the happiest I've ever seen them!

(Syncopated:)

ORPHEUS.	**EURYDICE.**
Think of things we did	Everything is so gray—
	it looks familiar—
	like home—
we went ice-skating—	our house was—
	gray—with a red door—
I wore a red sweater—	we had two cats
	and two dogs
	and two fish
	that died—

ORPHEUS. Will you talk to me!

EURYDICE. The train looks like
  the opposite of a train—

ORPHEUS. Eurydice!
  WE'VE KNOWN EACH OTHER FOR CENTURIES!
  I want to **reminisce**!
  Remember when you wanted your name in a song
  so I put your name in a song—
  When I played my music
  at the gates of hell
  I was singing your name
  over and over and over again.
  Eurydice.

(He grows quiet.
They walk away from each other on extended lines until they are out of sight.)

reminisce
remember;
recollect

Scene 3

THE STONES. Finally.
  Some peace.
LOUD STONE. And quiet.
THE STONES. Like the old days.
  No music.
  No conversation.
  How about that.

(A pause)

FATHER. With Eurydice gone it will be a second death for me.

LOUD STONE. Oh, please, sir—

BIG STONE. We're tired.

FATHER. Do you understand the love a father has for his daughter?

LOUD STONE. Love is a big, funny word.

BIG STONE. Dead people should be seen and not heard.

(The FATHER looks at the STONES.
He looks at the string room.
He dismantles the string room, matter-of-fact.
There's nothing else to do.
This can take time.
It takes time to dismantle a room made of string.
Music.
He sits down in what used to be the string room.)

FATHER. How does a person remember to forget.
  It's difficult.

LOUD STONE. It's not difficult.

LITTLE STONE. We told you how it works.

LOUD STONE. Dip yourself in the river.

LITTLE STONE. Dip yourself in the river.

BIG STONE. Dip yourself in the river.

FATHER. I need directions.

LOUD STONE. That's ridiculous.

BIG STONE. There are no directions.

(A pause. The FATHER thinks.)

FATHER. I remember.
  Take Tri-State South 294—
  to Route 88 West.
  Take Route 88 West to Route 80.
  You'll go over a bridge.

Go three miles and you'll come
to the exit for Middle Road.
Proceed three to four miles.
Duck Creek Park will be on the right.
Take a left on Fernwood Avenue.
Continue straight on Fernwood past
two intersections.
Go straight.
Fernwood will curve to the right leading
you to Forest Road.
Take a left on Forest Road.
Go two blocks.
Pass the first entrance to the alley on the right.
Take the second entrance.
You'll go about a hundred yards.
A red brick house will
be on the right.
Look for Illinois license plates.

Go inside the house.
In the living room,
look out the window.
You'll see the lights on the Mississippi River.
Take off your shoes.
Walk down the hill.
You'll pass a tree good for climbing on the right.
Cross the road.
Watch for traffic.
Cross the train tracks.
Catfish are sleeping in the mud, on your left.
Roll up your jeans.
Count to ten.
Put your feet in the river
and swim.

(He dips himself in the river.
A small metallic sound of forgetfulness—ping. The sound of water.
He lies down on the ground, curled up, asleep.)

(EURYDICE returns and sees that her string room is gone.)

EURYDICE. Where's my room?

(The STONES are silent.)

   (To the STONES) WHERE IS MY ROOM?

   Answer me!

LITTLE STONE. It's none of our business.

LOUD STONE. What are you doing here?

BIG STONE. You should be with your husband.

LOUD STONE. Up there.

EURYDICE. Where's my father?

(*The* STONES *point to the* FATHER.)

(*To the* STONES) Why is he sleeping?

(*The* STONES *shrug their shoulders.*)

(*To her father*) I've come back!

LOUD STONE. He can't hear you.

LITTLE STONE. It's too late.

EURYDICE. What are you talking about?

BIG STONE. He dipped himself in
  the River.

EURYDICE. My father did not dip himself in the River.

THE STONES. He did!
  We saw him!

LOUD STONE. He wanted some peace and quiet.

EURYDICE (*to the* STONES). HE DID NOT!

  (*To her father*) Listen. I'll teach you the words. Then we'll know each other
  again. Ready? We'll start with my name. Eurydice. E, U, R, Y . . .

BIG STONE. He can't hear you.

LOUD STONE. He can't see you.

LITTLE STONE. He can't remember you.

EURYDICE (*to the* STONES). I hate you! I've always hated you!
  Shut up! Shut up! Shut up!

(*To her father*) Listen. I'll tell you a story.

LITTLE STONE. He can't hear you.

BIG STONE. He can't see you.

LOUD STONE. He can't remember you.

LITTLE STONE. Try speaking the language of stones.

LOUD STONE. It's a very quiet language.
  Like if the pores in your
  face opened up and wanted to talk.

EURYDICE. Stone.
  Rock.
  Tree. Rock. Stone.

(*It doesn't work.*
She holds her father.)

LOUD STONE. Didn't you already mourn for your father, young lady?

LITTLE STONE. Some things should be left well enough alone.

BIG STONE. To mourn twice is excessive.

LITTLE STONE. To mourn three times a sin.

LOUD STONE. Life is like a good meal.

BIG STONE. Only gluttons want more food when they finish their helping.

LITTLE STONE. Learn to be more moderate.

morbid
gloomy

BIG STONE. It's weird for a dead person to be **morbid**.

LITTLE STONE. We don't like to watch it!

LOUD STONE. We don't like to see it!

BIG STONE. It makes me uncomfortable.

(EURYDICE *cries.*)

THE STONES. Don't cry!
   Don't cry!

BIG STONE. Learn the art of keeping busy!

EURYDICE. IT'S HARD TO KEEP BUSY WHEN YOU'RE DEAD!

THE STONES. It is not hard!
   We keep busy
   And we like it
   We're busy busy busy stones
   Watch us work
   Keeping still
   Keeping quiet
   It's hard work
   To be a stone
   No time for crying.
   No no no!

EURYDICE. I HATE YOU! I'VE ALWAYS HATED YOU!

(*She runs toward the* STONES *and tries to hit them.*)

THE STONES. Go ahead.
   Try to hit us.

LITTLE STONE. You'll hurt your fist.

BIG STONE. You'll break your hand.

THE STONES. Ha ha ha!

(*Enter the* CHILD.
He has grown.
He is now at least ten feet tall.
His voice sounds suspiciously like the NASTY INTERESTING MAN'S.)

CHILD. Is there a problem here?

THE STONES. No, sir.

CHILD (to EURYDICE). You chose to stay with us, huh? Good.

(*He looks her over.*)

Perhaps to be my bride?

EURYDICE. I told you. You're too young.

CHILD. I'll be the judge of that.

I've grown.

EURYDICE. Yes—I see that.

CHILD. I'm ready to be a man now. I'm ready—to be—a man.

EURYDICE. Please. Leave me alone.

CHILD. I'll have them start preparing the satins and silks. You can't refuse me.
I've made my choice. I'm ready to be a man now.

EURYDICE. Can I have a moment to prepare myself?

CHILD. Don't be long. The wedding songs are already being written. They're
very quiet. **Inaudible**, you might say. A dirt-filled orchestra for my bride.
Don't trouble the songs with your music, I say. A song is two dead bodies
rubbing under the covers to keep warm.

inaudible
not able to
be heard

(*He exits.*)

THE STONES. Well, well, well!

LITTLE STONE. You had better prepare yourself.

EURYDICE. There is nothing to prepare.

BIG STONE. You had better comb your hair.

LOUD STONE. You had better find a veil.

EURYDICE. I don't need a veil. I need a pen!

LITTLE STONE. Pens are forbidden here.

EURYDICE. I need a pencil then.

LOUD STONE. Pencils, too.

EURYDICE. Damn you! I'll dip you in the River!

BIG STONE. Too late, too late!

EURYDICE. There must be a pen. There are. There must be.

(*She remembers the pen and paper in the breast pocket of her father's coat. She takes
them out.*
She holds the pen up to show the STONES.
She gloats.)

A pen.

(*She writes a letter:*)

Dear Orpheus,

I'm sorry. I don't know what came over me. I was afraid. I'm not worthy of you. But I still love you, I think. Don't try to find me again. You would be lonely for music. I want you to be happy. I want you to marry again. I am going to write out instructions for your next wife.

To My Husband's Next Wife:
Be gentle.
Be sure to comb his hair when it's wet.
Do not fail to notice
that his face flushes pink
like a bride's
when you kiss him.
Give him lots to eat.
He forgets to eat and he gets cranky.

When he's sad,
kiss his forehead and I will thank you.
Because he is a young prince
and his robes are too heavy on him.
His crown falls down
around his ears.
I'll give this letter to a worm. I hope he finds you.

Love,
Eurydice

(She puts the letter on the ground.
She dips herself in the River.
A small metallic sound of forgetfulness—ping.
The sound of water.
She lies down next to her father, as though asleep.)

(The sound of an elevator—ding.
ORPHEUS appears in the elevator.
He sees EURYDICE.
He is happy.
The elevator starts raining on ORPHEUS.
He forgets.
He steps out of the elevator.
He sees the letter on the ground.
He picks it up. He scrutinizes it.
He can't read it.
He stands on it.
He closes his eyes.
The sound of water.
Then silence.)

THE END

AFTER YOU READ

Eurydice

Think and Discuss

1. What causes Orpheus to turn and look back at Eurydice?

2. What does the inclusion of Eurydice's father add to Ruhl's version of the myth?

3. At her wedding party, Eurydice says, "a wedding is for a father and a daughter. They stop being married to each other on that day." How do these lines **foreshadow** the central **conflict** in the play?

4. In what ways does the **character** of Eurydice in this play differ from Eurydice in Betty Bonham Lies' retelling of the myth (pages 531–536)? Explain.

5. In two places in Scene 2 of the Third Movement, the lines for Orpheus and Eurydice are set side by side on the page. What does this suggest to the actors performing the play? What does this indicate to the reader or viewer about Orpheus and Eurydice?

6. Create a chart like the one below and use it to compare the important characters in Betty Bonham Lies' retelling of the myth with the characters in Sarah Ruhl's play. List each character. Then write a brief description of the character. If a character doesn't exist in one version, leave the space blank.

Character	Orpheus and Eurydice	Eurydice
Orpheus		
Eurydice		
Hymen		
Nasty Interesting Man		
Eurydice's Father		
Hades / Lord of the Underworld		

Write to Understand: Focused Freewriting

Explore through focused freewriting Sarah Ruhl's re-invention of the Orpheus and Eurydice myth in her play *Eurydice*. Look over the graphic organizer you completed. In your Writer's Notebook, begin writing freely about what you recorded in your organizer. Try to answer the question: "How has Ruhl re-invented the story of Orpheus and Eurydice?" Use the information about the characters you included in the organizer to help answer that question. Keep your pen moving for at least 10 minutes.

Writers on Writing

BEFORE YOU READ

Introduction to
We Goddesses: Athena, Aphrodite, Hera

Meet the Author: Doris Orgel

From the time she was a young child, Doris Orgel (born 1929) wanted to be a writer. She has vivid memories from Vienna, Austria, where she lived until she was nine years old, of imagining herself to be a duck or an elephant. She writes, "Imagining how it might feel to be an elephant or duck is thinking oneself into other lives. And isn't that what writers do?" In high school she loved reading the ancient myths of the goddesses. That interest returned to her later in life when she wrote the book from which the following excerpt is taken, *We Goddesses: Athena, Aphrodite, Hera*. In this book, each goddess tells her story in her own voice, from her own point of view. Orgel has also written three other books about goddesses as well as a novel, *The Devil in Vienna*, about her childhood home.

Build Background: Gender Differences in Ancient Greek Culture

As in many ancient cultures, men and women in ancient Greece lived very different kinds of lives, with very different opportunities. Boys from wealthy families, for example, were educated in music, sports, philosophy, and military skills. They usually did not marry until they were in their 30s. Girls, in contrast, learned only the domestic arts—cooking, making clothing, and taking care of a home. Girls often married at age 15 and went to live in the house of their husband's family. They were not permitted in public places.

Yet the goddesses in Greek mythology, unlike the real women in ancient Greece, were much revered. In the introduction to her book *We Goddesses*, Orgel looks for a way to understand the mixed views about females.

As you read, think about the following:

• What can people today learn by reading myths about the gods and goddesses?

• In what ways does your gender influence your opportunities and expectations?

PALLAS ATHENA, Franz von Stuck, 1898

Introduction to
We Goddesses: Athena, Aphrodite, Hera

DORIS ORGEL

Introduction to
WE GODDESSES: ATHENA, APHRODITE, HERA

Doris Orgel

HOW AND WHY I WROTE THIS BOOK

First I met with three young girls I knew: Cara, Beth, and Rachel (not their real names), ages eleven, twelve, thirteen. I wanted to discover how they felt about mythology.

Cara started: "It bugs me when authors use old-fashioned language just to give you the idea that the myths are from ancient times."

Beth and Rachel agreed that the writing should sound natural, not stuffy, but not slangy, either.

I asked them why they thought Greek myths have been retold so often and still are popular.

Because they're exciting, with lots of action and few boring stretches when nothing's happening, my consultants said.

We talked about goddesses. They thought Athena[1] was awesome; Aphrodite,[2] amazing; and they did *not* like Hera.[3]

"But it's unfair that *she* gets blamed for being the possessive, jealous wife, and Zeus[4] gets away with being unfaithful, having lots of love affairs, and no one blames him," Rachel said.

This led to a lively discussion about attitudes toward women, then and now.

Toward the end of our meeting I asked, "What do you like *best* about myths?"

"That anything can happen," Cara answered. "Like, Zeus can be a cuckoo, and a horse can fly. It's cool. You never know what's coming next."

---

1 **Athena:** an armed warrior goddess and protector of Odysseus

2 **Aphrodite:** goddess of love and beauty

3 **Hera:** queen of all the gods, wife of Zeus and mother of Heracles (Hercules)

4 **Zeus:** the supreme ruler of the gods on Mount Olympus

Next I asked, "What do you like *least*?"

"That anything can happen," Cara answered with equal conviction. "Because it can't, in real life. So you can't relate to the characters it happens to."

The others nodded.

Rachel said, "I mind that myths don't let you in on the characters' private thoughts. So you don't get to know them that well."

"And you can't get as emotionally involved with them as you do with characters in novels," Beth added.

"Yes, but still, I love goddess stories," Cara said. "They give me a special feeling, I mean, a kind of *glow* . . . ."

I'd taken notes, but hardly needed them. My consultants' comments stayed clearly in my mind, and helped me as I worked.

In my reading—Homer, Hesiod, Virgil, Ovid,[5] and later myth retellings— I'd come across more incidents about Athena, Aphrodite, and Hera than I could ever possibly retell. Besides, the ancient sources often disagree. (For instance, Hesiod's Aphrodite was born of sea foam, but in Homer she's the daughter of Zeus and the little-known goddess Dione!) Which ones should I choose?

I mulled them over, gave them room in my imagination.

Eventually certain incidents *felt* right. Then my task was to combine the incidents **sequentially** into story order (which required groping my way through the blurry timelessness of myth to try and sort out what happened when); and to build three separate, but connected narratives.

My hope was that, if I worked well, each goddess would reveal herself in **undiminished** splendor, with her personality as fascinating now as it was in classic times.

Working well meant keeping faith with my sources: staying true to Hesiod and Homer (who "wrote the book" on ancient Greek beliefs), even while I made the leaps required to stir the emotions and imaginations of present-day young readers.

All along, I listened for Athena's voice, and Aphrodite's, Hera's, in the way that writers listen, as I'd always listened before when trying to get inside fictional characters' heads. It had worked with *human* characters. But these were goddesses. . . . That gave me pause. It seemed a nervy undertaking. And was it even nervier to write their stories in *their* voices?

sequentially
in a sequence or order

undiminished
not lessened

---

5 **Hesiod, Virgil, Ovid:** Hesiod was a Greek poet who lived about the same time as Homer. Virgil and Ovid were Latin poets. All are sources of stories about the gods and goddesses.

Introduction to *We Goddesses: Athena, Aphrodite, Hera*   587

Every generation can only tell the ancient myths anew out of its own needs and concerns, and in its own writing styles. Hesiod and Homer (whom nobody called nervy!) claimed to be writing down *verbatim*[6] what the Muses (goddesses!) personally sang into their human ears. And Virgil claimed it too, eight hundred years later, when hardly anyone believed in the Muses anymore, at least not literally. I thought about all that, and gave myself permission to go ahead and give my goddesses their say.

When I was eleven or twelve I fell in love with everybody up on Mount Olympus, especially the goddesses. Athena lent me courage to be brainy, although I was a girl. Aphrodite, queen of love, romance, and everything I lay awake nights trying to imagine, thrilled me to the core. Hera I disliked, of course. The myths I read all said she was a shrew.[7] And no girl back then (it was long ago) would have thought to argue, Yes, but Zeus was bad to her. . . .

Anyway, I wanted, needed, *craved* more goddess stories. I hung around the library, hoping every day some myth book I hadn't read yet would turn up. And I wished its title would be *Goddesses of Ancient Greece*.

That never happened. All the goddess stories—too few! too short!—were tucked away in books with male *Gods-and-Heroes* kinds of titles. We girls got the message: Females, even goddesses, don't rate titles of their own.

That's how it was. That's how it stayed. To the best of my knowledge, this is the only book exclusively about the goddesses of ancient Greece.

I wrote my book to fill this need, and because, in Cara's words, "I still love goddess stories. They give me a special feeling, I mean, a kind of *glow*."

THE PARADOX:
EXALTED GODDESSES, DEBASED WOMEN

Paradox—I looked it up: "From Greek, *paradoxos*, conflicting with expectation," my dictionary says.

Ancient Greece honored its goddesses and treated women not much better than slaves—yes, that does conflict with expectation.

It is a glaring contradiction.

Yet, classics scholars writing earlier than 1980 didn't even mention, much less question, it.

---

6 **verbatim:** word for word

7 **shrew:** a scolding, complaining woman

Bronze head of a goddess, probably Aphrodite, Hellenistic Greek period, 4th to 1st century B.C.

Introduction to *We Goddesses: Athena, Aphrodite, Hera*.   589

Scholars writing since the eighties give two explanations. First, the ancient Greeks made a categorical distinction[8] between goddesses and mortal females, considering them as unrelated species. You may not find this too convincing, especially when you look at any classical goddess statue and note how very woman-like or young-girl-like, only still more beautiful, it is.

Second, some **anthropologists** and mythologists[9] believe that powerful goddesses are **remnants** of a much more ancient culture that was ruled by women and in which men were oppressed. Later men rebelled and took over. According to this theory, *misogyny* (mis-AH-jin-ee—hating and **debasing** women) conceals men's deep-rooted fear that women might rise up and take men's power away.

This theory has never been proved.

Someday someone—maybe you—will resolve the paradox. In the meantime, here is what it says to me:

How women were treated in ancient Greece tells only half, the bad half, of the story. The other half, the shining half about the goddesses, holds out this vision: Women—the mortal counterparts of goddesses—and men embracing as equals; misogyny fading into the dim past.

anthropologists
people who study the origins and cultures of humans

remnants
leftovers; remains

debasing
lowering the value of

---

8 **categorical distinction:** a way of looking at two things that separates them into different categories

9 **mythologists:** people who study myths

AFTER YOU READ

Introduction to
We Goddesses: Athena, Aphrodite, Hera

Think and Discuss

1. What was Orgel's **purpose** for writing about these goddesses?

2. Who is Orgel's **audience**? How well do you think Orgel reaches her intended audience?

3. How does Orgel explain the apparent paradox of "exalted goddesses" and "debased women"?

4. All the selections in this unit draw on ancient myths. Which selection made the most sense to you, or communicated in the strongest way? In your Writer's Notebook, make a graphic organizer like the one below and use it to gather your thoughts.

Literary Work	Type	Use of Myth	What I Learned
Odyssey	epic poem	gods are part of the story and play an active role in people's lives	there were lots of good fights, and it gave me an outlook on how the ancient Greeks saw things
Ithaka			
Siren Song			
Ancient Gesture			
The Penelopiad			
Orpheus and Eurydice			
Eurydice			
We Goddesses			

Write to Understand: Retelling the Story

The *Odyssey* has inspired many other works. James Joyce uses the structure of the *Odyssey* for his book *Ulysses* but sets it in Ireland in the early 1900s. The movie *O Brother, Where Art Thou?* (released in 2000) sets The *Odyssey* in the rural South during the Depression. Look over your graphic organizer and think about the myths and treatments of them that meant the most to you. Choose one of the stories and retell it, but set it in a fresh time and place to bring out the special meaning it has for you.

A Writer's WORKSHOP

SUMMARY

You provide summaries in everyday life all the time—in response to questions about the plot of a movie, for example, or about what happened during your day. Summarizing requires you to highlight only the most important points and know what to leave out. For this reason, the ability to write summaries also sharpens your ability to understand as you read. Writing summaries of some of the selections in this unit will help you understand and remember what you have read.

Prewriting

WORKING IN GROUPS

Work in four small groups. Each group will summarize one of the following: *Odyssey* Part I, *Odyssey* Part II, *Odyssey* Part III, or *The Penelopiad*.

COOPERATIVE LEARNING: REVIEWING TRAITS OF GOOD SUMMARIES

With your group, discuss what makes a summary effective. Remember that a summary is not a line-by-line paraphrasing. Instead, a good summary digests the most important meaning and presents it in original words. Summaries are shorter than the original, and they do not include as many details. After your discussion, decide how to divide up the task of summarizing your group's selection.

IDENTIFYING THE MAIN IDEA

If your group is summarizing part of the *Odyssey*, you will probably want to work section by section. That is, read a group of lines and then stop to summarize when you come to a space before the next group of lines. If your group is summarizing *The Penelopiad*, you will probably want to work paragraph by paragraph, at least at first. Here is one strategy for finding the main idea or event.

- Ask yourself, "What happens in the section I just read?" Answer that question in one sentence.

- Ignore descriptive details that are not necessary to the plot.

- Create a general, overall action instead of repeating its several smaller parts. For example, instead of saying, "In the land of the Cyclopes, Odysseus's men suggest that they should just take cheeses, put them on board the ship, come back, let the livestock out, drive the livestock onto the boat, and set sail," you can substitute a more general action: "Odysseus's men urge him to take what they can from the land of the Cyclopes and make a getaway."

TAKING NOTES

Re-read the selection while you take notes. In your notes, record only the most important points. For example:

Original	Summary notes
"What shall I say first? What shall I keep until the end? The gods have tried me in a thousand ways. But first my name: let that be known to you, and if I pull away from pitiless death, friendship will bind us, though my land lies far. I am Laertes' son, Odysseus. Men hold me formidable for guile in peace and war: this fame has gone abroad to the sky's rim. My home is on the peaked sea-mark of Ithaca under Mount Neion's wind-blown robe of leaves, in sight of other islands—Dulichium, Same, wooded Zacynthus—Ithaca being most lofty in that coastal sea, and northwest, while the rest lie east and south. A rocky isle but good for a boy's training; I shall not see on earth a place more dear, though I have been detained long by Calypso, loveliest among goddesses, who held me in her smooth caves, to be her heart's delight, as Circe of Aeaea, the enchantress, desired me, and detained me in her hall. But in my heart I never gave consent. Where shall a man find sweetness to surpass his own home and his parents? In far lands he shall not, though he find a house of gold.	<ul><li>introduces himself as the son of Laertes and a man known for his skills in peace and war</li></ul><ul><li>says that he is from Ithaca, which he holds dear</li></ul> <ul><li>mentions he was detained by Calypso but that he always thought of home, which he values more than "a house of gold"</li></ul>

Drafting

Use your own or your group's notes to draft your summary or your portion of it. Remember to use your own words and to make the summary shorter than the original. When you finish your first draft, go back over it and trim away unnecessary detail.

Revising and Editing

A good summary is lively to read even without a lot of details. One way to achieve a lively summary is to choose strong, active verbs and clear nouns and adjectives.

USING A WORD PROCESSOR

If you highlight a word in your document and then either right-click or go to the Tools menu and select "Thesaurus," you will be able to find synonyms. The right-click menu will contain synonyms or let you link to the Thesaurus. In the Tools menu, if you choose "Language," you will see another menu that includes "Thesaurus." (Tools→Language→Thesaurus) You can check the synonyms or thesaurus for ideas for making your word choice as strong as possible.

READING WITH AN EDITOR'S EYE

When you summarize literary works, you use the "literary present" tense. That just means that you relate the events as if they were happening at the moment. When you are telling the events in the order they happened, you use the simple present tense.

SIMPLE PRESENT   Penelope *finds* herself in the Underworld and *feels* she can at last tell her story.

However, in the course of summarizing, you may need to refer to events that happened before the beginning of the part you are summarizing. In that case you may need to use a different tense.

PAST PERFECT   Odysseus had always *been* so plausible.

As you edit your summary, check to make sure that the sentences telling the main narrative events are in the simple present tense. Make sure any other tenses are used for a clear reason.

USING A CHECKLIST

When you are satisfied with your word choice and use of tenses, use the Six-Trait checklist on the next page to improve your summary even more.

Six Traits of Writing: Summary

Content and Ideas
- the main ideas and main plot events are included
- many details from the original have been left out

Organization
- the summary has a clear introduction that states the author of the work, title, and, if appropriate, the section of the work
- the ideas in the body are presented in a logical order; if you are summarizing a play or narrative, chances are you summary will be organized in chronological order

Voice or Style
- the voice is clearly distinct from the original author's voice
- the voice is more formal than speech

Word Choice
- the writer uses original words
- key quotes from the original may be used sparingly
- words are strong and active

Sentence Fluency
- sentences are complete
- sentence length and sentence beginnings are varied and purposeful
- transitions between ideas and sections are clear and smooth

Conventions
- in a summary of a literary work, the present tense is used (for example, "Odysseus returns to Ithaca.")
- the essay is free of errors in usage, spelling, capitalization, and punctuation
- works referred to are presented according to the style required by the school (for example, titles of short stories are in quotes)

USING A WORD PROCESSOR

When all groups have assembled their final summaries, make a "Reader's Digest," a booklet of all the summaries, using a word processor. Think of a name for the booklet, and design a cover and a table of contents. Print out and circulate the completed booklet so everyone in class can read it, or upload it to the school's Web site.

The Dark Side

"... What I felt was a—a mental chill—a sort of sudden dread."

Richard Connell, from
"The Most Dangerous Game"

BEFORE YOU READ

The Most Dangerous Game

Meet the Author: Richard Connell

Richard Connell (1893-1949) began writing stories and reporting on baseball games for the Poughkeepsie *News-Press* when he was ten years old. By the time he finished high school he was working as the paper's city editor. Connell wrote no matter what else he was doing. He contributed to the *Harvard Lampoon* in college, wrote news articles in the army during World War I, and wrote advertising copy until he sold his first short story. He carved out a successful career as a screenwriter and was nominated for an Academy Award for his script for the film *Meet John Doe*. Still, he remains best known for his short stories, especially "The Most Dangerous Game."

Build Background: Weak and Strong, Right and Wrong

The "survival of the fittest" has become an accepted part of our language and outlook since Charles Darwin's published his 1859 book, *On the Origin of Species*. His theory of natural selection proposed that, by natural law, the strong survive and the weak perish in competition with the strong. Hunters justify their sport with this sense of natural "superiority" to non-reasoning creatures; dictators have justified unthinkable crimes using a warped interpretation of Darwin's theory. Right and wrong, misinterpreted in this way, seem no longer to exist.

Think about the questions below as you read "The Most Dangerous Game."

- Do you think the strong have an obligation to protect the weak? Think of some examples to help you answer this question.

- What qualities separate humans from animals?

STORM, Henri Rosseau, 1891

The Most Dangerous Game

RICHARD CONNELL

THE MOST DANGEROUS GAME

Richard Connell

"**Off** there to the right—somewhere—is a large island," said Whitney. "It's rather a mystery—"

"What island is it?" Rainsford asked.

"The old charts call it 'Ship-Trap Island,'" Whitney replied. "A suggestive name, isn't it? Sailors have a curious dread of the place. I don't know why. Some superstition—"

"Can't see it," remarked Rainsford, trying to peer through the dank tropical night that was **palpable** as it pressed its thick warm blackness in upon the yacht.

palpable
capable of being felt

"You've good eyes," said Whitney, with a laugh, "and I've seen you pick off a moose moving in the brown fall bush at four hundred yards, but even you can't see four miles or so through a moonless Caribbean night."

"Nor four yards," admitted Rainsford. "Ugh! It's like moist black velvet."

"It will be light enough in Rio," promised Whitney. "We should make it in a few days. I hope the jaguar guns have come from Purdey's. We should have some good hunting up the Amazon. Great sport, hunting."

"The best sport in the world," agreed Rainsford.

"For the hunter," amended Whitney. "Not for the jaguar."

"Don't talk rot, Whitney," said Rainsford. "You're a big-game hunter, not a philosopher. Who cares how a jaguar feels?"

"Perhaps the jaguar does," observed Whitney.

"Bah! They've no understanding."

"Even so, I rather think they understand one thing at least—fear. The fear of pain and the fear of death."

"Nonsense," and Rainsford laughed. "This hot weather is making you soft, Whitney. Be a realist. The world is made up of two classes—the hunters and the hunted. Luckily, you and I are hunters. Do you think we've passed that island yet?"

"I can't tell in the dark. I hope so."

"Why?" asked Rainsford.

"The place has a reputation—a bad one."

"Cannibals?" suggested Rainsford.

"Hardly. Even cannibals wouldn't live in such a God-forsaken place. But it's gotten into sailor lore, somehow. Didn't you notice that the crew's nerves seem a bit jumpy today?"

"They were a bit strange, now you mention it. Even Captain Nielsen—"

"Yes, even that tough-minded old Swede, who'd go up to the devil himself and ask him for a light. Those fishy blue eyes held a look I never saw there before. All I could get out of him was, 'This place has an evil name among seafaring men, sir.' Then he said to me, very gravely, 'Don't you feel anything?'—as if the air about us was actually poisonous. Now, you mustn't laugh when I tell you this—I did feel something like a sudden chill.

"There was no breeze. The sea was as flat as a plate-glass window. We were drawing near the island then. What I felt was a—a mental chill—a sort of sudden dread."

"Pure imagination," said Rainsford. "One superstitious sailor can taint the whole ship's company with his fear."

"Maybe. But sometimes I think sailors have an extra sense that tells them when they are in danger. Sometimes I think evil is a **tangible** thing—with wave lengths, just as sound and light have. An evil place can, so to speak, broadcast vibrations of evil. Anyhow, I'm glad we're getting out of this zone. Well, I think I'll turn in now, Rainsford."

"I'm not sleepy," said Rainsford. "I'm going to smoke another pipe up on the afterdeck."[1]

"Good night, then, Rainsford. See you at breakfast."

"Right. Good night, Whitney."

There was no sound in the night as Rainsford sat there but for the muffled throb of the engine that drove the yacht swiftly through the darkness, and the swish and ripple of the wash of the propeller.

Rainsford, reclining in a steamer chair, **indolently** puffed on his favorite **brier.** The sensuous drowsiness of the night was on him. "It's so dark," he thought, "that I could sleep without closing my eyes; the night would be my eyelids—"

> "There was no breeze. The sea was as flat as a plate-glass window. We were drawing near the island then. What I felt was a—a mental chill—a sort of sudden dread."

tangible
able to be touched or felt

indolently
lazily

brier
a tobacco pipe made from the stems and roots of a shrub

---

1 **afterdeck:** the rear deck on a ship, toward the stern

An abrupt sound startled him. Off to the right he heard it, and his ears, expert in such matters, could not be mistaken. Again he heard the sound, and again. Somewhere, off in the blackness, someone had fired a gun three times.

Rainsford sprang up and moved quickly to the rail, mystified. He strained his eyes in the direction from which the reports had come, but it was like trying to see through a blanket. He leaped upon the rail and balanced himself there, to get greater elevation; his pipe, striking a rope, was knocked from his mouth. He lunged for it; a short, hoarse cry came from his lips as he realized he had reached too far and had lost his balance. The cry was pinched off short as the blood-warm waters of the Caribbean Sea closed over his head.

He struggled up to the surface and tried to cry out, but the wash from the speeding yacht slapped him in the face and the salt water in his open mouth made him gag and strangle. Desperately he struck out with strong strokes after the receding lights of the yacht, but he stopped before he had swum fifty feet. A certain coolheadedness had come to him; it was not the first time he had been in a tight place. There was a chance that his cries could be heard by someone aboard the yacht, but that chance was slender and grew more slender as the yacht raced on. He wrestled himself out of his clothes and shouted with all his power. The lights of the yacht became faint and ever-vanishing fireflies; then they were blotted out entirely by the night.

doggedly
with great
determination

Rainsford remembered the shots. They had come from the right, and **doggedly** he swam in that direction, swimming with slow, deliberate strokes, conserving his strength. For a seemingly endless time he fought the sea. He began to count his strokes desperately; he could do possibly a hundred more and then—

Rainsford heard a sound. It came out of the darkness, a high screaming sound, the sound of an animal in an extremity of anguish and terror.

He did not recognize the animal that made the sound; he did not try to; with fresh vitality he swam toward the sound. He heard it again; then it was cut short by another noise, crisp, **staccato.**

staccato
a musical
term meaning
detached and
separated
notes

"Pistol shot," muttered Rainsford, swimming on.

Ten minutes of determined effort brought another sound to his ears—the most welcome he had ever heard—the muttering and growling of the sea breaking on a rocky shore. He was almost on the rocks before he saw them; on a night less calm he would have been shattered against them. With his remaining strength he dragged himself from the swirling waters. Jagged crags appeared to jut up into the **opaqueness**; he forced himself upward, hand over hand. Gasping, his hands raw, he reached a flat place at the top. Dense jungle came down to the very edge of the cliffs. What perils that tangle of trees and underbrush might hold for him did not concern Rainsford just then. All he knew was that he was safe from his enemy, the sea, and that utter weariness was on him. He flung himself down at the jungle edge and tumbled headlong into the deepest sleep of his life.

When he opened his eyes he knew from the position of the sun that it was late in the afternoon. Sleep had given him new vigor; a sharp hunger was picking at him. He looked about him, almost cheerfully.

"Where there are pistol shots, there are men. Where there are men, there is food," he thought. But what kind of men, he wondered, in so forbidding a place? An unbroken front of snarled and ragged jungle fringed the shore.

He saw no sign of a trail through the closely knit web of weeds and trees; it was easier to go along the shore, and Rainsford floundered along by the water. Not far from where he landed, he stopped.

Some wounded thing, by the evidence, a large animal, had thrashed about in the underbrush; the jungle weeds were crushed down and the moss was **lacerated**; one patch of weeds was stained crimson. A small, glittering object not far away caught Rainsford's eye and he picked it up. It was an empty cartridge.

"A twenty-two," he remarked. "That's odd. It must have been a fairly large animal, too. The hunter had his nerve to tackle it with a light gun. It's clear that the brute put up a fight. I suppose the first three shots I heard was when the hunter flushed his **quarry** and wounded it. The last shot was when he trailed it here and finished it."

He examined the ground closely and found what he had hoped to find—the print of hunting boots. They pointed along the cliff in the direction he had been going. Eagerly he hurried along, now slipping on a rotten log or a loose stone, but making headway; night was beginning to settle down on the island.

Bleak darkness was blacking out the sea and jungle when Rainsford sighted the lights. He came upon them as he turned a crook in the coastline; and his first thought was that he had come upon a village, for there were many lights. But as he forged along he saw to his great astonishment that all the lights were in one enormous building—a lofty structure with pointed towers plunging

opaqueness
quality of being difficult to see through

lacerated
cut; sliced

quarry
prey; something to be hunted

upward into the gloom. His eyes made out the shadowy outlines of a palatial château;[2] it was set on a high bluff, and on three sides of it cliffs dived down to where the sea licked greedy lips in the shadows.

"Mirage," thought Rainsford. But it was no mirage, he found, when he opened the tall spiked iron gate. The stone steps were real enough; the massive door with a leering gargoyle[3] for a knocker was real enough; yet above it all hung an air of unreality.

He lifted the knocker, and it creaked up stiffly, as if it had never before been used. He let it fall, and it startled him with its booming loudness. He thought he heard steps within; the door remained closed. Again Rainsford lifted the heavy knocker, and let it fall. The door opened then—opened as suddenly as if it were on a spring—and Rainsford stood blinking in the river of glaring gold light that poured out. The first thing Rainsford's eyes discerned was the largest man Rainsford had ever seen—a gigantic creature, solidly made and black bearded to the waist. In his hand the man held a long-barreled revolver, and he was pointing it straight at Rainsford's heart.

---

2 **palatial château:** palace-like country home

3 **gargoyle:** a grotesque carving of a human or animal

Out of the snarl of beard two small eyes regarded Rainsford.

"Don't be alarmed," said Rainsford, with a smile which he hoped was **disarming**. "I'm no robber. I fell off a yacht. My name is Sanger Rainsford of New York City."

disarming
no cause for alarm

The menacing look in the eyes did not change. The revolver pointed as rigidly as if the giant were a statue. He gave no sign that he understood Rainsford's words, or that he had even heard them. He was dressed in uniform—a black uniform trimmed with gray astrakhan.[4]

"I'm Sanger Rainsford of New York," Rainsford began again. "I fell off a yacht. I am hungry."

The man's only answer was to raise with his thumb the hammer of his revolver. Then Rainsford saw the man's free hand go to his forehead in a military salute, and he saw him click his heels together and stand at attention. Another man was coming down the broad marble steps, an erect, slender man in evening clothes. He advanced to Rainsford and held out his hand.

In a cultivated voice marked by a slight accent that gave it added precision and deliberateness, he said, "It is a very great pleasure and honor to welcome Mr. Sanger Rainsford, the celebrated hunter, to my home."

Automatically Rainsford shook the man's hand.

"I've read your book about hunting snow leopards in Tibet, you see," explained the man. "I am General Zaroff."

Rainsford's first impression was that the man was singularly handsome; his second was that there was an original, almost bizarre quality about the general's face. He was a tall man past middle age, for his hair was a vivid white; but his thick eyebrows and pointed military mustache were as black as the night from which Rainsford had come. His eyes, too, were black and very bright. He had high cheekbones, a sharp-cut nose, a spare, dark face, the face of a man used to giving orders, the face of an aristocrat. Turning to the giant in uniform, the general made a sign. The giant put away his pistol, saluted, withdrew.

"Ivan is an incredibly strong fellow," remarked the general, "but he has the misfortune to be deaf and dumb. A simple fellow, but I'm afraid, like all his race, a bit of a savage."

"Is he Russian?"

---

4 **astrakhan:** fabric with curly, looped pile from the wool of young lambs

"He is a Cossack,"[5] said the general, and his smile showed red lips and pointed teeth. "So am I."

"Come," he said, "we shouldn't be chatting here. We can talk later. Now you want clothes, food, rest. You shall have them. This is a most restful spot."

Ivan had reappeared, and the general spoke to him with lips that moved but gave forth no sound.

"Follow Ivan, if you please, Mr. Rainsford," said the general. "I was about to have my dinner when you came. I'll wait for you. You'll find that my clothes will fit you, I think."

It was to a huge, beam-ceilinged bedroom with a canopied bed big enough for six men that Rainsford followed the silent giant. Ivan laid out an evening suit, and Rainsford, as he put it on, noticed that it came from a London tailor who ordinarily cut and sewed for none below the rank of duke.

The dining room to which Ivan conducted him was in many ways remarkable. There was a medieval magnificence about it; it suggested a baronial hall of feudal times with its oaken panels, its high ceiling, its vast **refectory** table where twoscore[6] men could sit down to eat. About the hall were mounted heads of many animals—lions, tigers, elephants, moose, bears; larger or more perfect specimens Rainsford had never seen. At the great table the general was sitting, alone.

> **refectory**
> dining hall

"You'll have a cocktail, Mr. Rainsford," he suggested. The cocktail was surpassingly good; and, Rainsford noted, the table appointments were of the finest, the linen, the crystal, the silver, the china.

They were eating *borsch*, the rich, red soup with sour cream so dear to Russian palates. Half apologetically General Zaroff said, "We do our best to preserve the **amenities** of civilization here. Please forgive any lapses. We are well off the beaten track, you know. Do you think the champagne has suffered from its long ocean trip?"

> **amenities**
> comforts and
> conveniences

"Not in the least," declared Rainsford. He was finding the general a most thoughtful and **affable** host, a true cosmopolite.[7] But there was one small trait of the general's that made Rainsford uncomfortable. Whenever he looked up from his plate he found the general studying him, appraising him narrowly.

> **affable**
> friendly

---

5 **Cossack:** a Czarist military man from southeastern Russia

6 **twoscore:** A score is twenty of something. Two score equals forty.

7 **cosmopolite:** a sophisticated, well-traveled person

"Perhaps," said General Zaroff, "you were surprised that I recognized your name. You see, I read all books on hunting published in English, French, and Russian. I have but one passion in my life, Mr. Rainsford, and it is the hunt."

"You have some wonderful heads here," said Rainsford as he ate a particularly well-cooked filet mignon. "That Cape buffalo is the largest I ever saw."

"Oh, that fellow. Yes, he was a monster."

"Did he charge you?"

"Hurled me against a tree," said the general. "Fractured my skull. But I got the brute."

"I've always thought," said Rainsford, "that the Cape buffalo is the most dangerous of all big game."

For a moment the general did not reply; he was smiling his curious red-lipped smile. Then he said slowly, "No. You are wrong, sir. The Cape buffalo is not the most dangerous big game." He sipped his wine. "Here in my preserve on this island," he said in the same slow tone, "I hunt more dangerous game."

Rainsford expressed his surprise. "Is there big game on this island?"

The general nodded. "The biggest."

"Really?"

"Oh, it isn't here naturally, of course. I have to stock the island."

"What have you imported, General?" Rainsford asked. "Tigers?"

The general smiled. "No," he said. "Hunting tigers ceased to interest me some years ago. I exhausted their possibilities, you see. No thrill left in tigers, no real danger. I live for danger, Mr. Rainsford."

The general took from his pocket a gold cigarette case and offered his guest a long black cigarette with a silver tip; it was perfumed and gave off a smell like incense.

"We will have some capital hunting, you and I," said the general. "I shall be most glad to have your society."

"But what game—" began Rainsford.

"I'll tell you," said the general. "You will be amused, I know. I think I may say, in all modesty, that I have done a rare thing. I have invented a new sensation. May I pour you another glass of port, Mr. Rainsford?"

"Thank you, General."

The general filled both glasses, and said, "God makes some men poets. Some He makes kings, some beggars. Me He made a hunter. My hand was made for the trigger, my father said. He was a very rich man with a quarter of

ardent
passionate

a million acres in the Crimea,[8] and he was an **ardent** sportsman. When I was only five years old he gave me a little gun, specially made in Moscow for me, to shoot sparrows with. When I shot some of his prize turkeys with it, he did not punish me; he complimented me on my marksmanship. I killed my first bear in the Caucasus[9] when I was ten. My whole life has been one prolonged hunt. I went into the army—it was expected of noblemen's sons—and for a time commanded a division of Cossack cavalry, but my real interest was always the hunt. I have hunted every kind of game in every land. It would be impossible for me to tell you how many animals I have killed."

The general puffed at his cigarette.

debacle
a sudden and
violent social
collapse or
disaster

imprudent
unwise

"After the **debacle** in Russia I left the country, for it was **imprudent** for an officer of the Czar to stay there. Many noble Russians lost everything. I, luckily, had invested heavily in American securities, so I shall never have to open a tea-room in Monte Carlo or drive a taxi in Paris. Naturally, I continued to hunt—grizzlies in your Rockies, crocodiles in the Ganges, rhinoceroses in East Africa. It was in Africa that the Cape buffalo hit me and laid me up for six months. As soon as I recovered I started for the Amazon to hunt jaguars, for I had heard they were unusually cunning. They weren't." The Cossack sighed. "They were no match at all for a hunter with his wits about him and a high-powered rifle. I was bitterly disappointed. I was lying in my tent with a splitting headache one night when a terrible thought pushed its way into my mind. Hunting was beginning to bore me! And hunting, remember, had been my life. I have heard that in America businessmen often go to pieces when they give up the business that has been their life."

"Yes, that's so," said Rainsford.

The general smiled. "I had no wish to go to pieces," he said. "I must do something. Now, mine is an analytical mind, Mr. Rainsford. Doubtless that is why I enjoy the problems of the chase."

"No doubt, General Zaroff."

"So," continued the general, "I asked myself why the hunt no longer fascinated me. You are much younger than I am, Mr. Rainsford, and have not hunted as much, but you perhaps can guess the answer."

"What was it?"

---

8 **Crimea:** a peninsula in southern Ukraine, which extends into the Black Sea

9 **Caucasus:** a region between the Black Sea and the Caspian Sea. It is bordered on the north by Russia and on the south by Iran. It constitutes the "border" between Asia and Europe.

"Simply this: hunting had ceased to be what you call 'a sporting proposition.' It had become too easy. I always got my quarry. Always. There is no greater bore than perfection."

The general lit a fresh cigarette.

"No animal had a chance with me any more. That is no boast; it is a mathematical certainty. The animal had nothing but his legs and his instinct. Instinct is no match for reason. When I thought of this it was a tragic moment for me, I can tell you."

Rainsford leaned across the table, absorbed in what his host was saying.

"It came to me as an inspiration what I must do," the general went on.

"And that was?"

The general smiled the quiet smile of one who has faced an obstacle and surmounted it with success. "I had to invent a new animal to hunt," he said.

> The general smiled the quiet smile of one who has faced an obstacle and surmounted it with success. "I had to invent a new animal to hunt," he said.

"A new animal? You are joking."

"Not at all," said the general. "I never joke about hunting. I needed a new animal. I found one. So I bought this island, built this house, and here I do my hunting. The island is perfect for my purposes—there are jungles with a maze of traits in them, hills, swamps—"

"But the animal, General Zaroff?"

"Oh," said the general, "it supplies me with the most exciting hunting in the world. No other hunting compares with it for an instant. Every day I hunt, and I never grow bored now, for I have a quarry with which I can match my wits."

Rainsford's bewilderment showed in his face.

"I wanted the ideal animal to hunt," explained the general. "So I said, 'What are the attributes of an ideal quarry?' And the answer was, of course, 'It must have courage, cunning, and, above all, it must be able to reason.'"

"But no animal can reason," objected Rainsford.

"My dear fellow," said the general, "there is one that can."

"But you can't mean—" gasped Rainsford.

"And why not?"

"I can't believe you are serious, General Zaroff. This is a grisly joke."

"Why should I not be serious? I am speaking of hunting."

"Hunting? Good God, Zaroff, what you speak of is murder."

The general laughed with entire good nature. He regarded Rainsford quizzically. "I refuse to believe that so modern and civilized a young man as you seem to be harbors romantic ideas about the value of human life. Surely your experiences in the war—" He stopped.

"Did not make me condone cold-blooded murder," finished Rainsford stiffly.

droll
oddly amusing
or comical

Laughter shook the general. "How extraordinarily **droll** you are!" he said. "One does not expect nowadays to find a young man of the educated class, even in America, with such a naive, and, if I may say so, mid-Victorian point of view.[10] It's like finding a snuffbox in a limousine. Ah, well, doubtless you had Puritan ancestors. So many Americans appear to have had. I'll wager you'll forget your notions when you go hunting with me. You've a genuine new thrill in store for you, Mr. Rainsford."

"Thank you, I'm a hunter, not a murderer."

"Dear me," said the general, quite unruffled, "again that unpleasant word. But I think I can show you that your **scruples** are quite ill founded."

scruples
concerns;
qualms

"Yes?"

"Life is for the strong, to be lived by the strong, and, if needs be, taken by the strong. The weak of the world were put here to give the strong pleasure. I am strong. Why should I not use my gift? If I wish to hunt, why should I not? I hunt the scum of the earth: sailors from tramp ships—lascars,[11] blacks, Chinese, whites, mongrels—a thoroughbred horse or hound is worth more than a score of them."

"But they are men," said Rainsford hotly.

"Precisely," said the general. "That is why I use them. It gives me pleasure. They can reason, after a fashion. So they are dangerous."

"But where do you get them?"

The general's left eyelid fluttered down in a wink. "This island is called Ship-Trap," he answered. "Sometimes an angry god of the high seas sends them to me. Sometimes, when Providence is not so kind, I help Providence a bit. Come to the window with me."

Rainsford went to the window and looked out toward the sea.

"Watch! Out there!" exclaimed the general, pointing into the night.

---

10 **mid-Victorian point of view:** beliefs held during the reign of England's Queen Victoria centered on self-help, moral values, and the importance of institutions

11 **lascars:** sailors from India employed on European vessels

Rainsford's eyes saw only blackness, and then, as the general pressed a button, far out to sea Rainsford saw the flash of lights.

The general chuckled. "They indicate a channel," he said, "where there's none: giant rocks with razor edges crouch like a sea monster with wide-open jaws. They can crush a ship as easily as I crush this nut." He dropped a walnut on the hardwood floor and brought his heel grinding down on it. "Oh, yes," he said casually, as if in answer to a question, "I have electricity. We try to be civilized here."

"Civilized? And you shoot down men?"

A trace of anger was in the general's black eyes, but it was there for but a second, and he said, in his most pleasant manner, "Dear me, what a righteous young man you are! I assure you I do not do the thing you suggest. That would be barbarous. I treat these visitors with every consideration. They get plenty of good food and exercise. They get into splendid physical condition. You shall see for yourself tomorrow."

"What do you mean?"

"We'll visit my training school." The general smiled. "It's in the cellar. I have about a dozen pupils down there now. They're from the Spanish bark *San Lucar* that had the bad luck to go on the rocks out there. A very inferior lot, I regret to say. Poor specimens, and more accustomed to the deck than to the jungle."

He raised his hand, and Ivan, who served as waiter, brought thick Turkish coffee. Rainsford, with an effort, held his tongue in check.

"It's a game, you see," pursued the general blandly. "I suggest to one of them that we go hunting. I give him a supply of food and an excellent hunting knife. I give him three hours' start. I am to follow, armed only with a pistol of the smallest caliber and range. If my quarry eludes me for three whole days, he wins the game. If I find him—" the general smiled—"he loses."

"Suppose he refuses to be hunted?"

"Oh," said the general, "I give him his option, of course. He need not play that game if he doesn't wish to. If he does not wish to hunt, I turn him over to Ivan. Ivan once had the honor of serving as official knouter[12] to the Great White Czar, and he has his own ideas of sport. Invariably, Mr. Rainsford, invariably they choose the hunt."

---

12 **knouter:** a person who flogs or punishes people

"And if they win?"

The smile on the general's face widened. "To date I have not lost," he said.

Then he added, hastily, "I don't wish you to think me a braggart, Mr. Rainsford. Many of them afford only the most elementary sort of problem. Occasionally I strike a tartar.[13] One almost did win. I eventually had to use the dogs."

"The dogs?"

"This way, please. I'll show you."

The general steered Rainsford to a window. The lights from the windows sent a flickering illumination that made grotesque patterns on the courtyard below, and Rainsford could see moving about there a dozen or so huge black shapes; as they turned toward him, their eyes glittered greenly.

"A rather good lot, I think," observed the general. "They are let out at seven every night. If anyone should try to get into my house—or out of it—something extremely regrettable would occur to him." He hummed a snatch of song from the Folies Bergère.[14]

"And now," said the general, "I want to show you my new collection of heads. Will you come with me to the library?"

"I hope," said Rainsford, "that you will excuse me tonight, General Zaroff. I'm really not feeling at all well."

"Ah, indeed?" the general inquired solicitously. "Well, I suppose that's only natural, after your long swim. You need a good, restful night's sleep. Tomorrow you'll feel like a new man, I'll wager. Then we'll hunt, eh? I've one rather promising prospect—"

Rainsford was hurrying from the room.

"Sorry you can't go with me tonight," called the general. "I expect rather fair sport—a big, strong, black. He looks resourceful—Well, good night, Mr. Rainsford; I hope you have a good night's rest."

The bed was good, and the pajamas of the softest silk, and he was tired in every fiber of his being, but nevertheless Rainsford could not quiet his brain with the opiate of sleep. He lay, eyes wide open. Once he thought he heard stealthy steps in the corridor outside his room. He sought to throw open the

---

13 **tartar:** a Turkish or Mongolian fighter who invaded Western Asia and Eastern Europe during the Middle Ages. The general is using the term as a slur against any Turk or Mongol.

14 **Folies Bergère:** Parisian music hall popular from the 1890s until World War II

door; it would not open. He went to the window and looked out. His room was high up in one of the towers. The lights of the château were out now, and it was dark and silent; but there was a fragment of **sallow** moon, and by its wan light he could see, dimly, the courtyard; there, weaving in and out in the pattern of shadow, were black, noiseless forms; the hounds heard him at the window and looked up, expectantly, with their green eyes. Rainsford went back to the bed and lay down. By many methods he tried to put himself to sleep. He had achieved a doze when, just as morning began to come, he heard, far off in the jungle, the faint report of a pistol.

sallow
sickly yellow color

General Zaroff did not appear until luncheon. He was dressed faultlessly in the tweeds of a country squire. He was **solicitous** about the state of Rainsford's health.

solicitous
politely concerned

"As for me," sighed the general, "I do not feel so well. I am worried, Mr. Rainsford. Last night I detected traces of my old complaint."

To Rainsford's questioning glance the general said, "Ennui. Boredom."

Then, taking a second helping of crêpes suzette,[15] the general explained, "The hunting was not good last night. The fellow lost his head. He made a straight trail that offered no problems at all. That's the trouble with these sailors; they have dull brains to begin with, and they do not know how to get about in the woods. They do excessively stupid and obvious things. It's most annoying. Will you have another glass of Chablis,[16] Mr. Rainsford?"

"General," said Rainsford firmly, "I wish to leave this island at once."

The general raised his thickets of eyebrows; he seemed hurt. "But, my dear fellow," the general protested, "you've only just come. You've had no hunting—"

"I wish to go today," said Rainsford. He saw the dead black eyes of the general on him, studying him. General Zaroff's face suddenly brightened.

He filled Rainsford's glass with **venerable** Chablis from a dusty bottle. "Tonight," said the general, "we will hunt—you and I."

venerable
commanding respect; impressive

Rainsford shook his head. "No, General," he said. "I will not hunt."

The general shrugged his shoulders and delicately ate a hothouse grape. "As you wish, my friend," he said. "The choice rests entirely with you. But may I not venture to suggest that you will find my idea of sport more diverting than Ivan's?"

He nodded toward the corner to where the giant stood, scowling, his thick arms crossed on his hogshead of chest.

---

15 **crêpes suzette:** dessert pancakes served warm, sometimes flaming, with an orange sauce
16 **Chablis:** white wine

"You don't mean—" cried Rainsford.

"My dear fellow," said the general, "have I not told you I always mean what I say about hunting? This is really an inspiration. I drink to a foeman worthy of my steel—at last."

The general raised his glass, but Rainsford sat staring at him.

"You'll find this game worth playing," the general said enthusiastically. "Your brain against mine. Your woodcraft against mine. Your strength and stamina against mine. Outdoor chess! And the stake is not without value, eh?"

"And if I win—" began Rainsford huskily.

"I'll cheerfully acknowledge myself defeated if I do not find you by midnight of the third day," said General Zaroff. "My sloop will place you on the mainland near a town."

The general read what Rainsford was thinking.

"Oh, you can trust me," said the Cossack. "I will give you my word as a gentleman and a sportsman. Of course you, in turn, must agree to say nothing of your visit here."

"I'll agree to nothing of the kind," said Rainsford.

"Oh," said the general, "in that case— But why discuss it now? Three days hence we can discuss it over a bottle of Veuve Clicquot,[17] unless—"

The general sipped his wine.

Then a businesslike air animated him. "Ivan," he said to Rainsford, "will supply you with hunting clothes, food, a knife. I suggest you wear moccasins; they leave a poorer trail. I suggest too that you avoid the big swamp in the southeast corner of the island. We call it Death Swamp. There's quicksand there. One foolish fellow tried it. The deplorable part of it was that Lazarus followed him. You can imagine my feelings, Mr. Rainsford. I loved Lazarus; he was the finest hound in my pack. Well, I must beg you to excuse me now. I always take a siesta after lunch. You'll hardly have time for a nap, I fear. You'll want to start, no doubt. I shall not follow till dusk. Hunting at night is so much more exciting than by day, don't you think? *Au revoir,* Mr. Rainsford, *au revoir.*"[18] General Zaroff, with a deep, courtly bow, strolled from the room.

From another door came Ivan. Under one arm he carried khaki hunting clothes, a haversack[19] of food, a leather sheath containing a long-bladed hunting

---

17 **Veuve Clicquot:** a very good brand of champagne

18 *Au revoir:* French for "Good-bye"

19 **haversack:** backpack

knife; his right hand rested on a cocked revolver thrust in the crimson sash about his waist. . . .

Rainsford had fought his way through the bush for two hours. "I must keep my nerve. I must keep my nerve," he said through tight teeth.

He had not been entirely clear-headed when the château gates snapped shut behind him. His whole idea at first was to put distance between himself and General Zaroff, and, to this end, he had plunged along, spurred on by the sharp rowels[20] of something very like panic. Now he had got a grip on himself, he had stopped, and was taking stock of himself and the situation.

He saw that straight flight was futile; inevitably it would bring him face to face with the sea. He was in a picture with a frame of water, and his operations, clearly, must take place within that frame.

> He saw that straight flight was futile; inevitably it would bring him face to face with the sea. He was in a picture with a frame of water, and his operations, clearly, must take place within that frame.

"I'll give him a trail to follow," muttered Rainsford, and he struck off from the rude path he had been following into the trackless wilderness. He executed a series of intricate loops; he doubled on his trail again and again, recalling all the lore of the fox hunt, and all the dodges of the fox. Night found him leg-weary, with hands and face lashed by the branches, on a thickly wooded ridge. He knew it would be insane to blunder on through the dark, even if he had the strength. His need for rest was imperative and he thought, "I have played the fox, now I must play the cat of the fable." A big tree with a thick trunk and outspread branches was nearby, and taking care to leave not the slightest mark, he climbed up into the crotch and, stretched out on one of the broad limbs, rested after a fashion. Rest brought him new confidence and almost a feeling of security. Even so **zealous** a hunter as General Zaroff could not trace him there, he told himself; only the devil himself could follow that complicated trail through the jungle after dark. But, perhaps, the general was a devil—

zealous
fanatic

An apprehensive night crawled slowly by like a wounded snake, and sleep did not visit Rainsford, although the silence of a dead world was on the jungle. Toward morning when a dingy gray was varnishing the sky, the cry of some startled bird focused Rainsford's attention in that direction. Something

---

20 **rowels:** small spiked wheels at the end of spurs

was coming through the bush, coming slowly, carefully, coming by the same winding way Rainsford had come. He flattened himself down on the limb, and through a screen of leaves almost as thick as tapestry, he watched. The thing that was approaching him was a man.

It was General Zaroff. He made his way along with his eyes fixed in utmost concentration on the ground before him. He paused, almost beneath the tree, dropped to his knees and studied the ground. Rainsford's impulse was to hurl himself down like a panther, but he saw that the general's right hand held something small and metallic—an automatic pistol.

The hunter shook his head several times, as if he were puzzled. Then he straightened up and took from his case one of his black cigarettes; its pungent incense-like smoke floated up to Rainsford's nostrils. Rainsford held his breath. The general's eyes had left the ground and were traveling inch by inch up the tree. Rainsford froze there, every muscle tensed for a spring. But the sharp eyes of the hunter stopped before they reached the limb where Rainsford lay; a smile spread over his brown face. Very deliberately he blew a smoke ring into the air; then he turned his back on the tree and walked carelessly away, back along the trail he had come. The swish of the underbrush against his hunting boots grew fainter and fainter.

The pent-up air burst hotly from Rainsford's lungs. His first thought made him feel sick and numb. The general could follow a trail through the woods at night; he could follow an extremely difficult trail; he must have uncanny powers; only by the merest chance had the Cossack failed to see his quarry.

Rainsford's second thought was even more terrible. It sent a shudder of cold horror through his whole being. Why had the general smiled? Why had he turned back?

Rainsford did not want to believe what his reason told him was true, but the truth was as evident as the sun that had by now pushed through the morning mist. The general was playing with him! The general was saving him for another day's sport! The Cossack was the cat; he was the mouse. Then it was that Rainsford knew the full meaning of terror.

"I will not lose my nerve. I will not."

He slid down from the tree, and struck off again into the woods. His face was set and he forced the machinery of his mind to function. Three hundred yards from his hiding place he stopped where a huge dead tree leaned precariously on a smaller, living one. Throwing off his sack of food, Rainsford took his knife from its sheath and began to work with all his energy.

The job was finished at last, and he threw himself down behind a fallen log a hundred feet away. He did not have to wait long. The cat was coming again to play with the mouse.

Following the trail with the sureness of a bloodhound came General Zaroff. Nothing escaped those searching black eyes, no crushed blade of grass, no bent twig, no mark, no matter how faint, in the moss. So intent was the Cossack on his stalking that he was upon the thing Rainsford had made before he saw it. His foot touched the protruding bough that was the trigger. Even as he touched it, the general sensed his danger and leaped back with the agility of an ape. But he was not quite quick enough; the dead tree, delicately adjusted to rest on the cut living one, crashed down and struck the general a glancing blow on the shoulder as it fell; but for his alertness, he would have been smashed beneath it. He staggered, but he did not fall; nor did he drop his revolver. He stood there, rubbing his injured shoulder, and Rainsford, with fear again gripping his heart, heard the general's mocking laugh ring through the jungle.

"Rainsford," called the general, "if you are within sound of my voice, as I suppose you are, let me congratulate you. Not many men know how to make a Malay man-catcher. Luckily for me, I too have hunted in Malaya. You are proving interesting, Mr. Rainsford. I am going now to have my wound dressed; it's only a slight one. But I shall be back. I shall be back."

When the general, nursing his bruised shoulder, had gone, Rainsford took up his flight again. It was flight now, a desperate, hopeless flight, that carried him on for some hours. Dusk came, then darkness, and still he pressed on. The ground grew softer under his moccasins; the vegetation grew ranker, denser; insects bit him savagely. Then, as he stepped forward, his foot sank into the ooze. He tried to wrench it back, but the muck sucked viciously at his foot as if it were a giant leech. With a violent effort, he tore his foot loose. He knew where he was now. Death Swamp and its quicksand.

His hands were tight closed as if his nerve were something tangible that someone in the darkness was trying to tear from his grip. The softness of the earth had given him an idea. He stepped back from the quicksand a dozen feet or so and, like some huge prehistoric beaver, he began to dig.

Rainsford had dug himself in in France when a second's delay meant death. That had been a placid pastime compared to his digging now. The pit grew deeper; when it was above his shoulders, he climbed out and from some hard saplings cut stakes and sharpened them to a fine point. These stakes he planted in the bottom of the pit with the points sticking up. With flying fingers he wove a rough carpet of weeds and branches and with it he covered the mouth of the pit. Then, wet with sweat and aching with tiredness, he crouched behind the stump of a lightning-charred tree.

He knew his pursuer was coming; he heard the padding sound of feet on the soft earth, and the night breeze brought him the perfume of the general's cigarette. It seemed to Rainsford that the general was coming with unusual swiftness; he was not feeling his way along, foot by foot. Rainsford, crouching there, could not see the general, nor could he see the pit. He lived a year in a minute. Then he felt an impulse to cry aloud with joy, for he heard the sharp crackle of the breaking branches as the cover of the pit gave way; he heard the sharp scream of pain as the pointed stakes found their mark. He leaped up from his place of concealment. Then he cowered back. Three feet from the pit a man was standing, with an electric torch in his hand.

"You've done well, Rainsford," the voice of the general called. "Your Burmese tiger pit has claimed one of my best dogs. Again you score. I think, Mr. Rainsford, I'll see what you can do against my whole pack. I'm going home for a rest now. Thank you for a most amusing evening."

At daybreak Rainsford, lying near the swamp, was awakened by a sound that made him know that he had new things to learn about fear. It was a distant sound, faint and wavering, but he knew it. It was the baying of a pack of hounds.

Rainsford knew he could do one of two things. He could stay where he was and wait. That was suicide. He could flee. That was postponing the inevitable. For a moment he stood there, thinking. An idea that held a wild chance came to him, and, tightening his belt, he headed away from the swamp.

The baying of the hounds drew nearer, then still nearer, nearer, ever nearer. On a ridge Rainsford climbed a tree. Down a water-course, not a quarter of a mile away, he could see the bush moving. Straining his eyes, he saw the lean figure of General Zaroff; just ahead of him Rainsford made out another figure whose wide shoulders surged through the tall jungle weeds; it was the giant Ivan, and he seemed pulled forward by some unseen force; Rainsford knew that Ivan must be holding the pack in leash.

They would be on him any minute now. His mind worked frantically. He thought of a native trick he had learned in Uganda. He slid down the tree. He caught hold of a springy young sapling and to it he fastened his hunting knife,

with the blade pointing down the trail; with a bit of wild grapevine he tied back the sapling. Then he ran for his life. The hounds raised their voices as they hit the fresh scent. Rainsford knew now how an animal at bay feels.

He had to stop to get his breath. The baying of the hounds stopped abruptly, and Rainsford's heart stopped too. They must have reached the knife.

He shinnied excitedly up a tree and looked back. His pursuers had stopped. But the hope that was in Rainsford's brain when he climbed died, for he saw in the shallow valley that General Zaroff was still on his feet. But Ivan was not. The knife, driven by the recoil of the springing tree, had not wholly failed.

Rainsford had hardly tumbled to the ground when the pack took up the cry again.

"Nerve, nerve, nerve!" he panted, as he dashed along. A blue gap showed between the trees dead ahead. Ever nearer drew the hounds. Rainsford forced himself on toward the gap. He reached it. It was the shore of the sea. Across a cove he could see the gloomy gray stone of the château. Twenty feet below him the sea rumbled and hissed. Rainsford hesitated. He heard the hounds. Then he leaped far out into the sea. . . .

When the general and his pack reached the place by the sea, the Cossack stopped. For some minutes he stood regarding the blue-green expanse of water. He shrugged his shoulders. Then he sat down, took a drink of brandy from a silver flask, lit a perfumed cigarette, and hummed a bit from *Madame Butterfly*.[21]

General Zaroff had an exceedingly good dinner in his great paneled dining hall that evening. With it he had a bottle of Pol Roger and half a bottle of Chambertin.[22] Two slight annoyances kept him from perfect enjoyment. One was the thought that it would be difficult to replace Ivan; the other was that his quarry had escaped him; of course, the American hadn't played the game—so thought the general as he tasted his after-dinner liqueur. In his library he read, to soothe himself, from the works of Marcus Aurelius.[23] At ten he went up to his bedroom. He was deliciously tired, he said to himself, as he locked himself in. There was a little moonlight, so, before turning on his light, he went to the window and looked down at the courtyard. He could see the great hounds, and he called, "Better luck another time," to them. Then he switched on the light.

A man, who had been hiding in the curtains of the bed, was standing there.

"Rainsford!" screamed the general. "How in God's name did you get here?"

"Swam," said Rainsford. "I found it quicker than walking through the jungle."

The general sucked in his breath and smiled. "I congratulate you," he said. "You have won the game."

Rainsford did not smile. "I am still a beast at bay," he said, in a low, hoarse voice. "Get ready, General Zaroff."

The general made one of his deepest bows. "I see," he said. "Splendid! One of us is to furnish a **repast** for the hounds. The other will sleep in this very excellent bed. On guard, Rainsford. . . ."

He had never slept in a better bed, Rainsford decided.

repast
meal; banquet

---

21 *Madame Butterfly:* an opera by Giacomo Puccini that was hugely popular when first performed in the early 1900s, remaining a favorite to this day

22 **Pol Roger and Chambertin:** brands of expensive champagne and burgundy (red wine)

23 **Marcus Aurelius:** a philosopher and one of ancient Rome's last great emperors; in his *Meditations* he writes that "everything is by nature made but to die."

AFTER YOU READ
The Most Dangerous Game

Think and Discuss

1. Compare and contrast Zaroff's and Rainsford's philosophies on hunting and human life. Refer to the text to support your answers.

2. What choices does Rainsford have at the very end of the story when he is back in Zaroff's house?

3. Does the choice Rainsford makes at the end of the story support Zaroff's philosophy or Rainsford's? Give reasons for your answer.

4. How is the terror that Rainsford will face **foreshadowed** early in the story? (For a definition of *foreshadowing*, see the Glossary of Literary Terms.)

5. Rainford's crewmate Whitney serves as a **foil**, or point of comparison, by which to measure General Zaroff and also Rainsford. Copy the following graphic organizer into your Writer's Notebook. Note the arguments Whitney makes and how Rainsford responds to them. Repeat the double-column writing, this time about what Zaroff says and how Rainsford answers him.

When Whitney Says:	Rainsford Answers:
When Zaroff Says:	**Rainsford Answers:**

6. Whose "dark side" is this story about? Give reasons for your answer.

Write to Understand: Tracing Character Development

Review your graphic organizer with a special focus on how Rainsford's ideas at the beginning of the story compare to his ideas later in the story. Also consider Rainsford's actions throughout the story. Does Rainsford change? Write freely exploring if and how the character of Rainsford develops through the experiences he has in the story.

BEFORE YOU READ
Variations on the Death of Trotsky

Meet the Author: David Ives

David Ives (born 1950) is an American playwright known especially for his crisp and witty one-act plays. A Polish American, he grew up in a working-class neighborhood on the south side of Chicago, which he has memorialized in a play called *Polish Joke*. Although some of his work is serious, Ives is a master of comedy. The theatre, he says, "isn't work, it's play, and you're playing with a lot of other smart and funny kids. . . . This is why they call these things 'plays'." The play that follows is from a collection of one-act plays by David Ives called *All in the Timing*.

Build Background: Burlesque . . . and the Russian Revolution?

The Russian Revolution in the early 1900s was fueled by the indifference of Russian rulers to the poor living conditions of the workers (the proletariat). V. I. Lenin headed the Bolsheviks, the leading revolutionary faction, with Leon Trotsky as second in command. Tsar Nicholas II was overthrown in 1917 and Lenin became the leader of the new Soviet states. When he died in 1924, Joseph Stalin prevailed in a power struggle with Trotsky for leadership and expelled his rival. Trotsky and his wife settled in Coyoacan, Mexico, where Trotsky was murdered in 1940.

The revolution and the death of Trotsky hardly seem like comic topics. But *Variations on the Death of Trotsky* falls into a category of dramatic comedy called **burlesque**, in which serious subjects are treated frivolously. Ives uses **irony**, the contrasting of what appears to be with what really is, to set this offbeat comedy spinning. The comedy comes in when his characters respond to dark events in unexpectedly matter-of-fact ways.

As you read the play, think about these questions:

• Where do you see irony in the play?

• What is the effect of treating serious subjects so lightly?

Variations on the Death of Trotsky

DAVID IVES

VARIATIONS ON THE DEATH OF TROTSKY

David Ives

TROTSKY's[1] study in Coyoacan, Mexico. A desk, covered with books and papers. A mirror hanging on the wall. A doorway, left, louvered[2] windows upstage, through which we can glimpse lush tropical fronds and greenery. A large wall calendar announces that today is August 21, 1940. Lights up on TROTSKY sitting at his desk, writing furiously. He has bushy hair and a goatee, small glasses, a dark suit. The handle of a mountain-climber's axe is sticking out of the back of his head.

VARIATION ONE

proletariat the laboring class, especially industrial workers

Trotsky (as he writes). "The **proletariat** is right. The proletariat must always be right. And the revolution of the proletariat against oppression must go on . . . forever!"

(MRS. TROTSKY enters, grandmotherly and sweet, in an ankle-length dress and high-button shoes. She is holding a large book.)

MRS. TROTSKY. Leon.

TROTSKY. "And forever and forever . . . !"

MRS. TROTSKY. Leon, I was just reading the encyclopedia.

TROTSKY. The heading?

MRS. TROTSKY. "Trotsky, Leon."

TROTSKY. Good. It's about me.

MRS. TROTSKY. Listen to this. *(Reads)* "On August 20th, 1940, a Spanish Communist named Ramon Mercader smashed a mountain-climber's axe into Trotsky's skull in Coyoacan, a suburb of Mexico City. Trotsky died the next day."

---

1 **Trosky, Leon:** Russian Communist who lived from 1879 to 1940

2 **louvered:** having shutters with horizontal boards

TROTSKY. What is the year of that encyclopedia?

MRS. TROTSKY *(Checks the spine).* 1999. *(Or whatever year it happens to be now)*

TROTSKY. Strange.

MRS. TROTSKY. Yes.

TROTSKY. But interesting. I am Trotsky.

MRS. TROTSKY. Yes, dear.

TROTSKY. And this is our house in Coyoacan.

MRS. TROTSKY. Yes.

TROTSKY. And we have a Spanish gardener named Ramon—?

MRS. TROTSKY. Mercader. Yes.

TROTSKY. Hmm . . . There aren't any *other* Trotskys living in Coyoacan, are there?

MRS. TROTSKY. I don't think so. Not under that name.

TROTSKY. What is the date today?

MRS. TROTSKY *(Looks at the calendar).* August 21st, 1940.

TROTSKY. Then I'm safe! That article says it happened on the twentieth, which means it would've happened yesterday.

MRS. TROTSKY. But Leon . . .

TROTSKY. And I'd be dead today, with a mountain-climber's axe in my skull!

MRS. TROTSKY. Um—Leon . . .

TROTSKY. Will the **capitalist** press never get things right? *(He resumes writing.)*

MRS. TROTSKY. But Leon, isn't that the handle of a mountain-climber's axe, sticking out of your skull?

TROTSKY *(Looks into the mirror).* It certainly does look like one . . . And you know, Ramon was in here yesterday, telling me about his mountain-climbing trip. And now that I think of it, he was carrying a mountain-climber's axe. I can't remember if he had it when he left the room . . . (TROTSKY *considers all this.*) Did Ramon report to work today? (TROTSKY *dies, falling face forward onto his desk.*)

(A bell rings.)

capitalist
related to an economic system built on the principle of private ownership and the forces of the marketplace

VARIATION TWO

*(*TROTSKY *resumes writing.)*

TROTSKY. "No one is safe. Force must be used. And the revolution of the proletariat against oppression must go on forever and forever . . ."

MRS. TROTSKY. Leon . . .

TROTSKY. "And forever!"

MRS. TROTSKY. Leon, I was just reading the encyclopedia.

TROTSKY. Is it the *Britannica*?

MRS. TROTSKY. Listen to this.

TROTSKY *(To audience)*. The universe as viewed by the victors.

MRS. TROTSKY. "On August 20th, 1940, a Spanish Communist named Ramon Mercader smashed a mountain-climber's axe into Trotsky's skull in Coyoacan, a suburb of Mexico City. Trotsky died the next day."

TROTSKY *(Impatient)*. Yes? And?

MRS. TROTSKY. I *think* that there's a mountain-climber's axe in your own skull right now.

TROTSKY. I knew *that*! When I was shaving this morning, I noticed a handle sticking out of the back of my head. For a moment I thought it was an ice pick, so at first I was worried.

MRS. TROTSKY. No, it's not an ice pick.

TROTSKY. Don't even say the word! You know my recurring nightmare.

MRS. TROTSKY. Yes, dear.

TROTSKY. About the ice pick that buries itself in my skull.

MRS. TROTSKY. Yes, dear.

TROTSKY. That is why I have forbidden any of the servants to allow ice picks into the house.

MRS. TROTSKY. But Leon—

TROTSKY. No one may be seen with an ice pick in this house. *Especially* not Spanish Communists.

MRS. TROTSKY. But Leon—

TROTSKY. We'll do without ice. We'll drink our liquor neat and our Coca-Cola warm. Who cares if this *is* Coyoacan in August? Hmm. Not a bad song title, that. "Coyoacan in August." *(Writes it down)* Or we'll get ice, but we just won't pick at it. Ice will be allowed into the house in blocks, but may not be picked or chipped under any circumstances—at least, not with ice picks. Ice-cube trays will also be allowed, if they've been invented yet. I'll bet this article doesn't say anything about an *ice-cube tray* in my skull, does it?

MRS. TROTSKY. No . . .

TROTSKY. Does it?

MRS. TROTSKY. No.

TROTSKY. HA! I've outsmarted **destiny**! *(To audience)* Which is only a capitalist explanation for the **status quo**!

MRS. TROTSKY. Leon . . .

TROTSKY. Also—look at this. *(Opens a desk drawer and takes out a skull)* Do you know what this is?

MRS. TROTSKY. No.

TROTSKY. It's a skull.

MRS. TROTSKY. Well I knew that, but—

TROTSKY. I bought this skull. I own this skull. So what does that make this?

(Pause)

MRS. TROTSKY AND TROTSKY *(Together)*. Trotsky's skull.

TROTSKY. If some Spanish-Communist-posing-as-a-gardener wants to bury anything in my skull, be it a *(he is about to say "ice pick")* you-know-what or anything else—this will be here as a decoy. He'll see this skull, recognize it as my skull, bury something in it, and he'll go his way and I'll go mine. Is that ingenious?

MRS. TROTSKY. Up to a point.

TROTSKY. Fifty more years of Trotsky!

MRS. TROTSKY. I have some very bad news for you, Leon. *(Shows him the entry in the encyclopedia)*

TROTSKY. A mountain-climber's axe . . . ? Ingenious! *(TROTSKY dies.)*

(Bell)

> **destiny**
> fate; a predetermined force of events
>
> **status quo**
> the existing state of affairs

VARIATION THREE

TROTSKY. Funny. I always thought it was an ice pick.

MRS. TROTSKY. A mountain-climber's axe! A mountain-climber's axe! CAN'T I GET THAT THROUGH YOUR SKULL?

(TROTSKY *dies.*)

(*Bell*)

VARIATION FOUR

(TROTSKY *begins to pace.*)

TROTSKY. This is very bad news. This is serious.

MRS. TROTSKY. What is serious, Leon?

TROTSKY. I have a mountain-climber's axe buried in my skull!

MRS. TROTSKY. Smashed, actually. It says Mercader "smashed" the axe into your skull, not "buried"—

TROTSKY. All right, all right. What am I going to do?

MRS. TROTSKY. Maybe a hat would cover the handle. You know. One of those cute little Alpine hats, with a point and a feather . . . ? (*Sees the look on his face, and stops.*)

TROTSKY. The encyclopedia says that I die today?

MRS. TROTSKY. The twenty-first. That's today.

TROTSKY. Does it say what time?

MRS. TROTSKY. No.

TROTSKY. So much for the usefulness of that encyclopedia. All right, then, I have until midnight at the latest.

MRS. TROTSKY. What should I tell Cook about supper?

TROTSKY. Well, she can forget the soup course. (TROTSKY *falls to the floor and dies.*)

MRS. TROTSKY. *Nyet,*[3] *nyet, nyet!*

(*Bell*)

---

3 **Nyet:** Russian word for "no"

VARIATION FIVE

TROTSKY. But this man is a gardener.

MRS. TROTSKY. Yes.

TROTSKY. At least he's been *posing* as a gardener.

MRS. TROTSKY. Yes.

TROTSKY. Doesn't that make him a member of the proletariat?

MRS. TROTSKY. I'd say so.

TROTSKY. Then what's he doing smashing a mountain-climber's axe into my skull?

MRS. TROTSKY. I don't know. Have you been oppressing him?

TROTSKY. Why would Ramon have done this to me? *(He holds up the skull, Hamlet-like.)*

MRS. TROTSKY. Maybe he's a literalist.

TROTSKY. A what?

MRS. TROTSKY. A literalist. Maybe Ramon ran into Manuel yesterday. You know—Manuel? The head gardener?

TROTSKY. I know who Manuel is.

MRS. TROTSKY. I know you know who Manuel is.

TROTSKY *(Ralph Kramden[4])*. One of these days, Mrs. Trotsky . . . Bang! Zoom!

MRS. TROTSKY. Maybe Ramon asked him, "Will Mr. Trotsky have time to look at the nasturtiums[5] today?" And maybe Manuel said, "I don't know—axe Mr. Trotsky." HA HA HA HA HA Ha!

TROTSKY. Very funny.

MRS. TROTSKY. Or maybe he was just hot-to-trotsky.

TROTSKY. Oh very, very funny.

MRS. TROTSKY. Or maybe he just wanted to pick your brain! HOO HOO HEE HEE HAA HAA!

TROTSKY. Stop it! Stop it! *(He dies.)*

MRS. TROTSKY. HA HA HA HA HA HA!

(Bell)

---

4 **Ralph Kramden:** a character in the early TV show *The Honeymooners*. He would often say these words to his wife, Alice, in frustration and annoyance.

5 **nasturtiums:** brightly colored yellow, red, and orange flowers

VARIATION SIX

TROTSKY. Call Ramon in here.

MRS. TROTSKY. Ramon!

TROTSKY. You'd better get him quickly. I have a mountain-climber's axe in my skull.

MRS. TROTSKY. Ramon! Come quickly!

(RAMON *enters: sombrero, serape, huaraches,*[6] *and guitar.*)

TROTSKY. Good morning, Ramon.

RAMON. Good morning, señor. (*They shake hands.*)

TROTSKY. Have a seat, please. (*To* MRS. TROTSKY) You see? We have very good employer-employee relations here. (*To* RAMON) Ramon, did you bury this mountain-climber's axe in my skull?

RAMON. I did not bury it, señor. I smashed it into your skull.

TROTSKY. Excuse me?

RAMON. You see? You can still see the handle.

MRS. TROTSKY. It's true, Leon. The axe is not entirely out of sight.

RAMON. So we cannot say "buried," we can only say "smashed," or perhaps "jammed"—

TROTSKY. All right, all right. But why did you do this?

RAMON. I think I read about it in an encyclopedia.

TROTSKY (*To audience*). The power of the printed word!

RAMON. I wanted to use an ice pick, but there weren't any around the house.

TROTSKY. But why? Do you realize who I am? Do you realize that you smashed this axe into the skull of a major historical figure? I helped run the Russian Revolution! I fought Stalin! I was a major political theorist! Why did you do this? Was it political disaffection? Anti-counterrevolutionary backlash?

RAMON. Actually—it was love, señor.

MRS. TROTSKY. It's true, Leon. (*She and* RAMON *join hands.*) I'm only sorry you had to find out about it this way.

TROTSKY. No.

MRS. TROTSKY. Yes.

TROTSKY. No.

---

6 **sombero, serape, huaraches:** Mexican wearing apparel: a large straw hat, a multicolored shawl, and leather sandals

RAMON. Sí!

TROTSKY. Oh God! What a fool I've been! *(He dies.)*

(Bell)

VARIATION SEVEN

TROTSKY. Why did you really do this, Ramon?

RAMON. You will never know, Señor Trotsky.

TROTSKY. This is a nightmare!

RAMON. But luckily for you—your night will soon be over.

(TROTSKY *dies.*)

(Bell)

VARIATION EIGHT

TROTSKY. All right, Ramon. Thank you. You may go.

(RAMON *starts out. Stops.*)

RAMON. Señor Trotsky—?

TROTSKY. Yes?

RAMON. Do you think you will have time to look at the nasturtiums today? They are really very beautiful.

TROTSKY. I don't think so, Ramon. But I'll try.

RAMON. Thank you, señor. *Hasta la vista.* Or should I say, *buenas noches. (Exits)*

TROTSKY. Well. All right then. The twenty-first of August, 1940. The day I'm going to die. Interesting. And to think that I've gone over so many twenty-firsts of August in my life, like a man walking over his own grave . . .

MRS. TROTSKY. It's been wonderful being married to you, Leon.

TROTSKY. Thank you, Mrs. Trotsky.

MRS. TROTSKY. Though it was a burden at times, being married to a major historical figure.

TROTSKY. I'm sorry I was away from home so often, tending the revolution.

MRS. TROTSKY. I understand.

TROTSKY. And I'm sorry I couldn't have been more in touch with my feelings.

MRS. TROTSKY *(Gentle protest).* No . . . please . . .

TROTSKY. And that I often had such trouble expressing my emotions.

MRS. TROTSKY. Oh, I haven't been everything I should have been.

TROTSKY. Well, it's a little late for regrets, with a mountain-climber's axe buried in one's skull.

MRS. TROTSKY. Smashed, actually.

TROTSKY. So it wasn't old age, or cancer, or even the ice pick that I feared for years. It was an axe wielded by a Spanish Communist posing as a gardener.

MRS. TROTSKY. You really couldn't have guessed that, Leon.

TROTSKY. So even an assassin can make the flowers grow. The gardener was false, and yet the garden that he tended was real. How was I to know he was my killer when I passed him every day? How was I to know that the man tending the nasturtiums would keep me from seeing what the weather will be like tomorrow? How was I to know I'd never get to see *Casablanca*, which wouldn't be made until 1942 and which I would have despised anyway? How was I to know I'd never get to know about the bomb, or the eighty thousand dead at Hiroshima? Or rock and roll, or Gorbachev, or the state of Israel? How was I supposed to know I'd be erased from the history books of my own land . . . ?

MRS. TROTSKY. But reinstated, at least partially, someday.

TROTSKY. Sometime, for everyone, there's a room that you go into, and it's the room that you never leave. Or else you go out of a room and it's the last room that you'll ever leave. *(He looks around.)* This is my last room.

MRS. TROTSKY. But you aren't even here, Leon.

TROTSKY. This desk, these books, that calendar . . .

MRS. TROTSKY. You're not even here, my love.

TROTSKY. The sunshine coming through the blinds . . .

MRS. TROTSKY. That was yesterday. You're in a hospital, unconscious.

TROTSKY. The flowers in the garden. You, standing there . . .

MRS. TROTSKY. This is yesterday you're seeing.

TROTSKY. What does that entry say? Would you read it again?

MRS. TROTSKY. "On August 20th, 1940, a Spanish Communist named Ramon Mercader smashed a mountain-climber's axe into Trotsky's skull in Coyoacan, a suburb of Mexico City. Trotsky died the next day."

TROTSKY. It gives you a little hope about the world, doesn't it? That a man could have a mountain-climber's axe smashed into his skull, and yet live on for one whole day . . . ? Maybe I'll go look at the nasturtiums.

(TROTSKY dies. The garden outside the louvered window begins to glow.)
The Lights Fade

AFTER YOU READ
Variations on the Death of Trotsky

Think and Discuss

1. What about the manner and timing of Trotsky's death might have appealed to Ives as the subject of a burlesque play?

2. Two variations rely on puns and word plays for humor. Which two are those, and what are the word jokes?

3. This play is one of the so-called "bell" plays by David Ives, plays that feature a ringing bell at certain times during the action. What **dramatic function** does the bell serve?

4. **Burlesque** goes to great lengths to make fun of its subject—using mockery, impersonations, jokes, and asides to the audience. Identify places in the play where these techniques are used.

5. How is this play like and unlike other plays that you know?

6. In Unit 1, you read about the work of Elisabeth Kübler-Ross with dying patients. (See page 73.) She identified five stages that people who know they are dying go through. Does the character of Trotsky go through those stages, even in a comic way? Copy the graphic organizer below into your Writer's Notebook. In the right hand column, quote passages from the play that demonstrate each stage. If you think he doesn't go through a stage, explain why you think that.

Five Stages	Passages in Play that Demonstrate Stages
Denial and isolation: Trying not to think or talk about what's happening	
Anger: Raging against your bad fortune	
Bargaining: Trying to figure out a way to avoid the inevitable	
Depression: Realizing and mourning the inevitable	
Acceptance: Finally making peace with what it is happening	

Write to Understand: Creating a New Variation

Review your graphic organizer. Is there one of the stages that Trotsky skips or passes through very quickly? If you think there is, write a new variation showing his passage through that stage. Keep your variation in the burlesque style, making fun of as much as possible. If you think Trotsky already goes through all the stages completely, write a ninth variation continuing the story.

BEFORE YOU READ

The Cask of Amontillado

Meet the Author: Edgar Allan Poe

Born in 1809, Edgar Allan Poe was a poet, essayist, and fiction writer whose troubled life was marked by the death of his parents and wife. His work often drew on subjects from the dark side. His own life was darkened by excessive drinking and gambling and by mental illness, including a suicide attempt. Poe died in 1849, at age 39, of unknown causes. Although he was considered a literary outsider for most of his life, especially in the United States, he is now widely respected. Many regard him as the first to write the modern short story, and the genres of crime and detective fiction can trace their roots back to Poe.

Build Background: Rivalry and Revenge

Shunned by literary society in New York, Poe was the subject of insult and ridicule in print by another writer, Thomas Dunn English. Poe won a libel lawsuit against English in 1846. After that, English ridiculed Poe less directly, through satire and parody, especially in a novel published that same year that parodied Poe as a drunken, lying character named Marmaduke Hammerhead who wrote poems about black birds and lost loves. Poe's "The Cask of Amontillado," also published in 1846, is in part literary revenge against English, with references to a number of details from English's novel.

"The Cask of Amontillado" is about a character determined to exact revenge for an insult. By its nature, revenge suggests "settling a score" outside of the law. It contains an element of justice, but is much darker. In fact, definitions of revenge often include the idea of hatred as a motive. Still, readers bring their own strong ideas of justice to tales of revenge and develop sympathies with the characters they regard as wronged.

As you read the story, think about these questions:

- Whose side are you on? Why?

- What other stories, books, or movies do you know that portray a character determined to get revenge?

I said to him—"My dear Fortunato, you are luckily met. How remarkably well you are looking today! But I have received a pipe[5] of what passes for Amontillado, and I have my doubts."

"How?" said he, "Amontillado? A pipe? Impossible? And in the middle of the carnival!"

"I have my doubts," I replied; "and I was silly enough to pay the full Amontillado price without consulting you in the matter. You were not to be found, and I was fearful of losing a bargain."

"Amontillado!"

"I have my doubts."

"Amontillado!"

"And I must satisfy them."

"Amontillado!"

"As you are engaged, I am on my way to Luchresi. If any one has a critical turn, it is he. He will tell me"—

"Luchresi cannot tell Amontillado from Sherry."[6]

"And yet some fools will have it that his taste is a match for your own."

"Come, let us go."

"Whither?"

"To your vaults."

"My friend, no; I will not impose upon your good nature. I perceive you have an engagement. Luchresi"—

"I have no engagement; come."

"My friend, no. It is not the engagement, but the severe cold with which I perceive you are afflicted. The vaults are insufferably damp. They are encrusted with nitre."[7]

"Let us go, nevertheless. The cold is merely nothing. Amontillado! You have been imposed upon. And as for Luchresi, he cannot distinguish Sherry from Amontillado."

Thus speaking, Fortunato possessed himself of my arm; and putting on a mask of black silk and drawing a *roquelaire*[8] closely about my person, I suffered

---

5 **pipe:** a large cask, the equivalent of 52.5 imperial gallons or about 238 liters

6 **Sherry:** a Spanish wine

7 **nitre:** the mineral form of potassium nitrate, also known as saltpeter; a critical component of gunpowder and explosives and also used in embalming

8 *roquelaire:* a knee-length cloak, buttoned in front

him to hurry me to my palazzo.[9]

absconded
left

There were no attendants at home; they had **absconded** to make merry in honor of the time. I had told them that I should not return until the morning and had given them explicit orders not to stir from the house. These orders were sufficient, I well knew, to insure their immediate disappearance, one and all, as soon as my back was turned.

I took from their sconces two flambeaux,[10] and giving one to Fortunato, bowed him through several suites of rooms to the archway that led into the vaults. I passed down a long and winding staircase, requesting him to be cautious as he followed. We came at length to the foot of the descent, and stood together upon the damp ground of the **catacombs** of the Montresors.

catacombs
network of caves, grottos, or underground passages; originally, a burial district in Rome said to be used by early Christians

The gait of my friend was unsteady, and the bells upon his cap jingled as he strode.

"The pipe," he said.

"It is farther on," said I; "but observe the white webwork which gleams from these cavern walls."

He turned towards me and looked into my eyes with two filmy orbs that distilled the **rheum** of intoxication.

rheum
watery or thin mucus discharge, as one gets when one has a cold

"Nitre?" he asked, at length.

"Nitre," I replied. "How long have you had that cough!"

"Ugh! ugh! ugh! —ugh! ugh! ugh! —ugh! ugh! ugh! —ugh! ugh! ugh! —ugh! ugh! ugh!

My poor friend found it impossible to reply for many minutes.

"It is nothing," he said, at last.

"Come," I said, with decision, "we will go back; your health is precious. You are rich, respected, admired, beloved; you are happy as once I was. You are a man to be missed. For me it is no matter. We will go back; you will be ill and I cannot be responsible. Besides, there is Luchresi" —

"Enough," he said; "the cough is a mere nothing; it will not kill me. I shall not die of a cough."

"True—true," I replied; "and, indeed, I had no intention of alarming you unnecessarily—but you should use all proper caution. A draught of this Medoc[11] will defend us from the damps."

---

9 **palazzo:** An Italian palace or townhouse

10 **flambeaux:** candelabras

11 **Medoc:** a prestigious wine from southwestern France

Here I knocked off the neck of a bottle which I drew from a long row of its fellows that lay upon the mold.

"Drink," I said, presenting him the wine.

He raised it to his lips with a leer. He paused and nodded to me familiarly, while his bells jingled.

"I drink," he said, "to the buried that repose around us."

"And I to your long life."

He again took my arm, and we proceeded.

"These vaults," he said, "are extensive."

"The Montresors," I replied, "were a great and numerous family."

"I forget your arms."[12]

"A huge human foot d'or,[13] in a field azure; the foot crushes a serpent rampant whose fangs are imbedded in the heel."

"And the motto?"

"*Nemo me impune lacessit.*"[14]

"Good!" he said.

The wine sparkled in his eyes and the bells jingled. My own

Casks in an Italian winery

fancy grew warm with the Medoc. We had passed through long walls of piled skeletons, with casks and **puncheons** intermingling, into the inmost recesses of the catacombs. I paused again, and this time I made bold to seize Fortunato by an arm above the elbow.

puncheons
casks containing 84 or 120 gallons

"The nitre!" I said; "see, it increases. It hangs like moss upon the vaults. We are below the river's bed. The drops of moisture trickle among the bones. Come, we will go back ere it is too late. Your cough—"

"It is nothing" he said; "let us go on. But first, another draught of the Medoc."

---

12 **arms:** coat of arms; family crest

13 **foot d'or:** foot of gold

14 *Nemo me impune lacessit:* Latin for "No one provokes me with impunity"

flagon
cruet;
ceramic, or
metal beaker,
such as
the pitcher
used in the
Christian
Eucharist

gesticulation
set of gestures

I broke and reached him a **flagon** of De Grâve.[15] He emptied it at a breath. His eyes flashed with a fierce light. He laughed and threw the bottle upwards with a **gesticulation** I did not understand.

I looked at him in surprise. He repeated the movement—a grotesque one.

"You do not comprehend?" he said.

"Not I," I replied.

"Then you are not of the brotherhood."

"How?"

"You are not of the Masons."[16]

"Yes, yes," I said, "yes! yes."

"You? Impossible! A Mason?"

"A Mason," I replied.

"A sign," he said, "a sign."

"It is this," I answered, producing from beneath the folds of my *roquelaire* a trowel.

"You jest," he exclaimed, recoiling a few paces. "But let us proceed to the Amontillado."

"Be it so," I said, replacing the tool beneath the cloak, and again offering him my arm. He leaned upon it heavily. We continued our route in search of the Amontillado. We passed through a range of low arches, descended, passed on, and descending again, arrived at a deep crypt, in which the foulness of the air caused our flambeaux rather to glow than flame.

At the most remote end of the crypt there appeared another less spacious. Its walls had been lined with human remains piled to the vault overhead, in the fashion of the great catacombs of Paris. Three sides of this interior crypt were still ornamented in this manner. From the fourth side the bones had been thrown down, and lay **promiscuously** upon the earth, forming at one point a mound of some size. Within the wall thus exposed by the displacing of the bones, we perceived a still interior crypt or recess, in depth about four feet, in width three, in height six or seven. It seemed to have been constructed for no especial use within itself, but formed merely the interval between two of the colossal supports of the roof of the catacombs, and was backed by one of their **circumscribing** walls of solid granite.

promiscuously
in a disordered
way; haphazardly

circumscribing
enclosing and
limiting

15 **De Grâve:** wine from Point De Grâve, the northernmost tip of the Medoc Peninsula

16 **Masons:** or Freemasons; a worldwide fraternity (which has included George Washington, Benjamin Franklin, and Paul Revere) for personal wisdom, self-improvement, and the betterment of humankind. Pope Clement XII, in 1738, condemned Freemasonry as a pagan religion and a threat to the Church.

It was in vain that Fortunato, uplifting his dull torch, endeavored to pry into the depth of the recess. Its termination the feeble light did not enable us to see.

"Proceed," I said; "herein is the Amontillado. As for Luchresi" —

"He is an ignoramus," interrupted my friend, as he stepped unsteadily forward, while I followed immediately at his heels. In an instant he had reached the extremity of the niche, and finding his progress arrested by the rock, stood stupidly bewildered. A moment more and I had **fettered** him to the granite. In its surface were two iron staples, distant from each other about two feet, horizontally. From one of these depended a short chain, from the other a padlock. Throwing the links about his waist, it was but the work of a few seconds to secure it. He was too much astounded to resist. Withdrawing the key I stepped back from the recess.

"Pass your hand," I said, "over the wall; you cannot help feeling the nitre. Indeed it is *very* damp. Once more let me *implore* you to return. No? Then I must positively leave you. But I must first render you all the little attentions in my power."

"The Amontillado!" ejaculated my friend, not yet recovered from his astonishment.

"True," I replied; "the Amontillado."

As I said these words I busied myself among the pile of bones of which I have before spoken. Throwing them aside, I soon uncovered a quantity of building stone and mortar. With these materials and with the aid of my trowel, I began vigorously to wall up the entrance of the niche.

I had scarcely laid the first tier of the masonry when I discovered that the intoxication of Fortunato had in a great measure worn off. The earliest indication I had of this was a low moaning cry from the depth of the recess. It was *not* the cry of a drunken man. There was then a long and obstinate silence. I laid the second tier, and the third, and the fourth; and then I heard the furious vibrations of the chain. The noise lasted for several minutes, during which, that I might hearken to it with the more satisfaction, I ceased my labors and sat down upon the bones. When at last the clanking subsided, I resumed the trowel, and finished without interruption the fifth, the sixth, and the seventh tier. The wall was now nearly upon a level with my breast. I again paused, and holding the flambeaux over the mason-work, threw a few feeble rays upon the figure within.

A succession of loud and shrill screams, bursting suddenly from the throat of the chained form, seemed to thrust me violently back. For a brief moment I hesitated, I trembled. Unsheathing my **rapier,** I began to grope with it about

fettered
bound by chains

rapier
a slender sword

clamored
shouted;
roared

the recess; but the thought of an instant reassured me. I placed my hand upon the solid fabric of the catacombs, and felt satisfied. I reapproached the wall. I replied to the yells of him who **clamored**. I re-echoed—I aided—I surpassed them in volume and in strength. I did this, and the clamorer grew still.

It was now midnight, and my task was drawing to a close. I had completed the eighth, the ninth, and the tenth tier. I had finished a portion of the last and the eleventh; there remained but a single stone to be fitted and plastered in. I struggled with its weight; I placed it partially in its destined position. But now there came from out the niche a low laugh that erected the hairs upon my head. It was succeeded by a sad voice, which I had difficulty in recognizing as that of the noble Fortunato. The voice said—

"Ha! ha! ha!—he! he! he!—a very good joke, indeed—an excellent jest. We will have many a rich laugh about it at the palazzo—he! he! he!—over our wine—he! he! he!"

"The Amontillado!" I said.

"He! he! he!—he! he! he!—yes, the Amontillado. But is it not getting late? Will not they be awaiting us at the palazzo, the Lady Fortunato and the rest? Let us be gone."

"Yes," I said, "let us be gone."

"For the love of God, Montresor!"

"Yes," I said, "for the love of God!"

hearkened
listened

But to these words I **hearkened** in vain for a reply. I grew impatient. I called aloud—

"Fortunato!"

No answer. I called again—

"Fortunato!"

No answer still. I thrust a torch through the remaining aperture[17] and let it fall within. There came forth in return only a jingling of the bells. My heart grew sick; it was the dampness of the catacombs that made it so. I hastened to make an end of my labor. I forced the last stone into its position; I plastered it up. Against the new masonry I re-erected the old **rampart** of bones. For the half of a century no mortal has disturbed them. *In pace requiescat!*[18]

rampart
hill

---

17 **aperture:** opening

18 *In pace requiescat:* Latin for "May he rest in peace!"

AFTER YOU READ
The Cask of Amontillado

Think and Discuss

1. Does Montresor succeed in getting revenge "with impunity"? Explain.

2. What parts of the story tell you how Montresor feels about what he has done?

3. Why do you think Fortunato becomes silent at the end except for the ringing of the bells on his fool's hat?

4. This story features a **first-person narrator**. A **reliable** narrator says and believes things the reader feels are true. An **unreliable** narrator says and believes things that the reader doubts or disbelieves completely. Is Montresor a reliable or unreliable narrator? Use examples from the story to support your answer.

5. Through what technique does Poe move along the **plot** of this story?

6. In your Writer's Notebook, make a cluster diagram like the one below to compare and contrast Montresor and Fortunato.

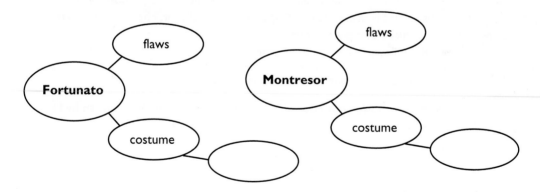

Write to Understand: Casting Call

Suppose you wanted to dramatize this story. In your Writer's Notebook, write a description of the characters and what you would look for in an actor for each part. Refer to your graphic organizer for ideas.

BEFORE YOU READ
Poems of Darkness

Meet the Author: Edgar Allan Poe

Poe's unhappy life (see page 634) found expression in his poems. Both "Annabel Lee" and "The Raven" are poems of mourning for a dead lover. "The Raven," published in 1845, made Poe famous—it was hugely popular and was reprinted many times. "The Bells" was inspired by Fordham University's bell tower, which is still standing in New York City's Bronx. Poe published four volumes of poetry in his lifetime; a fifth was published after his death.

Build Background: Poetry as a Mathematical Problem?

While Poe's poetry touches on madness and opens the door to the dark side, it was not, according to Poe himself, composed in a "fine frenzy" of intuition as he says other poets claim about their inspired writing. Quite the opposite, as he explains in an essay about how he composed "The Raven." He indicates that nothing in it is there by "accident or intuition"—that the work proceeded step by step, to its completion, with the "precision and rigid consequence of a mathematical problem."

Poe's belief about poetry—in fact about all literature that would be experienced in a single "sitting," including short stories—is that every detail in the work should support "a unity of impression." That is, creating one single overall effect is the purpose of artistic writing. Once that effect is decided on, the specific details of plot, character, and setting can be chosen to achieve that precise effect.

As you read the following poems, ask yourself:

• What impression forms in your mind as you read each poem?

• Based on what you know about Poe, what would you expect these poems to be like?

Poems of Darkness

EDGAR ALLAN POE

The Bells

EDGAR ALLAN POE

sledges
horse-drawn
sleighs

Hear the **sledges** with the bells—
Silver bells!
What a world of merriment their melody foretells!
How they tinkle, tinkle, tinkle,
In the icy air of night!   5
While the stars, that oversprinkle
All the heavens, seem to twinkle

crystalline
having
characteristics
of or made of
crystals

With a **crystalline** delight;
Keeping time, time, time,
In a sort of Runic[1] rhyme,   10
To the tintinnabulation[2] that so musically wells
From the bells, bells, bells, bells,
Bells, bells, bells—
From the jingling and the tinkling of the bells.

Hear the mellow wedding bells,   15
Golden bells!
What a world of happiness their harmony foretells!

balmy
soothing, mild,
and pleasant,
like balm

Through the **balmy** air of night
How they ring out their delight!
From the molten-golden notes,   20
And all in tune,
What a liquid ditty[3] floats

euphony
pleasing,
harmonious
sounds

To the turtle-dove that listens, while she gloats
On the moon!
Oh, from out the sounding cells,   25
What a gush of **euphony voluminously** wells!

voluminously
with great
volume; loudly

How it swells!
How it dwells

---

1 **Runic:** an allusion to ancient characters used by Germanic people during the Middle Ages.
In this context, the word refers to any kind of mysterious inscription.

2 **tintinnabulation:** the ringing of bells

3 **ditty:** little song

On the Future!—how it tells
Of the rapture that impels   30
To the swinging and the ringing
Of the bells, bells, bells,
Of the bells, bells, bells, bells,
Bells, bells, bells—
To the rhyming and the chiming of the bells!   35

Hear the loud alarum[4] bells,
Brazen bells!
What a tale of terror, now, their turbulency tells!
In the startled ear of night
How they scream out their affright!   40
Too much horrified to speak,
They can only shriek, shriek,
Out of tune,
In a clamorous appealing to the mercy of the fire,
In a mad expostulation[5] with the deaf and frantic fire,   45
Leaping higher, higher, higher,
With a desperate desire,
And a resolute endeavor
Now—now to sit or never,
By the side of the palefaced moon.   50
Oh, the bells, bells, bells!
What a tale their terror tells
Of Despair!

---

4 **alarum:** alarm

5 **expostulation:** expression of protest or reproof

How they clang, and clash, and roar!
What a horror they outpour   55
On the **bosom** of the palpitating air!
Yet the ear it fully knows,
By the twanging
And the clanging,
How the danger ebbs and flows;   60
Yet the ear distinctly tells,
In the jangling
And the wrangling,
How the danger sinks and swells—
By the sinking or the swelling in the anger of the bells,   65
Of the bells,
Of the bells, bells, bells, bells,
Bells, bells, bells—
In the clamor and the clangor[6] of the bells!

Hear the tolling of the bells,   70
Iron bells!
What a world of solemn thought their **monody** compels!
In the silence of the night
How we shiver with affright
At the melancholy menace of their tone!   75
For every sound that floats
From the rust within their throats
Is a groan.
And the people—ah, the people—
They that dwell up in the steeple,   80
All alone,
And who tolling, tolling, tolling,
In that muffled monotone,
Feel a glory in so rolling
On the human heart a stone—   85

bosom
(in poetic
terms) a place
of loving care

monody
voice or tone

---

6 **clangor:** clang

They are neither man nor woman—
They are neither brute nor human—
They are Ghouls:
And their king it is who tolls;
And he rolls, rolls, rolls,   90
Rolls
A paean[7] from the bells!
And his merry bosom swells
With the paean of the bells!
And he dances, and he yells;   95
Keeping time, time, time,
In a sort of Runic rhyme,
To the paean of the bells—
Of the bells:
Keeping time, time, time,   100
In a sort of Runic rhyme,
To the throbbing of the bells,
Of the bells, bells, bells—
To the sobbing of the bells;
Keeping time, time, time,   105
As he **knells**, knells, knells,
In a happy Runic rhyme,   **knells**
To the rolling of the bells—   rings slowly
Of the bells, bells, bells: and solemnly
To the tolling of the bells—   110
Of the bells, bells, bells, bells,
Bells, bells, bells—
To the moaning and the groaning of the bells.

---

7 **paean:** an expression of praise or appreciation

Annabel Lee

EDGAR ALLAN POE

It was many and many a year ago,
In a kingdom by the sea,
That a maiden there lived whom you may know
By the name of Annabel Lee;
And this maiden she lived with no other thought   5
Than to love and be loved by me.

I was a child and *she* was a child,
In this kingdom by the sea:
But we loved with a love that was more than love—
I and my Annabel Lee;   10
With a love that the winged **seraphs** of Heaven
Coveted her and me.

seraphs
heavenly beings
having three
pairs of wings

coveted
longed to
possess

And this was the reason that, long ago,
In this kingdom by the sea,
A wind blew out of a cloud, chilling   15
My beautiful Annabel Lee;
So that her high-born kinsmen came
And bore her away from me,
To shut her up in a **sepulcher,**
In this kingdom by the sea.   20

sepulcher
a cave or
room used as
a burial site

The angels, not half so happy in Heaven,
Went envying her and me—
Yes!—that was the reason (as all men know,
In this kingdom by the sea)
That the wind came out of the cloud by night,   25
Chilling and killing my Annabel Lee.

But our love it was stronger by far than the love
Of those who were older than we—
Of many far wiser than we—
And neither the angels in Heaven above,   30
Nor the demons down under the sea,
Can ever **dissever** my soul from the soul   **dissever**
Of the beautiful Annabel Lee;   divide; sever

For the moon never beams without bringing me dreams
Of the beautiful Annabel Lee;   35
And the stars never rise but I feel the bright eyes
Of the beautiful Annabel Lee;
And so, all the night-tide, I lie down by the side
Of my darling—my darling—my life and my bride,
In the sepulcher there by the sea—   40
In her tomb by the sounding sea.

YOUNG WOMAN AT THE BEACH,
Philip Wilson Steer

The Raven

EDGAR ALLAN POE

Once upon a midnight dreary, while I pondered, weak and weary,
Over many a quaint and curious volume of forgotten lore—
While I nodded, nearly napping, suddenly there came a tapping,
As of someone gently rapping, rapping at my chamber door.
"'Tis some visitor," I muttered, "tapping at my chamber door—   5
Only this, and nothing more."

Ah, distinctly I remember it was in the bleak December,
And each separate dying ember **wrought** its ghost upon the floor.
Eagerly I wished the morrow; vainly I had sought to borrow
From my books **surcease** of sorrow—sorrow for the lost Lenore—   10
For the rare and radiant maiden whom the angels name Lenore—
Nameless here forevermore.

And the silken, sad, uncertain rustling of each purple curtain
Thrilled me—filled me with fantastic terrors never felt before;
So that now, to still the beating of my heart, I stood repeating,   15
"'Tis some visitor entreating entrance at my chamber door—
Some late visitor entreating entrance at my chamber door; —
This it is and nothing more."

Presently my soul grew stronger; hesitating then no longer,
"Sir," said I, "or Madam, truly your forgiveness I implore;   20
But the fact is I was napping, and so gently you came rapping,
And so faintly you came tapping, tapping at my chamber door,
That I scarce was sure I heard you"—here I opened wide the door—
Darkness there, and nothing more.

Deep into that darkness peering, long I stood there wondering, fearing,   25
Doubting, dreaming dreams no mortal ever dared to dream before;
But the silence was unbroken, and the stillness gave no token,
And the only word there spoken was the whispered word, "Lenore?"
This I whispered, and an echo murmured back the word, "Lenore!"
Merely this, and nothing more.   30

wrought
made and
shaped

surcease
an end or stop
to something

Back into the chamber turning, all my soul within me burning,
Soon again I heard a tapping somewhat louder than before.
"Surely," said I, "surely that is something at my window **lattice**;
Let me see, then, what thereat is, and this mystery explore—
Let my heart be still a moment and this mystery explore;   35
'Tis the wind and nothing more!"

Open here I flung the shutter, when, with many a flirt and flutter,
In there stepped a stately Raven of the saintly days of yore;
Not the least **obeisance** made he; not a minute stopped or stayed he;
But, with **mien** of lord or lady, perched above my chamber door—   40
Perched upon a bust of Pallas[1] just above my chamber door—
Perched, and sat, and nothing more.

Then this ebony bird **beguiling** my sad fancy into smiling,
By the grave and stern decorum of the countenance it wore.
"Though thy crest be shorn and shaven, thou," I said, "art sure no craven,   45
Ghastly grim and ancient Raven wandering from the Nightly shore—
Tell me what thy lordly name is on the Night's Plutonian shore!"[2]
Quoth the Raven, "Nevermore."

Much I marveled this ungainly fowl to hear discourse so plainly,
Though its answer little meaning—little relevancy bore;   50
For we cannot help agreeing that no living human being
Ever yet was blest with seeing bird above his chamber door—
Bird or beast upon the sculptured bust above his chamber door,
With such name as "Nevermore."

But the Raven, sitting lonely on the **placid** bust, spoke only   55
That one word, as if his soul in that one word he did outpour.
Nothing further then he uttered, not a feather then he fluttered—
Till I scarcely more than muttered, "Other friends have flown before;
On the morrow *he* will leave me, as my hopes have flown before."
Then the bird said, "Nevermore."   60

lattice
a framework
of overlapping
materials

obeisance
bending in
respect or
obedience

mien
manner or
appearance

beguiling
enchanting

placid
peaceful;
serene

---

1 **Pallas:** a reference to Pallas Athena, the Greek goddess. Athena is pale and contrasts with
the dark raven on her shoulder.

2 **Plutonian shore:** In Greek mythology, the shore of the River Styx, on the other side of
which is the underworld (Hades) ruled by Pluto

Startled at the stillness broken by reply so aptly spoken,
"Doubtless," said I, "what it utters is its only stock and store,
Caught from some unhappy master whom unmerciful disaster
Followed fast and followed faster till his songs one burden bore—

melancholy
gloominess;
sense of
sadness

Till the dirges of his hope that **melancholy** burden bore   65
Of 'Never—nevermore'."

But the Raven still beguiling all my fancy into smiling,
Straight I wheeled a cushioned seat in front of bird, and bust, and door;
Then, upon the velvet sinking, I betook myself to linking
Fancy unto fancy, thinking what this ominous bird of yore—   70

gaunt
very thin;
bony;
worn-
looking

What this grim, ungainly, ghastly, **gaunt,** and ominous bird of yore
Meant in croaking "Nevermore."

This I sat engaged in guessing, but no syllable expressing
To the fowl whose fiery eyes now burned into my bosom's core;
This and more I sat divining, with my head at ease reclining   75
On the cushion's velvet lining that the lamplight gloated[3] o'er,
But whose velvet violet lining with the lamplight gloating o'er,
She shall press, ah, nevermore!

Then, methought, the air grew denser, perfumed from an unseen censer[4]
Swung by seraphim whose footfalls tinkled on the tufted floor.   80
"Wretch," I cried, "thy God hath lent thee—by these angels he hath sent thee

respite
relief

Respite—respite and nepenthe[5]—from thy memories of Lenore!
Quaff, oh quaff this kind nepenthe and forget this lost Lenore!"
Quoth the Raven, "Nevermore."

---

3 **gloated:** a rare meaning of the word, possibly indicating light being reflected from the side

4 **censer:** a container in which incense is burned

5 **nepenthe:** a drug that induces forgetfulness of sorrow; forgetfulness, especially of sorrow

"Prophet!" said I, "thing of evil!—prophet still, if bird or devil!   85
Whether Tempter sent, or whether tempest tossed thee here ashore,
Desolate yet all undaunted, on this desert land enchanted—
On this home by horror haunted—tell me truly, I implore—
Is there—is there balm in Gilead?[6]—tell me—tell me, I implore!"
Quoth the Raven, "Nevermore."   90

"Prophet!" said I, "thing of evil—prophet still, if bird or devil!
By that Heaven that bends above us, by that God we both adore,
Tell this soul with sorrow laden if, within the distant Aidenn,[7]
It shall clasp a sainted maiden whom the angels name Lenore—
Clasp a rare and radiant maiden whom the angels name Lenore."   95
Quoth the Raven, "Nevermore."

---

6 **Is there balm in Gilead?:** an allusion to the Biblical Jeremiah, who seeks a balm for the
   suffering of his people; Gilead is a mountainous region east of the Jordan River

7 **Aidenn:** an Arabic term for Paradise

"Be that word our sign in parting, bird or fiend!" I shrieked upstarting.
"Get thee back into the tempest and the Night's Plutonian shore!
Leave no black plume as a token of that lie thy soul hath spoken!
Leave my loneliness unbroken!—quit the bust above my door!   100
Take thy beak from out my heart, and take thy form from off my door!"
Quoth the Raven, "Nevermore."

And the Raven, never flitting, still is sitting, *still* is sitting

pallid
extremely
pale

On the **pallid** bust of Pallas just above my chamber door;
And his eyes have all the seeming of a demon's that is dreaming,   105
And the lamplight o'er him streaming throws his shadow on the floor;
And my soul from out that shadow that lies floating on the floor
Shall be lifted—nevermore!

AFTER YOU READ
Poems of Darkness

Think and Discuss

1. Does Poe succeed in establishing one main impression in "The Bells"? Explain.

2. What does the speaker's explanation for the death of his beloved in "Annabel Lee" tell you about him?

3. Why do you think "The Raven" became such a popular poem?

4. Poe uses a number of poetic techniques such as **consonance** and **alliteration** to add a musical quality to his poems. Copy the following graphic organizer into your Writer's Notebook. Fill it in with examples from the poems you have just read. (For definitions of *consonance, alliteration,* and other poetic techniques, see the Glossary of Literary Terms.)

Technique	The Bells	Annabel Lee	The Raven
Consonance (repeating internal vowel sounds, such as the short *e* sound in "Hear the mellow wedding bells.")			
Alliteration (repeating initial consonants, such as the letter *d* in "Doubting, dreaming dreams no mortals ever dared to dream before.")			
Repetition of Phrases and Lines			

5. Which poem in this lesson do you find most effective? What mood or feeling does the poem produce in you?

6. Were your expectations of the kinds of poems you would read in this lesson fulfilled? Explain.

Write to Understand: Poetry vs. Prose

Rewrite either "Annabel Lee" or "The Raven" as narrative prose. Try to achieve the same overall impression Poe achieves in his poems. Also try to recast some of the poetic techniques you recorded in your graphic organizer, using fresh, original wording. Compare your prose piece with the poetry and decide if you have achieved your goal.

BEFORE YOU READ

Dozens of Roses

Meet the Author: Virginia Euwer Wolff

Born in 1937, Wolff grew up in a pear and apple orchard in Portland, Oregon. Her father died when she was only five years old. She describes her childhood as "pretty messed up," but Wolff found solace in playing the violin. When she was older, she attended Smith College. After raising two children, she began teaching high school, where she accumulated material for many of her stories. She is the award-winning author of *Make Lemonade* and its sequel, *True Believer.*

Build Background: The Function of the Chorus

Ancient Greek drama is the foundation for Western dramatic writing. Greek comedies and tragedies featured a chorus that was both part of the action and separate from it. The chorus was often costumed to represent townspeople. Its songs or poems opened and closed most scenes and also voiced the playwright's perspective on the action. In addition, the chorus signaled to the audience members how they should respond to events in the play. In ancient Greek drama, the chorus was usually sympathetic to the hero of the play.

As you read the following play, ask yourself:

• Is the chorus in this drama used in the traditional way?

• Which of your friends, family, and acquaintances would you choose if you were casting a chorus to comment on your life?

Dozens of Roses

VIRGINIA EUWER WOLFF

DOZENS OF ROSES

Virginia Euwer Wolff

VOICES: Lucy
       Chuck
       Chorus
       The Rememberer

Chorus: They are bloodred, floating on long stems, stiffened with invisible wire so they stand up straight among maidenhair ferns, and there are a dozen of them.

LUCY: I don't want them.

CHORUS: But they came for you! A dozen red roses! Delivered by a florist's messenger! Right to the school office! An announcement came over the air, through the walls, into all the hallways, asking for you to come to the office!

LUCY: I don't want them. Please don't make me take them.

THE REMEMBERER: I used to know her when we were little. She was full of energy then. We had picnics and we played jump rope. She had pep.

CHORUS: Who sent them to you?

LUCY: Please don't make me say.

CHORUS: You can't ignore flowers. There they are, standing up straight in a vase full of water, right in front of the secretary's desk. It's really a sight to see: the dull old school office, with the tan walls and the tan filing cabinets and bad lighting—And those dozen romantic, red roses.

CHUCK: She'll know how I feel about her when she sees the roses.

LUCY: I can't go get them.

CHORUS: That's ridiculous. Of course you can go get them. Who would turn down such a gift?

LUCY: You don't understand.

CHORUS: Oh—you mean your sprained ankle? They must be get-well roses.

LUCY: I don't care what kind of roses they are.

THE REMEMBERER: Something has taken the fire out of her. She isn't the same.

CHORUS: Take a friend with you. To help carry them while you limp along. Read the card and tell us who sent them.

CHUCK: She'll love them. That's a lot of money I spent.

CHORUS: Whoever he is, he must adore you.

LUCY: I won't look at them. I won't go to the office. I won't read the card.

CHUCK: She'll forget she was mad.

CHORUS: You're a lucky girl.

LUCY: My ankle hurts.

CHORUS: People who feel sorry for themselves aren't any fun at all.

CHUCK: She fell.

LUCY: I can't leave my math class.

CHUCK: She fell right over the end of the chair.

LUCY: Please, somebody, take the roses home with you.

CHORUS: You must be crazy.

CHUCK: She had her weight distributed the wrong way. I barely touched her.

Maybe it was that cut on her forehead last fall. Maybe it did something to her brain. Maybe the emergency room was a shock to her system.

CHORUS: She must be very stubborn.

CHUCK: She looked at him. I saw her look at him. Making plans to meet him behind my back.

LUCY: I need to do my math.

THE REMEMBERER: Maybe it was that cut on her forehead last fall. Maybe it did something to her brain. Maybe the emergency room was a shock to her system.

CHORUS: She's so ungrateful.

LUCY: Please don't make me talk about it.

CHUCK: She'll know when she gets the roses. How much I feel for her.

LUCY: I want to stay in class, where I can breathe.

CHUCK: I need her. She'll know when she gets the roses.

THE REMEMBERER: That *was* it. When she had to go to the hospital that time. With the cut on her forehead. She's been different ever since.

LUCY: Can math class please go on forever?

CHORUS: There's a time to be moody and a time to snap out of it. She should snap out of it.

CHUCK: I can't live without her. She'll know when she gets the roses.

THE REMEMBERER: She got a dozen roses that other time, too.

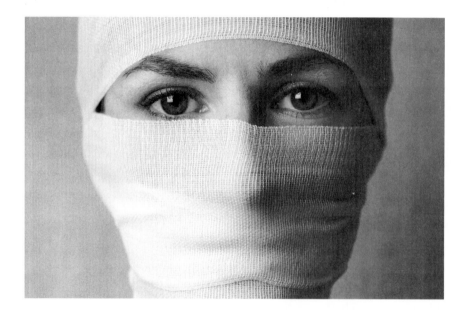

AFTER YOU READ
Dozens of Roses

Think and Discuss

1. At the beginning of the play, how do you feel about Lucy's unwillingness to get the roses?

2. At what point in the play do you understand why Lucy does not want the flowers?

3. In this play, Wolff invented a chorus that opposes, rather than supports, her protagonist. What effect does the **oppositional chorus** have on the audience? (One way to try to answer that is to imagine the play with a supportive chorus and think about that effect; then compare the two.)

4. Compare the role and perspective of the chorus in this play to that in the play *Eurydice* in Unit 6.

5. What **inferences** can you draw from the details of this play about the relationship between Lucy and Chuck? (For a definition of *inference* see the Glossary of Literary Terms.)

6. Copy the following graphic organizer into your Writer's Notebook. Write down each statement Lucy makes and each statement Chuck makes. Compare the subjects of the sentences and explain why Wolff might have constructed the statements that way.

Lucy's Statements	Chuck's Statements

Write to Understand: The Function of the Chorus

Dramatize a conflict you have experienced, observed, or read about. Include in your dramatization characters representing both sides of the conflict. Refer to your graphic organizer for ideas on how to make the lines for each character carry as much meaning as possible. Also include a chorus to represent your point of view about the conflict.

BEFORE YOU READ
The Lottery

Meet the Author: Shirley Jackson

Shirley Jackson (1919-1965) was drawn to writing even as a child. She won a poetry contest when she was twelve and kept a diary in high school about her writing. She graduated from Syracuse University in 1940 and married another writer and literary critic. Even in the midst of raising their four children, Jackson faithfully wrote 1,000 words a day. She wrote for magazines ranging from *Weird Tales* to *Good Housekeeping* to *The New Yorker*. She also published novels. She suffered from bouts of depression throughout her life and died of heart failure at age 46.

Build Background: Slow Revelation

Some literature from the dark side makes its darkness known from the beginning. "Once upon a midnight dreary," the opening words of Poe's poem "The Raven," sets a scene in which the worst can be expected. Other tales, however, are slow to reveal their dark side. They may draw readers in with a story of ordinary days and lives, making us feel right at home. A turn toward darkness, when it happens, becomes all the more disturbing since there had been no bolt of lighting, crash of thunder, or villainous laugh to lead readers to expect trouble.

The following story is Jackson's most famous. As you read:

- Let your mind create images of the people and setting Jackson describes on the clear, sunny day of June 27th.

- Call to mind what you know about lotteries.

- Jot down any questions you have while reading.

The Lottery

SHIRLEY JACKSON

THE LOTTERY

Shirley Jackson

profusely
abundantly

boisterous
noisy and
unruly

reprimands
scoldings

The morning of June 27th was clear and sunny, with the fresh warmth of a full-summer day; the flowers were blossoming **profusely** and the grass was richly green. The people of the village began to gather in the square, between the post office and the bank, around ten o'clock; in some towns there were so many people that the lottery took two days and had to be started on June 26th, but in this village, where there were only about three hundred people, the whole lottery took less than two hours, so it could begin at ten o'clock in the morning and still be through in time to allow the villagers to get home for noon dinner. The children assembled first, of course. School was recently over for the summer, and the feeling of liberty sat uneasily on most of them; they tended to gather together quietly for a while before they broke into **boisterous** play, and their talk was still of the classroom and the teacher, of books and **reprimands**. Bobby Martin had already stuffed his pockets full of stones, and the other boys soon followed his example, selecting the smoothest and roundest stones; Bobby and Harry Jones and Dickie Delacroix—the villagers pronounced this name "Dellacroy"—eventually made a great pile of stones in one corner of the square and guarded it against the raids of the other boys. The girls stood aside, talking among themselves, looking over their shoulders at the boys, and the very small children rolled in the dust or clung to the hands of their older brothers or sisters.

Soon the men began to gather, surveying their own children, speaking of planting and rain, tractors and taxes. They stood together, away from the pile of stones in the corner, and their jokes were quiet and they smiled rather than laughed. The women, wearing faded house dresses and sweaters, came shortly after their menfolk. They greeted one another and exchanged bits of gossip as they went to join their husbands. Soon the women, standing by their husbands, began to call to their children, and the children came reluctantly, having to be called four or five times. Bobby Martin ducked under his mother's grasping hand and ran, laughing, back to the pile of stones. His father spoke up sharply, and Bobby came quickly and took his place between his father and his oldest brother.

The lottery was conducted—as were the square dances, the teenage club, the Halloween program—by Mr. Summers, who had time and energy to devote to civic activities. He was a round-faced, **jovial** man and he ran the coal business, and people were sorry for him because he had no children and his wife was a scold. When he arrived in the square, carrying the black wooden box, there was a murmur of conversation among the villagers, and he waved and called, "Little late today, folks." The postmaster, Mr. Graves, followed him, carrying a three-legged stool, and the stool was put in the center of the square and Mr. Summers set the black box down on it. The villagers kept their distance, leaving a space between themselves and the stool, and when Mr. Summers said, "Some of you fellows want to give me a hand?" there was a hesitation before two men, Mr. Martin and his oldest son, Baxter, came forward to hold the box steady on the stool while Mr. Summers stirred up the papers inside it.

jovial
merry; jolly

The original **paraphernalia** for the lottery had been lost long ago, and the black box now resting on the stool had been put into use even before Old Man Warner, the oldest man in town, was born. Mr. Summers spoke frequently to the villagers about making a new box, but no one liked to upset even as much tradition as was represented by the black box. There was a story that the present box had been made with some pieces of the box that had preceded it, the one that had been constructed when the first people settled down to make a village here. Every year, after the lottery, Mr. Summers began talking again about a new box, but every year the subject was allowed to fade off without anything's being done. The black box grew shabbier each year; by now it was no longer completely black but splintered badly along one side to show the original wood color, and in some places faded or stained.

paraphernalia
miscellaneous equipment and tools

Mr. Martin and his oldest son, Baxter, held the black box securely on the stool until Mr. Summers had stirred the papers thoroughly with his hand. Because so much of the ritual had been forgotten or discarded, Mr. Summers had been successful in having slips of paper substituted for the chips of wood that had been used for generations. Chips of wood, Mr. Summers had argued, had been all very well when the village was tiny, but now that the population was more than three hundred and likely to keep on growing, it was necessary to use something that would fit more easily into the black box. The night before the lottery, Mr. Summers and Mr. Graves made up the slips of paper and put them in the box, and it was then taken to the safe of Mr. Summers' coal company and locked up until Mr. Summers was ready to take it to the square next morning. The rest of the year, the box was put way, sometimes one place, sometimes another; it had spent one year in Mr. Graves's barn and another year underfoot in the post office, and sometimes it was set on a shelf in the Martin grocery and left there.

There was a great deal of fussing to be done before Mr. Summers declared the lottery open. There were the lists to make up—of heads of families, heads of households in each family, members of each household in each family. There was the proper swearing-in[1] of Mr. Summers by the postmaster, as the official of the lottery; at one time, some people remembered, there had been a recital of some sort, performed by the official of the lottery, a **perfunctory**, tuneless chant that had been rattled off duly each year; some people believed that the official of the lottery used to stand just so when he said or sang it, others believed that he was supposed to walk among the people, but years and years ago this part of the **ritual** had been allowed to lapse. There had been, also, a ritual salute, which the official of the lottery had had to use in addressing each person who came up to draw from the box, but this also had changed with time, until now it was felt necessary only for the official to speak to each person approaching. Mr. Summers was very good at all this; in his clean white shirt and blue jeans, with one hand resting carelessly on the black box, he seemed very proper and important as he talked **interminably** to Mr. Graves and the Martins.

Just as Mr. Summers finally left off talking and turned to the assembled villagers, Mrs. Hutchinson came hurriedly along the path to the square, her sweater thrown over her shoulders, and slid into place in the back of the crowd. "Clean forgot what day it was," she said to Mrs. Delacroix, who stood next to her, and they both laughed softly. "Thought my old man was out back stacking wood," Mrs. Hutchinson went on, "and then I looked out the window and the kids was gone, and then I remembered it was the twenty-seventh and came a-running." She dried her hands on her apron, and Mrs. Delacroix said, "You're in time, though. They're still talking away up there."

Mrs. Hutchinson craned her neck to see through the crowd and found her husband and children standing near the front. She tapped Mrs. Delacroix on the arm as a farewell and began to make her way through the crowd. The people separated good-humoredly to let her through; two or three people said, in voices just loud enough to be heard across the crowd, "Here comes

perfunctory
routine; cursory

ritual
customary practice or codified set of actions

interminably
endlessly

I **swearing-in:** administering an oath to make someone's role official.

your Missus, Hutchinson," and "Bill, she made it after all." Mrs. Hutchinson reached her husband, and Mr. Summers, who had been waiting, said cheerfully, "Thought we were going to have to get on without you, Tessie." Mrs. Hutchinson said, grinning, "Wouldn't have me leave m'dishes in the sink, now, would you, Joe?," and soft laughter ran through the crowd as the people stirred back into position after Mrs. Hutchinson's arrival.

"Well, now," Mr. Summers said soberly, "guess we better get started, get this over with, so's we can go back to work. Anybody ain't here?"

"Dunbar," several people said. "Dunbar, Dunbar."

Mr. Summers consulted his list. "Clyde Dunbar," he said. "That's right. He's broke his leg, hasn't he? Who's drawing for him?"

"Me, I guess," a woman said, and Mr. Summers turned to look at her. "Wife draws for her husband," Mr. Summers said. "Don't you have a grown boy to do it for you, Janey?" Although Mr. Summers and everyone else in the village knew the answer perfectly well, it was the business of the official of the lottery to ask such questions formally. Mr. Summers waited with an expression of polite interest while Mrs. Dunbar answered.

"Horace's not but sixteen yet," Mrs. Dunbar said regretfully. "Guess I gotta fill in for the old man this year."

"Right," Mr. Summers said. He made a note on the list he was holding. Then he asked, "Watson boy drawing this year?"

A tall boy in the crowd raised his hand. "Here," he said. "I'm drawing for m'mother and me." He blinked his eyes nervously and ducked his head as several voices in the crowd said things like "Good fellow, Jack," and "Glad to see your mother's got a man to do it."

"Well," Mr. Summers said, "guess that's everyone. Old Man Warner make it?"

"Here," a voice said, and Mr. Summers nodded.

A sudden hush fell on the crowd as Mr. Summers cleared his throat and looked at the list. "All ready?" he called. "Now, I'll read the names—heads of families first—and the men come up and take a paper out of the box. Keep the paper folded in your hand without looking at it until everyone has had a turn. Everything clear?"

The people had done it so many times that they only half listened to the directions: most of them were quiet, wetting their lips, not looking around. Then Mr. Summers raised one hand high and said, "Adams." A man disengaged himself from the crowd and came forward. "Hi, Steve," Mr. Summers said, and

Mr. Adams said, "Hi, Joe." They grinned at one another humorlessly and nervously. Then Mr. Adams reached into the black box and took out a folded paper. He held it firmly by one corner as he turned and went hastily back to his place in the crowd, where he stood a little apart from his family, not looking down at his hand.

"Allen." Mr. Summers said. "Anderson. . . . Bentham."

"Seems like there's no time at all between lotteries any more," Mrs. Delacroix said to Mrs. Graves in the back row.

"Seems like we got through with the last one only last week."

"Time sure goes fast," Mrs. Graves said.

"Clark. . . . Delacroix."

"There goes my old man," Mrs. Delacroix said. She held her breath while her husband went forward.

"Dunbar," Mr. Summers said, and Mrs. Dunbar went steadily to the box while one of the women said. "Go on, Janey," and another said, "There she goes."

"We're next," Mrs. Graves said. She watched while Mr. Graves came around from the side of the box, greeted Mr. Summers gravely and selected a slip of paper from the box. By now, all through the crowd there were men holding the small folded papers in their large hands, turning them over and over nervously. Mrs. Dunbar and her two sons stood together, Mrs. Dunbar holding the slip of paper.

"Harburt. . . . Hutchinson."

"Get up there, Bill," Mrs. Hutchinson said, and the people near her laughed.

"Jones."

"They do say," Mr. Adams said to Old Man Warner, who stood next to him, "that over in the north village they're talking of giving up the lottery."

Old Man Warner snorted. "Pack of crazy fools," he said. "Listening to the young folks, nothing's good enough for *them*. Next thing you know, they'll be wanting to go back to living in caves, nobody work any more, live *that* way for a while. Used to be a saying about 'Lottery in June, corn be heavy soon.' First thing you know, we'd all be eating stewed chickweed and acorns. There's *always* been a lottery," he added **petulantly**. "Bad enough to see young Joe Summers up there joking with everybody."

"Some places have already quit lotteries," Mrs. Adams said.

petulantly
in a pouting manner

"Nothing but trouble in *that*," Old Man Warner said **stoutly**. "Pack of young fools."

stoutly
resolutely; with determination

"Martin." And Bobby Martin watched his father go forward.

"Overdyke. . . . Percy."

"I wish they'd hurry," Mrs. Dunbar said to her older son. "I wish they'd hurry."

"They're almost through," her son said.

"You get ready to run tell Dad," Mrs. Dunbar said.

Mr. Summers called his own name and then stepped forward precisely and selected a slip from the box. Then he called, "Warner."

"Seventy-seventh year I been in the lottery," Old Man Warner said as he went through the crowd. "Seventy-seventh time."

"Watson." The tall boy came awkwardly through the crowd. Someone said, "Don't be nervous, Jack," and Mr. Summers said, "Take your time, son."

"Zanini."

After that, there was a long pause, a breathless pause, until Mr. Summers, holding his slip of paper in the air, said, "All right, fellows." For a minute, no one moved, and then all the slips of paper were opened. Suddenly, all the women began to speak at once, saying, "Who is it?," "Who's got it?," "Is it the Dunbars?," "Is it the Watsons?" Then the voices began to say, "It's Hutchinson. It's Bill." "Bill Hutchinson's got it."

"Go tell your father," Mrs. Dunbar said to her older son.

People began to look around to see the Hutchinsons. Bill Hutchinson was standing quiet, staring down at the paper in his hand. Suddenly, Tessie Hutchinson shouted to Mr. Summers, "You didn't give him time enough to take any paper he wanted. I saw you. It wasn't fair."

"Be a good sport, Tessie," Mrs. Delacroix called, and Mrs. Graves said, "All of us took the same chance."

"Shut up, Tessie," Bill Hutchinson said.

"Well, everyone," Mr. Summers said, "that was done pretty fast, and now we've got to be hurrying a little more to get done in time." He consulted his next list. "Bill," he said, "you draw for the Hutchinson family. You got any other households in the Hutchinsons?"

"There's Don and Eva," Mrs. Hutchinson yelled. "Make *them* take their chance!"

"Daughters draw with their husbands' families, Tessie," Mr. Summers said gently. "You know that as well as anyone else."

"It wasn't *fair*," Tessie said.

"I guess not, Joe," Bill Hutchinson said regretfully. "My daughter draws with her husband's family; that's only fair. And I've got no other family except the kids."

"Then, as far as drawing for families is concerned, it's you," Mr. Summers said in explanation, "and as far as drawing for households is concerned, that's you, too. Right?"

"Right," Bill Hutchinson said.

"How many kids, Bill?" Mr. Summers asked formally.

"Three," Bill Hutchinson said. "There's Bill, Jr., and Nancy, and little Dave. And Tessie and me."

"All right, then," Mr. Summers said. "Harry, you got their tickets back?"

Mr. Graves nodded and held up the slips of paper. "Put them in the box, then," Mr. Summers directed. "Take Bill's and put it in."

"I think we ought to start over," Mrs. Hutchinson said, as quietly as she could. "I tell you it wasn't *fair*. You didn't give him time enough to choose. *Everybody* saw that."

Mr. Graves had selected the five slips and put them in the box, and he dropped all the papers but those onto the ground, where the breeze caught them and lifted them off.

"Listen, everybody," Mrs. Hutchinson was saying to the people around her.

"Ready, Bill?" Mr. Summers asked, and Bill Hutchinson, with one quick glance around at his wife and children, nodded.

"Remember," Mr. Summers said, "take the slips and keep them folded until each person has taken one. Harry, you help little Dave." Mr. Graves took the hand of the little boy, who came willingly with him up to the box. "Take a paper out of the box, Davy," Mr. Summers said. Davy put his hand into the box and laughed. "Take just *one* paper," Mr. Summers said. "Harry, you hold it for him." Mr. Graves took the child's hand and removed the folded paper from the tight fist and held it while little Dave stood next to him and looked up at him wonderingly.

"Nancy next," Mr. Summers said. Nancy was twelve, and her school friends breathed heavily as she went forward switching her skirt, and took a slip daintily from the box. "Bill, Jr.," Mr. Summers said, and Billy, his face red and his feet overlarge, near knocked the box over as he got a paper out. "Tessie," Mr. Summers said. She hesitated for a minute, looking around defiantly, and then set her lips and went up to the box. She snatched a paper out and held it behind her.

"Bill," Mr. Summers said, and Bill Hutchinson reached into the box and felt around, bringing his hand out at last with the slip of paper in it.

The crowd was quiet. A girl whispered, "I hope it's not Nancy," and the sound of the whisper reached the edges of the crowd.

"It's not the way it used to be," Old Man Warner said clearly. "People ain't the way they used to be."

"All right," Mr. Summers said. "Open the papers. Harry, you open little Dave's."

Mr. Graves opened the slip of paper and there was a general sigh through the crowd as he held it up and everyone could see that it was blank. Nancy and Bill, Jr., opened theirs at the same time, and both beamed and laughed, turning around to the crowd and holding their slips of paper above their heads.

"Tessie," Mr. Summers said. There was a pause, and then Mr. Summers looked at Bill Hutchinson, and Bill unfolded his paper and showed it. It was blank.

"It's Tessie," Mr. Summers said, and his voice was hushed. "Show us her paper, Bill."

Bill Hutchinson went over to his wife and forced the slip of paper out of her hand. It had a black spot on it, the black spot Mr. Summers had made the night before with the heavy pencil in the coal-company office. Bill Hutchinson held it up, and there was a stir in the crowd.

"All right, folks," Mr. Summers said. "Let's finish quickly."

Although the villagers had forgotten the ritual and lost the original black box, they still remembered to use stones. The pile of stones the boys had made earlier was ready; there were stones on the ground with the blowing scraps of paper that had come out of the box. Mrs. Delacroix selected a stone so large she had to pick it up with both hands and turned to Mrs. Dunbar. "Come on," she said. "Hurry up."

Mrs. Dunbar had small stones in both hands, and she said, gasping for breath, "I can't run at all. You'll have to go ahead and I'll catch up with you."

The children had stones already. And someone gave little Davy Hutchinson a few pebbles.

Tessie Hutchinson was in the center of a cleared space by now, and she held her hands out desperately as the villagers moved in on her. "It isn't fair," she said. A stone hit her on the side of the head. Old Man Warner was saying, "Come on, come on, everyone." Steve Adams was in the front of the crowd of villagers, with Mrs. Graves beside him.

"It isn't fair, it isn't right," Mrs. Hutchinson screamed, and then they were upon her.

AFTER YOU READ
The Lottery

Think and Discuss

1. At first, what did you think the lottery might be for? Explain why you thought that.

2. Why do the villagers hold the lottery every year?

3. Mrs. Hutchinson declares that the lottery is unfair. In what ways is she right, and in what ways is she wrong?

4. What effect did Jackson's **withholding information** about the purpose of the lottery have on your response to the story?

5. This story features **stock characters**, characters who represent certain types of people. The story feels universal as well as local. Copy the following graphic organizer into your Writer's Notebook and document the qualities of the stock characters in the story. One way to describe a character's qualities is to imagine the description you might write as a playwright when listing your cast of characters.

Stock Character	Qualities

6. This story is startling because its horrifying events take place in a village populated by people everyone can recognize. How are the people in your community like and unlike the villagers in the story? Use examples from the story to illustrate your comparisons.

Write to Understand: A Short Story

Now that you have identified different stock characters in *The Lottery* and thought about how people in your community may or may not be like them, write a short story that illustrates your thoughts and uses stock characters appropriate to your setting.

Writers on Writing

BEFORE YOU READ
The Morning of June 28, 1948, and "The Lottery"

Meet the Author: Another Look at Shirley Jackson

Though "The Lottery" (1948) and her novel *The Haunting of Hill House* (1959) represent the kind of quiet horror Shirley Jackson is best known for, she wrote in other styles as well. For example, her comic tales of life with four children, based on her own experiences, were popular in women's magazines. Some critics today feel that those works resulted in a loss of critical respect for Jackson as a serious writer. Even the "fierce visions . . . of cruelty and terror" that gave life to her best known works were incorrectly seen as "personal, even neurotic fantasies," according to her husband. Many critics today see those visions not as personal, troubled fantasies but instead as faithful reflections, by a timeless writer, of the horrors of the World War II era.

Build Background: The Draw of the Dark Side

What draws people to read and write about the dark side? Why does Stephen King, who admired Shirley Jackson and felt influenced by her, channel his talents into his dark tales, and why do people line up in bookstores to buy his latest books or see the movies based on them? Although each reader and writer may have somewhat different answers, the most fundamental reason might have to do with a desire to understand and manage those parts of ourselves—and of the people around us—that haunt or trouble us.

As you read the following article by Shirley Jackson about letters she received from readers, ask yourself:

- How did most of the people who wrote to Jackson after the publication of "The Lottery" view her?

- How did Jackson view them?

The Morning of June 28, 1948, and "The Lottery"

SHIRLEY JACKSON

THE MORNING OF JUNE 28, 1948, AND "THE LOTTERY"

Shirley Jackson

On the morning of June 28, 1948, I walked down to the post office in our little Vermont town to pick up the mail. I was quite casual about it, as I recall—I opened the box, took out a couple of bills and a letter or two, talked to the postmaster for a few minutes, and left, never supposing that it was the last time for months that I was to pick up the mail without an active feeling of panic. By the next week I had had to change my mailbox to the largest one in the post office, and casual conversation with the postmaster was out of the question, because he wasn't speaking to me. June 28, 1948, was the day *The New Yorker* came out with a story of mine in it. It was not my first published story, nor my last, but I have been assured over and over that if it had been the only story I ever wrote or published, there would be people who would not forget my name.

I had written the story three weeks before, on a bright June morning when summer seemed to have come at last, with blue skies and warm sun and no heavenly signs to warn me that my morning's work was anything but just another story. The idea had come to me while I was pushing my daughter up the hill in her stroller—it was, as I say, a warm morning, and the hill was steep, and beside my daughter the stroller held the day's groceries—and perhaps the effort of that last fifty yards up the hill put an edge to the story; at any rate, I had the idea fairly clearly in my mind when I put my daughter in her playpen and the frozen vegetables in the refrigerator, and, writing the story, I found that it went quickly and easily, moving from beginning to end without pause. As a matter of fact, when I read it over later I decided that except for one or two minor corrections, it needed no changes, and the story I finally typed up and sent off to my agent the next day was almost word for word the original draft. This, as any writer of stories can tell you, is not a usual thing. All I know is that when I came to read the story over I felt strongly that I didn't want to fuss with it. I didn't think it was perfect, but I didn't want to fuss with it. It was, I thought, a serious, straightforward story, and I was pleased and a little surprised at the ease with which it had been written; I was reasonably proud of it, and hoped that my agent would sell it to some magazine and I would have the gratification of seeing it in print.

My agent did not care for the story, but—as she said in her note at the time—her job was to sell it, not to like it. She sent it at once to *The New Yorker*, and about a week after the story had been written I received a telephone call from the fiction editor of *The New Yorker*; it was quite clear that he did not really care for the story, either, but *The New Yorker* was going to buy it. He asked for one change—that the date mentioned in the story be changed to coincide with the date of the issue of the magazine in which the story would appear, and I said of course. He then asked, hesitantly, if I had any particular interpretation of my own for the story; Mr. Harold Ross, then the editor of *The New Yorker*, was not altogether sure that he understood the story, and wondered if I cared to enlarge upon its meaning. I said no. Mr. Ross, he said, thought that the story might be puzzling to some people, and in case anyone telephoned the magazine, as sometimes happened, or wrote in asking about the story, was there anything in particular I wanted to them to say? No, I said, nothing in particular; it was just a story I wrote.

*M*y agent did not care for the story, but—as she said in her note at the time—her job was to sell it, not to like it.

I had no more preparation than that. I went on picking up the mail every morning, pushing my daughter up and down the hill in her stroller, anticipating pleasurably the check from *The New Yorker*, and shopping for groceries. The weather stayed nice and it looked as though it was going to be a good summer. Then, on June 28, *The New Yorker* came out with my story.

Things began mildly enough with a note from a friend at *The New Yorker*: "Your story has kicked up quite a fuss around the office," he wrote. I was flattered; it's nice to think that your friends notice what you write. Later that day there was a call from one of the magazine's editors; they had had a couple of people phone in about my story, he said, and was there anything I particularly wanted him to say if there were any more calls? No, I said, nothing particular; anything he chose to say was perfectly all right with me; it was just a story.

cryptic
short and
puzzling

I was further puzzled by a **cryptic** note from another friend: "Heard a man talking about a story of yours on the bus this morning," she wrote. "Very exciting. I wanted to tell him I knew the author, but after I heard what he was saying I decided I'd better not."

One of the most terrifying aspects of publishing stories and books is the realization that they are going to be read, and read by strangers. I had never fully realized this before, although I had of course in my imagination dwelt lovingly upon the thought of the millions and millions of people who were going to be uplifted and enriched and delighted by the stories I wrote.

It had simply never occurred to me that these millions and millions of people might be so far from being uplifted that they would sit down and write me letters I was downright scared to open; of the three-hundred-odd letters that I received that summer I can count only thirteen that spoke kindly to me, and they were mostly from friends. Even my mother scolded me: "Dad and I did not care at all for your story in *The New Yorker*," she wrote sternly, "it does seem, dear, that this gloomy kind of story is what all you young people think about these days. Why don't you write something to cheer people up?"

By mid-July I had begun to perceive that I was very lucky indeed to be safely in Vermont, where no one in our small town had ever heard of *The New Yorker*, much less read my story. Millions of people, and my mother, had taken a pronounced dislike to me.

The magazine kept no track of telephone calls, but all letters addressed to me care of the magazine were forwarded directly to me for answering, and all letters addressed to the magazine—some of them addressed to Harold Ross personally; these were the most vehement—were answered at the magazine and then the letters were sent me in great batches, along with carbons of the answers written at the magazine. I have all the letters still, and if they could be considered to give any accurate cross section of the reading public, or the reading public of *The New Yorker*, or even the reading public of one issue of *The New Yorker*, I would stop writing.

Judging from these letters, people who read stories are gullible, rude, frequently illiterate, and horribly afraid of being laughed at. Many of the writers were positive that *The New Yorker* was going to ridicule them in print, and the most cautious letters were headed, in capital letters: NOT FOR PUBLICATION or PLEASE DO NOT PRINT THIS LETTER, or, at best, THIS LETTER MAY BE PUBLISHED AT YOUR USUAL RATES OF PAYMENT. Anonymous letters, of which there were a few, were destroyed. *The New Yorker* never published any comment of any kind about the story in the magazine, but did issue one publicity release saying that the story

> By mid-July I had begun to perceive that I was very lucky indeed to be safely in Vermont, where no one in our small town had ever heard of *The New Yorker*, much less read my story.

had received more mail than any piece of fiction they had ever published; this was after the newspapers had gotten into the act, in midsummer, with a front-page story in the San Francisco *Chronicle* begging to know what the story meant, and a series of columns in New York and Chicago papers pointing out that *New Yorker* subscriptions were being canceled right and left.

Curiously, there are three main themes which dominate the letters that first summer—three themes which might be identified as bewilderment, speculation, and plain old-fashioned abuse. In the years since then, during which the story has been anthologized, dramatized, televised, and even—in one completely mystifying transformation—made into a ballet, the tenor of letters I receive has changed. I am addressed more politely, as a rule, and the letters largely confine themselves to questions like what does this story mean? The general tone of the early letters, however, was a kind of wide-eyed shocked innocence. People at first were not so much concerned with what the story meant; what they wanted to know was where these lotteries were held and whether they could go there and watch.

AFTER YOU READ

The Morning of June 28, 1948, and "The Lottery"

Think and Discuss

1. In what ways is this accounting of Jackson's summer of 1948 like the story that caused all the fuss?

2. What did Jackson feel good about after writing the story?

3. How would you describe the **tone** of this article?

4. Jackson writes: "I have all the letters still, and if they could be considered to give any accurate cross section of the reading public, or the reading public of *The New Yorker*, or even the reading public of one issue of *The New Yorker*, I would stop writing." What **inferences** can you draw about why she would stop writing?

5. Who seems to have the darker side—Jackson, who thought up the story, or the people who wrote her letters? Give reasons for your answer.

6. Look back over the selections in this unit. Decide which, in your opinion, is the darkest, and why. Use the graphic organizer below to help you explore your thoughts.

Selection	Villain or Antagonist	Scariness	Message or Theme
The Most Dangerous Game			
Variations on the Death of Trotsky			
The Cask of Amontillado			
The Bells			
Annabel Lee			
The Raven			
Dozens of Roses			
The Lottery			

Write to Understand: Evaluating and Persuading

Use the ideas you came up with in your graphic organizer to write a QuickDraft of a persuasive essay explaining which selection in this unit is, in your opinion, the darkest. Refer to specific criteria such as those in the graphic organizer as well as those you might come up with on your own. Try to have at least three good reasons for your choice, and use details from the stories to back up your opinion. Share your work with a partner and provide and receive feedback.

A Writer's WORKSHOP

PERSUASIVE CRITICAL ESSAY: LITERATURE FROM THE DARK SIDE

Horror writer Elizabeth Peake says, "We horror writers will go into any dark dwelling, any crawl space, anywhere the reader dare not venture. We will take a good, hard look at your fear; then we'll come back and tell you all about it." Take a critical look at what the dark side writers in this unit have brought back to "tell you all about" and decide which has done the best job. Express your opinion in a persuasive critical essay.

Prewriting

REVIEWING IDEAS

You have already written in response to the selections in this unit. Review your Writer's Notebook and skim back over the selections. Circle any ideas in your notebook that you think will help you choose the selection you found most effective. Review the QuickDraft you wrote to see if you still agree with it. (See page 683.)

COOPERATIVE LEARNING: IDENTIFYING TRAITS OF STRONG DARK SIDE WRITING

In a small group, discuss what makes some works of literature from the dark side better than others. In your discussion, consider some of the following:

- Plot: what makes a good story?

- Character: what do you want to know about the characters, and how lifelike should they be?

- Setting: how important is the setting, and which settings are especially effective?

- Suspense: how much do you want?

- Descriptive details: are there ever too many?

- Creativity: how important is originality?

- Twists: how important are surprise endings?

Make a list of the qualities you come up with. Choose three qualities you feel are most important and rank them in order of importance. These are the qualities you will use as criteria in your essay.

DEVELOPING YOUR IDEAS

Copy the following graphic organizer into your Writer's Notebook. Fill in the first row with the strongest examples you can from your chosen work. Fill in the second row with examples from at least two of the other selections.

Quality #1:	Quality #2:	Quality #3:
Proof that my chosen selection exhibits this quality strongly • • •	Proof that my chosen selection exhibits this quality strongly • • •	Proof that my chosen selection exhibits this quality strongly • • •
Examples of how the other selections fall short on this quality • • •	Examples of how the other selections fall short on this quality • • •	Examples of how the other selections fall short on this quality • • •

SKETCHING OUT YOUR ORGANIZATION

Visualize how you will organize your essay. You can use an outline, or you can use a graphic representation such as the following:

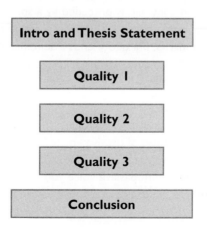

Intro and Thesis Statement

Quality 1

Quality 2

Quality 3

Conclusion

Drafting

Using your outline or graphic representation and your QuickDraft if it is still relevant, draft your persuasive essay. Remember that in a persuasive essay the thesis statement is a statement of opinion and the body must back it up with sound examples.

COOPERATIVE LEARNING: PEER REVIEW

Share your draft with a partner. Ask for feedback, and accept any input graciously. Offer feedback on your partner's work.

Revising and Editing

Reread your essay. Is it persuasive? Be sure you provide strong support for your position.

READING WITH AN EDITOR'S EYE

Critical essays usually call for quoting passages from a work. You might write:

In "The Most Dangerous Game," Connell takes a long time to establish the situation, beginning with a ship passing an island that is "rather a mystery." Rainsford [1] and Whitney discuss their philosophies of hunting before any real action takes place. Not realizing he will soon be hunted himself, Rainsford says, "Who cares how a jaguar [2] feels?" In "The Cask of Amontillado," in contrast, Poe heads directly into the story with the opening sentence: "The thousand injuries of Fortunato I had borne as I best could, but when he ventured upon insult, I vowed revenge." [3]

Check that you have handled the quotation marks correctly. For example, the quote by [1] finishes the sentence and does not include a speaker tag. For that reason, there is no comma preceding it. The end mark, in this case a period, goes inside the quotation marks. The quote by [2], in contrast, is preceded by a speaker tag (Rainsford says), so it is separated from the tag with a comma. Since the question mark is part of the quote, it goes inside the quotation marks. If a quote ends a sentence that is a question, but does not contain a question itself, the question mark goes outside the quotation marks. The quote by [3] shows just one way to lead into an entire quoted sentence—with a colon.

USING A WORD PROCESSOR

Keep your writing active and lively by avoiding the passive voice. Your word processor can alert you to the use of passive voice. Search the help menu of your word processor for "Display readability statistics." The search results will tell you how to see what percentage of sentences with passive voice you have used in the open document. If you have a high percentage, go back over your essay and replace passive constructions with active ones.

USING A CHECKLIST

Use the Six-Trait checklist on page 687.

Six Traits of Writing: Persuasive Critical Essays

Content and Ideas
- the main idea is an opinion about the strongest work of literature in the unit
- the body of the essay shows how the chosen work exhibits the three most important qualities and how the others fall short
- the ideas in the body are supported by details, examples, and quotes from the text(s)

Organization
- the essay has a clear introduction with an opinion thesis statement, a body in which the opinion is supported, and a conclusion that drives home the argument
- the ideas in the body are presented in a logical order

Voice or Style
- the voice sounds natural, not forced
- the voice is more formal than speech

Word Choice
- the writer uses specific and vivid nouns and adjectives
- the writer avoids the passive voice

Sentence Fluency
- sentences are complete
- sentence length and sentence beginnings are varied and purposeful
- transitions between ideas and sections are clear and smooth

Conventions
- the essay is free of errors in usage, spelling, capitalization, and punctuation
- works referred to are presented according to the style required by the school (for example, titles of short stories are in quotes)

What Has Value?

Soon the word spread through Gee's Bend that there was a crazy white man in town paying good money for raggedy old quilts.

Amei Wallach, from "Fabric of Their Lives"

BEFORE YOU READ

The Gift of the Magi

Meet the Author: O. Henry

William Sydney Porter (1862–1910) was an avid reader as a child, a talented artist, and a gifted musician. He worked at a variety of jobs but always wrote stories on the side. Shortly after taking a writing job at the *Houston Post*, he was found guilty of embezzlement at a bank he had worked at in Austin, Texas, though he denied the charges. Because he was also a licensed pharmacist, Porter became the night druggist in the prison hospital and had a room there. While in jail, he wrote and published stories under the pen name O. Henry. After he was released from prison, he moved to New York City and wrote full time. The optimism, cleverness, and craft of his stories led critics to honor O. Henry as the writer who made the short story into an art form.

Build Background: Allusion in "The Gift of the Magi"

The title of this story is an **allusion**, or reference to another text. Authors use allusion to enhance and deepen meaning. When readers come upon an allusion to another literary work, they recall the meaning and emotional impact of that other text and carry those associations over to the work they are reading.

The allusion in "The Gift of the Magi" is to the biblical story of the birth of Jesus. According to that story, especially as it is told in the New Testament book of Matthew, Jesus was born in a lowly manger in Bethlehem. The birth of a child of God had been foretold, and when news of the birth spread, "wise men" from the east, known as magi, followed a bright star to pay honor to the newborn. They came with valuable gifts suitable for a king: gold, frankincense (a kind of incense), and myrrh (a body oil used in rituals). According to this story, the magi started the tradition of giving gifts at Christmas.

This story, like all the other selections in this unit, raises questions about what has value. As you read this story, ask yourself:

- Do you agree with the saying, "It's better to give than to receive"?

- What present have you received that has had the greatest value to you?

Jo, La Bella Irlandaise, Gustave Courbet, 1866

The Gift of the Magi

O. HENRY

THE GIFT OF THE MAGI

O. Henry

One dollar and eighty-seven cents. That was all. And sixty cents of it was in pennies. Pennies saved one and two at a time by bulldozing the grocer and the vegetable man and the butcher until one's cheeks burned with the silent **imputation** of **parsimony** that such close dealing[1] implied. Three times Della counted it. One dollar and eighty-seven cents. And the next day would be Christmas.

There was clearly nothing to do but flop down on the shabby little couch and howl. So Della did it. Which **instigates** the moral reflection that life is made up of sobs, sniffles, and smiles, with sniffles **predominating**.

While the mistress of the home is gradually subsiding from the first stage to the second, take a look at the home. A furnished flat at eight dollars per week. It did not exactly **beggar** description, but it certainly had that word on the lookout for the mendicancy squad.[2]

In the vestibule below was a letter-box into which no letter would go, and an electric button from which no mortal finger could coax a ring. Also appertaining thereunto[3] was a card bearing the name "Mr. James Dillingham Young."

The "Dillingham" had been flung to the breeze during a former period of prosperity when its possessor was being paid thirty dollars per week. Now, when the income was shrunk to twenty dollars, the letters of "Dillingham" looked blurred, as though they were thinking seriously of contracting to a modest and unassuming D. But whenever Mr. James Dillingham Young came home and reached his flat above he was called "Jim" and greatly hugged by Mrs. James Dillingham Young, already introduced to you as Della. Which is all very good.

Della finished her cry and attended to her cheeks with the powder rag. She stood by the window and looked out dully at a gray cat walking a gray fence in a gray backyard. Tomorrow would be Christmas Day, and she had only one

imputation
implication, especially of something negative

parsimony
stinginess

instigates
advises and encourages

predominating
leading in number or strength

beggar
to go beyond the limits or definition of

---

1 **close dealing:** making deals or purchases with a very careful accounting of every penny

2 **mendicancy squad:** a portion of a police force assigned to arrest mendicants, or beggars

3 **appertaining thereunto:** belonging to

dollar and eighty-seven cents with which to buy Jim a present. She had been saving every penny she could for months, with this result. Twenty dollars a week doesn't go far. Expenses had been greater than she had calculated. They always are. Only one dollar and eighty-seven cents to buy a present for Jim. Her Jim. Many a happy hour she had spent planning for something nice for him. Something fine and rare and **sterling**—something just a little bit near to being worthy of the honor of being owned by Jim.

> *S*uddenly she whirled from the window and stood before the glass. Her eyes were shining brilliantly, but her face had lost its color within twenty seconds.

There was a pier glass[4] between the windows of the room. Perhaps you have seen a pier glass in an eight-dollar flat. A very thin and very agile person may, by observing his reflection in a rapid sequence of **longitudinal** strips, obtain a fairly accurate conception of his looks. Della, being slender, had mastered the art.

Suddenly she whirled from the window and stood before the glass. Her eyes were shining brilliantly, but her face had lost its color within twenty seconds. Rapidly she pulled down her hair and let it fall to its full length.

Now, there were two possessions of the James Dillingham Youngs in which they both took a mighty pride. One was Jim's gold watch that had been his father's and his grandfather's. The other was Della's hair. Had the Queen of Sheba[5] lived in the flat across the airshaft, Della would have let her hair hang out the window some day to dry just to **depreciate** Her Majesty's jewels and gifts. Had King Solomon[6] been the janitor, with all his treasures piled up in the basement, Jim would have pulled out his watch every time he passed, just to see him pluck at his beard from envy.

So now Della's beautiful hair fell about her rippling and shining like a cascade of brown waters. It reached below her knee and made itself almost a garment for her. And then she did it up again nervously and quickly. Once she faltered for a minute and stood still while a tear or two splashed on the worn red carpet.

On went her old brown jacket; on went her old brown hat. With a whirl of skirts and with the brilliant sparkle still in her eyes, she fluttered out the door and down the stairs to the street.

sterling
of the highest quality

longitudinal
straight, usually vertical

depreciate
belittle; reduce the value of

---

4 **pier glass:** long mirror

5 **Queen of Sheba:** a biblical queen who tested the wisdom of King Solomon

6 **King Solomon:** a biblical king known for his great wisdom

Where she stopped the sign read: "Mme. Sofronie. Hair Goods of All Kinds." One flight up Della ran, and collected herself, panting. Madame, large, too white, chilly, hardly looked the "Sofronie."

"Will you buy my hair?" asked Della.

"I buy hair," said Madame. "Take yer hat off and let's have a sight at the looks of it."

Down rippled the brown cascade.

"Twenty dollars," said Madame, lifting the mass with a practiced hand.

"Give it to me quick," said Della.

Oh, and the next two hours tripped by on rosy wings. Forget the hashed metaphor. She was ransacking the stores for Jim's present.

She found it at last. It surely had been made for Jim and no one else. There was no other like it in any of the stores, and she had turned all of them inside out. It was a platinum fob chain[7] simple and chaste in design, properly proclaiming its value by substance alone and not by **meretricious** ornamentation—as all good things should do. It was even worthy of The Watch. As soon as she saw it she knew that it must be Jim's. It was like him. Quietness and value—the description applied to both. Twenty-one dollars they took from her for it, and she hurried home with the eighty-seven cents. With that chain on his watch Jim might be properly anxious about the time in any company. Grand as the watch was, he sometimes looked at it on the sly on account of the old leather strap that he used in place of a chain.

When Della reached home her intoxication gave way a little to prudence and reason. She got out her curling irons and lighted the gas and went to work repairing the ravages made by generosity added to love. Which is always a tremendous task, dear friends—a mammoth task.

Within forty minutes her head was covered with tiny, close-lying curls that made her look wonderfully like a truant schoolboy. She looked at her reflection in the mirror long, carefully, and critically.

"If Jim doesn't kill me," she said to herself, "before he takes a second look at me, he'll say I look like a Coney Island chorus girl.[8] But what could I do—oh! what could I do with a dollar and eighty-seven cents?"

meretricious
showy in a vulgar way

---

7 **fob chain:** chain for a pocket watch

8 **Coney Island chorus girl:** entertainers at the seaside resort area in Brooklyn, New York, now known mostly for its amusement park. Chorus girls of the period cut their hair short, into a style called the bob. Most respectable women kept their hair long.

At seven o'clock the coffee was made and the frying pan was on the back of the stove hot and ready to cook the chops.

Jim was never late. Della doubled the fob chain in her hand and sat on the corner of the table near the door that he always entered. Then she heard his step on the stair away down on the first flight, and she turned white for just a moment. She had a habit of saying little silent prayers about the simplest everyday things, and now she whispered: "Please God, make him think I am still pretty."

The door opened and Jim stepped in and closed it. He looked thin and very serious. Poor fellow, he was only twenty-two—and to be burdened with a family! He needed a new overcoat and he was without gloves.

Jim stopped inside the door, as immovable as a setter at the scent of quail. His eyes were fixed upon Della, and there was an expression in them that she could not read, and it terrified her. It was not anger, nor surprise, nor disapproval, nor horror, nor any of the sentiments that she had been prepared for.

He simply stared at her fixedly with that peculiar expression on his face. Della wriggled off the table and went to him.

"Jim, darling," she cried, "don't look at me that way. I had my hair cut off and sold because I couldn't have lived through Christmas without giving you a present. It'll grow out again—you won't mind, will you? I just had to do it. My hair grows awfully fast. Say 'Merry Christmas!' Jim, and let's be happy. You don't know what a nice—what a beautiful, nice gift I've got for you."

"You've cut off your hair?" asked Jim, laboriously, as if he had not arrived at that **patent** fact yet even after the hardest mental labor.

patent
obvious

"Cut it off and sold it," said Della. "Don't you like me just as well, anyhow? I'm me without my hair, ain't I?"

Jim looked about the room curiously.

"You say your hair is gone?" he said, with an air almost of idiocy.

"You needn't look for it," said Della. "It's sold, I tell you—sold and gone, too. It's Christmas Eve, boy. Be good to me, for it went for you. Maybe the hairs of my head were numbered,"[9] she went on with sudden serious sweetness, "but nobody could ever count my love for you. Shall I put the chops on, Jim?"

Out of his trance Jim seemed quickly to wake. He enfolded his Della. For ten seconds let us regard with discreet scrutiny some inconsequential object in the other direction. Eight dollars a week or a million a year—what is the difference? A mathematician or a wit would give you the wrong answer. The Magi brought valuable gifts, but that was not among them. This dark assertion will be illuminated later on.

Jim drew a package from his overcoat pocket and threw it upon the table.

"Don't make any mistake, Dell," he said, "about me. I don't think there's anything in the way of a haircut or a shave or a shampoo that could make me like my girl any less. But if you'll unwrap that package you may see why you had me going a while at first."

White fingers and nimble tore at the string and paper. And then an ecstatic scream of joy; and then, alas! a quick feminine change to hysterical tears and wails, necessitating the immediate employment of all the comforting powers of the lord of the flat.

---

9 **Maybe the hairs of my head were numbered:** Della is using a pun. In popular culture, saying one's days are numbered means that one's life is nearly over.

Pearl, enamel, and gold comb made in Chicago, Illinois © 1905

For there lay The Combs—the set of combs, side and back, that Della had worshiped long in a Broadway window. Beautiful combs, pure tortoise shell, with jeweled rims—just the shade to wear in the beautiful vanished hair. They were expensive combs, she knew, and her heart had simply craved and yearned over them without the least hope of possession. And now, they were hers, but the tresses that should have adorned the coveted adornments were gone.

But she hugged them to her bosom, and at length she was able to look up with dim eyes and a smile and say: "My hair grows so fast, Jim!"

And then Della leaped up like a little singed cat and cried, "Oh, oh!"

Jim had not yet seen his beautiful present. She held it out to him eagerly upon her open palm. The dull precious metal seemed to flash with a reflection of her bright and ardent spirit.

"Isn't it a dandy, Jim? I hunted all over town to find it. You'll have to look at the time a hundred times a day now. Give me your watch. I want to see how it looks on it."

Instead of obeying, Jim tumbled down on the couch and put his hands under the back of his head and smiled.

"Della," said he, "let's put our Christmas presents away and keep 'em a while. They're too nice to use just at present. I sold the watch to get the money to buy your combs. And now suppose you put the chops on."

The Magi, as you know, were wise men—wonderfully wise men—who brought gifts to the Babe in the manger. They invented the art of giving Christmas presents. Being wise, their gifts were no doubt wise ones, possibly bearing the privilege of exchange in case of duplication. And here I have lamely related to you the uneventful chronicle of two foolish children in a flat who most unwisely sacrificed for each other the greatest treasures of their house. But in a last word to the wise of these days let it be said that of all who give gifts these two were the wisest. Of all who give and receive gifts, such as they are wisest. Everywhere they are wisest. They are the Magi.

AFTER YOU READ
The Gift of the Magi

Think and Discuss

1. According to this story, what has value? Find some quotes from the story that support your answer.

2. The narrator of this story calls Della and Jim both foolish and wise. In what ways are they foolish, and in what ways are they wise?

3. What is the **tone** of this story? In other words, what is the narrator's attitude toward his characters and subject?

4. What is the **plot twist** in this story? (For a definition of *plot twist*, see the Glossary of Literary Terms.)

5. One way authors set up readers for a plot twist is to misdirect the reader's attention so that, when it comes, the twist seems like a surprise. Along the way, though, there are likely to be hints that lead to the twist. How does O. Henry misdirect the reader, and what hints does he plant that a surprise ending is to come?

6. Copy the following graphic organizer into your Writer's Notebook to explore the concept of value in "The Gift of the Magi." Skim the story. As you do, list everything that is mentioned that has value in the large column. When you've finished, use the smaller boxes to categorize, or group the items logically. Think of a name for each category and write it in the small box; then list the items included in that category.

Things with Value:	Category:
	Category:
	Category:

Write to Understand: Commercial Script

Maybe you've seen this commercial on TV: A zookeeper tending an elephant sneezes and looks stuffy. The elephant grabs the man's credit card and goes into town to get supplies. He brings them back to the man's house and wraps his trunk gently around the man's head. The voice-over narrator says, "hot soup: $4; cold medicine: $11; blanket: $24; making it all better: priceless. There are some things that money can't buy." And then the product is identified. Write a new commercial script using a similar approach, basing it on "The Gift of the Magi" and the ideas from your graphic organizer. Sketch out a storyboard to go with your commercial.

BEFORE YOU READ
Everyday Use

Meet the Author: Alice Walker

Alice Walker (born 1944) was the youngest of eight children in a family of poor Georgia sharecroppers. When she was eight years old, she was blinded in one eye. Her injury made it hard for her to do chores, so her mother gave her a typewriter so she could keep busy in a meaningful way by writing. She was an outstanding student, the valedictorian of her high school class. In college, she traveled to Africa as an exchange student. She published her first volume of poetry in 1968 and her first novel in 1970. She won the Pulitzer Prize for her novel *The Color Purple* in 1982. Throughout her writing career, Walker has also been an activist for civil rights and women's rights. Much of her writing is about black women.

Build Background: Value in Heritage

Few things are more valuable than one's identity and heritage. The following story, set in the late 1960s or early 1970s, features an African American college student from the rural South who is attempting to connect with her African roots. During the 1960s and under the influence of Martin Luther King, Jr., Malcolm X, and other African American activists, an Afrocentric movement emerged in the United States. Afrocentrists hoped to correct the Eurocentric, or European-based, bias in American culture. So they pointed out and celebrated the culture and achievements of Africans and African Americans.

- To what ethnic, racial, geographic, or religious group(s) do you trace your roots?

- What part of your heritage has had the greatest influence on your identity?

Everyday Use

ALICE WALKER

EVERYDAY USE

Alice Walker

I will wait for her in the yard that Maggie and I made so clean and wavy yesterday afternoon. A yard like this is more comfortable than most people know. It is not just a yard. It is like an extended living room. When the hard clay is swept clean as a floor and the fine sand around the edges lined with tiny, irregular grooves, anyone can come and sit and look up into the elm tree and wait for the breezes that never come inside the house.

Maggie will be nervous until after her sister goes: she will stand hopelessly in corners, homely and ashamed of the burn scars down her arms and legs, eying her sister with a mixture of envy and awe. She thinks her sister has held life always in the palm of one hand, that "no" is a word the world never learned to say to her.

You've no doubt seen those TV shows where the child who has "made it" is confronted, as a surprise, by her own mother and father, tottering in weakly from backstage. (A pleasant surprise, of course: What would they do if parent and child came on the show only to curse out and insult each other?) On TV mother and child embrace and smile into each other's faces. Sometimes the mother and father weep; the child wraps them in her arms and leans across the table to tell how she would not have made it without their help. I have seen these programs.

Sometimes I dream a dream in which Dee and I are suddenly brought together on a TV program of this sort. Out of a dark and soft-seated limousine I am ushered into a bright room filled with many people. There I meet a smiling, gray, sporty man like Johnny Carson[1] who shakes my hand and tells me what a fine girl I have. Then we are on the stage and Dee is embracing me with tears in her eyes. She pins on my dress a large orchid, even though she has told me once that she thinks orchids are tacky flowers.

In real life I am a large, big-boned woman with rough, man-working hands. In the winter I wear flannel nightgowns to bed and overalls during the day. I can kill and clean a hog as mercilessly as a man. My fat keeps me hot in

---

I **Johnny Carson:** a stylish and popular television talk-show host

zero weather. I can work outside all day, breaking ice to get water for washing; I can eat pork liver cooked over the open fire minutes after it comes steaming from the hog. One winter I knocked a bull calf straight in the brain between the eyes with a sledgehammer and had the meat hung up to chill before nightfall. But of course all this does not show on television. I am the way my daughter would want me to be: a hundred pounds lighter, my skin like an uncooked barley pancake. My hair glistens in the hot bright lights. Johnny Carson has much to do to keep up with my quick and witty tongue.

But that is a mistake. I know even before I wake up. Who ever knew a Johnson with a quick tongue? Who can even imagine me looking a strange white man in the eye? It seems to me I have talked to them always with one foot raised in flight, with my head turned in whichever way is farthest from them. Dee, though. She would always look anyone in the eye. Hesitation was no part of her nature.

But that is a mistake. I know even before I wake up. Who ever knew a Johnson with a quick tongue? Who can even imagine me looking a strange white man in the eye?

"How do I look, Mama?" Maggie says, showing just enough of her thin body enveloped in pink skirt and red blouse for me to know she's there, almost hidden by the door.

"Come out into the yard," I say.

Have you ever seen a lame animal, perhaps a dog run over by some careless person rich enough to own a car, sidle up to someone who is ignorant enough to be kind to him? That is the way my Maggie walks. She has been like this, chin on chest, eyes on ground, feet in shuffle, ever since the fire that burned the other house to the ground.

Dee is lighter than Maggie, with nicer hair and a fuller figure. She's a woman now, though sometimes I forget. How long ago was it that the other house burned? Ten, twelve years? Sometimes I can still hear the flames and feel Maggie's arms sticking to me, her hair smoking and her dress falling off her in little black papery flakes. Her eyes seemed stretched open, blazed open by the flames reflected in them. And Dee. I see her standing off under the sweet gum tree she used to dig gum out of; a look of concentration on her face as she watched the last dingy gray board of the house fall in toward the red-hot brick chimney. Why don't you dance around the ashes? I'd wanted to ask her. She had hated the house that much.

I used to think she hated Maggie, too. But that was before we raised money, the church and me, to send her to Augusta to school. She used to read to us without pity; forcing words, lies, other folks' habits, whole lives upon us two, sitting trapped and ignorant underneath her voice. She washed us in a river of make-believe, burned us with a lot of knowledge we didn't necessarily need to know. Pressed us to her with the serious way she read, to shove us away at just the moment, like dimwits, we seemed about to understand.

organdy
crisp, transparent material made of cotton or silk

Dee wanted nice things. A yellow **organdy** dress to wear to her graduation from high school; black pumps to match a green suit she'd made from an old suit somebody gave me. She was determined to stare down any disaster in her efforts. Her eyelids would not flicker for minutes at a time. Often I fought off the temptation to shake her. At sixteen she had a style of her own—and knew what style was.

I never had an education myself. After second grade the school was closed down. Don't ask me why: in 1927 colored asked fewer questions than they do now. Sometimes Maggie reads to me. She stumbles along good-naturedly but can't see well. She knows she is not bright. Like good looks and money, quickness passes her by. She will marry John Thomas (who has mossy teeth in an earnest face) and then I'll be free to sit here and I guess just sing church songs to myself. Although I never was a good singer. Never could carry a tune. I was always better at a man's job. I used to love to milk till I was hooked in the side in '49. Cows are soothing and slow and don't bother you, unless you try to milk them the wrong way.

I have deliberately turned my back on the house. It is three rooms, just like the one that burned, except the roof is tin; they don't make shingle roofs any more. There are no real windows, just some holes cut in the sides, like the portholes in a ship, but not round and not square, with rawhide holding the shutters up on the outside. This house is in a pasture, too, like the other one. No doubt when Dee sees it she will want to tear it down. She wrote me once that no matter where we "choose" to live, she will manage to come see us. But she will never bring her friends. Maggie and I thought about this and Maggie asked me, "Mama, when did Dee ever *have* any friends?"

furtive
sneaky; cautious and secretive

lye
harsh liquid used in making soap

She had a few. **Furtive** boys in pink shirts hanging about on washday after school. Nervous girls who never laughed. Impressed with her they worshiped the well-turned phrase, the cute shape, the scalding humor that erupted like bubbles in **lye**. She read to them.

When she was courting Jimmy T she didn't have much time to pay to us, but turned all her faultfinding power on him. He *flew* to marry a cheap city girl from a family of ignorant flashy people. She hardly had time to recompose herself. When she comes I will meet—but there they are!

Maggie attempts to make a dash for the house, in her shuffling way, but I stay her with my hand. "Come back here," I say. And she stops and tries to dig a well in the sand with her toe.

It is hard to see them clearly through the strong sun. But even the first glimpse of leg out of the car tells me it is Dee. Her feet were always neat-looking, as if God himself had shaped them with a certain style. From the other side of the car comes a short, stocky man. Hair is all over his head a foot long and hanging from his chin like a kinky mule tail. I hear Maggie suck in her breath. "Uhnnnh" is what it sounds like. Like when you see the wriggling end of a snake just in front of your foot on the road. "Uhnnnh." Dee next. A dress down to the ground, in this hot weather. A dress so loud it hurts my eyes. There are yellows and oranges enough to throw back the light of the sun. I feel my whole face warming from the heat waves it throws out. Earrings gold, too, and hanging down to her shoulders. Bracelets dangling and making noises when she moves her arm up to shake the folds of the dress out of her armpits. The dress is loose and flows, and as she walks closer, I like it. I hear Maggie go "Uhnnnh" again. It is her sister's hair. It stands straight up like the wool on a sheep. It is black as night and around the edges are two long pigtails that rope about like small lizards disappearing behind her ears.

"Wasuzo-Teano!"[2] she says, coming on in that gliding way the dress makes her move. The short stocky fellow with the hair to his navel is all grinning and he follows up with "Asalamalakim,[3] my mother and sister!" He moves to hug Maggie but she falls back, right up against the back of my chair. I feel her trembling there and when I look up I see the perspiration falling off her chin.

"Don't get up," says Dee. Since I am stout it takes something of a push. You can see me trying to move a second or two before I make it. She turns, showing white heels through her sandals, and goes back to the car. Out she peeks next with a Polaroid.[4] She stoops down quickly and lines up picture after picture of

---

2 **"Wasuzo-Teano!":** a greeting used by the Buganda people of Uganda, in East Africa

3 **"Asalamalakim":** an Arabic greeting used mostly in North Africa and on the Arabian peninsula

4 **Polaroid:** a camera that takes and prints instant pictures

me sitting there in front of the house with Maggie cowering behind me. She never takes a shot without making sure the house is included. When a cow comes nibbling around the edge of the yard she snaps it and me and Maggie *and* the house. Then she puts the Polaroid in the back seat of the car, and comes up and kisses me on the forehead.

Meanwhile Asalamalakim is going through motions with Maggie's hand. Maggie's hand is as limp as a fish, and probably as cold, despite the sweat, and she keeps trying to pull it back. It looks like Asalamalakim wants to shake hands but wants to do it fancy. Or maybe he don't know how people shake hands. Anyhow, he soon gives up on Maggie.

"Well," I say. "Dee."

"No, Mama," she says. "Not 'Dee,' Wangero Leewanika Kemanjo!"[5]

"What happened to 'Dee'?" I wanted to know.

"She's dead," Wangero said. "I couldn't bear it any longer, being named after the people who oppress me."

"You know as well as me you was named after your aunt Dicie," I said. Dicie is my sister. She named Dee. We called her "Big Dee" after Dee was born.

"But who was *she* named after?" asked Wangero.

"I guess after Grandma Dee," I said.

"And who was she named after?" asked Wangero.

"Her mother," I said, and saw Wangero was getting tired. "That's about as far back as I can trace it," I said. Though, in fact, I probably could have carried it back beyond the Civil War through the branches.

"Well," said Asalamalakim, "there you are."

"Uhnnnh," I heard Maggie say.

"There I was not," I said, "before 'Dicie' cropped up in our family, so why should I try to trace it that far back?"

He just stood there grinning, looking down on me like somebody inspecting a Model A car. Every once in a while he and Wangero sent eye signals over my head.

"How do you pronounce this name?" I asked.

"You don't have to call me by it if you don't want to," said Wangero.

"Why shouldn't I?" I asked. "If that's what you want us to call you, we'll call you."

---

5 **Wangero Leewanika Kemanjo:** a blend of West African names from different peoples.

"I know it might sound awkward at first," said Wangero.

"I'll get used to it," I said. "Ream it out again."

Well, soon we got the name out of the way. Asalamalakim had a name twice as long and three times as hard. After I tripped over it two or three times he told me to just call him Hakim-a-barber.[6] I wanted to ask him was he a barber, but I didn't really think he was, so I didn't ask.

"You must belong to those beef-cattle peoples down the road," I said. They said "Asalamalakim" when they met you, too, but they didn't shake hands. Always too busy: feeding the cattle, fixing the fences, putting up salt-lick shelters, throwing down hay. When the white folks poisoned some of the herd the men stayed up all night with rifles in their hands. I walked a mile and a half just to see the sight.

Hakim-a-barber said, "I accept some of their doctrines, but farming and raising cattle is not my style." (They didn't tell me, and I didn't ask, whether Wangero (Dee) had really gone and married him.)

We sat down to eat, and right away he said he didn't eat collards, and pork was unclean. Wangero, though, went on through the chitlins and corn bread, the greens and everything else. She talked a blue streak over the sweet potatoes. Everything delighted her. Even the fact that we still used the benches her daddy made for the table when we couldn't afford to buy chairs.

"Oh, Mama!" she cried. Then turned to Hakim-a-barber. "I never knew how lovely these benches are. You can feel the rump prints," she said, running her hands underneath her and along the bench. Then she gave a sigh and her hand closed over Grandma Dee's butter dish. "That's it!" she said. "I knew there was something I wanted to ask you if I could have." She jumped up from the table and went over in the corner where the churn stood, the milk in it clabber[7] by now. She looked at the churn and looked at it.

"This churn top is what I need," she said. "Didn't Uncle Buddy whittle it out of a tree you all used to have?"

"Yes," I said.

"Uh huh," she said happily. "And I want the **dasher**, too."

"Uncle Buddy whittle that, too?" asked the barber.

Dee (Wangero) looked up at me.

dasher
the tool used to agitate the milk in a churn

---

6 **Hakim-a-barber:** a corruption of the Muslim name Hakim al Baba

7 **clabber:** spoiled

"Aunt Dee's first husband whittled the dash," said Maggie so low you almost couldn't hear her. "His name was Henry, but they called him Stash."

"Maggie's brain is like an elephant's," Wangero said, laughing. "I can use the churn top as a centerpiece for the alcove table," she said, sliding a plate over the churn, "and I'll think of something artistic to do with the dasher."

When she finished wrapping the dasher, the handle stuck out. I took it for a moment in my hands. You didn't even have to look close to see where hands pushing the dasher up and down to make butter had left a kind of sink in the wood. In fact, there were a lot of small sinks; you could see where thumbs and fingers had sunk into the wood. It was beautiful light yellow wood, from a tree that grew in the yard where Big Dee and Stash had lived.

After dinner Dee (Wangero) went to the trunk at the foot of my bed and started rifling through it. Maggie hung back in the kitchen over the dishpan. Out came Wangero with two quilts. They had been pieced by Grandma Dee and then Big Dee and me had hung them on the quilt frames on the front porch and quilted them. One was in the Lone Star pattern. The other was Walk Around the Mountain. In both of them were scraps of dresses Grandma Dee had worn fifty and more years ago. Bits and pieces of Grandpa Jarrell's Paisley shirts. And one teeny faded blue piece, about the size of a penny matchbox, that was from Great Grandpa Ezra's uniform that he wore in the Civil War.

"Mama," Wangero said sweet as a bird. "Can I have these old quilts?"

I heard something fall in the kitchen, and a minute later the kitchen door slammed.

"Why don't you take one or two of the others?" I asked. "These old things was just done by me and Big Dee from some tops your grandma pieced before she died."

"No," said Wangero. "I don't want those. They are stitched around the borders by machine."

"That'll make them last better," I said.

"That's not the point," said Wangero. "These are all pieces of dresses Grandma used to wear. She did all this stitching by hand. Imagine!" She held the quilts securely in her arms, stroking them.

"Some of the pieces, like those lavender ones, come from old clothes her mother handed down to her," I said, moving up to touch the quilts. Dee (Wangero) moved back just enough so that I couldn't reach the quilts. They already belonged to her.

"Imagine!" she breathed again, clutching them closely to her bosom.

"The truth is," I said, "I promised to give them quilts to Maggie, for when she marries John Thomas."

She gasped like a bee had stung her.

"Maggie can't appreciate these quilts!" she said. "She'd probably be backward enough to put them to everyday use."

"I reckon she would," I said. "God knows I been saving 'em for long enough with nobody using 'em. I hope she will!" I didn't want to bring up how I had offered Dee (Wangero) a quilt when she went away to college. Then she had told me they were old-fashioned, out of style.

"But they're *priceless!*" she was saying now, furiously; for she has a temper. "Maggie would put them on the bed and in five years they'd be in rags. Less than that!"

"She can always make some more," I said. "Maggie knows how to quilt."

Dee (Wangero) looked at me with hatred. "You just will not understand. The point is these quilts, *these* quilts!"

"Well," I said, stumped. "What would *you* do with them?"

"Hang them," she said. As if that was the only thing you *could* do with quilts.

Maggie by now was standing in the door. I could almost hear the sound her feet made as they scraped over each other.

"She can have them, Mama," she said, like somebody used to never winning anything, or having anything reserved for her. "I can 'member Grandma Dee without the quilts."

I looked at her hard. She had filled her bottom lip with checkerberry snuff[8] and gave her face a kind of dopey, **hangdog** look. It was Grandma Dee and Big Dee who taught her how to quilt herself. She stood there with her scarred hands hidden in the folds of her skirt. She looked at her sister with something like fear but she wasn't mad at her. This was Maggie's portion. This was the way she knew God to work.

hangdog
downcast;
oppressed

When I looked at her like that something hit me in the top of my head and ran down to the soles of my feet. Just like when I'm in church and the spirit of God touches me and I get happy and shout. I did something I never done before: hugged Maggie to me, then dragged her on into the room, snatched

---

8 **checkerberry snuff:** a powder from the checkerberry plant, a creeping shrub that produces wintergreen oil

the quilts out of Miss Wangero's hands and dumped them into Maggie's lap. Maggie just sat there on my bed with her mouth open.

"Take one or two of the others," I said to Dee.

But she turned without a word and went out to Hakim-a-barber.

"You just don't understand," she said, as Maggie and I came out to the car.

"What don't I understand?" I wanted to know.

"Your heritage," she said. And then she turned to Maggie, kissed her, and said, "You ought to try to make something of yourself, too, Maggie. It's really a new day for us. But from the way you and Mama still live you'd never know it."

She put on some sunglasses that hid everything above the tip of her nose and chin.

Maggie smiled; maybe at the sunglasses. But a real smile, not scared. After we watched the car dust settle I asked Maggie to bring me a dip of snuff. And then the two of us sat there just enjoying, until it was time to go in the house and go to bed.

AFTER YOU READ
Everyday Use

Think and Discuss

1. Who, in your opinion, has the closer tie to her heritage, Dee or Maggie? Explain, using details from the text.

2. Why is Dee so willing to take the objects and Maggie so willing to give them?

3. Who is the **main character** in this story? Explain why you think so.

4. Explain how clothing is a **motif,** or recurring theme, in this story and what the different kinds of clothing say about the characters.

5. Make a spider map like the one below in your Writer's Notebook. On the horizontal lines, write a main idea about the kinds of things Maggie, Dee, and Hakim-a-barber value. Then make diagonal lines that indicate the details from the story that support each main idea. Mama's values are identified.

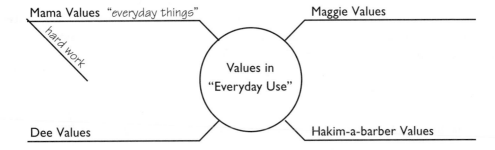

6. Compare your reaction to this story with your reaction to "The Gift of the Magi." Which stirred stronger feelings? Why?

Write to Understand: Extend the Story

Choose an event that is mentioned somewhere in the story (such as the fire, or the time when Grandma Dee and Big Dee taught Maggie how to quilt), or imagine an event that could have come before the story or afterwards. Write up that event so that it flows from or fits smoothly into the story. Use your spider map to remind you of what the characters value, and in your writing bring out the values of the characters by "showing, not telling."

BEFORE YOU READ
Fabric of Their Lives

Meet the Author: Amei Wallach

Amei Wallach was the chief art critic for *New York Newsday* for 26 years. She was also a regular art commentator on the "MacNeil/Lehrer NewsHour," a popular show on public television. Her father was a doctor but also wrote poetry and novels, which were published after his death. Her mother ran an art gallery. Wallach inherited her parents' love of writing and art and combined them to build her career as an art critic. She has published in a wide variety of newspapers and magazines, written a book, made a film, and mounted an award-winning exhibit featuring art that treats catastrophe through humor.

Build Background: The Quilts of Gee's Bend

The short story "Everyday Use" (pages 701–710) is a fictional account of a mother and her two daughters and their feelings about some quilts that have been in the family for a long time. Like most fiction, however, it draws its inspiration from real life. The article that follows is about real-life quilters in Gee's Bend, Alabama, who carry on a tradition they inherited from the generations before them. Their quilts have been put on display in art exhibits that traveled around the nation from one art museum to another. The first exhibit of "The Quilts of Gee's Bend" took place at the Museum of Fine Arts, Houston, in 2002. Later exhibits toured the nation.

- How does the information in this article affect your understanding of the story "Everyday Use"?

- What homemade items do you treasure above store-bought goods?

a quilt on display from the Gee's Bend collection exhibition

Fabric of Their Lives

AMEI WALLACH

FABRIC OF THEIR LIVES

Amei Wallach

Annie Mae Young is looking at a photograph of a quilt she pieced together out of strips torn from well-worn cotton shirts and polyester pants. "I was doing this quilt at the time of the civil rights movement," she says, contemplating its jazzy,[1] free-form squares.

Martin Luther King Jr. came to Young's hometown of Gee's Bend, Alabama, around that time. "I came over here to Gee's Bend to tell you, You are somebody," he shouted over a heavy rain late one winter night in 1965. A few days later, Young and many of her friends took off their aprons, laid down their hoes and rode over to the county seat of Camden, where they gathered outside the old jailhouse.

"We were waiting for Martin Luther King, and when he drove up, we were all slappin' and singin'," Young, 78, tells me when I visit Gee's Bend, a small rural community on a peninsula at a deep bend in the Alabama River. Wearing a red turban and an apron bright with pink peaches and yellow grapes, she stands in the doorway of her brick bungalow at the end of a dirt road. Swaying to a rhythm that nearly everyone in town knows from a lifetime of churchgoing, she breaks into song: "We shall overcome, we shall overcome. . . ."

"We were all just happy to see him coming," she says. "Then he stood out there on the ground, and he was talking about how we should wait on a bus to come and we were all going to march. We got loaded on the bus, but we didn't get a chance to do it, 'cause we got put in jail," she says.

Many who marched or registered to vote in rural Alabama in the 1960s lost their jobs. Some even lost their homes. And the residents of Gee's Bend, 60 miles southwest of Montgomery, lost the ferry that connected them to Camden and a direct route to the outside world. "We didn't close the ferry because they were black," Sheriff Lummie Jenkins reportedly said at the time. "We closed it because they *forgot* they were black. . . ."

---

1 **jazzy:** vibrant and colorful; related to jazz music, a form of music with an improvisational, or spontaneous, style, developed by African Americans

The bold drama of the quilt Young was working on in 1965 is also found in a quilt she made out of work clothes 11 years later. The central design of red and orange corduroy in that quilt suggests prison bars, and the faded denim that surrounds it could be a comment on the American dream. But Young had more practical considerations. "When I put the quilt together," she says, "it wasn't big enough, and I had to get some more material and make it bigger, so I had these old jeans to make it bigger."

Collector William Arnett was working on a history of African-American **vernacular art** in 1998 when he came across a photograph of Young's work-clothes quilt draped over a woodpile. He was so knocked out by its originality, he set out to find it. A couple of phone calls and some creative research later, he and his son Matt tracked Young down to Gee's Bend, then showed up unannounced at her door late one evening. Young had burned some quilts the week before (smoke from burning cotton drives off mosquitoes), and at first she thought the quilt in the photograph had been among them. But the next day, after scouring closets and searching under beds, she found it and offered it to Arnett for free. Arnett, however, insisted on writing her a check for a few thousand dollars for that quilt and several others. (Young took the check straight to the bank.) Soon the word spread through Gee's Bend that there was a crazy white man in town paying good money for raggedy old quilts. . . .

vernacular art
art made by people who do not regard themselves as artists and who have no formal art training

Arlonzia Pettway lives in a neat, recently renovated house off a road plagued with potholes. The road passes by cows and goats grazing outside robin's-egg blue and brown bungalows. "I remember some things, honey," Pettway, 83, told me. "I came through a hard life. Maybe we weren't bought and sold, but we were still slaves until 20, 30 years ago. The white man would go to everybody's field and say, 'Why you not at work?'" She paused. "What do you think a slave *is*?"

As a girl, Pettway would watch her grandmother, Sally, and her mother Missouri, piecing quilts. And she would listen to their stories, many of them about Dinah Miller, who had been brought to the United States in a slave ship in 1859. "My great-grandmother Dinah was sold for a dime," Pettway said. "Her dad, brother, and mother were sold to different people, and she didn't see them no more. My great-grandfather was a Cherokee Indian. . . ." In addition to Pettway, some 20 other Gee's Bend quiltmakers are Dinah's descendants.

Arlonzia Pettway discusses her Gee's Bend quilt

The quilting tradition in Gee's Bend may go back as far as the early 1800s, when the community was the site of a cotton plantation owned by a Joseph Gee. Influenced, perhaps, by the patterned textiles of Africa, the women slaves began piecing strips of cloth together to make bedcovers. Throughout the **post-bellum** years of tenant farming and well into the 20th century, Gee's Bend women made quilts to keep themselves and their children warm in unheated shacks that lacked running water, telephones and electricity. Along the way they developed a distinctive style, noted for its lively **improvisations** and geometric simplicity. . . .

In 1941, when Pettway was in her late teens, her father died. "Mama said, 'I'm going to take his work clothes, shape them into a quilt to remember him, and cover up under it for love.'" There were hardly enough pants legs and shirttails to make up a quilt, but she managed. A year later, Arlonzia married Bizzell Pettway. They had 12 children, but no electricity until 1964 and no running water until 1974. A widow for more than 30

postbellum
literally, "after war," from the Latin. The term usually refers to the period following the Civil War.

improvisations
effects made with materials that are on hand

years, Arlonzia still lives in that same house. Her mother, Missouri, who lived until 1981, made a quilt she called "Path Through the Woods" after the 1960s freedom marches. A quilt that Pettway pieced together during that period, "Chinese Coins," is a medley of pinks and purples—a friend had given her purple scraps from a clothing factory in a nearby town.

"At the time I was making that quilt, I was feeling something was going to happen better, and it did," Pettway says. "Last time I counted I had 32 grandchildren and I think between 13 and 14 great-grands. I'm blessed now more than many. I have my home and land. I have a deepfreeze five feet long with chicken wings, neck bones and pork chops."

. . . Loretta Pettway, 64, Arlonzia Pettway's first cousin, made her early quilts out of work clothes. "I was about 16 when I learned to quilt from my grandmamma," she says. "I just loved it. That's all I wanted to do, quilt.. . . When I finished my chores, I'd sit down and do like I'm doing now, get the clothes together and tear them and piece. And then in summer I would quilt outside under the big oak." She fingers the fabric pieces in her lap. "I thank God that people want me to make quilts," she says. . . .

In 1962 the U.S. Congress ordered the construction of a dam and lock on the Alabama River at Miller's Ferry, just south of Gee's Bend. The 17,200-acre reservoir created by the dam in the late 1960s flooded much of Gee's Bend's best farming land, forcing many residents to give up farming. "And thank God for *that*," says Loretta. "Farming wasn't nothing but hard work. At the end of the year you couldn't get nothing, and the little you got went for cottonseed."

Around that time, a number of Gee's Bend women began making quilts for the Freedom Quilting Bee, founded in 1966 by civil rights worker and Episcopalian priest Francis X. Walter to provide a source of income for the local community. For a while, the bee (which operated for about three decades) sold quilts to such stores as Bloomingdale's, Sears, Saks and Bonwit Teller. But the stores wanted assembly-line quilts, with orderly, familiar patterns and precise stitching—not the individual, often impro-vised and unexpected patterns and color combinations that characterized the Gee's Bend quilts.

"My quilts looked beautiful to me, because I made what I could make from my head," Loretta told me. "When I start I don't want to stop until I finish, because if I stop, the ideas are going to go one way and my mind another way, so I just try to do it while I have ideas in my mind."

"*My* quilts looked beautiful to me, because I made what I could make from my head," Loretta told me.

Loretta had been too ill to attend the opening of the first exhibition [of "The Quilts of Gee's Bend"] in Houston. But she wore a bright red jacket and a wrist corsage of roses to the opening of the second show last spring. Going there on the bus, "I didn't close my eyes the whole way," she says. "I was so happy, I had to sightsee." In the new show, her 2003 take on the popular "Housetop" pattern—a variant of the traditional "Log Cabin" design—is an explosion of red polka dots, zany stripes and crooked frames within frames (a dramatic change from the faded colors and somber patterns of her early work-clothes quilts). Two other quilts made by Loretta are among those represented on a series of Gee's Bend stamps issued this past August by the U.S. Postal Service. "I just had scraps of what I could find," she says about her early work. "Now I see my quilts hanging in a museum. Thank God I see my quilts on the wall, I found my way."

AFTER YOU READ
Fabric of Their Lives

Think and Discuss

1. Explain how quilts are important to each of these three women: Annie Mae Young, Arlonzia Pettway, and Loretta Pettway.

2. Are the quilts of Gee's bend items of art or items of everyday use? Explain.

3. The **structure** of this article resembles a quilt in that it is made of several **narratives** pieced together. What gives each narrative its distinctiveness?

4. What unifying **theme** holds the article together and adds to the story's meaning?

5. Design a quilt that represents the journey undertaken by the quilters of Gee's Bend. Make each major element of your design represent an important principle the quilters believe in, an important event in their lives, or one of the quilters featured in this article. Use smaller elements to represent supporting details from the article. In your Writer's Notebook, draw a quilt grid like the one below to plan your design.

Write to Understand: Inspiration Explanation
Write an explanation of your quilt design, explaining the meaning of each element. Then use your quilt design to do a QuickWrite of a short story about fictional characters inspired by the real-life people in Gee's Bend.

BEFORE YOU READ

Poems of Working People

Meet the Authors

Marge Piercy Born in 1936, Piercy grew to become a political poet, short story writer, and novelist. Her work grows from close observations of people and the landscape in which they live. Her work in civil rights, anti-war, feminist, and Jewish movements is central to her writing.

Walt Whitman An American poet, essayist, short story writer, educator, printer, and publisher, Whitman (1819–1892) lived and worked during a time when the nation was young, growing, and in the process of defining its character. His exuberant style, which contained free verse and prose, is considered distinctly American, especially in the way it expresses the beauty found in common, everyday life. His style continues to inspire and influence poets in the United States and around the world.

Build Background: The Work Ethic

In many ancient cultures, including Greece and Rome, work was considered demeaning—a curse. Many believed that only leisure had value, that the more leisure people had, the more moral and worthy they were, since they could devote themselves to study and thought. Even in early Christianity, work was believed to be a punishment for the disobedience humans showed to God in the Garden of Eden. However, when Protestantism rose in the 1500s, work became a valued way to serve God, to serve the human community, and even to ensure grace after death. The Puritans brought this "work ethic" with them to North America, and it has become a foundation of the "American Dream": through hard work, anybody can succeed and reap the rewards of labor.

- What kind of work makes you feel good when you do it?

- What is the value of hard work?

METALLURGY, Jules Didier

Poems of Working People

To be of use

MARGE PIERCY

The people I love the best
jump into work head first
without dallying in the shallows
and swim off with sure strokes almost out of sight.
They seem to become natives of that element,   5
the black sleek heads of seals
bouncing like half-submerged balls.

I love people who harness themselves, an ox to a heavy cart,
who pull like water buffalo, with massive patience,
who strain in the mud and the muck to move things forward,   10
who do what has to be done, again and again.

I want to be with people who submerge
in the task, who go into the fields to harvest
and work in a row and pass the bags along,
who are not parlor generals[1] and field deserters   15
but move in a common rhythm
when the food must come in or the fire be put out.

---

1 **parlor generals:** people who, from the safety and comfort of living rooms, direct others
who are fighting in the trenchesa

The work of the world is common as mud.
Botched, it smears the hands, crumbles to dust.
has a shape that satisfies, clean and evident.
But the thing worth doing well done
Greek **amphoras** for wine or oil,
Hopi vases that held corn, are put in museums
but you know they were made to be used.
The pitcher cries for water to carry
and a person for work that is real.

20

25

amphoras
ceramic vases
with handles
and a narrow
neck

I Hear America Singing   WALT WHITMAN

I hear America singing, the varied carols I hear,
Those of mechanics, each one singing his, as it should be
        blithe and strong;
The carpenter singing his as he measures his plank or beam,
The mason singing his as he makes ready for work, or leaves off work,   5
The boatman singing what belongs to him in his boat,
        the deck-hand singing on the steamboat deck,
The shoemaker singing as he sits on his bench, the
        hatter singing as he stands,
The wood-cutter's song, the ploughboy's, on his way in the morning,   10
        or at noon intermission or at sundown,
The delicious singing of the mother, or of the young wife at work,
        or of the girl sewing or washing,
Each singing what belongs to him or her and to none else,   15
The day what belongs to the day—at night the party of young fellows,
        robust, friendly,
Singing with open mouths their strong melodious songs.

AFTER YOU READ
Poems of Working People

Think and Discuss

1. According to "To be of use," what is the value of "work that is real"?

2. What **metaphors** does Piercy use to represent the strength of people who throw themselves into their work? (For a definition of *metaphor*, see the Glossary of Literary Terms.)

3. Imagine for yourself the song each one of the workers in Whitman's poem might sing. Choose one worker and write the lyrics—and, if possible, the music—for that worker's song.

4. Whitman's poetry broke new ground by using **common speech patterns** and **rhythms**; **repetitions**; "**catalogs**," or lists of things, and the spirit of popular music. How are these elements represented in "I Hear America Singing"? (For definitions of these highlighted words, see the Glossary of Literary Terms.)

5. Do Piercy's and Whitman's poems seem to support the same idea about the rewards of work? Explain.

6. Create a double-column organizer in your Writer's Notebook like the one below. In one column, write what you think the last four lines mean in "To be of use." In the other column, explain whether that meaning agrees or disagrees with the message in "Everyday Use" (pages 701–710).

Meaning of Last Four Lines of Piercy's Poem	Like or Unlike "Everyday Use"?

Write to Understand: Freewriting to Synthesize Meaning
Re-read the poems in this lesson and skim back over "Everyday Use." Then use your graphic organizer to reflect on the value of work as represented in these selections. After explaining the views of the texts, continue writing to discover how you feel about the value of work. Relate how you feel to the attitudes in the other works.

BEFORE YOU READ

The Necklace

Meet the Author: Guy de Maupassant

Guy de Maupassant (1850–1893) grew up in a middle-class family that lost its fortune during wartime. He began writing as an escape from the boredom of his job as a government clerk. The first short story he wrote made him famous, and he became a professional writer, publishing 200 articles, almost 300 stories, and several novels in just ten years. Unfortunately, de Maupassant, who lived as extravagantly as he wrote, contracted syphilis. As the disease progressed, he grew increasingly withdrawn and fearful. He was considered insane at the age of forty and died only two years later.

Build Background: Realism

Realism in literature, as its name suggests, is the treatment of a subject in a realistic, plausible way, focusing on the observable here and now. It contrasts with the use of fantastic, other-worldly elements, as in Poe's work, and the glorifying of the past, both of which were characteristic of literature from the Romantic period. Like a realistic film, literary realism tries to capture people just as they are, letting the details speak for themselves. Realistic literature often focuses on social classes—the rich, the working class, and the middle class between them, with its longing for upward mobility.

The story that follows, published in 1884, is an early example of realism and is one of de Maupassant's most famous stories.

• If you were writing a realistic story or making a realistic film, what view of people would you convey?

• Would your story or film have a happy ending? Explain.

The Bruker Family, Giuseppe Tominz, detail

The Necklace

GUY DE MAUPASSANT

THE NECKLACE

Guy de Maupassant

prospects
chances for
success or
wealth

She was one of those pretty and charming girls, born, as if by an accident of fate, into a family of clerks. With no dowry, no **prospects**, no way of any kind of being met, understood, loved, and married by a man both prosperous and famous, she was finally married to a minor clerk in the Ministry of Education.

She dressed plainly because she could not afford fine clothes, but was as unhappy as a woman who has come down in the world; for women have no family rank or social class. With them, beauty, grace, and charm take the place of birth and breeding. Their natural poise, their instinctive good taste, and their mental cleverness are the sole guiding principles which make daughters of common people the equals of ladies in high society.

disconsolate
unhappy;
offering no
comfort

She grieved incessantly, feeling that she had been born for all the little niceties and luxuries of living. She grieved over the shabbiness of her apartment, the dinginess of the walls, the worn-out appearance of the chairs, the ugliness of the draperies. All these things, which another woman of her class would not even have noticed, gnawed at her and made her furious. The sight of the little Breton girl[1] who did her humble housework roused in her **disconsolate** regrets and wild daydreams. She would dream of silent chambers, draped with Oriental tapestries and lighted by tall bronze floor lamps, and of two handsome butlers in knee breeches, who, drowsy from the heavy warmth cast by the central stove, dozed in large overstuffed armchairs.

She would dream of great reception halls hung with old silks, of fine furniture filled with priceless curios,[2] and of small, stylish, scented sitting rooms just right for the four o'clock chat with intimate friends, with distinguished and sought-after men whose attention every woman envies and longs to attract.

When dining at the round table, covered for the third day with the same cloth, opposite her husband, who would raise the cover of the soup tureen, declaring delightedly, "Ah, a good stew! There's nothing I like better . . . ," she

---

1 **Breton girl:** girl from Brittany, an area in northwestern France

2 **curios:** unusual, rare, or intriguing objects

would dream of fashionable dinner parties, of gleaming silverware, of tapestries making the walls alive with characters out of history and strange birds in a fairyland forest; she would dream of delicious dishes served on wonderful china, of gallant compliments whispered and listened to with a sphinxlike[3] smile as one eats the rosy flesh of a trout or nibbles at the wings of a grouse.

She had no evening clothes, no jewelry, nothing. But those were the things she wanted; she felt that was the kind of life for her. She so much longed to please, be envied, be fascinating and sought after.

She had a well-to-do friend, a classmate of convent-school days, whom she would no longer go to see because she would feel so distressed on returning home. And she would weep for days on end from **vexation**, regret, despair, and anguish.

Then one evening, her husband came home proudly holding out a large envelope.

"Look," he said, "I've got something for you."

She excitedly tore open the envelope and pulled out a printed card bearing these words:

"The Minister of Education and Mme. Georges Rampounneau beg M. and Mme. Loisel to do them the honor of attending an evening reception at the Ministerial Mansion on Friday, January 18."

Instead of being delighted, as her husband had hoped, she scornfully tossed the invitation on the table, murmuring, "What good is that to me?"

"But, my dear, I thought you'd be thrilled to death. You never get a chance to go out, and this is a real affair, a wonderful one! I had an awful time getting a card. Everybody wants one; it's much sought after, and not many clerks have a chance at one. You'll see all the most important people there."

She gave him an irritated glance and burst out impatiently, "What do you think I have to go in?"

He hadn't given that a thought. He stammered, "Why, the dress you wear when you go to the theater. That looks quite nice, I think."

He stopped talking, dazed and distracted to see his wife burst out weeping. Two large tears slowly rolled from the corners of her eyes to the corners of her mouth; he gasped, "Why, what's the matter? What's the trouble?"

By sheer willpower she overcame her outburst and answered in a calm voice while wiping the tears from her wet cheeks:

---

3 **sphinxlike:** mysterious; hard to understand

"Oh, nothing. Only I don't have an evening dress and therefore I can't go to that affair. Give the card to some friend at the office whose wife can dress better than I can."

He was stunned. He resumed. "Let's see, Mathilde. How much would a suitable outfit cost—one you could wear for other affairs too—something very simple?"

She thought it over a few seconds, going over her allowance and thinking also of the amount she could ask for without bringing an immediate refusal and an exclamation of dismay from the thrifty clerk.

Finally, she answered hesitatingly, "I'm not sure exactly, but I think with four hundred francs[4] I could manage it."

He turned a little pale, for he had set aside just that amount to buy a rifle so that, the following summer, he could join some friends who were getting up a group to shoot larks on the plain near Nanterre.

However, he said, "All right. I'll give you four hundred francs. But try to get a nice dress."

As the day of the party approached, Mme. Loisel seemed sad, moody, and ill at ease. Her outfit was ready, however. Her husband said to her one evening, "What's the matter? You've been all out of sorts for three days."

And she answered, "It's embarrassing not to have a jewel or a single gem—nothing to wear on my dress. I'll look like a **pauper**; I'd almost rather not go to that party."

pauper
very poor
person

He answered, "Why not wear some flowers? They're very fashionable this season. For ten francs you can get two or three gorgeous roses."

She wasn't at all convinced. "No. . . There's nothing more humiliating than to look poor among a lot of rich women."

But her husband exclaimed, "My, but you're silly! Go see your friend, Mme. Forestier and ask her to lend you some jewelry. You and she know each other well enough for you to do that."

She gave a cry of joy, "Why, that's so! I hadn't thought of it."

predicament
a difficult,
embarrassing,
or unpleasant
situation

The next day she paid her friend a visit and told her of her **predicament**.

Mme. Forestier went toward a large closet with mirrored doors, took out a large jewel box, brought it over, opened it, and said to Mme. Loisel, "Pick something out, my dear."

---

4 francs: the basic monetary unit in France and many other countries before the Euro was adopted

At first her eyes noted some bracelets, then a pearl necklace, then a Venetian[5] cross, gold and gems, of marvelous workmanship. She tried on these adornments in front of the mirror, but hesitated, unable to decide which to part with and put back. She kept on asking, "Haven't you something else?"

"Oh, yes, keep on looking. I don't know just what you'd like."

All at once she found, in a black satin box, a superb diamond necklace; and her pulse beat faster with longing. Her hands trembled as she took it up. Clasping it around her throat, outside her high-necked dress, she stood in ecstasy looking at her reflection.

All at once she found, in a black satin box, a superb diamond necklace; and her pulse beat faster with longing. Her hands trembled as she took it up. Clasping it around her throat, outside her high-necked dress, she stood in ecstasy looking at her reflection.

Then, she asked, hesitatingly, pleading, "Could I borrow that, just that and nothing else?

"Why, of course."

She threw her arms around her friend, kissed her warmly, and fled with her treasure.

The day of the party arrived. Mme. Loisel was a sensation. She was the prettiest one there, fashionable, gracious, smiling, and wild with joy. All the men turned to look at her, asked who she was, begged to be introduced. All the Cabinet officials wanted to waltz with her. The minister took notice of her.

She danced madly, wildly, drunk with pleasure, giving no thought to anything in the triumph of her beauty, the pride of her success, in a kind of happy cloud composed of all the **adulation**, of all the admiring glances, of all the awakened longings, of a sense of complete victory that is so sweet to a woman's heart.

> **adulation** excessive admiration or praise

She left around four o'clock in the morning. Her husband, since midnight, had been dozing in a small empty sitting room with three other gentlemen whose wives were having too good a time.

He threw over her shoulders the wraps he had brought for going home, modest garments of everyday life, whose shabbiness clashed with the stylishness of her evening clothes. She felt this and longed to escape, unseen by the other women who were draped in expensive furs.

---

5 **Venetian cross:** a necklace with a cross made in Venice, Italy

Loisel held her back—

"Hold on! You'll catch cold outside. I'll call a cab."

But she wouldn't listen to him and went rapidly down the stairs. When they were on the street, they didn't find a carriage; and they set out to hunt for one, hailing drivers whom they saw going by at a distance.

They walked toward the Seine,[6] disconsolate and shivering. Finally on the docks they found one of those carriages that one sees in Paris only after nightfall, as if they were ashamed to show their drabness during the daylight hours.

It dropped them at their door in the Rue des Martyrs,[7] and they climbed wearily up to their apartment. For her, it was all over. For him, there was the thought that he would have to be at the Ministry at ten o'clock.

Before the mirror, she let the wraps fall from her shoulders to see herself once again in all her glory. Suddenly she gave a cry. The necklace was gone.

Her husband, already half-undressed, said, "What's the trouble?"

despairingly
without hope

She turned toward him **despairingly**, "I . . . I . . . I don't have Mme. Forestier's necklace!"

"What? You can't mean it! It's impossible!"

They hunted everywhere, through the folds of the dress, through the folds of the coat, in the pockets. They found nothing.

He asked, "Are you sure you had it when leaving the dance?"

"Yes, I felt it when I was in the hall of the Ministry."

"But if you had lost it on the street, we'd have heard it drop. It must be in the cab."

"Yes. Quite likely. Did you get its number?"

"No. Didn't you notice it either?"

"No."

aghast
full of horror
and shock

They looked at each other, **aghast**. Finally Loisel got dressed again.

"I'll retrace our steps on foot," he said, "to see if I can find it."

And he went out. She remained in her evening clothes, without the strength to go to bed, slumped in a chair in the unheated room, her mind a blank.

Her husband came in about seven o'clock. He had had no luck.

He went to the police station, to the newspapers to post a reward, to the cab companies, everywhere the slightest hope drove him.

---

6 **Seine:** the river that flows through Paris

7 **Rue des Martyrs:** French for Martyrs Street, located on the Right Bank in Paris

That evening Loisel returned, pale, his face lined; still he had learned nothing.

"We'll have to write your friend," he said, "to tell her you have broken the clasp and are having it repaired. That will give us a little time to turn around."

She wrote to his dictation.

At the end of a week, they had given up all hope.

And Loisel, looking five years older, declared, "We must take steps to replace that piece of jewelry."

The next day they took the case to the jeweler whose name they found inside. He consulted his records. "I didn't sell that necklace, madame," he said. "I only supplied the case."

Then they went from one jeweler to another hunting for a similar necklace, going over their recollections, both sick with despair and anxiety.

They found, in a shop in Palais Royal, a string of diamonds which seemed exactly like the one they were seeking. It was priced at forty thousand francs. They could get it for thirty-six.

They asked the jeweler to hold it for them for three days. And they reached an agreement that he would take it back for thirty-four thousand if the lost one was found before the end of February.

Loisel had eighteen thousand francs he had inherited from his father. He would borrow the rest.

He went about raising the money, asking a thousand francs from one, five hundred from another, a hundred here, sixty there. He signed notes, made **ruinous** deals, did business with loan sharks, ran the whole **gamut** of moneylenders. He **compromised** the rest of his life, risked his signature without even knowing if he'd be able to honor it, and then, terrified by the outlook for the future, by the blackness of despair about to close around him, by the prospect of all the **privations** of the body and tortures of the spirit, he went to claim the new necklace with the thirty-six thousand francs which he placed on the counter of the shopkeeper.

When Mme. Loisel took the necklace back, Mme. Forestier said to her frostily, "You should have brought it back sooner; I might have needed it."

She didn't open the case, an action her friend was afraid of. If she had noticed the substitution, what would she have thought? What would she have said? Would she have thought her a thief?

ruinous
disastrous; destructive

gamut
the complete range or scope

compromised
weakened or exposed to disrepute or danger

privations
losses of qualities normal to one's well-being

Mme. Loisel learned the horrible life the needy live. She played her part, however, with sudden heroism. That frightful debt had to be paid. She would pay it. She dismissed her maid; they rented a garret[8] under the eaves.

She learned to do the heavy housework, to perform the hateful duties of cooking. She washed dishes, wearing down her shell-pink nails scouring the grease from pots and pans; she scrubbed dirty linen, shirts, and cleaning rags, which she hung on a line to dry; she took the garbage down to the street each morning and brought water, stopping on each landing to get her breath. And,

A WOMAN IRONING, Edgar Degas, 1873

---

8 **garret:** an attic room, especially a small, dismal one

clad like a peasant woman, basket on arm, guarding sou by sou[9] her scanty allowance, she bargained with the fruit dealers, the grocer, the butcher, and was insulted by them.

Each month notes had to be paid, and others renewed to give more time.

Her husband labored evenings to balance a trademan's accounts, and at night, often, he copied documents at five sous a page.

And this life went on for ten years.

Finally, all was paid back, everything including the **exorbitant** rates of the loan sharks and accumulated compound interest.

Mme. Loisel appeared an old woman, now. She became heavy, rough, harsh, like one of the poor. Her hair untended, her skirts **askew**, her hands red, her voice shrill, she even slopped water on her floors and scrubbed them herself. But, sometimes, while her husband was at work, she would sit near the window and think of that long-ago evening when, at the dance, she had been so beautiful and admired.

What would have happened if she had not lost that necklace? Who knows? Who can say? How strange and unpredictable life is! How little there is between happiness and misery!

Then one Sunday when she had gone for a walk on the Champs Elysées[10] to relax a bit from the week's labors, she suddenly noticed a woman strolling with a child. It was Mme. Forestier, still young-looking. still beautiful, still charming.

Mme. Loisel felt a rush of emotion. Should she speak to her? Of course. And now that everything was paid off, she would tell her the whole story. Why not?

She went toward her. "Hello, Jeanne."

The other, not recognizing her, showed astonishment at being spoken to so familiarly by this common person. She stammered. "But . . .madame . . . I don't recognize . . . You must be mistaken."

"No, I am Mathilde Loisel."

Her friend gave a cry, "Oh, my poor Mathilde, how you've changed!"

"Yes, I've had a hard time since last seeing you. And plenty of misfortunes— and all on account of you!"

"Of me? . . . How do you mean?"

exorbitant
unreasonably high

askew
not in a straight or level position

---

9 **sou:** a French coin of small value

10 **Champ Elysées:** a famous wide boulevard in Paris

"Do you remember that diamond necklace you loaned me to wear to the dance at the Ministry?"

"Yes, but what about it?"

"Well, I lost it."

"You lost it! But you returned it."

"I brought you another just like it. And we've been paying for it for ten years now. You can imagine that wasn't easy for us who had nothing. Well, it's over now, and I am glad of it."

Mme. Forestier stopped short, "You mean to say you bought a diamond necklace to replace mine?"

"Yes. You never noticed, then? They were quite alike."

And she smiled with proud and simple joy.

Mme. Forestier, quite overcome, clasped her by the hands. "Oh, my poor Mathilde. But mine were only paste.[11] Why, at most it was worth only five hundred francs!"

---

11 **paste:** a hard, glassy composition used to make imitation gems

AFTER YOU READ

The Necklace

Think and Discuss

1. Does this story seem realistic to you? Explain why or why not.

2. Do you feel the same way about Loisel as you feel about his wife? Refer to the text to support your answer.

3. What **details** reinforce the sense of shabbiness that Mme. Loisel feels in her surroundings?

4. What details paint the picture of Mme. Loisel's desired life?

5. At what moments in the **plot** did the Loisels make choices that influenced the outcome of their story? Using the following graphic as an example, draw a plot line in your Writer's Notebook. Identify the points at which Mme. Loisel and her husband make fateful choices. One is done for you.

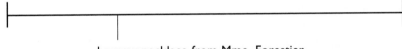

borrow necklace from Mme. Forestier

6. The question is asked near the end of the story, "What would have happened if she had not lost that necklace?" What do you think would have happened? Explain, relating your answer to theme of "what has value."

Write to Understand: Exploring "What If"

Look over your graphic organizer. Identify a spot on the plot outline at which the Loisels might have made a different choice that would have been as realistic. Sketch out how the story would have ended if they had made that other choice.

BEFORE YOU READ
The Man to Send Rain Clouds

Meet the Author: Leslie Marmon Silko

Leslie Marmon Silko (born 1948) has mixed Laguna, Pueblo, Mexican, and white ancestry. She grew up with several generations of relatives on the Laguna Pueblo reservation. She has lived and taught in New Mexico, Arizona, and Alaska. Silko's stories draw from the oral tradition she inherited from her grandparents and focus on the experience of indigenous people in America. She has written a number of novels, short stories, poetry collections, and essays and is considered one of the most prominent Native American writers today.

Build Background: North American Missionaries

Beginning in the sixteenth century, Christian missionaries in North America sought to lead indigenous people away from their traditional faiths and toward Christianity. Some missionaries used cruelty and force. Most, however, emphasized education and service. Catholic missionaries often founded missions, or religious outposts, which usually included a church, a school, and a center for labor such as farming, ranching, and weaving. Some of these missions have become world heritage sites.

The following story tells about a death in a Pueblo community near a mission and the rituals surrounding the death.

As you read, think about these questions:

- What traditions and rituals does your family or community find meaningful?

- Recall a time when you have been a visitor or newcomer at a traditional event. What did you appreciate about the event? What was difficult to accept or understand?

Geronimo Giyuatle, Apache

The Man to Send Rain Clouds

LESLIE MARMON SILKO

THE MAN TO SEND RAIN CLOUDS

Leslie Marmon Silko

ONE

They found him under a big cottonwood tree. His Levi jacket and pants were faded light blue so that he had been easy to find. The big cottonwood tree stood apart from a small grove of winterbare cottonwoods which grew in the wide, sandy **arroyo**. He had been dead for a day or more, and the sheep had wandered and scattered up and down the arroyo. Leon and his brother-in-law, Ken, gathered the sheep and left them in the pen at the sheep camp[1] before they returned to the cottonwood tree. Leon waited under the tree while Ken drove the truck through the deep sand to the edge of the arroyo. He squinted up at the sun and unzipped his jacket—it sure was hot for this time of year. But high and northwest the blue mountains were still deep in snow. Ken came sliding down the low, crumbling bank about fifty yards down, and he was bringing the red blanket.

Before they wrapped the old man, Leon took a piece of string out of his pocket and tied a small gray feather in the old man's long white hair. Ken gave him the paint. Across the brown wrinkled forehead he drew a streak of white and along the high cheekbones he drew a strip of blue paint. He paused and watched Ken throw pinches of corn meal and pollen into the wind that fluttered the small gray feather. Then Leon painted with yellow under the old man's broad nose, and finally, when he had painted green across the chin, he smiled.

"Send us rain clouds, Grandfather." They laid the bundle in the back of the pickup and covered it with a heavy tarp before they started back to the **pueblo**.

They turned off the highway onto the sandy pueblo road. Not long after they passed the store and post office they saw Father Paul's car coming toward them. When he recognized their faces he slowed his car and waved for them to stop. The young priest rolled down the car window.

> **arroyo**
> a deep gully or gulch that has been cut by a stream

> **pueblo**
> once a village made of adobe and rock, now any village inhabited by people who once lived in pueblos

1 **sheep camp:** the place where the sheep graze and the herder camps

"Did you find old Teofilo?" he asked loudly.

Leon stopped the truck. "Good morning, Father. We were just out to the sheep camp. Everything is O.K. now."

"Thank God for that. Teofilo is a very old man. You really shouldn't allow him to stay at the sheep camp alone."

"No, he won't do that any more now."

"Well, I'm glad you understand. I hope I'll be seeing you at Mass this week—we missed you last Sunday. See if you can get old Teofilo to come with you." The priest smiled and waved at them as they drove away.

TWO

Louise and Teresa were waiting. The table was set for lunch, and the coffee was boiling on the black iron stove. Leon looked at Louise and then at Teresa.

"We found him under a cottonwood tree in the big arroyo near the sheep camp. I guess he sat down to rest in the shade and never got up again." Leon walked toward the old man's bed. The red plaid shawl had been shaken and spread carefully over the bed, and a new brown flannel shirt and pair of stiff new Levis were arranged neatly beside the pillow. Louise held the screen door open while Leon and Ken carried in the red blanket. He looked small and shriveled, and after they dressed him in the new shirt and pants he seemed more shrunken.

It was noontime now because the church bells rang the Angelus.[2] They ate the beans with hot bread, and nobody said anything until after Teresa poured the coffee.

Ken stood up and put on his jacket. "I'll see about the gravediggers. Only the top layer of soil is frozen. I think it can be ready before dark."

Leon nodded his head and finished his coffee. After Ken had been gone for a while, the neighbors and clanspeople came quietly to embrace Teofilo's family and to leave food on the table because the gravediggers would come to eat when they were finished.

---

2 **Angelus:** a devotional prayer said or sung at morning, noon, and night in honor of Mary, the mother of Jesus

THREE

The sky in the west was full of pale-yellow light. Louise stood outside with her hands in the pockets of Leon's green army jacket that was too big for her. The funeral was over, and the old men had taken their candles and medicine bags[3] and were gone. She waited until the body was laid into the pickup before she said anything to Leon. She touched his arm, and he noticed that her hands were still dusty from the corn meal that she had sprinkled around the old man. When she spoke, Leon could not hear her.

"What did you say? I didn't hear you."

"I said that I had been thinking about something."

"About what?"

"About the priest sprinkling holy water[4] for Grandpa. So he won't be thirsty."

Leon stared at the new moccasins that Teofilo had made for the ceremonial dances in the summer. They were nearly hidden by the red blanket. It was getting colder, and the wind pushed gray dust down the narrow pueblo road. The sun was approaching the long mesa where it disappeared during the winter. Louise stood there shivering and watching his face. Then he zipped his jacket and opened the truck door. "I'll see if he's there."

FOUR

Ken stopped the pickup at the church, and Leon got out; and then Ken drove down the hill to the graveyard where people were waiting. Leon knocked at the old carved door with its symbols of the Lamb. While he waited he looked up at the twin bells from the king of Spain with the last sunlight pouring around them in their tower.

The priest opened the door and smiled when he saw who it was. "Come in! What brings you here this evening?"

The priest walked toward the kitchen, and Leon stood with his cap in his hand, playing with the earflaps and examining the living room—the brown sofa, the green armchair, and the brass lamp that hung down from the ceiling

---

3 **medicine bags:** containers for items with religious power or significance. Some items in a medicine bag also are used for healthcare.

4 **holy water:** water that has been blessed by a Catholic priest for use in religious rituals

by links of chain. The priest dragged a chair out of the kitchen and offered it to Leon.

"No thank you, Father. I only came to ask you if you would bring your holy water to the graveyard."

The priest turned away from Leon and looked out the window at the patio full of shadows and the dining room windows of the nuns' **cloister** across the patio. The curtains were heavy, and the light from within faintly penetrated; it was impossible to see the nuns inside eating supper. "Why didn't you tell me he was dead? I could have brought the Last Rites[5] anyway."

Leon smiled. "It wasn't necessary, Father."

The priest stared down at his scuffed brown loafers and the worn hem of his **cassock**. "For a Christian burial it was necessary."

His voice was distant, and Leon thought that his blue eyes looked tired.

"It's O.K. Father, we just want him to have plenty of water."

The priest sank down into the green chair and picked up a glossy missionary magazine. He turned the colored pages full of lepers[6] and pagans[7] without looking at them.

"You know I can't do that, Leon. There should have been the Last Rites and a funeral Mass at the very least."

Leon put on his green cap and pulled the flaps down over his ears. "It's getting late, Father. I've got to go."

When Leon opened the door Father Paul stood up and said, "Wait." He left the room and came back wearing a long brown overcoat. He followed Leon out the door and across the dim churchyard to the adobe steps in front of the church. They both stooped to fit through the low adobe entrance. And when they started down the hill to the graveyard only half of the sun was visible above the mesa.

The priest approached the grave slowly, wondering how they had managed to dig into the frozen ground; and then he remembered that this was New Mexico, and saw the pile of cold loose sand beside the hole. The people stood

cloister
a residence that is also a place of seclusion

cassock
a black or brown ankle-length robe often worn by priests

---

5 **Last Rites:** a Catholic sacrament, or sacred ritual, performed on the ill and the dying

6 **lepers:** people who suffer from leprosy. In ancient times, people with any skin disease were known as lepers. Jesus was said to have cured lepers, and missionaries often worked among them.

7 **pagans:** people who worship their own local gods. Christians often define any non-Christian as pagan.

close to each other with little clouds of steam puffing from their faces. The priest looked at them and saw a pile of jackets, gloves, and scarves in the yellow, dry tumbleweeds that grew in the graveyard. He looked at the red blanket, not sure that Teofilo was so small, wondering if it wasn't some perverse Indian trick[8]—something they did in March to ensure a good harvest—wondering if maybe old Teofilo was actually at sheep camp corralling the sheep for the night. But there he was facing into a cold dry wind and squinting at the last sunlight, ready to bury a red wool blanket while the faces of his parishioners were in shadow with the last warmth of the sun on their backs.

His fingers were stiff, and it took him a long time to twist the lid off the holy water. Drops of water fell on the red blanket and soaked into dark icy spots. He sprinkled the grave and the water disappeared almost before it touched the dim cold sand; it reminded him of something—he tried to remember what it was, because he thought if he could remember he might understand this. He sprinkled more water; he shook the container until it was empty, and the water fell through the light from sundown like August rain that fell while the sun was still shining, almost evaporating before it touched the wilted squash flowers.

The wind pushed at the priest's brown Franciscan[9] robe and swirled away the corn meal and pollen that had been sprinkled on the blanket. They lowered the bundle into the ground, and they didn't bother to untie the stiff pieces of new rope that were tied around the ends of the blanket. The sun was gone, and over on the highway the eastbound lane was full of headlights. The priest walked away slowly. Leon watched him climb the hill, and when he had disappeared within the tall, thick walls, Leon turned to look up at the high blue mountains in the deep snow that reflected a faint red light from the west. He felt good because it was finished, and he was happy about the sprinkling of the holy water; now the old man could send them big thunderclouds for sure.

---

8 **Indian trick:** what some Christian missionaries called an Indian rite or ritual

9 **Franciscan:** relating to the order of priests, nuns, and others devoted to St. Francis of Assisi and dedicated to the principles of poverty, chastity, and service

AFTER YOU READ
The Man to Send Rain Clouds

Think and Discuss

1. What value does the holy water have to Teofilo's family? Explain.

2. Do Father Paul's feelings about the holy water change during the story? Explain your answer with details from the text.

3. This story is told by a **third-person omniscient narrator** who can describe the thoughts of each character. How would the story change if it were told from only one character's point of view? Explain by using an example.

4. What does the **image** of the holy water disappearing "almost before it touched the dim cold sand" suggest about the value of the ritual?

5. Father Paul and the villagers measure time very differently. Copy the following graphic organizer into your Writer's Notebook to track each reference to the passing of time. A few examples are done for you.

Time as Represented by Father Paul and Catholic Traditions	Time as Referred to by the Villagers
• Mass this week • missed you last Sunday	• hot for this time of year • sun was approaching the long mesa where it disappeared during the winter

6. Do you think Father Paul is a helpful, harmful, or neutral influence? Explain, using details from the story to support your understanding.

Write to Understand: A Statement Exploring Worldviews

A *worldview* is a body of beliefs and attitudes about the world and the place of humans in it. Look over your graphic organizer and "add up" the details related to time in each column to form a main idea about the worldviews of Father Paul and the villagers. In other words, what does the characters' perceptions of time suggest about how they view the world and their place in it? Freewrite to discover ideas. When your thoughts have become clear, write a main idea statement expressing the differences or similarities between Father Paul's worldview and that of the villagers.

BEFORE YOU READ
Marigolds

Meet the Author: Eugenia Collier

Eugenia Collier (born 1928) began her working life as a social worker but then followed in her mother's footsteps in the field of education. Collier graduated from Howard University with high honors and went on to attain advanced degrees from Columbia University and the University of Maryland. She became a professor, scholar, and writer. When she retired from teaching, Collier focused on publishing essays, short stories, poems, and scholarly articles. She has also co-edited an anthology of African American writing.

Build Background: "Mary's Gold"

The bright, golden color of the flowering calendula plant inspired the common name for the flowers that are in the title of this story. The flower's brilliant color made it seem a fitting offering to the Virgin Mary, whom Christians revere as the mother of Jesus. So the flower was called "Mary's Gold." Over time the name changed into *marigold*. Because of their connection to the Virgin Mary, marigolds were believed to bring good luck and to keep away evil and witchery.

In the following story, an old woman who lives in dire poverty grows marigolds each spring. She values them so highly that she spends all her energy and care on them.

- Think of a project on which you have lavished attention and care. Why was the project important to you?

- When do people often give flowers to someone else, and why?

WOMAN SOWING, Robert Gwathmey

Marigolds

EUGENIA COLLIER

MARIGOLDS

Eugenia Collier

When I think of the hometown of my youth, all that I seem to remember is dust—the brown, crumbly dust of late summer—arid, sterile dust that gets into the eyes and makes them water, gets into the throat and between the toes of bare brown feet. I don't know why I should remember only the dust. Surely there must have been lush green lawns and paved streets under leafy shade trees somewhere in town; but memory is an abstract painting—it does not present things as they are, but rather as they *feel*. And so, when I think of that time and that place, I remember only the dry September of the dirt roads and grassless yards of the **shantytown** where I lived. And one other thing I remember, another **incongruency** of memory—a brilliant splash of sunny yellow against the dust—Miss Lottie's marigolds.

Whenever the memory of those marigolds flashes across my mind, a strange **nostalgia** comes with it and remains long after the picture has faded. I feel again the chaotic emotions of adolescence, **illusive** as smoke, yet as real as the potted geranium before me now. Joy and rage and wild animal gladness and shame become tangled together in the multicolored **skein** of fourteen-going-on-fifteen as I recall that devastating moment when I was suddenly more woman than child, years ago in Miss Lottie's yard. I think of those marigolds at the strangest times. I remember them vividly now as I desperately pass away the time waiting for you, who will not come.

I suppose that **futile** waiting was the sorrowful background music of our impoverished little community when I was young. The Depression that gripped the nation was no new thing to us, for the black workers of rural Maryland had always been depressed. I don't know what it was that we were waiting for; certainly not for the prosperity that was "just around the corner," for those were white folks' words, which we never believed. Nor did we wait for hard work and thrift to pay off in shining success—as the American Dream promised—for we knew better than that, too. Perhaps we waited for a miracle, **amorphous** in concept but necessary if one were to have the grit to rise before dawn each day and labor in the white man's vineyard until after dark, or to

shantytown
a slum neighborhood of shanties, or rundown shacks

incongruency
the putting together of things that normally don't fit together

nostalgia
a longing for a past that seems, in memory, very desirable

illusive
illusory; an illusion

skein
a coil of yarn

futile
useless

amorphous
without shape

wander about in the September dust offering one's sweat in return for some meager share of bread. But God was **chary** with miracles in those days, and so we waited—and waited.

chary
sparing; not
generous

We children, of course, were only vaguely aware of the extent of our poverty. Having no radios, few newspapers, and no magazines, we were somewhat unaware of the world outside our community. Nowadays we would be called "culturally deprived" and people would write books and hold conferences about us. In those days everybody we knew was just as hungry and ill-clad as we were. Poverty was the cage in which we all were trapped, and our hatred of it was still the vague, undirected restlessness of the zoo-bred flamingo who knows that nature created him to fly free.

Nowadays we would be called "culturally deprived" and people would write books and hold conferences about us. In those days everybody we knew was just as hungry and ill-clad as we were.

As I think of those days I feel most poignantly the tag end of summer, the bright, dry times when we began to have a sense of shortening days and the imminence of the cold.

By the time I was fourteen my brother Joey and I were the only children left at our house, the older ones having left home for early marriage or the lure of the city, and the two babies having been sent to relatives who might care for them better than we. Joey was three years younger than I, and a boy, and therefore vastly inferior. Each morning our mother and father trudged wearily down the dirt road and around the bend, she to her domestic job, he to his daily unsuccessful quest for work. After our few chores around the tumbledown shanty, Joey and I were free to run wild in the sun with other children similarly situated.

For the most part, those days are ill-defined in my memory, running together and combining like a fresh watercolor painting left out in the rain. I remember squatting in the road drawing a picture in the dust, a picture which Joey gleefully erased with one sweep of his dirty foot. I remember fishing for minnows in a muddy creek and watching sadly as they eluded my cupped hands, while Joey laughed uproariously. And I remember, that year, a strange restlessness of body and of spirit, a feeling that something old and familiar was ending, and something unknown and therefore terrifying was beginning.

One day returns to me with special clarity for some reason, perhaps because it was the beginning of the experience that in some inexplicable way marked the end of innocence. I was loafing under the great oak tree in our yard, deep in some **reverie** which I have now forgotten, except that it involved some secret, secret thoughts of one of the Harris boys across the yard. Joey and a bunch of kids were bored now with the old tire suspended from an oak limb, which had kept them entertained for a while.

"Hey, Lizabeth," Joey yelled. He never talked when he could yell. "Hey, Lizabeth, let's go somewhere."

I came reluctantly from my private world. "Where at? What you want to do?"

The truth was that we were becoming tired of the formlessness of our summer days. The idleness whose prospect had seemed so beautiful during the busy days of spring now had degenerated to an almost desperate effort to fill up the empty midday hours.

"Let's go see can we find us some locusts on the hill," someone suggested.

Joey was scornful. "Ain't no more locusts there. Y'all got 'em all while they was still green."

The argument that followed was brief and not really worth the effort. Hunting locust trees wasn't fun any more by now.

"Tell you what," said Joey finally, his eyes sparkling. "Let's us go over to Miss Lottie's."

The idea caught on at once, for annoying Miss Lottie was always fun. I was still child enough to scamper along with the group over rickety fences and through bushes that tore our already raggedy clothes, back to where Miss Lottie lived. I think now that we must have made a tragicomic spectacle, five or six kids of different ages, each of us clad in only one garment—the girls in faded dresses that were too long or too short, the boys in patchy pants, their sweaty brown chests gleaming in the hot sun. A little cloud of dust followed our thin legs and bare feet as we tramped over the barren land.

When Miss Lottie's house came into view we stopped, **ostensibly** to plan our strategy but actually to reinforce our courage.

Miss Lottie's house was the most ramshackle of all our ramshackle homes. The sun and rain had long since faded its rickety frame siding from white to a sullen gray. The boards themselves seemed to remain upright not from being nailed together but rather from leaning together like a house that a child might have constructed from cards.

A brisk wind might have blown it down, and the fact that it was still standing implied a kind of enchantment that was stronger than the elements. There it stood and as far as I know is standing yet—a gray, rotting thing with no porch, no shutters, no steps, set on cramped lot with no grass, not even weeds—a monument to decay.

In front of the house in a squeaky rocking chair sat Miss Lottie's son, John Burke, completing the impression of decay. John Burke was what was known as "queer-headed." Black and ageless, he sat rocking day in and day out in a mindless stupor, lulled by the monotonous squeak-squawk of the chair. A battered hat atop his shaggy head shaded him from the sun. Usually John Burke was totally unaware of everything outside his quiet dream world. But if you disturbed him, if you intruded upon his fantasies, he would become enraged, strike out at you, and curse at you in some strange enchanted language which only he could understand. We children made a game of thinking of ways to disturb John Burke and then to elude his violent **retribution.**

But our real fun and our real fear lay in Miss Lottie herself. Miss Lottie seemed to be at least a hundred years old. Her big frame still held traces of the tall, powerful woman she must have been in youth, although it was now bent and drawn. Her smooth skin was a dark reddish brown, and her face had Indian-like features and the stern **stoicism** that one associates with Indian faces. Miss Lottie didn't like intruders either, especially children. She never left her yard, and nobody ever visited her. We never knew how she managed those necessities which depend on human interaction—how she ate, for example, or even whether she ate. When we were tiny children, we thought Miss Lottie was a witch and we made up tales that we half believed ourselves about her exploits. We were far too sophisticated now, of course, to believe the witch nonsense. But old fears have a way of clinging like cobwebs, and so when we sighted the tumbledown shack, we had to stop to reinforce our nerves.

"Look, there she is," I whispered, forgetting that Miss Lottie could not possibly have heard me from that distance. "She's fooling with them crazy flowers."

"Yeh, look at 'er."

Miss Lottie's marigolds were perhaps the strangest part of the picture. Certainly they did not fit in with the crumbling decay of the rest of her yard. Beyond the dusty brown yard, in front of the sorry gray house, rose suddenly and shockingly a dazzling strip of bright blossoms, clumped together in enormous mounds, warm and passionate and sun-golden. The old black witch-woman worked on them all summer, every summer, down on her creaky knees, weeding and cultivating and arranging, while the house crumbled and John Burke rocked. For some perverse reason, we children hated those marigolds. They

retribution
just
punishment

stoicism
indifference
to pleasure
or pain

interfered with the perfect ugliness of the place; they were too beautiful; they said too much that we could not understand; they did not make sense. There was something in the vigor with which the old woman destroyed the weeds that intimidated us. It should have been a comical sight—the old woman with the man's hat on her cropped white head, leaning over the bright mounds, her big backside in the air—but it wasn't comical, it was something we could not name. We had to annoy her by whizzing a pebble into her flowers or by

yelling a dirty word, then dancing away from her rage, reveling in our youth and mocking her age. Actually, I think it was the flowers we wanted to destroy, but nobody had the nerve to try it, not even Joey, who was usually fool enough to try anything.

"Y'all git some stones," commanded Joey now and was met with instant giggling obedience as everyone except me began to gather pebbles from the dusty ground. "Come on, Lizabeth."

I just stood there peering through the bushes, torn between wanting to join the fun and feeling that it was all a bit silly.

"You scared, Lizabeth?"

I cursed and spat on the ground—my favorite gesture of phony bravado. "Y'all children get the stones, I'll show you how to use 'em." I said before that we children were not consciously aware of how thick were the bars of our cage. I wonder now, though, whether we were not more aware of it than I thought. Perhaps we had some dim notion of what we were, and how little chance we had of being anything else. Otherwise, why would we have been so preoccupied with destruction? Anyway, the pebbles were collected quickly, and everybody looked at me to begin the fun.

"Come on, y'all."

We crept to the edge of the bushes that bordered the narrow road in front of Miss Lottie's place. She was working placidly, kneeling over the flowers, her dark hand plunged into the golden mound. Suddenly zing—an expertly aimed stone cut the head off one of the blossoms.

"Who out there?" Miss Lottie's backside came down and her head came up as her sharp eyes searched the bushes. "You better git!"

We had crouched down out of sight in the bushes, where we stifled the giggles that insisted on coming. Miss Lottie gazed warily across the road for a moment, then cautiously returned to her weeding. Zing—Joey sent a pebble into the blooms, and another marigold was beheaded.

Miss Lottie was enraged now. She began struggling to her feet, leaning on a rickety cane and shouting. "Y'all git! Go on home!" Then the rest of the kids let loose with their pebbles, storming the flowers and laughing wildly and senselessly at Miss Lottie's **impotent** rage. She shook her stick at us and started shakily toward the road crying, "Git 'long! John Burke! John Burke, come help!"

Then I lost my head entirely, mad with the power of **inciting** such rage, and ran out of the bushes in the storm of pebbles, straight toward Miss Lottie, chanting madly, "Old witch, fell in a ditch, picked up a penny and thought she was rich!" The children screamed with delight, dropped their pebbles, and joined the crazy dance, swarming around Miss Lottie like bees and chanting, "Old lady witch!" while she screamed curses at us. The madness lasted only a moment, for John Burke, startled at last, lurched out of his chair, and we dashed for the bushes just as Miss Lottie's cane went whizzing at my head.

I did not join the merriment when the kids gathered again under the oak in our bare yard. Suddenly I was ashamed, and I did not like being ashamed. The child in me sulked and said it was all in fun, but the woman in me flinched at the thought of the malicious attack that I had led. The mood lasted all afternoon. When we ate the beans and rice that was supper that night, I did not notice my father's silence, for he was always silent these days, nor did I notice my mother's absence, for she always worked until well into evening. Joey and I had a particularly bitter argument after supper; his exuberance got on my nerves. Finally I stretched out upon the **pallet** in the room we shared and fell into a fitful doze.

When I awoke, somewhere in the middle of the night, my mother had returned, and I vaguely listened to the conversation that was audible through the thin walls that separated our rooms. At first I heard no words, only voices.

My mother's voice was like a cool, dark room in summer—peaceful, soothing, quiet.

I loved to listen to it; it made things seem all right somehow. But my father's voice cut through hers, shattering the peace.

"Twenty-two years, Maybelle, twenty-two years," he was saying, "and I got nothing for you, nothing, nothing."

impotent
helpless; lacking power or ability

inciting
provoking

pallet
a straw-filed mattress, usually placed on the floor

Marigolds   753

"It's all right, honey, you'll get something. Everybody out of work now, you know that."

"It ain't right. Ain't no man ought to eat his woman's food year in and year out, and see his children running wild. Ain't nothing right about that."

"Honey, you took good care of us when you had it. Ain't nobody got nothing nowadays."

"I ain't talking about nobody else, I m talking about *me*. God knows I try." My mother said something I could not hear, and my father cried out louder, "What must a man do, tell me that?"

"Look, we ain't starving. I git paid every week, and Mrs. Ellis is real nice about giving me things. She gonna let me have Mr. Ellis's old coat for you this winter—"

"Damn Mr. Ellis's coat! And damn his money! You think I want white folks' leavings?"

"Damn, Maybelle"—and suddenly he sobbed, loudly and painfully, and cried helplessly and hopelessly in the dark night. I had never heard a man cry before. I did not know men ever cried. I covered my ears with my hands but could not cut off the sound of my father's harsh, painful, despairing sobs. My father was a strong man who could **whisk** a child upon his shoulders and go singing through the house. My father whittled toys for us, and laughed so loud that the great oak seemed to laugh with him, and taught us how to fish and hunt rabbits. How could it be that my father was crying? But the sobs went on, unstifled, finally quieting until I could hear my mother's voice, deep and rich, humming softly as she used to hum to a frightened child.

The world had lost its boundary lines. My mother, who was small and soft, was now the strength of the family; my father, who was the rock on which the family had been built, was sobbing like the tiniest child. Everything was suddenly out of tune, like a broken accordion. Where did I fit into this crazy picture? I do not now remember my thoughts, only a feeling of great bewilderment and fear.

Long after the sobbing and humming had stopped, I lay on the pallet, still as stone with my hands over my ears, wishing that I too could cry and be comforted. The night was silent now except for the sound of the crickets and of Joey's soft breathing. But the room was too crowded with fear to allow me to sleep, and finally, feeling the terrible aloneness of 4 A.M., I decided to awaken Joey.

"Ouch! What's the matter with you? What you want?" he demanded disagreeably when I had pinched and slapped him awake.

whisk
to pick up in a sweeping motion

"Come on, wake up."

"What for? Go 'way."

I was lost for a reasonable reply. I could not say, "I'm scared and I don't want to be alone," so I merely said, "I'm going out. If you want to come, come on."

The promise of adventure awoke him. "Going out now? Where to, Lizabeth? What you going to do?"

I was pulling my dress over my head. Until now I had not thought of going out. "Just come on," I replied tersely.

I was out the window and halfway down the road before Joey caught up with me.

"Wait, Lizabeth, where you going?"

I was running as if the Furies[1] were after me, as perhaps they were—running silently and furiously until I came to where I had half known I was headed: to Miss Lottie's yard.

The half-dawn light was more eerie than complete darkness, and in it the old house was like the ruin that my world had become—foul and crumbling, a grotesque caricature. It looked haunted, but I was not afraid, because I was haunted too.

"Lizabeth, you lost your mind?" panted Joey.

I had indeed lost my mind, for all the smoldering emotions of that summer swelled in me and burst—the great need for my mother who was never there, the hopelessness of our poverty and degradation, the bewilderment of being neither child nor woman and yet both at once, the fear unleashed by my father's tears. And these feelings combined in one great impulse toward destruction.

"Lizabeth!"

I leaped furiously into the mounds of marigolds and pulled madly, trampling and pulling and destroying the perfect yellow blooms. The fresh smell of early morning and of dew-soaked marigolds spurred me on as I went tearing and mangling and sobbing while Joey tugged my dress or my waist crying, "Lizabeth, stop, please stop!"

I **Furies:** from Greek and Roman mythology, goddesses of vengeance, with snakes for hair and blood dripping from their eyes. They punished crimes and caused offenders to go mad.

And then I was sitting in the ruined little garden among the uprooted and ruined flowers, crying and crying, and it was too late to undo what I had done. Joey was sitting beside me, silent and frightened, not knowing what to say. Then, "Lizabeth, look!"

I opened my swollen eyes and saw in front of me a pair of large, calloused feet; my gaze lifted to the swollen legs, the age-distorted body clad in a tight cotton nightdress, and then the shadowed Indian face surrounded by stubby white hair. And there was no rage in the face now, now that the garden was destroyed and there was nothing any longer to be protected.

"M-miss Lottie!" I scrambled to my feet and just stood there and stared at her, and that was the moment when childhood faded and womanhood began. That violent, crazy act was the last act of childhood. For as I gazed at the immobile face with the sad, weary eyes, I gazed upon a kind of reality which is hidden to childhood. The witch was no longer a witch but only a broken old woman who had dared to create beauty in the midst of ugliness and sterility. She had been born in **squalor** and lived in it all her life. Now at the end of that life she had nothing except a falling-down hut, a wrecked body, and John Burke, the mindless son of her passion. Whatever **verve** there was left in her, whatever was of love and beauty and joy that had not been squeezed out by life, had been there in the marigolds she had so tenderly cared for.

Of course I could not express the things that I knew about Miss Lottie as I stood there awkward and ashamed. The years have put words to the things I knew in that moment, and as I look back upon it, I know that that moment marked the end of innocence. Innocence involves an unseeing acceptance of things at face value, an ignorance of the area below the surface. In that humiliating moment I looked beyond myself and into the depths of another person. This was the beginning of compassion, and one cannot have both compassion and innocence.

The years have taken me worlds away from that time and that place, from the dust and squalor of our lives, and from the bright thing that I destroyed in a blind, childish striking out at God knows what. Miss Lottie died long ago and many years have passed since I last saw her hut, completely barren at last, for despite my wild contrition she never planted marigolds again. Yet, there are times when the image of those passionate yellow mounds returns with a painful poignancy. For one does not have to be ignorant and poor to find that his life is as barren as the dusty yards of our town. And I too have planted marigolds.

squalor
poor and grubby condition

verve
liveliness, enthusiasm

AFTER YOU READ
Marigolds

Think and Discuss

1. How old is the narrator in this story, and how does she feel about her life in the present? Explain with details from the story.

2. The narrator of this story suggests several reasons why she and the other children taunt Miss Lottie. Identify at least three reasons for their actions and explain which reason or reasons you find most convincing.

3. What does the **allusion** to the Furies communicate about the narrator's destructive act?

4. Collier uses a number of **metaphors** to describe adolescence. Choose a metaphor and explain why it is an apt description.

5. This story traces the narrator's journey to adulthood. Copy the following graphic organizer into your Writer's Notebook. List the actions and emotions that fall on the childhood side of the organizer and those that fall on the adult side of the organizer.

6. In the conversation Lizabeth overhears, what does the reader learn about the things that have value for Lizabeth's father?

Write to Understand: Interpreting Story Events

Look over your graphic organizer. Identify the event that signals the shift from childhood to adulthood. Write an explanation of how the events in the childhood column led up to that point and how the events in the adulthood column grew out of that point. Share your writing with a partner and discuss your interpretations.

Writers on Writing

BEFORE YOU READ
Polaroids

Meet the Author: Anne Lamott

Anne Lamott (born 1954) grew up in northern California, the daughter of a writing father and a mother who read everything she could get her hands on. It is no wonder, then, that Lamott turned to writing at an early age. In *Bird by Bird: Some Instructions on Writing and Life*, she describes herself as a scrawny, anxious child who was often teased. All of that changed, though, when she "got funny." She developed her keen sense of humor and before long realized she had a gift for telling stories in a vivid and comic style. She has written six novels and a number of nonfiction books that are largely autobiographical. In them she has explored the challenges of parenthood, her battles with alcoholism, and, in *Bird by Bird*, her life as a writer.

Build Background: First Drafts

The selections in this unit have explored the question of what has value. Lamott feels that the way writers get at what has value—the way they find the story that is worth telling—is through exploratory writing. In *Bird by Bird* she shares her methods for finding value. In one chapter, she explains an exercise she uses with her writing students. She directs them to focus their attention on the contents of their lunch bag and to write about that for a full half hour. She participates in the exercise as well and reports her experience.

Lamott relates how once, when she was doing the exercise along with her students, she remembered that kids used to judge each other's lunches. If yours were too "weird" you might end up like the boy who was always standing alone at the fence. Unexpectedly, the image of the boy at the fence grabbed Lamott's attention and started to come into clearer view for her. She had found a subject of value to write about, which she refers to in the following selection. "Polaroids" continues the theme of studying a focus point long and carefully enough to find the real value in it. She compares first draft writing to photographs that develop right before your eyes.

As you read, think about these questions:

- Have you ever discovered through writing an idea you did not know you had?

- What subjects have value for you to write about?

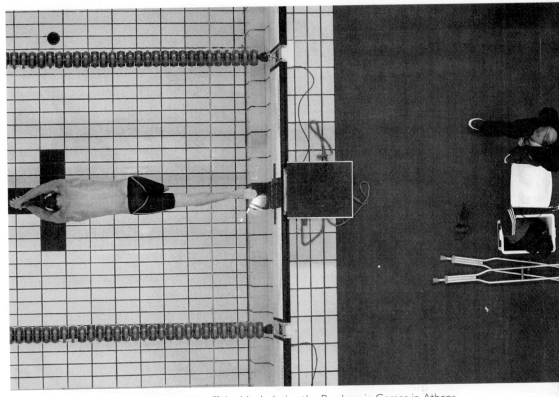

Mark Barr starts off the block during the Paralympic Games in Athens

Polaroids

ANNE LAMOTT

POLAROIDS

Anne Lamott

Writing a first draft is very much like watching a Polaroid develop. You can't—and, in fact, you're not supposed to—know exactly what the picture is going to look like until it has finished developing. First you just point at what has your attention and take the picture. In the last chapter, for instance, what had my attention were the contents of my lunch bag. But as the picture developed, I found I had a really clear image of the boy against the fence. Or maybe *your* Polaroid was supposed to be a picture of that boy against the fence, and you didn't notice until the last minute that a family was standing a few feet away from him. Now, maybe it's his family, or the family of one of the kids in his class, but at any rate these people are going to be in the photograph, too. Then the film emerges from the camera with a grayish green murkiness that gradually becomes clearer and clearer, and finally you see the husband and wife holding their baby with two children standing beside them. And at first it all seems very sweet, but then the shadows begin to appear, and then you start to see the animal tragedy, the baboons baring their teeth. And then you see a flash of bright red flowers in the bottom left quadrant that you didn't even know were in the picture when you took it, and these flowers evoke a time or a memory that moves you mysteriously. And finally, as the portrait comes into focus, you begin to notice all the props surrounding these people, and you begin to understand how props define us and comfort us, and show us what we value and what we need, and who we think we are.

You couldn't have had any way of knowing what this piece of work would look like when you first started. You just knew that there was something about these people that compelled you, and you stayed with that something long enough for it to show you what it was about.

Watch this Polaroid develop:

Six or seven years ago I was asked to write an article on the Special Olympics. I had been going to the local event for years, partly because a couple of friends of mine compete. Also, I love sports, and I love to watch athletes, special or otherwise. So I showed up this time with a great deal of interest but no real sense of what the finished article might look like.

Things tend to go very, very slowly at the Special Olympics. It is not like trying to cover the Preakness.[1] Still, it has its own exhilaration, and I cheered and took notes all morning.

The last track-and-field event before lunch was a twenty-five-yard race run by some unusually handicapped runners and walkers, many of whom seemed completely confused. They lumped and **careened** along, one man making a snail-slow break for the stands, one heading out toward the steps where the winners receive their medals; both of them were shepherded back. The race took just about forever. And here it was nearly noon and we were all so hungry. Finally, though, everyone crossed over the line, and those of us in the stands got up to go—when we noticed that way down the track, four or five yards from the starting line, was another runner.

She was a girl of about sixteen with a normal-looking face above a **wracked** and **emaciated** body. She was on metal crutches, and she was just plugging along, one tiny step after another, moving one crutch forward two or three inches, then moving a leg, then moving the other crutch two or three inches, then moving the other leg. It was just excruciating. Plus, I was starving to death. Inside I was going, Come on, come on, come on, swabbing at my forehead with anxiety, while she kept taking these two-or-three-inch steps forward. What felt like four hours later, she crossed the finish line, and you could see that she was absolutely stoked,[2] in a shy, girlish way.

A tall African American man with no front teeth fell into step with me as I left the bleachers to go look for some lunch. He tugged on the sleeve of my sweater, and I looked up at him, and he handed me a Polaroid someone had taken of him and his friends that day. "Look at us," he said. His speech was difficult to understand, thick and slow as a warped record. His two friends in the picture had Down's syndrome. All three of them looked extremely pleased with themselves. I admired the picture and then handed it back to him. He stopped, so I stopped, too. He pointed to his own image. "That," he said, "is one cool man."

And this was the image from which an article began forming, although I could not have told you exactly what the piece would end up being about. I just knew that something had started to emerge.

careened
rushed recklessly

wracked
wrecked; ruined

emaciated
as thin as a starving person

---

1 **Preakness:** a very fast, very famous horse race

2 **stoked:** filled with energy, as a locomotive engine is stoked with firewood

After lunch I wandered over to the auditorium, where it turned out a men's basketball game was in progress. The African American man with no front teeth was the star of the game. You could tell that he was because even though no one had made a basket yet, his teammates almost always passed him the ball. Even the people on the *other* team passed him the ball a lot. In lieu of any scoring, the men stampeded in slow motion up and down the court, dribbling the ball thunderously. I had never heard such a loud game. It was all sort of crazily beautiful. I imagined describing the game for my article and then for my students: the loudness, the joy. I kept replaying the scene of the girl on crutches making her way up the track to the finish line—and all of a sudden my article began to appear out of the grayish green murk. And I could see that it was about tragedy transformed over the years into joy. It was about the beauty of sheer effort. I could see it almost as clearly as I could the photograph of that one cool man and his two friends.

The auditorium bleachers were packed. Then a few minutes later, still with no score on the board, the tall black man dribbled slowly from one end of the court to the other, and heaved the ball up into the air, and it dropped into the basket. The crowd roared, and all the men on both teams looked up wide-eyed at the hoop, as if it had just burst into flames.

You would have loved it, I tell my students. You would have felt like you could write all day.

AFTER YOU READ
Polaroids

Think and Discuss

1. The subtitle of Lamott's book is "Some Instructions on Writing and Life." In what ways might this selection contain instructions on life?

2. What is the effect of the humor in this selection? Refer to specific examples.

3. In the introduction to her book, Lamott says that she writes because she wants to and she's good at it. Find passages in this selection that show her writing **craft.**

4. What **inferences** can you draw about how Lamott feels about her students? Explain.

5. In another chapter in her book, Lamott writes: "If you find that you start a number of stories or pieces that you don't ever bother finishing, that you lose interest or faith in them along the way, it may be that there is nothing at their center about which you care passionately. You need to put yourself at their center, you and what you believe to be true or right. The core, ethical concepts in which you most passionately believe are the language in which you are writing." Discuss which "core, ethical concepts," such as kindness, fairness, and the value of hard work, mean the most to you.

6. Look back over the selections in this unit. What are the "core, ethical concepts" that form the foundation of each piece? In your Writer's Notebook, make a graphic organizer like the one below to help you identify the values underlying each selection. In the left-hand column, list all the selections in the unit. In the right-hand column, identify the core value expressed in the piece. One is done to show you how.

Selections	Ethical Concepts/Values
The Gift of the Magi	Giving is better than receiving; material goods are not as important as love and sacrifice

Write to Understand: Exploring What You Value

Think back to your earlier discussion and look over the graphic organizer you completed. Write a brief, informal essay explaining which ethical concept or value from your graphic organizer is most important to you. Also discuss how the work of literature that is associated with that value succeeds in getting it across. Use specific references to the text.

A Writer's WORKSHOP

REFLECTIVE ESSAY: IN GOOD COMPANY

As a reader, you spend time in the company of the author's mind, and authors can become almost like friends. Like real friends, some help bring out the best in you. In this unit you have been in the company of a number of different authors. Reflect now on which ones seemed the best company, which ones expanded your way of thinking and imparted a sense of value to your life. You can express your ideas in a reflective essay.

Prewriting

REVIEWING IDEAS

Review your Writer's Notebook and skim back over the selections to remind you of the responses you had to the selections in this unit.

COOPERATIVE LEARNING:
REVIEWING WORKS OF LITERATURE THROUGH DISCUSSION

In a small group, discuss each selection in this unit with a focus on the kind of company the author provides. What is each author's worldview? What did you learn from each author? Which author did you enjoy the most?

To help you understand an author's worldview, discuss the following questions.

FICTION
• Does the main character's "good" side triumph?
• Do the people with the most social power behave admirably?
• What does the main character learn about the way the world works?

POETRY
• Does the poem celebrate some aspect of life, or is it mainly critical?
• What do you think the speaker's emotions are?
• What is the speaker communicating?

NONFICTION
• Is there any bias, or slanted viewpoint, you can detect?
• If so, what does that bias suggest about the author's view of the world?
• Is the subject matter uplifting or depressing?

DEVELOPING YOUR IDEAS

Select three of the authors from this unit whose company was most rewarding to you. Copy the following graphic organizer into your Writer's Notebook. Use it to explore what you valued in the company of each author.

Author #1:	Author #2:	Author #3:
What I appreciated about that author's company • • •	What I appreciated about that author's company • • •	What I appreciated about that author's company • • •
What I learned about life from that author • • •	What I learned about life from that author • • •	What I learned about life from that author • • •

PLAN YOUR ORGANIZATION

Review your completed graphic organizer. Rank your author companions as good, better, or best. Then outline or sketch out your plan for organizing your essay. For example, will you start with the good author and work your way up to the best, using ascending order of importance? Or will you begin with the most important and work your way down? Or will you take the two main topics from the graphic organizer—things you appreciate about the author and life lessons learned—and make those the main parts of your essay?

Drafting

Using your outline or graphic representation, draft your reflective essay. Remember that a reflective essay, as its name suggests, should present a good reflection of your thoughts about yourself and your reaction to the readings and to the authors.

USING A WORD PROCESSOR

If you get bogged down while composing your first draft at the computer, save what you have and open a new document. Clear your mind by writing freely and creatively. For example, imagine yourself in the actual physical company of the authors, over breakfast, for example. What would you talk about? When you feel ready to get back to your drafting, save the writing you just did. Maybe you could use it to add sparkle to your essay.

Revising and Editing

Use the Six-Trait checklist to help you revise your reflective essay.

When you have finished a first draft, possibly with some of your "sparkle" worked into it, put it aside for a while. Then read it with fresh eyes as you try to make it better.

READING WITH AN EDITOR'S EYE

Thoughtful, easy-to-read writing uses a variety of sentence lengths, types, and patterns. Note the sentence variety in the following passage.

Six or seven years ago I was asked to write an article on the Special Olympics. I had been going to the local event for years, partly because a couple of friends of mine compete. Also, I love sports, and I love to watch athletes, special or otherwise. So I showed up this time with a great deal of interest but no real sense of what the finished article might look like. —from "Polaroids"

The first sentence is a short, simple sentence, and it begins with an adverbial phrase. The second sentence is longer, it begins with the subject, and it is a complex sentence. The third sentence begins with a conjunction and is a compound sentence. The final sentence is somewhat long and is another complex sentence. In your essay, check that you have a similar degree of sentence variety—in sentence beginnings, length, and types. Also check to make sure you punctuate each type of sentence correctly.

USING A CHECKLIST

When you are satisfied with your reflective essay, use the Six-Trait checklist on the next page to double check each trait.

Six Traits of Writing: Reflective Essays

Content and Ideas
- the main idea expresses the satisfaction felt in the company of three authors whose works are in this unit
- the body of the essay discusses each of the three authors
- the ideas in the body are supported by details, examples, and quotes from the text that explain why the authors provided good company

Organization
- the essay has a clear introduction with a thesis statement, a body in which the thesis is supported, and a conclusion that creates a strong and fitting end to the reflections
- the ideas in the body are presented in a logical order

Voice or Style
- the voice sounds natural, not forced
- the voice may be as informal as speech or may be more formal; in either case it carries a reflective quality

Word Choice
- the writer uses specific and vivid words
- the writer avoids the passive voice

Sentence Fluency
- sentences are complete
- sentence length and sentence beginnings are varied and purposeful
- transitions between ideas and sections are clear and smooth

Conventions
- the essay is free of errors in usage, spelling, capitalization, and punctuation
- works referred to are presented according to the style required by the school (for example, titles of short stories are in quotes)

Glossary of Literary Terms

action
the events that take place in a story or on a stage

alliteration
the repetition of initial consonants, as the letter *d* in "Doubting, dreaming dreams no mortals ever dared to dream before"

allusion
a reference to another literary work or to a familiar person, place, or event

andecdote
a minor incident used to illustrate a point in a larger work

article
a nonfiction prose work that can stand alone and is part of a longer publication

assonance
the repetition of vowel sounds in stressed syllables (for example, the long *a* sound in "They came, they played)."

audience
the readers (or viewers, in the case of a play) of a work of literature

autobiographical narrative
a story of an experience that took place in the writer's life, usually focusing on details

autobiography
the true story of someone's life, written by the person himself or herself

background information
information provided that fills the reader in on parts of the subject necessary to understand before being able to grasp the author's main idea

biography
the true story of someone's life, written by someone else

burlesque
a category of dramatic comedy in which serious subjects are treated frivolously

catalog
a literary device used to list things and ideas; by grouping them in one "catalog," the author can cast meaning on each one by suggesting the characteristics it shares with other items in the group

character	a person or animal who is part of the action of a literary work
characterization	the ways in which a writer shapes the reader's understanding of a character
character development	the way a character changes throughout a work of literature
character sketch	a brief description of a character that emphasizes just the most important points
character type	a model of a kind of standard character, from which copies are often made
character trait	a quality of personality that helps define a character
chart	one kind of visual graphic that conveys information in a way that shows relationships among the data
chorus	a group of actors who comment on the action of a play
chronological order	the arrangement of events according to when they happened, with the earliest coming first
classic hero	a male character who exhibits courage and strength and who is favored by the gods
common speech patterns	a consistent style of talking in everyday conversation
conflict	a struggle between two forces. A struggle can be between two or more characters, between a character and nature, or between opposing feelings or drives within a character.
consonance	the repetition of internal vowel sounds, such as the short e sound in "Hear the mellow wedding bells"
craft	the skill or art in a task
critical essay	a composition in which the writer interprets a work of fiction, drama, or poetry
descriptive details	details that help paint a vivid picture, often by appealing to the five senses

details	specific examples, events, facts, statistics, comparisons, and other kinds of information that support a bigger idea
diagram	a drawing or other kind of graphic that shows how something works or how the parts relate to the whole
dialect	the style of speech used by people in a certain region of social group
dialogue	the exact words characters say to each other in a literary work
diction	the author's choice of words
dramatic chorus	(See **chorus**.)
dramatic function	the purpose of a technique used in a play, such as the ringing bell in some of the plays of David Ives
entertain	one of many possible purposes for writing
epic poem	a long narrative poem, highly stylized, that tells a story of heroic events
epic simile	an extended simile that elaborates on a comparison in great detail
essay	a short composition on only one subject
examples	one of several main types of supporting details used especially in nonfiction; specific instances of a more general idea
extended metaphor	a comparison in which a number of qualities of two unlike things are shown to be similar
facts	statements that can be proved true
fairy tale	a story, often intended for children, about imaginary and magical places and beings
feature article	an article that is especially prominent in a newspaper or magazine
field notes	written record of observations made by a researcher, usually at the site of the observations